More Like Lions Than Men

Sir William Brereton and the Cheshire Army of Parliament, 1642–46

Andrew Abram

Helion & Company

Helion & Company Limited
Unit 8 Amherst Business Centre
Budbrooke Road
Warwick
CV34 5WE
England
Tel. 01926 499 619
Email: info@helion.co.uk
Website: www.helion.co.uk
Twitter: @helionbooks
Blog: https://helionbooks.wordpress.com/

Published by Helion & Company 2020
Designed and typeset by Mach 3 Solutions Ltd (www.mach3solutions.co.uk)
Cover designed by Paul Hewitt, Battlefield Design (www.battlefield-design.co.uk)

ISBN 978-1-913118-82-2

British Library Cataloguing-in-Publication Data.
A catalogue record for this book is available from the British Library.

For details of other military history titles published by Helion & Company Limited contact the above address or visit our website: http://www.helion.co.uk.

We always welcome receiving book proposals from prospective authors.

Contents

Lists of Illustrations

List of Maps

List of Tables

List of Abbreviations

AA	Aston Archive, unlisted warrants and receipts, 1643-5.
A&O	C. H. Firth and R. S., Rait (eds), *Acts and Ordinances of the Interregnum, 1642-1660*, 3 vols(London: HMSO, 1911).
BCA	Birmingham City Archives.
BL	The British Library, London.
BLB	R. N. Dore (ed.), *The Letter Books of Sir William Brereton*, 2 vols, RSLC, 123, 128 (1984, 1990).
Bod. Lib.	Bodleian Library, Oxford.
BU	Bangor University.
CH	*Cheshire History.*
CJ	*Journals of the House of Commons.*
CL	Chetham's Library, Manchester.
CPCM	M. A. Everett Green (ed.), *Calendar of Proceedings of the Committee for the Advancement of Money*, 3 vols (London: HMSO, 1888).
CRO	Cheshire Archives (Record Office), Chester.
CS	*Cheshire Sheaf.*
CS	Chetham Society.
CSPD	*Calendar of Sate Papers Domestic.*
CWS	Ivor Carr and Ian Atherton (eds), *The Civil War in Staffordshire in the Spring of 1646: Sir William Brereton's Letter Book, April-May 1646*, Collections for a History of Staffordshire, Fourth Series, 21 (SRS, 2007).
CWTC	James Atkinson, *Tracts Relating to the Civil War in Cheshire, 1641-1659* (Manchester: Chetham Society, 1909).
CWTL	George Ormerod (ed.), *Tracts Relating to Military Proceedings in Lancashire during the Great Civil War*(Manchester: CS, 1844).
DRO	Derbyshire Record Office, Matlock.
DWL	Dr Williams's Library, London.
ECWNQ	*English Civil War Notes & Queries.*
EHR	*English Historical Review.*
ERA	East Riding Archives, Beverley.
HLJO	House of Lords, Journal Office, London.
HMC	Historical Manuscripts Commission.
HR	*Historical Research.*

IHS	*Irish Historical Studies.*
JAAS	*Journal of the Arms and Armour Society.*
JBS	*Journal of British Studies.*
JCAS	*Journal of the Chester Archaeological Society.*
JRL	John Rylands Library (The University of Manchester Library), Manchester.
JSAHR	*Journal of the Society for Army Historical Research.*
Lancaster	John Lewis (ed.), *The Siege of Chester: Nathaniel Lancaster's Narrative* (Nottingham: Raider Books, 1987).
LCL	Lichfield Cathedral Library.
LCRS	Lancashire and Cheshire Record Society.
Lich. RO	Lichfield Record Office, Lichfield.
LJ	*Journals of the House of Lords.*
LRO	Lancashire Record Office, Preston.
Malbon	James Hall (ed.), *Memorials of the Civil War in Cheshire and the adjacent counties by Thomas Malbon, of Nantwich, Gent., and Providence improved by Edward Burghall,* Lancashire and Cheshire Record Society, 19 (1889).
MC	*Montgomeryshire Collections.*
MH	*Midland History.*
MS	Manuscript.
MSS	Manuscripts.
MS Add.	Manuscript Additional in the BL.
NH	*Northern History.*
NLW	National Library of Wales, Aberystwyth.
ODNB	*Oxford Dictionary of National Biography.*
P&P	*Past and Present.*
RSLC	Record Society of Lancashire and Cheshire.
RHS	Royal Historical Society.
RMA	Rijksmuseum, Amsterdam.
SA	Sheffield Archives, Sheffield.
SRO	Staffordshire Record Office, Stafford.
SRS	Staffordshire Record Society.
SS	Surtees Society.
TLAHS	*Transactions of the Leicestershire Archaeological and Historical Society.*
THSLC	*Transactions of the HistoricSociety of Lancashire and Cheshire.*
TLCAS	*Transactions of the Lancashire and Cheshire Antiquarian Society.*
TSAS	*Transactions of the Shropshire Archaeological Society.*

Acknowledgements

Any project of this scope owes a debt of gratitude to various institutions and people. In particular, much generous assistance has been received from the archivists and librarians at the Cheshire Archives, John Rylands Library, Philadelphia Museum of Art, the British Library and the National Archives. I am also particularly grateful to the following: Christine Talbot for allowing me access to original documents in the Aston Archive, and to publish images of them; Dr Fergus Wilde of Chetham's Library, the Centre for Heritage Imaging and Collection Care at the University of Manchester, and Philadelphia Museum of Art for their friendly advice and allowing the use of images from their collections. Moreover, I am further indebted to Dr David Wykes, director of Dr Williams's Library for providing photographs of cornets and agreeing to their replication. Personal thanks are due to Gary Ashby for furnishing his knowledge of Sir Thomas Aston's regiments of horse and dragoons. I also wish to recognize the generosity of David Evans in sharing his research on soldier's clothing and equipment, as well as Ian Dicker, who freely imparted his considerable knowledge of early-modern tailoring and reconstructions of military garments of the period. Thanks also to Paul Wright, whose friendship and conversations (over many pints of beer and meals), as well as civil war sight visits over the years have considerably added to my knowledge and proved inspirational in the writing of this book.

Last, but certainly not least, I want to thank my wife Dr Kathryn Hurlock for patiently listening to my many descriptions of civil war units and battles, as well as looking for bullet marks in church walls, whilst seemingly possessing an aversion to most forms of military history. Importantly also, Kathryn allowed me much needed breathing (and thinking) space from child-care duties, particularly when pulling the final parts of the book together. This book is dedicated, with love, to her.

Explanatory Notes and Conventions

Although dates prior to 1752 are recorded with the year beginning 25 March, modern dating is used throughout, with the New Year being taken to start on 1 January. Spellings in contemporary manuscripts and printed sources (which varied considerably during the seventeenth century) have been modernised, while where appropriate, current forms of punctuation have been added to period accounts.

According to the Imperial system, contemporary monetary values have been quoted throughout. Hence, 12 pennies (12d.) = 1 shilling (1s.); 20 shillings = one pound sterling (£1); £1 = 240d. Moreover, lengths and distances are given in inches, feet, yards, ells and miles; weights in pounds (lb), 112lb = a hundredweight (cwt), 20 cwt = 1 ton.

In this book Cheshire corresponds with the historical boundaries that were lost to the new metropolitan authorities of Merseyside and Greater Manchester in 1974.

Chronology

Summary of the main events in Cheshire during the First Civil War, 1642–6

1642

August	Charles I visits Chester. Commission of Array musters trained bands. Sir William Brereton attempts to recruit for Parliament.
September	Royalist regiments raised in Cheshire join the king's main army.
December	Royalists seize Beeston Castle. Bunbury Peace Treaty signed.

1643

January-April	Brereton arrives in county with military forces and places headquarters at Nantwich. Chester defended for the king. Sir Thomas Aston defeated at Middlewich. Parliamentarian authority established in north and east Cheshire. Sir William Brereton appointed commander-in-chief of forces in Cheshire. Lord Capel's royalists threaten Nantwich.
May-August	Cheshire parliamentarian army defeats Capel at Whitchurch. Brereton's forces assist in the capture of Warrington. Halton Castle surrenders to them.
July	Parliamentarians probe Chester defences at Boughton.
November	Invasion of North Wales launched from Nantwich. Arrival of 3,000 royalist troops from Ireland compels Brereton to abandon operations and remove his soldiers into garrisons.
December	Parliamentarian forces defeated at Second Battle of Middlewich.

1644

January	Royalist siege of Nantwich. Byron's army vanquished by combined parliamentarian forces and town relieved.
February	Sir William Brereton called to Westminster. Royalist garrisons in Cheshire fall to parliamentarian forces.
May	Prince Rupert advances through Cheshire, crossing into Lancashire at Stockport.
June	Brereton returns to Cheshire.
July	Rupert briefly at Chester before retreating to the Welsh borders.
August	Cheshire parliamentarians defeat royalists at Tarvin and Malpas.
November	Siege operations begin formally against Chester.

1645

January	Parliamentarians victorious at Christleton. Assaults made on Chester's walls, but unsuccessful.
February	Prince Maurice briefly relieves city and attacks Brereton's troops at Farndon.
March	Combined forces of Maurice and Rupert compel parliamentarians to temporarily forsake the Chester Leaguer.
May	Siege is resumed, but Brereton's forces again forced to withdraw as the king's main army approaches Cheshire. Sir William Brereton returns to London.
August	Siege of Beeston Castle resumed by Cheshire parliamentarians.
September	Eastern suburbs of Chester taken by Brereton's forces. Charles I arrives at city, but royalists suffer catastrophic reversal at Rowton Heath.
October	Parliamentarians launch 'Great Assault' of the city, which is partially successful.
November	Beeston Castle surrenders. Chester bombarded by mortars, causing heavy damage to the city defences and lowers morale of citizens. Parliamentarians crush a royalist relief force under Sir William Vaughan in North Wales.

1646

January	With Chester effectively cut off, Byron enters into negotiations for the surrender of the city.
February	Garrison of Chester capitulates.

Introduction

Drawing on a range of contemporary sources – a number of which have neither been studied nor published before – this book aims to provide a focused study of the military operations, organisation, leadership, pay and equipping of the Cheshire army of Parliament between the autumn of 1642 and spring of 1646. Thus, there is no intention to offer a standard 'battle book' (that is, one largely describing campaigns and battles). Although the first three chapters provide a necessary overview of the somewhat broad military campaigns, and the regional and more widespread strategy of the Civil War as it effected Sir William Brereton's army, the book concentrates on the leadership, context and nature of the regiments under his overall command, whilst casting light upon the composition, supply, clothing, financing and effectiveness of what would rapidly become a seasoned and important fighting force, albeit mainly on a local or regional stage. Such important aspects are covered in some detail in subsequent chapters. The aim is to add significantly to our knowledge of the Parliamentarian war effort and Civil War forces in the North West and beyond, whilst locating the Cheshire army in its wider military and strategic context. The approach taken here offsets the more traditional view of military historians of the English Civil Wars that they were a national conflict, and the contention that considerations of counties and regions 'has led to an exaggeration of the view that the war was nothing more than a disconnected series of petty local struggles'.[1]

Works, such as Ronald Hutton's *Royalist War Effort*, Roy Sherwood's *The Civil War in the Midlands*, Brian Stone's *Derbyshire in the Civil War*, Malcolm Gratton's *The Parliamentarian and Royalist War Effort in Lancashire* and Jonathan Worton's *To Settle the Crown: Waging Civil War in Shropshire* offer commendable studies of the war effort of both sides in a county or regional context, whilst illustrating the potential of differing, yet complimentary approaches to common issues.[2] Moreover, the early modern sense of 'locality'

1 A.H. Burne and P. Young, *The Great Civil War: A Military History of the First Civil War 1642–1646* (London: Eyre & Spottiswoode, 1959), pp.xi–xii.

2 Ronald Hutton, *The Royalist War Effort, 1642–46* (Upper Saddle River, NJ: Prentice Hall Press, 1984); Roy Sherwood, *The Civil War in the Midlands 1642–1651* (Stroud: Sutton, 1992 edn); Brian Stone, *Derbyshire in the Civil War* (Matlock: Scarthin Books, 1992); J.M. Gratton, *The Parliamentarian and Royalist War Effort in Lancashire 1642–1651* (Manchester: CS, 2010);

or 'regionalism' depended to a great extent on the county, although as R.N. Dore and Clive Holmes suggest, the notion of 'country' did not always refer to county but sometimes to smaller and/or more less defined areas in the locality.[3] Few attempts have been made so far, to reconstruct the composition and organisation of provincial Parliamentarian armies, even though, in comparison to their Royalist counterparts, sources are relatively forthcoming and potentially provide a rich seam of material for research. Similarly, Holmes's in-depth *The Eastern Association in the English Civil War* provides something of a model for this approach, while Tony Brighton's exploration of the Parliamentarian and Royalist regiments raised in Derbyshire, and Gratton's work on Lancashire utilised untapped manuscript sources from local and central archives.[4]

The value of studying provincial armies is clear – in the case of Cheshire, the strengths and compositions of regiments, individual troops, companies and other sub-units are contained in a range of sources, including muster rolls, financial accounts and the correspondence of Brereton and others. Crucially also, the analysis of such material serves to identify a greater number of Parliamentarian officers holding more junior commands, as well as non-commissioned officers and in some instances, common soldiers. Even though the sources have their limitations in that entries are sometimes patchy and occasionally inaccurate or contradictory, and there remain inherent problems of identification, the potential of such research and analysis is considerable. With this in mind, in his study of the origins and careers of Royalist officers in Lancashire P.R. Newman asserts:

> The simple counting of names is pointless: the officers must be identified, given verifiable social status or whatever, for any analysis to have meaning ... It is not enough to accept the existence of rival armies, historians are obliged to treat the personnel of those armies with as much careful scrutiny as is devoted, for example, to membership of the Long Parliament or to the courtiers of Charles I and his queen.[5]

Geographically small and of modest prosperity, the county of Cheshire during the first half of the seventeenth century boasted a population of about 75–85,000. Considerable enclosure of woodland, heath and waste had changed the agricultural landscape, although cattle farming (above all, the production of cheese, but also leather goods) and salt remained historically important industries. However, lack of internal water communication

Jonathan Worton, *To Settle the Crown: Waging Civil War in Shropshire, 1642–1648* (Solihull: Helion & Co., 2016).

3 *BLB*, I, p.15; Clive Holmes, 'The County Community in Stuart Historiography', *JBS*, 19(2) (1980), pp.54–73.

4 Clive, Holmes, *The Eastern Association in the English Civil War* (Cambridge: Cambridge University Press, 2008); T.J. Brighton, *Royalists and Roundheads in Derbyshire* (Bakewell: Bakewell and District Historical Society, 1981); Gratton, *Parliamentarian and Royalist War Effort in Lancashire*.

5 P.R. Newman, 'Aspects of the Civil War in Lancashire', *TLCAS*, 82 (1983), pp.113–120 (pp.115–16).

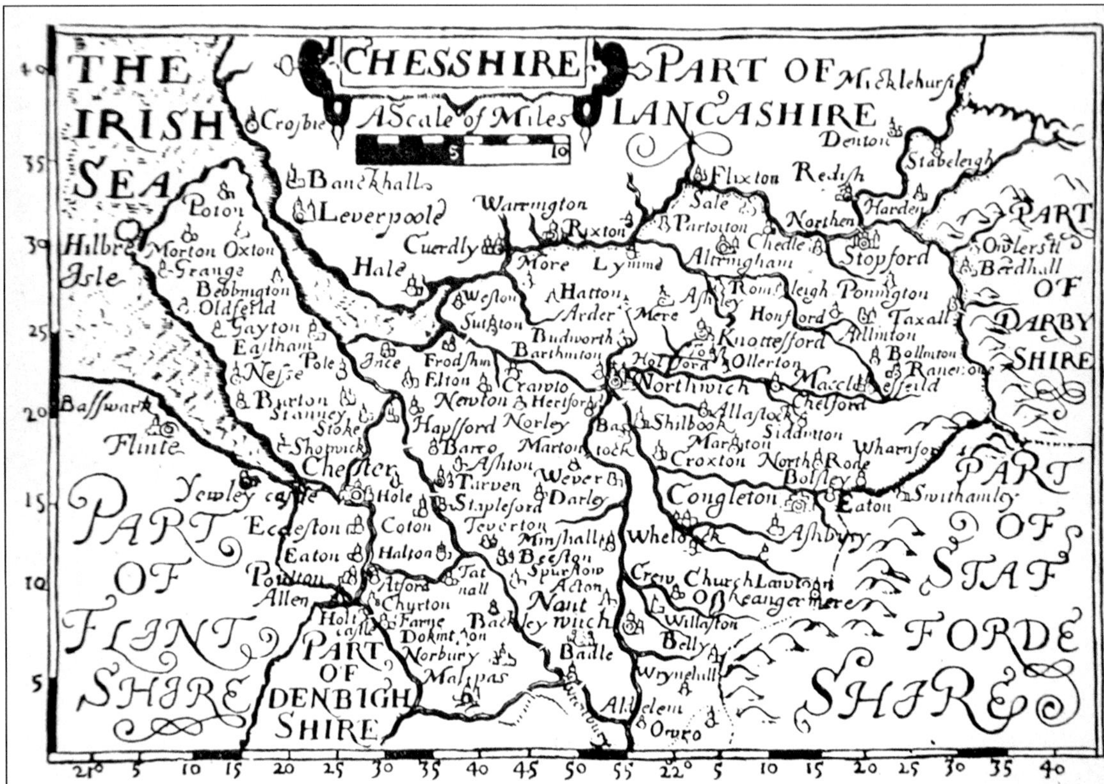

Contemporary map of seventeenth-century Cheshire. John Bill, *The Abridgement of Camden's Britannia* (1626).

restricted Cheshire and its neighbour, Lancashire – the Dee was not navigable above Chester, whereas the Weaver above Frodsham and the Mersey past Runcorn could be used for transporting goods. In terms of national affairs, Chester was the only town in the North West considered important in terms of its size and proximity to Ireland. The second town in the county in terms of size and importance was Nantwich. Crucially, Cheshire was a seaboard county, although the silting of the Dee had begun to affect Chester as far back of the fourteenth century. In the meantime by the 1640s the port of Liverpool had begun to capture much of the trade with Ireland, although it was yet to rival Cheshire in importance.

The early modern period witnessed a development of population and industry in north-east Cheshire. A flourishing textile industry centred on Stockport had important links to Manchester, while the market towns of Knutsford, Congleton, Middlewich and Northwich increased the mercantile prosperity of the region. With this went a particular level of religious and educational distinction. Puritanism, which reached many commercial hubs, had been encouraged as a counterbalance to papist west Lancashire.[6] Burgeoning educational standards for sons of the local gentry and growing middling classes resulted in the foundation of grammar schools in Stockport

6 Dorothy Sylvester and Geoffrey Nulty, *The Historical Atlas of Cheshire* (Chester: Cheshire Community Council, 1958), pp.36–8; Norman Lowe, *The Lancashire Textile Industry in the Sixteenth Century*, CS, 20, Third Series (Manchester, 1972), pp.1–3.

and Macclesfield, and of Brasenose College, Oxford, which had specific provisions for students from northern Cheshire and southern Lancashire. All of these features were relevant to the course of the Civil War in the county and the nature of the fighting there.

The Civil War in Cheshire – and some of the military aspects of its associated campaigns and sieges – have received the varied attention of historians.[7] Particular credit must be given, however, to Norman Dore, whose enthusiasm and erudition placed Civil War Cheshire under the microscope of modern scholarship from the mid 1960s onwards. His groundbreaking *The Civil Wars in Cheshire* (1966), two-volume *The Letter Books of Sir William Brereton* (1984, 1990) and a string of journal articles remain a model of scholarship. Significant works on warfare and commanders in Cheshire from a more Royalist perspective are welcomed. The Cheshire army of Parliament is well served by contemporary sources, many of which have received little attention or have remained unknown to researchers. Perhaps the most important are the various military documents among the State Papers in The National Archives (principally SP28), as well as the copious (yet incomplete) financial accounts of sequestration committees and army officers in the British Library (mainly MS Harley series). Moreover, various documents, such as depositions, petitions, commonplace books and Quarter Sessions records exist in county and other repositories, both in the north-west of England and further afield.

The five surviving letter books of Sir William Brereton – in chronological order, Cheshire Archives, DDX/428; BL, MS Add. 11331–3; and Birmingham City Archives, MS 595611 – cover roughly the periods February–April 1645, April–May 1645, October–December 1645, and December 1645–January 1646 respectively, while the last volume spans April–May 1646. Whilst the gaps pose a number of chronological and continuity problems, and MS 595611 covers the period when Brereton was conducting a campaign in the midlands, the scope of MS Add. 11332–3 is undoubtedly narrower than the rest in that it is focused on the siege of Chester itself. The letter books remain invaluable to our understanding of the scope, and day-to-day operations of Sir William and the forces under his command, while shedding further light on his relationship with his military and civilian colleagues, as well as his political masters. The analysis of a range of sources allows for a detailed reconstruction of the composition, strength and nature of the army as a whole, as well as its various fighting units and supporting elements. However, although the letter books have been reproduced in calendared form, the majority of other material pertaining to Cheshire remains unpublished.[8]

---

7 See in particular, J.R. Phillips, *Memoirs of the Civil War in Wales and the Marches, 1642–1649*, 2 vols (London: Longmans, 1874); P.H. Lawson (ed.), R.H. Morris, *The Siege of Chester, 1643–1646*, ed. P.H. Lawson (Chester: G.R. Griffith, 1924); John Morrill, 'Sir William Brereton and England's Wars of Religion', *JBS*, 24:3 (1985), pp.311–32; John Barratt, *The Battle of Nantwich 1644* (Bristol: Stuart Press, 1993); *The Great Siege of Chester* (Stroud: Tempus, 2003); Peter Gaunt, 'The Parliamentary War Effort in Cheshire', *CH*, 32 (1993), pp.6–14.

8 R.N. Dore (ed.), *The Letter Books of Sir William Brereton*, 2 vols, RSLC, 123, 128 (1984, 1990); Ivor Carr and Ian Atherton (eds), *The Civil War in Staffordshire in the Spring of 1646: Sir William Brereton's Letter Book, April–May 1646*, Collections for a History of Staffordshire,

Although the National Archives material has received the attention of some historians, it presents an invaluable, if largely unexploited source for the centralised pay, equipping and composition of the Parliamentarian armed forces of Cheshire. Equally, although John Morrill made sterling use of some of the Harley material in his authoritative *Cheshire 1630–1660* (1974), as did Malcolm Wanklyn in going some way in understanding the wider aspects of Brereton's relationship with other county organisations and the social origins of the Parliamentarian regiments in Cheshire in his doctoral thesis, 'Landed Society and Allegiance in Cheshire and Shropshire in the First Civil War' (1976). Yet the scope of their work did not allow for a broader study of this crucial material, which provides a valuable insight into the financing, supply and maintenance of the army in a local context, in addition to a glimpse into the relationship between military units and often overworked Parliamentarian officials in Civil War Cheshire. A number of contemporary narratives of the war in Cheshire are especially informative, as are various newsbooks, and published London-based reports of campaigns and sieges.[9] Of a somewhat different and more local complexion, the private collection of unlisted warrants and receipts, dating to between 1643 and 1645 from the Aston Archive, has been studied and published for the first time. This invaluable material not only provides a wealth of military and financial information, but offers a unique snapshot of the relationship between Parliamentarian forces and local constables in microcosm.

As a 'provincial' or 'regional' force, Sir William Brereton's army was not only engaged in the siege and capture of the city of Chester (described by Nathaniel Lancaster as 'the key to Ireland'), but carried out the war aims of the Parliament in its own county, as well as a wide range of areas across the North West, Midlands and Welsh borders. Yet by its very nature, his regiments and sub-units – sometimes brigaded with others – operated in a much wider strategic and geographical context, and also in conjunction when required, with Parliamentarian troops from other commands. Although the Cheshire army of Parliament was not called upon to participate in major engagements on the scale of Edgehill or Marston Moor, it nevertheless fought in a number of sizeable and regionally important hard-fought battles, including Nantwich, Montgomery and Rowton Heath, in addition to various lesser actions and sieges in many theatres of war. Cheshire and the North West were no backwaters during the First Civil War, and on occasion Brereton's forces became embroiled in events of a more national complexion, such as the landing of the Royalist army from Ireland in late 1643, the advance of Prince Rupert through the Welsh borders, Cheshire and Lancashire during the summer of 1644, and the shadowing of the Royalist Oxford Army during the Naseby campaign of 1645. Led predominantly by experienced and

Fourth Series, 21 (SRS, 2007); Joseph McKenna (ed.), *A Journal of the English Civil War: The Letter Book of Sir William Brereton, Spring 1646* (Jefferson, NC: McFarland and Co., 2012).

9 John Lewis (ed.), *The Siege of Chester: Nathaniel Lancaster's Narrative* (Nottingham: Raider Books, 1987); James Hall (ed.), *Memorials of the Civil War in Cheshire and the adjacent counties by Thomas Malbon, of Nantwich, Gent., and Providence improved by Edward Burghall*, LCRS, 19 (1889); James Atkinson, *Tracts Relating to the Civil War in Cheshire, 1641–1659* (Manchester: CS, 1909).

talented officers, it quickly became an experienced, flexible and resilient fighting force which drew the admiration of allies and enemies alike.

Sir William Brereton, commander-in-chief of the Parliamentarian forces in Cheshire (1601–64). John Vicars, *England's Worthies, Under Whom all the Civill and Bloody Warres since Anno 1642, to Anno 1647, are related* (London, 1647).

Sir William Brereton (1604–61) was the eldest son of William Brereton of Handforth, Cheshire and Margaret, daughter and co-heiress of Richard Holland of Denton, Lancashire. He matriculated at Brasenose, Oxford in 1621 and was a student of Gray's Inn in 1623. It is probable that William owned around 3,000 acres and that his annual income approached £1,000. On 10 March 1627 he was created a baronet, and during the 1630s served as a local magistrate. At this time he also toured Scotland, Ireland, the United Provinces, the Spanish Netherlands and France. Brereton also became a member of the Massachusetts Bay Company and built a commercial duck decoy on his property at Saltney Marshes. The diary he kept of his travels affords interesting information regarding the social condition of Scotland and England, but also reveals his developing religious outlook. His natural leaning towards puritanism was probably further confirmed by his marriage to Susanna, fourth daughter of Sir George Booth of Dunham Massey, and by association with his near neighbours, Robert Duckenfield and Henry Bradshaw. According to Clarendon, he was 'most considerable for a known averseness to the government of the Church'.[10] Sir William was elected MP for Cheshire in 1628–9 and 1640–53. In 1640–1 he entered into a pamphlet and petition war with Sir Thomas Aston (his later Civil War adversary) over the nature of the Established Church.

As war approached Brereton put himself at the head of the Parliamentarian movement in Cheshire. In August 1642 the Houses of Parliament drew up instructions to him as one of the deputy lieutenants of the county, and subsequently he was appointed commander-in-chief of the Cheshire army of Parliament from March 1643 onwards, and had this extended to the command of the wider forces of the Leaguer of Chester from March to May 1645, and October 1645 to February 1646. Between May and October 1645 he temporarily surrendered his military commands under the terms of the Self-Denying Ordinance. Brereton was also commissioned captain of a troop of harquebusiers, and colonel of regiments of horse, foot and dragoons. As a war leader Sir William Brereton was devout, energetic and strategically astute, and remains one of Parliament's most underrated military commanders. Although he may not have possessed the flair of Sir Thomas Fairfax, he was highly respected and trusted by his men, and well-regarded by most of the civilian population from whom he obtained much advantage from their readiness to supply him with intelligence. Brereton's greatness as a soldier was his ability for strategy, organisation, the ability to interpret intelligence and to select (and place his confidence in) the professional expertise of subordinates

10 Edward, Earl of Clarendon, *The History of the Rebellion and Civil Wars in England* (Oxford: Clarendon Press, 1888), vi, p.270.

of the calibre of James Lothian and Michael Jones. He also had a hand in choosing some of his native officers – men like Robert Venables, William Massey and Gilbert Gerard revealed themselves as highly competent field commanders.

Although his initial victory in Cheshire was tempered with a slice of luck, Brereton had the tactical and strategic awareness to capitalise on both this, and the subsequent success at Middlewich to engage in mutual operations with his Parliamentarian allies. Sir William's biographer has observed, 'He waged an aggressive and relentless war throughout the north Midlands. At different times he took his troops into each of the seven counties that are contiguous with Cheshire and led joint operations with local commanders there'.[11] During all of this he worked tirelessly in securing recruits, and lobbying Westminster for money and supplies for the Cheshire forces. If Brereton was never in a position to undertake grand strategic designs, the abundant documentation of the war in the North West illustrates that he continuously exercised strategic options and organised his troops skilfully to meet the constantly fluctuating circumstances of local warfare. Despite the view that most 'secondary' campaigns during the war showed 'as little co-ordinated purpose as ducks on a pond', the day-to-day record of military operations during the siege of Chester shows in the words of Dore, that 'this was emphatically not so where Brereton was in command. He knew very well what he was doing and why he was doing it'.[12]

Lastly, in considering Sir William Brereton's military record it would be very misleading to see him predominantly as a methodical, desk-bound administrator who existed far from the heat of combat. Such a notion has led some writers to suggest that he lacked courage on the battlefield. Most recently Barratt contends that 'Brereton was better as an administrator than a field commander, facing persistent if unproven accusations of personal cowardice'.[13] The jibe of Lord Byron that Brereton 'never greatly loved' danger may have some truth, but he never promoted himself as a hard-fighting soldier. Moreover, Byron's account of Sir William's actions in May 1645 when he greatly endangered his own troops on the Welsh side of the Chester leaguer by prolonging the siege of Hawarden until Rupert's forces were on the borders of Cheshire before withdrawing, is a gross misrepresentation.[14] Byron himself was a ruthless commander who gloried in war, and on more than one occasion shifted the blame for defeat onto the shoulders of others, notably his own Anglo-Irish soldiers at Nantwich.

Furthermore, Sir John Meldrum's somewhat uncharitable remark that during the Battle of Montgomery Brereton had spent time 'standing by the cannon whilst others were in a fight, at a very far distance from any danger',

11 John Morrill, 'Brereton, Sir William, first Baronet (1604–61)', *ODNB*, 7, pp.471–3.

12 Ivan Roots, *The Great Rebellion: A Short History of the English Civil War and Interregnum 1642–60* (London: The History Press, new edn, 2009), p.75; *BLB*, II, p.51.

13 John Barratt, *The Last Army: The Battle of Stow-on-the-Wold and the end of the Civil War in the Welsh Marches, 1646* (Solihull: Helion & Co., 2018), p.27.

14 Lord Byron, 'Account of the Siege of Chester', Rawlinson MS 210 in Bodleian Library, reprinted as 'John Byron's Account of the Siege of Chester 1645–1646', *CS*, 4th series, 6 (1971), pp.1–25 (pp. 4–5).

probably came out of jealousy that the Cheshire commander had received too much credit for the victory.[15] Sir William more likely had over-seen the late deployment of the Parliamentarian guns during the crucial point in the battle, as the Royalist foot disintegrated when confronted with a comprehensive counter-attack. Besides, Meldrum later reported that 'The personal carriage and endeavours of Sir William Brereton and Sir Thomas Myddelton hath been exceeding great in the advancement of this service', while the conduct of the Cheshire foot was praised by each of the Parliamentarian commanders.[16] Evidence shows that as the siege of Chester intensified Brereton spent increasing periods at Tarvin, his army's forward base on the English side of the Dee, and Dodleston, the new base on the Welsh side. When he returned from Westminster in October 1645 he was for most of his time at the new forward headquarters in the eastern suburbs, within close proximity to the city walls.

15 *CSPD 1644–5*, pp.5–6; Worton, *Montgomery*, p.90.

16 *Letters from Sir William Brereton, Sir Thomas Myddelton, Sir John Meldrum, of the Great Victory (by God's providence), given them in raising the siege from before Montgomery Castle* (London: 18 September 1644); Phillips, *Memoirs*, II, p.206.

Part I

Military Operations of the Cheshire Army of Parliament

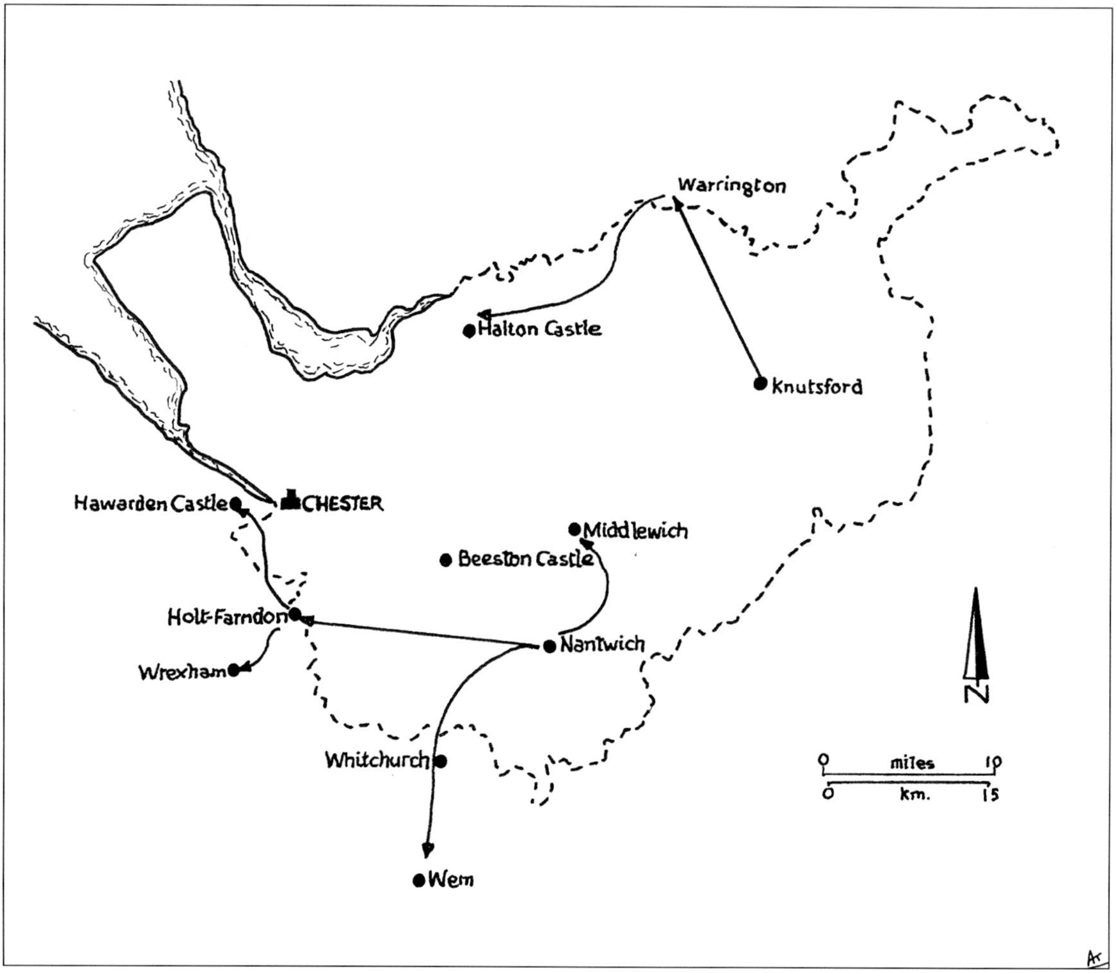

Map 1 Parliamentarian Military Operations in Cheshire and on its borders 1642, 1643.

1

'Some old soldiers for sergeants would do wonderous well': Autumn 1642–December 1643

Sir William Brereton's arrival in Cheshire on or about 25 January 1643 in command of two troops of horse, his own company of foot (consisting of 180–200 men) and three companies of dragoons brought about the first phase of military operations in the county, and established Parliamentarian control over most it. In July 1642 a general assembly of Chester citizens had declared their opposition to the impending war, while on 8 August Brereton and Alderman Edwards attempted to recruit for Parliament in the city. A 'great tumult' ensued, causing the mayor to call the citizens to arms. Sir William was arrested in accordance with the commission of array, but allowed to leave, although his supporters were imprisoned.[1] Popular enthusiasm in Chester was indifferent towards either side, although on 6 September levies were raised for the repair of gates and walls, while during a flying visit on 23 September Charles I was greeted with great ceremony and escorted into the city by musketeers of the trained bands. On 6 December 1642 the assembly decided to band together in a mutual association for the protection of the city. Following his expulsion from Chester Sir William Brereton went to London. There he was created commander-in-chief of Parliamentarian forces of Cheshire, while he recruited men and raised finance for the purchase of arms, equipment and horses. At Westminster Brereton was backed by Sir Henry Vane the younger and Oliver St John, the leaders at this time of the party demanding decisive military action. His most important contact, however, was William Ashurst, MP for Newton in Lancashire, who acted as Brereton's agent throughout the First Civil War.

The Parliamentarian army for Cheshire would be equipped initially for the most part from the pockets of the captains of its various troops and companies, although some grants were obtained from Parliament. Captain John Bramhall's initial outlay in pay for his officers and soldiers expended in

1 Randle Holme's Account (BL, MS Harley 2155), reprinted in Rupert H. Morris, *The Siege of Chester, 1643–1646*, ed. P.H. Lawson (Chester, 1923), p.215.

London and on the march northwards amounted to £53 15s.[2] On 3 December 1642 it was ordered that 400 muskets and 300 firelocks were procured, 'to be employed for the safety of the county of Chester', and that Sir William Brereton should 'have liberty to raise 300 horses in the several counties where they shall be brought in voluntarily, upon Propositions'.[3] In November 1642 Sir William Brereton's troop and Bramhall's dragoons participated in the skirmish at Brentford and the defence of the city.[4] Although their role was probably limited it provided an opportunity for newly recruited officers and soldiers to experience combat. Brereton left for Cheshire around 4 January 1643. Five days later the deputy lieutenants of the county (of which he was one) received instructions from Parliament to take command of the militia and put the county on a war footing:

> fight with, kill, and slay, all such as shall by force oppose you, or any of you, in the execution of this or any other order or ordinance of both Houses of Parliament, and all other their assistants, aiders, and abettors; and you, or any one or more of you, shall levy such other forces of horse and foot; as his excellency the Earl of *Essex* shall by his commission give you power to levy, under such colonels, commanders, and other officers, as shall be by him appointed or directed; and you shall pursue the said traitors and rebels, and their adherents, in the said county of *Chester*, or in any other places or counties of the kingdom into which they shall retire themselves; and you shall defend and protect His Majesty's good subjects from violence and oppression, by the illegal commission of array or otherwise; and you shall hinder and forbid the execution of that illegal commission, and, in all places, to the utmost of your power, endeavor to restore and preserve the peace of the kingdom.[5]

Such measures effectively strangled the Bunbury peace agreement. The strategic situation in north-west England was somewhat fluid during the autumn and winter of 1642–3. Lancashire, Shropshire and Staffordshire looked divided and uncertain, although Manchester (the 'London of the north') had been garrisoned for Parliament and came under attack from Lancashire forces under Lord Derby in September 1642. Furthermore, the Lancashire town of Warrington, an important hub of communications on the road from London and northwards towards Preston and Lancaster, and commanding one of only two major crossings over the Mersey, had been guarded by the Royalists since the previous autumn.[6] In Cheshire, areas of Royalist and Parliamentarian support were overshadowed by an amount of apathy and neutralism, although this was about to change as the county was rapidly brought into the conflict. Whilst quartered at Derby in mid January 1643 Sir William Brereton received a request from Sir John Gell and Lord Grey

---

2 BL, MS Harley 2128, fols 20r.–21r.

3 *CJ*, II, p.874.

4 BL, MS Add. 11332, fol. 43r.; *BLB*, II, 809.

5 *LJ*, V, pp.535, 538–41.

6 Malcolm Gratton, 'The Earl of Derby's Catholic Army', *THSLC*, 137 (1988), pp.25–54; Ronald Hutton, 'The Failure of the Lancashire Cavaliers', *THSLC*, 129 (1980), pp.47–57.

King Charles I (1600–49). Cornelis van Dalen, *Ruiterportret van Karel I, Konig van Engeland* (1626–65). (Amsterdam, Rijksmuseum, CC0 1.0 Universal (CC0 1.0) Public Domain Dedication)

to join the Derbyshire forces in attacking Ashby-de-la-Zouch. On 17 January Brereton's own troop (part of a greater force of about 2,000 men) forced the Royalists from the town's outer defences towards the castle and fortified church. However, the intended siege was abandoned when a report arrived that Prince Rupert was marching from Banbury towards Leicestershire with substantial forces.[7] It is likely that Brereton's freedom from the spectre of a potentially time-consuming siege and temporary subjection to Grey's command came as a relief. The Cheshire forces departed from Derby (during bitter, snowy weather), marching north-west via Ashbourne and Leek, where they disrupted a rendezvous ordered by Thomas Comberford, the newly installed Royalist governor of Stafford.

At Oxford on 19 January 1643 Charles I appointed Sir Thomas Aston as major general with orders to take his cavalry regiment to Shropshire, where he was to raise forces of horse and foot with the intention of safeguarding Cheshire against the Parliamentarian force heading to the county under the command of Sir William Brereton. He was instructed to seize arms and ammunition for the King's use, and 'put into execution the laws and customs martial upon all offenders ... for the better preventing of disorders, plunderings and outrages which are often committed by soldiers'.[8] The Cheshire commissioners of array received explicit orders to assist Aston with all means necessary. When Sir William Brereton arrived in the Cheshire town of Congleton on 25 January the governor of Chester ordered the defence of the city with about 1,000 Welsh foot. Brereton was joined by three newly raised troops of horse and some infantry companies recruited in the eastern part of the county by Robert Duckenfield. The Cheshire foot was led by the Scottish professional, Sergeant Major James Lothian, whose experience and skill would quickly be utilised.

---

7 DRO, D803/MZ9, fol. 52r.; *Mercurius Aulicus, 21 January 1643;*HMC, *Fifteenth Report*, II, p.88; Eliot Warburton, *Memoirs of Prince Rupert, and the Cavaliers* (London: S. & J. Bentley and Henry Fley, 1849), II, p.96.

8 BL, MS Add. 36913, fols 105r.–14v.

In a letter to the Committee of Accounts on 3 November 1645 Brereton claimed pay from the date of his earliest commissions and mentioned the activities of his initial forces:

> I understand by my servant whom I left to wait upon you that you should make scruple of admitting pay from the date of the commissions. Wherein I desire not to be mistaken for it is no part of my expectation or desire to insist upon the demand of pay any other ways as is by the rule and appointment of Parliament allowed unto others that serve them. To this end I thought good to give you this further information. The first time I was out with my troop upon service was at Brentford. The certainty of the time I cannot now remember but you may easily call to mind by that eminent business at Brentford. As for my foot regiment I had my field officers and divers captains before the date of my commission. So had I also my own company consisting near of nine score or two hundred divers months before the date of my commission, before which time as also before my coming down, they did perform good service. I also raised and took down with me in December these companies of dragoons: Captain Bramhall, Captain Goldegay and Captain Lea which, together with my horse and all the force with me, were put upon service by the way and the first night after we came into Cheshire. It is true that my regiment of foot was not completed until my coming down into the country. It is as true I had a good regiment of horse a full twelvemonth before I had my commission for that regiment. All which I willingly submit unto the constant rule whereby you are guided in the accounts of others. I shall desire no more than not to be mistaken nor misunderstood as though I made any demand from any time certain but only computed what was the pay from the date of the commissions, if by the state it ought to be allowed. And now that I have truly informed you, I refer to yourselves to state the account from which time as you think fit.[9]

During the early months of 1643 the Cheshire Parliamentarians set about establishing a strong foothold in the county. They largely out-manoeuvred and out-fought their enemy during a series of operations, beginning with a confused dusk action at Nantwich on 28 January. Brereton despatched a party of horse and dragoons to secure the town ahead of Aston, who was commanding his own cavalry and Corbet's inexperienced Shropshire dragoons. The Royalists panicked and fled when the Parliamentarian soldiers discharged two small field guns. Clearing a lane of Aston's troops, 'Captain Goldegay dismounted his dragooners, and turned his horses upon them, which brought them into confusion, and charged upon them very sore'.[10] Goldegay was wounded, and his lieutenant and two soldiers were killed. Showing their inexperience, the dragoons neglected to leave anyone to hold their mounts – which fortuitously were taken by the Royalists for charging cavalry. It was a sound beginning that enabled Brereton to establish Nantwich as his base of operations. Nantwich was the second town in Cheshire in size

---

9 BL, MS Add. 11332, fol. 43r.; *BLB*, II, 809.

10 *Cheshire's Successe since their pious and truly valiant Colonel, Sir William Brereton, Baronet, came to their rescue, &c.* (London, 20 March 1643); Malbon, p.20; Phillips, *Memoirs*, II, pp.49–51.

and importance, and a far better communications centre than its only rival, Macclesfield. As Chester was firmly in Royalist possession, Nantwich was the only viable alternative as a permanent headquarters. Brereton's decision to safeguard the town led to the establishment of Parliamentarian control over the majority of the county, except for Chester, and the western hundreds of Broxton and Wirral.

Previously raised units and new recruits continued to add to the build-up of the Cheshire army of Parliament. Malbon reports that on 30 January 'Mr Mainwaring and other great forces armed, came in aid of the town [of Nantwich] to Sir William Brereton. And the next week following came unto him also at Nantwich Captain Duckenfield, Captain Hyde, Captain Marbury and many other captains, and commanders with a good number of both horse and foot'.[11] By the end of spring the Cheshire forces would number about 2,000 men. On 10 February 1643 Brereton wrote to a London contact, Captain Francis Rowe:

> We have near upon five troops of horse in this county, but because they are independent troops and not subjected to command it was and is my desire that there may be a major sent down, and honest and conscionable man. We are much disadvantaged for want of such an officer, who is able to order a regiment of horse and if you please to send me a commission to command them I shall be thereby enabled the better to serve you and shall expect no increase of pay ... I am much weakened for by reason of the thronging in of foreign forces out of Shropshire and Wales, and Lancashire, the Earl of Derby being now at Chester and making his strongest design for Chester, and the Manchester forces not attempting to divert him, we must be constrained to raise another regiment, and therefore we could much desire some more commanders, otherwise for want of more forces the country will be in danger to be overrun and our forces disabled ... Take care I pray that there may be a major to order a regiment of horse with some officers of foot sent down, for we have a great need of them, a lieutenant-colonel and sergeant major of foot and some lieutenants of foot ... some old soldiers for sergeants would do wonderous well.[12]

In a broader sense, Sir William sought military assistance from his allies in the Welsh marches. During February 1643 he petitioned Parliament to urge Sir John Corbet and Sir Thomas Myddelton to raise forces, and advance into Shropshire and Denbighshire respectively.[13] Brereton further expected to procure recruits from these areas. In May 1643 Colonel Thomas Mytton was commissioned by the Earl of Essex to raise regiments of horse, foot and dragoons – these, and others commanded by the Earl of Denbigh were established in London and departed from the capital in late August. Similarly, Myddelton was appointed major general of North Wales, and recruited a small infantry regiment and a few troops of horse in the south-east. These constituted the 'great force' that reached Nantwich in August 1643. As the

11 Malbon, pp.36–7.

12 HMC, *Portland*, I, pp.94–5.

13 HMC, *Thirteenth Report, App. I*, pp.94–6; *CJ*, III, p.155.

events of the summer would show, Sir William Brereton could rely on some Shropshire and Denbighshire forces, which combined with his Cheshire troops, would represent an experienced and flexible power in the region. Following the action at Nantwich Brereton and the deputy lieutenants issued warrants, summoning men between the ages of sixteen and 60 to attend musters at Tarporley and Frodsham on 21 February. The commissioners of array in Chester responded by ordering troops under Sir Thomas Aston to march through winter snows and quagmire roads to intercept Brereton en route to Tarporley. Save for a brief exchange of musketry and a mounted clash near Beeston and Tiverton, 'both sides retreated without any more harm doing, the one party to Chester, and the other to Nantwich where they continued that week until they had fortified all the town round about with strong trenches, and mud walls of clods of earth'.[14]

However, Brereton's attempts at recruiting were stymied for the present. The previous day (20 February) the Parliamentarian forces garrisoned Beeston Castle with between 200 and 300 men under Captain Steele. Sir William 'caused the breaches to be made up with mud walls, the well of the outer ward to be cleansed, and a few rooms erected'.[15] Brereton was now in a position to consolidate his grip on central and eastern Cheshire. On 25 February 1643 he led a combined force of horse and foot, numbering 500 men to Knutsford and the market town of Northwich, which were garrisoned for Parliament. These garrisons had recently been formed at Northwich with volunteers from the hundreds of Northwich, Bucklow and Eddisbury. Captain (later Lieutenant Colonel) Gilbert Gerard received a commission to raise a company on 14 February 1643 and was appointed governor of Northwich on 1 March, whilst defensive earthworks were constructed about both towns.[16] Eleven miles to the north-west, Norton House, the home of Henry Brooke, had come under siege from Royalist forces under Earl Rivers. The Brookes were the only major Parliamentarian supporters in upper Bucklow Hundred by early 1643, being direct neighbours of Rivers and Aston, both of whom raised forces for Charles I during the early months of the war, but had lately been ordered back to Cheshire from the King's Oxford Army. During the previous November Rivers had garrisoned Rocksavage and Halton (the latter under Captain Primrose), and going by Parliamentarian reports, plundered and intimidated Brooke's tenants.[17]

The Norton garrison (consisting of members of the Brooke family, but probably not Henry himself, who is likely to have been with the county committee at Nantwich) contained 80 men drawn from among his supporters and estate tenants. It was prepared for defence with a good stock of ammunition and provisions, although its chief strength was probably the recently constructed defensive works that augmented the pre-existing system of moats and ponds of the former monastic site. During the days preceding

14 Malbon, p. 38.

15 R.N. Dore, 'Beeston Castle in the Great Civil War, 1643–46', *TLCAS*, 75–6 (1965–6), pp.103–22 (p.104).

16 TNA, SP28/152/4, unfol.; SP28/208, fols 33v.–4r.

17 CRO, DCH/X/15/14.

the main Royalist assault on 28 February Rivers threatened the lady of the house, Henry's mother Katherine, while his soldiers pilfered livestock from the estate.[18] As Lancaster reported, Norton held, although afterwards the Royalists 'plundered Mr Brooke's tenants, and returned home with same and hatred of all the country'.[19] This small, yet significant victory gave the Parliamentarian war effort in Cheshire a vital boost as the garrison of Halton withdrew into the castle and Parliamentarian forces in the area (in the shape of Brooke's troop of horse and regiment of foot) continued to build up their power and isolated Royalist outposts.

On 13 March Brereton's forces inflicted a second defeat on Sir Thomas Aston at Middlewich. The Royalist commander had entered the town two days before with 500 horse and 'many companies of foot' as part of a wider incursion into central Cheshire, extending over the River Weaver. According to Parliamentarian sources Aston's men plundered Weaverham and the villages round about, although in his letter to William Ashurst, Sir William Brereton regarded the Royalist occupation of Middlewich 'of most dangerous consequence'.[20] Sir Thomas Aston's stay, in awaiting a rendezvous with Lord Brereton, was meant to be brief since he was aware of how vulnerable his troops were in an 'open' (undefended) town, in an exposed position between the Parliamentarian garrisons of Nantwich and Northwich.[21] The uncertainties and limitations of the sources for the battle (including Sir Thomas's detailed sketch plan), as well as post-Civil War redevelopments of the town and its environs have been explored in depth by Peter Gaunt in his recent appraisal of events.[22] On the evening of 11 March Brereton sent some horse from nearby Northwich. Who gave them alarm', and the next day led his cavalry and dragoons in a reconnaissance in force against the Royalist dispositions to the west of Middlewich. Cautious of launching a full attack on a well-prepared enemy, Sir William seems to have planned a two-pronged assault for the Monday morning involving attacks on the western portion of the town by troops from Northwich, while a larger body of infantry would press on from Nantwich.

With a force of 300 or so soldiers, Brereton made a number of audacious attacks across the River Dane and the rough country about it, and even though Aston claimed to have despatched successful counter-strikes with his horse, these were driven back. The Parliamentarians were, however, isolated, and as Malbon noted of this opening phase of the encounter, 'the fight continuing long between them equal'. By late morning, with the Nantwich

18 *Certaine Informations from severall parts of the Kingdome, for the satisfaction of all sorts of people that desire to be truly informed*, 8 March 1643; Malbon, pp.38–9.

19 *CWTC*, pp.24–5.

20 *Cheshire's Successe*; Malbon, pp.38–9; BL, MS Add. 34253, fols 23r.–v.

21 BL, MS Add. 36913, fols 120r.–1v.; MS Harley 2135, fols 102r.–3v.; Phillips, *Memoirs*, II, pp.56–61.

22 Peter Gaunt, '"Wedged up in the church like billets in a woodpile": New light on the battle of Middlewich, 13 March 1643', Ismini Pells (ed.), *New Approaches to the Military History of the English Civil War*, Proceedings of the First Helion and Company 'Century of the Soldier' Conference, 2015 (Solihull: Helion & Co., 2016), pp.27–56. Aston's plan is contained in BL, MS Add. 36913, fols 129v.–30r.

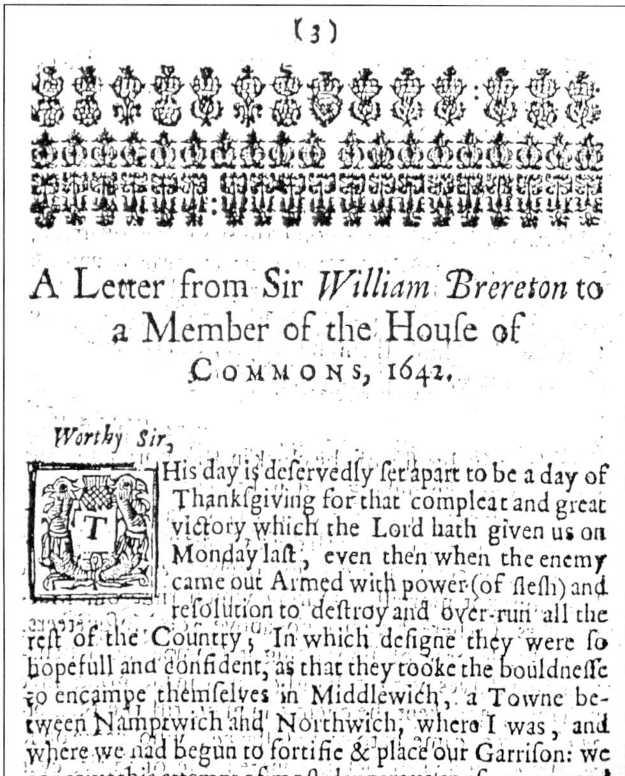

(3)

A Letter from Sir *William Brereton* to a Member of the Houſe of COMMONS, 1642.

Worthy Sir,

This day is deſervedly ſet apart to be a day of Thankſgiving for that compleat and great victory which the Lord hath given us on Monday laſt, even then when the enemy came out Armed with power (of fleſh) and reſolution to deſtroy and over-run all the reſt of the Country; In which deſigne they were ſo hopefull and confident, as that they tooke the bouldneſſe to encampe themſelves in Middlewich, a Towne between Namptwich and Northwich, where I was, and where we had begun to fortifie & place our Garriſon: we

Sir William Brereton's account of the Parliamentarian victory at Middlewich, 13 March 1643. *Two Letters of Great Consequence to the House of Commons: the one from Aylesbury in Buckinghamshire … The other from Sir William Brereton to a Member of the House of Commons, of a Great Victory he obtained the 15 of March, at a town called Middlewich.* (Author's collection)

companies yet to arrive and Brereton's powder supply dwindling (partly by accidental spillage), some of his officers advised a withdrawal, yet the author of the Nantwich-derived *Cheshire's Successe* recounted that 'Sir William was resolute not to retreat, but to send to Northwich for more powder, and to keep them in play as well as they could until the powder came, which accordingly they did'. When the Nantwich contingent of perhaps 800 foot did arrive, it immediately attacked from the south of the town. Here Aston had positioned two trained band companies, seconded by a cavalry troop, 120 musketeers lining the narrow road and a cannon, described by Malbon as 'a good brass piece of ordnance'. It was a relatively brief and confusing fight. The Parliamentarian cavalry, including Colonel George Booth's troop, stood firm against the Royalist gun as fired over their heads, and the main body of musketeers – probably 300 of them led by the experienced Sergeant Major Lothian– fought their way up Booth Lane.

Two days after the battle Brereton reported, '[they] came on so resolutely, and with such undauntedness of spirit, even to the amazement and admiration of the enemy, whom they beat from their works, and from their cannon'.[23] Aston's troops rapidly withdrew into the middle of the town. Sir Thomas's fragmented account presents a picture of orderly redeployment about the churchyard, but as Gaunt suggests, 'the reality was probably more disorganised and *ad hoc*, as chaos increasingly overtook the Royalist forces'.[24] Aston would later claim that the majority of his musketeers suffered a collapse in morale and 'all instantly forsook their stand and ran away', although (according to him) in contrast the Royalist horse stood their ground bravely.[25] The actuality of the situation was that with the Parliamentarians advancing on three sides, the Royalists disintegrated. In contrast, the Nantwich writer stressed the energy and bravery of the garrison's foot, especially 'our major (a right Scottish blade), in fighting through the streets 'upon the mouth of the cannon, and storm of the muskets'. The Royalist infantry, including a number of officers, held out in the church for about an hour, the defenders losing

23 *Two Letters of Great Consequence to the House of Commons: the one from Aylesbury in Buckinghamshire … The other from Sir William Brereton to a Member of the House of Commons, of a Great Victory he obtained the 15 of March, at a town called Middlewich* (London: 24 March 1643), p.4.

24 Gaunt, 'Wedged up in the church', p.53.

25 BL, MS Add. 36913, fols 120r.–1v.; MS Harley 2135, fols 102r.–3v.

heart and 'they cried for quarter, which was granted them'. Casualties were surprisingly light, although following Aston's escape with some of his horse, a rich cache of prisoners, including Colonel Ellis, 11 captains, six lieutenants and 'not many fewer than 500 prisoners', with copious weapons, powder and money, fell into the hands of Brereton's soldiers. Although the battle was disorderly and ultimately one-sided, it resulted in a complete Parliamentarian victory. The military and strategic impact of Sir William Brereton's triumph and the campaign overall is noted by Gaunt:

> The Battle of Middlewich of mid-March, which ended with another street fight, is best seen as the culmination of this series of events; the final, biggest and most decisive battle of this six-week campaign, which saw Brereton's Parliamentarians secure most of the county, including establishing garrisons in the newly-fortified towns of Nantwich and Northwich, and a forward base at Beeston Castle, overlooking Chester, west Cheshire and the Dee valley, which remained in Royalist hands.[26]

Brereton's attention now shifted to Staffordshire, where the local Parliamentarian forces under Lord Brooke had captured Lichfield (although he was shot through the eye and killed during attempts to storm the city on 2 March, leaving something of power vacuum in the county). From Stafford Sir William quickly despatched a letter from to Sir John Gell, in which he suggested a joint attack on Lichfield. Gell's force of around 1,500 men, including about 450 horse and 500 Derbyshire foot, rendezvoused with the Cheshire troops at Hopton Heath on 19 March 1643, with two troops of Cheshire cavalry and three dragoon companies. Sir John also had the mortar from Lichfield and assorted ordnance. Here, around 3:00 p.m., they encountered a Royalist force under the Earl of Northampton, on the march from Stafford of about 1,100 horse, a small body of foot and some artillery, including a large piece known as 'Roaring Meg'. Following and opening bombardment, during which the great cannon slayed 'six of their men and hurt four more', the Royalists attacked with horse and dragoons, the latter attempting to clear the hedges on the right flank of the Parliamentarian army. Brereton later wrote:

> These came on with great resolution and boldness, and in very good order. [He continued] there were five companies of dragoons, whereof I brought three, some of which did extraordinary good service. There were near one hundred of the dragoons slain in the place where the dragoons skirmished, and I cannot discern that we lost more than two or three. And yet they fought so long, and so fiercely, until all their powder and bullet was spent. Afterwards they joined, and fell to it pell mell, one upon another, with the stocks of their muskets. These were Captain Bramhall's men, who behaved themselves well at Brentford, and also at Middlewich, upon Monday March 13.[27]

---

26 Gaunt, 'Wedged up in the church', p.30.

27 Greenslade, M.W. and Baugh, G.C. (intro.), *The History and Antiquities of Staffordshire, by Stebbing Shaw* (East Ardsley: E.P. Publishing, 1976), I, pp.80–1.

The battlefield of Hopton Heath from the Royalist position. (Photograph courtesy of Paul Wright)

Within 15 minutes most of the Parliamentarian horse had been repulsed. Brereton reported, 'the greatest part of our horse were disordered', while Gell confirmed, 'all our horse fled except for 240 of the Lord Brooke's reformado troop, who behaved themselves very gallantly'.[28] During the charge Northampton was mortally wounded, and the second mounted assault was repelled by the musket fire of Sir John's Gell's infantry, who had been reinforced by 200 Cheshire foot following their forced march from Newcastle-under-Lyme. The Royalists decided against another attack and encamped for the night, although their losses had been around 600 killed and an unknown number wounded. While the skill and leadership of Northampton's troops undoubtedly deserves credit, the poor performance of the Parliamentarian horse at Hopton Heath could have been partly down to their imperfect deployment. Sir William Brereton complained that 'Both our horse [placed on either wing] and foot were unhappily disposed [and] divided into small bodies'. This was probably not helped by the rancour that existed between the two commanders – Brereton's report of the battle made no mention of Gell's part in it. Instead he ascribed the flight of his troopers to 'the wisdom and goodness of Divine Providence', as the Royalists were thereby encouraged to charge the foot, with disastrous consequences for themselves. However, Sir William admitted that the bodies of the enemy soldiers were stripped and plundered, and that the Earl of Northampton's remains were treated in a shameful manner.

28 DRO, D258/60/59.

Following this setback, Brereton withdrew his men to Nantwich. Keeping constantly on the move, however, his attention quickly turned to Lancashire and the Royalist-held town of Warrington. During early 1643 Royalist garrisons had been established at Preston, Wigan, Warrington and Liverpool, with smaller forces at Lathom House. They formed a network of strongholds and communication centres in south-west Lancashire. Moreover, Lord Derby was becoming more active south of the Mersey until the arrival on 9 February of Sir John Seaton, in commanded 1,600 men, who captured Wigan and Preston. The loss of Preston in particular caused Derby to launch a series of counter-attacks against his opponents. Having previously agreed a rendezvous with a force from Manchester in order to assault Warrington, Sir William Brereton's force reached Stockton Heath on the Cheshire side of the Mersey before the supporting Lancashire troops arrived. On 5 April 1643 they were caught by a party of Royalists who sallied out. According to *Mercurius Aulicus*, 'Brereton being well-beaten at the first onset, with the loss of many of his men and some of his colours, had no mind to go away till he had perfected the Earl's victory and his own overthrow, and therefore drew into the field again with the accession from some new forces from Manchester to play double or quits'.[29] Malbon added:

> Upon Monday in Easter week Captain Arderne and some other captains on the parliament's side with a reasonable company did face the town. But the earl [of Derby] perceiving their strength, but small, and neither Colonel Brereton nor Manchester men come up, issued further with great forces over the bridge into Cheshire where the said Captain Arderne and the other captains and soldiers were. The earl setting upon them with his forces slew some of them, and took other some of them prisoners, and had been likely to have slain and routed them all, had not Colonel Brereton with Manchester forces just come to their aid, which when the earl perceived (being then on Stockton Heath in Cheshire where the battle was) his lord in all haste with all his forces returned back in to Warrington with some loss of men likewise. And towards the middle of that week (greater forces came forth of Lancashire) Colonel Brereton with all their forces beset the town around, and fiercely and violently assaulted the same. And having gotten Sankey Bridges and a fair house of Mr Bridgeman's, and some of their own works, had with a small time won the town, which the earl perceiving did set the middle of the town on fire, protesting he would burn the whole town before Brereton should have it. So that the fire increasing and they perceiving his cruelty, to save the town from utter desolation, Colonel Brereton raised the siege and withdrew his forces away, after they had lain against it three days'.[30]

Parliament had appointed Sir William Brereton as 'commander-in-chief of the forces in *Cheshire*' on 25 March 1643.[31] The county had been grouped into the Northern Association under Lord Fairfax and then the West Midland Association led by the Earl of Denbigh.

29 *Mercurius Aulicus*, 8 April 1643.
30 Malbon, pp.44–5.
31 *CJ*, III, p.19.

Basil Fielding, 2nd Earl of Denbigh (*c.* 1608–75). Drawn by an unknown artist and engraved by R.S. (Richard Sawyer?), *A Series of Four Hundred and Six Historical Portraits to Illustrate Granger's Biographical History of England* (London, 1890).

Yet although the second allocation was never cancelled, with Brereton's appointment Parliament recognised that Cheshire was in a special position and that Sir William himself (particularly after his victories of spring 1643) was peculiarly well placed to undertake its own strategic aims in the wider region. Alliance with adjacent counties was a priority from the moment that Sir William arrived back in Cheshire in January 1643. He achieved this in Lancashire through his links with the Parliamentarian colonels, while the geographical positions of the two counties, with common links across the Mersey and the importance of the port of Liverpool to their fortunes in the North West, made cooperation between them a sensible policy. Thus, in the spring of 1643 Brereton was placed on the committee for both counties.

There was no time for rest, however. On 21 April Prince Rupert, advancing north following his capture of Birmingham, retook Lichfield after a siege of 11 days, and was expected to cut through the north Midlands by moving on the Parliamentarian garrisons of Coventry, Burton-on-Trent and Derby. Yet Rupert, hastily recalled by the King to counter Essex's army in the Thames Valley, was unable to exploit his position, and leaving a garrison in Burton he returned with his troops to Oxford.[32] Burton was quickly retaken by Sir John Gell, although his priority remained the security of Derbyshire and parts of the East Midlands. The importance of maintaining a strong Parliamentarian presence in north Staffordshire came within the orbit of Brereton's ambitions, and in the late summer of 1643 he oversaw the establishment of a county committee there. In typical fashion, during the early hours of 16 May he broke the stranglehold of Royalist power in the region by capturing Stafford. His own troop of horse and Captain Bramhall's dragoons, supported by companies of Staffordshire foot, 'took the town by *scalado*, with the loss of very few men on both sides, some sentinels only excepted, for the cavaliers in the town seeing themselves too desperately and suddenly surprised, had not the power to make any opposition'. Prisoners to the number of 300 were reportedly taken, besides arms and horses, and '42 were men of note and quality'.[33]

Brereton now capitalised on his success by capturing Wolverhampton, employing the same tactics he had used at Stafford, 'about three o'clock in the morning without any opposition or resistance'. Part of the booty included cannonballs and moulds which had been intended for Lichfield.[34] It had been a rapid and fruitful few weeks that achieved all its objectives, both in a military and political sense in terms of increasing Sir William's influence in the region. While elements of the Cheshire army of Parliament were engaged in Staffordshire, the Lancashire Parliamentarians besieging

32 *Certaine Informations*, 1 May 1643.

33 *Ibid.*, 18 May 1643; Malbon, pp.54–5.

34 *Antiquities of Staffordshire*, I, p.55.

the Earl of Derby's headquarters at Warrington were reinforced by further troops and the addition of six cannon. On 21 May 1643 they were joined by Brereton with 'all his horse … and some considerable forces out of Cheshire'. The Parliamentarians bombarded the town for seven days, and although the defenders held their own, they were ill-prepared for a protracted siege as supplies of ammunition and victuals were low.[35] Moreover, they learnt that Lord Goring and his forces coming to their aid had suffered a defeat at the hands of Sir Thomas Fairfax's Northern Army at Wakefield. The garrison capitulated on 27 May, *Perfect Diurnal* reporting, 'What prize they have got in the taking of Warrington is not yet informed, but it must needs be of considerable worth. Some reports they took there 14 pieces of ordnance, 1,100 prisoners and great store of arms'.[36]

The benefits gained by the capture of Stafford and Warrington were enormous. 'With the supposedly impregnable rock fortress of Beeston also in his hands,' states Dore, 'Stafford gave Brereton control of the Midland Gap, while Warrington completed the tally of the Mersey bridges, and left the Lancashire and Cheshire Royalists no links save the uncertain fords and ferries below the town.'[37] Before 15 March 1643 Arthur, Lord Capel was appointed Royalist lieutenant general of North Wales and Shropshire, and by 23 March he was in Shrewsbury to take up his command.[38] However, the area had been drained of military resources by the King's army, and Capel's attempts to press recruits and money in Flintshire and Denbighshire were far from popular. Thus, Ronald Hutton asserts that Capel 'possessed certain long-term advantages which might prove potent if he were an able leader'.[39] For a number of weeks Royalist patrols ranging from Capel's forward headquarters at Whitchurch had harassed while Brereton's forces, which by the early summer were proving formidable. Royalist soldiers pilfered livestock and goods from several villages across the Cheshire border, while on 17 May 1643, with 'a great company of cavaliers both of Whitchurch and Shropshire, and other places to the number of 1,500 or more', Lord Capel made a perfunctory attack on Nantwich.[40]

A few days later he was ordered by Rupert to go to the aid of the Royalist defenders of Warrington, but as Capel marched he was unaware that the garrison had recently fallen. Forewarned, Brereton sidestepped the Royalist commander and 'with the horse and all the foot in Nantwich' destroyed Capel's base at Whitchurch and another recently begun at Market Drayton. During the early morning of 30 May the Cheshire forces stormed Whitchurch, Malbon reporting, 'The Nantwich foot soldiers firing very fiercely upon them, and they in the town did the like, maintaining their works and town

35 Malbon, pp.54, 56–7.

36 *Perfect Diurnall*, 5 June 1643. For further accounts of the two stages of the Parliamentarian siege of Warrington, see *Exceeding Joyful News out of Lancashire* (London, 1643); *Lancashire's Valley of Achor* (London, 1643); William Beamont (ed.), Edward Robinson, *A discourse of the warr in Lancashire* (Manchester: CS, 1864), pp.31, 112–24.

37 Dore, *Civil Wars in Cheshire*, p.29.

38 *Certaine Informations*, 18 April 1643.

39 Hutton, *Royalist War Effort*, p.60.

40 Malbon, p.55; *Mercurius Aulicus*, nineteenth week 1643.

very bravely'.[41] The defenders, commanded by Sergeant Major Michael Woodhouse, were overcome and the town was seized with a substantial amount of military supplies and additional plunder. A week later Brereton's soldiers returned to remove back to Nantwich what remained, although (according to Malbon) seizing 'no man's goods but only the cavaliers'.[42] On 12 June 1643 Parliament appointed Sir Thomas Myddelton as sergeant major general and commander-in-chief of the six North Wales counties – largely a paper command – but although he brought barely a handful of troops, perhaps more importantly he had seven great pieces of ordnance, four cases of drakes, and 40 carriages of arms and ammunition.[43] These were the 'great forces' generously described by Malbon that arrived at Nantwich on 19 August.[44]

Nonetheless, because of their mutual strategic objectives, co-operation with Brereton's forces and the Shropshire Committee might bring about the Parliamentarian conquest of the county and provide a bridgehead into North Wales. Also the Earl of Denbigh was created commander-in-chief in the Midlands, although he was delayed in taking up his command by accusations of disloyalty and it would be mid November before he was exonerated. On 12 June, with Sir William Brereton in Liverpool with his own troop overseeing the delivery of a consignment of ordnance and ammunition from London, dragoons (including Bramhall's company) undertook a foraging expedition towards the Welsh border. They disrupted the market at Farndon and returned via Shocklach, where they rounded up nearly 100 cattle and a number of horses. However, acting on faulty intelligence, Brereton's and Bulkeley's troops, with 'many other troopers and dragoons', were ambushed at Hanmer in Flintshire on 20 June by local Royalist forces under Capel. A number were killed and taken prisoner, but the biggest loss was the capture of Captain-Lieutenant Zankey, of which Malbon rued, 'the worst day's work that ever Nantwich forces had from the beginning'.[45] According to *Mercurius Aulicus*, in the breeches of one of the Parliamentarian prisoners was discovered the surplice of Hanmer Church.[46]

In north-west Cheshire events also developed rapidly during mid 1643. Halton Castle, located atop a steep promontory dominating Runcorn Gap and the Mersey, was garrisoned for the King in November 1642 by a company of foot of Rivers' regiment. Savage's opponent, Henry Brooke, later complained that although the Earl was steward of Halton, he had garrisoned the stronghold without commission from the King. Furthermore, Brooke reported that Royalist soldiers had plundered his tenants 'and many of the county round about'. The deputy lieutenant Thomas Marbury also stated that, 'The said [Earl Rivers] did fortify Halton Castle and Rocksavage House, and there kept two garrisons against the Parliament, which garrisons did

41 Malbon, pp.56–60.

42 HMC, *Twelfth Report, App. IX*, pp. 39–40; Malbon, p.60.

43 *LJ*, VI, pp.90–2, 102, 80.

44 Malbon, p.71; R.N. Dore, 'Sir Thomas Myddelton's Attempted Conquest of Powys, 1644–5', *MC*, 57 (1961–2), pp.91–118 (p. 92).

45 Malbon, p.63.

46 *Mercurius Aulicus*, twenty-sixth week, 1643.

Halton Castle from the south-west. (Author's photograph)

much did much against the parliament's party. Therefore of the said earl did imprison those well affected to the parliament and did take their horses and cattle to a very great value.'[47] Due to the close proximity of Halton to Warrington (and being barely a mile from the Parliamentarian garrison of Norton) was therefore vital that the stronghold was seized. Shortly after the surrender of Warrington on 27 May the blockade of Halton Castle commenced, the *Mercurius Aulicus* reporting: 'They have now procured several pieces of ordinance from Warrington, threatening to batter the castle walls; but the captain hangs out his flag of defiance, resolving to lose his life rather than the castle [of Halton].'[48]

The Parliamentarian siege lasted about six weeks. A guard post placed opposite the castle gatehouse was reported by a Royalist source, and trenches and gun embrasures are likely to have been constructed by the besiegers, perhaps at the 'mount', positioned to the south-east. Details of the siege and its subsequent surrender are provided by contemporary accounts, including *Mercurius Aulicus*, which recounted:

47 CRO, DCH/X/15/14.
48 *Mercurius Aulicus*, 25 June 1643.

> This day it was advertised, that on Monday last Captain Walter Primrose (whom the earl Rivers appointed to keep Halton Castle in Cheshire for His Majesty) apprehending an opportunity that the rebels who had besieged the castle were gone to their old trade of plundering: the captain issued 32 of his soldiers out of the castle, fell upon the house where the rebels kept their sentries, killed one of them, the other fled; took from them 20 good muskets, their provisions of match, powder, and bullet, besides good store of victual, which they out of zeal had robbed from His Majesty's good subjects. The rebels finding that castle was relieved, which they for a month before had strongly besieged, and being enraged to see anything which concerned His Majesty undestroyed, they with fresh forces approached and faced the fort, but were so entertained by this valiant captain, that they all fled, leaving some of their friends dead on the place. On Tuesday evening they appeared again before the castle, but received better welcome than before, for the soldiers forth of the castle killed 10 of them presently, and made the rest fly; which their commanders perceiving, comforted themselves with some new plunder, which is their chief errand. They have now procured several pieces of ordinance from Warrington, threatening to batter the castle walls; but the captain hangs out his flag of defiance, resolving to lose his life rather than the castle.

The garrison surrendered on 20 July 1643. This was immediately capitalised upon by the storming of Rocksavage House, Captain (later Lieutenant Colonel) Richard Brooke claiming its goods as a prize.[49] Such gains were crucial to the Parliamentarian war effort in both a local and wider strategic context. A final end was brought to the activities in Cheshire of Earl Rivers and his troops, whilst Halton Castle in particular (which was straightaway garrisoned for Parliament), was part of a broader network of defences on the Mersey at Hale Ford and Warrington. Moreover, it enabled fortified positions to be established at Frodsham Bridge and ditch, and a ford at Dutton, and for the safeguarding of Runcorn dock (an important link in the supply chain between the port of Liverpool and the army in Cheshire). During Prince Rupert's advance through Cheshire in May 1644 Colonel Brooke placed the bulk of his regiment (and possibly his cavalry troop) in the Halton and Norton garrisons, while locally raised dragoons patrolled what was considered by the Parliamentarians as a 'safe area'.[50]

Assessing why the Cheshire and Lancashire Parliamentarian forces were so successful during the spring and summer of 1643, when in most other theatres the Royalists were carrying all before them is crucial to understanding the wider strategic situation in north-west England and the Welsh borders. The military capacity of the Royalist war effort in Cheshire had been reduced by the marching away of five locally raised (although not all complete) regiments with Charles I to Edgehill in the autumn of 1642, and except for some of Sir Thomas Aston's cavalry, they never returned. The Royalists were also at a disadvantage because their adversaries were located

49 HLJO, HL/PO/JO/10/1/224 (Surrender document of the Royalist garrison); BL, MS Harley 2128, fols 144r.–v., 201r.; 2137, fol. 200v.

50 AA, unlisted warrants, dated 18 June, 1, 6, 10, 13, 14, 18, 19 July 1644; BL, MS Harley 2128, fol. 166r.

in a wedge stretching from northern Staffordshire through eastern Cheshire into south-east Lancashire, controlling the interior lines of communications (dominated by a number of local garrisons). Additionally, the King's forces were scattered around the margins of Shropshire, North Wales, the Wirral and west Lancashire, while the city of Chester was to a significant extent isolated from the wider course of events in the region. In terms of gaining assistance from the main Royalist armies, except for Sir Thomas Aston's setbacks at Nantwich and Middlewich, and Rupert's appearance at Lichfield, the King was far too occupied engaging Essex's army during the Reading campaign and forging links with Hopton's forces in the West. The Earl of Newcastle promised, but never sent, troops across the Pennines, while the deterioration of the Earl of Derby's fortunes in southern Lancashire was little short of spectacular.[51]

The quality of leadership in the Cheshire Parliamentarian army during the early phases of the war must have been another contributory factor. Clarendon said, 'Sir William Brereton and other gentlemen of that party executed their commands with notable sobriety and indefatigable industry, insomuch as the best soldiers that encountered with them had no cause to despise them'.[52] Soon after his arrival in Cheshire in January 1643 Brereton had requested 'a major to order a regiment of horse with some officers of foot sent down, for we have a great need of them, a lieutenant-colonel and sergeant major of foot and some lieutenants of foot … some old soldiers for sergeants would do wonderous well'.[53] Although most of Sir William's earliest supporters in the county were local gentlemen, during the first months of the conflict figures such as George Booth, William Massey, Robert Venables, John Bramhall and Henry Bradshaw were quickly proving to be resourceful and courageous officers, while one of Brereton's closest allies, Robert Duckenfield had raised and equipped a cavalry troop and foot company made up of volunteers from east Cheshire in mid 1642, and by the following year had a full infantry regiment.

Moreover, Jerome Zankey, Brereton's 'preaching captain' led the commander's own troop with much skill. From the start the army was boosted by experienced professionals, including Sergeant Major James Lothian and the dragoon captain, William Goldegay. Similarly, Parliamentarian commanders in Lancashire, in contrast to the Earl of Derby who was 'essentially a reactive commander who dealt in knee-jerk responses to particular crises, rather than initiating aggressive moves himself', frequently took the initiative, although they only tended to go onto the offensive when outside influences such as the Northern Association and Sir William Brereton prompted them to do so.[54] Also a critical factor in the success of Brereton's forces during the spring and

51 Ann Hughes, 'The King, the Parliament, and the Localities during the English Civil War', *JBS*, 24:2 (April 1985), pp.236–63; P.R. Newman, 'Aspects of the Civil War in Lancashire', *TLCAS*, 82 (1983), pp.113–120; Gratton, 'Earl of Derby's Catholic Army', pp.25–54.

52 Macray, W.D. (ed.), Edward Hyde, Earl of Clarendon, *The History of the Rebellion and Civil Wars in England* (Oxford: Clarendon Press, 1888), II, p.471.

53 HMC, *Portland*, I, pp.94–5.

54 Malcolm Gratton, 'The Parliamentarian and Royalist War Effort in Lancashire 1642–1651', PhD thesis (Manchester, 1998), p.448.

early summer of 1643 was the support of much of the civilian population in Cheshire. The Earl of Clarendon, no Parliamentarian, noted, 'Whereby it was in their power not to grieve and oppress the people; and thereby (besides the spirit of faction that much governed) the common people were more devoted to them [the Parliamentarians], and gave them all intelligence of what might concern them'.[55]

With the success of the surprise assaults on Stafford and Wolverhampton, on 18 July Sir William Brereton's troops made a night probe against the defences of Chester. Occupying Boughton, to the south-east of the city, and 'intending to have entered their outworks before they had been aware and so done', they spent two days firing on the Royalists. On 21 July the Parliamentarians made a perfunctory attack on the outworks at Cow Lane, but this was merely a diversionary tactic to cover their withdrawal to Tarvin.[56] Although this 'reconnaissance in force' might have momentarily encouraged the defenders, Brereton ordered the destruction of property, the felling of trees and clearing of hedges around the Boughton turnpike in order to deny them to the enemy, and in preparation for future siege operations against the city. Following Parliament's commissions in the Midlands, Brereton and Myddelton could not push any farther west until they had neutralised Eccleshall Castle, which protected the approaches to Shropshire. Following a lengthy blockade of the castle its garrison deserted on 29 August. The Cheshire dragoon companies of Bramhall, Lea and Cheswis were present and benefitted from the sale of goods with other Cheshire and Staffordshire troops.[57]

A small number of Royalists who had fled the skirmish in the town rode hastily to beckon the assistance of Colonel Hastings at Tutbury Castle. Not realising that Eccleshall had been taken, he came to its aid, but was spotted by Brereton's scouts. According to a contemporary report, 'Sir William understanding the whole design, made as speedy preparations to meet [Hastings], and upon notice of his near approach, placed his ambuscades very secretly behind hedges, and afterwards faced the colonel with a small party of horse, skirmished a little with him, and then made a seeming retreat.'[58] The Royalist horse continued its pursuit, only to encounter the Cheshire dragoons, who were lying in ambush. Opening fire, they annihilated Hastings and his soldiers, who were 'put to an absolute rout, about 100 of his horse slain in the place, and about as many were taken prisoners; himself wounded, and with a few of his ragged troops escaped, and fled to Tutbury Castle'.[59] The loss of Eccleshall dented Royalist control of Staffordshire in late summer 1643 and in turn exposed much of neighbouring Shropshire to Parliamentarian activity.

55 Clarendon, *History of the Rebellion*, II, pp.272–3.

56 Malbon, p.64. See also Randle Holme's narrative of events.

57 CRO, ZCR63/2/702, fol. 24r. – Petition of the widow of the Royalist governor, Captain Thomas Bird, who was killed during operations there (HMC, *Seventh Report*, p.121).

58 *A Perfect Diurnall of some Passages in Parliament*, 7 September 1643.

59 John Vicars, *Gods Ark overtopping the World's Waves* (London, 1646), p.63.

Church of St Michael, Loppington. (Author's photograph)

Operations in Shropshire largely occupied Brereton's field army throughout the next few months. The immediate objective of the combined Parliamentarian force was the town of Wem. Malbon mentions that an advance guard belonging to the Cheshire army left Nantwich on 8 September along the London road and quartered overnight at Blakenhall, Doddington 'and the towns thereabouts'. They were joined at Market Drayton by the bulk of Brereton's and Myddelton's forces the next day, and with Colonel Thomas Mytton took possession of Wem unopposed on 11 September. As Malbon relates, the new garrison was supplemented on 29 September by the Nantwich Hundred trained bands, a company from Sir William Brereton's regiment led by the experienced Captain Thomas Croxton.[60] They also fortified a number of outlying garrisons. Lord Capel, leading a Royalist force of about 2,000 men, began its march to relieve the garrison but became embroiled in an attack on Loppington, its earthwork defences being defended by three companies of Cheshire dragoons under Bramhall. Heavily outnumbered, they were forced to withdraw to the church, yet 'not so speedily but that the King's party had fired the church before relief came. And by that means enforced them in the church to issue forth, where Captain Bramhall, Thomas Mainwaring (his ensign), Sergeant Turner and others were taken prisoner.'[61]

The Royalists were driven off by a relieving force from Wem and withdrew under the cover of darkness. The encounter at Loppington temporarily blunted the effectiveness and morale of Capel's troops, and provided the Parliamentarians with a further breathing space during which they improved the defences of Wem, which included substantial earthworks.

In mid October 1643 Lord Capel marched his army of about 3,000 men north-eastwards from Shrewsbury. The defenders of Wem, anticipating an attack on the town, reported the Royalists 'came not as we expected'.[62] There developed a grim cat-and-mouse struggle as the Royalist commander, learning that Brereton had marched towards Wem, advanced by night towards the Parliamentarian headquarters at Nantwich, although his intentions at this point are far from clear. However, his troops became embroiled in

60 Malbon, pp.75–6, 78.

61 *Shropshires misery and mercie, Manifested in the defeat given to the Lord Capels ravenous and devouring Armie, by the forces of Cheshire and Shropshire* (November 1643); Malbon, pp.76–7.

62 HMC, *Thirteenth Report, Appendix I*, p.141.

combat at Acton Church, a mile from the town, when they were attacked by two companies of Cheshire foot and a party of dragoons that had sallied out. It was a bitter action in the churchyard and the Royalists were forced into the church, but failing to dislodge them, the Parliamentarians withdrew to the security of Nantwich. Arriving in Market Drayton at daybreak the following morning, Sir William Brereton and his officers allowed their exhausted soldiers a day's rest, although by then Capel had already disengaged from further skirmishing near Nantwich and was returning to Wem. With the bulk of his troops deployed at Prees Heath, near Whitchurch, Brereton ordered his weary warriors to pursue them. They just missed the Royalists in the dark as they slipped away towards Wem.

During 17 and 18 October the Royalists stormed the town defences, but Mytton's soldiers fought ferociously, a contemporary account claiming, 'they behaved themselves valiantly, dashed their brains upon the kids [faggots], and kept their town, and many a bloody kid there lay, and men gasping on the ground, of cavaliers, and drove them off'.[63] A Royalist observer stated, 'not withstanding all this, Wynn, colonel of the Welsh regiment being their settled colonel, Scriven of the trained bands, and Major Broughton of Sir Michael Woodhouse's regiment, being shot, all the example or persuasions of my Lord Capel could use to them did signify nothing, the soldiers would not fall on again'.[64] In the meantime Brereton and Myddelton's had arrived to relieve Mytton at Wem. Wishing to avoid what might have been a one-sided action in favour of the Parliamentarians, Capel engaged in a fighting retreat, but his battered army was outpaced at Leigh Bridge, south-east of Wem during the late afternoon of 18 October. Malbon mentions that 'they fired on both side, one at another, which continued for a great space'. Royalist losses are unclear, although it was reported that the Brereton's soldiers sustained six killed and 15 wounded.[65] That night the victorious Parliamentarians continued their route to Wem.

The following evening the Cheshire forces marched the nine miles back to Whitchurch, where they demanded a ransom of £300, 'being a cavalier place to save it from plundering'.[66] On 20 October 1643 the bulk of the army arrived back in Nantwich, although Brereton despatched some of the horse to Churton, near the Welsh border, intelligence having reached him that a detachment of Royalist horse was in the vicinity. Pursuing them to Aldford, Sir William's troopers captured a number of officers and the following day returned with them to Nantwich. Albeit brief, the campaign in Shropshire and the borders had been a gruelling and frustrating one. Capel's defeated army was thrown into turmoil, and while save for the Royalist garrison at Chester Parliamentarian military authority was strongly established in the region, which would soon be extended by an incursion by Brereton and Myddelton into Denbighshire. For the Cheshire forces the manoeuvrings

63 *A True Relation of a great Victory obtained by the Parliament's Forces against the Cavaliers near Chester* (London: 27 November, 1643).

64 HMC, *Thirteenth Report, Appendix I,* p.141.

65 Malbon, p.83; *A True Relation of a great Victory*.

66 Malbon, p.84.

in Cheshire and Shropshire during September and October 1643 were something of a 'proving ground', not only in terms of the key development of flexibility of leadership, and military resilience and endurance, but in forging high morale among both officers and men.

The next phase of operations was the Parliamentarian invasion of North Wales. Brereton's logistical situation had been greatly improved by the arrival of a ship carrying ordnance and ammunition at Liverpool in June 1643, the arrival of Sir Thomas Myddelton at Nantwich with 40 cases of weapons and munitions, though few soldiers, and the taking of one of Capel's war chests. To enhance the Cheshire army Brereton could rely on troops from Lancashire, who had conquered their entire county except for Latham Hall and Greenhalgh Castle, and were under no great strain from Newcastle's men across the Pennines. The appeal of an infiltration into North Wales by the Cheshire Parliamentarian commanders centred on the strategic necessity of cutting off the vital support given to Chester by Royalist supporters in the area. The commissioners of array at Chirk (the captured home of Sir Thomas Myddelton) encountered problems in raising the trained bands for the King's service, writing in mid August that the hundred of Bromfield had found 124 musketeers 'to guard the passages upon the River Dee', and provided £150 for a month's pay for them. Moreover, the commissioners recommended that Chirk might contribute 100 men and £100 to support them. Similarly, On 6 November, on the eve of Brereton's raid, John Edwards wrote to Sir Richard Lloyd and the other commissioners, 'I have hastened the soldiers you desired, the delay has been caused by the illness of Mr John Trevor, who could not assist me … I have no arms with which to furnish the men.'[67]

The following evening the combined forces under Brereton and Myddelton embarked from Nantwich. Approaching Farndon, on the Dee on 9 November 1643 they rendezvoused with Lancashire foot troops, thus creating a combined force of about 2,000 men. In order to open the door into North Wales the capture of the medieval bridge separating English Farndon and Welsh Holt was imperative. Sir William Brereton's account of the ensuing action offers a detailed picture:

> We drew out upon Tuesday last five Cheshire foot companies and three or four troops of horse, and three or four companies of country dragooners, wherewith they joined five companies of Lancashire foot and one or two troops of horse, and one or two companies of dragooners under the command of Colonel John Booth and Lieutenant Colonel Peter Egerton, and about 200 foot and one troop of horse of Sir Thomas Myddelton's, with which we advanced that night to Farne over against the Holt in Wales wherein the enemy kept a garrison in the castle, and had contracted all the strength and power of Wales for our resistance, for which purpose they rung their bells backward and fired the beacons throughout Wales, for which end they had also made a tower and drawbridge, and strong gates upon the bridge so as both they and we conceive it very difficult if not altogether impossible to make way for our passage over the bridge, and in the

67 Margaret Mahler, *The History of Chirk Castle and Chirkland* (London: G. Bell and Sons, 1912), pp.165–6.

Bridge crossing the Dee between Farndon and Holt. (Author's photograph)

> meantime to attempt by boats to land over some of our foot ... To interrupt and prevent which intended design of our's they brought their foot all along the riverside so far remote from the bridge as that they gave us the opportunity to make a desperate assault upon the bridge by placing ladders to the top of the drawbridge and cutting the ropes. Which being done and the [draw]bridge falling down we had access to the gates and casting over some hand grenades amongst the Welshmen – which struck such terror into them as that they all run away and could not be obtained to relieve. Whereby we had a very fair opportunity to force open the gates: which being done, the enemy was without much difficulty beaten from their double works within the gates.[68]

The Parliamentarians captured about 40 common soldiers, one captain, four or five lieutenants and one cornet, while a lieutenant colonel was also mentioned among the prisoners. Brereton stated further that his men pursued Colonel Ellice's foot, Major Trevor's horse 'and all the forces which could be arranged in all the adjoining parts of Wales', adding 'about six o'clock Thursday evening we entered Wrexham ... the enemy fly apace and begin to remove all their goods out of these parts, but Holt Castle holds out, but is

68 HMC, *Portland*, I, p.151.

besieged'. It was a lightening advance. Malbon added, 'after they had taken Holt [bridge and town] and left a considerable party there, they marched to Wrexham where they were well-entertained and quartered there that night'.[69] With his characteristic energy, on 11 November Brereton with Myddelton led 'nine troops of horse and two small foot companies' to Hawarden Castle, where upon their arrival the governor, Colonel Thomas Ravenscroft opened the gates without a shot being fired. There were mutterings of 'treachery' among the Royalists, especially as he had borrowed a barrel of black powder from Chester. According to Royalist sources, the next day Sir William Brereton despatched a summons to surrender to the governor of Chester, accompanied by numerous threats in the case of refusal. Holme (whose chronology at his point is suspect), added, 'the city now in a manner all about (at a little distance), and for fear of a closer beleaguering, the town of Handbridge was commanded from the governor to be forthwith pulled down and fired'.[70] This occurred on 16 November 1643 and the day after Overleigh Hall, Bache Hall and Flookersbrook Hall were burnt by the Royalists 'to prevent the enemy from sheltering themselves there if they should come to attack the city'.[71]

Even so, on 20 November Royalist troops marched out of the city eastwards as far as Stamford Bridge, where they clashed with Captain Gerard's company of Colonel Leigh's Cheshire regiment quartered at nearby Tarvin. A firefight ensued before troops from Cholmondeley House arrived and assisted the Parliamentarian soldiers in driving the Royalists as far as the Gorse Stacks to the south-east of Chester. In the words of Malbon, the Parliamentarians 'slew some of them, and marched back to Tarvin without loss of any, only one a little wounded'.[72] Across the Dee, with Holt Castle circumvented, and Wrexham and Hawarden taken, Brereton's troops overran much of Denbighshire and Flintshire, severing communications, and as Randle Holme put it, 'very discommodious to the city of Chester by stopping of corn, coals, lime and all sort of victuals which by the Welsh was brought in while that side was open'.[73] At Oxford Brereton's triumphant foray so alarmed the council of war that Lord John Byron was despatched to Chester with a relief force, including his own regiment, while orders were sent for the Lancastrian units serving with Prince Rupert to march with him. Expecting to unite with Capel at Shrewsbury, Byron left Oxford on 21 November in command of 1,000 foot and 300 horse.[74] He was duly appointed commander-in-chief of the Royalist forces in Lancashire and Cheshire.

Sir William Brereton's strategy now suffered a severe setback as events of a more national complexion began to unfold, and the counties of Lancashire

69 Malbon, p.87.

70 BL, MS Harley 2155; reprinted in Morris, *Siege of Chester*, p.219.

71 CRO, DCC/26 ('An account of the Siege of the city of Chester, by or after William Cowper, 1764'), fol. 4r.

72 Malbon, p.88.

73 BL, MS Harley 2155; reprinted in Morris, *Siege of Chester*, p.219.

74 Eliot Warburton, *Memoirs of Prince Rupert, and the Cavaliers* (London: S. & J. Bentley and Henry Fley, 1849), II, pp.355–6; Thomas Carte, *The Life of James, Duke of Ormond* (Oxford: Oxford University Press, 1851), V, p.521.

Tower of the church of St Giles, Wrexham. (Author's photograph)

and Cheshire were thrust into prominence. The signing in September 1643 of both the Solemn League and Covenant between the Parliamentarian and Scottish Covenanters, and the Cessation between Charles I and the Irish Confederates meant that troops from both Scotland and Ireland were about to enter England. In late November the consignment of royal troops being mustered in Dublin for despatch to the North West (earlier and smaller bodies had been sent to the South West) was hurried across the Irish Sea and landed at Mostyn on the Flintshire coast. These consisted of around 3,000 foot. The majority of these 'Irishmen' were English soldiers who had enlisted for service in Ireland, yet the spectre of an 'army of papists' arriving on their doorstep alarmed Parliamentarian commanders, who had in recent months witnessed the collapse of the Royalist army in the North West.

Brereton helped circulate the rumour that the enemy were Irish Catholics. Whilst from Hawarden Castle on 15 November 1643 he told Speaker Lenthall:

> The whole country hereabouts tremble and dare not make any opposition, and Colonel Davies and Colonel Mostyn are fled and their commanders dispersed. The bishop of York, bishops of Chester, St Asaph and Bangor, and the grandees of the country are at Conway, which they have exceedingly fortified, expecting the landing of the Irish army under the command of the Earl of Ormonde.[75]

Moreover, Sir William and some of the Lancashire Parliamentarian commanders, recognising the quality and experience of such troops, petitioned officers under Sir Michael Ernle, who were sailing from Ireland, to come over to their cause.[76] Upon their arrival, two companies, supported by around 600 Welshmen who had joined them, were detached from the main force in order to besiege Hawarden Castle. It was garrisoned by 120 men

75 HMC, *Thirteenth Report*, p.153.
76 *Mercurius Aulicus*, 2 December 1643.

under the command of a captain. On 22 November he rejected a summons to surrender, prompting a brief, yet bitter siege. A week later the main body of somewhat ragged troops from Ireland reached Chester, shortly in advance of Byron's arrival from Oxford. They were quickly joined by the group from Hawarden, and on 6 December the second contingent from Ireland, numbering 1,200 infantry and 140 cavalry, disembarked in Flintshire. Byron would take overall charge as commander-in-chief of Royalist forces in Lancashire and Cheshire.

The question as to why Sir William Brereton did not attack the troops from Ireland – as was his original intention – on disembarkation is an interesting one. During late November 1643 he commanded roughly 3,000 troops, but although he estimated the enemy at 500 fewer than his own, Brereton possessed intelligence that more than 10,000 more were on their way.[77] However, his Lancashire allies, anxious that the Mersey and south Lancashire, rather than the Dee and Cheshire might be the first target of the invasion, insisted on going home. Faced with reports of Byron's advance and powder in short supply, Sir William's options quickly became limited, and although the Parliamentarian retreat from North Wales was executed with some promptness, Malbon reported:

> Colonel Brereton and the rest of the Parliament's forces remaining in Wales, where they prospered well (having many gentlemen and others resorting unto them), but having intelligence that great forces were come from Ireland and landed in Wales to the number of 2,500, they all marched back again to Holt, and on Friday 24 November sent their ordnance back to Nantwich. And upon Saturday they all marched, some to Nantwich, others some to Northwich, and Lancashire men into Lancashire with all their carriage without fight or battle with the enemy, leaving Holt Castle unrelieved.[78]

Brereton, with a small body of horse, left a substantial garrison in Nantwich its garrison and rode to Manchester to raise more forces. However, some of the Cheshire Parliamentarian units continued to hold strongpoints in the north and east of the county, including Knutsford, Northwich and Halton. Warnings were issued to the constables of various townships by Parliamentarian army officers and local officials in December 1643 against 'aiding any papist', and 'the violence and cruelty of the papists and the rest of their adherents of the array, who have used all possible means for the gathering of great forces towards the affecting of their malicious designs'. Further warrants instructed them to turn out soldiers billeted upon them 'for the speedy raising of men and arms to be in readiness in *extremis exigence* and urgent necessity within divers townships … with god's blessing to resist the enemy who otherwise will be ready to make much intrusion, waste and spoil in the country', while the deputy lieutenants authorised them to press men, carts and horses for the service of Parliament 'as the enemy is now

77 HMC, *Thirteenth Report*, p.153.
78 Malbon, pp.88–9.

advanced into the bowels of this county, threatening the same hereof with fire and sword'.[79]

Although the Parliamentarian headquarters at Nantwich were Byron's main objective, his initial task was to neutralise each of the garrisons in the vicinity. Hawarden Castle, whether through lack of food and water or not, capitulated on 2 or 3 December. However, during an incident that marked the advent of a more brutal phase of the war, upon departing from the castle the Parliamentarian soldiers were attacked and injured by Welsh troops who had broken the terms of surrender. The Royalist officer, Captain Harry Byrch, admitted that 'the articles were not so well performed as I could have wished, but our men profess they could not help it, but it was the fault of the Lord Cholmondeley's men, who bid them remember Reading'.[80] On 13 December Captain Thomas Steele surrendered Beeston Castle to Captain Sandford and eight of his firelocks (although the garrison was 60 strong), who got into the upper ward. Steele capitulated on terms which allowed him and his men to march away with their colours and arms, having received and dined with his adversary in his quarters, and sent beer up to the Royalists in the upper ward. To Malbon, the surrender 'was wickedly and treacherously performed by the said Captain Steele. And the same day at night, they all came to Nantwich, where the said Steele was presently imprisoned, and kept close for fear the soldiers would have killed him'.[81] He was later shot for treachery.

On 17 December 1643 a detachment of Cheshire Parliamentarian horse inflicted damage on the forward elements of Byron's army at Barbridge, near Nantwich. During the action, however, Sergeant Major Lothian, an officer of considerable experience, who had been left as chief military advisor to the Parliamentarian garrison was taken prisoner.[82] Leaving troops to harass the fortified town of Nantwich five days later, Byron's army crossed the River Weaver, swinging in a wide arc towards Northwich in an attempt to sever communications between Nantwich and the Parliamentarian stronghold of Manchester. Three days later, on Christmas Day, after ravaging much of the countryside, Royalist troops occupied the village of Barthomley. Here civilians, all male and possibly armed, took refuge in the tower of St Bertoline's Church. They were smoked out, stripped and 12 of them killed. Although Byron and some of his officers claimed that having requested and been granted quarter, the villagers fired on his men, killing one of them. One evidently shocked Royalist officer reported, 'divers of the Parliamentarian party, which were most barbarously used and murdered in cold blood', while Malbon stated that Major Connaught 'most barbarously and contrary to the laws of arms, murdered, stabbed and cut the throats of twelve of them'.[83] Sir Robert Byron's brief account omits to mention that those killed were non-combatants.[84] Moreover, Lord Byron's boast to the Marquess of Newcastle on

79 AA, unlisted warrants, dated 4, 13 and 20 December 1643.

80 Carte, *Letters* I, p.32.

81 Malbon, pp.91–2, 117–8; R. Parkinson (ed.), Henry Newcome, *The Autobiography of Henry Newcome M.A.* (CS, 26, 1852), I, p.95.

82 Malbon, pp.92–3.

83 BL, MS Harley 2125, fol. 135v.; Malbon, pp.94–5.

84 Carte, *Letters* I, p.34.

26 December that he had 'put them all to the sword, which I find to be the best way to proceed with these kind of people, mercy to them is cruelty', coupled with the harsh conduct of some of his officers and continued plundering in the villages along the army's line of march, revealed him to Parliamentarians and Royalists alike as a ruthless man, and further fuelled the resentment of his enemies against his soldiers.[85]

The Second Battle of Middlewich on 26 December 1643 has received little attention from historians. This is partly because the sources are imperfect, but more because the strategic results of the loss at Middlewich in particular, were nullified by Byron's comprehensive defeat at Nantwich a month later. With a force of 200 horse and 1,500 foot (the latter including the Cheshire regiment of Colonel Duckenfield, and the Lancashire commands of Colonel Assheton and Rigby) Brereton advanced with his main body as far as Sandbach, some 10 miles north-east of Nantwich. There appears, however, to have been at least one clash to the north-west, because Captain Anthony Booth's company of Duckenfield's foot fought either a defensive or delaying action at Acton Bridge, where the Warrington road crosses the Weaver. Booth was reimbursed soon afterwards the sum of 2s. 'for the expending of shot and powder for the first work at Acton Bridge'.[86] This action makes sense in that by autumn 1643 the Parliamentarians had secured the bridges and fords at Frodsham, while local companies of foot and dragoons had been mustered for the defence of the area during the preceding week.[87] Additionally, Malbon mentioned that the 'Nantwich army (saving those left to tend the town) [that is, the troops with Brereton] being at or about Middlewich and Holmes Chapel marched towards Sandbach'.[88]

The fullest and most accurate account of the subsequent fighting was written by Robert Byron, the commander of the Royalist vanguard. On 25 December he had intelligence that elements of Brereton's forces were at Sandbach, and quickly advanced to engage them there. The Royalists encountered 200 Parliamentarian cavalry and perhaps Assheton's Lancashire foot outside the town, who 'drew themselves off and away', allowing Byron's men to occupy Sandbach unopposed.[89] The author of a pamphlet describing the whole Nantwich campaign (probably Nathaniel Lancaster) confirms this, reporting 'Sir William Brereton with some Lancashire forces came to our aid, drew up to Sandbach, but on the enemy's appearance … they left that place to their enemies, and fell down to Middlewich three miles lower'.[90] The following morning Royalist scouts reported that the Parliamentarians were concentrated at Middlewich. 'When we came nearer the town [wrote Byron], the enemy were drawn out twice musket shot from the town, and had placed themselves in hedges and ditches to as much advantage as can be'.

85 HMC, *Portland*, I, p.34; Peter Gaunt, 'Four Churches and a River: The Civil War in Cheshire', *Cromwelliana*, Fifth Series, 5 (2008), pp.31–48 (pp.21–2); Geoffrey Hudson, 'Northern Civil War Atrocity at Barthomley Church, 1643, Revisited', *NH*, 46:2 (2009), pp.329–32.

86 BL, MS Harley 2128, fol. 43r.

87 AA, unlisted warrants, 6 October, 11 November, 13 and 20 December 1643.

88 Malbon, p.96.

89 Carte, *Letters*, I, pp.34–6; Phillips, II, pp.116–18.

90 *A Relation of some of the Remarkable Passages*; *CWTC*, pp.100–1.

Although three Royalist foot regiments were present, for reasons unknown, only his regiment engaged with Brereton's soldiers in a firefight that continued for over an hour. At this point in the battle Sir Robert Byron received a musket wound. The arrival part of Colonel Gibson's regiment appears to have turned the tide and the Parliamentarians engaged in a fighting retreat (they 'gave fire as they went, till they came to the town'). Outnumbered by three to one, about 300 of them took refuge in Middlewich Church, while the rest ran through the streets fiercely pursued by the Royalist cavalry. Ultimately, they managed to break contact, but only after they were dispersed in confusion over a broad area. Those in the church were granted quarter and taken prisoner. It had been a desperate fight – Malbon mentions 'many slain and wounded on both sides; it was reported that the Parliament party slain and taken prisoners were about 200'.[91] Robert Byron, who was himself wounded, admitted that four Royalist officers and 41 soldiers were injured, and 15 killed, with Parliamentarian losses of 300 dead and 274 captured.

Although both sides may have been guilty of exaggeration, in the Parliamentarians' case to minimise the scale of their defeat, while Byron wanted to overstress his part in the encounter, Brereton's losses were verified by Colonel Duckenfield, who reported later that his regiment had lost many weapons, and 'two clerks of my own and Captain William Duckenfield's company did lose their accounts at the fight at Middlewich'. He expended the sum of £80 for arming and refitting his regiment after the defeat, where he lost over 200 arms.[92] During the action Brereton's foot, although initially holding their advantage in terms of a prepared defensive position, were not only outnumbered, but in the effective absence of Parliamentarian horse lacked manoeuvrability, especially during their retreat. Only Robert Byron mentions the presence of 200 Parliamentarian cavalry, but merely their arrival at and retreat from Sandbach the previous evening. Their involvement at Middlewich – and indeed that of the bulk of the Cheshire horse, which had been so effective in the lightning campaign into Wales only weeks before – appears to have been ineffectual or even lacking. It can only be assumed then, that most of the Cheshire troops had been withdrawn to garrisons, perhaps as far away as Manchester.

Sir William's actions during the brief campaign are hard to fathom. To attack Lord Byron's main army with little more than the residue of his own force, once a significant part of it had been withdrawn into garrisons, and with the addition of a small number of Lancashire troops implies rashness, or at the least poor intelligence gathering. Yet even the worst of Brereton's critics never suggested that recklessness was one of his characteristics. The actions of his cavalry at Sandbach and the swift tactical withdrawal to Middlewich do indicate that he grossly underestimated the strength of Byron's force. This would tend to be borne out by the Parliamentarian report that his men realised they were 'too weak to encounter so great a power', and thus were unable to withdraw effectively in time. Sir William's strategy,

91 Malbon, p.97.

92 TNA, SP28/128/10, fols 8r., 9r.; SP28/196/3, fol. 15r.

however, would make sense if he was anticipating further assistance, either from the strong garrison at Nantwich (which was not under attack at that time, but would intervene so successfully in the battle itself a month later), or from the Committee of Stafford.

The latter is distinctly possible because on 23 December 1643 Colonel Rugeley was instructed 'now in this time of danger to go to Newcastle[-under-Lyme]' to take command of the horse and to raise forces, which he was to employ 'for the safety of Newcastle[-under-Lyme] and Leek for the assistance of Sir William Brereton in Cheshire'.[93] As Brereton was a leading member of this committee it is possible that he was expecting to be reinforced by Rugeley, who commanded regiments of Staffordshire horse and foot, and who had co-operated with the Cheshire forces at Stafford, Chillington and Eccleshall only months before. Although costly in terms of casualties and Parliamentarian morale, the Second Battle of Middlewich was only serious defeat that Sir William Brereton's forces ever suffered. However, the premature end of Sir William's campaign in North Wales and the defeat at Middlewich left an indelible mark. As Dore suggests, 'the eventual triumph at Nantwich did not erase for Brereton the trauma of the preceding weeks. The long period of absence from his command after Nantwich can only be explained by his determination to see that he was never put in such a position again'.[94] Brereton retreated with the remnants of his force to Manchester, from where he urgently appealed to the Committee of Both Kingdoms for reinforcements.

93 D.H. Pennington and I.A. Roots (eds and intro.), *The Committee at Stafford, 1643–1645* (Manchester: Manchester University Press, 1957), p.21.

94 *BLB*, II, p.40.

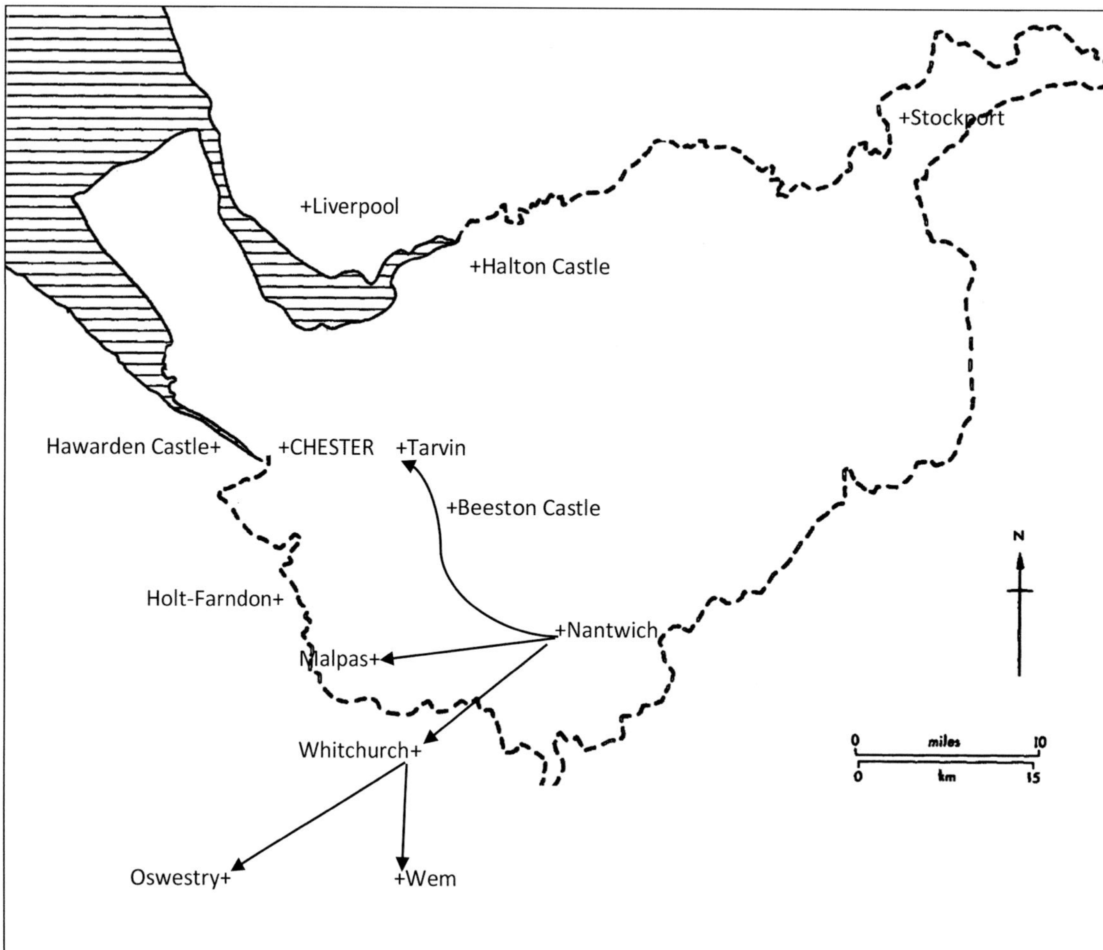

Map 2 Parliamentarian military operations in Cheshire 1644.

2

'More like lions than men': January–November 1644

On 10 January 1644 the Royalist commander, Lord Byron issued the first of two summonses to surrender to the town of Nantwich, which was well fortified with earthworks. His officers supposed that the garrison was inadequately provisioned and its morale low. As Sir Nicholas Byron had assured Rupert, the assault would prove easy and the army could therefore turn its attention to the reduction of Lancashire.[1] The summons was defiantly rebuffed, however, but anticipating a sudden attack the defenders continued to man their posts, whilst the townswomen rushed to put out fires caused by the subsequent bombardment. On 16 January Byron, ever the opportunist, sent a further missive, in which he accused the town corporation of misleading the inhabitants, although as events would prove, they were immune to such propaganda. The Royalist assault, when it came, was fierce and targeted against five different points, while artillery directed its close-range fire at the town. Such attacks were repulsed with heavy casualties. Among the dead was Captain Sandford, whose 'big letter' had intimidated the defenders of Hawarden before their capitulation, and was repeated at Nantwich with threats to the garrison with dire punishments if it refused to surrender. Further bombardments failed to break the defenders' morale and Byron consequently settled upon starving them into submission. It was probably his best policy to persist – his troops were fully committed, and as Malbon reported, things were becoming desperate for the defenders.[2]

In response to Sir William Brereton's urgent appeal for reinforcements, the Committee of Both Kingdoms ordered Sir Thomas Fairfax, who was wintering in Lincolnshire, to come to Nantwich's assistance. Fairfax had already shown himself a fine commander, capable of inspiring the affection and respect of his men. When he arrived in Manchester he found some reluctance among the gentry (probably the Lancashire Committee), although to their credit the Lancashire and Cheshire foot, albeit ill clad, were eager to march. On 16 January 1644, five days before departing from Manchester,

1 Warburton, *Memoirs of Prince Rupert and the Cavaliers*, II, pp.355–6.
2 Malbon, p.110.

the Cheshire forces were issued with the following order to forbear from plundering by their officers:

> Forasmuch a great complaint is made unto us of the outrageous pilfering and plundering that many captains, officers and soldiers (who yet pretend themselves to be and stand for the service of king and parliament), do make and use contrary to a former order of the Council and Committee at Nantwich straightly forbidding such courses. It therefore this day ordered and appointed that every captain, lieutenant, officer, common soldier and other person whatsoever upon sight of this order shall forbear to seize upon the person of any man or plunder or take the goods of any upon any pretence whatsoever (without showing special order for the same) upon pain of being proceeded against by martial law.[3]

Crucially, the wider strategic balance seems to have assisted the Parliamentarians because on the same day as Byron's abortive attack on Nantwich, a 20,000-strong Covenanting army had crossed the English border through deep snow drifts, causing the Earl of Newcastle to withdraw from Lancashire to meet them. The broader context of the developing campaign in Cheshire and the north-west of England is adequately summarised by Clarendon:

> It cannot be denied the reducing of that place [Nantwich] at that time would have been of unspeakable importance to the king's affairs, there being between that and Carlisle no one town of moment (Manchester only excepted) against the king: and those two populous counties of Cheshire and Lancashire (if they had been united against the Parliament) would have been a strong bulwark against the Scots.[4]

On 21 January 1644 Fairfax left Manchester, making slow progress in difficult conditions through Northwich towards Nantwich. Sir Thomas, assisted by Brereton and some of the Lancashire commanders, had at his disposal a composite force comprising 1,800 horse, including troops from the regiments of Sir Thomas Fairfax, Sir William Fairfax, Colonels Lambert and Bethell, and Sir William Brereton. There were also 500 dragoons under Colonel Morgan. The 3,000-strong foot was drawn from the Cheshire regiments of Brereton, Duckenfield, Mainwaring and George Booth, plus the Lancashire commands of John Booth, Assheton, Holland and Rigby, and Bright's Yorkshire and Lancashire infantry.[5] It is uncertain how much Lord Byron was apprised of the situation, but he seems to have anticipated that Fairfax would not be able to mount a relief for some time. On 24 January patrols of Parliamentarian cavalry and dragoons made contact with a Royalist blocking force at Delamere Forest, before concentrating at Tilston Heath, about eight miles from Nantwich. That night, however, saw a rapid thaw which caused the

3 *Ibid.*, p.250.
4 Clarendon, *History of the Rebellion*, IV, p.427.
5 Malbon, pp.116–7; John Barratt, *The Battle of Nantwich 1644* (Bristol: Stuart Press, 1993), p.25.

Weaver to flood. Byron ordered his infantry and artillery to shift to the west bank of the Weaver around Acton, where the ground was drier, but the bridge at Beambridge was then swept away by the floodwater while Byron himself and his 1,800 horse were still on the east bank. He was forced to make a march of six miles by way of another crossing at Shrewbridge to support his regiments of foot at Acton, although this enterprise did not get underway until 8:00 a.m. the following morning.

Sir Thomas Fairfax (1612–72). Vicars, *England's Worthies*.

As the Parliamentarian army approached, the opportunity presented itself of striking at Acton Church before the other half of the Royalists could rendezvous with them, but their council of war determined to pursue the most direct route to the town and to effect a link-up with the garrison, with an expectation to enforce a battle the following day. Besides, Fairfax's rear was yet to come up. We know from Fairfax's *Memorials* that his troops had been in battle-order for 24 hours by that stage. One major threat was a possible attack by Byron's veteran foot, which the Parliamentarian commander regarded as strong in number and of high quality. Although speed was essential, the enclosed terrain presented a serious challenge, but as Sir Thomas reported, 'we resolved to make our way with pioneers though the hedges, and so to the town to relieve it, and by it, to enable us better to fight with them'.[6] Lord Byron's version of events is misleading and suggests a coordinated response by his officers. Probably more reliably, Robert Byron reported, 'our army was drawn in several enclosures, there our horse (which we are superior in) could do no good, nor we help one another, by reason of the great distance from one and other'.[7]

About 3:00 p.m. Robert Byron's foot, which had joined Gibson's regiment at Acton, wheeled to its right, striking the Parliamentarian column in the rear. Probably shortly afterwards the Royalist right wing, which had thrust forward to interpose itself between the town and the enemy, closed on Fairfax's front and flank. Lord Byron probably exaggerated in reporting that Gibson and his brother made significant progress against the regiments opposing them, seizing many of their colours, but Parliamentarian reports confirm the effectiveness of their attack. Yet the hard-pressed vanguard of Cheshire and Lancashire foot (commended by Fairfax for performing 'very good service') was closely supported by detachments of horse fighting along the lanes and hedges.[8] The Royalist cavalry appears to have remained immobile. Quickly, it seems, events swung decisively in favour of Fairfax's army. On the Royalist

6 Thomas Fairfax, 'A Short Memorial of the Northern Actions in which I was engaged (1642–4)', *JSAHR*, 5 (1926), pp.119–25 and 160–74 (p.162); *CWTC*, pp.107–12; R.N. Dore and John Lowe, 'The Battle of Nantwich, 25 January 1644', *THSLC*, 113 (1961), pp.97–124 (p.108).

7 Carte, *Letters* I, pp.36–7, 41; Phillips, *Memoirs*, II, pp.130–2.

8 Fairfax, 'Short Memorial', p.164.

left Warren's regiment disintegrated when it came into close contact with the Parliamentarians, especially their pike blocks.

Byron, willing to blame everyone but himself, reported that they 'retreated almost without fighting a stroke', with his brother adding, 'Warren's regiment, though they had their beloved Colonel Monk in the head of them, was no sooner charged but they broke, and being rallied again, the next charge ran quite away'. Robert Byron also mentioned a rumour that 60 of Warren's soldiers changed sides, although what might have been a lost account of Sir William Brereton verified that the battle 'was bravely performed on both sides and the day doubtful for a good space [of time], but at last upon an instant unexpected the enemy [Warren's] gave ground'.[9] Barratt suggests that part of the failure of Warren's soldiers may have been down to running short of ammunition, although the courage of Brereton's pikemen could have caught them by surprise.[10]

The Royalist centre collapsed around 4:00 p.m., just as 800 or so musketeers of the Nantwich garrison sallied out of the western suburbs, overrunning Byron's ordnance in Acton churchyard, before assailing Ernle's regiment in the rear. Even though Robert Byron's foot and most of the horse managed to extricate themselves, the Parliamentarian victory was complete. Over 200 Royalists were reported killed, whilst a number of officers were also taken. Critically also, about a third of the prisoners took the Covenant accepted service in the Parliamentarian army. On 13 February a day of thanksgiving was held for Nantwich's deliverance. It had been a decisive defeat for Byron's army, and although reinforcements arrived from Ireland in February, he never completely reconstituted his field force. Even though the fighting had been ferocious on both sides, the importance of the sortie by the Nantwich soldiers to the overall outcome was clear. The intervention was not lost on Brereton, who in October 1645 when prosecuting the siege of Chester, urged the Committee of Both Kingdoms that when Sir William Vaughan's forces were advancing to the relief of the city, they should be engaged at a distance, so that the besieging troops were not attacked in the rear. He wrote, 'We learnt this by experience upon our enemy, the Irish army at Nantwich battle. For our soldiers (when the battle was in hot dispute, the success being very doubtful) issued out of the town and put a period to the debate, fell upon the rear, routed that part of the enemy and made way for a glorious victory'.[11] Brereton would repeat these sentiments in November 1645 when he led a taskforce to Whitchurch, in response to intelligence reports of Royalist troops under Vaughan and Sir Jacob Astley approaching from the Welsh borders.

On 2 February 1644 Sir William rode south with the most important of the prisoners taken at Nantwich, where he received something near a Roman triumph in the streets of London and the thanks of the Commons for his 'great and faithful services'. Fairfax remained in temporary command over the forces of Lancashire and Cheshire. Outwardly, Sir William Brereton got

9 *The Parliament Scout*, 26 January–2 February 1644; Dore and Lowe, 'Battle of Nantwich', pp.110–11.

10 Barratt, *Nantwich*, p.18.

11 BL, MS Add. 11332, fol. 35v.; *BLB*, II, 790.

his share of the credit for the rescue of Nantwich, which represented the first clear-cut victory won by the Parliament's forces since the beginning of the war. It must be said, however, that much of this recognition was engineered by himself, even though he and the Cheshire forces had played a significant role in the Nantwich campaign. Nevertheless, Parliamentarian dominance in the north-west of England was all but complete. Despite his dissatisfaction with the support he received in both Lancashire and Cheshire, within a month of the Battle of Nantwich Sir Thomas Fairfax not only reversed all Byron's efforts but made the Parliamentarian position in Cheshire stronger than it had ever been before.

Very quickly, a number of minor strongholds fell into the hands of the Cheshire army. On 5 February Crewe Hall, which had been used a base for attacks on Nantwich by Byron's forces, was taken. Malbon reported that the governor, Captain Fisher, with 120 prisoners and all their arms were marched to Nantwich, although Fisher 'carried himself so basely towards the neighbourhood thereabout that the country people would have killed him when he was come forth, had he not been preserved by those to whom he had yielded up the house'. Two days later Doddington Hall was bombarded and assaulted by Brereton's troops, and following a parley, most of the Royalist prisoners change sides, Malbon writing, 'the greatest part of them came to Nantwich, where they were entertained'. They left behind 'almost 200 arms, and good store of victuals, powder, match and bullets'.[12] In north-eastern Cheshire, Colonel Robert Duckenfield's soldiers, having returned from the relief of Nantwich, captured Adlington Hall on 16 February after a two-week siege. A detachment of 30 men under the command of Captain Adams had also besieged Wythenshawe Hall, the home of the Royalist Robert Tatton since 21 November 1643. Although they occupied a commanding position on Lawton Moor, near Northenden village, deep snow and a determined defence by a well-supplied garrison made operations particularly arduous.

The siege came to an end on 27 February 1644 after a brief bombardment and exchange of musketry, during which Adams and three soldiers were killed.[13] A reported 700 arms, 15 barrels of powder and 140 prisoners of war were taken.[14] The following month the officers and soldiers of Duckenfield's regiment were paid £213 4s. 'out of the goods at Wythenshaw, which was a lawful prize', while Colonel Robert received £50 as a gratuity.[15] There was little rest, however. On the same day that Adlington yielded, the energetic Duckenfield led the remainder of his foot regiment on a four-day march with the cavalry troops of Captain Philip Mainwaring and another under the command of a captain 'from London' [possibly Vivers], to Biddulph Hall, near Leek. Due to the especially cold conditions the Cheshire men were supplied with cooked meat and burnt ale by the corporation of Congleton.[16]

12 Malbon, pp.120–1.

13 JRL, Tatton of Wythenshawe Papers, deposition of James Brownhill, October 1646; Jill Groves, *The Impact of Civil War on a Community: Northenden and Etchells in Cheshire 1642–1660* (Northern Writers Advisory Service: Sale, 1992), pp.11–16.

14 Malbon, pp.121–2.

15 TNA: SP28/128/10, fol. 6v.

16 Anon., 'Extracts from the Corporation Books', pp.367–8.

Colonel Robert Duckenfield (1619–89). Chetham's Library, Bridgewater Scrapbook 248. (Copyright of Chetham's Library)

With Colonel Assheton's Lancashire foot, on 20 February the Cheshire forces joined the siege of Biddulph, which had been in place for a month. Vigorously assaulted by such experienced soldiers and 'much battered with great ordnance', within 24 hours the defenders were granted quarter, yielding up as prisoners Lord and Lady Brereton, four officers and 150 men.[17]

Sir William Brereton's stay in Westminster during the spring and early summer of 1644 was important enough to keep him from his command and duties in Cheshire, which he was normally so conscientious about performing. Although evidence is far from forthcoming as there survive no letters from or to him during this period, entries in the journals of houses of the Lords and Commons reveal that his objectives included the strengthening of his authority in Cheshire, the removal of obstructions to it, and the safeguarding of adequate supplies of money, arms and ammunition. On 20 March he was allowed the funds to obtain powder, match, arms and accoutrements for 1,500 musketeers, though it was well into May before there was evidence that these weapons had actually been provided.[18] Similarly, a parliamentary grant of £5,000 from the revenues of the Court of Wards and Liveries on 12 April 1644 was followed by a further sum of £2,125, which was granted on 7 May 1644.[19] This secured the purchase from London suppliers of arms, saddles and armour for 500 cavalry. As will be seen in later chapters, there is little doubt that a considerable expansion of the Cheshire army of Parliament occurred at this time and in the months to come.

In supplementing these sums Brereton had been permitted to receive rents of such concealed estates of papists and delinquents as he could discover within a 20-mile radius of the city, and this grant of 26 March 1644 was renewed for a further three months on 3 June.[20] On 10 June Sir William was placed onto the Committee for Salop, thus adding to his membership of the Staffordshire Committee, which he had held since the previous spring.[21] Brereton was accompanied to London by one of his colonels, Henry Brooke, who on 7 May was granted £1,000 towards the completion of his regiment of foot and troop of horse. Brooke's authority increased on 13 September 1644 when he was appointed high sheriff of Cheshire by parliamentary ordinance.[22] In London too was Sir Thomas Myddelton, who had missed the Nantwich campaign, but spent this period raising money, recruits, horses

17 Malbon, pp.122–3; Sherwood, *Civil War in the Midlands*, p.87.
18 *LJ*, VI, pp.446, 474, 479.
19 *CJ*, III, p.484; *LJ*, VI, p.551.
20 *CJ*, III, p.515; *LJ*, VI, pp.486, 573, 576; VII, p.336.
21 *LJ*, VI, p.586.
22 *JHC*, III, pp.439, 484, 610; R.S. Rait and C.H. Firth (eds), *Acts and Ordinances of the Interregnum, 1642–1666* (HMSO, 1911), I, pp.503–5.

and arms in the capital for his return to North Wales. Still, by April 1644 the absence of Brereton and Myddelton from their commands drew the attention of several newssheets. The *Scottish Dove* for 19 April called the two 'brave and gallant gentlemen who deserve love and honour, yet I rather wish they were with their charge ready for action rather than in London'. On 30 April the *Kingdome's Weekly Intelligencer* said that 'if they were so supplied with necessaries as to be fit to go, they would not stay a minute'.[23]

As spring approached and the main campaigning season began, the fortunes of the Parliamentarians in the north-west of England and the Welsh borders became perilous once more. Fairfax had left for Yorkshire in early March 1644, and on 11 April with his father, inflicted a crushing defeat at Selby which forced the Marquess of Newcastle to abandon field operations in the north and close himself up in York. At the end of the month Sir Thomas and the Earl of Leven, commanding the Scots Covenanters, advanced from Tadcaster to York, where they began a blockade of the city. By the end of May they were joined by the Earl of Manchester's army. Following Byron's defeat at Nantwich the task of reorganising and consolidating Royalist power in Wales and its borders fell to Prince Rupert. Taking advantage of the departure of Fairfax, Brereton and Myddelton, he arrived at Shrewsbury on 19 February with a commission as President of Wales and the Marches. Whilst briefly at Chester, Rupert was ordered to the relief of Newark, the vital communications point between the Oxford Army and the north. He subsequently undertook a lightning campaign that resulted in the relief of garrison and one considered by historians as one of his most notable achievements.

During this period also, the Royalists defeated Mytton's Shropshire forces in a series of engagements, thus by late April the Parliamentarians were restricted to a small area in the north of the county. Since his appearance in the borders Rupert had received a number of appeals from the Earl of Derby to come to the rescue of Lathom House, the only Royalist stronghold remaining in Lancashire.[24] Prince Rupert's force left Shrewsbury on 16 May. It rendezvoused with troops from Chester and North Wales commanded by Lord Byron at Market Drayton, bringing the combined army to about 2,500 horse and 5–6,000 foot. On the 19th they crossed into Cheshire near Audlem and for the next week marched through the county. It would seem that the Parliamentarian response to Rupert's march through Cheshire was ineffectual, considering that the forces of the entire area, if combined, would have been not far below the strength of the Royalists. It seems that the Mersey and its environs were considered the best line of defence, 'but the prince's speed, the uncertainty as to his point of crossing and the absence of any dominant local leader prevented any concentration of forces in time'.[25] Malbon mentions that on 20 May about 1,000 Parliamentarian troops marched from Nantwich, but failed to make contact with the Royalists. He adds, 'but the prince's army was returned again to Audlem, so that they were not met withal'.

23 *Scottish Dove*, 17–23 April 1644; *Kingdome's Weekly Intelligencer*, 24–30 April 1644.

24 Warburton, *Memoirs of Prince Rupert and the Cavaliers*, II, p.304.

25 Dore, *Civil Wars in Cheshire*, p.42.

This might suggest that given the reputation of the Nantwich garrison, whose role in the Royalist defeat of 25 January 1644 had been crucial, Rupert's commanders avoided a fight with them and withdrew. Three days later the Doddleston garrison skirmished with the Royalists, 'and did take about twenty of them prisoners, and some of them were slain as they passed'.[26] Rupert's line of march was governed to some extent, however, by his need to avoid further Parliamentarian strongholds, such as Northwich and Macclesfield, as well as the garrisons of Halton and Norton. Based on the misreading of a summary of a letter from Lord Goring to Rupert by the nineteenth-century writer William Beamont, tradition has it that Halton Castle fell to the Royalists as the Prince traversed the county in May 1644 and was reclaimed by the Parliamentarians in early July.[27] Written at Leigh on 5 June the despatch noted, 'Colonel Fenwick's quarters at Alton beaten up this night by those of Warrington, beseeches Prince Rupert to send some musketeers, or to remove their quarters'.[28] In her biography of Goring, Florence Memegalos affirms that:

> During the first few weeks of June, [he] was not quartered with the prince, but rather had based at Leigh, between Manchester and Liverpool, where his men were involved in several skirmishes with local Parliamentarian troops. After the quarters of one of his colonels was overrun, George asked Rupert for some musketeers or the removal of their quarters to a safer location'.[29]

Alton is actually Westhoughton, near Wigan, and the officer in question was Colonel John Fenwick, who commanded a regiment in Langdale's horse and was killed at Marston Moor.[30]

The Aston warrants illustrate that Halton Castle, and nearby Norton Hall were part of a wider strategic network of defences centred on the Mersey at Hale Ford and Warrington, as well as defensive positions at Frodsham Bridge and a series of outposts up the Weaver valley as far as Acton Bridge. Prior to Rupert's advance Colonel Brooke had maintained the bulk of his regiment and cavalry troop (perhaps 250 men) at Halton and Norton, while dragoons patrolled what was considered by the Parliamentarians as a secure area. Warrants were specifically issued by Lieutenant Colonel Brooke from Halton 18 May, 30 May and 18 June 1644.[31] Thus, the notion that Halton Castle changed hands in mid 1644 cannot be sustained. In addition to this, the crossing into Lancashire at Warrington Bridge was barred to Prince Rupert by the town's Parliamentarian garrison. The next major crossing of

---

26 Malbon, pp.129–30.

27 William Beamont, *A History of the Castle of Halton and the Priory or Abbey of Norton* (Warrington: Percival Pearse, 1873), pp.117–8.

28 Warburton, *Memoirs of Prince Rupert and the Cavaliers*, II, p.519.

29 Florence S. Memegalos, *George Goring (1608–1657): Caroline Courtier and Royalist General* (London: Routledge, 2007), p.170 – quoting Bod. Lib., MS Clarendon 28, fol. 134; MS Firth C7, fols 289, 302.

30 *The Diary of Sir Henry Slingsby* (London: Longman, 1836), p.114; Peter Wenham, *The Great and Close Siege of York* (York: Roundwood, 1970), pp.87–8.

31 AA, unlisted warrants, dated 18 and 30 May, 3 and 18 June, 1, 6 and 10 July 1644.

the Mersey was at Stockport, roughly 20 miles to the east. When Rupert's force reached the town on 25 May it encountered a 3,000-strong force, consisting of Duckenfield's and Mainwaring's Cheshire regiments and some trained band units, blocking its passage. Initially the Parliamentarians held off Rupert's cavalry, but according to a Royalist account:

> When his foot came up (which was about six of the clock in the evening) the cunning rebels withdrew themselves, and lined the hedges through which he was to pass with their musketeers. Which being perceived by the prince, he commanded Colonel Washington with some dragoons to scour those hedges; he performed the service with such speed and courage, that the rebels in great affright fled towards the town; whom the prince followed so close upon the heels, that he entered pellmell with them, and so took the town, together with all their cannon, most of their arms and ammunition, and 800 prisoners.[32]

Colonel Thomas Mytton (1597–1656). Vicars, *England's Worthies*.

Colonels Duckenfield and Mainwaring, with the remainder of their men, withdrew to Manchester. The way into Lancashire was thus opened for the Royalists. Rupert would swing west towards Liverpool and the town of Bolton. Somewhat ambiguously, on 14 June Charles urged him to march to the relief of York, and as his forces began their march they left behind a county that was almost entirely in Royalist hands.

The Committee of Both Kingdoms – the joint council of the Parliament and the Scots who had taken control of the strategic direction of the war since the arrival of the Covenanting army – was enormously anxious about the situation. Instead of viewing Lancashire and Cheshire as a sideshow to the struggle developing in Yorkshire, they recognised that Rupert's control of them presented the King with considerable advantages. There were many Royalist supporters who might unite with Rupert in Lancashire, the most papist county in the kingdom, while his possession of the port of Liverpool would bring in supplies from Ireland. On 13 June 1644 the Committee issued unrealistic instructions for a new army under the Earl of Denbigh, comprising troops from the Midlands, Cheshire and North Wales 'to hinder Prince Rupert's return out of Lancashire', yet at the time of writing the Committee was unaware that Bolton and Liverpool were lost. Hence Brereton and Myddelton were ordered back from London to join Denbigh with all the forces they could muster.[33] At Stourbridge on 15 June Sir William Brereton, in company with Denbigh, Mytton and other commanders warned the Committee of Both Kingdoms:

> The king and prince's forces left without any army to oppose them will speedily destroy the whole remainder of Lancashire, deprive us of that great strength of

32 *Mercurius Aulicus*, 2 June 1644.

33 *LJ*, VI, p.476; *CJ*, III, pp.440, 449; *CSPD 1644*, pp.149–50.

> foot and those numbers of arms that yet we have in Manchester and Warrington. The encouragement the ill-affected within the counties of Salop, Cheshire and Staffordshire will receive by the presence of the king's person and his forces, with the discouragements that will fall upon your friends by the retreat and absence of that power [which] might preserve them, will lay necessity upon those in Wem, Nantwich and Stafford, to quit their garrisons as not able (after ten weeks' lying under the power of a strong army in the field) to bear the shock of their assaults.[34]

Brereton arrived back at Nantwich on midsummer's day (24 June).[35] When Denbigh's combined force assembled at Knutsford Heath five days later it comprised 12,000 men – the largest army yet seen in Cheshire. However, with inconsistent orders arriving daily from London and York, and continuing rumours as to Rupert's whereabouts, few immediate actions were undertaken. Amidst this, Denbigh and Sir Thomas Myddelton received news that upwards of 2,000 Royalists from Shrewsbury and Chester were at Oswestry, and had begun to bombard the town. Denbigh allowed Myddelton with his own horse and three regiments of Cheshire foot to march to the garrison's relief. Denbigh rode to Manchester, where he arranged with its governor, Sir John Meldrum to despatch Brereton with most of the Cheshire horse, including his own troop, led by Sergeant Major Zankey and some Lancashire cavalry to go to the assistance of their Parliamentarian allies across the Pennines. Sir William arrived at Marston Moor on 2 July, the day after the battle. Denbigh's next move was to follow Myddelton with the remainder of the troops under his command to Shropshire.[36] By the spring of 1644, if not earlier, the Cheshire foot had gained a reputation as a steadfast, well-led, flexible and efficient fighting force. During this period Parliament had determined to assemble a force to undertake operations in Shropshire, and in particular, the relief of Wem. On 8 March letters were despatched to Colonel Duckenfield 'for two companies of his foot and his horse'; to Lieutenant Colonel Massey for two companies of Colonel George Booth's foot; to Sergeant Major Croxton 'to assign one or two companies as many stand with the safety of the garrison of Nantwich'; and to Colonel Mainwaring and Major Phillip Mainwaring for their troops of horse.[37]

Moreover, it instructed on 10 April that the Lancashire foot regiments of Colonels Booth and Holland, consisting of 2,000 musketeers to assemble for the same design, and 'that Cheshire do contribute 600 musketeers and all their horse for this service of the relief of Wem'. An entry in Duckenfield's accounts for April 1644 records a payment of £38 3s. 4d. 'to a party of my foot regiment that went to meet the Earl of Denbigh'.[38] This confirms that his soldiers joined the composite force of foot, horse and dragoons under the overall command of Fielding that was defeated by Prince Rupert's troops

34 *CSPD 1644*, pp.237–8.

35 Malbon, p.131.

36 *Great Victories obtained by the Earl of Denbigh at Shrewsbury, Chulmely and other parts of Cheshire* (London, 1644); *CWTC*, pp.122–3.

37 *CSPD 1644*, pp.41, 106.

38 TNA, SP28/128/10, fol. 4r.

near Longford in Shropshire on 25 March. Some Cheshire forces stayed with him until late April, while others remained at the garrison of Wem, which remained under siege. In late June 1644 the regiments of George Booth and Mainwaring, and most of the Nantwich companies joined Myddelton's taskforce that returned to Shropshire to counter increasing Royalist threats in the Welsh borders, and against the Parliamentarian garrison of Oswestry in particular. Described by Sir Thomas as 'the key which opens the door to Wales', the walled town was defended by a castle under the command of Colonel Edward Lloyd.[39] The fast-paced events were related in Myddelton's post-battle report:

> May it please you to be advised that the town of Oswestry, late taken by the forces of Parliament, under my brother, Colonel Mytton's command, was upon Saturday last begun to begirt, and since strictly besieged by the king's forces, consisting of about 1,500 horse and 3,500 foot under the command of Colonel *Marrow. And that thereupon*, in pursuance of a Council of War's determination, occasioned by an earnest and importunate letter from by brother, Colonel Mytton, directed me for speedy relief and raising of the siege of the said town, I did upon the Lord's day last past, with such forces of horse and foot as I then had with me, and the foot forces of Cheshire, all of us then at *Knutsford* (intending to have marched for *Manchester*, and for service in the north, according to enjoinment of the Committee of both Kingdoms), return and re-advance with all my said forces to a place called *Spurstow* Heath, where that night we quartered, and thence advanced upon Monday towards Whitchurch. We quartered that night likewise in open fields, at a place called *Fens [Hall]* in *Flintshire*, whence yesterday we marched towards Ellesmere, and so *Oswestry*, where the enemy endeavoured, by battering and storming of the same, violently to have carried it. About two o'clock in the afternoon we came in sight of the town, and within three miles of it, where the enemy having got intelligence of our approach were prepared to receive us. The chief forces of our enemy consisted of the most valiant commanders and soldiers drawn out of the garrisons of Chester, Cheshire, Shrewsbury, Shropshire, Ludlow, Derbyshire and Flintshire, and other places. The enemy had taken up the passage of water near Whittington, and very furiously assaulted and charged us, but were repulsed, and forced to retire through the courage of our horse, who most courageously entertained the enemy. Three several times the skirmish was doubtful, either side being forced so often to retreat; but in the end, our foot forces coming up relived the horse, beat back the enemy, and pursued them with much force that the horse, thereby encouraged, which indeed was formerly weary, joining with the foot, they put the enemy to an absolute flight, in which we pursued them five miles towards Shrewsbury, to a place called Felton Heath, and where we remained after the fight again masters of the field.[40]

39 *Copy of a Letter sent from Sir Thomas Myddelton, to the Honourable, William Lenthal Esq; Speaker of the House of Commons, Concerning the Siege of Oswestree* (London: 3 July 1644).

40 *A Copy of a Letter sent from Sir Thomas Myddelton* (London, 10 July 1644); Phillips, *Memorials*, II, pp.179–81.

During what was a hard fight, in which 200 Parliamentarian foot stormed the parish church, situated in a suburb outside Oswestry. Grateful for the skill and experience of the Cheshire foot, Sir Thomas added:

> I had to my aid three regiments of foot, viz., Colonel George Booth's regiment, a gallant regiment, led by himself on foot to the face of the enemy. Another led by Colonel Mainwaring, and the third by Colonel [*sic* – Sergeant Major] Croxton; all of them stout and gallant commanders, and the rest of the officers and soldiers full of courage and resolution. Major Lothian, Adjutant-General, that brave and faithful commander, to whom I cannot ascribe too much honour, brought up the rear that day.

The following day (23 June) Myddelton's command was joined by the Earl of Denbigh, who had arrived from Manchester with reinforcements. The Parliamentarians in the locale now numbered between 3,500 and 4,000 men. After a botched attempt to burn the castle gates using pitch, as the senior commander Denbigh accepted the surrender of the castle. The Parliamentarians reported about 240 prisoners and 100 muskets taken.[41] Such a loss represented a major setback for the Royalists as it opened a route into Mid Wales for the Parliamentarians and severed direct communications between the garrisons of Chester and Shrewsbury. On 4 July operations recommenced with an assault on Montford Bridge, to the south of Shrewsbury. A number of troops of Shropshire and Cheshire horse seconded the forlorn hope, one eyewitness reporting:

> early next morning we marched towards Montford Bridge where the enemy kept garrison, and a drawbridge over the Severn, our men fell on gallantly … in a quarter hour's-time the enemy fled, upon which my lord [the Earl of Denbigh] sent Captain Keme to call the forlorn hope of horse, and after other horse which he did, and we came so hastily on, that one Captain Shepley a gallant man, not having patience to stay till the drawbridge was let down, ventured over the river after him, rent the forlorn hope.[42]

In support was a fast-moving body of infantry that advanced across heathland before engaging Royalist horse, dragoons and foot defending more enclosed ground near Shrewsbury. An anonymous writer related:

> We drew up till our army came up on a heath on this side of Shrewsbury a mile, the enemies came in parties up ambuscadoes, the lanes we beat them from them. Colonel Booth led his regiment of foot on valiantly, and my Lord's own horse, his lifeguard commanded by Captain Tovy a gallant man pursued to pistol shot of the works, Marrow came out, and Major Manley, and fought us; and there was a hot bout for two hours and above … We made good the ground within musket shot

41 *Two Great Victories: On[e] Obtained by the Earl of Denbigh as Oswestry […] The Other by Colonel Mytton* (London: June 1644).

42 *Great Victories obtained by the Earl of Denbigh at Shrewsbury, Chulmely and other parts of Cheshire* (London, 1644); *CWTC*, pp.123–4.

> of their works till night: then seeing our little army was not able to sit down before it, my Lord drew off and we retreated that night to the heath.[43]

At the western suburbs the Cheshire foot engaged in a two-hour firefight until ordered off as darkness began to descend. Denbigh reported that:

> Upon facing of the town, and viewing the large circumference, and the strength of their works (from where it did appear they did not want men by their shooting of 100 muskets in a volley several times), and our forces in no way proportionable in number to the greatness of the design, I held it unsafe to engage these forces in a siege, and so drew off back to the heath, where we quartered that night; but with much difficulty brought off the Cheshire foot, who could by no order be withdrawn from firing against the town.[44]

It has been suggested that Denbigh's description of his 'difficulties' in ordering the Cheshire soldiers to withdraw points to a certain level of indiscipline among Brereton's ranks, but it is likely that, given their usual aggressiveness and application under fire, they were extremely reluctant to break contact with the enemy, especially given their success at Oswestry a few days previously.[45] Besides, there is evidence that having experienced the Earl's indifferent leadership and reversals in the Midlands only months before, the Cheshire foot, like others, mistrusted his judgement. Denbigh admitted that 'at Whitchurch Major Lothian moved me from the Cheshire commanders to take Cholmondeley House in my way, which I willingly consented unto'. Of the assault on the Royalist garrison on 8 July he recounted:

> I ordered the giving on in several places to storm it, having intelligence they had few men to maintain the works. But finding the Cheshire commanders who had engaged me very backward, some absent, and those that were present not unmindful of a former disgrace and repulse they had received there with great loss, could not, except Major Lothian, be persuaded that the attempt was feasible. In the end I declared that if they would not assist me in the service of their own county, I would make a trial only with the Staffordshire regiment of foot, which consisted but of 200 musketeers which way of emulation brought back the Cheshire foot to their accustomed forwardness and valour which they have expressed on all occasions. The Staffordshire foot led the way, seconded by some Cheshire foot, and the rest of the Cheshire foot were disposed of to give on in two other several parts, and in places where the moat was conceived most fordable. The assault was so fierce upon their works, and at the same time out men endeavouring to get down the drawbridge behind those works, bred such a distraction in the enemy that they quit their works and retired into the house, and the governor himself looking out of the window demanded quarter, which was then granted by Major Lothian, and after by me, informed the governor, caused the bridge to be let down, our men entered.[46]

---

43 *Great Victories obtained by the Earl of Denbigh*; *CSPD, 1644,* pp.332, 337–8; Malbon, p.138.

44 *Letter sent from Sir Thomas Myddelton*; Phillips, *Memorials*, II, pp.182–6.

45 Worton, *Montgomery*, p.87.

46 *Great Victories obtained by the Earl of Denbigh at Shrewsbury.*

Denbigh's parting comment that 'Upon retiring to a convenient place, whither I had called a Council of War before we were assembled, both horse and foot and train of artillery marched away without order, and I forced to follow after to Nantwich', is particularly telling in that it insinuates that unlike the more popular Myddelton and their own officers, the Cheshire foot had experienced what some modern historians and psychologists refer to as 'leadership malpractice', wherein soldiers suffer combat stress through a lack of confidence in their commander.[47] Denbigh's failures and unpopularity with the Shropshire Committee in particular, hastened his departure in autumn 1644. Sir William Brereton's dispute with him is beyond this book, suffice to say that it was part of a wider quarrel within the associated counties between Denbigh who sought a negotiated settlement with Charles I, and his hard-line opponents.[48] Also, as Worton puts it, Brereton also endeavoured to 'extend his influence as de facto regional commander in Shropshire and Staffordshire'.[49] Back in Cheshire, Denbigh received word from Sir William Brereton of the shattering Royalist defeat at Marston Moor, and in view of Rupert's return march towards Lancashire, he urged him to keep his army together in order to prevent the Prince's forces from uniting with the King.[50] But the Earl remained immobile: always reluctant to take decisive action, he was pressed by Myddelton – who had recently acquired men and materiel in London – to undertake an invasion of Wales, but was under pressure from county committees to return their troops.

On 16 July the Committee of Both Kingdoms sanctioned Sir Thomas Myddelton to undertake military operations in Mid Wales, with the stipulation that he was expected to cooperate with his fellow regional commanders. Having reached Marston Moor on 2 July, the day after the battle with Meldrum and some troops of Cheshire cavalry, Brereton acquired 500 captured muskets. After briefly joining the siege of York, he led his men to the magazine at Hull, where cavalry pistols and carbines were procured.[51] Sir William's party arrived back in Cheshire soon afterwards. Following a difficult passage back through Lancashire, Rupert reached Chester on 25 July, having recrossed the Mersey at Hale Ford. The difficulties he faced in restoring order and morale in the city were reflective of a wider disintegration of Royalist fortunes in the northern Marches. Writing from Nantwich to the Committee of Both Kingdoms on 3 August Sir William Brereton said of the Prince's forces:

> we conceive they are in much want of ammunition and arms, because they are so little active, and quarter their horse and foot, except those in the city of Chester, upon the Welsh side beyond the Dee, and in Wirral, which is a corner of this county and almost a peninsular, whither we cannot have access to their quarters.

47 Jonathan Shay, *Odysseus In America: Combat Trauma and the Trials of Homecoming* (New York: Scribner, 2002), p.225; Mary Catherine McDonald, 'Haunted by a Different Ghost: Rethinking Moral Injury', *Philosophy Faculty Publications*, 35 (2017), pp.1–16.

48 *Committee at Stafford*, pp.lxxiv–lxxxii; Hughes, 'Militancy and Localism', pp.51–68.

49 Worton, *To Settle the Crown*, pp.97–8.

50 *CSPD 1644*, p.338.

51 Malbon, *Memorials*, p.140; TNA, SP28/152/7, fols 8r.–v.; *BLB*, II, 796.

> But when the intended and expected forces come to join with us, wherever the [enemy] may be, I hope we will find them out.[52]

By the beginning of August 1644 the Montgomeryshire town of Welshpool, itself of little strategic importance, had become an objective for Sir Thomas Myddelton and his brother-in-law Colonel Mytton. This assumed greater significance, however, when intelligence reported the presence of eight troops of Royalist horse (half of which were from Rupert's own regiment) billeted in and around the unfortified town. Although their temporary commander, Sir Thomas Dallison, was nervous about his exposed position, the presence of this force had mobilised Royalist support in the area, while the commissioners of array for the county were to issue pay and clothing to his soldiers on 5 August.[53] As Myddelton's despatch relates, during the previous afternoon he left Oswestry with Mytton and a force of 300 horse and dragoons, supported by 250 Cheshire infantry.[54] A contemporary London newsbook described the latter as 'two colours of Nantwich foot'.[55] The taskforce executed a night march of around 17 miles 'round about the mountains to gain the town, lest that the lit matches should discover us … compassing and gaining the town about break of day'.[56]

Events would unfold unexpectedly quickly, however. In the half-light the forward Parliamentarian horse ran into enemy outposts, and after a brief firefight pushed them into the town. The main force was overrun and scattered, but with Myddelton's infantry still deploying the majority of the Royalists managed to get away, though not without substantial losses in men and horses.[57] After securing the town and prisoners, and mindful of a counter-attack from Royalist reinforcements, within a few hours Myddleton and Mytton retraced their steps to Oswestry. Although Sir Thomas, like his fellow commanders, remained concerned about the continuing threat posed by Rupert in the region, the Welshpool operation had proven that the Parliamentarians were capable of undertaking destructive sorties into Wales. In the meantime the Committee of Both Kingdoms had initiated strategic plans to counter the danger of Prince Rupert's forces before they could concentrate in the Welsh borders. This would involve a rapid march of the Earl of Manchester's army of the Eastern Association and troops from the East Midlands, but the scheme did not materialise, partly because Manchester, whose troops were to form the core of this force, refused to co-operate. Besides, the threat receded on 20 August 1644 with Rupert's departure from Chester and the passing of his army to the Royalist garrison at Bristol, which he made his new headquarters.

Yet Royalist forces escaping after Marston Moor had continued to stream into Lancashire. The bulk of this 3,000-strong force comprised Sir Marmaduke

---

52 *CSPD 1644*, p.394.

53 *The True Informer*, 10–17 August 1644; Phillips, *Memorials*, II, p.195.

54 *CSPD 1644*, pp.405–6. See also Malbon, pp.140–1.

55 *Mercurius Civicus*, 15 August 1644.

56 *Wareham taken by the Parliament Forces. Also Colonel Mytton's valiant Exploits certified by two several Letters dated at his Quarters* (London: 1644).

57 *Mercurius Civicus*, 15 August 1644.

Langdale's Northern Horse, and cavalry under Sir Thomas Tyldesley, Lord Molyneux and Lord Byron.[58] The latter had assumed overall command in the county since Rupert's exodus from Chester. Yet as Barratt suggests, 'judging by friction which quickly arose between Langdale and the Royalist leaders in Lancashire, it seems likely that the Northern Horse had no intention of being absorbed into Byron's forces, and were already determined on maintaining their independent identity, and ultimately their own agenda'.[59] This would play out during the next week or so. The newsbook *Perfect Diurnall* reported that on 12 August Sir William Brereton 'sent a party of 1,500 foot to join the Lancastrians in beleaguering the town of Liverpool'.[60] The town had been taken by Rupert on 12 June during his operations in Lancashire. Sir John Meldrum's call for a rendezvous for Lancashire and Cheshire forces on Penwortham Moor, south of the Ribble at Preston on the morning of 19 August, was initially declined by Brereton, although his soldiers were sent from their siege positions following pressure from the Committee of Both Kingdoms.

In his account Major Edward Robinson, he began his account of Meldrum's attacks by saying: 'He quartered his army in Preston about Saturday and Sunday. Upon Saturday late at night came up to him a regiment carrying all black colours that came out of Cheshire.'[61] Although this might have been Colonel John Booth's Lancashire regiment, Meldrum's later report mentioned that there was a 'want of ammunition for the Cheshire forces', thus suggesting further that these were Brereton's men.[62] However, it was noon before they all appeared. Meldrum now advanced towards the Royalists, who were on the north side of the river, but his troops were impeded by the boggy ground and by the time his men engaged with them they had managed to cross the broad estuary at Hesketh Bank at low tide and escaped southwards.[63] Sir John gleaned from local intelligence that Langdale's men were heading for Cheshire, although the Royalist main force paused at Ormskirk. After spending the night at Preston, Meldrum's troops followed 'before the enemy was aware of him'.[64]

Although accounts of the battle are muddled and contradictory, it is clear that Byron's army was caught out at Ormskirk. According to one Parliamentarian source, Meldrum's foot immediately attacked, and after 'Colonel Booth's [possibly John Booth's Lancashire regiment] had given fire on them', the Royalist horse was routed from the field.[65] Byron and Molyneux purportedly evaded capture by hiding in a cornfield. The speed and effectiveness of the attack was confirmed by Langdale, who in placing the blame for the defeat on his fellow commanders informed Rupert the

58 *CWTL*, pp.204–6; *CSPD 1644*, p.440.
59 John Barratt, *A Rabble of Gentility: The Royalist Northern Horse, 1644–45* (Solihull: Helion & Co., 2017), p.25.
60 *Perfect Diurnall*, 12 August 1644; *CWTL*, p.204.
61 Robinson, *Discourse of the War in Lancashire*, p.55.
62 *CSPD 1644*, p.440.
63 *CWTL*, p.106.
64 Robinson, *Discourse of the War in Lancashire*, p.58.
65 *Perfect Occurrences*, 28 August 1644; *CWTL*, p.110.

following day, 'The enemy came fast on and the moor was straight so that they with the help of their horse and foot forced them to retreat to another moor where the rest of the horse were drawn up in good order ready to receive them'.[66]

On 21 August, the same day that Langdale's cavalry rode into Cheshire, Sir William Brereton ordered a body of Cheshire horse under the command of the redoubtable Lieutenant Colonel Jones, and a force of Cheshire foot – consisting of Lieutenant Colonel Brooke's men and companies from Colonel Leigh's regiment under Sergeant Major John Trevis (perhaps numbering 400 infantry overall) – to march to Frodsham, where it was believed that Royalist troops under Colonel Marrow were located. Their enemy had withdrawn, but some of the Northwich foot encountered Marrow at Sandiway where the Royalist commander received a mortal wound and 14 of their own soldiers were captured. When Jones and Trevis reached the village of Ashton they realised that their prey was now in Tarvin, barely four miles from the Royalist stronghold of Chester. Spurring onwards, the Cheshire horse surprised the Royalist pickets and drove the remaining cavalry headlong towards the city. Of the action it was reported:

> Some fled into the church, others out of the town towards Chester, but were pursued gallantly by Captain Sankey who commands Sir William Brereton's own troop within pistol shot of the walls of Chester. A gentleman of Sir William Brereton's troop, named Mr Dury, killed one of the enemy close at the works of Chester. And while these were in pursuit of the enemy towards Chester, the rest were not idle in Tarvin; for that worthy and valiant Lieutenant Colonel Jones, who commanded the horse, behaved himself gallantly, as did Major Trevor who commanded the foot. The enemy fired very fast out of the church; they took some horses into the church. The service being very hot there was one brave horse they could not get in; but one of the enemy held him in his hands under the church wall. A corporal of Sir William Brereton's troop, named John Cooper, seeing the horse, ventured to fetch him; but they fired so fast out of the church that he retreated twice, but the third time he ventured up, he pistoled the enemy and brought away the horse, which horse was valued worth four score pounds.[67]

Malbon added that 200–300 horses and 45 prisoners were captured, and the Parliamentarians had 'killed about fifteen of them, only with loss of one man'.[68] It had been a fast-moving and tenacious performance on the part of Brereton's troops, made possible for the most part by determined leadership and skillful horsemanship, but also by the doggedness of the Cheshire foot, most of which had marched upwards of 18 miles and fought twice in a single day.

On the evening of 24 August reports reached Sir William Brereton at Nantwich that Langdale's horse, who had escaped from Lancashire in

---

66 Bod. Lib., MS Firth C7, fol. 146r.

67 *A True Relation of two great Victories obtained of the enemy: the one by Sir William Brereton in Cheshire, etc.* (London, August 1644); Phillips, *Memoirs*, II, pp.196–7.

68 Malbon, p.142.

Battlefield of Malpas from the south-west. (Author's photograph)

unfavourable condition and were haemorrhaging deserters, had crossed into Cheshire from Flintshire, intent on removing themselves to Shrewsbury and the Welsh borders. Although he himself was recently returned from a meeting with Meldrum in Lancashire and caught at a temporary disadvantage, Brereton got word to the bulk of the Cheshire horse – reorganising at Middlewich 11 miles to the north-east, after the triumph at Tarvin – and speedily assembled a force of 800–900 horse and foot under Lieutenant Colonel Jones. The assembled force left Nantwich next evening. Characteristic of Sir William's strategic judgement, he aimed to arrive just before daybreak and catch the enemy unawares, as he had done successfully at Stafford and elsewhere. However, the Royalists, as the Parliamentarian writer Malbon recounted, 'took their ground on Oldcastle Heath [south-west of Malpas], awaiting Colonel Brereton's coming'.[69]

Without hesitation Jones, with Brereton's own troop in the van, charged the considerably stronger Royalist force, while the remaining three troops of Parliamentarian horse and the entire foot pressed forward. Although the lieutenant colonel was hit in the thigh by musket shot, he regrouped and launched a determined second attack on the faltering Royalists. Langdale's formations initially scattered, yet the bitter fighting continued. The clearest account is provided by Sir William Brereton:

69 *Ibid.*, pp.143–4.

Two or three of our troops came not in, which made the assault heavier on the rest, which, together with some seven companies of our foot (whereof three or four were of my own regiment, one of Colonel Brooke's, and the rest of Colonel Duckenfield's regiment) marched out of Nantwich upon the Sabbath day, in the evening, about six of the clock, and came to Malpas in the next morning about the spring of day, where my troop charged the enemy about three or four times, the other troops which followed not being able to come up in the narrow lanes. The enemy were judged to be about forty colours, and betwixt two and three thousand in number. Their commanders thereof, there being many of them papists (for this was the remainder of the Earl of Newcastle's army sometime commanded by Goring) did fight and come on us very gallantly, but their leaders never went back again. There was in the front of my troop divers officers who behaved themselves very gallantly, as Lieutenant Colonel Jones, Captain Sankey, Captain Finch, Captain Church, Lieutenant Burroughs and divers others. When we came to the top of the hill (around Hampton Heath) we discovered the enemy to stand in six or seven bodies, or divisions, in very good order. But before this time we had killed divers of their colonels and great officers. It was not thought fit to pursue any further, we having beaten two strong parties of them through Malpas town. Nor was it safe to engage a hundred against so great a number, and we could not retreat without losing all.

Therefore, it was resolved that we should stand in the mouth of the lane till the foot came up to relieve them, which were commanded by Major Lothian and [Lieutenant] Colonel Venables, which was accordingly done. But before the foot came up, our horse were spent, having received three of four fresh charges by several fresh brigades or divisions, wherein was neither man nor one foot of ground lost, but rather gained every charge. And when the foot came up they performed very good execution; yet they were all in danger to be surrounded by the enemy, who, as they were sufficiently strong, so they wanted not opportunity, when God delivered up so many of their commanders into our hands, who were killed, wounded, and taken prisoners, as will appear by the enclosed.

Their common soldiers, upon the loss of so many of their commanders, retreated, and we were not able to pursue them far. But had we five hundred horse, we might (by God's blessing) have wholly destroyed this army, whereof there may still be about 2,000 remaining, which with the addition of Sir William Vaughan's regiment, and Colonel Trevor's and the remainder of the Prince's regiment or horse, they cannot be above 3,000. They were then on their way to Shrewsbury, and so to the king, but fled back towards Chester, where they could not be admitted, but were looked upon very scornfully, because they were beaten back by so inconsiderable a number, which they exceeded above ten-fold.

The enemy still being numerous can still overmatch us, it is not improbable they may force their passage to join the king's army: therefore it were to be much desired that what horse and foot is intended us may be speeded unto these parts. It is uncertain where Prince Rupert is, but some say he is gone towards Shrewsbury, but some say to the king, but it is not known to many in Chester. Lieutenant Colonel Jones, Captain Sankey, Captain Finch, Captain Church and others, showed much courage and resolution in standing so valiantly, not shrinking a foot at several charges by the enemy, which did so much amaze the enemy that

> some of them swore 'they were devils not men'. Hereof, I desire God may have the glory.[70]

In excess of 150 Royalists were reported killed, while a number of senior officers were taken prisoner. As Barratt puts it, 'Though the Northern Horse had perhaps been unfortunate in coming up against some of the best of Parliament's regional forces, their rather sorry display had forced them off their direct line of march to Oxford.'[71] In his assessment of the situation, the Royalist Arthur Trevor at Chester informed Ormonde in Dublin that 'Many of the Northern commanders of good account lie here of the hurts they received in the retreat; and among them Sir Marmaduke Langdale, a person of great courage and much prudence. The disorderly retreat, the disasters and the ill-discipline used by the Northern Horse when they were here, hath procured some scandal and much prejudice to his Majesty's affairs here'.[72]

Sir William Brereton now began to plan his army's part in the siege of Liverpool, which had begun in earnest soon after the victory at Ormskirk and would continue for the space of 10 weeks. Whilst the strategic necessity for the recapture of one of the remaining Royalist garrisons in the north was clear, the port of Liverpool had been a major point of supply for the Cheshire forces. Their involvement may also have been intended to bolster the local Parliamentarians who lacked enthusiasm for the operation. The Lancashire colonels were split by internal problems, such as disputes over the financing and the prosecution of the war. Moreover, after the Montgomery campaign Sir John Meldrum reported, 'I have had much to do to bring back the Lancashire foot to their quarters before Liverpool, in regard to their want of obedience even to their own officers, the unseasonable weather, and the time of harvest'.[73] But this was a frustrating time for Brereton, as the Committee of Both Kingdoms made frequent operational demands on his army. On 30 August 1644 he was asked to supply 500 foot for the garrisons of Wem and Oswestry because Sir Thomas Myddelton was attempting to extract his forces from the Shropshire strongholds to raise the siege before Montgomery Castle.[74]

In a letter to the Committee on 9 September Sir William Brereton reported, 'I had sent to Wem part of three companies lately raised under the command of Lord Calvin, one of my captains, Lieutenant Colonel Coote and Captain Finch, which I had not time to complete'.[75] Malbon testified that on 30 August 'all the forces at Nantwich, except Major Croxton's and the town companies marched forth to Middlewich, where they quartered that night. And the next day to Northwich and Great Budworth, and then to Tarvin, which they fortified with strong works, made it a market town and therein put a garrison'.[76] Further garrisons were established as Brereton consolidated

70 *The Success of Our Cheshire Forces, as they came Related by Sir William Brereton's own pen* (London: August 1644); Phillips, *Memoirs*, II, pp.198–200.

71 Barratt, *Rabble of Gentility*, p.35.

72 Carte, *Letters*, I, pp.60–1.

73 *CSPD 1644–5*, p.5.

74 *CSPD 1644*, p.462.

75 *Ibid.*, pp.484–5.

76 Malbon, p.145.

the army's positions around Nantwich and south-west of Chester. On 8 September 1644 the three Cheshire companies previously despatched to Wem and Oswestry spearheaded the capture of Moreton Corbet with their Shropshire compatriots. The following day Sir William Brereton recounted, 'they had been the night before very successful, and have with about 80 musketeers, whereof most were Cheshire men, and about 50 horse taken Morton Corbet garrison. This party was commanded by Lieutenant Colonel Reinking and Lord Calvin, who assaulted the garrison, and after an hour's fight it was delivered up'.[77] Malbon credited the success to the Cheshire foot and dragoons, stating, 'the Lord Calvin, Lieutenant Colonel Coote and Captain Finch with all their companies (being come a little before to Wem from Nantwich), did march to Moreton Corbet House and by assault took it, and in the same three score and odd prisoners'.[78]

These were officers of considerable ability who had previously served in Ireland – Calvin and Coote were among those who refused to serve the King when the Cessation of Arms was signed, while Finch had been a Royalist who was captured at Nantwich and changed sides. As Worton asserts, 'Not only was Brereton's army a reliable source of timely reinforcements, by the secondment or transfer of a number of officers it also provided the Shropshire forces with experienced leadership'.[79] Eventually the Cheshire forces joined Meldrum's troops before Liverpool. On 10 September the *London Post* reported, 'There are but two garrisons only which resist the Parliament, which are the garrisons of Liverpool and Lathom.'[80] Four days later a relief force mustered by the Earl of Derby was intercepted on its way to Liverpool by Brereton's soldiers who killed or captured 500 of them 'and put the rest to flight'.[81] The Parliamentarian blockade of the town was pressed by sea by Colonel Moore's fleet and by land by Meldrum's combined forces. On 22 September Trevor informed Ormonde, 'This last night the enemy possessed themselves of Birkenhead in Wirral; wherein we had a small garrison for the securing of the passage from hence to Liverpool, which will now be much more straightened than formerly, and I am afraid will not long hold out.'[82]

Further south, on 4 September 1644 Sir Thomas Myddelton had intercepted a convoy of ammunition at Newtown sent from Bristol by Prince Rupert for the Shrewsbury, Chester and Liverpool garrisons. Myddleton ordered its transportation to the castle at Montgomery where it could be stored in immediate safety before it could be disposed of. Later in the day with his whole force he entered the walled town of Montgomery. The castle was held by Lord Herbert of Cherbury, but 'he lacked both the commitment and physical stamina to actively defend the place'.[83] Sir Thomas sent out a foraging party out for provisions for what could be an uncertain period of occupation. Sir John Meldrum described the castle later as 'one of the

77 *CSPD 1644*, p.485.
78 Malbon, *Memorials*, p.146.
79 Worton, *To Settle the Crown*, p.97.
80 *London Post*, 10 September 1644.
81 *Perfect Diurnall*, 9–16 September 1644; *LJ*, VI, p.715.
82 Carte, *Letters*, I, p.65.
83 Worton, *Montgomery*, p.37.

goodliest and strongest places I ever looked upon'.[84] By the following day the Royalist commanders in the region had become aware of Myddelton's presence, while Sir Michael Ernle, together with Sir Michael Woodhouse and Sir Lewis Kirke (the governor of Bridgnorth) resolved to send forces to relieve Herbert, which were drawn from various garrisons in the Welsh borders, and contained a mixture of experienced troops from the war in Ireland and raw recruits. Although the extent of their force is unknown, it considerably outnumbered Myddelton's brigade.

Early on 8 September the Royalists attacked Myddelton's skirmishers, causing him to withdraw his infantry into the castle. Ernle confirmed this by reporting, 'I drew out a considerable force of horse and foot, who marched thither, where they beat Sir Thomas Myddelton, and forced both his horse and foot into the castle and kept them in ten days.'[85] Sir Thomas, however, got off with his cavalry and dragoons, reporting 'some small loss of stragglers that lay loitering behind'.[86] Following the arrival of the main body of foot under Colonel Broughton the Royalists commenced besieging the castle. Sir Thomas Myddelton now rode northwards to procure relief. On 9 September he met Brereton at Tarvin. He requested his immediate support, and although the bulk his horse was still resting after the action at Malpas and his troops were already serving in Lancashire, Cheshire and Shropshire, Brereton agreed to commit a substantial part of his army to the design. Although Brereton's and Myddelton's personal relationship was occasionally strained over competing war aims, the latter had a constructive understanding with the Cheshire officers and had been supported by three of their foot regiments at the relief of Oswestry a few months before.

The two commanders went to Lancashire, where they met Meldrum. He agreed in principle to come to the aid of his allies. He had a large amount of horse at his disposal – not only Lancastrian, but the Yorkshire regiment of Sir William Fairfax – and combined with Brereton's cavalry might number roughly 1,600 horsemen. On 14 September the Committee of Both Kingdoms advised Brereton, and the Lancashire and Shropshire forces that:

> Sir Thomas Myddelton has done very good service in Montgomeryshire, which will be of a very great consequence if he be enabled to make it good. But we are informed that great forces are going against him, and that he is there in some straits, wherein we earnestly desire that he with all expedition be relieved. We desire to send him what forces you can and such provisions as he may need, in order that he may be enabled to keep those parts.[87]

As the most experienced of the commanders Sir John Meldrum led the force, although Brereton provided the largest contingent. The Parliamentarians

84 *LJ*, VI, p.715.

85 Warburton, *Memoirs of Prince Rupert and the Cavaliers*, III, p.25; Phillips, *Memoirs*, II, p.208.

86 *Letters from Sir William Brereton, Sir Thomas Myddelton, Sir John Meldrum, of the Great Victory (by God's providence), given them in raising the siege from before Montgomery Castle* (London: 18 September 1644); Phillips, *Memoirs*, II, pp.201–7.

87 *Ibid.*, pp.500, 505.

promptly headed towards their distance objective. Passing through Shropshire they picked up more Cheshire foot from Wem and Welshpool, the forward units coming within sight of Montgomery Castle on the evening of Tuesday 17 September. Meldrum's force numbered about 3,900 horse, dragoons and foot. They deployed in open ground slightly north of where the Welshpool road crosses the River Camlad and a little over two miles from the town and castle of Montgomery.[88] Loosely positioned across the north and north-east of the town, the Royalists had been joined by Lord Byron with forces from Chester. Yet upon the arrival of Meldrum's troops Byron, who had assumed overall command of the roughly 4,400-strong army, withdrew to the high ground adjacent to the castle, perhaps because the Royalist commanders were unsure as to their opponents' strength and cognisant of a substantial garrison in the castle to their rear. In his account Myddelton outlined the overnight situation and developments the following morning:

> We lay that night in the field that was most advantageous for us, which the enemy had possessed themselves of before, and deserted at our coming thither, placing themselves on the mountain above the castle, a place of great advantage for them. We resolved not to go to them but endeavour the victualling of the castle, whereupon we sent out our parties for the bringing in of provisions.[89]

Early on the morning of 18 September 1644, possibly realising that a large part of the Parliamentarian horse was absent on foraging duties, Byron ordered a general attack. Myddelton stated that the Royalists 'came up to our ground and gave us battle'. Almost immediately Colonel Trevor's regiment charged headlong into the Parliamentarian horse, forcing them back in some confusion. The Yorkshire commander, Sir William Fairfax, who had previously been at the relief of Nantwich, rallied some of his own troops and counter-attacked, but he became isolated and taken prisoner. Mortally wounded, Fairfax died the next day. Meanwhile the infantry battle was developing in earnest. As the Royalist foot advanced in good order the Parliamentarians seem to have immediately opened fire, but probably at too great a distance to be effective. A London source, probably drawing on a first-hand account, mentioned: 'At the first advance of the enemy they discharged their muskets at too much distance, by reason of which our first impression failed of the execution which was expected. On this they with noise and violence pressed upon us and firing close upon our men they made them in some disorder to retreat.'[90]

As Worton implies, the 1,400-strong Cheshire foot, consisting of Brereton's, Booth's and Duckenfield's regiments, 'had fired by three-rank salvoes, in order to quickly deliver a weight of fire to bring the Royalist advance to a halt'.[91] This they had recently delivered with great skill at

88 Andrew Abram, *The Battle of Montgomery 1644* (Bristol: Stuart Press, 1993), p.9.

89 *Letters from Sir William Brereton*; *LJ*, VI, p.715.

90 *The London Post*, 24 September 1644.

91 Worton, *Montgomery*, p.87. The presence of Colonel Duckenfield's men is confirmed by an entry in his accounts, referring to a payment of £100 made in September 1644 'sent to my

Oswestry and Malpas. It seems there was a further exchange of shot, although at some points the lines closed, with Sir William Brereton reporting, 'it came to push of pike [weapons being 'charged' and thrust horizontally at the enemy], wherein they were much too hard for us, having many more pikes'.[92] The formidable offensive capacity of the pike had been witnessed by Sir John Meldrum in October 1643, when leading a sally from the besieged garrison of Hull. He wrote later: 'The violence of our soldiers was abated by 100 pikes of the enemy, who charged the van of our foot, scattered and in disorder did drive us backward again … and enforced us all to a shameful retreat.'[93]

The 'push of pike' technique is described by Sir John Smythe, who wrote in 1595:

> [When the pikes are] ready to encounter with another … letting fall the points of their pikes and carry them close breast high with both hands steadily and firmly, the points full in the face of their enemies. And the second rank likewise straightening and closing themselves by rank and front, and joining themselves to the back of the first rank, and following them step with step carrying their pikes above hand over the shoulders of the first rank, the points of their pikes likewise towards the face of the enemy's.[94]

Brereton's comments may signify the numerical advantage of the Royalist foot, or as seems more probable, they possessed a higher proportion of pikes to shot than the Parliamentarians. Before long though, numbers began to tell as the Parliamentarian foot were forced back. Brereton added that 'We were so very hard tasked by the multitude of our enemies … as that, if the commanders and soldiers had not engaged and behaved themselves very gallantly, or if we had wanted any part of our forces, it might have hazarded our army, for it was very dubious and uncertain which way the Lord would incline the victory.'

The Royalist foot – superior in numbers – pressed forward and began to threaten the Parliamentarian right flank and seize the bridge over the Camlad behind them. With the loss of such a route of retreat Meldrum's army might have faced annihilation. But the tide of battle was about to turn. Meldrum's horse, still intact, reformed and drove their counterparts in great disorder from the field. The Lancashire regiments of Tyldesley and Molyneux 'ran without a blow struck', while Colonel Trevor, who had courageously led the opening attack, was unhorsed, but managed to escape as the entire strength of the Royalist cavalry dissolved and fled. Simultaneously, at the hands of their officers, men of great experience and tenacity such as James Lothian, Robert Venables and a number of captains, the Cheshire foot rallied and counter-attacked. The Royalist regiments – whose fragile morale had evaporated with

---

regiment as they marched to Montgomery and into Wirral by Sir William Brereton's order' (TNA, SP28/128/10, fol. 6v.).

92 *Letters from Sir William Brereton*; *LJ*, VI, p.715.

93 *A True and Exact Relation of the Great Victories Obtained by the Earl of Manchester and the Lord Fairfax Against the Earl of Newcastle's Army in the North* (London, 1643).

94 Sir John Smythe, *Instructions, Observations and Orders Mylitare* (London: 1595), pp.25–6.

the rout of their horse – broke and the soldiers not immediately killed or taken were routed. The Royalist Arthur Trevor lamented the cowardice of Byron's foot, 'who ran shamefully when they had no cause of so great fear'.[95] According to Brereton, 'The Lord so guided and encouraged our men, that with a fresh and valiant charge we routed, and put to retreat and flight their whole army, pursued them many miles, even in the mountains, and did perform great execution upon them.' Watching on, the garrison of the castle sallied out and overran the Royalist entrenchments, taking many prisoners in the process.

The conduct of Brereton's infantry drew the admiration of his fellow commanders. Myddelton, who had previously served with them at Oswestry and described them then as 'soldiers full of courage and resolution', reported: 'Sir William Brereton with the Cheshire foot did most bravely behave themselves that day, and did beat the best foot in England, as they the very enemies confess, being all Prince Rupert's foot, and the chosen foot out of all their garrisons.' Similarly, Meldrum wrote, 'The Cheshire foot, with their officers, carried themselves more like lions than men, especially Major Lothian, who commanded as major-general.'[96] Within the space of little more than an hour Byron's army had suffered colossal damage. From a total of around 4,500 men, the Royalists likely sustained 500 dead and over 1,500 captured, including a high number of officers, although many of these may have been lost during the pursuit phase of the battle. Later Parliamentarian reports mention that Byron retreated to Shrewsbury with about 300 cavalry and some foot, and others reached safety, most of the Royalist infantry had gone. The Parliamentarians may have sustained up to 200 casualties, although their greatest loss was the death of Fairfax.[97]

The victory before Montgomery had been a joint victory. Myddelton gave credit to the bravery of all the commanders and soldiers, while Brereton praised the army as a whole, giving credit for their triumph to God. Yet Meldrum possessed some ill feeling towards Sir William, who had been initially reluctant to assist him at Ormskirk and in his view, taken much of the credit for this and other successes. Sir John greatly wanted the glory from the fight at Montgomery to offset his humiliating surrender at Newark some six months earlier, when he was out-generalled by Rupert, and was forced to capitulate and march away in defeat.[98] Within days of the fight at Montgomery the Parliamentarian army began to return northwards, leaving Myddelton there with his foot and two troops of Cheshire horse to help bring in supplies.[99] By 21 September Meldrum and Brereton had reached Oswestry, but because the hastily assembled taskforce that had gone to Montgomery had not had much logistical support, and the soldiers at some distance from their regular sources of rations and pay expressed their discontentment, they were

95 Carte, *Letters*, I, p.64.

96 *Letters from Sir William Brereton*; *LJ*, VI, p.715.

97 Worton, *Montgomery*, pp.91–2.

98 Hutton, *Royalist War Effort*, p.134.

99 *CSPD 1644–5*, pp.5–6.

compelled to move northwards.[100] Besides, the security and provisioning of the 1,500 or more prisoners of war was problematic, even if some of them changed sides or were released on parole. Brereton recommended that any prepared to take the Covenant could be shipped from Liverpool once it had fallen, to fight in Ireland. Nevertheless, four Parliamentarian deserters were 'hanged at Nantwich, being so adjudged by the Council of War, for running from their colours to the enemy'.[101]

Meldrum's focus remained on the reduction of Liverpool. He reported to the Committee of Both Kingdoms, 'There is good hope that Liverpool, by famine, will soon be reduced, and that Shrewsbury and Chester will be at the last gasp, whereof, by God's assistance, there shall be a short trial made.'[102] Sir William Brereton reached Nantwich on 23 September 1644, but within days Meldrum was making further demands upon them. On 29 September Sir John complained of persistent Royalist activity in the Wirral and related how he had ridden to Brereton's headquarters at Tarvin to seek his assistance. There he met Colonel George Booth, who informed him that cavalry from Chester were plundering in Wirral and making the provisioning of his soldiers difficult.[103] Meldrum continued:

> This being so, and finding that there were more of the scattered horse which had escaped from Montgomery come over to Wirral by fording the Dee, I desired Sir William Brereton to send his horse that night to Wirral, so that they, joining with the Yorkshire horse, might fall on the Chester horse the next day. Contrary to my expectation his horse never came to Wirral, but he went that night to Eccleshall Castle in Staffordshire, without giving me notice, although I had commanded all this journey in-chief. Whereupon I resolved to withdraw to Liverpool, leaving Cheshire side to Sir William Brereton, which he had formally undertaken.

On 22 September 1644 Birkenhead fell to the Parliamentarians, while six days later the Royalist gun battery on the banks of the Birket, north of the town, which had bombarded the besiegers at Liverpool and disrupted ferry crossings over the Mersey, was neutralised and its ordnance transported across the river.[104] During the ensuing weeks, elements of the Cheshire army undertook provisioning operations, which in turn denied such resources to their enemy. On 26 October they seized cattle outside Beeston Castle, which resulted in an ambush of a Royalist sally from the garrison by troops under Lieutenant Colonel Massey at Tilston Heath. A few days later Gimbert's dragoons carried out a similar raid, during which 37 oxen were taken, while 'two or three nights afterwards' Croxton's company requisitioned 60 beasts and returned with them to Nantwich. Likewise, Brereton's soldiers in the Wirral seized 100 cattle during the same period.[105] In continuing

100 *CSPD 1644*, pp.505, 524.
101 Malbon, p.149.
102 *Letters from Sir William Brereton*; *LJ*, VI, p.715.
103 *CSPD 1644*, pp.543–4.
104 HMC, *Fourth Report*, I, p.270; Malbon, pp.148–9.
105 Malbon, pp.150–2; *CSPD 1644–5*, p.67.

operations, on 28 October Sir William Brereton reported to the Committee of Both Kingdoms from his outpost at Great Neston, 'we find the inhabitants very well affected to the Parliament, except the gentry, most of whom have deserted the country and are in Chester and Wales'.[106] Hooton House, located five miles north of Chester, was fortified by Brereton's troops, while more were positioned in the area 'that they may assist Sir John Meldrum and the Lancashire forces against the town [of Liverpool]'.

Brereton also engaged in psychological warfare by sending over Lieutenant Colonels Jones and Coote, who had formerly served in Ireland and were known to many in the Liverpool garrison (particularly those in Sir Robert Byron's regiment). They encouraged 60 of them to desert the Cheshire army. On 29 October, anticipating the final act in the drama, Sir John Meldrum requested that 500 Cheshire foot be sent 'for the storming of Liverpool', to which Brereton agreed.[107] Three days later the 'Irish' soldiers, on being promised their lives by Meldrum seized their officers and surrendered the town to the Parliamentarians. In his report on 2 November Sir William Brereton proclaimed Sir John's part in the victory, but also drew the Parliament's attention to the possibility of assigning the 3–4,000 Scots foot 'towards the taking in of Chester and clearing these parts' that had been besieging Newcastle until its fall on 21 October.[108] He could finally concentrate on the great strategic prize of Chester, the last major Royalist garrison in the North West. Brereton had now been joined before the city by Sir Thomas Myddelton, who although keen to launch his own strike into Wales, endorsed the Cheshire commander's appeal to Parliament for more resources for the success of the venture:

> Chester is at present in great want of gunpowder, ammunition and other necessaries, so if you would give the order for three or four regiments of Scots to be sent to Sir William Brereton and myself I doubt not but in a short time to give you a good account of that city, and also of North Wales.[109]

By the autumn of 1644 the Cheshire army of Parliament had emerged from a series of demanding and geographically wide-ranging challenges, during which at key moments the very survival of the Parliamentarian cause in county had seemed close to extinction, while its own survival was uncertain. Yet in a series of bloody and fiercely fought battles, and at times exhausting marches, Brereton's soldiers had also won some decisive victories, none less than their outstanding performance at Malpas and Montgomery. Although the demands placed upon its regiments were heavy – and at times must have felt constant – during the two years of its existence it had developed into a resilient, flexible and dependable fighting force, led by a cadre of experienced and intrepid officers.

---

106 TNA, SP21/17, fols 63v.–5r.; *CSPD 1644–5*, p.67.
107 *CSPD 1644–5*, p.80.
108 *Ibid*., pp.90–1; *Perfect Diurnall*, 4–11 November 1644.
109 *CSPD 1644–5*, p.126.

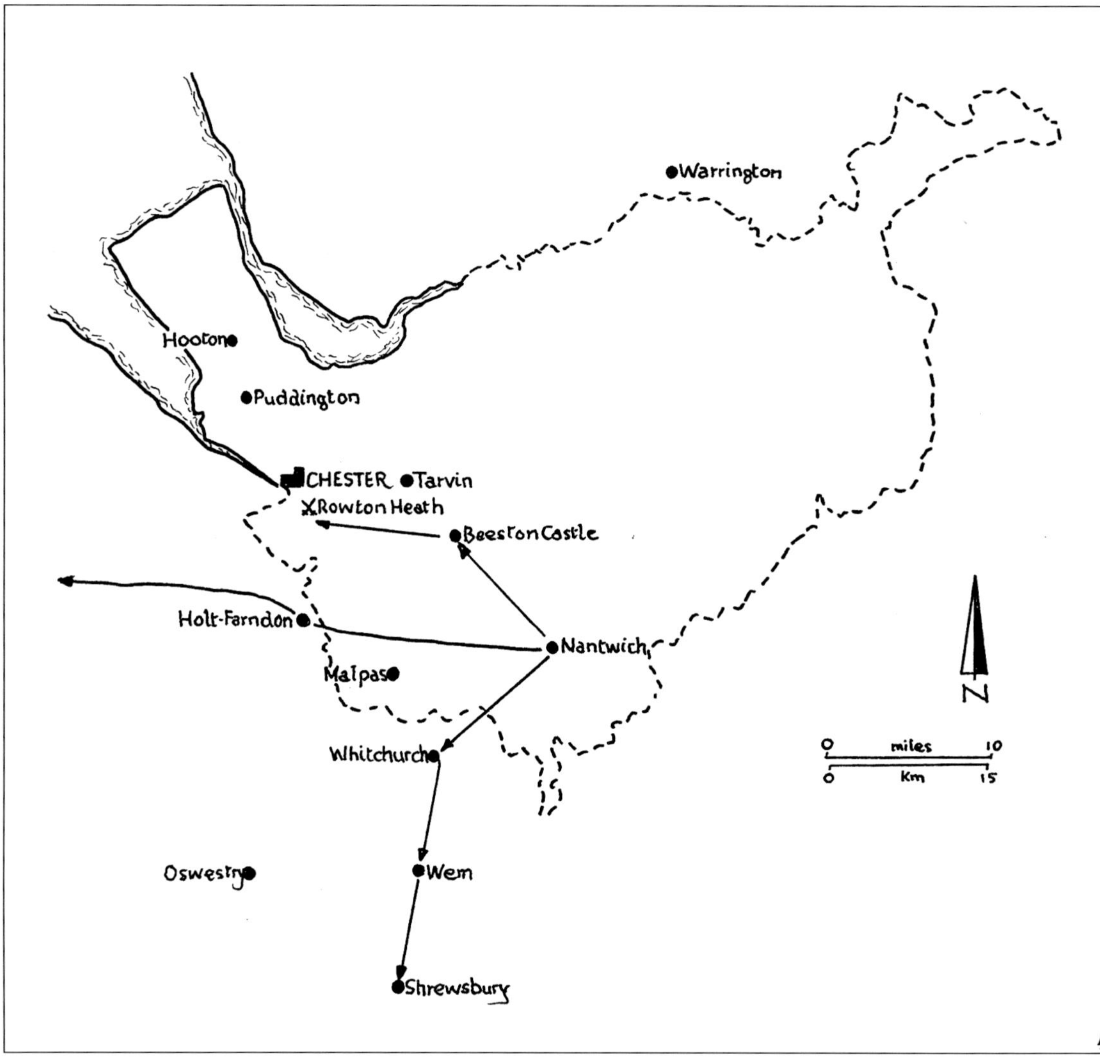

Map 3 Parliamentarian Military Operations in Cheshire and beyond its borders 1645, 1646

3

'The present expedition against Chester': January 1645–February 1646

The reduction of Chester remained the principal operational focus of Brereton's army until the surrender of its garrison in February 1646. Although a detailed study of the siege or 'leaguer' (to use its contemporary name) is beyond the scope of this book, studies by Morris, Dore, Barratt and Ward in particular have gone a considerable distance in elucidating various aspects of the siege from a military, political and strategic perspective, including some of the key phases of the struggle.[1] Three of the four surviving letter books of Sir William Brereton cover the period of February to May 1645 and October 1645 to February 1646. Moreover, a range of other contemporary sources, both Royalist and Parliamentarian, offer key evidence of the prosecution of the sieges of Chester and other garrisons, and attempts to disrupt them, as well as the experience of the defenders. By January 1645 Sir William Brereton had begun to tighten the blockade of Chester by establishing a series of outposts to the south and east of the city. From his forward base at Tarvin, which had been established the previous summer, a force had been placed outside Beeston and another in Farndon at the Cheshire end of the Dee Bridge, to try to prevent raiding on the backs of the besiegers. New garrisons had also been established at Aldford, Oulton, Huxley, Tattenhall, Hawarden, Bridge Trafford, Barrow and Upton, while by early January a strong base had been pushed forward to Christleton, barely a mile from the eastern suburb of Chester at Boughton.

However, the Cheshire Parliamentarian army, even with the additional support of some Staffordshire and Lancashire troops, still did not possess

1 P.H. Lawson (ed.), Rupert H. Morris, *The Siege of Chester, 1643–1646* (Chester, 1923); Dore, *The Civil Wars in Cheshire*; 'Beeston Castle'; 'Sir William Brereton's siege of Chester and the campaign of Naseby', *TLCAS*, 67 (1957), pp.17–44; *BLB*, I and II, intros; John Barratt, *The Great Siege of Chester* (Stroud: Tempus, 2003); *Rabble of Gentility*, chapter 6; *The Last Army: The Battle of Stow-on-the-Wold and the end of the Civil War in the Welsh Marches, 1646* (Solihull: Helion & Co., 2018), chapters 1, 2 and 5; Simon Ward, *Excavations at Chester: Civil War Siegeworks 1642–46* (Grosvenor Museum Chester, 1987).

the numbers for an all-out assault of Chester at this point. Moreover, the operational and logistical challenges faced by Brereton's commanders in prosecuting the siege, against a large garrison behind formidable defences, were enormous. Lord Byron immediately attacked their recently established outposts – some of which were in isolated locations – with some success. At Tattenhall on the night of 9 January 1645 the Royalists 'took many of Colonel Leigh's horses, arms, and some men of his troop, being of the parliament side in their quarters, and took them to Chester', while two days later Brooke's troopers were surprised in their quarters at Aldford.[2] On 16 January Sir William Brereton appealed to the Committee of Both Kingdoms, 'We hear the king's forces are garrisoning Evesham and Campden House, whence they may more opportunely and undiscovered fall upon these parts. We trust you will not suffer us, who have been upon constant hard duty since the battle of York, to be overpowered by numbers of fresh forces from the king's army.'[3] Forty-eight hours later the Royalist garrison at Chester attempted its most audacious operation to date by attacking Christleton. This was part of a plan that included the relief of Beeston Castle. Lancaster takes up the story:

> One memorial achievement fell out in the time of this leaguer, the enemy from Chester with a body of 1,500 horse and foot, endeavoured the surprisal of Christleton, while they were at dinner. After notice of their approach by a sentry on the steeple, in a quarter of an hour's space, Colonel Jones drew up the horse and Adjutant Lothian 700 foot. The enemy laid a strong *ambuscado* of above 300 foot in the hedges [and] the body of their horse advanced towards their foot in a fair broad lane near Boughton. Colonel Jones with his own troop, and Major Zankey with his, charged through their *ambuscado*, which so terrified the enemy that many of them cast down their arms. Then they routed their horse, against whom the city shut their gates, lest by their retreat they should lose all their foot. Adjutant Lothian divided his foot, and drew them into the fields to fall on the enemy's foot on both sides the lane, whom we utterly routed, chasing them within musket shot of their own works. Our horse being but few not seconded by the reserve, the enemy's horse many, and compelled by the citizens to face about, we were necessitated to drive away the prisoners we could with safety, and whom we could not bring off we cut and slashed miserably, which caused many to supplicate themselves prisoners, that they might escape wounds. Many escaped from us down a steep hill by the river, others got into boggy places.[4]

Brereton, praising his officers, added:

> Lieutenant Colonel Jones led on the horse with much judgement, valour and success. I do not hear of any of our commanders being slain, but Captain Blackwell is missing and Captain Zankey, who is a very valiant man and commands my own troop, being without his arms, was wounded, but it is hoped not mortally. This

2 Malbon, p.154; Lancaster, p.11.
3 *CSPD 1644–5*, p.255.
4 Lancaster, p.12.

> may have good effect on Beeston Castle, and we will endeavour to improve time and advantage by all means in our power.[5]

The defeat, which forced the Royalists onto the defensive, was followed by Byron's appointment as governor of Chester. Brereton, encouraged by the Christleton fight, launched an attack on the Northgate turnpike on the morning of 27 January 1645. Malbon reported that before light and 'approaching near the same unto their works, they perceived the walls by the light of their matches, well-guarded with soldiers'.[6] However, when the assault was made with scaling ladders, the Royalists 'did shoot very vehemently at them, but the Lord preserved them all from any harm'. Three days later, a force from the Wirral crossed the Dee into North Wales and cleared the passage over Farndon/Holt Bridge. These moves were menacing enough for Prince Maurice, and then Rupert to move up to relieve both Beeston and Chester. As Maurice left Shrewsbury, the ever-vigilant Mytton received intelligence of the debilitated state of the town and quickly requested reinforcements. From the Shropshire garrisons he was joined by 250 horse and 250 foot, and elicited from Sir William Brereton the assistance of 400 Cheshire and Staffordshire horse, 300 Staffordshire foot and a company of his own infantry regiment. About 5:00 a.m. on 22 February around 40 to 50 of Captain Finch's Cheshire dragoons stealthily led the storming of Shrewsbury's town wall, whereupon:

> the soldiers helping one another got over, and slew the sentinels, and surprised the soldiers in the court of guard, and from thence went to the magazine, and their chief works, and possessed themselves of them before they opened the gates to the rest of the foot, and the governor and many of the great ones surprised the garrison were surprised in their beds, and when they had made all sure, the opened the castle gate, and let in all the horse and the rest of the foot.[7]

As Maurice arrived before Chester on 20 February, effecting a rather tenuous relief, Brereton's troops were forced to fall back while their works at Christleton (described by Lancaster as having been 'secured from horse by slight mud walls') and Farndon were destroyed.[8] Also given up was Beeston Hall, the main Parliamentarian base for the investment of the castle.[9] On 23 February Maurice's troops, augmented by garrison forces from Shrewsbury and North Wales, assaulted Brereton's outpost on the Dee at Farndon. Of this Vicars later reported:

> a notable defeat given to the forces of Prince *Maurice,* by a party of Sir *William Brereton's* at *Holt Bridge,* in *Cheshire,* under the command of valiant Lieutenant Colonel *Jones,* the manner whereof was thus. Prince *Maurice,* being still greatly vexed in his mind at the sad loss of *Shrewsbury,* and as vigilantly as possibly he

5 *CSPD 1644–5*, p.260.
6 Malbon, p.159.
7 *Shrewsbury taken, a copy of Sir William Brereton's Letter to the Parliament* (London, 1645).
8 Lancaster, p.11.
9 Malbon, pp.167–8; Lancaster, p.30.

could, watching to catch and lay hold on all opportunities to be revenged on the Parliament's party, at last resolved upon one, and therefore sent a party of foot over the River *Dee,* which parts *Cheshire* and *Wales,* and about thirteen companies got over the said river, by laying over it a bridge of canvas dipped in pitch, over which three men might march abreast. These all being thus past over, intended in a dark night, to have surprised Sir *William's* said garrison at *Holt Bridge,* and to have forced their passage that way to some other further design; which garrison, the prince understood was maintained by only two companies of firelocks under the command of Lieutenant Colonel *Jones,* who being thus, now, suddenly assaulted by the said numerous enemy, yet had his men in order and readiness to receive them, and entertained them with such a successful volley of shot, and with such valour and gallantry, that at the very first encounter and giving of fire, he put them to the rout and swift retreat, killed in the pursuit, Colonel *Owen* a knight, and about an 100 officers and common soldiers, took divers prisoners and arms, and five colours, forced the enemy back again in great confusion over the river, in which passage many were drowned; and in which service we lost only six men that were slain, and among them, Major *Jackson* a valiant man and brave commander.[10]

Bullet marks in the north wall of the tower of St Peter's Church, Farndon. (Author's photograph)

10 Vicars, *Magnalia Dei*, p.122.

Maurice left Chester on 13 March and rendezvoused with Rupert at Ellesmere three days later. With a combined force of around 7,000 men they returned to Cheshire. Despite repeated appeals by Brereton and the Committee of Both Kingdoms for substantial assistance from Lord Fairfax, as well as the committees of Lancashire and various Midland counties, this arrived too late to prevent the lifting of the siege.[11] The Scots, whose help Sir William prized most of all, came too late and on 16 March the Cheshire forces were compelled to abandon their positions, and, except for his main headquarters at Nantwich, withdraw, 'where the Cheshire foot – except those that returned to garrisons for the defence thereof – quartered until the Scotch army returned [that is, retreated]'.[12] This must have comprised the best part of Duckenfield's, Booth's and Mainwaring's regiments, with the companies from the Tarvin garrison (Brereton's, Hardware's, William Daniell's and Gerard's), and maybe a few others. In the event, the Princes returned as swiftly as they had come, for their purpose had not only been the relief of Chester, but to remove the last of the regiments from Ireland to strengthen their own forces.[13] Byron was disconsolate, although Brereton reported joyfully that 'the princes have left Chester in a worse condition than they found it'.[14]

Attempts by Sir William Brereton and the County Committee to raise an additional force of 2–3,000 infantry from Cheshire during the spring of 1645 are evident from his letter books, although understanding what its immediate purpose was, from whence such recruits would be drawn and how they were meant to be maintained is far from easy. On 10 April Brereton wrote to the deputy lieutenants, committees and sequestrators of the county:

> I would not so often have visited you with the necessity of procuring 2–3,000 more foot and the speedy levying of the money assessed. Both of these I believe may well be done and deserve the utmost endeavour of every well-affected Cheshire man. To this end I desire the head constables of every hundred may be speedily called to a strict account of want moneys they have received and that the same may be paid to Treasurer James Croxton, and that they may be hastened to the levying of what remains. In the next place I desire all the firemen [musketeers] and all the horsemen in the country to be sent unto us, whom we shall endeavour to marshal so that they be most useful and serviceable. If this be not done and we be constrained to rise from this most hopeful design, I cannot suspect much misery and calamity is destined to the country who may now (though God's mercy) in a short time rescue themselves, if they will but rise as one man and bring their provisions along with them. It is hoped that this may not be any long work, for I am informed that they in Chester have put themselves upon a strict diet of one meal a day, and hereof I can assure you that they have every reason to be very provident in the distribution of what they have, because they have little or

11 *CSPD 1644–5*, pp.294, 344, 351–2.

12 BL, MS Add. 11331, fol. 47r.; *BLB*, I, 141

13 Phillips, *Memoirs*, II, p.246.

14 *CSPD 1644–5*, p.435; H.G. Tibbut (ed.), *The Letter Books of Sir Samuel Luke* (London: HMSO, 1963), p.1178.

> nothing brought in unto them, our men being quartered at Dodleston, Eccleston, Pulford, Hawarden, Bretton, Broughton and Lache.[15]

It appears that the 'country companies' were to be called up, but also there was to be a levy en masse of the full county militia (not just the trained bands). This notion is supported by the Tarvin Committee's instructions to Sir George Booth, sent on 4 April 1645, that he was to 'summon in the country especially all that are enlisted or well-armed', and Booth's sending on of the instructions to Colonel Leigh with the comment that he had told Captains Alcocke and Grantham to call up their (country) companies, but had refrained from:

> [raising the] country people because they were sewing their seeds and had been burdened by frequent call-ups to little apparent purpose. Soon afterwards William Marbury request that the colonels of the volunteer foot regiments should not make any claim to the men who came to the muster, and that they should be put under such captains as 'we' (that is, the deputy lieutenants) shall think fit and 'return home free men when the design was over.[16]

None of this could apply to the country companies who were already enlisted under the colonels, had their officers named and were on a permanent war footing. Finally, if we were to tot up the numbers given to the country companies in Brereton's army list of 30 April 1645, it amounts to a little over 1,000, nothing like the 2–3,000 he said he wanted to add to his army.

It seems that Sir William intended these soldiers as a permanent addition to the Cheshire forces, but one that could be raised as a temporary force to help block up the English side of Chester now that he had withdrawn part of his regular force in order to shore up the Welsh side. The Tarvin Committee stated that this was the intention in their letter to Sir George Booth, and Brereton repeated it in on 10 April 1645.[17] Brereton was hoping for a quick surrender of Chester before the Princes could gather troops to effect another relief, as Maurice had done barely a month or so earlier. With the difficulties over adequate pay and provision, and mounting discontent in some quarters that Brereton was already experiencing with those already under his command, the question of how he could have maintained them remains a valid one. The next eight months were to show that he had underestimated the staying power of the defenders of the city of Chester. In early April Brereton had retained his 'auxiliaries' (Assheton's regiment of Lancashire foot, two regiments of Yorkshire horse and some Staffordshire units), enough with the Cheshire forces to strike into North Wales, pausing only to blockade Hawarden, before continuing onwards towards Mold. Of the developing operations before Hawarden, Byron reported:

15 CRO, DDX/428, fols 76r.–v.; *BLB*, I, 194.

16 CRO, DDX/428, fols 87v., 95r.; *BLB*, I, 162–3, 232.

17 CRO, DDX/428, fol. 95r.; *BLB*, I, 193.

> At the same time likewise Lothian, a Scotchman, adjutant-general to Sir William Brereton, had straightly beleaguered Hawarden Castle in Flintshire (distant four miles from Chester) and both by mines and battery had made several attempts upon it, but (by the good encouragement Sir William Neale's lady, who dwelt in the castle, gave the soldiers) was continually repulsed with loss.[18]

With Brereton intensifying his attacks on Chester and Hawarden, Lieutenant Colonel Jones led an audacious raid deep into Denbighshire, although there were several accusations that he allowed his soldiers to indulge in plundering property and livestock. An estimated 6,000 sheep and 500 cows were brought back to Cheshire.[19] On 29 April Jones wrote:

> a party of 500 horse and 400 foot marched to St Asaph twenty miles distant from Chester where they heard the enemy was. But finding it impossible by reason of their mountains and castles to overtake them being fled thence, the county was driven by the assent of Sir Thomas Myddelton for the gaining of provisions for the army, which in manner until that time was provided for by Cheshire, most of which cattle, the whole number of good cows not amounting to 400 nor the sheep to 2,000 being not fit to be slain.[20]

Confident that the fall of Chester was within his grasp, Brereton continued to tighten the leaguer. To sever the link with Wales, Assheton's Lancashire regiment was brought to Eccleston Ford above Chester and a detachment was placed in the marshes at Lache. Garrisons under Lieutenant Colonel Coote were established at Puddington and Hooton, both intended to observe any crossings over the Dee to the Wirral. Hawarden, where Lothian was laying a mine, might fall at any moment, while Beeston was enclosed by a ditch and mount. Thus, Chester, though less isolated, could only survive for a short while longer. Yet Brereton repeatedly stipulated that this increasing grip on the city depended on the prevention of major Royalist aid from arriving. To add to his concerns, his officers were experiencing considerable difficulties in maintaining their combined forces – in April and May 1645 elements of the Cheshire foot, in particular Duckenfield's regiment and some of the trained band companies brought up to the leaguer, were in significant arrears of pay. Moreover, the Yorkshire and Lancashire troops were close to mutiny and consuming the county's limited supplies.[21]

Considering the protracted resistance of Chester until 1646 Brereton's reports during this period were probably over optimistic, but nevertheless, they were sufficient for the King's army in Oxford to be troubled. This can only have been heightened by Byron's despondent appeal to Lord Digby on 26 April, stating that 'any misfortune that should befall me before relief come, it may appear how little accessory I have been to it; and for these poor means

18 Byron, 'Account of the Siege of Chester', p.13.

19 BL, MS Add. 11331, fol. 23r.; *BLB*, I, 362.

20 *Ibid.*, fol. 38r.; *BLB*, I, 375; Morris, *Siege of Chester*, pp.97–100.

21 *Letter Books of Sir Samuel Luke*, p.505; CRO, DDX/428, fol. 88r.–v.; BL, MS Add. 11331, fols 78r., 81v.–4v., 92v.–5r.; *BLB*, I, 362. *BLB*, I, 202, 469, 474–5, 486, 499–501.

I have left to maintain this place'.[22] The preservation of Chester, as Dore asserts, 'was more vital as ever as Royalist hopes of turning the tide of war came to depend more and more on intervention from Ireland and Scotland'.[23] On 9 May 1645 Charles marched northwards with the 12,000-strong Oxford Army. The Committee of Both Kingdoms informed Sir William Brereton that he should 'have an eye to the king's motions so as not to be surprised'.[24] Again, evidence from his letter books reveals that with his army's position in Cheshire extremely vulnerable as the King's army approached, he suggested that if Cromwell, commanding 7,000 New Model foot in Oxfordshire might quickly unite with Lord Fairfax's northern forces and the Scots they could defeat Charles before his troops became too numerous.[25] On 16 May it was found that the enemy had discovered Lothian's mine at Hawarden, and the same day a council of war voted to forsake it and all siege operations there.[26] Brereton waited until the last possible moment until the King's troops were marching on Market Drayton barely 12 miles from Nantwich before abandoning the leaguer.

Following the cessation of Sir William's military commissions in early 1645 under the Self-Denying Ordinance, on 12 May he was allowed to continue his command of the army for a further 40 days.[27] From his base at Nantwich Brereton corresponded with Lords Fairfax and Leven, and the Committee, the outcome being an agreement for a rendezvous of their forces at Barlow Moor, an open heath on the north bank of the Mersey, south of Manchester.[28] The link-up with Cromwell failed to materialise, however, because the prevaricating Committee of Both Kingdoms had debated whether Sir Thomas Fairfax with the bulk of the New Model Army should besiege Oxford or follow the King. Determining that the Scots, the northern Parliamentarians and forces of various Midland counties could deal with the Royalist threat, it decided that Fairfax should stay put and instructed Cromwell that if the King continued northwards to wheel about and join Sir Thomas in besieging the Royalist capital.[29] Cromwell wrote to Brereton on 18 May, 'no man is more troubled (that I cannot advance to the assistance of friends) than myself. I must obey commands and truly, Sir, I am just now by my orders which I received this day to return back upon important service'.[30]

While Charles I was at Market Drayton Lord Byron arrived from Chester with a party of horse, bringing news that the siege of the city and its satellite

22 Morris, *Siege of Chester*, pp.78–9.

23 *BLB*, II, p.47.

24 *CSPD 1644–5*, p.471.

25 Glenn Foard, *Naseby: The Decisive Campaign* (Barnsley: Pen & Sword, 2004 edn), p.99. For an overview of the events of the summer of 1645 in relation to the Chester leaguer and wider military events, see Dore, 'Sir William Brereton's siege of Chester and the campaign of Naseby', pp.17–44.

26 BL, MS Add. 11331, fols 112v.–13r., 130r.; *BLB*, I, 551–2, 565.

27 *CJ*, IV, p.139; BL, MS Add. 11131, fols 123v., 131r.

28 BL, MS Add. 11331, fols 127v., 158r., 133r.–34v., 144r., 139v.–40r.; *BLB*, I, 572, 578–82, 597–9; *CSPD 1644–5*, pp.504, 506, 509, 512.

29 *CSPD 1644–5*, pp.506, 509, 512.

30 John Rushworth, *Historical Collections of Private Passages of State* (London: D. Browne, 1722), VI, pp.29–30; BL, MS Add. 11331, fols 145r.; *BLB*, I, 583.

garrisons had been raised. With little alternative, especially since the Scots had failed to appear, a council of war held on 17 May at Dodleston, attended by Brereton and some of the army's most senior officers, ordered that:

> all the forces now on the Welsh side [of] the river do draw together into a body tomorrow at such time as Lieutenant Colonel Jones and Major Lothian shall think most convenient, and shall march into Cheshire as they shall think fittest. It is left to the direction of Lieutenant Colonel Jones and Major Lothian whether Colonel Ashton's regiment march to the body or march over the boat at Eccleston and so to Huntingdon, or shall march to Dodleston and Hawarden and so with the rest of the army.[31]

On hearing this the Royalist army veered eastwards, and although Charles was yet to make up his mind about Chester, it began a march to the south towards the East Midlands and distant objectives in Yorkshire. At Knutsford on 22 May Sir William Brereton informed Leven that due to the proximity of the King's army to his own headquarters at Nantwich, 'I can bring no more foot than one regiment and some choice dragoons – firelocks that were in Ireland lately mounted.' Besides, when they arrived at Barlow Moor later in the day the combined forces gathered there amounted to barely 1,000 foot and 300 horse. Leven and Lord Fairfax had not come, and the Lancashire appeared to be in disarray.[32] Brereton continued about the area over a number of days, hoping for more troops to assemble. On 27 May he informed his associate and fellow MP in London, William Ashurst:

> Herein I shall not presume to advise but shall deliver my judgement that if Sir Thomas Fairfax or some other be not speedily sent down with a powerful army, you hazard all the north; yea and York itself. I have been five or six days about Barlow Moor to provide the conjunction of the forces that were to be united for such service as Lords Leven and Fairfax should order, and have brought up the Cheshire horse and dragoons, and what foot could possibly be spared (which was Colonel Duckenfield's regiment) and now have sent for more foot. There were two regiments of Lancashire foot appointed, Colonel Holland's and Colonel Ashton's. Colonel Holland's regiment … was in high mutiny and Colonel Ashton's on Monday last were few of them come up, but have undertaken to be in readiness. Nut in as much as these have received no orders, there could be now scarce time enough to interpose between the king and York, because the king marches on swiftly and without interruption.[33]

Brereton continued to receive intelligence reports of the King's movements from his scouts in the Midlands. During the last week of May he informed the Committee of Both Kingdoms, Leven and Lord Fairfax that the Oxford Army had skirted Newark, from whence it drew reinforcements, and was moving towards Ashby-de-la-Zouch. His prediction that the Royalists were

31 BL, MS Add. 11331, fol. 130r.; *BLB*, I, 565.
32 BL, MS Add. 11331, fols 142r.–v; 144v., 150r., 156r.; *BLB*, I, 610–14, 621.
33 BL, MS Add. 11331, fols 169r.–v.; *BLB*, I, 651.

fixed on attacking the East Anglian counties was confirmed by reports from other quarters.[34]

In addition to this, Sir William Brereton and the Committee at Nantwich gathered a sizeable force, led by Lothian and Jones, to follow the movements of the King's army east of Market Drayton, and then south-east to Leicester and Naseby in late May 1645. On the evening of 29 May, two days before Leicester was stormed, sacked and many of the garrison massacred by Rupert's troops, Brereton was met at Middlewich by Adjutant Lothian, with 885 Cheshire and Staffordshire foot, and some dragoons. The force consisted of 80 soldiers of Lothian's own company, 80 men under Captains Cotton and Baskerville (of Mainwaring's regiment), 60 foot led by Captain French, 20 under Sergeant Major Daniell (of Booth's regiment), 300 from Duckenfield's regiment, 120 of Leigh's regiment, 200 Staffordshire foot under Sergeant Major Snow and 25 dragoons of Holt's company. In his note to Sir William, Lothian further requested the payment of '10s. a man for my company and proportionable for my officers'.[35] A letter from Jones to Brereton in November 1645 concerning outstanding pay for 'the troops that were at Leicester' under his command, lists the cavalry troops of Duckenfield, Brooke, Shepley and Carter, plus Captain Gimbert's dragoon company.[36]

The force was assembled before Sir William left for London on 13 June 1645. Lancaster mentions what happened subsequently. According to his account, besides Lothian 'with a considerable body of foot', there was Jones with 500 horse and dragoons.[37] If the numbers are accurate, then Brereton's army list of 30 April 1645 indicates that more horse (perhaps Jones's own troop) and other companies of dragoons were present.[38] Lancaster further mentions that when they reached Bakewell on 6 June, the horse, with other northern Parliamentarian cavalry were instructed to unite with Gell, who was to be under Fairfax's command and assist at the rear of the Royalist army.[39] Yet because of the Derbyshire commander's ineffectiveness they reached Naseby too late for the decisive battle. Joshua Sprigge reported acerbically in his account of the campaign, 'it was the wonder of all men how they [the King's army] (being in such a tired and distracted condition) could escape Sir John Gell's horse, who the same day were on their march from Nottingham towards Leicester'.[40] However, the combined forces under Lothian and Jones would reach Leicestershire, where they supported Fairfax in his retaking of the town. Among the army remaining in Cheshire though, vigilance against Royalist threats remained paramount. On 9 June 1645 Captain John Glegg's troop found itself caught up in an incursion from Chester, intent

34 BL, MS Add. 11331, fols 144r., 150r., 156r., 157v.; *BLB*, I, 614–7.

35 BL, MS Add. 11331, fols 165r.–v; *BLB*, I, 653–4.

36 BL, MS Add. 11332, fol. 105r.; *BLB*, II, 897.

37 Lancaster, p.16.

38 BL, MS Add. 11331, fol. 45r.; *BLB*, I, 385.

39 *CSPD 1644–5*, p.569.

40 Sprigge, Joshua, *Anglia Rediviva or England's Recovery* (London, 1647), p.47. For recent assessments of Gell's conduct during and after the Naseby campaign, see Slack, *Man at War*, chapter 9; Stone, *Derbyshire in the Civil War*, chapter 8.

on disrupting various Parliamentarian garrisons about the besieged city. According to Lancaster:

> The enemy encouraged hereby issued out of Chester with three hundred foot, and one hundred and twenty horse (the design not yet known to us), passed near Tarvin, so through Barrow, and accidently fell upon Captain Glegg's quarters at Helsby. [They] took him, all his troop, and some country men prisoners, [and] marched towards Beeston, intending to pass home by Holt. Upon intelligence, Tarvin sent out, under command of Lieutenant Colonel Venables with 200 horse (most of which by special providence happened to be there at the time) and 190 foot. They hastened towards the enemy, whom they encountered in Eaton town, rescued Captain Glegg, all his men, the country men, and some of his horse, slew seven, many escaped by counterfeiting themselves dead, took three captains, many officers, two hundred and twenty soldiers, and all their plunder. [We] lost not a man on the ground but four died of their wounds not long after.[41]

Malbon reported similarly, adding:

> The parliament side took two captains and officers, and common soldiers about two hundred and ten, and slew ten of them (only with the loss of three which were slain and taken prisoners), besides one barrel and many bags of powder, and some arms, about three hundred. And on Tuesday morning, fourscore and seven of the prisoners were removed from Tarvin to Nantwich.[42]

With Brereton at Westminster under the terms of the Self-Denying Ordinance during most of the summer, the County Committee – a body of notable Parliamentarian gentry, some with and some without commissions – oversaw the general direction of the war in Cheshire. On 10 May Parliament had ordered that 'Sir George Booth, Sir William Brereton, Colonel George Booth, Colonel Henry Brooke, Colonel Robert Duckenfield, Colonel John Leigh, the governor of Nantwich for the time being, or any three of them, are at the end of 40 days [the extension to Brereton's commission] to order and direct the carrying on of war within the county of Chester, and to govern the forces under the command of Sir William Brereton until Parliament shall make further notice'.[43] Another directive instructed that at the end of 40 days Lieutenant Colonel Jones to succeed to the command of Brereton's regiment of horse, and Sergeant Major Lothian to lead his regiment of foot. This arrangement, although pleasing to the mainly Presbyterian faction who opposed to Brereton, lacked his religious motivation, verve and capacity for decisive action.

41 Lancaster, p.15.

42 Malbon, pp.172–3.

43 *CJ*, IV, p.139; BL, MS Add. 11131, fols 123v., 131r.

South view of Beeston Castle by Samuel and Nathaniel Buck, 1727.

By the beginning of August Lothian and Jones had begun to reconstitute the siege of Beeston, within seven days redigging the line of trenches and constructing a strong fort within musket range of the gate to the outer ward. They also fetched over a barn, which they stored with provision and munitions.[44] Crucially, the Royalist garrison was blocked up, its only succour being a strong enough relieving force that might drive off the besiegers. The new fortifications around Beeston could be maintained by a small force of 100 men, thus a significant portion of the Cheshire Parliamentarian army could be utilised against Chester. Once more though, wider military events interrupted it and drew on its resources. Following the Royalist disaster at Naseby the King's army retreated via Hereford to South Wales. Here he hoped to rebuild his foot – most of which had been lost – and meet up with Rupert and Goring in the South West. Increasingly desperate, Charles looked towards Ireland for military assistance, but this failed to materialise. Royalist hopes were shattered again at Langport on 10 July, while the King envisaged a meeting with Montrose's army to the north. Within three weeks his exhausted forces returned, the Scottish project having proved as much a mirage as the new army.

Now in Raglan, the hapless King was shadowed by the Northern Association horse commanded by Colonel General Sydenham Poyntz, who had been tasked with pursuing him since the northern march. Rupert's surrender of Bristol to Fairfax's army on 10 September 1645 was catastrophic in that it exposed the entire West Country and made Chester the only major seaport connecting the Royalists with Ireland. On 18 September Charles, with a force of around 3,000 cavalry, marched towards Denbighshire and Chester, from where Byron had petitioned him for assistance. Lancaster mentions that in countering the King's march the Cheshire foot were deployed 'to secure the garrisons from surprise', and that Jones, with 400 cavalry and dragoons, rode into the south of the county 'to fall upon the rear of the enemy, and to fight if occasion should require'.[45] He adds that Jones was 'drawn by

44 Lancaster, p.16; Malbon, p.180.
45 Lancaster, p.17.

authority' to a longer march than was intended, expecting to be engaged towards Doncaster or Newark. Such moves correlate with instructions from the Committee of Both Kingdoms on 12 September to the Derby horse, and those of Colonels Rossiter and Greaves to join with Poyntz in engaging the King's force, which was reported to be at Bridgnorth.[46] Back in Cheshire, Lothian and Jones executed the second phase of their plan to bring about the reduction of Chester. Somewhat dramatically, Lancaster wrote:

> This work so advanced, their thoughts were upon Chester, though it seemed a design most impossible in the judgement of man, for all visible means was gone, the commander-in-chief [gone] to Parliament, all the auxiliaries dispersed to their own countries, and we, a small despised inconsiderable force, not only engaged in the Leaguer of Beeston, but hard put to it by the incursions of Holt Castle (a bad neighbour) besides other forces out of Wales and Chester, daily infesting some part of the county, but, laying to heart the reproach cast upon us by some of our pretended friends, as if all out works were to lie idle in the Leaguer, and considering it was all one with God to work with many or few, we resolved to storm the city.[47]

Thus, on 19 September, amidst great secrecy, a detachment of 500 horse, 700 foot and 200 dragoons drew off from their assembly point at Beeston in a probing attack on the riverside mount at Boughton. In the early hours of the following morning, carrying scaling ladders, Gimbert's dragoons spearheaded the assault that took the defenders completely by surprise. As Lancaster relates:

> Captain Gimbert was the first that entered, his ladder being too short, he lift up his man to the mount (near the riverside) from the top of it, his man drew him up by the hand and then they cried 'a town, a town', immediately they cleared that mount, slew Lieutenant Aldersley, the captain of the watch, and put the rest, about six men, to flight. Then others set to their ladders, possessed themselves of all the mounts of that side of the city, and with the instruments we brought with us, broke open the gates: then all the horse entered, with the remainder of the foot, with loud shouts, which utterly daunted the enemy. The next work was to take the Barra, being the fortification for the Forest Street, which was effected speedily, by entering at the back of some houses, not far from the gate. So we fell upon that guard in the rear, who fled in all haste into the city. That while our men opened the gate into the Forest Street, which we entered with a full body of horse and foot, and some close pursued the guard, that they were near entering the city with them. Master Mayor very difficultly got into the city, but made such haste, that he left the sword and mace at his house in the suburbs.[48]

During the relative lull of 21 September, the Parliamentarians positioned two or more cannon in a battery near St John's Church, and the next day

46 *CSPD 1645–7*, pp.132–3.

47 Lancaster, p.16.

48 *Ibid.*, pp.17–18.

Stephano della Bella, *Soldaten die kannon afvuren* (*c.* 1640), depicting an artillery battery firing. (Amsterdam, Rijksmuseum, CCO 1.0 Universal (CCO 1.0) Public Domain Dedication)

unleashed a determined bombardment upon the city wall. One the defenders reported, 'the east side of our walls near the Newgate received a visit from their artillery ... 32 shots were made and by them a breach at which ten men abreast may enter'.[49] At eight o'clock that evening 500 of Brereton's troops attempted to storm the city through the breach (which by modern estimates was 25 feet wide). During close-quarter fighting the dragoons, leading the attack, suffered most of the casualties – Captain Finch and a number of his men were wounded, while Gimbert and his lieutenant, John Turner, received injuries. Malbon states that they were forced to retreat, however, because the foot seconding them were slow coming up.[50] Byron conceded that the assault troops came on with 'great boldness', but:

> those in the Newgate and the houses adjoining to the breach, annoyed the enemy with their shot, so did the grenadoes and the fire pikes, which were used by very stout men, and placed upon the flanks of the breach ... Thrice that night the enemy was upon the top of the wall, but at last quite beaten off, seven of them were killed upon the top of the wall, who afterwards fell into the street, and were the next day buried by us. They were some of them taken alive, much hurt, and much drunk, that the scent of them was very offensive.[51]

On 23 September the King entered Chester by the Handbridge across the Dee. He brought with him an escort of around 500 horsemen, including

49 Morris, *Siege of Chester*, p.223.
50 Malbon, p.182.
51 Byron, 'Account of the Siege of Chester', p.8.

Stephano della Bella, *Slagveld met soldaten te paard in gevecht* (*c.* 1640), illustrating cavalry in battle. (Amsterdam, Rijksmuseum, CCO 1.0 Universal (CCO 1.0) Public Domain Dedication)

his Lifeguard and Lord Gerard's cavalry. Earlier in the day some 2,500 men under Sir Marmaduke Langdale had crossed the Dee eight miles south of Chester at Holt Bridge. Langdale was to approach Chester from the south-east with orders to either trap the besiegers in Chester's suburbs or intercept them as they retreated to their base at Tarvin. The Parliamentarians within the suburbs were faced with a dilemma upon learning of the King's approach, in that if they withdrew they sacrificed their gains, but if they remained they risked destruction. The Royalists, however, were unaware that Poyntz was advancing towards them with about 3,000 horse of the Northern Association and Midland counties. On the night of 23 September he was met at Whitchurch by messengers from the Cheshire army, requesting his assistance. Leading the vanguard during a night pursuit, at about 6:00 a.m. Poyntz encountered Langdale's troops arrayed on Miller's Heath some three miles south of Chester. Due to the nature of the terrain the Parliamentarians had some difficulty deploying, but they 'immediately drew into order, and advanced upon them (though all his force were not yet come up)'.[52]

A brief summary of events was supplied by Poyntz to the Speaker of the House of Commons, the day after the battle:

> Yesterday we discovered the enemy on Miller's heath within three miles of Chester, whereupon I sent to Chester for some foot, which was very seasonably sent me, and in my advance towards them we unawares met a body of them in a narrow pass on the top of the heath, where we had a very violent encounter, wherein we cut off many of the king's Lifeguard and routed the rest, then we retreated to our main body, and toward four of the clock in the afternoon we advanced toward them, and finding the enemy ready for battle we presently fell upon them, killed, took, wounded, and routed the whole army, and I am confident they never received a greater blow.[53]

52 Lancaster, p.19.

53 *A True Relation of the great Fight and Routing the Kings forces on Rowton Heath* (London: September 1645).

However, the Royalists had the better of the initial action. The Parliamentarians holding the suburbs of the city heard unpromising reports of the fighting, and it was probably these that prompted the deployment during the early afternoon of 350 horse under Jones and 400 commanded musketeers led by Colonel John Booth to assist Poyntz. Their remaining forces (numbering about 1,000 foot and 150 horse) under Lothian remained in position to await events. Meanwhile, Langdale had retreated about a mile north-eastwards to Rowton Heath, but soon found himself in a difficult situation. Perhaps realising that Jones and Booth were likely to take Landgale's men in the flank, Lord Gerard led a body of around 500 Royalist cavalry and 500 foot from Chester, via the Northgate and the northern suburbs, intending to attack them in the rear, but in actuality most of them were fired upon by their own men from the city walls. During the ensuing, confused fight on Hoole Heath the Parliamentarian musketeers disrupted the Royalist advance under cover of the hedgerows and 'so galled their horse, that the rear fled, perceiving their loss by them, upon whom they made no execution'.[54] Captain Daniell of Brooke's regiment was particularly commended for his conduct in leading 200 Cheshire foot.

The arrival of Lothian's force of '200 horse and as many foot', led by Lieutenant Colonel Coote completed the destruction of Gerard's men, while from the walls of Chester Royalist musketeers fired indiscriminately into the massed ranks, killing both friend and foe.[55] Jones probably approached the battlefield from the west, having taken the Saighton road from Chester. In this way he struck Langdale's horse in the flank, compelling him to abandon his position at the southern end of Miller's Heath. Poyntz then launched a frontal attack, which joined with the Chester troops 'in the enemy's ground'. Parliamentarian accounts portray the action as fierce and closely contested. One of Poyntz's officers recounted, 'A little before five o'clock, we joined a terrible storm, firing in the faces of one and other hacking and slashing with our swords, neither party gained or lost a foot of ground, as if everyone were resolved there to breathe their last.'[56] In describing the effect of the Parliamentarian mounted assault, Lancaster placed the emphasis on Jones and his troopers:

> the greatest burden lay upon the Cheshire Horse, because they were fresh for service, the rest being very much wearied with an incessant march and long fasting. Colonel Jones encouraged his soldiers with such language, that he drew tears from their eyes, and vows from their mouths, that they would stick fast to him, whether in life or death, which they faithfully performed. The rest also buckled themselves to the service in hand, and to give their due, they performed their work with as much vigour and resolution as could be expected from men. But God owning his own cause, made the Parliament party victorious, who slew them with a great slaughter on the ground, and chased them all over the country.[57]

54 Morris, *Siege of Chester*, p.119.
55 Carte, *Letters*, I, p.98.
56 Morris, *Siege of Chester*, p.119.
57 Lancaster, p.20.

The Royalists suffered an overwhelming defeat at Rowton Heath with many survivors scattering northwards and westwards where a number were captured. Their casualties, variously estimated, included about 600 killed and 800 captured. Among the dead was the King's cousin, the Earl of Lichfield, while about 50 of the Lifeguard were also lost. Lancaster admitted to a Parliamentarian loss of 'not 30 men on the ground', although among the Cheshire horse Captain Hugh Culme, and Captain-Lieutenant Grant of Jones's troop were killed.[58] The overall figure was doubtless higher, given that some of the Yorkshire officers were reported dead or 'sore wounded'. Charles extricated himself from Chester on 25 September, taking refuge in Denbigh Castle, while his remaining troops tried to regroup in the local area. The defeat of Rowton Heath, followed by the swift departure of the King brought about a plunge in morale among the Chester garrison, while Byron was hardly consoled by his subsequent assurances of relief and supply of provisions.

Encouraged by the victory outside the walls of Chester, on 25 September 1645 the deputy lieutenants requested the Committee of Both Kingdoms to send summonses to the counties of Staffordshire, Shropshire and Lancashire to send forces to aid Lothian and Jones before Chester.[59] The next few days saw a quickening in the pace of Parliamentarian operations. Poyntz was ordered by the Committee to continue pursuing the King, but also to provide assistance in completing the seizure of Chester. On 27 September Byron informed Digby that 'At this instant the enemy's horse appear before the town on the Cheshire side, tomorrow, as one who comes from amongst them assures me, Poyntz passes over into Wales; so that unless the king's horse be very active in beating up their quarters and cutting off provisions from the enemy this town will be enforced to a parley'.[60] Lancaster mentions that 1,000 Lancashire foot and 500 Cheshire foot accompanied Poyntz's forces, which had been reorganising after Rowton Heath, during this operation, adding:

> We quartered that night near Chester, on Monday night at Wrexham, endeavouring to inform ourselves of the king's motion, and to follow him as opportunity might serve. Upon Wednesday 1 October the intelligence was that the king marched towards Hereford, thereupon General Poyntz that day marched after him from Wrexham to Ellesmere and Colonel Jones towards Chester, to make good the Leaguer there.[61]

In the meantime, a great brass piece and three other guns had been brought up to the siege.

On 27 September a concerted bombardment was opened on Chester's defences. Two days later the Royalist garrison received reports of undermining, while the besiegers were preparing a new battery at St John's

58 TNA, SP28/224/2, fol. 72r.; SP28/224/3, fols 249r.–v.; SP28/252/1, fol. 1v.; Lancaster, p.20.

59 *CSPD 1645–7*, pp.158, 162–4.

60 *Ibid.*, p.164; Morris, *Siege of Chester*, p.124.

61 Lancaster, p.21.

South-west prospect of the city of Chester, Nathaniel and Samuel Buck (1728), showing the castle, St John's Church and Dee Bridge. The advantage which the capture of the tower of the church gave to the Parliamentarians is clear.

Church and were manoeuvring troops to close off the Welsh side of the city.[62] On 4 October 24 cannon shots were discharged at the old breach near the Newgate and a Royalist battery was suppressed, while further measures were taken to bring breastworks on the Welsh side to within musket range.

Following a four-day pause, preparations for a major assault of the city were complete. Later that day the commanders at the Leaguer summoned the garrison to surrender. Stalling for time, Byron answered, 'We have received his Majesty's express command for the keeping thereof: and cannot without his knowledge break so great a trust laid upon us. And therefore must require liberty of fourteen days, to give his Majesty an account of your demands and to receive his further pleasure.'[63] The proposal was rejected the following day. Poyntz warned Byron that 'If you will not treat upon any other conditions you must expect (what you desire) the fury of enraged soldiers.' In their last answer, Byron and Mayor Charles Walley stated, assured the citizens that his request had been rejected because the Parliamentarians knew that the King was hastening to their relief, but cautioned them, 'We have received your refusal of our reasonable offer, which argues you intended not what you pretended, sparing the effusion of Christian blood. We are therefore ready to defend ourselves to the utmost of your rage, not doubting of God's blessing and protection upon us.'

62 Byron, 'Account of the Siege of Chester', pp.12–13; Malbon, p.185; Morris, *Siege of Chester*, pp.226–7.

63 Byron, 'Account of the Siege of Chester', pp.13–14; BL, MS Add. 11332, fols 92v–93r.; *BLB*, II, 671–4.

From batteries placed at Brewers Hall, situated in the northern suburbs, the Parliamentarian gunners opened a heavy bombardment of the Northgate and line of walls extending to the Goblin Tower. Lancaster observed that the wall:

> proved so thick, and the ball so brittle, that not more than the battlements were beaten down, whilst the besieged endeavoured to make up the breach by packs, father-beds, etc., and to line the wall all along: our cannon on the Welsh side made great execution, swords, arms, legs, whole bodies were seen to fly in the air, cart loads of bodies drawn off, and the horse in the rear driving up men and women to make up the breach.[64]

According to Byron:

> A breach was made near the Goblin's Tower, but not easy to be assaulted by reason of a dry ditch under the wall, which they were to pass before they came to the breach. Their other battery near the Newgate, made not that effect they expected by reason of the rampier newly cast up which had made the wall cannon-proof.[65]

Overall the Parliamentarian bombardments had expended 40 barrels of powder, although before they had begun the Cheshire gentlemen had offset some of the cost by raising £400 on credit.[66]

Before sunset the Cheshire army commenced its assault. Of the desperate hand-to-hand fighting Lancaster reported:

> That night, a little before sunset, we stormed the city upon the new breach, and the old breach near the Newgate, and by scaling betwixt the Eastgate and the Phoenix Tower. The storm was very hot for two hours together, some of ours carried it very stoutly, fighting in the breach, and on the tops of the ladders. Had they been suitably seconded, the town in all possibility had been ours that night. In conclusion, we made good our retreat in the dark. We lost twenty-seven men on the ground, of those, no officers but a sergeant and a corporal. About 60 [were] wounded; amongst them Lieutenant Colonel Venables, and Captain Massey, brother to the renowned Massey of Gloucester, but neither of them dangerously.[67]

On 20 October Jones and Lothian were commended by the Speaker for 'the great service you have performed from time to time with much valour and resolution, and of your industry, diligence and care in this present service'. They were each allowed £200 out of the £10,000 granted to the Cheshire forces.[68]

Sir William Brereton arrived back in Cheshire on 26 October 1645, having had his commission as commander-in-chief of the army renewed for a period of four months. He was met by his senior officers, along with the complaints of soldiers of two months' arrears of pay. Brereton immediately

64 Lancaster, p.22.
65 Byron, 'Account of the Siege of Chester', p.14.
66 *Ibid.*, fol. 117r.; *BLB*, II, 1248.
67 Lancaster, p.22.
68 *CJ*, IV, p.308; BL, MS Add. 11332, fol. 54v.; *BLB*, II, 711.

Repaired breach in Chester's city wall near the New Gate. (Author's photograph)

reproached the head constables of the hundreds of Macclesfield, Northwich, Bucklow and Nantwich for their failure to collect the weekly assessments meant for the regular payment of his soldiers.[69] In attempting to address the practical and sensitive issue of soldiers' pay the sum of £10,000 had been voted by the Commons 'for such forces as are drawn together about Chester and North Wales'.[70] Anxious to forward money to his men at the earliest opportunity, during his journey from the capital Sir William had instructed his London agents to immediately forward £2,000 to Cheshire in specially made leather satchels 'to be disposed of there for the service of the forces united against Chester'.[71]

Whilst Brereton was heading towards Cheshire, Lothian and Jones had continued to tighten the Parliamentarian grip around Chester, although the Welsh side still proved challenging. On 18 October a bridge of boats spanning the river at the foot of Dee Lane and eventually protected on the Welsh side by two mounts, was completed.[72] This would enable them to reinforce their forces on either bank more quickly. Moreover, a new battery sited below St John's Church inflicted damage on the Dee Mills, opposite Handbridge. During this period further operations to secure the Welsh approaches to Chester opened up the possibility of obtaining supplies and

69 *CSPD 1645–7*, p.158; BL, MS Add. 11332, fols 27r.–v., 119v.; *BLB*, II, 780–1, 931.
70 *CJ*, IV, pp.293, 302; BL, MS Add. 11332, fols 2r., 99r.–v.; 11333, fol. 32r.; *BLB*, II, 667, 886–7, 1057.
71 SP28/35/2, fol. 260r.; BL, MS Add. 11332, fols 1r., 3v.; *BLB*, II, 700–2.
72 Malbon, p.186; Lancaster, p.22; Ward, *Excavations at Chester*, pp.12–13, 33–7.

money from North Wales, where there remained reluctance to support the Parliamentarian cause. On 20 October Lieutenant Colonel Jones led a successful attack on Holt Castle, capturing Lieutenant Colonel William Byron and according to Lancaster, 'had the forlorn hope observed the command, to keep within musket shot of the body, in all probability, we had entered the castle before they had drawn up the bridges.[73]

Soon afterwards, Jerome Zankey, who had been authorised by Poyntz to lead a mounted force of horse and dragoons 'to fetch out of Wales so many cattle as shall serve for the aforesaid purpose', targeted the town of Hawarden, 10 miles to the north-west, 'which would not contribute to the Leaguer'. Zankey laid an ambush 'within pistol shot of the castle', taking 12 prisoners as well as 42 head of cattle, 52 sheep belonging to the governor, 14 horses and a bear (which 'roared upon the man that laid hold on him'). Lancaster concluded by adding, 'Thenceforth the town contributed, and we restored the cattle. This became a good precedent to the Welsh, who above 20 miles off follow their example'.[74] Although such raids were successful from a Parliamentarian perspective, the possibility of a Royalist relief of Chester from the vicinity of the Welsh borders remained. On 24 October 1645 news reached the commanders at the leaguer from the Shropshire Committee that Sir William Vaughan, a soldier of experience of Continental and Irish warfare, was at Ludlow with a force of 1,500 horse and foot, intent on the marching to the relief of the city. Other reports, however, put the number at 3,000, and rumoured that Vaughan was to be joined by troops from North Wales and possibly from Ireland.[75] But although Byron had advised him that 'the enemy for the present being both weak and much discouraged since their loss upon the last assault', the Parliamentarians enjoyed a distinct numerical advantage and could be relatively confident of resisting any relief force.[76]

Brereton had arrived in Nantwich on 26 October as Vaughan's advance guard was nearing Chirk and his main body passing Oswestry.[77] He cautioned Jones and Lothian against premature contact and urged that they fight at a distance from Chester itself, 'since they in the city may by issuing out much annoy you by falling on your rear as the Nantwich [garrison] did by falling on the Irish army'.[78] On 27 October Jones, commanding the leaguer on the Welsh side of the Dee, assured Brereton:

> I find the horse under my command so gallantly resolved that were there no expectation of foot, yet I should give the enemy a meeting. However, I pray haste up all the forces you can that, the siege being secured, we may chase the enemy out of Wales and these parts. Were there 500 men commanded with spades, shovels and mattocks, I am confident that in four days to cast such a trench and outworks

73 Lancaster, p.23.

74 BL, MS Add. 11332, fol. 47v.; *BLB*, II, 676; Lancaster, *Narrative*, p.23.

75 BL, MS Add. 11332, fols 13v. 14r., 21v.–22r.; *BLB*, II, 717–8, 726–8.

76 BL, MS Add. 11332, fol. 81r.; *BLB*, II, 683.

77 C.E. Long (ed.), *Diary of the Marches of the Royal Army during the Great Civil War; kept by Richard Symonds*, CS, Old Series, 74 (1859), p.276.

78 BL, MS Add. 11332, fol. 20r.; *BLB*, II, 750.

> on this side of Chester from water to water that, if the enemy were master of the field, he should not relieve the city.[79]

He also asked Lothian, in command on the English side, to send over Duckenfield's regiment and any other available foot, 'for it may be we shall fight this day'.[80] Jones's cavalry patrols had reported Vaughan first at Ruabon and then at Ruthin, but by 29 October he reasoned that he was aiming to meet with Welsh troops somewhere in the Clwyd Valley. Allowing a day's pause to allow the Shropshire troops who had arrived exhausted from a forced march to rest, and to enable Lothian to coordinate the foot about to march from the Leaguer, the taskforce got under way. According to a list of 'those forces that marched under the command of Jones and Lothian' this consisted of roughly 1,350 horse (the figure for the reformadoes is not given) and 1,250 foot. In response to promptings by the Committee of Both Kingdoms the Cheshire army had been reinforced before Chester by around 2,000 horse and 1,350 foot from the counties of Yorkshire, Shropshire, Warwickshire, Derbyshire, Staffordshire and Lancashire.[81] The 200-strong reformado unit had come from London with Sir William Brereton. Lancaster gives 1,400 horse and 1,000 foot, while Symonds estimates the Parliamentarian infantry at '1,500 at least'.[82] Additionally, the Cheshire horse is described as participating in the forthcoming battle and probably rendezvoused with the taskforce at Ruthin, where on 31 October the Parliamentarians learned of Vaughan's presence near Strata Marcella (Whitchurch).

Although the Royalists were already drawn up, they were thrown off guard by the rapid approach of the Parliamentarian troops before noon on 1 November. Symonds mentions, 'Saturday at noon we had the alarm, for they were at Whitchurch below the town'. Byron confirmed this by stating, 'The alarm being given, the foot were sent down a lane, by which the enemy was to pass'.[83] Lancaster's report to the Speaker, written the same day, offers the clearest account of the campaign and decisive battle:

> Sir William Brereton upon his return to Cheshire found the work for reducing Chester and Beeston Castle in a good posture. Bust the enemy, esteeming Chester the masterpiece of the kingdom, extended their utmost endeavours for the relief thereof, gathering into a body about Denbigh waiting for an opportunity for the effecting of that high design without which they must give up these parts as utterly lost. Sir William, reserving a competent strength to make good both leaguers, sent away Colonel Jones and Adjutant Lothian, dextrous and trusty men, with the Cheshire forces and auxiliaries of the counties of Lancashire, Derbyshire, Warwickshire, Montgomeryshire and Salop, the whole being 1,400 horse and 1,000 foot, the cream of all these parts. The enemy, under the command of Sir William Vaughan (as our best intelligence by the prisoners gives us), were about

79 BL, MS Add. 11332, fols 25r.–v.; *BLB*, II, 757.
80 BL, MS Add. 11332, fol. 22v.; *BLB*, II, 745.
81 BL, MS Add. 11332, fol. 32v.; *BLB*, II, 791.
82 Lancaster, p.24; Symonds, *Diary*, p.258.
83 Symonds, *Diary*, p.258; Byron, 'Account of the Siege of Chester', p.17.

> 1,700 horse and 400 foot. On Thursday night we marched to Mold, on Friday to Ruthin, where, having intelligence the enemy were at Denbigh (reported to be a far greater number), we hastened on Saturday 1 November, accompanied by that active gentleman General Mytton and part of his auxiliaries, the rest being left at Chester.
>
> The forlorn hope, forty out of every regiment, was commanded by Captain Otter, captain of the reformadoes, a gallant soldier, and Captain Edwards, a Cheshire captain and well deserving gentleman. Coming to Whitchurch, a mile from Denbigh, they were in a lane flanked by the enemy's horse and dragoons, so that they were forced to make good that pass with the forlorn hope and Cheshire dragoons, under the command of Captains Finch and Holt, stout and resolute men. These with the forlorn hope behaved themselves gallantly and maintained the pass until the foot came up, the most part of which with the Warwickshire and Derbyshire horse, commanded by Majors Saunders and Hawkesworth, seconded the forlorn hope and bore the burden of the day, whiles the reformadoes, Cheshire horse and 400 Lancashire foot were intended for a greater service. For the commanders, finding that strait lane too difficult a pass to fall through upon the enemy who were marshalled in an open field, these last mentioned (by the advice of those who knew the country) were drawn thence to Denbigh Green (a way near four miles in compass) to fall upon the enemy upon even ground. While these were drawn off the foot (exceedingly forward to engage themselves) beat the enemy out of the lane, and routed both horse and foot, driving them under the command of the castle where they rallied themselves. But the forlorn hope, Derby and Warwickshire horse with the foot encountered them again, and utterly routed them, whom the horse chased eight miles in the way to Conwy, making great execution on them in the way, taking many prisoners and 5–600 horse, and so long pursuing them that not above fourscore were left together. To give everyone his due in this service would savour too much of vainglory, but I may modestly report that everyone endeavoured to exceed each other in gallantry, whose spirits God hath raised to so high a pitch as might to suit to a work of so high a nature. It is conjectured by those best able to give an account herein that about 100 of the enemy were slain and about 400 taken prisoners with divers men of quality. It is not known that any of ours are slain and few wounded.[84]

On 15 November the Royalist garrison at Beeston Castle capitulated after almost a year's siege. News that Royalist horsemen carrying provisions and ammunition were approaching from Holt assisted the governor, Captain William Vallett, in obtaining good terms. Vallett and his men were to march out with drums beating, colours flying, matches lit, each soldier with a proportion of musket ammunition. Those who wished to lay down their arms and return home could do so provided that they lived quietly and peaceably there.[85] According to Malbon 56 soldiers surrendered with Vallett, 20 of whom departed for their homes. Brereton estimated that about 50 men

---

84 *A True Relation of a Great Victory obtained by the Parliament Forces in Cheshire, under Sir William Brereton, against the King's Forces, under the command of Sir William Vaughan, near Denbigh* (London: 1 November 1645); BL, MS Add. 11332, fols 76r.–v.; *BLB*, II, 801; Phillips, *Memoirs*, II, pp.282–3.

85 BL, MS Add. 11332, fols 90r.–v., 101v.–2r.; *BLB*, II, 868–72.

were permitted to 'march away on foot with their arms to Flint and so to Denbigh or Beaumaris. There remained about 40, who laid down their arms and submitted themselves, desiring liberty to live at home.'[86] Intriguingly, Symonds reported 'the captain and his company marched out with all their baggage, arms, match lighted, bullet in mouth, etc. Their ammunition was so spent that the enemy gave the soldiers many shots of powder to make their conditions good.'[87] This author had no reason to be predisposed towards the Parliamentarians, but he seemingly recorded a rare show of respect to the surrendered garrison on the part of Brereton's soldiers.

Vallett was an officer of Lord Byron's regiment of horse, and given that a number of Royalist prisoners switched sides after Nantwich, there may have been some earlier contact in Ireland. All were agreed that at the time of the surrender the garrison was facing starvation. Lancaster remarked, 'They were brought so low that they had eaten their cats and had not provision for that night', whereas according Malbon 'There was neither meat, ale or beer found in the castle, save only a piece of turkey pie, two biscuits, a live peacock and a peahen.'[88] Of the general conditions, Sir William Brereton wrote:

> The castle was left well strengthened and in very neat order, and in good repair. I do believe a great part of what they had exacted and collected from the country was bestowed upon the reparation of the castle, wherein we found above four-score muskets, little provision and less ammunition. The greatest part of the soldiers within the castle laid down their arms, and desired liberty to go home and live in peace.[89]

On the day after the surrender Brereton ordered the provisions and ammunition to be removed from the fort outside the castle's gate, and the building itself and all the siegeworks to be dismantled. On 18 November he went from Nantwich to the Chester suburbs from which he summoned the city, but the terms expected by the garrison were rejected.[90]

The commanders at the leaguer remained resolute. By early November 1645 they had received a mortar piece from the Shropshire Committee, and there is evidence that others came from the same source.[91] These were soon put into action with devastating effect. The bombardment of Chester had begun in earnest by 10 November. On this day the Royalist eye-witness, Randle Holme wrote:

> By this time they have unmuzzled death and swear they will let them loose amongst us, a wide-mouthed mortar piece in which like the mouth of Etna spits little mountains in our faces and grinds our dwellings into dust and ashes, three of these bombards or huge stones light amongst us, and the day following three

86 Malbon, pp.188–9; BL, MS Add. 11332, fol. 92r.; *BLB*, II, 875.
87 Symonds, *Diary*, p.276.
88 Lancaster, p.25; Malbon, p.189.
89 BL, MS Add. 11332, fols 100r.–v.; *BLB*, II, 885.
90 BL, MS Add. 11332, fols 91r., 93r.; *BLB*, II, 875, 878.
91 BL, MS Add. 11332, fol. 51r.; *BLB*, II, 832.

> more, the uncapped houses crouch for fear, and beg forbearance on their bended knees, but it seems these forerun a greater judgement. Two great granadoes are by this time mounted, one of which being filled too full of spirit becomes its own executioner, by bursting in the air, the other lights in a back side without doing any harm at all.[92]

The barrage continued sporadically over the next few days. During the night of 25 November the Royalists made strong attempts to burn the Parliamentarian bridge of boats, while simultaneously a sally came out to attack the siegeworks south of the river. About this time Brereton informed the Speaker that within Chester, 'The better sort eat beef and bacon, but little cheese … the poorer sort of the city that are not soldiers are ready to starve, they are compelled to eat horseflesh.'[93] On 10 December the mortar and artillery bombardment resumed, compelling Sir William to report:

> We have made use of some mortar pieces, which we borrowed from Shrewsbury, whereby great execution hath been done. On 10 December fired in the night three several places in the city, and killed and wounded several in their beds. Yet this does nothing at all work upon them but they seem still as stubborn as formerly, so as we judge it more easy to fire and destroy than reduce that strong city.[94]

The march of a taskforce from the Leaguer of Chester to Whitchurch in December 1645 was Sir William Brereton's counter to the last serious attempt to relieve the city. Although his troops would not directly encounter any Royalists, the operation would ultimately usher in final phase of the Parliamentarian siege of the city. In March and May 1645, when the appearance of the princes and marches of the Oxford Army threatened the security of the Cheshire army, Brereton had acted on the orders of the Committee of Both Kingdoms, while in October he was on his way back to Cheshire, and the preparations that led to the Denbigh fight had been made before his arrival by his military subordinates and the deputy lieutenants.[95] There is every reason to believe that the Whitchurch march was undertaken largely by Sir William's own initiative. The welter of correspondence – both Parliamentarian and Royalist – during the weeks running up to the launch of the taskforce on 21 December 1645 provides a valuable insight into both the reports of Royalist movements targeted at the relief of Chester, and the strategic outlook of Brereton and other leaders at the Leaguer during this period.

On 6 December Sir Jacob Astley was commissioned by the King as Lieutenant General of Worcestershire, Herefordshire, Salop and Staffordshire, his primary mission being to raise and army for the spring campaign of 1646.[96] He hoped to rejuvenate the Royalist cause in the area, while relieving Chester in preparation for a force of Catholic rebels from Ireland, which

92 Morris, *Siege of Chester*, pp.231–2.
93 *Ibid.*, p.149.
94 BL, MS Add. 11333, fol. 14r.–v.; *BLB*, II, 997.
95 *CSPD 1645–7*, pp.435, 471.
96 Clarendon, *History of the Rebellion*, IV, p.152.

was reportedly preparing to cross to Chester and North Wales. However, Sir William Vaughan's enterprise into Denbighshire, aimed at harassing the logistical arteries of the Parliamentarian Leaguer of Chester and the abandonment of the siege had backfired with shattering consequences at Denbigh Green on 1 November with the defeat of his army. On 16 December the crucial garrison of Hereford was lost and the remaining Royalist garrisons in the Welsh borders were in disorder. Astley would not arrive at Worcester to take up his command until Christmas Day, and he was not able to muster sufficient troops to stage any relief of Chester until late January 1646. Nevertheless, during the first weeks of December Parliamentarian intelligence reports related that Royalist forces were on the move. On 15 December 1645 Brereton was informed by the Committee of Both Kingdoms that 'all the horse of the garrison of Oxford and parts adjacent to the number of 1,000–1,200 – some say 1,400 – are under the command of Bamfield or Astley are marching towards Chester'.[97] The following day reports suggested that the King and his nephews were at Worcester, and that there was a build-up of men, arms and provisions there.[98] Equally, Sir Charles Gerard, who commanded the remnants of his troops from South Wales (those not captured at Denbigh) was rumoured to be with Vaughan and planning to march towards Chester.[99]

By around 18 December 1645 more certain information about troop movements was being received by Brereton and the Shropshire Committee by the governors of Shropshire garrisons. The Committee passed on reports that a about 3,000 Royalist troops had marched from Bridgnorth towards Wellington and Shifnal, which they were likely to reach that night.[100] This was confirmed by Byron, who mentioned that he had received a letter from Vaughan dated 19 December, informing him that he was at Wellington 'in the van of the Lord Astley'.[101] The next day the Shropshire Committee reported to Brereton, 'We know not which way they will march, but some speeches have been given out that they will come through Newport, and then it is likely they will march by Whitchurch. We are bold to put you in mind to look to your guards, for it is generally whispered amongst them that they will make way for the besieged to sally out to relieve themselves, and so prolong your business.'[102] Crucially also, two intercepted letters from Sir Richard Lloyd at Holt and the report of one of Brereton's 'intelligencers' at Worcester revealed the prospect of diversionary strikes on the Cheshire army of Parliament's headquarters at Nantwich and Tarvin. The impact of this, it was assumed, would so unsettle the besiegers at Chester that they would abandon their positions and by consequence enable the garrison to achieve its own relief.[103]

97 BL, MS Add. 11333, fol. 45v.; *BLB*, II, 1009.
98 BL, MS Add. 11332, fols 115r.–v., 117v.–118r., 120r., 124r.; 11333, fols 7v., 13v., 15r.; *BLB*, II, 925–6, 933, 936–7, 939, 946, 971–2.
99 BL, MS Add. 11333, fol. 37v.; *BLB*, II, 1041; Symonds, *Diary*, p.264.
100 BL, MS Add. 11333, fol. 41v.; *BLB*, II, 1049.
101 Byron, 'Account of the Siege of Chester', p.20.
102 BL, MS Add. 11333, fols 24r.–v., 26r.–v., 28r., 37v., 39v., 41v.; *BLB*, II, 992–3, 1000, 1005–6, 1023, 1042, 1049.
103 BL, MS Add. 11333, fols 12r.–v., 43r.–v., 36v.–37r.; *BLB*, II, 983, 1007–8.

The next day the Parliamentarian council of war resolved:[104]

> That it may be most advantageous for the Leaguer, that, now the enemy is approaching, we should take out a considerable party and march towards them; so that we might rather fight with them at a distance than suffer them to come so near the city as that those in the city might join with them, or fall upon our rear whilst we were engaged. That Waverton Heath [that is, Rowton Heath] be the place appointed for the rendezvous tomorrow by nine o'clock for the forces that are in or about the Leaguer, and that the Warwickshire horse and one of the Lancashire regiments, and 200 of Mytton's foot and 200 of his horse meet the forces that come from Chester at Malpas about one o'clock, and that the Reformadoes regiment meet also at Malpas or else come with us to Whitchurch, where all the whole body following is appointed to quarter: viz.

Table 1: Whitchurch march: forces to march.

Foot:		**Horse:**		**Officers to march:**
Col. Brooke	0100	Reformadoes	0200	Adj. Lothian
Col. Massey	0100	Warwickshire	0200	Lt Col. Twistleton
Col. Croxton	0100	Derbyshire	0200	Lt Col. Gerard
Adj. Lothian	0100	Montgomeryshire	0200	Maj. Daniell
Lt Col. Gerard	0100	Staffordshire	0150	Capt. Daniell
Capt. William Daniell	0060	Cheshire	0300	Capt. Monke
Staffordshire	0100			Capt. Davenport
Salop	0100	**Sum**	1,250	
Lancashire	0200			
Montgomeryshire	0200	**Dragoons:**	[unstated]	
Sum	1,160			

Table 2: Whitchurch march: forces to stay.

Foot:		**Horse:**		**Commanders to stay:**
Col. Duckenfield	0230	Cheshire	0200	Col. Duckenfield
Lt Col. Venables	0090	Montgomeryshire	0150	Lt Col. Venables
Maj. Daniell& Capt. Brooke	0100	Salop	0150	Lt Col. Carrington
Capt. Grantham & Capt. Alcocke	0070	Staffordshire	0100	Lt Col. Brooke
Wirral foot	0150		0600	Lt Col. Mason
Birtles and Brereton	0060	Cheshire	0300	Maj. Downes
Staffordshire	0400			Capt. Stanley
Salop	0200	**Sum**	1,250	
Montgomeryshire	0200			
Lancashire	0200	**Dragoons:**	[unstated]	
Sum	1,700			

104 BL, MS Add. 11333, fols 45r.–v.; *BLB*, II, 1063.

The task of assembling the force and the bringing up of its replacements at the Leaguer were easier than at the time of the Denbigh campaign – Beeston Castle had fallen over a month previously and, leaving behind a small holding garrison, its besiegers had joined those before Chester.[105] In Brereton's absence, command of the Chester leaguer was left in the hands of two of his most trusted officers – Colonel Robert Duckenfield on the Cheshire side and Colonel Chidley Coote on the Welsh side. Before he left, Sir William wrote to the Committee of Both Kingdoms, explaining the reasons for the expedition and for the move and suggesting that it was their encouragement of 15 December which precipitated his march to encounter a relieving army before it reached Chester. To his Westminster colleague William Ashurst he stated specifically that he was maintaining the siege, before adding, 'We hear from Shrewsbury and those parts that Astley with his forces is advancing to join with Vaughan. And we hear some Irish are landed but the number we hear not certainly.'[106] Brereton remained anxious to reinforce the troops remaining at the leaguer. On 9 December the Committee of Both Kingdoms (prompted by his appeals) had decided that following the surrender of Lathom 2,000 horse and foot should march to Chester, and should be 'designed to lay in the way on this [English] side [of] Chester, in case any relief should be intended'.[107]

After waiting for a few days for Lancashire troops to arrive, on 21 December the taskforce marched. Meeting Mytton's Shropshire troops, the reformadoes and Warwickshire horse at Malpas, it made Whitchurch by nightfall. Brereton's troops remained in the town the next day 'in expectation of further intelligence of the enemy's motions', to which end cavalry patrols were sent out as far as Newtown. It was during this time that news arrived from the Worcestershire Committee of the surprisal of Hereford.[108] This had taken place on 19 December, two days before the Whitchurch march began, but the poor weather and Brereton's own movements prevented the letter reaching him sooner. Since August 1645 Hereford had been considered one of the safest of Royalist strongholds. When the panic died down, Vaughan and Astley began to push their unharmed troops into Worcestershire and Shropshire, and maintained that they had commanded an advance guard that had never been intended for Chester.[109] In realisation that instead of hearing of a Royalist advance they were hearing of a retreat, Brereton wrote to Mytton:

> Before I received yours from Wrexham dated one o'clock today I had given order, not only to the Montgomery horse but to my own dragoons to march back to the Leaguer to strengthen there according to your desire, and likewise have ordered some more foot to Colonel Duckenfield from Northwich and Tarvin. Nine troops of Lancashire horse, which came up to us yesterday, I sent back to the Leaguer to be employed where Colonel Duckenfield, Colonel Carter and the rest think

105 BL, MS Add. 11333, fols 90v.–91r.; *BLB*, II, 868, 874.
106 BL, MS Add. 11333, fols 46v.–47r.; *BLB*, II, 1066–7.
107 *CSPD 1645–7*, p.252; *Perfect Diurnall*, 1–8, 8–15 December 1645; Lancaster, p.26.
108 BL, MS Add. 11333, fols 48v.–49v.; *BLB*, II, 1072, 1055, 1079.
109 BL, MS Add. 11333, fols 50r., 65v., 71v.; *BLB*, II, 1080, 1120, 1131

> fittest and most conducive, both to the blocking up of the city and preserving the quarters on the Welsh side from any Welsh enemy ... We hear nothing of the enemy's advance, but rather of their retreat and dispersing themselves. So as we intend to stay here only so long as till we hear some confirmation of the news we hear of the enemy. Therefore at present we have not that occasion (which we expected) for your forces to be sent hither.[110]

On 26 December the taskforce was hurriedly withdrawn because during what was an exceptionally bitter winter the Dee had frozen, while a sudden thaw broke the bridge of boats, now the main link between the forces on the English side and the Welsh sides of Chester. Although Brereton's troops did not directly encounter any Royalists during the operation in Shropshire, it had shown that an effective and well-organised fighting force could be despatched with relative ease to disperse any potential relief of Chester, yet while confining the defenders inside the city walls. As Byron's hungry and desperate garrison hung onto the city during the final weeks of 1645 and 1646, what would prove to be a final series of attempts to force through provisions to Chester occurred. As Lancaster wrote:

> On Saturday night the enemy in Wales with about 150 horse of the Lord Byron's and others joined with his, marched beside our guards into the city, with some small relief of wheat, oatmeal, pies and moneys for the Welsh soldiers, which was collected for them towards Conwy. The next morning, with the assistance of Chester horse and about 600 foot, they forced their passage through the guard to Hawarden Castle, with the loss of a cornet, a corporal and one common soldier taken by the guard. Colonel Jones, perceiving the danger might ensue to the Leaguer on the Welsh side by this unhappy accident of the bridge broken, hasted that day over the ford with 600 horse [and] 100 dragoons, and appointed 100 foot to march after him, to dissipate that party, which was preparing relief for the city, and to ease those oppressed parts of the burden of free quarter. That night we quartered at Mold, then coasted about the country near Ridley, Denbigh and Ruthin, and returned to the Leaguer upon Saturday. In all the march we found the country well-affected to us, not wanting in courteous entertainment, rejoicing in our success, contributing freely to the relief of the Leaguer [and] tendering their assistance as opportunity might serve for reducing of the country. A people rather to be pitied for their ignorance (whose leaders have taught them to err) than spoiled for their malignity.[111]

The blocking of Hawarden was now especially crucial to Parliamentarian strategy. Jones led elements of the Cheshire and the Derbyshire horse, who 'took up their Leaguer quarters close by Hawarden Castle', while they were joined by Lieutenant Colonel Massey with about 400 foot, which proved 'very advantageous for the intercepting of all relief that might come from those parts of Wales to the city'.[112]

---

110 BL, MS Add. 11333, fol. 51v.; *BLB*, II,1078.

111 Lancaster, pp.27–8.

112 *Ibid.*, p.28.

Despite Byron's hopes, no assistance was forthcoming from hard-pressed Oxford, while any remaining notions of the arrival of Irish rebels had also evaporated. By 7 January 1646 Chester, almost entirely isolated, and its garrison and civilian occupants exposed to starvation, the bombardment eased as Brereton and Byron began to enter negotiations for its surrender. As a mark of their confidence in him, on 22 January the Lords and Commons renewed Sir William Brereton's commission as commander-in-chief of all the forces of Cheshire, Staffordshire, Lancashire, Derbyshire, Salop and North Wales for 40 days.[113] Following a series of acrimonious exchanges between the two commanders, commissioners for both sides agreed to terms for the surrender of the garrison. On 3 February the Royalists departed, passing the Dee bridge and bound for Wales, as Parliament's victorious troops entered the battered and exhausted city.[114] Recognising the significance of the event, Lancaster remarked: 'On Tuesday we were possessed of the city and castle, by which the Almighty (who ever-owned our undertakings) finished the great work of reducing this afflicted county almost spent under the incessant travail of a three-years war.'[115]

The Commons, when it received the news three days later, voted £50 to the messenger that delivered it, with special thanks to Sir William Brereton and his officers for their services.[116] Additionally, a day of thanksgiving was ordered in the cities of London and Westminster, with appropriate sermons preached by ministers. The 'present expedition against Chester' and the war in Cheshire came to an end as the Leaguer was broken up, and some of the besieging troops passed into garrisons in the city and Nantwich. The greater part of the Cheshire army of Parliament accompanied Mytton into North Wales, or remained with Brereton in the midlands, where the final siege of Lichfield Close and the defeat of Astley's forces at Stow-on-the-Wold awaited them.

113 *CSPD 1645–7*, p.317.

114 BL, MS Add. 11333, fols 101v.–2r.; 120v., 128r.–v.; *BLB*, II, 1197, 1200, 1207–8, 1257, 1260; Malbon, pp.194–201.

115 Lancaster, p.33.

116 *CJ*, IV, p.429.

Part II

Identifying, paying, equipping and feeding an army

4

Anatomy of an Army I: Recruitment and Organisation

Given its nature and base of operations as a provincial force, the majority of recruits for Brereton's army were obtained locally, although a great recruiting ground for Parliament during the Civil Wars was London. It was here that in the autumn of 1642 and the summer of 1644 in particular, that a number of men were drawn to enlist in Brereton's army. During the summer of 1642 Sir William Brereton attempted to raise a significant proportion of the trained bands, but was compelled to leave Cheshire for Westminster after unsuccessfully raising men and support for the Parliamentarian cause in Cheshire. However, a strong powerbase was established in Macclesfield Hundred among the 'puritan' towns of Stockport, Macclesfield, Knutsford and Northwich. Here there existed the ability to recruit in the area as it was beyond the power of the commission of array and relatively close to Manchester. Early Royalist demands for recruits for the Lancashire forces from this area had been largely unsuccessful. In August the Congleton corporation paid 'a boy to hold horses, until we had excused ourselves to the Earl of Derby in sending him no men'.[1]

In espousing the Parliamentarian cause in Cheshire, the puritan families of the eastern part of the county possessed a level of religious radicalism and independence that was far stronger here than anywhere else in the county. The 22-year-old Congregationalist, Robert Duckenfield, raised a company of foot and troop of horse for Parliament by mid summer 1642, while local gentlemen such as Ralph Arderne, Edward Hyde and William Duckenfield (Robert's brother) became company commanders in his regiment. Moreover, Robert Venables of Antrobus recruited and maintained a unit of volunteers from his own pocket, which saw active service in Cheshire and Lancashire, while Venables himself became captain-lieutenant of Brereton's own company. Others, such as George Booth, Henry Mainwaring, John Leigh of Norbury Booths, near Knutsford and Henry Brooke of Norton raised their

1 Anon, 'Extracts from the Corporation Books ', p.365.

own troops of horse and regiments of foot that would form an important part of the Cheshire army of Parliament.

Unquestionably, the religiosity of many Parliamentarians in Cheshire formed an essential motivation for recruitment and perception of religious war. As Morrill suggests, 'Those who mobilised for Parliament in 1642, as against those who threw in their lot with Parliament, were the religious militants, and this is at least as true of the provinces as it is of Westminster.'[2] Brereton's horse was a 'double-regiment', in many ways akin to Cromwell's horse of the Eastern Association and later New Model Army. Like them, the religious enthusiasm of Sir William's men (recruited and led to some extent by radicals such as Duckenfield and Brereton's 'preaching captain' of his own troop, Jerome Zankey) is likely to have provided a major impetus for their motivation.[3] Brereton deeply believed that he and like-minded men such as Cromwell were instruments of God's purpose, 'That God who is much glorified by working by the weakest and unworthiest interests.'[4] On 18 May 1645 the Lieutenant General wrote to him, 'God has set the way and time of putting a period to the miseries of this distressed kingdom. It is good for us to wait upon God and to seek his face which I am assured you do.'[5] In referring to the success of the Ironsides at Naseby, Foard remarks, 'Like Gustavus Adolphus before him, Cromwell had used the power of religion to weld his cavalry into an irresistible force. The belief that they were doing God's work was after all fundamental to many of the troops, as it had been in the Eastern Association, and this was for many of its members a godly army with a destiny to fulfil.'[6]

The success of both sides' recruiting drives lay to some extent in the backing each derived from the local population. Brereton maintained that he had the general support of the inhabitants of Cheshire, claiming in April 1645, 'I can do them no less right that give this testimony (which their actions abundantly confirm): that they have been generally willing to expend their estates and engage their persons to support the advance of this cause.' He also declared separately that 'the common people, who for the most part judge our cause by the demeanour of our army'.[7] The policy of winning popular support by Sir William and his commanders brought dividends from an early stage in terms of recruitment and material support for the army, although its implementation depended on the maintenance of good discipline, and the general principle was in opposition to seventeenth-century strategies of mobility, attrition and the denial of key objectives to an enemy. The Earl of Clarendon singled out Cheshire with Lancashire as

2 J.S. Morrill, 'Sir William Brereton and England's Wars of Religion', *JBS*, 24:3 (1985), pp.311–32 (p.329).

3 Leo F. Solt, *Saints in Arms: Puritanism and Democracy in Cromwell's Army* (Stanford: Stanford University Press, 1959), p.91; Keith Roberts, *Cromwell's War Machine: The New Model Army, 1645–1660* (Barnsley: Pen & Sword, 2005), p.174.

4 *Shrewsbury Taken.*

5 BL, MS Add. 11331, fol. 145r.; *BLB*, I, 573.

6 Foard, *Naseby*, p.245.

7 BL, MS Add. 11331, fols 4r.; 25r.; *BLB*, I, 283, 352.

Jacques Callot, *Rekruteren van soldaten* (1633), showing the recruitment or mustering of foot soldiers. (Amsterdam, Rijksmuseum, CCO 1.0 Universal (CCO 1.0) Public Domain Dedication)

an area where Parliamentarian support among the common people was enthusiastic and Royalist lukewarm, stating:

> the difference in the temper of the common people of both sides was so great, that they who inclined to the parliament left nothing unperformed that might advance the cause, and were incredibly vigilant and industrious to cross and hinder whatsoever might promote the king's: whereas they who wished well to him thought that they had performed their duty in doing so, and that they might have done enough for him that they had done nothing against him.[8]

He added, 'Whereby it was in their power not to grieve and oppress the people; and thereby (besides the spirit of faction that much governed) the common people were more devoted to them [the Parliamentarians], and gave them all intelligence of what might concern them.' In his account of the 1644 Nantwich campaign Sir Thomas Fairfax corroborated Clarendon's view, admitting that there was greater enthusiasm in Cheshire for the Parliamentarians among the common people.[9]

A number of writers, including Dore, Morrill and Hutton have concluded that the conduct of the King's soldiers in Cheshire not only helped to evaporate what residual support remained among the local population for them, but provided a ready recruiting sergeant for the Parliamentarian forces. During the first months of the war the commissioners of array were accused of being unable to control their troops. Malbon may have exaggerated when he reported that in August 1642 the troops turned out for the array at Northwich behaved boisterously in the neighbouring villages while the Parliamentarians departed peacefully.[10] But this idea of undisciplined and violent behaviour among the civilian population is confirmed to some degree by Aston's admission in early 1643, that he had not always been able to prevent his troops from plundering. Even so, following the Parliamentarian

8 Clarendon, *History of the Rebellion*, II, pp.272–3.
9 Fairfax, 'Short Memorial', p.169.
10 Malbon, pp.24–5.

victory at Middlewich Sir Thomas's defeated horse arrived at Chester, causing difficulties over the apportionment of money and supplies. Orlando Bridgeman, the Royalist commander of the city, overruled an arrangement between Aston and the commissioners of array, and seized these for his own troops, thus Aston's soldiers were compelled to pillage in order to survive.[11] There is also evidence of extreme sensitivity in Cheshire towards the dangers of ill discipline amongst troops since the passing through the county and the port of Chester to Ireland in the early months of 1642. On 22 April the mayor of Chester, Sir William Brereton (as MP for the county) and others informed the Speaker, 'We understand from their officers that several more regiments will soon pass this way and we have received divers complaints from the city and the country [county] that several sums of money are still owing, although some have been discharged, and there have been robberies and violence committed by soldiers who were put upon [quartered on] some persons without their consent.'[12]

Local resentment was also fuelled by the attack by Welsh soldiers with the Royalist 'Irish' companies on the departing garrison of Hawarden Castle in late November 1643, while the killing of civilians at Barthomley Church may have been intensified by Sir John Byron's reported boast that he had 'put them all to the sword; which I find to be the best way to proceed with these kind of people, mercy to them is cruelty.'[13] Writing after the relief of Nantwich in January 1644 he claimed that his soldiers from Ireland 'are so poisoned by the ill-affected people here that they grow very cold in the service.'[14] In terms of Parliamentarian recruiting, it is worth noting Dore's comment that 'None of these sources can be regarded as entirely reliable in the matter, but it is otherwise difficult to understand how Brereton could have established such a grip on the county at the very time that the Parliamentarian cause was suffering disaster after disaster elsewhere.'[15]

Because of the sparseness of direct and reliable evidence it is difficult to assess the levels of forced and voluntary recruitment by Brereton's army. The enlistment of tenants by regimental colonels was common from the outset, and many such recruits were included among the multitude of soldiers brought to Manchester in September 1642 under the Lancashire Parliamentarians, but also some of the gentlemen of Cheshire. The Royalist commanders Sir Edward Fitton and Earl Rivers raised a number of officers and men from their own tenants, while Sir Thomas Aston recruited men for his horse and dragoons in Cheshire and Lancashire, financing this partly by public subscription, not all of which was paid.[16] During 1642 the Colonel's and Bridgeman's troops of Aston's horse were recruited from the Aston estate, Frodsham, Over, Keckwick and other local areas. Similarly, in Lancashire the Earl of Derby made various attempts to recruit both from his own tenants

11 BL, MS Harley 6804, fols 139v.–40r.; Hutton, *Royalist War Effort*, p.99.

12 HMC, *Portland*, I, pp.32–3; BL, MS Add. 11333, fols 130v.–4r.; *BLB*, II, pp.539–40.

13 HMC, *Portland*, I, p.34.

14 Carte, *Collection*, I, p.39.

15 *BLB*, II, p.53.

16 BL, MS Add. 36913, fol. 101v.; Young, *Edgehill*, pp.22–3, 212–13.

and wider afield by coercive methods. The continued use of tenants (either willingly or not) and forced recruitment seems to indicate that recruitment by voluntary means was not altogether successful, however. Thus, Hutton observes that service out of duty rather than service out of conviction may have been a source of weakness rather than strength.[17]

Some indication of the conscious decisions made by some leaseholders is contained in a petition of William Davenport of Bramhall received from his tenants on 17 September 1642 in response to his call for their support in raising a regiment or troop, under his command and in the name of the King. They wrote:

> We your worshipful tenants … having these many days with sad spirits weighed not only the woeful distractions of our kingdom, but also the present standing that is betwixt your worship and ourselves, have thought it our duty, as well as for the working up of sweet union, as for the taking away of all jealousies among us, to present your worship with these few lines of our humble request. We therefore request that either you would be pleased to bend our intentions that way which we may with upright hearts and safe consciences cleave to you both in life and death … or else that your worship will not repute us ill-affected or false-hearted tenants in refusing to venture our lives and consciences do persuade us are not good or lawful, nor such as we dare safely and with good consciences maintain and defend you in. For, howsoever we would not for the world harbour a disloyal thought against his Majesty, yet we dare not lift up our hands against that honourable assembly of parliament, whom we are confidently assured do labour both for the happiness of his Majesty and all his kingdom.[18]

Davenport subsequently recorded in his diary, 'the very next day (and it being a Sabbath day too) not staying or belike caring much for me or my answer, they with some others of my tenants enrolled their names and enlisted themselves with Captain Hyde or Norbury [of Duckenfield's regiment] to become soldiers for the parliament under his command'. According to Morrill, 'If the tenants of many Royalists acted in such a fashion, it is not surprising that Parliament had raised by the spring of 1643 several regiments of foot and troops of horse, recruited quite independently of the trained and freehold bands.'[19]

Some tenants were also liable by the terms of their 'leases' (contracts or indentures) with their landlords for military service, especially in trained band units. In November 1645 Sir George Booth outlined to Brereton some of the difficulties in turning out such men. He stated that a leaseholder of his:

> upon knowledge of my letters and warrants for the calling of Captains Walker and Weld with 200 of my tenants by covenants in their leases and others in Ashton

17 Hutton, *Royalist War Effort*, pp.92–3. See also C.B. Phillips, 'Landlord–Tenant Relationships 1642–1660', R.C. Richardson (ed.), *Town and Countryside in the English Revolution* (Manchester, Manchester University Press, 1992), pp.224–50 (pp. 227–30, 232–3, 245).

18 CRO, ZCR63/2/19, fol. 88r.

19 Morrill, *Cheshire*, p.79.

> [-under-Lyne] parish to repair unto the said siege [of Chester] and further as they should be required, publicly declared before the congregation on the Sabbath day after my directions were read by Mr Harrison that the said service was not for the king's war, and my letters and warrants were such as were never heard [before] and that he for his part would not send forth any man.[20]

The alternative to forced recruiting was the enlistment of volunteers. On 20 May 1645 Colonel Duckenfield petitioned that he was:

> one of the first that took up arms for the parliament at assisting distressed Manchester at the first siege thereof, opposing the Commissions of Array and other parliament's charges within the parts where he lived, and from the beginning of the troubles hath had a full foot company and complete troop of horse, which were raised and from time to time recruited by him; and since November 1643 having a commission from the right honourable the Earl of Essex hath commanded a regiment of foot besides his troop of horse, and therewith done service [and that] he had order in January last from the deputy lieutenants of this county for recruiting and maintaining his regiment in the hundred of Macclesfield, where he lives.[21]

By 1643 Duckenfield's regiment consisted of 10 volunteer companies, each raised and commanded by local captains, including the Colonel's brother, and aldermen of Stockport and Macclesfield.[22] Evidence for voluntary recruiting is also widespread in Lancashire, if slightly exaggerated. In late November 1642 it was said that 3,000 men enlisted in a morning in response to Royalist aggression around Leigh, while *Mercurius Aulicus* reported that 'the country people to the number of 3,000, being wearied with the insolence and tyranny of the rebels came with great cheerfulness' to assist the Earl of Derby in his raid on Lancaster in March 1643.[23]

The parliamentary ordinance authorising county committees to impress soldiers, gunners and surgeons of 10 August 1643, decreed that recruits 'shall have so much impressed money, coat and conduct money, wages and entertainment, and other necessary charges and allowances, as shall be fit and convenient'.[24] Gathering together and guarding conscripted men was an arduous and costly task, and soldiers recruited in this fashion were liable to desert or be poached by officers of other commands. Hence, in Bucklow in February 1645 Captain Nathaniel French, assisted by a cadre of officers and non-commissioned officers, was employed in conducting them to their regiments.[25] In a similar way, 11 months later Captains Walker and Weld received letters and warrants from Sir George Booth for mustering and

20 BL, MS Add. 11332, fols 71v., 123r.; *BLB*, II, 846, 934.

21 TNA, SP/20/10/63, fol. 161r. (later copy in different hand in fol. 162r.).

22 *Ibid.*, fol. 163r.

23 *Mercurius Aulicus*, 20 March–2 April 1643. See also, *CWTL*, p.84; Joyce Malcolm, *Caesar's Due: Loyalty and King Charles, 1642–46* (London: RHS, 1983), p.122.

24 *CJ*, III, p.194.

25 BL, MS Harley 2137, fols 52v., 155v.; Harley 2128, fols 47v.–50r., 52r.; TNA: SP28/225/1, fol. 39r.

conducting 200 men of the Nantwich Hundred trained bands from Dunham Massey and Ashton-under-Lyne to the army about Chester.[26]

There seems no reason to think that Brereton would not have started implementing the parliamentary ordinance as soon as he received it. Malbon mentions much activity from Nantwich south to Market Drayton and eventually Wem in September 1643, and the sending out of warrants for a general muster 'in all that country'.[27] If that meant only in Salop, the area the Parliament controlled in that county was so small at that time, it would have appeared somewhat pointless and it is therefore likely that the Nantwich area would have been included as well. Although recruiting occurred constantly at a local level, as commanders of companies and troops of horse would strive to keep their numbers up in the face of losses through combat, disease and desertion, there would be special bursts of it, directed from above at county level (Brereton and his colonels) at particular times as danger from the enemy presented itself or opportunity arose. The last came about firstly when Sir William visited London (the greatest recruiting ground in the country), particularly during the initial build-up of his army in the autumn and winter of 1642, and the summer of 1644; when fresh areas of the county came under his control (for example, Wirral and Broxton after the retreat of Rupert and Goring southwards, and the Battle of Montgomery in August–September 1644; and the taking of a number of prisoners, particularly from the royal army in Ireland (in particular, after Nantwich in January 1644 and the recapture of Liverpool in 1644). These prisoners were always susceptible to the argument that Parliament was 'anti-popery', and in the case of Liverpool found they could re-enlist under their old commanders – Jones, Coote and Finch. It is possible that such soldiers would still be regarded as volunteers. They had the right of refusal and it is known that many prisoners from Ireland exercised it and remained in prison in Cheshire.

An effective starting point for assessing the organisation of Sir William Brereton's army is his 'army list' of 30 April 1645, and schedule of his own regiments of horse and foot, dated 18 October 1645.[28] Although slightly later than the operations in Cheshire, a muster roll of companies serving at the siege of Lichfield Close on 23 May 1646 provides valuable information on their composition, leadership and strengths.[29] This document was used to remunerate the common soldiers of the Cheshire foot and dragoons on 30 May, and the officers in early June 1646. Rather than being a previously existing unit, the force listed here was made up of companies drawn from the various regiments of the Cheshire army. This might have been the simplest way of assembling the numbers required, or perhaps Brereton had chosen officers he considered reliable. The brigaded companies were commanded overall at Bacon Hill by Lieutenant Colonel Gerard and Adjutant Lothian, two highly resourceful and dependable officers, while Sergeant Major William Daniell and a number of the captains had admirable records. As

26 BL, MS Add. 11332, fol. 71r.; *BLB*, II, 846.

27 Malbon, p.76.

28 BL, MS Add. 11331, fol. 45r.; 11332, fol. 3r.; *BLB*, I, 385; II, 703.

29 BCL, MS 595611, fols 252v.–3r.

is shown by other evidence, Sir William was anxious to have the dragoon companies with him, and they subsequently performed valuable service throughout the siege.

Table 3: Sir William Brereton's Regiment of Horse, 30 April 1645

Sir William Brereton's Regiment of Horse	Strength
Sir William Brereton's own troop under Major Sankey	100
Lieutenant Colonel Michael Jones	070
Colonel Duckenfield	060
Lieutenant Colonel Chidley Coote	050
Colonel Brooke	050
Captain Hawkbridge	050
Captain Stone	100
Captain Vivers	050
Captain Shepley	060
Captain Bulkeley	070
Captain Glegg	040
Captain Culme and Captain Edwards	050
Captain Carter	040
Total	790

Table 4: Sir William Brereton's Regiment of Foot, 30 April 1645

Sir William Brereton's own Regiment of Foot 'upon instant duty'	Strength
Sir William Brereton's own company under the conduct of Lt Colonel Venables	150
Lieutenant Colonel Coote	100
Sergeant Major Croxton	160
Lord Calvin, Captain about	100
Captain Finch about	070
Captain Sadler about	070
Captain Monke about	060
Captain Greene about	120
Captain Glegg (now disposed of) [and] Captain Birkenhead about	160
Captain Gimbert's Dragoons	060
Captains Hulse and [? at] Cholmondeley	060
Captain Rathbone	080
Captain Hardware	060
Captain Spicer	040
Captains William and Richard Coventry, and Captain Ball	150
Captain Holt's Firelocks	080
Total	1,520

Table 5: Adjutant Lothian's Company of Broxton Hundred, 30 April 1645

Adjutant Lothian's Company of Broxton Hundred	Strength
Adjutant Lothian's Company of Broxton Hundred	080

Table 6: Colonel George Booth's Regiment of Foot, 30 April 1645

Colonel George Booth's Regiment of Foot	Strength
his own company under Sergeant Major Daniell	070
Lieutenant Colonel Massey	160
Captain Alcocke and Captain Grantham	100
Captain George Massey and Captain Cartwright	100
Captain Wright and Captain Whitney	080
Two Nantwich companies of townsmen under Captain George and Captain Thomas Malbon	200
Total	710

Table 7: Colonel Henry Brooke's Regiment of Foot, 30 April 1645

Colonel Henry Brooke's Regiment of Foot	Strength
his own company under Sergeant Major Church of Bucklow Hundred	140
Lieutenant Colonel Richard Brooke	060
Captain John Brooke	070
Captain William Daniell	060
Captain Delves and Captain Bramhall, both of Nantwich Hundred	160
Lieutenant Touchet[30]	080
Total	570

Table 8: Colonel Robert Duckenfield's Regiment of Foot, 30 April 1645

Colonel Robert Duckenfield's Regiment of Foot	Strength
his own company	120
Sergeant Major Bradshaw	140
Captain Booth and Captain Watson	140
Captain Siddal and Captain Shelmerdine	120
Captain Smith[31]	060
Total	580

Table 9: Colonel John Leigh's Regiment of Foot, 30 April 1645

Colonel John Leigh's Regiment of Foot	Strength
his own company	100
Lieutenant Colonel Gerard	100
Captain Acton and Captain Whalley	120
Captain Pigott of the Town of Northwich	120
Lieutenant Birtles	080
Total	520

30 *Sic*: 'Captain'.

31 Captain William Duckenfield erased in manuscript, indicating that Captain William Smith had taken over his command by spring 1645.

Table 10: Colonel Henry Mainwaring's Regiment of Foot, 30 April 1645

Colonel Henry Mainwaring's Regiment of Foot	Strength
Captain Leadbeater	
Captain Cotton }about 160 all countrymen	
Captain Baskerville	
Captain Hancock	
Total	160

Table 11: Cheshire Army Strengths, 30 April 1645

Horse	790
Foot	4,140
Total	4,930

Table 12: Sir William Brereton's Regiment of Horse, 18 October 1645

Sir William Brereton's Regiment of Horse	Strength
Harquebusiers	
His own troop about	120
Lieutenant Colonel Jones's troop about	060
Colonel Duckenfield (colonel of foot) his troop about	060
Colonel Brooke (colonel of foot) his troop about	050
Colonel Leigh his troop	060
Lieutenant Colonel Coote (lieutenant colonel of foot) his troop	060
Captain Stone his troop	100
Captain Culme about	040
Captain Bulkeley and Captain Vivers about	120
Captain Edwards's troop	040
Captain John Glegg about	040
Captain Shepley his troop about	050
Captain Hawkbridge his troop	050
Total	910

Table 13: Sir William Brereton's Regiment of Foot, 18 October 1645

Sir William Brereton's Regiment of Foot	Strength
His own company	140
Lieutenant Colonel Coote's company	080
Sergeant Major Croxton's company	140
Captain Sadler about	060
Captain Rathbone and Captain Glegg about	120
Captain Monke about	050
Captain Spicer about	050
Captain Greene about	100
Captain Birkenhead about	100
Captain Hulse and Captain Brereton about	080
Captain Davies	080
Captain Hardware about	080
Total	1,080

Table 14: Muster Roll of Cheshire Forces at Lichfield Close, 23 May 1646

An abbreviate of the names of the several captains, their lieutenants and ensigns, with the number of other officers and whole companies who are now engaged in the siege against Lichfield Close. Mustered by Lieutenant Colonel Hunt on Cheshire side the leaguer the day above said, 23 May 1646	
Sergeant Major Daniell, Lieutenant Heath, Ensign Witter, 3 sergeants, 2 drums, 3 corporals, 1 gentleman of arms and 92 common soldiers	} These two make but one company and officers are allowed accordingly
Captain Booth, 1 sergeant, 1 drum, 2 corporals and 48 common soldiers; Captain Leadbeater, Lieutenant Norbury, Ensign Banniell, 1 sergeant, 1 drum, 2 corporals and 33 common soldiers	
Captain Rathbone, Lieutenant Browne, Ensign Wettmough, 3 sergeants, 1 clerk, 2 drums, 3 corporals and 60 common soldiers	
Captain Whalley, Lieutenant Bostock, Ensign Bradford, 2 sergeants, 1 drum, 2 corporals and 36 common soldiers	
Captain Finch, Lieutenant Mather, Cornet Sydes, 1 drum, 3 corporals and 76 common soldiers	
Captain Gimbert, Lieutenant Turner, Cornet Urmson, Quartermaster Bentley, 2 sergeants, 1 drum, 3 corporals and 65 common soldiers	
Captain Birtles, Ensign Cartwright, 2 sergeants, 1 drum, 2 corporals, 1 clerk and 52 common soldiers	
Captain Glegg, Lieutenant Swettenham, Ensign Ball, 3 sergeants, 1 clerk, 2 drums, 3 corporals and 69 common soldiers	
Captain Monke, Lieutenant Pargiter, 2 drums, 2 corporals and 36 common soldiers	
The number of captains, other officers and private soldiers: captains 10; lieutenants 8; ensigns 8; sergeants 19; clerks and quartermasters 4; drums 14; corporals 25; common soldiers 567	
Trained Bands besides:	
Colonel Croxton's company	about 140
Lieutenant Colonel Gerard's company	about 130
Total	270
Overall total	837

Estimating the composition and size of the Cheshire army of Parliament, probably at its zenith in 1645, requires some necessary calculations based upon Sir William Brereton's incomplete and slightly perplexing army lists of April and October 1645, as well as the use of other evidence. As a regional or county force it contained one regiment of horse, six regiments of foot, one independent company of foot, one regiment of dragoons and various supernumerary units. Going by the first list, dated 30 April 1645, the Cheshire horse comprised 790 troopers in 14 troops, although the schedule is incomplete and there are (for unexplained reasons) at least three troops omitted. Sir William's list of 10 October 1645 includes 910 troopers in 14 troops. In the latter, half of the increase of 120 men can be accounted for by the inclusion of Colonel Leigh's command, and the rest by the increases in the troops of Brereton himself, Lieutenant Colonel Coote and Captains Culme, Edwards and Carter. Against these must be set small reductions in the troops of Lieutenant Colonel Jones and Captain Shepley. However, there is evidence for the existence of at least 26 different troops of horse in the service of Parliament from Cheshire, although clearly not all of them were active concurrently as some were disbanded or fed into other commands during the course of the war. Various sources compute the Cheshire horse as 600-strong in November 1645 and April 1646, while the troops sent to participate in operations under Colonel Mytton in North Wales had an overall strength of 400 (some, such as Duckenfield's, having remained in Cheshire).

As a provincial force, Brereton's army prosecuted the extended war aims and strategy of the Parliament in Cheshire (and in particular, its primary objective, the reduction and capture of the Royalist stronghold of Chester). Yet by its very nature, his forces operated in a much wider strategic and geographical context, and also in conjunction when required, with Parliamentarian troops from other commands. When the situation demanded, the Cheshire troops conducted their own operations, both at regimental and sub-unit level. For instance, the foot regiments of Duckenfield and Mainwaring acted together at Stockport in May 1644, while Mainwaring's and George Booth's were part of Mytton's brigade in Shropshire during the summer of the same year. More generally though, outside the main marching armies, troops and companies were the typical level for deployments, with regiments fulfilling a mainly administrative function. Such units were often 'brigaded' together with others to constitute more effective combat formations. Such tactical formations were utilised at Rowton Heath and Denbigh Field, although at Montgomery the Cheshire army provided most of the foot. Brereton's commanders also had to adopt such an approach during the siege of Chester when tactical considerations, such as reacting to military threats from outside quarters and combining the forces of various satellite garrisons were common. Moreover, the Cheshire forces operated across a broad geographical area, serving in conjunction with other forces and under various regional commanders, throughout the North West, as well as the Midland counties, North Wales and elsewhere.

The blockading of the city and port of Chester was strategically vital, because it caused considerable disruption to Royalist strategy and supplies in the North West, the Welsh borders and wider afield. Brereton and his army undertook a protracted blockade of Chester against determined and skillful opposition, particularly over the winter of 1645 to 1646 when the weather and depredations suffered by the soldiers were severe. Additionally, detachments of Parliamentarian troops from a number of adjacent counties served with them as auxiliaries under Sir William's nominal command, even though at times frictions existed over differing responsibilities and disproportionate pay, as well as some of the county committees that sent them. Such flexibility in a broad sense was characteristic of the Cheshire army, as well as similarly 'small' regional forces in other counties. According to Gratton, 'The flexibility displayed by the Lancashire Parliamentarians was one of the reasons for their success'.[32] Additionally, Cheshire and the north-west of England in particular, were no backwaters during the First Civil War, and often Brereton's forces

32 Gratton, *Parliamentarian and Royalist War Effort in Lancashire*, p.400.

became embroiled in events of a more national complexion, such as the landing of the Royalist army from Ireland in late 1643, the advance of Prince Rupert through the Welsh Marches, Cheshire and Lancashire during 1644, and the pursuit of the Royalist army from Oxfordshire to Leicestershire in the summer of 1645.

When the wars began, both sides looked towards officers and men from the trained bands. At the national muster of the militia in 1638 Cheshire accounted for 599 men armed with 359 muskets and 240 corslets (body armour, denoting pikemen).[33] Moreover, in late July 1642 Sir William Brereton described that at the muster of the Northwich Hundred trained bands 'there was a full appearance about three hundred and twenty musketeers and four score pikemen well-armed, and near six hundred other volunteers, who, thought they brought not arms so complete yet I believe their hearts as well affected as the other to the safety and peace of the King and Parliament'.[34] Very few officers from Brereton's army can be identified with any degree of certainty to have had pre-war trained band service. Thomas Croxton led a company of Northwich Hundred trained bandsmen, who later became a 'semi-regular' unit quartered in Nantwich, also as part of Brereton's own regiment.[35] Even though trained band participation before 1642 could not equate with actual combat experience, it did provide some practice in the training, drilling and commanding of soldiers, so that when conflict began this was not unfamiliar to them. Croxton's war record shows him to have been a man of considerable skill and experience, and a rare example of seasoned and dependable home-grown soldiers, which by Brereton's own admission were much needed for his own regiments of horse and foot. It is possible also that the captains and junior officers who later led 'country companies' in the Cheshire army had served in those units before the war. Nine captains commanded such companies, while Captains Walker and Weld were tasked with the calling in of 200 men of the Nantwich Hundred trained bands from Dunham Massey and Ashton-under-Lyne in November 1645.[36]

Given the cohesive nature of gentry families in the social, economic and political life of the county of Cheshire, it would appear unreasonable to expect that military service was much different. Malcolm Wanklyn suggests that the army's regiments of foot possessed varying levels of 'social exclusiveness', adding that four of Colonel Brooke's companies were led by officers from 'middling landowning families'.[37] This may be so, but other regiments were also officered by locally exclusive gentlemen (and in some cases, yeomen). Brooke's regiment, raised from Bucklow Hundred, contained the Colonel's younger brothers as senior officers. Two of Colonel Robert Duckenfield's brothers acted as captains in his regiment, while Colonel John Leigh's cavalry troop was led by his brother as captain-lieutenant. This pattern was not

33 TNA, SP 16/381/66; SP16/409/216.

34 HMC, *Portland*, I, p.46

35 BL, MS Add. 12429, fol. 7r.; 11410, fols 56v.–7r.; MS Harley 2119, fols 211v.–13r.; *The latest printed News from Chichester, Windsor, Winchester, Chester and Manchester* (London, 1642); *Narrative of General Venables*, pp.1–2.

36 BL, MS Add. 11332, fol. 71r.

37 Wanklyn, 'Landed Society', p.239 and n. 3.

uncommon amongst Royalist and Parliamentarian regiments in county or regional forces. In Lancashire the Parliamentarian colonels Ralph Assheton and Richard Shuttleworth chose their sons as their lieutenant colonel, Alexander Rigby appointed his sons as lieutenant colonel and major, while Shuttleworth's regiment included his four sons.[38]

Among each of the Cheshire foot regiments in the First Civil War (except Brereton's own, which was more broadly recruited, and contained both urban and trained band soldiers) command structures depended to a great extent on officers who were related to their colonels by familial, religious and local ties. It would be a mistake, however, to view such 'country gentlemen' as parochial and inexperienced. In regard to the leading Parliamentarian leaders in Cheshire, Dore asserts, 'They were not men whose horizons were so limited that they would put 'country' meaning county above 'country' meaning nation. They were not 'mere country gentlemen', eschewing all office and opting for a life centred mainly round their estates ... A viewpoint limited to the horizons of the local community was hardly from such men.'[39] Thus, old Sir George Booth had campaigned in the Netherlands as a young man, and his extended family possessed social and political connections across the North West, in addition to Westminster. Likewise, Henry Brooke of Norton's wife came from Nottinghamshire and he spent time prior to the war living on her family's estates there, while a number of others, including Henry Mainwaring and John Marbury had marital interests in various counties.

Collective religious sensibilities also characterised some regiments. The captain-lieutenant of Sir William Brereton's troop, Jerome Zankey, was an independent 'preaching captain', who later became a senior officer in Ireland. Officers (and possibly soldiers) belonging to those raised by Brooke, Booth and Mainwaring tended to be mostly of the Presbyterian faith (although Captain William Daniell of Brooke's may not have been so, as he survived the later New Model Army purges and served as a colonel of foot in Scotland). Colonel Leigh's Anabaptist lieutenant colonel, Gilbert Gerard, shared his puritan outlook and probably most of his captains and junior commanders did too. Many of the company commanders under Duckenfield were further drawn together by similar Congregationalist views to their young colonel. Stemming largely from the Tameside area of east Cheshire, his officers also possessed a shared mercantile and urban identity. Although Captain Ralph Arderne belonged to a long-standing gentry family of Harden Hall, he was closely associated with the town of Stockport. Moreover, many of Duckenfield's captains and soldiers were of the emerging 'middling sort', who had joined in the defence of Manchester in 1642. These included Anthony Booth (alderman and mayor of Macclesfield

38 TNA, E121/351, unfol.; E121/4/43, fol. 12v., SP20/253A/40, fol. 18r.; *Discourse of the War*, pp.15, 42; J.H. Stanning (ed.), *The Royalist Composition Papers: being the proceedings of the Committee for Compounding, A.D. 1643–1660, so far as they relate to the County of Lancaster* (Manchester, 1891–1942), IV, p.76.

39 R.N. Dore, '1642: the coming of the Civil War to Cheshire: conflicting actions and impressions', *TLCAS*, 87 (1991), pp.39–63 (pp. 55–6).

for 1640–1, 1645 and 1649–50) and William Watson (mayor of the same town from 1643 to 1644). Additionally, two officers – Captains William Siddall and Edmund Shelmerdine – were tenants of the closet-Royalist William Davenport of Bramhall, but enlisted for the Parliamentarian cause when the opportunity arose.

The Cheshire foot is given as 4,100 common soldiers on 30 April 1645, with Brereton's own regiment 'upon instant duty' being listed as1,520 men in approximately 19 companies, but this includes 210 dragoons and thus should be calibrated to 1,310 soldiers in approximately 16 companies. The second strengths of 18 October 1645 shows Brereton's command as 1,080 in some 14 companies – the decrease of 230 is apparently explained by some reductions to its companies, but especially the non-appearance of the Wirral country companies of Captains William and Richard Coventry, and Captain Ball, although evidence from pay warrants indicates that some of these were still active in late 1645. Moreover, in the April list 'Adjutant Lothian's company of Broxton Hundred' is given as 80 common soldiers, whereas the foot regiments of Colonel George Booth appears as 710 soldiers, that of Colonel Henry Brooke as 570, that of Colonel Robert Duckenfield as 580, that of Colonel John Leigh as 520 and the one under the command of Colonel Henry Mainwaring as 'about 160 all countrymen'. The Cheshire foot is likely to have been larger than this earlier in the war, because Duckenfield's reportedly contained 10 companies (perhaps around 800 men) in 1643 and 1644, and by Spring 1645, Mainwaring's command seems to have been in some turmoil, with at least three of his volunteer companies (including his own, and those commanded by Major Robert Jackson and Captain John Baskerville) being no longer listed and probably disbanded.

As for the dragoons, the figure of 210 appears rather a modest one. Brereton commonly referred in correspondence to his 'three to four companies' – he certainly began 1643 with three firelock units, yet there is evidence of perhaps four other dragoon commands (led by Captains Cheswis, Littler, Kempton and Stockport) operating as part of the army at various times. Their number was estimated by the Royalist Richard Symonds in November 1645 at 400 dragoons, while 300 were known to be present at Chester in April 1646.[40] Necessarily, overall calculations of Brereton's horse, foot and dragoons must take into consideration the amount of officers and non-commissioned officers in the army's various sub-units, the troops and companies. Given that each of the roughly 17 troops of horse, and 54 companies of foot and dragoons present in mid 1645 or thereabouts, possessed 10 or more individuals above the rank of trooper or common soldier (in the case of a cavalry troop, for example, a captain, a lieutenant, a cornet, a quartermaster, three corporals and two trumpeters) this is likely to compute to around 710 officers and men. The problem of underestimating the size of civil-war units by the omission of officers and musicians is

40 BCA, MS 595611, fol. 60r.; Symonds, *Diary of the Marches*, p.263 – 'Colonel Jones lay at Dodleston with a regiment of 400 horse, and another 400 firelocks called Jones his regiments'.

acknowledged by various writers.[41] Whilst it is difficult to assess the numbers of 'supporting' troops, such as gunners, pioneers, surgeons, commissaries and 'supernumerary' regimental officers, perhaps 200–300 men fell into this category. In all then, it is possible to suggest a strength for the Cheshire army of somewhere between 5,500 and 6,000.

The Cheshire Horse

The principle mounted force of Sir William Brereton's army was the horse, being harquebusiers or 'light cavalry'. Compared with the heavily armed cuirassiers, the advantages of mobility and relative cheapness made them the normal type of cavalry from the early stages of the conflict. Notionally commanded by a captain, or in the case of a colonel's troop a captain-lieutenant, the troop was the fundamental unit of the cavalry, and typically consisted of a captain, a lieutenant, a cornet, a quartermaster, two trumpeters, three corporals, a saddler and a farrier (although the latter two rarely appear in muster rolls for Brereton's army), as well as common troopers. At the forefront of military operations between 1642 and 1646, the Cheshire horse saw action at (among other places) Malpas, Tarvin, Montgomery and Rowton Heath and Christleton, as well as various arduous sieges.

The Cheshire Foot

Constituting the mainstay of Civil War armies, the foot was divided into pike and shot (or musketeers). In 1642 the majority of the infantry in England comprised companies of the trained and freehold bands of each county under the direction of the lord lieutenant and deputy lieutenants, although very soon many units of volunteer and 'impressed' (conscripted) men were raised, equipped and trained. A particular problem faced by researchers, however, is accurately determining the size of units. In Lancashire some nine Royalist foot and 13 cavalry regiments were raised, although in 1642 most of the latter went off on the Edgehill campaign. Similarly, upwards of 12 regiments of foot were raised for Parliament, yet some were very small, and a distinct force of horse was not instituted until August 1645 when 10 troops were placed together under Colonel Shuttleworth. As in other counties, to some extent the 'Cheshire Foot' originated its trained band predecessors, and by mid 1645 accounted for roughly 70 percent of the army's strength. From his own testimony, when Sir William Brereton arrived in Cheshire from London in January 1643 at the head of a newly raised force of horse, foot and dragoons, he had 180–200 infantry with him, including a body of 40 volunteers commanded by Lieutenant Slade that met him at Derby.

However, a number of companies of volunteers had already been raised in Cheshire, especially those formed by Robert Duckenfield and his officers

41 Burne and Young, *The Great Civil War*, p.13; Foard, *Naseby*, pp.202–3, 206–7; Worton, *To Settle the Crown*, p.101.

in the Stockport–east Cheshire area up to six months earlier, while the trained bands of five of the seven Cheshire hundreds (Bucklow, Eddisbury, Nantwich, Northwich and Macclesfield) had been mobilised during summer of 1642 under the Militia Ordinance and later brought under the command of Brereton and the deputy lieutenants of the county. Although the survival and role of the 'country companies' in Brereton's army is not fully clear, there were attempts to assemble the militia at Northwich, Stockport, Nantwich and elsewhere in the summer and autumn of 1642.

The theoretical strength of an English foot regiment was 1,200 men divided into 10 companies. The colonel's company was to have 200 common soldiers, the lieutenant colonel's 160, the sergeant major's 140, and the remaining seven captains' companies 100 men each. In most armies, and certainly regional forces, it was hardly possible to adhere to such figures. In Brereton's army his own regiment numbered 1,310 soldiers in about 16 companies in April 1645 and 1,080 in 14 companies in October 1645, while in May of the same year the Cheshire deputy lieutenants certified that Colonel Duckenfield 'hath commanded a regiment of foot, raised within the said county, sometimes consisting of 10 companies but now of seven or eight full companies, which have also done very good service'.[42] Moreover, according to Brereton's army list Colonel Booth's regiment mustered 710 common soldiers, Colonel Brooke's 570, Colonel Duckenfield's 580, Colonel Leigh's 520 and Colonel Mainwaring's 160 'countrymen' (although by this period its former volunteer commands appear to have been disbanded).

Although there is little directly in the sources to corroborate this, it seems likely that Brereton's foot maintained a high proportion of shot and there are various reports of the effectiveness of their musketry on the battlefield. It may account also for the initial setback during the infantry engagement at Montgomery in September 1644, when their Royalist counterparts attacked them 'at push of pike' with a greater number of such weapons than they were used to. Other than Sir William Brereton's own regiment (which was originally raised in London and various parts of Cheshire) that of George Booth was drawn partly from eastern areas of the county, but also Nantwich town and hundred. Brooke's was recruited mainly from upper Bucklow Hundred, yet it also contained two companies of Nantwich townsmen; Duckenfield's regiment took recruits from eastern Macclesfield Hundred, Tameside, and the town of Stockport; Leigh's came from the town and hundred of Northwich, plus areas of Bucklow and Eddisbury hundreds, while Mainwaring's soldiers were drawn predominantly from Northwich Hundred and the Sandbach–Holmes Chapel area. Furthermore, an independent company was raised from Broxton Hundred in 1644–5, seemingly for special operations and in particular, siege warfare.

The Cheshire foot was organised, commanded and presumably trained by Sergeant Major James Lothian, an experienced Scots professional who came to Cheshire with Brereton in early 1643. He acted successively as sergeant major and adjutant general of the foot, which he commanded in numerous

42 TNA, SP/20/10/63, fol. 163r.

operations and battles. Lothian possessed superb fighting qualities, and as an authority on siege warfare he directed works at Beeston, Hawarden, Lichfield Close and elsewhere. As Dore asserts, 'There is little doubt that his professional knowledge and considerable ability had a great deal to do with the success of the Parliamentarian cause in Cheshire, particularly in 1643 when few of its leaders had any military experience'.[43] Lothian was captured at Burford, near Nantwich on 17 December 1643. He was released on 1 July 1644 – a London newsbook of mid July 1644 described him as 'Major Lothian, a gallant man lately come out of prison', while an entry in the accounts of Brereton's clerk, Ralph Judson, notes: 'Major Lothian out of prison on 1 July 1644'.[44]

The Cheshire Dragoons

Dragoons were an essential part of seventeenth-century armies, even though some contemporaries were uncertain about their precise role. Gervase Markham referred to them as 'a kind of footman on horseback', or mounted infantry who rode rather than walked to the battlefield.[45] They were mainly employed in flexible operations where mobility was essential, namely the seizing of bridges and strongholds, raiding, reconnaissance, patrolling and foraging. Brereton reported that on the day before the First Battle of Middlewich on 12 March 1643, he sent 'betwixt two and three companies of dragooners' to reconnoitre the strength and dispositions of the Royalists. Similarly, in October 1645 during the siege of Chester, elements of the Cheshire firelocks were ordered to accompany troops of horse in a sweeping foraging expedition, specifically, 'to fetch out of Wales so many cattle as shall serve for the aforesaid purpose.[46]

Dragoons were also used for holding hedges and passes, as well as providing covering fire for both the foot and horse. A typically ingenious and audacious use of dragoons occurred on 29 July 1645, when some of Colonel John Okey's men took Bath without firing a shot by creeping on their stomachs across the bridge to the town gate, where they seized the muzzles of the guards' muskets. They shouted to the defenders to accept quarter, whereupon they dropped their weapons and ran away. Okey's dragoons then blew open the gate, and the garrison quickly surrendered.[47] Increasingly, the role of dragoons in supporting the cavalry in battle became to be regarded as a crucial aspect of their work. To the professional soldier of the Thirty Years' War, Johann Jacobi von Wallhausen, writing in 1616 in *Kriegskunst zu Pferd* (*The Military Art Mounted*), dragoons were 'devised so that the infantry or a portion of it mounted on horse (since there a number of deeds which cannot be accomplished by cavalry alone), may promptly and

43 *BLB*, I, 91, n. 2.
44 TNA, SP28/196, fol. 17v.
45 Gervase Markham, *The Soldier's Accidence* (London, 1625), p.42.
46 Malbon, p.36; *Cheshire's Successe*; BL, MS Add. 11332, fol. 47r.; *BLB*, II, 676.
47 Sprigge, *Anglia Rediviva*, p.76; *A Full Relation of the Taking of Bath* (London, 1645).

rapidly come to the aid of the cavalry'.[48] An English contemporary view of the use of dragoons by Orrery relates to their tactical use alongside the cavalry:

Stephano della Bella, *Twee trommelars te paars* (c. 1640), probably depicting two dragoon drummers. (Amsterdam, Rijksmuseum, CCO 1.0 Universal (CCO 1.0) Public Domain Dedication)

> the seventh troop should be of *firelocks*, or *dragoons*, whose duty should be to guard the quarter of the regiment; to secure passes with celerity; to force passes possessed by the enemy; to assist the horse when they fight in enclosed countries; and in battles, to alight; and marching up in the outermost flank of the regiment, should in two ranks, the first kneeling, the second standing, a little before the squadrons charged, fire upon the enemy, their guns loaded with pistol bullets, which I have sometimes practised, and found it attended with great success; every tenth man while the rest were on such service, was to hold the horses of those who were thus employed; and if the enemy were routed, they were all to mount again, and to follow the execution.[49]

Dragoon regiments were organised in companies like the foot, with their officers and non-commissioned officers bearing infantry ranks, except the cornet, whose job was to carry the guidon or colour. In addition to acting as messengers, the drummers of the company transmitted commands, yet quite how this was done during varied and fast-paced dragoon actions remains open to question. The earliest muster roll of Bramhall's command (dated 24 January 1643) shows its establishment as one captain, one lieutenant, one cornet, two sergeants, three corporals, one drummer and one clerk, although by 20 May a second drummer was present.[50] In 1643 and 1644 no drummers are listed among Captain Littler's company, which comprised three officers, two sergeants, three corporals and 36 dragoons, while at Lichfield on 22 June Captain Finch's firelocks mustered one lieutenant, one cornet, two sergeants, one drummer, three corporals and 76 private soldiers.[51]

The Cheshire Forces and Parliamentarian 'Associations'

In July 1642 Parliament realised that by forming associations of neighbouring counties as co-operative military units, Royalist activity could be constrained. In a general sense, both sides deemed county armies to be too small to be effective militarily, either because the counties were too

48 Johann Jacobi von Wallhausen, *Kriegskunst zu Pferd* (Frankfurt, 1616), p.2.
49 Orrery, *Treatise of the Art of War*, pp.33–5.
50 BL, MS Harley 2128, fols 20v.–21r., 23v., 32r.
51 TNA, SP28/224, fol. 40v.; BCA, MS 595611, pp.203, 252–3.

minor or because they were too divided, and thus parliamentary ordinances were issued to the whole of England and Wales for their incorporation. This looked impressive on paper, but rarely translated into military effectiveness because they could not create an inter-county administration which would keep the various associations together. Only in the Eastern Association did this work successfully, and then only for about a year.[52] They had to seek assistance from each other and eventually received semi-official backing for this from the Committee of Both Kingdoms, which more and more took over the running of the Parliamentarian war effort. They built up Poyntz's new multi-county force before Newark and ordered troops from other counties to assist the leaguer of Chester. This acquired official recognition when Sir William Brereton's commission was renewed in January 1646, no longer as 'commander-in-chief of the forces of Cheshire' but as 'commander-in-chief of *all* the forces before Chester'.[53]

Several instances of inter-county collaboration among Parliamentarians in the North West are evident before the emergence of the Northern Association under the command of Lord Fairfax on 17 November 1642, when Cheshire was arbitrarily clustered with the counties of York, Lincoln, Nottinghamshire, Derby, Staffordshire, Lancashire, Northumberland, Cumberland, Westmorland, Durham and Newcastle. This was an expedient that was supposed to alleviate Parliament's fear that the 'papist malignants', and in particular, the Earl of Newcastle's northern forces would advance south to rendezvous with the King's Oxford Army to threaten London. During 1643, however, the Eastern Association secured East Anglia and cooperated with the Yorkshire Parliamentarians to hold back the northern Royalists.[54] Moreover, In December 1642 the counties of Leicestershire, Derbyshire, Nottinghamshire, Northamptonshire, Rutland, Bedfordshire, Buckinghamshire and Huntingdonshire were brought together under a single committee as the East Midland Association, to be commanded by the 19-year-old Lord Grey as major general. Due to 'inherent localism', however, this was ineffective and the Parliamentarian war effort in the region continued to be run by individual county committees.[55]

Whether they were officially 'associated' or not, perhaps the most noticeable example of cooperation between the Parliamentarian forces of Lancashire and Cheshire is the siege of Manchester in September 1642. Cheshire troops flocked to protect the town, which reflected its regional importance. Sir George Booth 'sent his only son with his friends, neighbours and tenants to the assistance of the said town against the Earl of Derby', while volunteer companies under Robert Duckenfield and Ralph Arderne were also present. Following the formation of the Northern Association Duckenfield and Henry Mainwaring lent further assistance to the Lancastrians in December and January 1643, including the sending of Duckenfield's troop of horse to the defence of Bolton against the Earl of Derby's forces. In return,

52 *CJ*, II, pp.649, 666; Holmes, *Eastern Association*, pp.1–4.

53 *CJ*, III, p.19; *LJ*, VIII, p.117.

54 *LJ*, V, pp.451, 466; Holmes, *Eastern Association*, p.62.

55 Lynn Beats, 'The East Midland Association 1642–1644', *MH*, 4(3) (1978), pp.160–174.

Manchester forces helped in the attack on Adlington Hall in December 1642. Gratton suggests that, 'It is this collaboration between Lancashire and Cheshire Parliamentarians which provides the most tangible evidence of mutual co-operation, outside the framework of an association'.[56]

Cooperation with adjacent counties was a priority from the moment that Sir William Brereton arrived back in Cheshire in January 1643. He achieved this in Lancashire through an alliance with the Parliamentarian colonels in the county who had ties of kinship with him or other Cheshire links, and besides, the geographical positions of the two counties made cooperation between them a sensible policy. In 1643 Brereton assisted in the capture of Liverpool and Warrington. This not only helped his Lancashire colleagues, but served his own interests, partly because the former was a vital link in his army's supply chain by sea from London. In response, the Lancashire forces (mainly Colonel John Booth's regiment) aided the Cheshire army in North Wales in October 1643, the Nantwich campaign in January 1644 (when demonstrating a considerable degree of co-operation under the auspices of the Northern Association, Sir Thomas Fairfax's contingent combined with those from Cheshire, Lancashire, Derbyshire and Staffordshire), operations in Staffordshire and the Battle of Montgomery in 1644, as well as the siege of Chester in 1645 and 1646. Yet co-operation between Brereton's forces and their Lancastrian neighbours did not always run smoothly. The ill feeling over the maintenance of Warrington garrison certainly challenged Sir William's patience, and he was vexed by what he regarded as the inconsistent performance of the Lancashire troops in North Wales in autumn 1643.

In February 1643 Cheshire was meant to be allied with the new East Midlands Association, while on 10 April the county was similarly affiliated with the new association for the six counties of North Wales under the command of Sir Thomas Myddelton.[57] Yet neither of these schemes came to anything. Part of Brereton's problem in the Midlands stemmed from the involvement of the Earl of Denbigh, whose loyalty was regarded by many Parliamentarians as highly suspect and his military leadership deficient. During the summer of 1644 when Sir William was returning from Yorkshire with the majority of his horse, a large contingent of the Cheshire foot, led by Adjutant Lothian, was obliged to serve under Fielding in Shropshire. Following the storming of Cholmondeley, Denbigh earmarked their 'forwardness and valour which they have expressed on all occasions', but he was somewhat critical of their performance at Oswestry, Shrewsbury and elsewhere. However, other accounts suggest that Lothian's men (principally the regiments of Mainwaring and Booth) acquitted themselves admirably and were reluctant to serve under Denbigh, marching away to Nantwich at the end of the fighting without his permission and without even informing him. It was Myddelton who rightly regarded the Cheshire foot as indispensable to the campaign, and recognised that the Parliamentarians would not have achieved the success they did without their involvement.

56 Gratton, *Parliamentarian and Royalist War Effort in Lancashire*, p.364.

57 *LJ*, V, p.708; *A&O*, I, pp.178–9; Dore, 'Sir Thomas Myddelton's Attempted Conquest of Powys, 1644–5', pp.91–118.

In January 1643 it was crucial to create a strong Parliamentarian presence in North Staffordshire, whose border was close to Nantwich where Brereton had recently established his army's headquarters. It also covered the important link between the Midlands with London. Thus, in August 1643 Sir William's horse and dragoons combined with Sir John Gell's troops in aiding the Staffordshire forces at Hopton Heath, and in capturing Stafford and Eccleshall castles, before placing garrisons across the towns of the county. Through using his military forces and personal influence both in Staffordshire and Shropshire, Brereton managed to get county committees established in both. He had himself placed on such committees by Parliament, then controlled them through a variety of means, some of them exceedingly devious. Thus when Josiah Rycraft called Sir William 'Major General for Lancashire, Cheshire and Staffordshire', it could be said that he was an early instance of an editor sacrificing strict accuracy for an effective headline. That he left out Shropshire is perhaps because he thought it might 'cramp his style' when he came to Mytton later.

Soldiers from Ireland in the Cheshire Army

The English regiments brought back from Ireland after Charles I's cessation of hostilities between October 1643 and February 1644 presented the Parliamentarian cause in the north-west of England and Welsh borders with a major challenge. This was felt none more so than in Cheshire, as it threatened both the future existence of Brereton's army and its reduction of the Royalist stronghold of Chester. Modern assessments have concentrated some of their energies on the military and psychological impact of the arrival of the army from Ireland to the King's cause.[58] However, Ian Gentles argues that both English and Irish alike were 'more of a liability than an asset'.[59] Although such soldiers were generally admired on account of their fighting ability and familiarity with harsh conditions, according to Lowe, they 'introduced licence and cruelty into the fighting in the North West which had hitherto been conducted with essential chivalry on both sides'.[60] Thus, adding to a more general fear of 'bloody Irish rebels' in their midst, they provided Parliament an enormous propaganda opportunity.

The first major defection of Royalist troops occurred after Byron's defeat at Nantwich on 25 January 1644, where over 70 officers and 1,500 common soldiers were taken prisoner by troops under Sir Thomas Fairfax and Sir William Brereton. The majority of these had previously served in

58 Lowe, 'Campaign of the Irish Royalist Army', pp.49–76; Lowe and Dore, 'Battle of Nantwich', pp.97–124; Malcolm, 'All the King's Men', pp.239–64; Ian Ryder, *An English Army for Ireland* (Leigh-on-Sea: Partizan Press, 1987); Pádraig Lenihan, *Confederate Catholics at War, 1641–49* (Cork: Cork University Press, 2001); Eamon Darcy, *The Irish Rebellion of 1641 and the Wars of the Three Kingdoms* (Woodbridge: Boydell, 2013).

59 Ian Gentles, *The English Revolution and War in Three Kingdoms, 1638–1652* (London: Routledge, 2007), pp.202–3. See also Andrew Hopper, *Turncoats and Renegadoes: Changing Sides during the English Civil Wars* (Oxford: OUP, 2012), pp.89–91.

60 Lowe, 'Campaign of the Irish Royalist Army', p.61.

Ireland. Writing of the catastrophe Lord Byron and his brother, Sir Robert, complained of the unreliability of some of their regiments. The latter asserted that 'Warren's regiment, though they had their beloved Colonel Monck in the head of them, was no sooner charged but they broke, and being rallied again, the next charge ran quite away. Some say they played foul-play and ran over to the enemy, at least 60 of them, and fired upon us.' Such criticisms remain unconfirmed, although Lord Byron later requested of Ormonde that if reinforcements were sent from Ireland, 'I wish they were rather Irish than English, for the English we have already are very mutinous, and being for the most part these countrymen are so poisoned by the ill-affected people here, that they grow very cold in the service.'[61]

Sir John Mennes, lieutenant general in North Wales, informed Rupert that 'several of the Irish prisoners, yea 500 men, have taken arms under the Parliament, besides 200 who ran to them before'.[62] Similarly, Robert Byron later admitted, 'We lost all our artillery, munition and baggage; all our colonels taken prisoner, and most of the rest of the officers … We hear many of the soldiers that were prisoners, especially of Warren's, have taken conditions with them.'[63] This is confirmed by Malbon, who reported that '1,500 or more' prisoners were taken, and many 'took up arms for the Parliament and were listed under several captains'.[64] On 11 November 1643 on the eve of their embarkation to England, Ormonde had warned that the reason why Royalist regiments needed to disciplined by their officers was not merely because they had been 'infected' with puritanism, but because, after long and arduous service in Ireland, they 'will be apt to fall into disorders, and will think themselves delivered from prison, when they come on English ground, and that they may make use of their liberty to go whither they will'.[65]

Four days after the relief of Nantwich Fairfax and Brereton wrote to Robert Monroe, the Covenanting general in Northern Ireland:

> We are possessed of far more prisoners than we are able to master, or this town (which hath been so long besieged, and thereby distressed, and hereby relieved) is able to maintain. Whilst these men were employed in Ireland they did perform very good service, and now they seem to be very willing to take up arms on this side … Part thereof are natural Irish, the rest English lately come out of Ireland … We took fourteen captains, twenty lieutenants, twenty-six ensigns, four sergeants, forty drummers, sixty-three corporals, two cornets, two quartermasters, four commanders and twenty gentlemen of companies [as well as 1,500 common soldiers].[66]

The Parliamentarian commanders also made it known that not all of the prisoners of war took the Covenant and change sides, arguing that some would not take up arms against Charles I in England, but they might be

61 Carte, *Letters*, I, p.39.
62 Warburton, *Memoirs*, II, p.371.
63 Carte, *Letters* I, p.42.
64 Malbon, p.115.
65 Thomas Carte, *The Life of James, Duke of Ormond* (Oxford: Oxford University Press, 1851), V, p.505; Phillips, *Memoirs*, II, pp.91–2.
66 HMC, *Tenth Report*, App. IV, pp.65–6.

persuaded to continue fighting against the Confederates in Ireland. Of the 1,500 soldiers from Ireland who surrendered at Nantwich, about 700 or 800 soldiers went over to the Parliament. Some of these were put into new garrisons in Shropshire and the Welsh borders. Captain Wood reportedly took 60 men from Nantwich to Longford Hall, near Market Drayton, 'they being prisoners taken from Lord Byron in Cheshire, and were in actual service with the said captain from 16 January 1644 until Prince Rupert came with his forces and surprised the garrison about the middle of April 1644'.[67] Similarly, writing in the February to her husband, Mrs Luke Lloyd reported, 'This week there are garrisons put in Feneshall and Bettisfield. We expect more to Hanmer. They are those men that came from Ireland that turned when they were taken prisoners at Wich [Nantwich]'.[68]

At least 600 prisoners from Nantwich enlisted in Brereton's army, where the majority of them were presumably scattered among existing units. Although there remains some doubt over their degree of commitment shown to the Royalist cause in England by some of these soldiers, there can be little doubt about their calibre, or the eagerness of Brereton and other commanders to enlist them. Fairfax, a man not known for wasting words, described them as 'men of great experience who had run through all sorts or services, and were not new to the policies of war … They were men acquainted with the greatest hardship, habituated to cold and want, and whatever suffering a winter siege could require … They were put in heart by their former successes, and that they would make them the more daring and desperate, and they were valiant before, being used to nothing but conquests'.[69] In March 1644 Colonel Robert Duckenfield spent the sum of £30 'for arms to furnish my Irish company and some clothes for them', thus suggesting that not only had a number of these veterans been recruited into his regiment, but perhaps most of them served in a single company. Duckenfield had previous experience of these soldiers during the Parliamentarian reversal at Middlewich in December 1643 and in the relief of Nantwich, and no doubt held them in high regard.[70]

Furthermore, Brereton made use of soldiers who had served in Ireland and North Wales in the former firelock companies of Captains Sandford and Langley. Sandford played a leading role in the capture of Hawarden Castle and with eight of his men took Beeston Castle in a surprise operation. He was killed leading Byron's unsuccessful attack on Nantwich on 17 January 1644.[71] It is likely that such soldiers were absorbed into Sir William Brereton's dragoons. He later talked about the Cheshire dragoons, 'which were soldiers in Ireland' as 'very serviceable' and 'well-accommodated'. Brereton also informed Lord Leven on 22 May 1645, 'I can bring no more foot than one regiment and some choice dragoons – firelocks which were soldiers in Ireland

67 *CSPD 1645–7*, p.298.

68 HMC, *Fourteenth Report*, App. IV, p.62.

69 'Short Memorial', pp.119–25; *CWTC*, pp.107–110.

70 TNA, SP28/128/10, fol. 7v.

71 HMC, *Fourteenth Report*, App. IV, pp.124, 131, 143; Malbon, pp.91–109. See also Lowe, 'Campaign of the Irish Royalist Army', pp.62, 65; Ryder, *An English Army for Ireland*, p.31; John Barratt, 'What Sanford's Firelocks Did Next', *English Civil War Notes & Queries*, 50 (Leigh-on-sea: Partizan Press, 1995), pp.18–21; Hopper, *Turncoats*, pp.89–90.

lately mounted'.[72] In addition to this, Simon Finch, the late captain in Ernle's regiment of foot was taken with other captured officers to London after the Battle of Nantwich, where he consequently accepted a commission as captain of dragoons in the Cheshire Parliamentarian army.[73] When the Cessation of Arms was signed in the summer of 1644, Anglo-Irish Protestant officers such as Michael Jones and Chidley Coote refused to fight against the Parliament and joined Brereton's forces. With them came Captains Culme, Hawkbridge, Lord Calvin, Gimbert and Holt. Culme was an Anglo-Irishman linked to Jones by marriage, Hawkbridge first appears with Jones in London recruiting their cavalry troops in London and on their way back to Cheshire, whereas Calvin was a Scot living in Ireland. The first three commanded troops of horse (Jones himself taking over the entire Cheshire Horse during Brereton's absence in London in 1645), while Calvin led a company in Sir William's own regiment of foot. On 9 September 1644 Brereton reported to the Committee of Both Kingdoms, 'I had sent to Wem part of three companies lately raised under the command of Lord Calvin, Lieutenant Colonel Coote and Captain Finch, which I had not time to complete.'[74]

Given the origins of such officers, it is likely that some of their commands contained former Royalist soldiers captured at Nantwich, as well as following the fall of Liverpool two months later. Mark Stoyle contends that of the approximately 9,000 men who were brought over to England and North Wales in 1643 and 1644, about 2,000 were native Irish.[75] There remains the possibility, given the blurred evidence surrounding the treatment by Parliament and its officers of captured soldiers from Ireland, that not only were native Irishmen among them, but as Dore suggests, 'it is possible that some who were Catholic in religion may have been induced for a time to take up service even under so avowed an anti-catholic as Brereton'.[76] The parliamentary ordinance of 24 October 1644 instructed its officers and soldiers that 'no quarter shall be given hereafter to any Irishman, nor any papist whatsoever born in Ireland, who shall be taken in hostility against the Parliament ... every officer that shall be remiss or negligent in observing the tenor of this ordinance shall be reputed a favourer of that bloody rebellion in Ireland'.[77] Yet this was rarely acted upon, and was effective only in England and Wales. Arguably, the reason for its issue was that it did not wish any of its officers to be 'refuted a favourer of that bloody rebellion in Ireland'. Moreover, such legislation appeared some 10 months after Nantwich, when a number of 'native-born' Catholics might have been recruited by the Cheshire Parliamentarian army. Although not in major numbers, it is clear that some 'native Irish' troops served in Royalist units in England.

In April 1644 about 500 men were transported to Chester to form part of Lord Byron's foot, and were placed under English and Welsh officers,

72 HMC, *Fourteenth Report*, App. IV, p.62; BL, MS Add. 11331, fol. 142; *BLB*, I, 610.

73 BL, MS Harley 2135, fols 69v.–71r.

74 *CSPD 1644*, pp.484–5.

75 Mark Stoyle, *Soldiers and Strangers: An Ethnic History of the English Civil War* (New Haven, CT: Yale University Press 2005), pp.209–10.

76 *BLB*, II, p.596.

77 *A&O*, I, pp.554–5; Lenihan, *Confederate Catholics*, p.211.

while as late as February 1646 attempts were still being made to recruit Irish soldiers for the relief of the city. There is firm evidence that at least Lieutenant Colonel Coote's company were bolstered by Irish Protestant (and perhaps even Catholic) soldiers who came over to him and Michael Jones from the siege of Liverpool in the autumn of 1644. On 29 September Meldrum reported to the Committee of Both Kingdoms, 'The enemy is stronger within the town of Liverpool than we are without, besides the advantages of very strong works. It is rumoured that the Irish here desire to return and serve in Ireland if they may have quarter. These propositions have been made by the Irish to Lieutenant Colonel Coote, son of Sir Charles Coote'.[78] Similarly, the following month Brereton told the same Committee:

> Upon today we removed to Tranmere near Liverpool in Wirral, opposite to Liverpool about half a mile from the waterside, where we have quartered these seven days expecting almost every day when the town would be delivered up, with whom Sir John Meldrum and the Lancashire Gentlemen have been in treaty these divers days, for which purpose Sir John Meldrum sent for my Lieutenant Colonel Coote (a son of Sir Charles Coote, to be employed in this treaty) whom I sent over for that end, but thought they did not make use of him yet diverse of those old soldiers in Ireland that knew him came out of the town over the works and came unto him. So also did some others to Lieutenant Colonel Jones, who reported that there are divers more would do the like if they can but find the opportunity – most of the soldiers within the town (except the papists, and those who are Irish and were in rebellion in Ireland) desire the town may be surrendered.[79]

The recruitment of such soldiers is confirmed by Sir William Brereton's report on the fight at Christleton on 18 January 1645, in which he mentioned, 'There were 500 or 600 Cheshire foot … those foot which came out of Liverpool, and are now under my Lieutenant Colonel Jones (some of which served in Ireland), did perform good service this day'.[80] During the final stages of the Parliamentarian siege of the town in November 1644 Brereton observed, 'those obstinate and hard-hearted rebels, who before would not accept better conditions than they deserved, are now most justly constrained and contented to deliver themselves to the mercy of the besiegers, the very Irish concurring in the mutiny against the commanders in the town because they would not deliver up the same, whereupon the common soldiers delivered up their commanders prisoners (1 November, about noon) to the end themselves might receive quarter'.[81] Moreover, Meldrum's negotiations for the surrender of Liverpool revealed that among the 140 officers and 700 common soldiers, besides 400 who had mutinied and gone over to the enemy, there were native Irish (and therefore probably Catholic) among the garrison.[82]

78 *CSPD 1644*, p.544.
79 TNA, SP21/17, fols 63v.–5r.; *CSPD 1644–5*, p.67.
80 *Perfect Passages*, 14, 22 January 1645; Phillips, *Memoirs*, II, p.226.
81 TNA, SP21/17, fols 106v.–107r.; *Letter Books of Sir Samuel Luke*, p.377.
82 *CSPD 1644–5*, pp.94–5; HMC, *Tenth Report*, App. IV, p.95.

5

Anatomy of an Army II: Leadership and the Machinery of War

Sir William Brereton's authority in Cheshire stemmed from two main ordinances. On 25 March 1643 Parliament decreed that 'it be recommended to my Lord General to grant a commission to Sir William Brereton, to command-in-chief the forces in Cheshire'. In March 1644 a further ordinance (which replaced that of January 1643) gave Brereton overall control over all decisions relating to the county. Crucially also, on 16 May 1644 his commission as commander-in-chief was extended:

> in the absence of the Lord Fairfax and Sir Thomas Fairfax, over the forces which are, or shall be, raised in the county of Chester, is very expedient to promote the public service. It is therefore ordered that Sir William Brereton, baronet shall command, and have the full power of a commander, in chief in the said county of Chester, in the absence of the said Lord Fairfax and Sir Thomas Fairfax. And that the Lord Fairfax shall be desired to grant a commission to the said Sir William Brereton, to command in chief the forces aforesaid; and to have power to lead, conduct, and carry the same, to such place as he shall think fit, for the defence of the said county, and counties adjacent; and likewise power to give the same orders and instructions, in the absence of the said superior officers, for regulating the soldiers which are or shall be under his command, as his excellency hath given to his army; and to use martial law, to compel obedience thereunto, as occasion shall require; and also power and authority to make and appoint colonels, captains, and other officers, for the leading and conducting the said forces, as he shall think fit.[1]

Following the cessation of his military commissions in early 1645 under the Self-Denying Ordinance, on 12 May Brereton (alongside Sir Thomas Myddelton and Oliver Cromwell) was allowed to continue his command of the army for a further 40 days. At the same time Parliament informed

1 *CJ*, III, pp.19, 494; *LJ*, V, pp.538–41; VI, p.486; Morrill, *Cheshire*, pp.80–1.

the deputy lieutenants of Cheshire that Sir George Booth and the four regimental colonels, or any three of them, were authorised at the end of this period to direct the war effort in the county, and to govern the forces under Brereton's command 'until Parliament shall make further notice'. Another order instructed that at the end of 40 days Colonel Mytton was to succeed Myddelton as major general for North Wales, Lieutenant Colonel Jones to succeed to the command of Brereton's regiment of horse, and Sergeant Major Lothian to lead his regiment of foot.[2]

Soon after his arrival in Cheshire in January 1643 Sir William Brereton reported, 'Take care I pray that there may be a major to order a regiment of horse with some officers of foot sent down, for we have a great need of them, a lieutenant-colonel and sergeant major of foot and some lieutenants of foot ... some old soldiers for sergeants would do wonderous well.'[3] Although most of Brereton's earliest supporters in the county were local gentlemen, the army contained officers from a range of backgrounds and experiences. Men such as Henry Mainwaring, George Booth and Edward Hyde raised troops for the Parliamentarian cause during the early stages of the conflict, while Robert Duckenfield turned out a foot company of volunteers at his own expense in mid 1642, and by the following year had recruited a full regiment and troop of horse.

Established Cheshire landowners, including Henry Brooke, John Leigh, Thomas Croxton, Robert Venables, William Massey, Henry Bradshaw and Gilbert Gerard became valuable and loyal commanders, while Brooke was appointed high sheriff in 1644. Yet following the expulsion of various 'disloyal' officers, including Colonels Mainwaring and Booth, by early 1645 all of Brereton's leading officers were either dependable local men, talented outsiders (such as Jerome Zankey and officers from Ireland), or professional soldiers. The quality of leadership in the Cheshire Parliamentarian army drew the attention of Clarendon. Hardly a supporter of their cause, he nonetheless declared, 'Sir William Brereton and other gentlemen of that party executed their commands with notable sobriety and indefatigable industry, insomuch as the best soldiers that encountered with them had no cause to despise them'.[4] By the close of the First Civil War, this group was at the centre of a body of experienced and trustworthy officers. As Morrill asserts, by early 1645 'Brereton's army was controlled by men who owed their advancement to him alone.'[5]

Brereton's force was boosted from the outset by the presence of experienced professionals, whose knowledge during the early months of the war in particular, were greatly in demand. In 1598 the soldier Robert Barret wrote of officers 'such as have seen wars, and borne office in the same, I mean honest and valiant men, not tapsterly praters, and ale-bench braggers, who know no point of soldiery in the world'.[6] Veterans returning

2 *CJ*, IV, p.139; BL, MS Add. 11131, fols 123v., 131r.
3 HMC, *Portland*, I, pp.94–5.
4 Clarendon, *History of the Rebellion*, II, p.471.
5 Morrill, *Cheshire*, p.81.
6 Robert Barret, *The Theorike and Practike of Moderne Warres discoursed in dialogue wise* (London, 1598), p.5.

from the wars in the Netherlands were often employed as muster-masters and sergeants, whose role was to train the English and Welsh militia and help to familiarise them with the 'modern fashion' of infantry drill. In 1626 the Privy Council stipulated that experienced soldiers were to 'be sent from the Low Countries hither, to be distributed into the several counties, there to teach the captains, lieutenants, ensigns, and other officers and leaders of files in each company the true use of arms and order of soldiers'.[7] It can be assumed that Parliamentarian officers (especially professionals) in Cheshire made use of up-to-date military manuals. The Derbyshire commander, Sir John Gell, served as a captain of trained bands between 1624 and 1634, and owned a copy of Thomas Styward's *The Pathwaie to Martiall Discipline*. The book is badly worn and bloodstained, suggesting that it was used during the Civil Wars. It is possible that Gell served 'two years in the borders of France under the late Duke of Buckingham'.[8]

Arriving in Cheshire with Brereton in January 1643 Sergeant Major James Lothian appears to have held range of skills including the training of recruits, organising and leading the Cheshire foot, and undertaking specialised siege operations. Brereton's chief engineer, Captain William Buchanan, was a fellow Scot and likely to have served with Lothian previously, while the army's master gunner, Captain John Arundel, was probably also a professional. Three of Brereton's dragoon captains, Goldegay, Gimbert and Holt probably had previous military service, as had another dragoon, Captain Finch, who was captured at Nantwich in 1644 and given a commission in the Cheshire forces. Moreover, Colonel Brooke recruited the likely professionals Robert Wynn to command his troop of horse, and John Church to act as captain-lieutenant of his own company (and presumably to help organise and train his regiment of foot). Robert Duckenfield also received 'advice about fortifying Stockport' from Lieutenant Colonel Rosworm, the Dutch or German engineer, who had constructed earthworks at Manchester, Liverpool and elsewhere in Lancashire.[9] Such officers were highly respected by both sides.

Some of the most effective officers in the Cheshire army were those who had previously served in Ireland. A number of Anglo-Irish and Anglo-Scots Protestant officers who refused to fight against Parliament also enlisted in the Cheshire forces. These included Michael Jones and Chidley Coote, who became lieutenant colonels in the Cheshire forces, and Captains Hugh Culme, Hawkbridge, Calvin, Gimbert and Joseph Holt. Some of these are also likely to have been professional soldiers. Coote was with Brereton, Mytton and Denbigh on 15 June 1644 at Stourbridge, reporting to the Committee of Both Kingdoms on the movements of Prince Rupert in the North West.[10] Moreover, Arthur Trevor informed the Marquess of Ormonde from Chester on 30 August that 'Chidley Coote, Michael Jones, Young Wingfield and many more are at Nantwich, and have taken

7 HMC, *Third Report*, p.445.
8 DRO, D3287/1043/4, D252/60/26c; Slack, *Man at War*, pp.34–6.
9 TNA, SP28/128/10, fol. 7v.; *CWTL*, pp.219–47.
10 *CSPD 1644*, pp.237–8.

conditions from Sir William Brereton, whose Lieutenant Colonel Michael Jones is'.[11] Trevor mentioned also that Captain Culme was 'betrayed to the enemy, and has since escaped hither'. This officer, along with Coote, Jones and Hawkbridge raised troops for Brereton's cavalry regiment in London during the summer and autumn of 1644. Sir William's own accounts show that on the way back from the capital into the Midlands in the June and July he disbursed further money for raising and arming additional troopers, as well as purchasing horses for them.[12]

Often competing notions of parliamentary and military authority in the North West and Midlands of England discussed previously were also related to the granting of commissions to army officers. About 250 commissioned officers from the rank of quartermaster up to colonel have been identified among the Cheshire army, although not all of them would have served at the same time. It may also be possible to unearth more names and ranks of junior officers from surviving documents. Evidence suggests that Brereton's officers received their commissions from three sources. It would seem that the sensible solution, at least during the early stages of the war was that the 'greater' commissions (that is, colonelcies) were issued by the Earl of Essex as captain general of Parliament's forces, and the lesser by Lord Fairfax. There was never the animosity between the two that there existed between Essex and Waller, major general of the south-western forces (and to a lesser degree between Essex and the Earl of Manchester), because Essex never felt threatened by Fairfax's command. Yorkshire and the north were too far distant from his own sphere of operations.

Sir William Brereton received his original commission as commander-in-chief of the Cheshire forces from the Earl of Essex, as well as those as colonel of regiments of foot, horse and dragoons on respectively 20 September 1642, 1 March 1643 and his 'first appearance in Cheshire in January 1643'.[13] Likewise, Robert Duckenfield was commissioned as colonel of a regiment of foot by Devereux on 7 November 1643.[14] This would suggest that the other Cheshire colonels received commissions from Essex, and probably about the same time as Duckenfield. Given the nominal inclusion of Cheshire in the Northern Association in 1642 and 1643, it is possible that the greatest number of early officer's commissions were issued by Lord Fairfax. Henry Bradshaw of Duckenfield's regiment of foot 'was sergeant major to the foresaid regiment from the said 10 March [1643], by virtue of a commission from the late Ferdinando, Lord Fairfax until the third day of February 1645[6]'.[15] On 2 March 1644 Captain John Brooke cited in a warrant that he was to be sent men and arms 'By virtue of an original commission to me granted by the right honourable Lord Fairfax, general of these counties.' Similarly, Robert Venables, captain-lieutenant of Brereton's own foot company served

11 Carte, *Letters*, III, p.349.

12 TNA, SP28/152/7, fol. 4r.–5v.

13 *CJ*, III, p.19; TNA, SP28/152/7, fol. 20r.

14 TNA, SP28/128/10, fol. 9v.; SP/20/10/63, fol. 161r.

15 BDL, MS Top Cheshire e 3, fols 1r.–v.; A. Craig Gibson, 'Every-Day Life of a Country Gentleman of Cheshire in the 17th Century', *THSLC*, 15 (1862–1863), pp. 67–92 (p. 71).

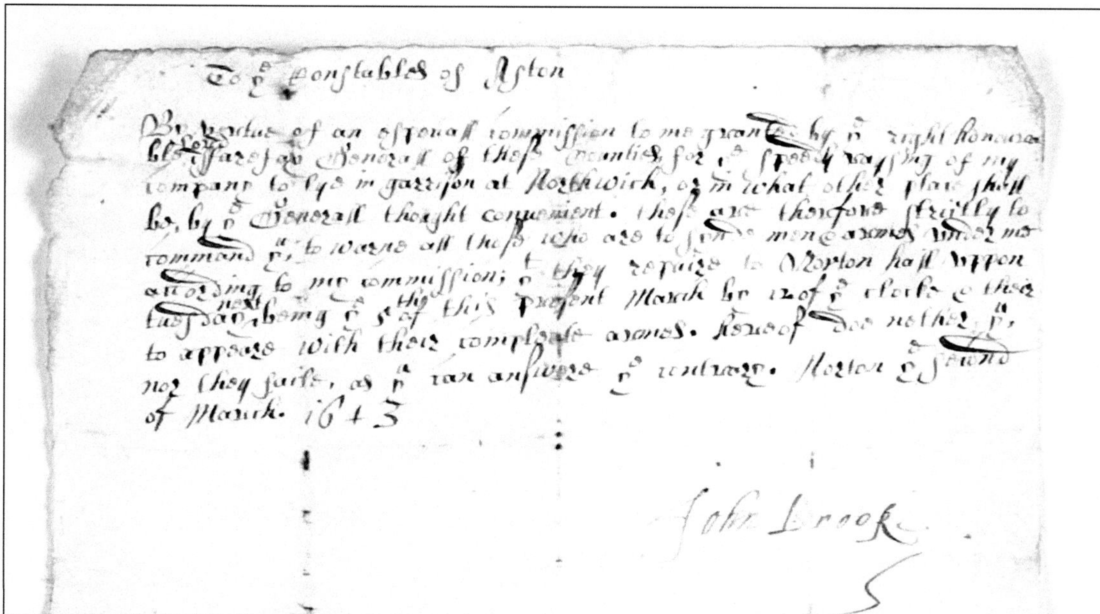

Warrant issued by Captain John Brooke to the constables of Aston, dated 2 March 1644. (Courtesy of Christine Talbot)

as lieutenant colonel as by Lord Fairfax's commission from 14 February 1644 until 1 March 1646.[16]

A further example of the commissioning of officers of the Northern Association by Fairfax is that of the Lancashire officer Thomas Birch, who received a commission as colonel of a regiment on 15 March 1643.[17] Robert Duckenfield stated that his commission as colonel came from the Earl of Essex, but the source of his commissions as captain of a troop of horse (granted on 26 November 1642) and of a company of foot (issued on 25 September 1642) is unclear, but given the dates it is possible that they came from Fairfax. Sir William Brereton's appointment on 25 March 1643 as 'command-in-chief the forces in Cheshire' gave him the authority to grant his own commissions, and it might be that as the war progressed a number of those issued to captains and 'junior officers' (lieutenants, cornets and ensigns) came from him. Thus William Wright served as lieutenant to Captain Littler's dragoon company, but on that officer's death was promoted in his stead. In his certificate of service Wright stated:

> My commission received date 11 April 1644, and within the space of four days I was in actual service, being sent by my colonel (with that party I received after Captain Littler his decease, being under his command in his lifetime) to quarter in Aston and maintain a force, to prevent the enemy from making incursion into safe places, where for some time I continued in service till my colonel's command was called for by the general, Sir William Brereton, which was the last of September *Anno Domini* 1644. So yet I served as captain under the command

16 AA, unlisted warrant, dated 2 March 1644; BL, MS Harley 1999, fols 58v.–63r.

17 *CJ*, VI, p.503; *Royalist Composition Papers*, I, p.18; *CWTL*, p.241.

> of Colonel Leigh from 11 April 1644 until the last of September in the same. I was absent four, before [I] marched to Aston as above.[18]

William Davies was commissioned by Brereton on 9 September 1644 'to be captain of one company of foot soldiers consisting of 100 men to be raised by you within the several townships of Tarvin, Ashton, Alvanley and Hartford, and anywhere your talents within the county of Chester, to serve in my own regiment of foot for the service of protestant religion, the king, parliament and kingdoms.' He served in that capacity until 'the latter end of September 1645.[19]

The Trained Bands

For researchers into questions of military organisation, finance and administration in Civil War Cheshire, the survival and nature of the trained bands is highly problematic. This is not helped by the often passing and vague references in documents to 'trained soldiers' and 'countrymen', in addition to confusion over the status of volunteer and trained band units, and difficulties in identifying both Royalist and Parliamentarian trained band officers in 1642. The trained and freehold bands were local militia units organised on a county and hundredal basis. They were controlled by the lords lieutenant of each county in England and Wales (as well as London). These were expected to appoint professional soldiers to provide the trained bands with basic military training, and periodically inspect their armour and weapons. Membership was compulsory for 'well-affected men', Protestant freeholders, landowners and householders, who were fit and able to serve. By 1642 the freehold bands were regarded as an elitist reserve, and saw themselves as their own territorial force, somewhat distinct from the county force. At Warrington on 21 October 1642 the Royalist leaders agreed that the Lancashire trained bands were to be maintained by the hundreds and the freeholders by gentlemen of the county. The 'whole' or 'county' militia remained possibly the largest force and were expected to turn out in time of war. A particular impediment with the trained bands, however, was their general unwillingness to serve away from their home areas.

In Cheshire during the summer of 1642 it was Sir William Brereton who saw in the Militia Ordinance a means to maintain local peace and order in the county. The trained bands of five of the seven Cheshire hundreds (Bucklow, Eddisbury, Nantwich, Northwich and Macclesfield) were mobilised and later brought under the command of Brereton and the deputy lieutenants of the county. Although the survival and role of the 'country companies' in Brereton's army is not fully clear, there were attempts to assemble the militia at Northwich, Stockport, Nantwich and elsewhere in 1642. On 30 June 1642 the head constable of Bucklow, Richard Worrall, at the instigation of

18 TNA, SP28/152/9, fol. 15r.; SP28/208, fol. 33v.; E121/351, fols 63r.–v.; BL, MS Harley 2128, fol. 166r.

19 BL, MS Harley 1970, fols 73v.–74r.

Thomas Jenner, *The Military Discipline* (1642), showing musket postures.

the Sir George Booth and other deputy lieutenants, summoned the trained band of the hundred to appear at Knutsford.[20] A few days later Sir William Brereton appears to have had two successful musters in the north of the county (probably in Macclesfield and Bucklow Hundreds). On 2 and 5 July he praised the obedience of the trained bands in turning out, stating 'they having more appearance in one hundred than the commission of array had in four and they had more volunteers three to one than the commissioners of

20 *LJ*, V, pp.200, 204.

array had'. Another muster followed in Northwich Hundred. In a letter to the Speaker on 30 July Brereton related:

> So soon as we were assisted by the addition of some other deputy lieutenants to join in the other hundreds we proceeded to assemble the hundred of Northwich upon Tuesday last at Northwich, where there was a full appearance about three hundred and twenty musketeers and four score pikemen well-armed, and near six hundred other volunteers, who, thought they brought not arms so complete yet I believe their hearts as well affected as the other to the safety and peace of the King and Parliament. And though the number was not so great as in the former Hundreds, which were much larger and more populous than this, wherein divers of the trained bands and some others charged with arms absented themselves by reason of their relation to the commissioners of array, that the number of those that were completely armed was double to those that are ordinarily charged with arms, besides the other 600 volunteers; so as you may be confirmed in the assurance of the good affection of many in this country if they receive encouragement and protection, and many more I am confident would discover themselves if they were not enawed by their remoteness from your assistance and exposed to more than ordinary peril in regard to the disaffected in Wales, Lancashire, Nottinghamshire, and some other neighbouring counties.[21]

Yet his attempt to organise a muster at Nantwich (the town that was expected to be, and later became the Parliamentarian headquarters in Cheshire) was prevented by the greater readiness of the Royalists, and the uncertain conduct of some deputy lieutenants and local justices. Sir William and his supporters were also violently treated by the citizens of Chester, and were only saved by the mayor.[22] The successful mustering of the larger part of the Cheshire trained bands by Parliamentarian leaders in 1642 has to be offset by the reported local activities of some of the leading Royalists. With his estates located at Rocksavage in Bucklow Hundred, Earl Rivers recruited heavily in the area for his regiment of foot, which later joined the Oxford Army. Furthermore, he maintained a gun battery which protected the crossing of the River Weaver at Frodsham, a Royalist newsbook reporting on 17 September 1642, 'The Earl of Rivers hath five pieces of ordnance, ten barrels of powder and sixty bullets landed at Frodsham.'[23]

In addition to garrisoning his own home, Rivers placed troops in Halton Castle and reportedly menaced his Parliamentarian neighbours, the Brooke family of Norton. Depositions given before the committee for sequestrations in Bucklow in March 1645 by Colonel Henry Brooke, and his relatives and tenants reveal that he also attempted to raise the local militia. According to Richard Jennings of Norton, 'in July or August 1642 John, Earl Rivers did recruit the commission of array in several places of the county, and did raise divers of the trained bands of this county, and so this person did credibly hear, did forth set forth his warrants for collecting of moneys, and did also

21 HMC, *Portland*, I, pp.46–7.

22 Malbon, pp.25–6; HMC, *Portland*, I, pp.51–2.

23 *The Latest Remarkable Truths*, 29 October 1642; Malbon, p.239.

as this person had heard, send several of the assorted plans to the people to inform and threaten others'. Likewise, John Fletcher of Weston said:

> the Earl Rivers in the year 1642 did recruit the commission of array and did by virtue of his commission muster and require the freehold bands of the county, and did about November in the said year cause the castle of Halton to be garrisoned with a company of foot soldiers, and did further raise a troop of horse, which horse and foot did plunder divers well affected persons to the parliament, and did take from them all their arms and divers other goods of great value.'[24]

The authority of the deputy lieutenants in Cheshire resulted in the survival of the trained bands. This was especially significant in this county because the lord lieutenant, William Fiennes, Lord Saye and Sele was absent from Cheshire during the war, although he raised a regiment of foot in Essex's army and was a member of the Committee of Both Kingdoms. In noting the existence of the deputy lieutenants, Morrill suggests that under the financial control of the deputy lieutenants, the trained bands were employed in garrison work while volunteers and 'listed' (pressed) men served in Sir William Brereton's field army. He concedes, however, that this pattern could not be maintained and that militia regiments maintained in the various hundreds of the county were brought up to the Chester leaguer on an intermittent basis.[25] Although this has been challenged by Dore, this appears to remain the prevailing view. As Dore notes more generally, 'Obviously much more research into the question of the survival of the trained bands is needed, as the principle writers on military organisation on the Parliamentarian side during the Civil War have assumed that their abandonment in the Civil War was nationwide.'[26]

Evidence from Brereton's army list of 30 April 1645 in particular, but also letters between Sir William and his fellow deputy lieutenants, pay warrants and muster rolls, suggests that to varying degrees, some regiments of foot in the Cheshire Parliamentarian army were a mixture of volunteers, pressed men and trained band companies. Although to be treated with caution, the marginal notes to the April 1645 list reveal companies from different regiments located in various parts of Cheshire and Shropshire, while the garrison of Nantwich comprised five companies from three different regiments, and three companies were billeted at Tarvin. Yet these and other army dispositions (including the manning of a range of outlying posts and garrisons by both horse and foot) during this period reflected Brereton's necessity of maintaining the blockade of Chester and response to wider tactical considerations elsewhere. Evidence from earlier in the war is less clear, but although sub-units were 'brigaded' into taskforces, complete regiments of Cheshire foot fought together on the battlefield. Examples include operations in Shropshire and the Welsh borders in 1643 and 1644,

---

24 CRO, DCH/X/15/14.

25 Morrill, *Cheshire*, pp.117–18.

26 *BLB*, I, pp.15–16. For works on the pre-war trained bands and assumptions over their later role, see Firth, *Cromwell's Army*, pp.15–18; Holmes, *Eastern Association*, pp.163–5; G.P. Higgins, 'The militia in early Stuart Cheshire', *JCAS*, 61 (1978), pp.39–49.

the defence of Stockport in May 1644, as well as the despatch of 1,500 to the aid of Meldrum in Lancashire and the Battle of Montgomery a few months later.

A particular issue is the terms 'country' or 'country companies', presumably applied to militia units in Cheshire. In general terms the marginal note 'country' in Brereton's list of his army refers to companies living at home and therefore certain to be trained bands, ready to be mustered for service by the deputy lieutenants. Yet as Dore and Holmes suggest, early modern notions of 'country' did not always refer to county but sometimes to smaller and/or more less defined areas in the locality.[27] Thus, certainly by the later part of the war in Cheshire such terminology may have been employed alternately to describe troops recruited and maintained in more remote parts of Cheshire, and regularly quartered at some considerable distance from the main area of operations of Brereton's army. An obvious example is the Wirral (effectively under Royalist control until the fall of Liverpool in autumn 1644), which was relatively isolated in terms of geography and Parliamentarian control. One of the Wirral companies in Brereton's foot regiment was listed as 'country' and hence probably a trained band unit, although it is virtually certain that the rest were volunteers.

The same marginal note 'country' given for Colonel George Booth's regiment refers to the known trained band commands of Captains Alcocke and Grantham, but it is further implied that soldiers under Captains Massey and Cartwright were of similar status. The latter is debatable though, partly because Massey was an officer of considerable experience, who on 9 October 1645 led his company in the assault on the new breach at the Newgate of Chester, where he was wounded.[28] To complicate matters further, in April 1645 there was an attempt by Sir William Brereton to call out the whole militia. The deputy lieutenants in the persons of Sir George Booth and William Marbury protested against this, although their response is indicative perhaps of their anger that their ultimate power over the raising, payment and mustering of the county force had been significantly challenged by the leading army officers. On 5 April Sir George Booth reported to Brereton that he had instructed Captains Alcocke and Grantham:

> to call their companies together and make their appearance. But for raising the country people I forbear, they are making their seedings, as also they have been so often called together and to so little purpose that they grow sensible that the country is burdened and opportunities offered neglected and no return made of them.[29]

William Marbury alleged that Brereton's colonels used the occasion to impress men in Bucklow Hundred from what was intended to be a temporary emergency call-up, in order to replenish their regiments, even though these

27 *BLB*, I, p.15; Clive Holmes, 'The County Community in Stuart Historiography', *JBS*, 19(2) (1980), pp.54–73.

28 Lancaster, p. 22.

29 CRO, DDX/428, fols 87v.–88v., 78v., 76v.; *BLB*, I, 162–3, 182–3, 194, 202, 232.

soldiers were originally thought to be trained bands drawn from various Cheshire hundreds. His comments also reveal something of the methods of calling up trained band soldiers. Writing to Sir William on 13 April 1645 Marbury stated:

> If all the colonel's companies are not called up [mustered], no countryman will appear, because of the evil examples of Colonel Duckenfield's men, who returned with their colours, and Colonel Leigh's, who lie still and will not stir, to the great retarding of our design. The day after they [Duckenfield's soldiers] marched through Northwich I received a letter from the Committee at Tarvin by your direction to summon in all the enlisted soldiers at Crabtree Green in the forest [of Delamere] upon Tuesday last. This summons I caused to be given in every congregation within this Hundred the Sabbath day before. On Tuesday, the day of the rendezvous, I went to Crabtree Green and stayed there until three in the afternoon. I saw not about four men that came in, nor with orders, or to take charge of those who in all probability might have come in.
>
> That which is the greatest grievance is the usage of those that were raised by me and the sequestrators (wherein no township was spared) [and we were] allowed to have them enlisted except [only] under such as we set over them and you approve of. Yet some colonels claimed them because they said they were raised in their divisions, which hath much troubled the country in regard of our promises that they should return home free men when the design was over. Methinks they [the colonels] are very slack in raising their regiments that have such number they know not of. They may very well think that though I be the servant to the state, which I am and will be, yet I shall forbear so far to trouble myself for the completing of their regiments. If you please to have any men raised in this hundred, you may well do to write to Sir George Booth, my cousin Mainwaring and me what number in this hundred you desire, and request the sequestrators to be with us to take notice who shall offend in slackness and proceed against them as enemies to the state. This we much desire, that all townships be proportionably charged and that no colonels make any claim to the men. But that they may be put under such captains as we shall think fit and return when the design is ended. Otherwise I believe we shall raise none.[30]

Evidence from various sources illustrates that a significant number of the Cheshire foot companies described as 'trained bands' were mustered for instant service, and commanded by 'regular' officers. In this case, their actual status must be questioned. Adjutant Lothian's company of foot was drawn from the Broxton Hundred trained and freehold bands in late 1644 and early 1645. This was permanently mustered, and appears to have been something of a specialist unit, operating it seems, in conjunction with engineers and fireworkers, particularly in undertaking siege warfare, and was thus indispensable to the army. Croxton's company of Brereton's own regiment was drawn from the Northwich Hundred trained bands and was quartered in

30 CRO, DDX/428, fols 95r.–v.; *BLB*, I, 232.

the town by early 1643. It was paid as a volunteer unit, the total disbursement from London sources to its officers and soldiers amounting to £1,243 19s.[31]

These officers and soldiers were experienced and reliable, and served in a number of operations in Cheshire and elsewhere. Also quartered in the garrison of Nantwich was a unit of the Nantwich Hundred trained and freehold bands led by William Massey, which constituted the lieutenant colonel's company of Colonel George Booth's regiment and operated essentially as a 'frontline' command. Malbon relates that in September 1643 the command received orders to advance towards the Shropshire town of Wem, whereupon:

> On Friday being Michaelmas day, the trained band of Nantwich Hundred marched towards Wem, in assistance of the Parliament's forces there, with a case of drakes; and quartered the first night at [Market] Drayton, and the next day after at Wem. And thence continued making works and fortifying the town. And many times sallied forth and gave alarms upon Shrewsbury, facing them in the town and tempting them to a set battle, but they ever fled and would not fight.[32]

Sergeant Major James Lothian's Company of Broxton Hundred

James Lothian was an experienced Scots professional soldier who came to Cheshire with Sir William Brereton in January 1643. As Dore asserts, 'There is little doubt that his professional knowledge and considerable ability had a great deal to do with the success of the Parliamentarian cause in Cheshire, particularly in 1643 when few of its leaders had any military experience'.[33] Lothian acted successively as sergeant major and adjutant-general of the Cheshire foot, whom he led with dexterity on numerous occasions. He also directed siegeworks at Beeston, Hawarden, Lichfield Close and other locations. Lothian's experience was invaluable to the success of the Cheshire army during the early months of 1643, which enabled Brereton to quickly and effectively gain control of much of the county. Sergeant Major Lothian was captured at Barbridge, near Nantwich on 17 December 1643 while attacking Byron's approaching troops, but by the following summer he was at the forefront of Parliamentarian operations in Cheshire, Shropshire and the Welsh borders, which culminated in victory at Montgomery (where he was commended for leading the Cheshire foot).

Placed in co-command of the army with Lieutenant Colonel Jones during Sir William Brereton's absence, Lothian fought skilfully at Christleton, and in April and May he oversaw the siege of Hawarden Castle. As commander of the Cheshire foot at the Chester leaguer James executed the assault on the city's eastern suburbs and played an important part in the victory of Rowton Heath on 24 September 1645. During the autumn and winter of 1645 he organised and led expeditions into North Wales, and was subsequently a

31 TNA, SP28/128/13, fol. 17r.

32 Malbon, p.78.

33 *BLB*, I, 91, n. 2.

commissioner for the surrender of the city of Chester. Following this Lothian commenced the reduction of Hawarden and Holt Castles, and played a leading role with Brereton and other seasoned Cheshire officers at the siege of Lichfield Close. On 17 July 1646 the Commons ordered that 'Adjutant-General Lothian shall have the sum of £200 bestowed upon him for his good service to the parliament at Lichfield and other places, and that the sum of £500 more be paid unto the said Adjutant General Lothian, by the Committee of Goldsmiths Hall, upon account.'[34]

During the Second Civil War Lothian was appointed colonel of the 'standing regiment of this county'. The regiment was mustered on 19 August and 2 September 1648, while a contemporary pay warrant identifies Ensign Croxton as having employed his officers and soldiers to collect assessments levied upon Wirral and Broxton hundreds.[35] The sum of £625 0s. 10d. was disbursed by treasurer Croxton to 'Colonel James Lothian, and to the officers and soldiers of a regiment of foot raised in the county under his command in 1648', with a further £14 3s. 6d. paid out for colours.[36] Though formed in Chester, Lothian's regiment assisted Mytton in defeating the Royalist uprising in North Wales, especially leading the assault on Beaumaris town and Castle on 1 October. In Lothian's own company Ensign Benjamin Croxton was commissioned as captain-lieutenant, the other inferior officers being Lieutenant James Smallwood and Ensign William Salmon. On 2 September there were 46 common soldiers.[37] In late August 1648 Lothian and the sheriff of Cheshire, Roger Wilbraham, took the surrender of the fleeing Scottish Army at Warrington, whilst on 7 October the Commons awarded him £1,000 out of the sequestrations of North Wales rebels involved in the Second Civil War. In May 1657 he was still pursuing his arrears of pay.[38]

In addition to acting as adjutant-general to the Cheshire foot during the First Civil War, Lothian commanded a company of the Broxton Hundred trained and freehold bands. Although this was ostensibly a militia unit, it appears to have been permanently mustered for duty. Owing to the Broxton area being in Royalist hands until 1644 and the large number of demands made on its inhabitants by troops of both sides, there was no more than one company raised for the Parliamentarian army from the area to the south of Chester. Writing from Hawarden to Sir William Brereton on 8 April 1645 Lothian expressed concerns about keeping his command up to strength, owing to his commander's policy of permitting other captains to draw recruits and provisions that might have gone to him:

> I wonder that you pass orders to so many captains to lie in Broxton Hundred to the undoing of it and consequently spoil my company by disabling the townships. Please you to withdraw your orders from Carter and Brereton, stop the current

34 *CJ*, IV, p.621.

35 TNA, SP28/224/2, fols 308v., 310r., 316v.

36 TNA, SP28/128/13, fol. 23r.

37 TNA, SP28/225/3, fol. 465r.; SP28/124, fols 189r., 192v.

38 TNA, SP28/224/2, fols 267v., 308v., 317v.–318r.; *CJ*, IV, pp.139, 621; V, pp.688–9; VI, pp.43–4, 46; VII, p.539; *LJ*, VI, pp.715, 609; X, p.533.

> Ridley warrant, let my company keep both Cholmondeley and Lea Halls, and so preserve the country for the conservation of these soldiers I have and sooner completing of my company. Whereas, on the country being abused, I shall both lose my soldiers and also the Hundred, which will be undone (if you take not this course) by those that are neither willing nor can do service.[39]

On 17 March 1646 Lothian's company mustered the following:

Lieutenant Robert Wright	Corporal Francis Bainley
Ensign Benjamin Croxton	Corporal Thomas North
Sergeant Thomas Davenport	Drummer Simon Moore
Sergeant Richard Huntingdon	Drummer John Brownhill
Corporal Ralph Gregory	Clerk Richard Hewitt[40]

Thomas Lawton replaced Huntingdon as sergeant to the company in April 1646.[41] Ensign Croxton had been captured in November 1645 delivering letters from Tarvin garrison to Tranmere, yet by 17 March 1646 he had returned to the ranks, and appears in a pay warrant of December, having employed his soldiers to collect assessments levied upon Wirral and Broxton hundreds.[42] The total paid to Lothian's officers and men from central sources was £2,666 19s. 5d.[43] Company strengths (common soldiers) were 80 on 30 April and 27 May 1645, 72 on 18 January 1646, 75 between 17 March and 13 April 1646, 94 on 8 August 1646 and 54 on 14 December 1646.[44]

Artillery

The Cheshire army of Parliament's commander of artillery was Captain John Arundel. He had served under Sir Thomas Myddelton during the storming of Powys Castle, when on 2 October 1644 the outer gate was blown in by a petard placed by 'Mr John Arundel, master-gunner'.[45] He had joined Brereton's forces by early January 1645, when payment was made to 'Captain Arundel for the Cheshire gunners'. On 12 August 1645 the sequestration agents for Broxton Hundred disbursed £20 to Arundel 'for himself and the cannoneers under him'. Additionally, treasurer Croxton laid out the sum of £413 1s. 9d., being the arrears of pay of 'the gunners, gunners' mates and matrosses'.[46] On 16 May 1645 James Lothian disclosed that the defenders of Hawarden Castle had discovered the mine shaft dug by the Parliamentarians, and had broken into the tunnel and blocked it. During the subsequent council of war Captain

39 CRO, DDX/428, fol. 79v.; *BLB*, I, 181.
40 TNA, SP28/124/1, fols 1r., 33v.; SP28/123/1, fol. 32v.
41 TNA, SP28/124/1, fol. 1v.
42 TNA, SP28/224/2, fol. 316r.
43 TNA, SP28/128/13, fol. 17r.
44 BL, MS Add. 11331, fols 45v., 165v.; TNA, SP28/124, fols 4r., 33v.–39r., 192v.; SP28/123/3, fol. 557v.
45 *The True Informer*, 2 October 1644; Phillips, *Memoirs*, II, pp.212–3.
46 TNA, SP28/224, fol. 85v.; SP28/128/13, fol. 20r.; BL, MS Harley 2128, fol. 92v.

Jan van de Velde, *Uittocht van het Spaanse leger uit Maastricht* (1632), illustrating an artillery train on the move. (Amsterdam, Rijksmuseum, CC0 1.0 Universal (CC0 1.0) Public Domain Dedication)

Arundel advised that the mine prepared by his men would not be repaired and ready for the next 20 days.[47]

Artillery and ordnance, in the shape of cannon and mortars, were an increasingly important (and mobile) form of warfare during the seventeenth century. Though their effects were firepower and destruction, ordnance logistics (the production, supply and storage of gunpowder, shot, grenadoes, petards, fuses and match, not to mention carriages, wagons and large numbers of draught animals) taxed most armies.[48] There were a great many sizes of cannon, the heavier types being regarded as 'siege or battering pieces'; those of smaller bore being more readily transportable, and regarded as 'field pieces'.

Table 15: Principal types of ordnance, from William Eldred, *The Gunner's Glasse* (1646)

Artillery piece	Calibre in inches	Weight of gun (lb)	Length of piece (feet)	Shot weight (lb)
Cannon Royal	8	8,000	8	63
Cannon	7	7,000	10	47
Demi Cannon	6	6,000	12	27
Culverin	5	4,000	11	15

47 BL, MS Add. 11331, fol. 113r.; *BLB*, I, 554.

48 Stephen Bull, '*The Furie of the Ordnance*': *Artillery in the English Civil War* (Woodbridge: Boydell, 2008), chapter 3.

Artillery piece	Calibre in inches	Weight of gun (lb)	Length of piece (feet)	Shot weight (lb)
Demi Culverin	4.5	3,600	10	9
Saker	3.5	2,500	9.5	5.25
Minion	3	1,500	8	4
Falcon	2.75	700	6	2.25
Falconet	2	210	4	1.25
Robinet	1.25	120	3	0.75

An important omission from the above is the drake, which fired a ball of about 3lbs and operated as light artillery. By the time the Civil War broke out these had become the standard infantry support weapon among Parliamentarian armies.[49] Brereton's troops brought two of these (known as a case) from London in January 1643, whereupon during the skirmish at Nantwich, the guns 'upon carriage ready charged, discharged the same upon the king's party, which did some execution and so affrighted them, that they were all scattered and quite routed'.[50] Artillery was deployed more effectively at Chillington Hall, near Wolverhampton, the fortified home of the Catholic Giffard family, on 10 August 1643. Arriving there in command of Cheshire and Staffordshire troops, Sir William Brereton, 'with three great pieces of ordnance and a set of drakes, besieged the same, and played with their ordnance against the said house for two days together, and made great breaches in the same. And about 4 o'clock on Friday evening they in the house, not able to endure any longer, yielded up the same, craving quarter, which was granted them'.[51] Similarly, Lancaster wrote that before Chester on 20 September 1645 'we brought in the artillery, prepared a battery that night, fell upon the whole the next day, made a wide breach by the Newgate, intending to storm the city at night'.[52] As far as the River Dee would allow, by late 1645 the Parliamentarians had to a great extent encompassed the city with gun batteries at Foregate Street, St John's churchyard opposite the Newgate, to the north-west of Morgan's Mount and Brewer's Hall Hill.

A particularly valuable resource in siege warfare, however, was the mortar, a weapon designed to fire projectiles (hollow spheres filled with black powder, known as granadoes or shells) at a high trajectory yet low velocity.[53] Commonly operated by engineers or 'firemasters', mortars were ideal for lobbing explosive projectiles over the top of fortifications. For those on the receiving end, the effects of mortar bombardments were often highly destructive and terrifying, especially 'fireballs' or incendiaries, which were designed to burn and obliterate buildings. However, their ammunition was expensive and intermittently supplied, while the method of ignition (by

49 Bull, '*Furie of the Ordnance*', p.141; Simon Marsh, 'A Case of Drakes – James Wemyss and Artillery Innovation in the Civil War', Serena Jones (ed.), *A New Way of Fighting: Professionalism in the English Civil War*, Proceedings of the 2016 Helion and Company 'Century of the Soldier' Conference (Solihull: & Co., 2017), pp.91–107.

50 Malbon, p.35.

51 *Ibid.*, p.71.

52 Lancaster, p.18.

53 Bull, '*Furie of the Ordnance*', p.12.

lighting the mortar using two matches – one to ignite the fuse of the shell, the other to set off the propelling charge) could be especially hazardous to their users, hence they were habitually sited in specially dug pits.

Table 16: Master-gunner and gunners, 16 March 1645 (TNA, SP28/225/2, fols 314v., 346r.)

Samuel Bennett, Master-gunner	
Tobias Dawkins	Robert Gambley
John Todd	Thomas Burke
Ralph Henfield	Simon Pettigrew
Evan Jones	John Chetham
Bartholomew Butler	James Vaughan

Appended to the list are payments for their equipment:

Paid for three dark lanterns – 7s. 6d.
One more lantern bought off Richard Venables, costing 2s. 6d.
One budge barrel, costing 2s. 2d.

Table 17: 'Gunners belonging to Stafford piece', 20 December 1645 (TNA, SP28/223/3, fol. 527v.)

Robert Wilden, master-gunner	
Robert Henman, gunner's mate	Robert Palthrop, matross
Abraham Ramsgate, quarter-gunner	John Walton, matross
Thomas Tew, commissary to the magazine at Stafford	James Smith, boy to the company
Richard Smith, carpenter and matross	John Smith, boy to the company
Abraham Jordon, matross	Humphrey Allot, wagoner
All allowed three weeks' pay. William Brereton, 14 January 1646	

Engineers

The art, science and practice of military engineering developed rapidly during the early modern period, particularly as artillery became more powerful and more mobile. Military engineering significantly revised the way fortifications were constructed in order to be better protected from enemy. New fortifications were also intended to increase the ability of defenders to bring fire onto attacking enemies. The great range of treatises published during the Thirty Years' War, with its many sieges, reflected the operational needs of armies and gave great impetus to the techniques, practices and methods of warfare during the period. Perhaps one of the better known military engineers of the English Civil Wars was the German John Rosworm. He had served on the Continent and in Ireland, previous to the outbreak of the Irish insurrection in 1641, and in the spring of 1642 supervised the works at Manchester. In his *Good Service* (1649) Rosworm related his service, which included accompanying Sir Thomas Fairfax to the siege of Nantwich and his appointment as master of the ordinance at Liverpool by Sir John Meldrum in August 1644.[54] In March 1644 he advised Colonel Robert Duckenfield on the fortification of Stockport, and given the number and type of the defensive works constructed at various Parliamentarian garrisons, as well as extensive siegeworks before Chester and Beeston, it is possible that Rosworm was influential in Cheshire.[55]

The challenges faced by Brereton and his commanders in not only constructing and maintaining substantial siegeworks in Cheshire and North Wales, but also in properly fortifying against sudden attack from reliving forces or from the besieged garrison sallying out, were immense. Garrisons and outposts to the west side of the Dee were particularly remote and prone to enemy attack. During the spring of 1645 this was exacerbated by the brief raising of the siege of Chester by Prince Maurice and the uncertain moves of Rupert in the Midlands. William Ashurst, one of Sir William's contacts in Westminster raised this issue on 22 April: 'I saw a letter from one Mr John [Captain John Jones of Myddelton's forces] of 14 April which informed me that you had not put a spade in the ground nor made any defence for yourselves or other work about Chester, but that they [your forces] did still lie in loose and open quarters.'

A week later Lieutenant Colonel Jones stated:

> It is true our remote quarters are not made defensible after the Low Country manner. But I am confident no city in England hath been closelier blocked up than this, considering the weakness of our army. On the Cheshire side they are kept in by three garrisons or quarters, each within half a mile of that city, all fortified. On the Welsh side there are five quarters, two of them not a mile distant from the city, of sufficient strength to oppose the enemy'. Moreover, Brereton himself responded to these 'unjust aspersions secretly vented against me' by outlining the offensive achievements of his limited forces, including the fortifications about Hawarden ('within 30 yards round the castle and drawing out of it'), and the defensive works constructed around various outlying garrisons.[56]

Sir William Brereton's chief-engineer was Captain William Buchanan. He had been a captain of foot under Denbigh from 6 March 1644 to 15 July 1644, before serving as an engineer in the Cheshire army from 6 August 1644 to 31 July 1646.[57] Buchanan is likely to have been a Scottish professional, and may have previously served with Sergeant Major James Lothian, given that officer's familiarity with siege warfare. Captain Buchanan was at forefront of siege operations before Chester and other sites, such as Beeston, and his skills were evidently much in demand at Lichfield Close and elsewhere

54 Lieutenant Colonel John Rosworm, *Good Service hitherto ill Rewarded or, An Historicall Relation of eighteen years Services for King and Parliament done in and about Manchester and those parts* (London: 1649), George Ormerod (ed.), *Tracts Relating to Military Proceedings in Lancashire during the Great Civil War* (Manchester: CS, 1844), pp.215–44.

55 TNA, SP28/128/10, fol. 7v.

56 BL, MS Add. 11331, fols 43r., 38r., 36r.–v.; *BLB*, II, 318, 375, 379.

57 TNA, SP28/253A/Letter Book B/5; SP28/224/1, fol. 85v.; SP28/134/5, fol. 86r.; SP28/134/10, fol. 237v.

in 1646. Whilst blockading the Royalist garrison at Tutbury on 16 April Colonel Bowyer requested of Brereton (who was at Lichfield), 'we desire you to send our own forces some ammunition and to give leave that Captain Buchanan may come over tomorrow to set out some works in case we agree not'.[58] On 6 March he was paid the sums of £5 as 'engineer in the leaguer at Lichfield upon account for pay (being in want of necessaries)', £2 with other 'fire-workers, mortars and engineers' on 10 April for work at Tutbury, with a further 5s. received at Lichfield for his services on 14 April.[59]

Mining operations, employed since the medieval period during sieges, were conducted by Parliamentarian forces at places such as Lathom House and Bridgnorth in 1644, as well as Hawarden Castle by Lothian's and Buchanan's men in 1645. At Lichfield Close in April 1643 Prince Rupert, a man experienced in military engineering, requested sappers and 'caused the colliers to come in, and they brought with them all their pick-axes to undermine it'.[60] Sometimes siege engines (known as 'sows' or 'boars' because of their shape) were used by attacking troops. These were wheeled vehicles covered with boards to protect those within from musket fire. At Corfe Castle in May 1643 the besiegers made their approach 'with more safety, they make two engines; one they call the Sow, the other the Boar, being made with boards lined with wool to dead the shot'.[61] In March 1645 Sir William Brereton took delivery of three 'movable breastworks' which were:

> fitted to storm any place or enter any breach, and will shelter from the enemy's shot eighteen musketeers who, wheeling off to right or left, can charge and discharge in an orderly manner and, on occasion, six can discharge at once. These also will be of use to barricade suddenly any bridge, lane or narrow pass. But then it will be necessary you add what formerly I had: three palisades of an ell [45 inches] long with pikes against the mid-rail of each breastwork, the palisades to be fixed in a piece of timber equal in bigness and length to the mid-rail by hinges or staples, which can be let down for carriage in wagons or raised breast-high for service against horse. Four-score of these will front the musketeers of a regiment of 1,000 foot, the pikes needing none of them. If these were used, we would need no pikes at all, which would add a third to the strength of an army.[62]

A Royalist diary giving Rupert's movements from 16–19 March 1645 mentions that when Brereton's troops quitted the siege of Beeston they 'left their works undemolished and a sow behind them, perhaps a musket-proof wooden tower, mounted on wheels and hauled by oxen.[63] Something akin to this was received on an unknown date from the carpenter William Monmouth by Sir Thomas Myddelton, who disbursed the sum of £10 'for timber and iron to make an engine, and to pay for working it'. Interestingly

58 BCA, MS 595611, p.37; *CWS*, 56.

59 TNA, SP16/513/1, fols 74r., 76Av., 79r.

60 *A Continuation of Certain Special Remarkable Passages*, 20 April–27 April 1643.

61 Bruno Ryves, *Mercurius Rusticus* (London: 1685), p.120.

62 CRO, DDX/428, fol. 13r.; *BLB*, I, 21.

63 CRO, DDX/428, fol. 141r.–v.; *BLB*, I, 142.

also, Sir Thomas was supplied with other siege-related equipment, which was presumably employed at Hawarden, Beeston, Chester and elsewhere. This included 12 ells of canvas (probably used for screens) procured in June 1643, whilst a year later seven chests of 'dragons' (caltrops, anti-personnel devices made of spikes arranged in such a manner that one of them always points upward from a stable base, but also employed for slowing horses), and 480 *palisadoes* (wooden obstacles that surmounted earthen barricades) were purchased from the London manufacturer Richard Kirby.[64]

Pioneers

The principal role of pioneers was the construction of earthwork defences and siege-fortifications, and any other manual tasks, such as the digging of trenches and building of bridges. Such duties were often performed by paid labourers (raised via quotas from hundreds and local townships), although soldiers and townspeople could also be pressed into service, especially in garrisons. Parties of pioneers might also be sent ahead of besieging forces to break up defences with axes. The Aston documents include various warrants issued to the constables of Aston and Aston Grange. On 21 March 1644 Captain-Lieutenant Francis Duckenfield instructed them to send 12 men with shovels and spades for the securing of the fords over the Weaver, while on 6 April the Aston officials were commanded to 'bring mattocks and other tools for digging' by Lieutenant Colonel Richard Brooke, the governor of Halton. Additionally, 10 days later the latter and his brother Captain John Brooke issued the following warrant to Thomas Bennet, one of the constables:

> These are to authorize and appoint you, Thomas Bennett, by virtue of these presentments to make your repair to the township of Aston tomorrow by five of the clock in the morning, and thereby the power to your committees to charge the constables of the same township to be aiding and assisting to your charging all the able inhabitants of the said township, or at the least out of every effort to repair to the ford, commonly called Byfleet, and the same to block up and spoil by sharp piles driven into the ground with a thorough decent hedge and ditch, with a breastwork fit for the certainty of soldiers, according to you and the soldiers and officers of all quick convenience, to which said the constables shall present all instruments conscientiously and they shall also cause the watches to bring provision of meat and bread for the workmen, for all wise and neatness you shall do in preparation of the intent of this commission, this shall be your warrant.[65]

The exact location of Byfleet ford and its defensive works remains unidentified, although it may have been on low-lying ground near Dutton, or conceivably the Runcorn side of Hale Ford, an important crossing on the River Mersey. Both were within the area of upper Bucklow and thus close to Aston.

64 TNA, SP28/346/1, unfol.

65 AA, unlisted warrants, dated 21 March, 6 April and 16 April 1644.

During operations in October 1645 to consolidate the Parliamentarian siegeworks before Chester, especially following the partially successful assaults on the eastern parts of the city, the committee at Tarvin described to Sir William Brereton that they had 'sent for many pioneers to be at Chester tomorrow early. Your own commands will be expected in this hundred [Eddisbury] and Wirral for the raising of them, else they will not be forward to come in'. On 27 October Lieutenant Colonel Jones expressed his concerns about the continuing danger caused by attempts to adequately blockade the Welsh side of the leaguer:

> I pray [he said] haste up all the forces you can that, the siege being secured, we may chase the enemy out of Wales and these parts. Were there 500 men commanded with spades, shovels and mattocks, I am confident in four days to cast such a trench and out-works on this side [of] Chester from water to water that, if the enemy were master of the field, he should not relieve the city.[66]

Two days later Brereton instructed the head constables of Northwich, Macclesfield, Bucklow and Northwich hundreds 'for 100 men to be at Chester on Friday next by ten o'clock and to bring with each of them a spade, mattock or shovel and six days' provision. To the Northwich officials he further added that he was:

> well assured that a considerable number of pioneers would in very short time make such works on the Welsh side as would not only keep in Chester men, but debar them of relief and then a great part of our army might march out and meet the enemy at a distance, and quarter in the enemy's quarters, which would be a great ease to this county.[67]

Captain John Whitworth was acting as captain of pioneers by August 1643, although there is evidence that he was also a special emissary to Sir William Brereton, as well as undertaking an executive role in the army. His responsibilities included representing the commander-in-chief outside the county, purchasing and transporting arms and ammunition, and discharging contractor's bonds. John also seems to have vetted muster rolls when troops and companies were paid. His role in military finance is demonstrated by his payment to various officers and commands, including Lieutenant Colonel Venables and Colonel Duckenfield, whose accounts survive for most of their service.[68] During September 1644 John Whitworth supervised the construction of defensive works at Tarvin, the Parliamentarian army's forward headquarters, for which he was later remunerated £37 6s. 8d., while at the siege of Chester he was similarly employed. During December 1645 Whitworth approved work carried out by Captain Holt's pioneers, who had

66 BL, MS Add. 11332, fol. 25r.; *BLB*, II, 757.

67 BL, MS Add. 11332, fols 15r., 30r.–v.; *BLB*, II, 733, 778–9.

68 BL, MS Harley 1999, fol. 62v.; 2128, fol. 61r.; MS Add. 11331, fols 44r., 105v., 115; 11332, fols 38r., 42r.; TNA, SP28/43/7, fol. 871r.; SP28/242/2, fol. 376v.; *BLB*, I, 385, 544, 556; II, 796, 806.

dug trenches and built barricades below the Old Newgate on the eastern side of the city.[69] Whitworth's distinct employment must explain why his own pay often appears in Brereton's own accounts with those of officers and soldiers of Sir William's own commands.[70]

Captain Hugh Holt may have begun his service in the Cheshire army as quartermaster to Captain Bramhall's dragoons. Probably in 1644 Holt succeeded Whitworth as captain of pioneers. His men played an integral role during the Chester leaguer. During a council of war at the siege of Hawarden Castle on 16 May 1645 he advised on the lack of readiness of a mine, whole he was paid £5 for overseeing workmen before Chester on 11 November, the warrant stating: 'He is captain of the pioneers now making the line about the town.'[71] Additionally, a voucher issued on 12 December 1645 was for 'payment to Captain Hugh Holt for work done about the Chester leaguer – for making of trenches and barricades below the Newgate and for barricading a house at Newgate'. Fourteen soldiers under the Shropshire officer, Captain Leighton Owen and six other men were paid a total of £3 14s. for carrying out these tasks. The document is signed by Hugh Holt and the work testified to by John Whitworth. Furthermore, the county treasurer, James Croxton laid out £195 2s. 1d. 'to workmen to make trenches at the leaguer before Chester, and other incidental charges in the leaguer, and repairing walls about the city after entrance'.[72] Perhaps unsurprisingly, Captain Holt served at the siege of Lichfield Close – on 25 May 1646 £1 10s. was distributed to him 'upon account of his arrears being to defray his charges to London upon public business'. Similarly, on the same day Lieutenant Colonel Gerard, one of the Cheshire commanders, received £5 'to pay workmen in the leaguer in Lichfield to work about the sconces and mounts against the Close'.[73]

Medical Services

During the seventeenth century combatants were under obligation to provide care for the sick and wounded of their own side (partly because fit men needed to be returned to the ranks) as well as their enemy in accordance with military convention, and the religious and moral values of the period.[74] Henry Hexham, writing in 1642, felt that each infantry company should possess 'a good *barber surgeon* ... to have skill in *surgery,* that when the company watches in approaches, and guards, where there is danger, he may be at hand (in the absence of the surgeon of the regiment) to bind up and

69 TNA, SP28/128/13, fol. 20r.; SP28/225/3, fols 582r.–v.

70 TNA, SP28/152/7, fols 24v.–26.

71 BL, MS Harley 2128, fol. 22v.; MS Add. 11331, fol. 113; TNA, SP28/224, fol. 52v.; *BLB*, I, 552.

72 TNA, SP28/225/3, fols 582r.–v.; SP28/128/13, fol. 20r.

73 TNA, SP28/16/513/1, fol. 84r.

74 Eric Gruber von Arni, *Justice to the Maimed Soldier: Nursing, Medical Care and Welfare for Sick and Wounded Soldiers and their Families during the English Civil Wars and Interregnum, 1642–1660* (London and New York: Routledge, 2001).

dress hurt, and wounded men'. Moreover, surgical treatises of the period, including Richard Wiseman's *A Treatise of Wounds*, reflected developments in battlefield surgery, especially the treatment of gunshot injuries.[75]

Richard Barrett served as surgeon general to the Cheshire Parliamentarian forces from 1 December 1642 to 22 February 1647. His three assistants, William Dunlop, Nathaniel Burrows and Peter Yates were present from 21 December 1642 to 30 November 1646, 21 December 1642 to 30 September 1646, and 21 December 1644 to 10 February 1647 respectively. Barrett's complete accounts, ending on 22 February 1647, include a range of moneys received by him and his assistants, and detail payments for medicines, surgeon's instruments and other necessaries.[76] On 18 December the sum of £100 was disbursed by treasurer Croxton 'to Mr Barrett, surgeon to the Cheshire forces, for himself and his mates, who was in want of salves for the wounded soldiers, having done gallant service and hath not received any pay for a long time, and must have more speedily'.[77] Moreover, a year later Croxton's own accounts record payments of £696 4s. 4d. to the 'surgeons and their mates', £34 18s. 8d. 'for quartering wounded soldiers, and other incidental charges', and a further £4 3s. for quartering injured men under the command of Sir Thomas Fairfax.[78]

Additional provisions were made by army officers for the care of wounded and sick men of both sides, as well as for the guarding of prisoners of war. In February 1643 two of Bramhall's dragoons were treated for injuries, possibly sustained during the recent skirmish with Aston's Royalists at Nantwich. The sum of 1s. was spent on a yard of cloth to wrap William Betts's hand, while the same amount was given to a woman for attending Ralph Finney, 'when he lost the use of his hand'.[79] Similarly, Colonel Robert Duckenfield disbursed 14s. for the wounded of Captain Arderne's company that had been mauled at Warrington on 5 April 1643, and for the burial of John Hay, presumably one of his soldiers. On 12 July 1643 Duckenfield also paid £8 to John Massey's wife 'for the relief of eight troopers, being prisoners at Shrewsbury'. Between July1643 and May 1644 a total of £20 3s. 10d. went on 'guarding the prisoners and for provision for them, and for the repair of the prison house [at Stockport], and for coals for guard'.[80]

75 Henry Hexham, *The First Part of the Principles of the Art Military* (Delft, 1642); Richard Wiseman's *A Treatise of Wounds* (London, 1672).

76 BL, MS Harley 2128, fols 67r.–69r. The 'Accounts of Mr Richard Barrett, surgeon', consist of one folio and only cover the period up to 26 May 1645 (TNA: SP28/30/7, fol. 695v.).

77 BL, MS Add. 11333, fols 30r., 118v.; *BLB*, II, 1040, 1235.

78 TNA, SP28/128/13, fols 20v., 18r., 27r. Croxton's payment to Barrett and his subordinates should be seen as roughly correlating with the figures outlined in the surgeon-general's accounts and not as additional sums.

79 BL, MS Harley 2128, fols 28v., 31r.

80 TNA, SP28/128/10, fols 4v., 6r.

Table 18: Regimental, troop, company and garrison surgeons

Mr Dunlop	Colonel Henry Brooke's regiment[81]
John Chadwick	Sir William Brereton's troop[82]
Thomas Harrington	Colonel Robert Duckenfield's troop.[83]
Elias Preston	Captain Hugh Culme's troop[84]
Humphrey Pearson	Sergeant Major Croxton's company[85]
Edmund Granger	Captain Anthony Booth's company.[86]
Francis Atwood	Surgeon to the Nantwich garrison and the Cheshire forces in 1645 and 1646[87]

As might be expected, given the Cheshire army of Parliament's active military experience, a number of officers received combat wounds. At Malpas on 26 August 1644 Lieutenant Colonel Michael Jones received a bullet wound to the leg whilst leading the Cheshire horse.[88] Sir William Brereton reported that during the victory at Christleton on 18 January 1645, 'Captain Zankey, who is a very valiant man, and commands my own troop, being without his armour, was wounded in the body, but we hope not mortally.'[89] Sankey had returned to active service by 26 March. Similarly, in describing the assault on the Chester's suburbs on 8 October 1645 Lancaster reported: 'we made good our retreat in the dark. We lost 27 men on the ground, of those, no officers but a sergeant and a corporal. About 60 wounded, amongst them Lieutenant Colonel Venables, and Captain Massey, brother to the renowned Massey of Gloucester, but neither of them dangerously.'[90] Malbon corroborates that by adding, 'Venables, a gallant man, received a wound in the arm but not dangerous.'[91]

Perhaps given the dangerous nature of their service (and leadership qualities) the rate of attrition among Brereton's dragoon officers was proportionally high. During the action at Nantwich on 28 January 1643 Captain William Goldegay was injured, and his lieutenant and two soldiers were killed. Malbon mentioned also that the Parliamentarians 'had many wounded'.[92] Likewise, according to his certificate of service, Captain John Lea was 'once shot through the body' during the attack on Eccleshall Castle on 30 August 1643. His absence from the records after this suggests that his wound was serious one and that he did not return to military service after November 1643.[93] Captain John Cheswis was killed in action at Oswestry on 20 July 1644 (his widow receiving a pension of £50 per annum), while leading the

81 TNA, SP28/225/4, fol. 714v.
82 *True Relation*; Phillips, *Memoirs*, II, pp.196–7.
83 TNA, SP28/225/4, fol. 747r.
84 TNA, SP28/123/3, fols 381v.–7r.
85 TNA, SP28/152/7, fol. 8r.
86 TNA, SP28/122/4, fol. 553r.
87 TNA, SP28/224/1, fols 30r., 171r.
88 *A True Relation of two great Victories*; *The Success of Our Cheshire Forces*; Malbon, p.144.
89 *Perfect Passages,* 22 January 1645; Lancaster, *Narrative*, p.12; Phillips, *Memoirs*, II, p.226.
90 Lancaster, p.22.
91 Malbon, p.186; HMC, *Thirteenth Report*, p.288.
92 *Cheshire's Successe*; Malbon, *Memorials*, p.20.
93 CRO, ZCR/63/2/702, fol. 24r.

attack on the Newgate breach at Chester during the night of 21 September 1645 Captain Finch and Lieutenant Mather both received wounds during close-quarter fighting.[94] In addition to these examples, whilst at the siege of Beeston in May 1645 Captain John Walker, Brereton's scoutmaster general was seriously hurt and taken prisoner. The somewhat irritated Royalist governor, Captain Vallett, subsequently informed Sergeant Major Thomas Croxton at Nantwich:

> As for Captain Walker, I perceive you conceive him mortally wounded, but there is no such danger. His surgeon gives him good encouragement, and he [Walker] is strongly opinionated of his abilities and says he will employ no other. I conceive his removal might prejudice his health, and I am sure my proposition for depositing the money is soldier-like and reasonable. In case (which I hope he will not) that he will be in danger, your request shall be granted.[95]

Quartermasters

Lieutenant Colonel Richard Bradshaw served as quartermaster general to the Cheshire forces and was one of Brereton's commissioners for the surrender of Chester in 1646.[96] From Aspull and Pennington, Lancashire, he was a Chester merchant in 1637, and related by marriage to Brereton and Sir George Booth. Richard acted as mayor of Chester and was a distinguished diplomatist for the Interregnum governments of 1650–60. Bradshaw has tended to be confused with the regicide John Bradshaw by modern historians, to whom he was not related, although Sergeant Major Henry Bradshaw of Duckenfield's regiment was John's elder brother. Richard appears regularly in Brereton's correspondence in connection with the supply and finance for arms and ammunition. A voucher, dated 24 November 1645 and endorsed by treasurer Croxton is made out to 'Lieutenant Colonel Richard Bradshaw, quartermaster general of the Cheshire army, paid for the carriage of ammunition.'[97]

Muster-Masters

The role of the muster-master general was to train and discipline the trained bands in accordance with Parliament's militia ordinance, although as a senior officer, Lieutenant Colonel Robert Hunt was also a valuable executive officer in Brereton's army. He is not to be confused with Lieutenant Colonel Thomas Hunt the Staffordshire cavalry officer and governor of Hooton, nor the captain of the same name who led a company of foot and a troop of horse

94 TNA, SP28/196/3, fol. 490v.; SP28/267/3, fol. 115r.; SP28/128/13, fol. 26r.; BL, MS Harley 2166, fol. 130r.; Lancaster, p.18.

95 BL, MS Add.11331, fols 34v., 135r.–v.; *BLB*, I, 357, 589.

96 TNA, SP28/252A/Letter Book B/case 45; *BLB*, I, 70, n. 2.

97 TNA, SP28/224/1, fol. 74r. For his activities in 1645 see CRO, DDX/428, fols 37r.–v., 45v., 79v.; BL, MS Add. 11332, fol. 118v.; 11333, fols 32r., 128r.; *BLB*, I, 70, 87, 159; II, 940, 1057, 1260.

in Colonel Mytton's forces. A voucher dated about 11 July 1644 includes a payment at Hull of £60 to Lieutenant Colonel Robert Hunt and Captain John Whitworth for the purchase of arms. A number of warrants for Hunt's pay survive, including the sum of £20 on 17 December 1644.[98] Robert must be the person who obtained £16 'in part of his pay' on 12 January 1646 as he appears in neither this, nor earlier lists of Staffordshire and Shropshire officers receiving pay at the Chester leaguer. Sometime later in the year James Croxton disbursed the sum of £116 to 'Lieutenant Colonel Hunt, muster-master general'.[99] William Davies was paid £72 by Croxton as 'muster-master' with Hunt in the same pay account and was thus probably his assistant.[100]

Assisting the muster-master general were officers whose duties charged with mustering and directing soldiers from local areas – these appear to have been predominately new recruits and trained bandsmen. Captain Nathaniel French was under the command of Colonel John Booth in the garrison of Warrington, before taking a commission in the Cheshire forces. From March 1644 onwards a series of payments were made by the Bucklow sequestrators to him, while during the same year the constables of Nether Whitley and Lymm provided various sums for the quartering of soldiers under his authority at Tarvin.[101] The latter in particular seems to relate to Nathaniel's duty of conducting Parliamentarian recruits raised in Bucklow Hundred to Tarvin and the Chester leaguer, for which he was paid in February 1645. He was assisted by a cadre of officers and non-commissioned officers, including Lieutenant Gandy and Sergeant French.[102] The problematic nature of directing soldiers from Bucklow to the main army in Cheshire are highlighted by following report to Brereton from the deputy lieutenants, dated 23 April 1645:

> Upon Saturday last the soldiers raised within this hundred of Bucklow to go under the command of Captain French, appearing to be in numbers far short of what they should have been and many townships in the Hundred having sent in none, there was a warrant signed by Sir George Booth and Mr Marbury, and delivered to Captain French to authorise him, with those soldiers he then had, to repair unto the several townships that had neglected to send their soldiers with their complete arms that they were charged with for the design in hand. Accordingly having gathered them together and being upon his march towards Tarvin with them yesterday, Lieutenant Alcocke of Warrington garrison came with a party of horse and foot from thence, took them from him and discharged them to their several homes.[103]

Captain French also participated in wider military operations, commanding 60 volunteer infantry as part of a taskforce of Cheshire and Lancashire troops

98 TNA, SP28/152/7, fols 10r.–v.; SP28/125/1, fol. 149r.; BL, MS Add. 11332, fol. 39; *BLB*, I, 790.
99 TNA, SP28/128/13, fol. 16v.; BL, MS Add. 11333, fol. 130v.; *BLB*, II, 1235.
100 TNA, SP28/128/13, fol. 16v.
101 BL, MS Harley 2137, fols 52v., 155v.; Harley 2128, fols 47v.–50r., 52r.
102 TNA, SP28/225/1, fol. 39r.; BL, MS Harley 2137, fol. 52v.
103 BL, MS Add. 11331, fol. 43v.; *BLB*, I, 330.

assembled by Sergeant Major Lothian, which was ordered to rendezvous at Middlewich on 4 May 1645 in advance of Brereton's temporary relinquishment of the siege of Cheshire during the King's march northwards.[104]

Captain John Warburton may have been related to Thomas Warburton, sequestration commissioner for Bucklow Hundred. He is included in pay warrants of 6 and 27 February 1644, while in early 1645 he received 2s. 6d. expenses from the constables of Nether Whitley 'for going with volunteers to the siege of Chester'.[105] His local links are emphasised by his capture on 11 January 1645 whilst serving as a gentleman trooper in Brooke's troop. In November 1645 Captains Walker and Weld received letters and warrants from Sir George Booth for the calling in of 200 men of the Nantwich Hundred trained bands from Dunham Massey and Ashton-under-Lyne.[106] These officers were probably local men, and appear to have been tasked with mustering and directing recruits from their local areas to the army at the Chester leaguer.

The responsibilities of Captains William Millington and Thomas Partington are more difficult to define. Captain Millington was from Millington, near Altrincham and first appears in December 1643.[107] His duties were seemingly diverse in nature. In April 1645 Millington was involved in the procurement of cattle and cloth from North Wales with other Cheshire troops. He received two payments of £14 8s. 2d. 'for the service he hath done the state' on 18 December 1645 and 12 January 1646 respectively.[108] During the siege of Lichfield Close he was paid with other 'fire-workers, mortars and engineers' the sum of £4.[109] Captain Partington hailed from Cotton Abbots, near Tarvin, although his identity is uncertain as there was a Thomas senior and Thomas junior (father and son). A Lieutenant Thomas Partington was paid in early 1645, while a Thomas Partington acted as a member of the Tarvin Committee. A letter from Colonel Robert Duckenfield to the committee, penned on 11 April 1645, refers the receipt of a despatch from them via a 'Captain Partington', but as Dore observes, he 'may not have been too careful about ascertaining his rank'.[110]

Military Intelligence

A vitally important aspect of warfare during the seventeenth century, as with other periods, was the reconnaissance and intelligence gathering efforts of military forces. Cavalry commanders, according to Cruso, 'must also procure to have spies, not only in the enemy's army, but also upon their frontiers,

104 BL, MS Add. 11331, fol. 165r.; *BLB*, I, 654.

105 TNA, SP28/196/1, fols 2v., 14r.; BL, MS Harley 2128, fol. 41r.

106 BL, MS Add. 11332, fol. 71r.; *BLB*, II, 846.

107 TNA, SP28/196/1, fol. 14v.

108 CRO, DDX/428, fol. 85; BL, MS Add. 11332, fol. 99; 11333, fol. 118; *BLB*, I, 199–200; II, 887, 1235.

109 TNA, SP16/513/1, fols 74r.

110 BL, MS Harley fol. 2136, fol. 9r.; MS Add. 11332, fol. 14r.; CRO, DDX/428, fol. 111v.; *BLB*, I, 206; II, 733.

to penetrate their designs and intentions, omitting no inventions which may stand him instead to avoid inconveniences; knowing that diligence is the mother of good fortune'.[111] Reconnaissance and the accumulation of intelligence were directed by its scoutmaster general, a role performed by Captain John Walker for the Cheshire army of Parliament. As part of their standard duties, the horse and dragoons participated in scouting in a purely combat sense, but they also questioned civilians about the whereabouts and numbers of enemy forces. Given the generally good disposition of the local population towards Brereton's forces, this was often fruitful. On 29 October 1645 Sergeant Major Sankey, who was left in Dodleston while Lieutenant Colonel Jones went to Chester to confer with Lothian on methods of dealing with Royalist relief from Vaughan's forces, reported on 'The intelligence that I have received from some that went forth with the party and from the common people', and that he would warn the dawn patrol to be ready to go out as usual.[112]

In early 1645 Captain Walker kept a detachment of horse at Ridley, near Holt, where he was governor. Although highly valuable to Brereton, Walker attracted the ire of Captain Luke Lloyd, who maintained a Parliamentarian garrison at neighbouring Willington. On 26 April 1646 he complained to Sir Thomas Myddelton:

> There is one Captain Walker that keeps garrison at Ridley whose horse doth much hurt in these parts. They pretend to be cavaliers when they go abroad to take men's horses out of the plough and harrow, and revile them so that they terrify the country exceedingly. They have plundered many in Dirtwich [Foulwich on the Cheshire–Shropshire border] and Worthenbury. I desire Sir William Brereton to be acquainted herewith, so that a course may be taken that the country not be abused.[113]

On 13 May 1645 Sir William Brereton instructed the Tarvin committee to 'Send for the scoutmaster's horse; keep one good scouter and also foot scouts, the want thereof was the loss of Shrewsbury'.[114] In February 1645, the surprise attack on the town was made against a weak point in the riverside fortifications identified to the Parliamentarians by two deserters from the garrison. A warrant dated 30 October 1645 was for the payment of Captain John Walker (described as 'scout-master' on the endorsement) the sum of £20, of which he engaged to pay £7 13s. to the marshal at Beeston Castle and the rest to go towards his arrears of pay to satisfy his surgeon. He had evidently been released by 12 January 1646, when the overall sum of £29 was disbursed 'to Captain Walker, who was prisoner in Beeston Castle, £20, and for nine of his men who were employed as scouts by the garrison at

111 Cruso, *Militarie Instructions*, p.6.
112 BL, MS Add.11332, fol. 32r.; *BLB*, II, 774.
113 BL, MS Add.11331, fol. 34v.; *BLB*, I, 357.
114 BL, MS Add.11331, fol. 88v.; *BLB*, I, 515. For this and Walker's other activities on the Welsh border see Malbon, *Memorials*, pp.169–70.

Nantwich, 20s. for a man'. Sometime afterwards treasurer Croxton disbursed £125 10s. 'to scoutmaster Walker and his men'.[115]

Sir William Brereton's letter books are scattered with references to his network of 'intelligencers' (spies), which kept him informed of Royalist movements in the Midlands, Welsh borders and farther afield, but they also provided information from inside Chester on aspects such as morale, strengths of military units and availability of rations. John Vernon was of the opinion that in their 'cloak and dagger' operations spies should be amply remunerated, 'which will cause them to expose themselves unto all hazards and dangers to give intelligence'.[116] In normal operational terms, deserters, prisoners and the interception of messengers provided sources of military intelligence, even if this was sometimes unreliable. Yet this was a double-edged sword, for on 30 October 1645 a trooper belonging to Captain Bulkeley 'went forth to scout and most treacherously betrayed those of his fellow soldiers into the hands of the enemy'.[117] He subsequently deserted and was recaptured by his former comrades, although his fate is unknown.

During late 1645 a number of Shropshire garrisons kept tabs on the activities of the three remaining Royalist bastions in the county and the movements of forces through it, processing information to Brereton and the Shropshire committee.[118] On 11 December Captain Francis Spicer, governor of Lilleshall and company commander in Sir William's own regiment, passed on detailed information on skirmishes around High Ercall, while two days later Captain Calvin, the governor of the Parliamentarian garrison at Broncroft Castle reported that he possessed 'an honest friend for intelligence' within Bridgnorth, and also employed an informant in the Royalist garrison of Worcester.[119] In early December 1645 one of Sir William Brereton's (unnamed) female intelligencers met Prince Maurice at Worcester and Sir William Vaughan in his quarters in Bridgnorth. Her report to Brereton illustrates the workings of such agents, whose clandestine encounters and conversations with leading Royalists yielded range of vital information.[120] They underline in particular, the lack of any strong sense of purpose among the Royalist leadership for the relief of Chester and the pursuit already of diversionary attacks to allow the garrison to relieve itself. A further interesting aspect of this particular intelligencer is that when off duty, she lodged in the quarters of Captain Anthony Booth, alderman and mayor of Macclesfield, and company commander in Duckenfield's regiment.

On 15 October 1645 Captain William Carter's troop was surprised at Eccleston when a body of Royalist horse sallied out and 'beat up a quarter of the rebels and took one horse colours and a trumpet, and Carter's lieutenant, and four troopers and about eight horses and some foot arms and (as they say) killed 30 upon the place'. The identity of the lieutenant was confirmed

115 TNA, SP28/224/1, fol. 37r.; SP28/128/13, fol. 20r.; BL, MS Add.11333, fol. 118; *BLB*, II, 1235.

116 Vernon, *The Young Horseman*, p.41.

117 BL, MS Add.11332, fol. 29r.; *BLB*, II, 786.

118 See BL, MS Add. 11332, fols 126v.–7r.; 11333, fols 7r., 24r.–v.; *BLB*, II, 951–3, 993–4.

119 BL, MS Add.11333, fols 16v., 24v.; *BLB*, II, 951–3, 997, 1000.

120 BL, MS Add.11333, fols 8v., 12r.–v., 43r.–v.; *BLB*, II, 963, 983.

two days later as Philemon Mainwaring.[121] According to Canon Morris, he was a spy in Chester during the siege and 'was very conveniently taken prisoner for that purpose and later recaptured by his own party'.[122] Dore suggests, however, that while Mainwaring was 'smuggling information about conditions inside the city to Brereton', no other evidence indicates that his capture was 'arranged', and adds 'so far from being recaptured by the Parliamentarians, he was still in prison in Chester and trying to effect an exchange less than three weeks from the final surrender'.[123]

Captain Thomas Steele

A cheese factor of Weston, near Barthomley, he was described by Lancaster as 'a rough-hewn man, no soldier'.[124] Steele may have gone to London with Sir William Brereton in August–September 1642 because he received pay for 40 volunteers at Derby during the army's march to Cheshire in January 1643. He also disbursed £2 5s. to workmen at Nantwich the following month, which suggests that Steele was acting as an executive officer.[125] Brereton must have had some faith in him as he was appointed governor of Beeston Castle on 20 February 1643, but he surrendered it to a small party of Royalist firelocks under Captain Sandford 10 months later. He was later court-martialled, and as Malbon put it, made a 'long confession and repentance of his sins', but nonetheless, 'disclaimed all treachery'.[126] Richard Sellers was paid as 'corporal, clerk and commissary under Captain Thomas Steele in the garrison of Beeston'.[127]

'Some godly and learned ministers'

In her study of religious ministers in the Parliamentarian army Ann Laurence concludes that 'Provincial army chaplains do not form a coherent subject of study because of the diversity of the forces in which they served and because there survive only fragmentary records for many of the provincial regiments.'[128] Based on her findings for the two main regional armies – the Northern army, commanded for much of the First Civil War by the Fairfaxes, and the Western forces of Edward Massey – she further suggests that due to the local connection ministers were not usually appointed to individual

121 BL, MS Add. 11332, fols 84r., 96r.; *BLB*, II, 684, 686. See also Randle Holme's account of the action, which corroborates the main details (MS Harley 2155, fol. 24v.).

122 Morris, *Siege of Chester*, pp.168–9.

123 *BLB*, II, 686, note 4. For the compelling evidence supporting this interpretation, see CRO, DDX 428, fols 115v., 4v., 80r., 90r.; *BLB*, II, 1242–4, 801, 960, 1071, 1155.

124 Lancaster, p.10.

125 TNA, SP28/196/3, fols 1r., 13r.

126 Malbon, *Memorials*, pp.117–8.

127 TNA, E121/5/7/351, fol. 39v.

128 Anne Laurence, *Parliamentary Army Chaplains, 1642–51* (Woodbridge: Royal Historical Society, 1990), p.36.

military units, but were often paid by county committees to preach to local troops. However, like the northern and western forces, some chaplains were appointed to the Cheshire army of Parliament. In the county a number of ministers were plundered by Royalists, and between 1643 and 1645 over half of the Cheshire clergy was suspended. Sir William Brereton himself was empowered by parliamentary ordinance to eject 'scandalous ministers'. Such a situation brought about a large quantity of itinerants, of which a number found employment with the army. The following are known to have ministered to Brereton's forces:

Nathaniel Lancaster

A Lancashire man, he was Presbyterian rector of Tarporley, admitted Brasenose 1618, BA 1622, BD 1634. During the war be was paid as chaplain to Brereton's regiment of horse and clerk to the Cheshire forces. Lancaster wrote a narrative of the Parliamentarian victory at Denbigh Green and *A More Exact Account of Chester's Enlargement*, which was accepted as the official account of the siege of the city. Although he complained about the conduct of the anti-Brereton faction among the deputy lieutenants, he appears to have fallen out with the commander-in-chief in early 1646.[129]

Mr Adams

He was paid on 6 May 1645 as 'minister to the Hooton garrison'.[130]

Mr Brennan

An itinerant preacher employed by the Cheshire army in December 1645.[131]

Samuel Eaton

As a radical Congregationalist Eaton was suspended from West Kirkby in 1631, and spent periods in Holland and New England before returning to Cheshire in 1640. He was patronised by Sir William Brereton, and especially Colonel Robert Duckenfield, who installed him at Duckenfield Hall and appointed him as chaplain to the Chester garrison in 1647. Samuel also succeeded Nathaniel Lancaster as chaplain to Brereton's regiment of horse and was present at the Chester leaguer in 1645.[132]

Ephraim Elcock

From Chester, BA Brasenose 1641, he signed the Attestation of Cheshire ministers in favour of the Covenant in 1648 as pastor of Runcorn. On 2 June 1645 Brereton authorised payment to 'Mr Elcock, minister and chaplain in the army, who was constant with us', while on 12 January 1646 he received

129 TNA, SP28/27/398, fol. 371v.; SP28/30, fols 654v., 722r.; SP28/42, fol. 698r.–v.; SP28/144, fols 9v., 17v., 20r., 65r.; SP28/196/1, fol. 6v.; *BLB*, I, 395, note 1; Laurence, *Parliamentary Army Chaplains*, pp.144–5.

130 TNA, SP28/225/4, fol. 834r.

131 BL, MS Add. 11333, fol. 34; *BLB*, II, 1038.

132 BL, MS Add. 11333, fol. 118; *BLB*, II, 1237 note 6; Earwaker, *East Cheshire*, II, pp.28–35; Morrill, 'Wars of Religion', p.319; Laurence, *Parliamentary Army Chaplains*, pp.122–3.

£5 'having been careful in the ministry before Chester'.[133] Given Elcock's link with Runcorn Church and its patrons, the Brookes of Norton, it seems likely that he served for some time at least with Colonel Henry's regiment of foot.[134]

Dr John Harding

Harding was an Anabaptist minister, who in May 1645 was a prisoner in Dublin Castle, but was exchanged following negotiations by Sir William Brereton. He was evidently with the Cheshire forces at the Chester leaguer, for he was paid for preaching on 12 January 1646.[135] After the fall of the city John replaced Lancaster as chaplain to the Cheshire army and served with it at Lichfield Close. On 9 April 1646 Harding was paid £20 as 'chaplain to the army, attending it and preaching constantly', and received further disbursements in June and July of the same year.[136]

Thomas Langley

As a non-conformist Langley became a lecturer at Middlewich in 1609, and had the living there between 18 March 1646 and his death in 1657. He received a licence to preach from the House of Commons in Chester in May 1642, but the Royalist control of the city must have made that impossible. In December 1645 Thomas was mentioned by Brereton with Samuel Eaton as being with the army outside Chester, while in 1648 he signed the attestation of Cheshire Presbyterian ministers.[137]

William Peartree

Presbyterian minister of Wybunbury from 1630 to *c.* 1643, he became an itinerant preacher based at the Nantwich garrison. Peartree acted as chaplain to Major Lothian in 1643, although a letter by Brereton, dated 13 May 1645 suggests that he was involved with intelligencers to the army.[138]

Francis Shelmerdine

Francis may have been related to Captain Edmund Shelmerdine. He was curate of Cheadle from 1636 to 1641, and most likely served as chaplain to Duckenfield's regiment of foot. He performed the same function in Colonel Bradshaw's regiment in 1650–1.[139]

Richard Smith

Smith was vicar of Wybunbury and minister to Sergeant Major Thomas Croxton, the governor of Nantwich. On 14 April 1645 he reported to Croxton and the deputy lieutenants a number of complaints from his parishioners

---

133 TNA, SP28/30/7, fol. 654r.; MS Add. 11333, fol. 118; *BLB*, II, 1235.

134 TNA, PROB 11/220/237; Laurence, *Parliamentary Army Chaplains*, p.124.

135 BL, MS Add. 11331, fols 86, 57; 11333, fol. 118; *BLB*, I, 396, 401; II, 1235.

136 TNA, SP16/513/1, fols 73r., 79r., 84r.–v., 89r.; SP28/152/9, fol. 1v.; Morrill, *Cheshire*, pp.164–5.

137 BL, MS Add. 11333, fols 136, 33; *BLB*, II, App. II, 1037 note 6; Morrill, *Cheshire*, p.167; Judith Maltby, *Prayer Book and People in Elizabethan and Early Stuart England* (Cambridge: Cambridge University Press, 1998), p.222.

138 TNA, SP28/196, fol. 6v.; BL, MS Add. 11331, fol. 88; *BLB*, I, 515.

139 Laurence, *Parliamentary Army Chaplains*, p.174.

about the threatening and violent conduct of members of the Yorkshire horse who were billeted amongst them.[140]

Ralph Stringer

Minister of Macclesfield, paid £2 10s. for his services by Colonel Duckenfield on 18 September 1643, and received a further £2 on 20 November 1645 from the Macclesfield hundred sequestration committee.[141]

William Swettenham

One of five ministers sponsored by Brereton between 1643 and 1646, he served as an army chaplain in Cheshire.[142]

140 BL, MS Add. 11333, fol. 102; *BLB*, I, 244.
141 TNA, SP28/128/10, fol. 6r.; BL, MS Harley 2130, fol. 212v.
142 Morrill, *Cheshire*, p.168.

6

The Sinews of War: Money, Ammunition and Provisions

Like other provincial forces, the financing and supplying of the Cheshire army of Parliament was a considerable and difficult task. On 31 October 1645 Sir William Brereton reported to the Committee of Both Kingdoms, 'we must complain to you of three main wants (the sinews of war): money, ammunition and provision'.[1] During the later stages of the siege of Chester Brereton's force, and the various auxiliary troops attached to it, were in dire need of pay, clothing and provisions. On 13 January 1646 Brereton and the deputy lieutenants thanked Parliament for their recent grant of £5,000, but added:

> We convey to you our serious consideration as an inducement to afford a larger supply of moneys in some measure proportionable to the work in hand to be speeded down so that we may be enabled to give some reasonable satisfaction to the army that grows every day more impatient in their hard duty and want of pay. Which necessity and impatience we believe is one of the city's great encouragements to hold out to the last, very many of our men daily falling sick, many leaving the Leaguer and many refusing to be otherwise disposed of, under pretence of want of pay, it being out of our power to satisfy them or the other necessities of the Leaguer without greater supplies and assistance, not only of moneys but of provisions also, this county being wholly exhausted.[2]

The following day Sir William reported from the suburbs of Chester that before his return to the county in November 1645 the army had been engaged at the second attempted storming of the city on 9 October, prior to which the Parliamentarian bombardment had consumed 40 barrels of powder. Though he added that his soldiers had subsequently received a further 70 barrels from London sources, Brereton outlined the demands placed upon his army by various other sieges and outlying garrisons, particularly on the Welsh side of the Dee, 'all of which are supplied with ammunition from hence; where we

1 BL, MS Add. 11332, fol. 35v.; *BLB*, II, 790.
2 BL, MS Add. 11333, fol. 116v.; *BLB*, II, 1245.

could not possibly be furnished with such other materials – granadoe shells for the mortar piece and the like'.[3]

The army received its funding from central (London) sources in the form of grants and loans authorised by Parliament, and local moneys, consisting of the weekly and monthly mize (tax assessment), as well as contributions from sequestrated Royalist estates. In addition to these, when faced with the prospect of unpaid and mutinous troops (particularly following the fall of Chester and during the final siege of Lichfield Close in 1646) Sir William Brereton and his fellow deputy lieutenants procured personal loans to provide for wages. Although the deputy lieutenants were responsible for the raising of funds locally and the maintenance of committees to control it, direct evidence for their activities remains fragmentary. More is known, however, of the activities of the group of agents and treasurers, recruited by Brereton to procure and distribute money for his army in London, and its transferral to Cheshire, as well as to represent his interests in the capital. Sir William principal agent in Westminster was William Ashurst, MP and member of the Lancashire Committee. Their partnership dated to before Brereton's original return to Cheshire during the winter of 1642–3. Following his election as MP for Stafford in October 1645 John Swinfen joined Ashurst as a major promoter of Brereton's efforts in London.

Another close contact was John Bradshaw, younger brother of Sergeant Major Henry Bradshaw and the later president of the Parliamentarian commission to try the King. John was jointly responsible with Richard Worrall for the collection of 'London moneys' and their transference to Cheshire. Henry Cockson acted as solicitor for the Cheshire Sequestration Committee, travelling constantly back forth between Cheshire and London. As county treasurer George Spurstowe acted until his removal in mid 1644. He was replaced by James Croxton, who remained in the post until July 1647. As a collector of loans for the Nantwich–Broxton area Ralph Judson also forwarded the Indictment of Cheshire Parliamentarians for the Committee of Compounding in London. John Brereton of Handforth (cousin to Sir William) and Nicholas Higginbotham of Stockport assisted Brereton secretarially and legally before and after the war, and both appear in documents distributing arms, clothing and rations to the Cheshire troops.[4] Lastly, Richard Stelfox appears frequently in Sir William's accounts and letter books. He is referred to as his 'servant', and from as early as October 1642 seems to have occupied a position of great trust as a kind of personal secretary and accountant.[5]

From the Excise, first levied by parliamentary ordinance in July 1643, Sir William Brereton was authorised to collect the tax on salt. In December 1643 Parliament ordered the receipts from the salt excise to be employed for the

3 BL, MS Add. 11333, fol. 117r.; *BLB*, II, 1248.

4 TNA, SP28/8, fol. 16r.; BL, MS Harley 2130, fols 88r., 91v.; CRO, DDX/428, fol. 41r.

5 See TNA, SP28/152/7 (Accounts of Sir William Brereton); SP28/152/8 (Accounts of Richard Worrall); SP28/128/13, SP28/224 (Accounts of James Croxton); SP28/196/1, SP28/208 (Accounts of Ralph Judson); SP28/196/3 (Accounts of Richard Stelfox).

payment of the Cheshire forces.[6] Entries in Croxton's account book (before he became county treasurer) contain incomplete records of the collection of the tax at Nantwich in late 1643, while in October the following year Brereton ordered all the proceeds to be paid to the townsmen who 'have been ready in the absence of the trained bands to watch for the safety and defence of the said town … and have never received any pay for their service'.[7] Further sources of army finance include the sum of £182 16s. obtained from assessments and loans secured on taxation from the parish of St Olave, Southwark in January 1643. Although Parliament employed direct taxation to fund its major field armies, it continued to use unsecured voluntary subscriptions to support the regional forces, for instance £148 for and £80 for Lord Brooke's Midlands troops.[8] Moreover, on 21 October 1643 Brereton petitioned Speaker Lenthall, 'that the King's, Queen's and Prince's revenues in Cheshire might be applied for the supply of the necessities of the soldiers there'.[9]

Doubtless the largest items in treasurer Croxton's receipts were the 'London moneys' (that is, parliamentary grants using City loans on security of Excise) procured for the Cheshire army, and in particular, the leaguer of Chester. Sums of £5,000 were received from this source in March and June 1644. On 13 March 1645, having narrowly missed capturing Chester, Brereton wrote to the Committee of Both Kingdoms:

> [I] humbly desire that some £4–5,000 be sent down for the pay of our soldiers, which demand is not proportionable to what is wanting but suitable to your necessity. I know not other ways faithfully to discharge that duty you have placed with me for I cannot for want of making you acquainted with our condition, suffer this army to break or disburse, which has been as little chargeable as any in the kingdom that has been in such constant employment'.[10]

In response, Parliament granted £5,000 loaned from the Livery Companies, although it seems unlikely that the money was ever received by the army, for no such receipt appears in the accounts of Brereton's or any of his agents, while the fragmentary and confused correspondence regarding its implementation in Brereton's letter books offers no confirmation either.[11]

In May 1645 Sir William Brereton received the outstanding sum of £835, ordered to be reimbursed to him for his purchase of saddles and weapons, from the grant of £2,125 from the revenue of the Court of Wards and Liveries, which had been authorised by Parliament on 7 May the year previously.[12]

---

6 *CJ*, III, p.331.

7 TNA, SP28/152/3, fols 1r.–2v.; SP28/225/1, unfol.

8 *A Perfect Diurnall*, 17–24 July 1643; TNA, 28/179, unfol.; Ben Coates, *The Impact of the English Civil War on the Economy London, 1642–50* (Routledge: London, 2004), p.97.

9 HMC, *Portland*, I, p.140.

10 CRO, DDX/428, fol. 19r.; *BLB*, I, 67. For further requests from Sir William and the deputy lieutenants during the spring of 1645, see fols 20r., 45r., 63v.–4r., 82r.; *BLB*, I, 66, 82, 122, 152–3, 195.

11 *CJ*, IV, pp.109, 122; CRO, DDX/428, fol. 101v.; BL, MS Add. 11331, fols 28r., 57r., 117v.; *BLB*, I, 219, 349–51, 364, 388, 406, 662.

12 *CJ*, III, p.484; *LJ*, VI, p.551; CRO, DDX/428, fols 79v., 94r.; *BLB*, I, 159, 406.

Plate A: Ensign of the Cheshire Foot. (Illustration by Alan Turon © Helion & Company 2019)
See Colour Plate Commentaries for further information.

Plate B: Trooper of Sir William Brereton's Own Troop. (Illustration by Alan Turon © Helion & Company 2019)
See Colour Plate Commentaries for further information.

Plate C: Musketeer. (Illustration by Alan Turon © Helion & Company 2019)
See Colour Plate Commentaries for further information.

Plate D: Dragoon. (Illustration by Alan Turon © Helion & Company 2019)
See Colour Plate Commentaries for further information.

Plate E: (Top) Cornet of Sir William Brereton. (Bottom) Cornet of Lieutenant Colonel Michael Jones.
(Illustrations by Dr Lesley Prince © Helion & Company 2019) See Colour Plate Commentaries for further information.

Plate F: (Top) Cornet of Colonel Robert Duckenfield. (Bottom) Cornet of Colonel George Booth.
(Illustrations by Dr Lesley Prince © Helion & Company 2019) See Colour Plate Commentaries for further information.

Plate G : (Top) Cornet of Colonel Henry Mainwaring. (Bottom) Cornet of Captain John Hawkbridge.
(Illustrations by Dr Lesley Prince © Helion & Company 2019) See Colour Plate Commentaries for further information.

Plate H : (Top) Cornet of Captain John Vivers. (Bottom) Cornet of Captain William Edwards.
(Illustrations by Dr Lesley Prince © Helion & Company 2019) See Colour Plate Commentaries for further information.

Plate I : John Speed's map of Chester, *The Theatre of the Empire of Great Britaine* (1611–12).

Plate J: Gerard ter Borch, Officer Writing a Letter, with Trumpeter (c. 1648–9).

Plate K: *Drie ruiters in gevecht* (Three riders in combat), Jan Martszen de Jonge, 1642–49.

Plate L: Reconstruction of grey russet soldier's coat by Ian Dicker and Barbara Robinson of *The 1642 Tailor*. (Author's photograph)

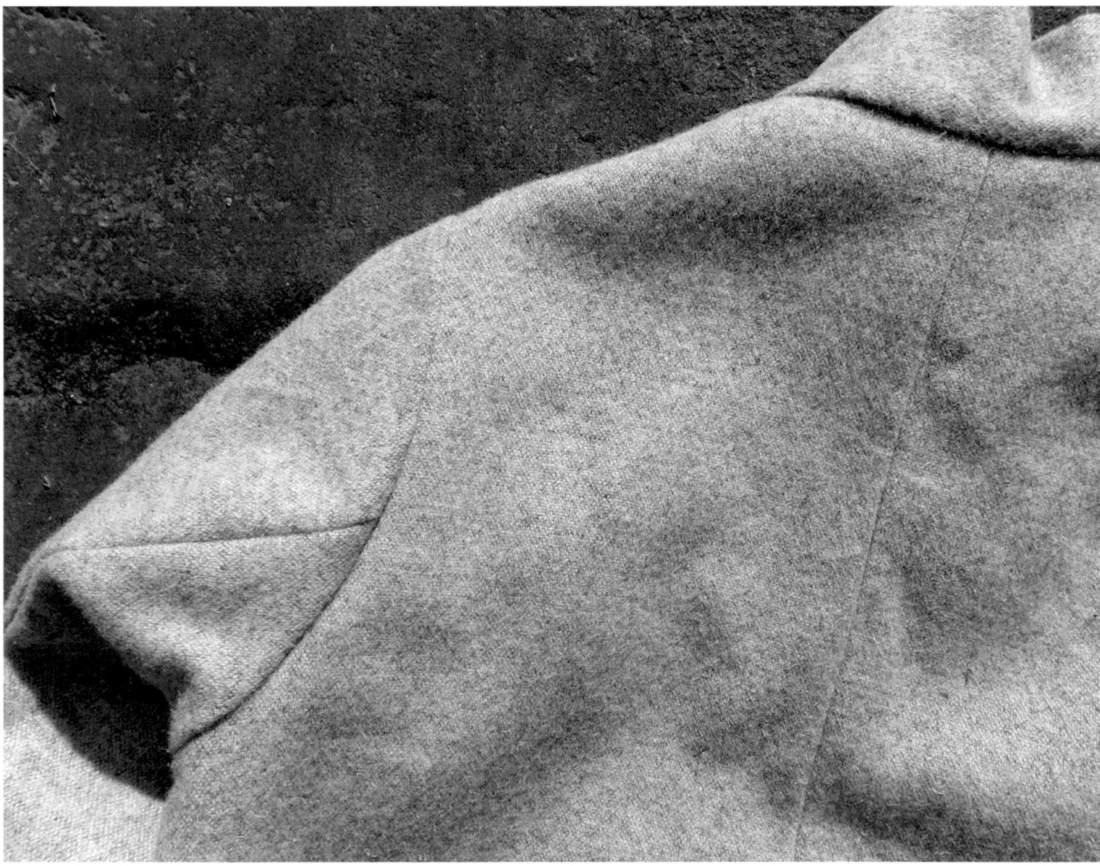

Plate M: Soldier's coat – detail. (Author's photograph)

Plate N: Reconstruction of cavalry and dragoon riding coat. (Courtesy of Ian Dicker)

Plate O: Riding coat – detail. (Courtesy of Ian Dicker)

Plate P: Mounted dragoon wearing riding coat. (Courtesy of Gary Ashby)

Probably the most significant grant of money was the £10,000 voted by the Commons 'for such forces as are drawn together about Chester and North Wales' in the autumn of 1645.[13] Writing from Northampton on 18 October 1645, during his journey back from London to Cheshire, Brereton instructed his London agents Bradshaw and Worrall to pay their colleague Henry Cockson £2,000 out of the £10,000. Cockson was immediately to carry the money into Cheshire 'to be disposed of there for the service of the forces united against Chester'.[14] A further grant of £12,000 was made by Parliament in September 1646, which was largely intended to settle the outstanding arrears of the Cheshire troops.[15]

The sums received in September and December 1645 in particular were predominantly for paying soldiers, although some cash went on settling the army's debts in London (mostly to cover the purchase of ammunition). Before mid 1645 Brereton had taken primary responsibility for the payment of his regiments, while the deputy lieutenants maintained the militia. Croxton's accounts are overwhelmingly concerned with the payment of troops from London moneys. His overall disbursements up to June 1647 amounted to £77,494 2s. 5d., of which £66,045 2s. 9d. was given to army officers as pay for themselves and their soldiers. This included payments to the Cheshire forces serving within and outside the county under the commander-in-chief. Thus, on 18 December 1645 £1,253 was distributed from the £10,000 grant from Parliament to 'the officers and soldiers of the Cheshire horse who have been constant upon duty and received no pay since August last 1645, as appears under the hands of Colonel Jones, Major Zankey, Captains Glegg, Wynn, Captain-Lieutenant Smith, Captain Edwards and the rest of the Cheshire officers that have received pay'.[16]

Additionally, sums from London sources were paid to the trained bands, whilst £20,000 went to troops from other counties who served at the Leaguer of Chester. The sum of £7,650 was spent on military items (including arms and powder), supernumeraries such as surgeons, scouts and pioneers, as well as clerks and chaplains. Moreover, Brereton's personal account book of his expenses discloses that he received money from different sources, in particular from London, including some of the funds granted for Cheshire in 1644.[17] Even though his top priority remained the payment of the Cheshire soldiers (in particular, finding sums in late 1645 and early 1646 to prevent troops from mutinying), his total expenditure of around £7,200 also covered key disbursements to intelligencers, messengers, scouts and other agents. Sir William also delved into this source of petty cash to render on the spot payments for soldiers' clothing and emergency supplies of ammunition.

As Morrill shows, the patchy accounts surviving for the sequestration committees, collectors and constables of individual Cheshire hundreds and

13 *CJ*, IV, pp.293, 302; BL, MS Add. 11332, fols 2r., 99r.–v.; 11333, fol. 32r.; *BLB*, II, 667, 886–7, 1057.

14 BL, MS Add. 11332, fols 1r., 3v.; *BLB*, II, 700–2.

15 TNA, SP28/128/13, fols 12r.–13r.; SP28/152/8 and 9, *passim*.

16 BL, MS Add. 11333, fols 30r.–v.; *BLB*, II, 1040.

17 TNA, SP28/152/7, *passim*.

townships offer a detailed and diverse picture of local funding. Such sources indicate that in addition to the estimated £100,000 raised in direct taxation and on the Propositions within the county by mid 1646, 'over £120,000 would have been expended on quarter and about £90,000 seized or destroyed in goods'.[18] Morrill further suggests that the total cost to the inhabitants and sequestered Royalists of Cheshire would have been in excess of £400,000. The most complex of all Parliament's attempts to procure funding was the administration of the sequestered estates of delinquents and papists, although for a number of reasons the Parliamentarian commissioners ultimately failed to raise revenue comparable with that of the same assets in the years before the war. A number of sequestration agents and local constables were issued standing orders for the upkeep of particular garrisons and military units. Hence, in early 1644 numerous payments were received by Colonel Leigh's regiment from the Northwich Hundred agents, while the constables of Nether Whitley expended 16s. on 'two bushels of oats brought to the Northwich garrison'.[19] Additionally, the Bucklow committee complied with an order from the deputy lieutenants by granting some of the profits of the sequestered goods of Peter Leycester of Tabley to Lieutenant Colonel Gerard and Captain Holford for the use of their soldiers.[20]

The most complicated and problematic arrangement for the payment, supply and recruiting of men for the Cheshire army from local sources involved Thomas Warburton, treasurer to the Bucklow sequestration committee. The foot regiments of Colonels Brooke and George Booth suffered from recruiting problems, and the procurement of supplies and pay due chiefly to an order from the Council of War at Nantwich, made in late 1643, which permitted the Lancashire colonel, John Booth, to draw money raised in the 29 townships of the upper division of Bucklow Hundred to be diverted towards his soldiers. John Booth's regiment formed the Parliamentarian garrison of Warrington, with responsibility for securing the eastern part of West Derby Hundred, as well as assisting Brereton in Cheshire.[21] But although its officers and soldiers served with distinction at Nantwich, Ormskirk and elsewhere, the conduct of its colonel was questionable. On 12 October 1643 West Derby Hundred was made liable for the upkeep of the garrisons of Liverpool and Warrington, while the leys and taxations raised within five South Lancashire parishes were allotted to the latter.

However concerned Sir William Brereton might have been that the Lancashire Committee (of which he was a member) should have taken complete responsibility for the maintenance of the Warrington garrison, its Cheshire neighbours remained liable for substantial contributions. Warburton's accounts show that to the end of April 1644 he paid £328 18s. 2d. to Colonel John Booth, almost half the total received from sequestrations in the whole hundred during the same period.[22] Additionally, in Warburton's

18 Morrill, Cheshire, pp.108–9.
19 BL, MS Harley 2128, fols 42r., 41v.
20 BL, MS Harley 2137, fols 55v., 95v., 114r.
21 *CJ*, III, p.157; HMC, *Tenth Report, App. IV*, p.68; *BLB*, I, 19n.
22 TNA, SP28/208, unfol.; BL, MS Harley 2137, fols 56v., 60v.–61r.

summary of his accounts, made on 28 June 1645, he highlighted the difficulty of maintaining garrisons at both Warrington and at Halton, in addition to funding the various military units raised from the area. Warburton and his collectors, he said, had been 'much obstructed in the service of sequestrators within the division ordered for the garrison of Warrington, and that there hath been great sums seized for the use of the garrison of Halton ... and that several soldiers have seized goods without our order, we conceive it cannot be, but something may be committed and some mistaken'.[23] Yet payments to Booth ceased, following an order of 2 March 1644 by Sir Thomas Fairfax, nominally commander-in-chief while Brereton was in London, that all sequestration money was to be paid directly to the county treasurer. Even though the concession to Colonel Booth was formally annulled by Parliament on 7 May 1644, evidence shows that money, recruits and supplies continued to be appropriated well into the following year.[24]

Occasionally Cheshire troops were paid for assisting local officials in the collection of arrears of tax or rent, the assumption being that they would be called upon to use force if necessary. On 10 March 1645 eight soldiers of Captain Hulse's company assisted the Nantwich sequestrators in seizing delinquents' goods. A total of 29s. was disbursed to 'Corporal Dudley and others of Major Zankey's troop the help the collectors to strain upon the unruly'. The accounts of William Penketh and John Wright, collectors for Bucklow Hundred, include the sum of 6s. 'paid to Captain John Brooke's soldiers distraining upon John Laughton's goods at two several times and carrying them to Daresbury'.[25] However, at times soldiers were faced with the opposition of reluctant civilians. On 5 May 1645 Brooke (temporarily commanding his brother's cavalry troop) reported to his commander-in-chief:

> I crave further leave to acquaint you in brief of an act of baseness which cannot be paralleled. I licensed a corporal of mine to go over into Cheshire out of Wales to collect pay, as well as for some soldiers in his squadron as for myself [John may have had temporary command of Colonel Brooke's troop at this time]. He accordingly went and came to demand some arrears due from the constables of Daresbury. They forthwith acquainted old Mr Daniell; wherefore he came, who immediately raised the township to oppose him from levying what was due to be paid. The townsmen beat my soldier in a shameful manner and Mr Daniell himself run violently to have stabbed him with a knife, which by God's providence fortuned upon a belly-piece on his doublet, otherwise he had either slain him or much endangered his life, being just opposite to his heart. Nor was he so sensible of God's mercy in presenting his intended mischief but attempted a second; being disarmed of his knife, he presently laid hold on a pair of shears and proffered with them, had he not been withheld by some standers-by, to have executed his bloody intent. His reason for so doing I cannot hear nor learn, unless some old spleen towards me still galls him and so he thought to revenge it. But I shall desire the

23 BL, MS Harley 2137, fol. 161r.
24 TNA, SP28/225/1, fols 51v.–2r.
25 BL, MS Harley 2166, fol. 130r.; 2136, fol. 39v.; 2128, fol. 119r.

> benefit of a Council of War to pass upon it, lest others (this passing unpunished) make it a precedent for them to act the like.[26]

Attacks on local officials were not uncommon, especially during the latter stages of the conflict. There were anti-excise riots in Warrington in 1645 and in south-west Lancashire in 1649. In April 1645 Colonel Moore was ordered to despatch companies to the town to settle taxes and punish defaulters.[27]

Ultimately, both the London moneys and funds obtained within Cheshire proved inadequate in meeting the army's financial requirements. On 15 January 1646 Brereton and the deputy lieutenants estimated that the cost of maintaining the siege of Chester during the previous 16 weeks (from 18 September) was in excess of £70,000, not including ammunition – a considerable sum.[28] Arrears of pay among the Cheshire army of Parliament reached near epidemic proportions in 1645 and 1646. On 18 December 1645 the Cheshire horse was some four months in want of pay, while elements of the foot suffered considerably.[29] Probably the hardest hit was Duckenfield's regiment. Duckenfield was fiercely loyal to his soldiers, who were amongst the earliest raised for Parliament in the county and from the farthest parts of Cheshire. On a number of occasion he petitioned various commanders (including Sir Thomas Fairfax) about their conditions and arrears of pay, which were acute. On 5 April 1645 he reported to Sir Samuel Luke:

> my regiment hath passed upon very hard duty for this twelvemonth, especially last winter at the siege of Beeston Castle, and in Wirral where many of my men were lost and maimed, for all which service they have received but a month's pay and now they begin to mutiny and will break presently, unless some competent means be allowed them.[30]

Parliamentary instructions were issued for the pay of the Cheshire forces at the siege of Lichfield Close, who had received nothing from the resources of their own county which had been exhausted by the protracted siege of Chester. The soldiers of the foot, who had been at Lichfield for 20 weeks without pay, were remunerated in June and December 'according to the new model', while the junior officers were paid in June and their company commanders in November.[31] At least the majority of them had received their Chester bounty from the deputy lieutenants of Cheshire before marching to Staffordshire in April 1646. Hence, the Cheshire Committee lobbied the Commons for the payment of an estimated figure of £80,000 owing to the

26 BL, MS Add. 11331, fol. 79v.; *BLB*, I, 457.

27 TNA, SP24/15/8; SP24/74.

28 BL, MS Add. 11333, fols 116r.–v.; *BLB*, II, 1250. Sent with a covering letter by the deputy lieutenants of Cheshire to the Speaker, dated 13 January 1646, but not sent until two days later, presumably when the above was completed (fol. 116r.; *BLB*, II, 1245).

29 BL, MS Add. 11333, fols 30r.–v.; *BLB*, II, 1040.

30 *Letter Books of Sir Samuel Luke*, p.505; *The Cheshire and Lancashire Historical Collector*, ed. T.W. Barlow (Manchester, 1853), pp.95–6.

31 TNA, SP28/16/513, fols 70r.–72r.; *CWS*, pp.325–8.

Cheshire army in arrears.[32] Such a sum is borne out by the petitions and corrected accounts of several of Brereton's officers. These indicate that their commands were owed in some instances more than half the total due to them since their establishment. By the summer of 1647 Duckenfield's regiment had received pay amounting to £5,444 17s. 7d., with £3,557 remaining outstanding. During a similar period Lieutenant Colonel Venables had received £561 out of £2,113 owing to the soldiers of Sir William Brereton's own company.[33] Additionally, the final arrears owing to Captain John Brooke were assessed on 15 September 1650 at £418 0s. 4d. In return for its payment he was able to procure the manor of Middlewich under the Act of 16 July 1649, which disposed of Crown lands in order to raise £600,000 to pay the army. In January 1651 Brooke further purchased properties in Hawarden for the sum of £100.[34] More striking, perhaps, are the figures for the company of dragoons and troop of horse commanded by John Bramhall. Between the end of 1642 and September 1645 his officers and men received £909 from the £6,880 to which they claimed to be allowed from central sources.[35] Since each of these claims were checked and certified by the Committee of Accounts there is no reason to suppose that they were significantly exaggerated.

Owing to the incomplete nature of the evidence and the varied sources of finance available to the Cheshire army, attempts to form a clear picture of the pay received by Brereton's officers and soldiers are not straightforward. How applicable common pay rates were among his regiments remains uncertain, particularly given the problems experienced in collecting the weekly or monthly mize, restrictions placed on funds sent via the London treasurers and the increasing demands of the prolonged siege of Chester. In mid 1645 there emerged among the Cheshire army a system of pay known as the 'new model' or 'Cheshire model'. Not to be confused with the New Model Army, this was according to Lancaster an attempt by Jones, Lothian and the deputy lieutenants to place the payment of the troops engaged at the Chester leaguer on firmer ground after Brereton left for Westminster in the June. He stated:

> These two soldiers laid the foundation to the work according to their own principles. First they endeavoured to appease the soldiers who were desperately mutinous, and the horse on their march to leave the county for want of pay, and because of their deep arrears. This the gentlemen performed by fair language, a month's pay in hand (borrowed and out of their own purses) and by deep engagements for a constant monthly pay. Then they put in execution the new model, by which the soldiers were reduced to such order that they passed muster every night upon the parade, and all that came not daily upon duty lost their pay. The country were as sensible of their own happiness, that they paid to none, but those that served, and that all free quarter to the foot was taken off.[36]

32 BCA, MS 595611, pp.57–9; *CWS*, 87–8.

33 TNA, SP28/128/10, fol. 1v.; SP28/224/2, fol. 232v.; BL, MS Harley 1999, fols 62v.–3r.

34 TNA, E121/1/5, fol. 307v.; NLW, Hawarden Deeds/325 (Glynne of Hawarden Estate Records).

35 BL, MS Harley 2128, fols 20r.–33v.

36 Lancaster, p.15.

When Sir William Brereton returned to Cheshire from London on 29 October 1645 and was met by Jones and Lothian, along with the complaints of soldiers of two months arrears of pay, he reproached the head constables of the hundreds of Macclesfield, Northwich, Bucklow and Nantwich that the problem was 'occasioned by the not bringing in of the weekly payment agreed upon at the framing of the last model'. Moreover, on 4 December Colonel George Booth reported that the custom of payments of units by individual townships and persons should have ended, thus implying that this was a further attempt to pass funds to a central source (presumably the county treasurer) before it was reallocated to the soldiers.[37] Warrants drawn up for a month's pay for the Cheshire cavalry troops of Jones, Zankey, Shepley, Glegg, Brooke, Duckenfield and Culme; the foot companies of Anthony Brereton, Whalley and John Daniell; and the dragoons of Gimbert, Holt and Finch, dating to between July and November 1645, not only show the 'new model' in operation, but record uniform rates of pay.[38] The system was also used to pay Cheshire troops at the siege of Lichfield in 1646.[39] Lancaster's mention of a 'constant monthly pay' must refer to the monthly assessment, but whether this was part of the 'model' and thus a portion of it was meant to go to the auxiliaries at the Chester leaguer is unclear. However, the scheme was authorised by Parliament and may have been initiated by it.

Pay arrears became acute in late 1645, particularly during Brereton's absence from the army under the Self-Denying Ordinance. On 30 October he observed, 'On Monday the Cheshire foot, who were two months in arrears for their pay, were in a high mutiny. But on my coming to them next morning, they were not only well appeased but seemed to be so well satisfied that none demanded any pay.' Twelve days later he mentioned 'But so often have I been there at my speaking to them they have been appeased and well satisfied.' A similar report by Colonels Brooke and Duckenfield of a partial revolt at the Chester leaguer, expressly states that, 'It is most certain that if moneys come not in, tomorrow in the morning the soldiers will again mutiny. Sir William Brereton's presence would much appease the fury of the soldiers until the moneys come and therefore we desire his speedy coming hither.'[40]

It must be concluded therefore that the troops appear to have been more liable to go to such lengths when Sir William was absent, and that he maintained considerable influence and authority among its soldiers. The author of *Shropshire's Miserie and Mercie* had recorded in October 1643 that 'Sir William Brereton who commands in Cheshire, and is colonel in, and hath a tender care of, and interest in the affections of the Staffordshire soldiers.'[41] In late October 1645 he had made several complaints about the lack of discipline amongst the troops during his absence as commander-in-chief, reporting to Ashurst in London, 'upon my coming to the army I found

37 BL, MS Add. 11332, fols 27r.–v., 119v.; *BLB*, II, 780–1, 931.

38 TNA, SP28/224/1, fols 32r., 33r.–v., 43r., 47r., 49r.–50v., 62r., 85r.–86r., 88r., 193r.–94v.

39 BCA, MS 595611, fols 252v.–3r.; TNA, SP16/513/1, fols 70r., 71r., 86v., 87v., 88r.

40 BL, MS Add. 11332, fols 29v., 59r., 128v.; 11333, fols 30r.–v.; *BLB*, II, 787, 821, 944, 1040.

41 *Shropshire's Miserie and Mercie. Manifested in the defeat given to Lord Capel's Armie by the forces under Sir William Brereton, Sir Thomas Middelton and Colonel Mitton* (London: 16 October 1643).

a great want of commission for the execution of martial law, without which the soldiers will not be kept in order.' Further letters reveal Brereton's anxiety that such a grant was slow to materialise, although Parliament finally allowed him a commission for the execution of martial law on 10 December 1645.[42]

In Cheshire there is evidence that faced with extreme wants and a string of broken promises of pay, some troops were reluctant to march and were engaged in organised desertion from early 1645 onwards.[43] With grievances overlooked the pilfering of food and clothing from civilians might provide an immediate solution when men had, to use words of one of Brereton's reformado officers, 'not wherewithal to cover their nakedness nor a penny money in their pockets, truly I confess if I had not been an eye-witness I should hardly have believed it'.[44] Moreover, on 10 April 1645 the 'deputy lieutenants and committees of Nantwich' drew Sir William's attention to bodies of 'wandering discontented soldiers, both of our own country and foreigners. These, under pretext of want of pay, wander up and down the country, rob and spoil it and will obey no orders of yours nor command of any officer, quarter were they will and remove when they will.'[45] Such gentlemen appear to have possessed little if any sympathy for the plight of the soldiery. A number of complaints from local people highlight the nature of these violations, although there is little sense of violence being used by soldiers and there was never a Clubman movement in the county.[46] In some instances officers either turned a blind eye or even joined in.

Many of the Cheshire soldiers grumbled that their conditions were aggravated by the payment of Parliamentarian troops from other counties at the Chester leaguer, something that caused Brereton and his senior officers some anxiety, although often they could do little to prevent it. Moreover, soldiers from the Macclesfield and Stockport area frequently moaned (with considerable reason) that outside forces were billeted on their homes and consumed vital resources. On 9 May 1645 Sergeant Major Bradshaw of Duckenfield's regiment stated:

> whilst they themselves are upon duty here [at Chester] and have nothing, strangers, having pay, doing no service, devour that which should sustain both them and theirs at home. Therefore, seeing their petition disregarded and hearing of the many outrages done by the Yorkshiremen, and in as much as they and theirs are so continually opposed, they are resolved to endeavour to help themselves.[47]

By the following year a major crisis was approaching, and in the summer of 1646 some of the soldiers took direct action by threatening and seizing local officials, from whom they attempted to extorted cash, often very small amounts. Various reports of these activities are contained in the accounts of

42 *LJ*, VIII, p.33; BL, MS Add. 11332, fols 8v., 29r.–v., 45v., 58r.; *BLB*, II, 712, 786, 825, 827.
43 J.S. Morrill, 'Mutiny and Discontent in English Provincial Armies 1645–1647', *P&P*, 56:1 (1972), pp.49–74.
44 BL, MS Add. 11332, fol. 107v.; *BLB*, II, 899.
45 CRO, DDX/428, fol. 88r.–v.; *BLB*, I, 202.
46 BL, MS Harley 2128, fol. 150v.; 2126, fol. 16r.; 1943, fol. 48v.
47 BL, MS Add. 11331, fol. 70v.; *BLB*, I, 453.

sequestration committees and township constables, such as those of Over Peover 'when Colonel Booth's soldiers came for the first time for moneys to Mobberley and took me with them to Bowden, and kept me there two days a prisoner'.[48]

However, in late June1646 troops revolted in Chester, while sequestrators and tax collectors were assaulted, the disturbances only being subdued by hurried loans on the part of the deputy lieutenants and the promise of £2,000 from London.[49] More severe was the mutiny by five companies of the Nantwich garrison on 14 July 1646, who according to Malbon:

> did by violence draw some of the committee of sequestrations for Nantwich hundred (being in peaceable manner executing their office for the state) forth of the office where all their books and records were, and fetched some of them (and one of the collectors) forth of several houses, wherein they were at dinner, and put them all in the common prison in Nantwich amongst cavaliers, common thieves and horse stealers (which were then there) having been the common prison from the first making the town a garrison … Neither would they allow them to have either meat or drink, or quarter in any other house or place, although it desired both by the high sheriff [Henry Brooke], and many of the deputy lieutenants and justices of the peace being then in town … neither would they suffer them to go further for doing of their needs during the whole space of 54 hours (laying nothing to their charge) but alleged that their wages were presently paid. Although they knew that the same committee never paid them, nor no other soldiers any, neither had they any warrant to pay them any, for they received their pay always from the treasurer, by warrant of the deputy lieutenants. But as some of them said, they would beat Jack for Jill, yet they would not deliver them further until Colonel Lothian and some other gentlemen had undertaken for their pay.[50]

Even though the town's governor was attacked and wounded when he endeavoured to intervene, and the justices and collectors forced to flee, it is significant that the soldiers put their faith in James Lothian (and a few others), who had led the Cheshire foot from the early days of the war. Still acting independently of their officers, the soldiers sent representatives to the county committee, although they backed their demands with veiled threats of further disorder. They had showed themselves capable in somewhat complex operations in defiance of their officers and had argued their case some eight months before the election of agitators in the New Model Army. At the end of July two cavalry troops quartered themselves on the homes of the deputy lieutenants Philip Mainwaring and Thomas Stanley, and when their calls for money were not met they forced each of the gentlemen to pay them £50–60. Disorder on the part of the Cheshire soldiers finally abated in mid 1647, although not before the provision of £12,000 from Parliament and the disbanding of the Nantwich garrison, as well as a further mutiny

48 BL, MS Harley 2126, fol. 103r.

49 *Perfect Occurrences*, 27 June–3 July 1646; *Kingdome's Weekly Intelligencer*, 28 July–4 August 1646.

50 Malbon, *Memorials*, pp.208–10.

in Chester during which Colonel Massey, the Parliamentarian governor and others had been arrested.[51]

Muster rolls, pay warrants, and the accounts of individual officers and sequestration committees contain examples of pay to the Cheshire horse. In September 1644 the constables of Weston provided Brooke's troop with the sum of £1 14s. 10d., while on 20 February 1644 the constables of Aston were ordered to provide £5 13s. 4d., and to render a further six weeks' pay at 13s. weekly per trooper.[52] This computes to fractionally above 2s. per day. Under the terms of the system of pay known as the 'Cheshire Model' or 'New Model', whilst serving at the Chester leaguer during the period 18 September 1645 to 15 January 1646, captains of horse were paid 39s. per week, whereas their brother captains in the foot received the sum of 20s.[53] Additionally, on 4 August 1646 the sum of £70 was disbursed to 57 troopers from Sir William Brereton's troop for their service at Lichfield Close, at the rate of 30s. each, amounting to one month's arrears of pay at just over 1s. per day.[54]

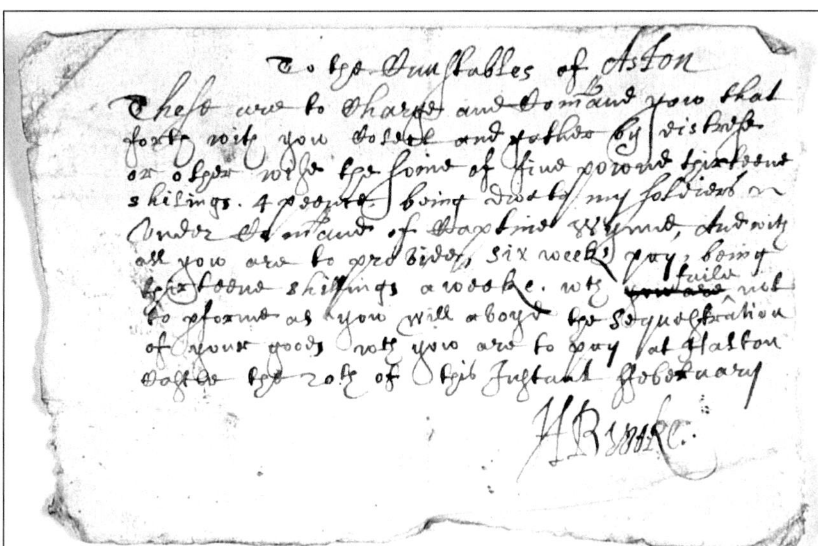

Warrant issued by Colonel Henry Brooke to the constables of Aston, dated 20 February 1644. (Courtesy of Christine Talbot)

The monthly rates of pay contained in army warrants of July to November 1645 include the following (in accordance with the 'Cheshire Model'): for the horse – captains received £7 16s.; lieutenants £4; cornets £2, quartermasters £2, corporals, trumpeters and clerks £1 12s.; and troopers 20s. For the foot – captains had £4; lieutenants £2 16s.; ensigns £2; sergeants and clerks £1 8s.; corporals and drummers £1 4s.; common soldiers 10s. For the dragoons – captains received £5; lieutenants £3; cornets £2 8s.; sergeants £1 12s.; clerks £1 10s.; corporals and drummers £1 8s.; dragoons 14s. Moreover, as commanders of the horse and foot, Jones and Lothian

51 Morrill, 'Revolt in the Provinces', pp.61–2.

52 BL, MS Harley 1970, fol. 150r.; AA, unlisted warrant, dated 20 February 1644.

53 BL, MS Add. 11333, fols 116r.–v.; *BLB*, II, 1250.

54 TNA, SP16/513/1, fol. 92r.

respectively, were paid the rate for colonels, being £40. Surgeon Chadwick of Brereton's regiment of horse received £3 4s., while Nathaniel Lancaster, chaplain to the regiment had £4.[55]

On 24 November 1645 a warrant instructed the delivery to Captain Holford's officers and troopers of one month's pay, while the same command received a further month's wages on 4 November 1646 'for gratuity promised them at the taking of Chester'.[56] Similarly, Captain Carter received £14 8s. in pay from the sequestrators of the upper division of Wirral Hundred on 23 May 1645, while his troop was mentioned as being in distinct arrears with other Cheshire horse and Captain Holt's dragoons on 6 November 1645.[57] Further illustrations of the level of pay arrears owing the Cheshire horse are those of Colonel Robert Duckenfield, whose outstanding pay as captain of a troop of horse, having served for 1,405 days at 39s. per day, amounted to £2,739 15s.[58] When Brereton's regiment of horse was disbanded in late 1646 its arrears of pay totalled £600.[59]

Standard daily rates of pay for the foot of other Parliamentarian armies offer some comparison. In April 1643 Lieutenant Colonel Thomas Gell paid his Derbyshire foot company the weekly rate of £1 10s. to the lieutenant; 13s. 8d. to the ensign; 10s. 6d. to the sergeants; 7s. to corporals, drummers and gentlemen of the arms; and 5s. 4d. (9d. per day) to the common soldiers.[60] As far as many armies were concerned, pay was infrequent and often in substantial arrears. According to Ron Slack, 'The wages paid to most of these Derbyshire troops were less than those quoted in an official list. Sergeant's, corporal's and dragoon's wages were about half the official figure.'[61] Holmes observes that in the Eastern Association the period up to mid 1644 'was marked by some confusion in the organisation of the pay of the infantry', but after this a uniform system was adopted. Moreover, during 1644 and 1645 the foot was more frequently remunerated than their brothers-in-arms in the horse, although this is probably explained by the fact that the infantry were generally less disciplined than the cavalry and more ready to mutiny or desert if their arrears were not met.[62] This pattern is broadly discernable in the Cheshire army during the later stages of the war when companies in Duckenfield's, Booth's and Brereton's own regiments refused to march if their back pay was not forthcoming, whilst at the same time (between August and December 1645) the majority of Brereton's horse was four months in arrears.

In March 1645 most of Captain Edward Glegg's company deserted at Tilston, causing the Nantwich Committee to report:

55 TNA, SP28/224/1, fols 32r., 33r.–v., 43r., 47r., 49r.–50v., 62r., 85r.–86r., 88r., 193r.–94v.

56 *Great Victories obtained by the Earl of Denbigh*; CRO, DDX/428, fol. 88v.; BL, MS Add. 11331, fol. 96v.; TNA, SP28/128/10, fol. 7v.; SP28/224, fol. 175v.

57 BL, MS Add. 11332, fol. 105v., *BLB*, II, 897.

58 TNA, SP28/128/10, fol. 9v.

59 TNA, SP28/51/1, fol. 118r.

60 DRO, D258/30/9; D803/MZ9, fol. 57r.

61 Slack, *Man at War*, p.77.

62 Holmes, *Eastern Association*, pp.145–6.

> They likewise pretend their harsh usage: removal from their own country (being trained bands) which is committed to the hands of strangers who look more after themselves than it: that, going out of their own estates, pay is denied them and paid to others who less deserve it. These are the reasons which, with the laying down of their captain's commission, make them resolute to be gone.[63]

The deputy lieutenants raised sums to find them a month's wages and a further month's pay (being its bounty due on the fall of Chester) when the company marched, nonetheless, the county treasurer found that 'because money was wanting' there was only enough to pay the common soldiers.[64] Similarly, the deputy lieutenants provided pay for Captain Brereton's company in May 1646, 'who (being something full) have undertaken to keep the bridge and Farndon Church where they now are, and are about to build a mount in the face of the castle [of Holt] on the Cheshire side.'[65]

Separating the pay of the trained bands from that of other soldiers in Brereton's army is another matter. Money for them should have come from pre-war taxation and been administered by the deputy lieutenants. Morrill suggests that it was kept separate from the wartime taxation used to pay the other troops until the summer of 1645, and evidence from a range of sources tends to bear this out in a general sense. The expected rate of weekly pay 'upon service' (and the mechanisms employed in raising it) for the trained bands of Cheshire is indicated by a warrant issued by Fairfax and other military officers at Nantwich on 28 February 1644 to provide a month's pay for trained soldiers. This was followed by a similar order from deputy lieutenants the following day:

> In regard that this county is very much impositioned by the oppression of providing by leys and other charges for the maintenance of this cause, whereby the gentry and others of the county are disabled to continue the full pay to the soldiers where with the stand responding charged as formerly, this therefore orders it every soldier of the trained and freehold band in this county shall from henceforth content himself with 4s. 8d. for a week's pay, the same by reason of the kingdom's impoverishment being as much as paid in any part of this our kingdom until this country shall be brought into a better condition and order to the contrary, which weekly pay every soldier to receive from the treasurer, George Spurstowe esquire, unto whom all constables and gentlemen shall forthwith pay in all the arrears of pay to those soldiers after the accustomed rates that the soldiers may be the better satisfied with that small portion hereby allotted to them. And to this end, notice may be given of this through this county a copy of the same is forthwith to be sent to every high constable within the county who are straightly commanded to send notice here of any petty constable within their respective sub-district.[66]

63 CRO, DDX/428, fol. 88; *BLB*, I, 202.

64 TNA, SP28/43/7, fols 863v.–4r.; SP28/123/4, fol. 618v.

65 BCA, MS 595611, fol. 197r.–v.

66 AA, unlisted warrants, dated 28 February and 1 March 1644.

Several other payments made to the trained and freehold bands by local sequestration committees and constables are known, and include the sum of 2s. 'for our trained soldiers' disbursed by the Northwich officials in 1643; in the same year the constables of Frodsham in Eddisbury Hundred paid £2 'to Lieutenant Colonel Gerard for the monthly pay of trained soldiers'; the figure of £4 2s. 8d. was distributed to the freehold bands of Bucklow Hundred in 1645 by George Leicester, clerk to Captain John Brooke. In addition to these, throughout the conflict the constables of Church Lawton maintained two trained band soldiers by fixed contribution at 1s. per week; also the constables of Lymm provided for 'three soldiers in the trained band at Nantwich under Colonel Brooke', totalling £54 12s. in 1643, £46 4s. in 1644 and £19 5s. in 1645.[67] The latter reference to trained bandsmen belonging to Colonel Henry Brooke is odd, however, as the two companies of his regiment quartered in Nantwich (commanded by Captains Delves and Francis Bramhall) are known from other sources to have been volunteer townsmen.

As with the issue of reasonably identifying the trained and freehold bands, the somewhat imprecise contemporary terminology surrounding the various sources of their pay creates additional problems. When Brereton spoke to the deputy lieutenants on 9–10 April 1645 about 'the late taxation', which was imposed three months before and still had to be collected, he referred to it first as a 'lay', then a 'lay or assessment' and once merely the 'late taxation', and thus it is difficult to establish exactly what form it took.[68] A confusing phrase from the army's commanders at the Chester leaguer to the deputy lieutenants of Cheshire on 6 December 1645 concerning the payment of troops, states: 'We are sensible that there are much arrears for pay to the soldiers of the trained and freehold bands of the weekly mize, intended by the Model for the horse and volunteer companies, uncollected in all the hundreds.'[69]

Dore asserts that:

> The first sentence, given exactly as it is in the MS, seems almost incomprehensible unless it is assumed that by this time the horse and the volunteer foot companies were included as part of the trained and freehold bands, although originally – by definition – they must be separate. If this is so, then the phrase 'trained and freehold bands', and even the word 'militia' now meant no more than the native forces of the county as opposed to 'auxilleries'.[70]

Comparisons are also valid between Brereton's comments of April 1645 to the Committee of Both Kingdoms 'concerning the condition of the country and soldiers, and my thoughts of such a way for the ordering and commanding of the militia', and his 'proposals for settling the militia', in addition to the use of the term 'country' in the list of Cheshire regiments with its assortment of

67 BL, MS Harley 2128, fols 41v., 48v.; 1999, fol. 75r.; 2137, fol. 203r.; 1943, fols 2r.–8r.
68 CRO, DDX/428, fols 78v., 76r.–v.; *BLB*, I, 183, 193–4.
69 BL, MS Add. 11332, fol. 128r.; *BLB*, II 944.
70 *BLB*, II, 944, note 2.

all classes of troops.[71] This further implies that this was the case as early as the spring of 1645, and before the introduction of what Lancaster and others referred to as the 'New Model', a financial reorganisation designed to provide the Cheshire army with more reliable system of pay.

By autumn 1645 Brereton and his senior officers were becoming increasingly concerned over the pay of their soldiers, especially from local sources. On 11 July George Manley, a Cheshire landowner, complained of:

> a poor and miserable country we live in, and if these Leaguers continue, it is like to be worse, if there be a possibility of being worse, for the taxes are so many, and the payments laid upon us, is more than our land is worth, our stocks all wasted and we are put into a way of ruin, not easily to be recovered but by great providence and length of time, the lord look down in a mercy upon his poor distressed people.[72]

Similarly, on 7 November 1645 Brereton, Brooke and Duckenfield stated, 'Our country is so much exhausted that it is not possible our army should subsist and be kept together without supply out of North Wales, according as by the Parliament is ordered.'[73] It is in this context that the Cheshire trained bands received payment from London moneys in lieu of funds raised locally. On the same day as the previous complaint, it was ordered by the commanders before Chester:

> For as much as the soldiers of the Trained and Freehold Bands are almost three months in arrears of their pay and that moneys are not brought in out of the country according to expectation: it is therefore for the prevention of present discontents (which may tend to the dissolution of the army) desired that so much moneys of those which are brought down from London may be lent as may pay the same soldiers of both the same bands one month's pay, and the same to be regained out of the first moneys that shall be brought in out of the country.[74]

A similar issue presented itself in June 1646 when trained band companies at the siege of Lichfield had pay from Cheshire sources (the deputy lieutenants), 'but the officers of the said companies had no pay from Cheshire so that they were paid in the like [proportion] as other officers of voluntary companies'.[75]

Some officers were careful or wealthy enough to expend sums on quartering their men. On the way from London in January 1643 Captain Bramhall paid £1 12s. 10d. at Ashbourne in Derbyshire 'for the discharge of my soldiers' quarters', whereas on 26 March and 22 May 1644 disbursements of £5 1s. 6d. and £2 16s. were made to Widow Harding for housing two of his soldiers in Nantwich.[76] Synonymous with pay was the issue of free quarter,

71 BL, MS Add. 11331, fols 4v., 44r.–45v.; *BLB*, I,283, 383–5.
72 TNA, SP23/197/39.
73 BL, MS Add. 11332, fol. 48r.; *BLB*, II, 831.
74 BL, MS Add. 11332, fol. 47v.; *BLB*, II, 830.
75 BL, MS 595611, fol. 71r.
76 BL, MS Harley 2128, fols 25r., 26r.

which both sides resorted to throughout the war. Officially the constables of each township were to keep a record in order that householders could be subsequently compensated when the soldiers' arrears were made up and the relevant amounts deducted from their pay. Whether in the majority of cases this was actually paid remains uncertain, although the survival of several constables' records indicate how much was spent in quarter and money lost in plunder. In Over the inhabitants disbursed £250 in quarter up to the summer of 1646, with £400 lost in plunder and destruction. Similarly, in Nether Whitley £372 was laid out on quartering troops up to the end of 1644.[77]

Nevertheless, several amounts were provided by officials in recompensing civilians for providing quarter, such as in August 1643 when elements of Colonel Brooke's regiment were billeted at Frodsham. Robert Ragin was paid 8d. by the Bucklow sequestration committee for housing two soldiers of Richard Brooke's company for a day and a night, while Thomas Modshall had 1s. 4d. for accommodating two men under Captain John Brooke for two days and two nights.[78] Less forthcoming are details for towns, such as Northwich, Nantwich and Tarvin, which housed full-time Parliamentarian garrisons. On 24 July 1645 Richard Hickock, a townsman of Nantwich, was given £1 5s. 'for the discharge of tickets for the quartering of soldiers, he being a poor man and not being able to forebear [the cost himself].[79]

Ammunition

The providing of arms and ammunition – and of ready money to pay for them and their transportation – was a major task for early modern armies. In Cheshire's case, this was something that could be materially assisted by Brereton's presence in Westminster during the spring and summer of 1644, and autumn 1645. His accounts reveal that during mid 1644 in particular, Sir William disbursed sums towards the recruiting and arming additional troopers for his cavalry regiment during his journey back via the Midlands.[80] The payment of moneys from London was slow, however. The £5,000 from the revenues of the Court of Wards, originally granted in April 1644 was finally authorised by the Commons Committee for Revenue on 3 May 1645.[81] Various quantities of gunpowder were supplied from London to the Cheshire army of Parliament. In November 1642 and November 1643 Colonel Duckenfield purchased powder for his regiment from London suppliers at the cost of £20 for each purchase.[82] Between December 1643 and June 1644 further quantities were procured in the capital for 14s. 4d. by James Croxton, and forwarded to Cheshire.[83] Substantial amounts of arms and munitions

77 BL, MS Harley 2126, fols 3r.–39r.; 2128, fols 4v.–15v.
78 BL, MS Harley 2137, fol. 75v.
79 BL, MS Harley 2166, fol. 132v.
80 TNA, SP28/152/7, fols 5v–11r.
81 BL, MS Add. 11331, fol. 94r.; *BLB*, I, 406.
82 TNA, SP28/128/10, fols 1r., 7v.
83 TNA, SP28/128/13, fol. 30r.

would reach the county overland through the Midlands from London – the main haulier being 'Shakeshaft the carrier' – although it would have been well known by Brereton and his agents that he would encounter at any time of the year, not only the danger of interception by Royalist garrisons, but also the possibility of having the carts waylaid by inclement conditions.[84]

Significantly, the Cheshire army was also supplied by sea. As Dore illustrates, 'The evidence shows that there was considerable maritime activity in the North West during the Civil War. Both sides spent energy and resources in trying to control the sea approaches to Chester and Liverpool, the Royalists sporadically and with only limited temporary success, the Parliamentarians throughout and with increasing effectiveness as the war progressed.'[85] It is clear that Parliamentarian commanders attached great significance to this mode of supply and that the Royalists were eager to prevent it by the capture of Liverpool. During the winter of 1643–4 the governor of Chester had stressed the importance of the port to Ormonde, who in succession pressed this upon Sir John Byron upon his arrival in the North West. In April 1644 Byron informed Rupert that its seizure would be the main benefit of the Prince's march to Lancashire.[86]

The Parliamentarian tract *Lancashire's Valley of Achor*, celebrating their success in the county in 1643, mentions a vessel that at the time of the siege of Warrington in May 1643 entered Liverpool waters and by its appearance aided Warrington's surrender. It was 'watching the friendly opportunity to unburden itself for Cheshire and supply us with powder, Liverpool readily giving entertainment'.[87] On 13 June 1643 Brereton was at Liverpool for the unloading of a ship 'which was come tither from London with his great ordnance and ammunition came with his troop of horse to Nantwich and brought with him … six loads of his own ammunition in safety, being accompanied with many brave captains and commanders'.[88] In the November Brereton reported to the Speaker that a fleet transporting Ormonde's troops from Dublin captured Captain Lurtine's ship, the *George*, which was carrying ammunition for him and the Lancashire commanders. Sir William also took the opportunity to request that:

> when you send a fleet to clear these coasts there may be sent down 100 pair of pistols, 200 muskets and 200 or 300 firelocks. These are not to be procured on any terms in this country wherein I could raise good store of men if I could arm them. We also desire some 30 or 40 barrels of powder, whereof we have great use, having been in continued action in Shropshire and Wales ever since Colonel Mytton came down.[89]

---

84 BL, MS Add. 11331, 117r.–v.; *BLB*, I, 472.

85 R.N. Dore, 'The Sea Approaches: the importance of the Dee and the Mersey in the Civil War in the North West', *THSLC*, 136 (1987), pp.1–26 (p.19).

86 Carte, *Letters*, V, p.525, VI, p.10; BL, MS Add. 18981, fol. 137r.

87 *Lancashire's Valley of Achor* (London: 1643); *CWTL*, p.138.

88 Malbon, p.61.

89 HMC, *Portland*, I, p.157.

In an attempt to alleviate Brereton's problems in keeping hold of such seaborne supplies, one of the ordinances he got the Commons to pass during the summer of 1644 prohibited the Lancashire Parliamentarians from appropriating arms, ammunition and ordnance directed through their county for the Cheshire forces.[90] In April 1645 16 barrels of powder, 20 barrels of corn powder (for priming muskets and cannons) and 30 hundredweight of match purchased in the capital by Brereton's London agent, Richard Worrall, were included in a consignment of arms and equipment despatch by sea to Liverpool aboard the *Sarah Bonaventura*.[91] Evidence that Sir William Brereton still distrusted his Lancashire colleagues is suggested by a letter to Worrall regarding the same consignment, in which he stated. 'I have given order that they (the cargo) shall not be landed until you send for them. Therefore I desire you to lay wait for the ship against her arrival in Liverpool. John Sandiford promised me that as soon as they arrived he would send Captain Rathbone word.'[92] Rathbone, himself a Wirral man, commanded a company in Brereton's own infantry regiment that was quartered at Upton, to the north of the Chester leaguer. It is possible that this particular shipment was brought by smaller craft to Tranmere, as it was from here that Sir William's cheeses had been embarked for Kinsale in March 1645.[93] On 25 October 1645 the Commons ordered that 50 barrels of powder were to be 'sent down to be employed for the service of the forces before Chester'. This was to be issued by Sir Walter Erle, lieutenant of the ordinance, although it is unclear whether the load went by road or sea.[94]

Abraham Casembroot, *Kamp van Roma* (1603–58), showing soldiers in camp. (Amsterdam, Rijksmuseum, CCO 1.0 Universal (CCO 1.0) Public Domain Dedication)

90 *CJ*, III, p.484.

91 CRO, DDX/428, fols 45r., 79v.–80r.; *BLB*, I, 87, 139, 159.

92 CRO, DDX/428, fol. 80r.; *BLB*, I, 159.

93 CRO, DDX/428, fols 41r.–v.; *BLB*, I, 37.

94 *CJ*, IV, p.32; BL, MS Add. 11332, fol. 55v.; *BLB*, II, 724.

The Cheshire army's chief magazine (for the storage of powder, ammunition and other military stores) was at Nantwich, although a subsidiary depot was established at Runcorn. The latter, an important tidal dock on the south bank of the Mersey, could supply the forces in northern and eastern Cheshire, but its main function was to provide a secure storage point for ammunition brought up-river from Liverpool and thence transported by wagon to Brereton's headquarters. Warrants signed by Lieutenant Colonel Brooke and Sir William Brereton on 5 September and 7 September 1644 respectively commanded the constables of Aston to provide wagons and 'two teams with four able horses or six oxen indeed led with carters and drivers, to be employed for carrying arms and ammunition for the service of this county' between Runcorn and Halton Castle.[95] Each garrison had a magazine, even if it was only a small one. Magazines were controlled by commissary officers and their assistants, who directed the procurement and distribution of supplies. Commissaries for the Cheshire forces included the commissary general, William Hinde; assistant commissary Robert Lunt; William Becket and Henry Rogers, commissaries in Nantwich; Ralph Metcalfe, commissary at Beeston Hall in early 1645. Edward Podmore acted as wagon master.[96] Between 1644 and 1646 they were materially assisted by Captain John Whitworth, an executive officer with a wide range of administrative roles, who was responsible for purchasing and transporting arms and ammunition, and discharging contractor's bonds.[97]

Shortages of powder and ammunition at the Chester leaguer and elsewhere were acute enough for the deputy lieutenants to purchase what they could locally upon account. Sir William Brereton was duly obliged to report to the Committee of Both Kingdoms on 31 October, 'we have not only borrowed from our neighbouring counties what supplies they can afford, but there is so much bought as the gentlemen here, according to their information, are indebted for £1,500 or £1,600'.[98] This appears to have had some effect because four days later Parliament granted him an extra 20 barrels of powder in addition to the previous 50, although on 6 November 1645 Brereton's close associate in London William Ashurst, warned that 'the stores are quite empty and so little means to furnish them', but following the issue of the 50 barrels he promised to send 20 more 'out of the first that comes'.[99] Four months later, on 15 April 1646 the Committee of Both Kingdoms sent 60 barrels of powder to Sir William's forces before Lichfield, with match and bullet proportionable.[100] During the same month, Thomas Guise of London, gunpowder maker, was employed by the army at Chester.[101] A further agreement was reached in July

95 AA, unlisted warrants, dated 5 September and 7 September 1644.

96 BL, MS Harley 2137, fol. 153r.; 2126, fols 129v.–130r.; 1943, fols 7r.; TNA, SP28/224, fols 25r., 223v.; E121/5/7/351, fol. 5v.

97 BL, MS Add. 11331, fols 44r., 105v., 115; 11332, fols 38r., 42r.; TNA, SP28/43/7, fol. 871r.; SP28/242, fol. 376v.; *BLB*, I, 385, 544, 556; II, 796, 806.

98 BL, MS Add. 11332, fol. 35v.; *BLB*, II, 790.

99 *CJ*, IV, p.333; BL, MS Add. 11332, fols 67r., 68v.; *BLB*, II, 814, 824.

100 *CSPD 1645–7*, p.412; BCA, MS 595611, pp.43–4.

101 BCA, MS 595611, p.53.

1646 with Thomas Browne of Cheapside for furnishing ammunition at a cost of £56 8s.[102]

Beyond London the Manchester dealer, William Sunderland was a leading distributor of gunpowder and ammunition. From 1644 he sold considerable amounts of munitions to the Parliamentarian forces of Cheshire, Lancashire, Shropshire and Staffordshire.[103] Sir William Brereton used this gunpowder and match at the Chester leaguer, one consignment in 1645 was worth £849 6s. 6d. Sunderland's commodities were much in demand. In comparison to the £4 10s. for a barrel of powder and 3d. for 1lb of match that the London munitions manufacturers charged, in April 1645 Sunderland's products retailed at £6 for gunpowder and 6d. for match. As Edwards suggests, 'the higher price probably reflects local shortages at a time when resources were being diverted to London to help provision the New Model Army'.[104] On 5 December 1645 Brereton's treasurers discharged the sum of £1,418 4s. to William Sunderland for provision of ammunition to the Cheshire forces.[105] This included £849 6s. 6d. for munitions, 'which he furnished for the service of the Leaguer before Chester upon entering the suburbs [20 September 1645]'. The outstanding figure of £568 17s. 6d. was settled via the payment of £268 17s. 6d. by treasurer Croxton, while the army's London officials were directed by the deputy lieutenants to make up the remaining £300. Both amounts were paid out of the £10,000 ordered for the service the leaguer before Chester.

The Cheshire army also secured the services of the Manchester supplier of gunpowder, Edward Johnson, the Macclesfield sequestrators paying him the sum of £10 on 20 November 1645.[106] Also, having been compelled to work with Sir John Gell to secure Staffordshire since early 1643, Brereton poached his gunpowder maker at Derby, George Bainbridge, for his own mill in Stafford.[107] An illustration of the quantities of musket and cannon ammunition consumed by Brereton's army and auxiliary troops at the siege of Chester (in addition to powder and match) is detailed in an account of 'Powder spent at the Leaguer 20 September to 16 December 1645':

> Since 20 September 1645 in entering the suburbs of Chester and since then in storming the city with cannon and muskets, and about the city in the Leaguer, at Dodleston and Eccleston and in the Foregate Street and at the Northgate: seven-score barrels of powder and bullets proportionable. And 40,000 weight of match, besides what ammunition hath been spent in this time at Tarvin and Beeston and the battle in Wales [Denbigh on 1 November] with the enemy. Remaining yet in

102 TNA, SP28/152/8, fol. 2r.

103 TNA, SP28/134/12, fol. 36r.; SP28/152/8, fol. 2v.; SP28/224, unfol.; SP28/225/3, fols 578r.–v.; SP28/225/4, fol. 824v.; *Committee at Stafford*, p.82.

104 Edwards, *Dealing with Death*, p.113; 'Turning Ploughshares into Swords: The Arms and Military Equipment Industries in Staffordshire in the First Civil War, 1642–1646', *MH*, 27 (2002), pp.52–79 (p. 56).

105 BL, MS Add. 11332, fol. 124v.; *BLB*, II, 935.

106 BL, MS Harley 2130, fol. 99v.

107 Slack, *Man at War*, p.97; Edwards, 'Ploughshares', p.61.

> powder at Tarvin and at the Leaguer: 30 barrels and bullets proportionable and 3,000 of match.[108]

Like the supply of powder to the Cheshire forces, considerable amounts of musket ammunition and match were also procured. On 27 September 1643 Colonel Robert Duckenfield spent £62 4s. 2d. on bullets for his regiment and a further £10 on its carriage, and on an unspecified date he also gave £18 10d. 'to William Bardsby [possibly the same local supplier] for ammunition'.[109] Similarly, one of Duckenfield's company commanders, Captain Anthony Booth, was reimbursed the sum of 2s. 'for the expending of shot and powder for the first work at Acton Bridge', one of the actions leading up to the Second Battle of Middlewich on 26 December 1643.[110] Sir William Brereton was supplied with musket bullets in January 1644 by Edward Johnson, while probably during the same autumn a ton of lead was forwarded to the Cheshire army from the mines in the Peak District.[111] Furthermore, on 20 November 1645 the sequestrators of Macclesfield Hundred disbursed £15 'to Thomas Sidebottom of Stockport, plumber, for bullets for the public by order of Sir William Brereton and others'.[112] A not uncommon method employed by infantry soldiers of both sides during the Civil War was that of replenishing stocks of ammunition by salvaging spent lead for remoulding into bullets. Thus, musketeers belonging to Captain John Marbury's company of Colonel Booth's Cheshire regiment were paid 4s. for collecting used musket balls at Cholmondeley House on 27 August 1643.[113]

Few direct references exist in the sources to the individual amounts of powder, bullet and match issued to Brereton's soldiers. On 4 December 1643 Lieutenant Colonel Brooke, the governor of Halton, instructed the constables of Aston to assist in seizing, taxing and levying of arms and ammunition upon their township, 'allowing for every musket 24 bullets and 2lb of powder'. A fortnight afterwards his brother, Captain John Brooke, directed the same officials to 'gather moneys for the buying of ammunition according to 3lb of powder, 12 yards of match, 60 bullets for every musket ... you shall be provided after the rates of 1s. 6d. powder the pound, match 8d. the pound, now for the better gathering of this money you are to understand that every whole plough, and every two half ploughs are to find a man, musket, sword and bandolier, and for you to gather proportionately'.[114] Such warrants were issued in response to the general muster of Parliamentarian forces faced with the recent disembarkation of Royalist troops from Ireland in Cheshire and North Wales, and it is interesting to note that Richard's soldiers were in the main, garrison troops, whereas his brother's company had mustered for field service (being 'equipped and trained in martial discipline'), thus suggesting

108 BL, MS Add. 11333, fol. 25r.; *BLB*, II, 1020.

109 TNA, SP28/128/10, fols 4r., 6r., 5v.

110 BL, MS Harley 2128, fol. 43r.

111 TNA, SP28/27/398; DRO, D258/34/10.

112 BL, MS Harley 2130, fol. 99v.

113 BL, MS Harley 1999, fol. 60r.

114 AA, unlisted warrants, dated 4, 18 and 13 December 1643.

that the 3lb of powder, 12 yards of match and 60 bullets was most common issue to musketeers in 'marching order'.

The issue of half a pound of powder to a pound of shot calculates as 10 bullets to the pound (of shot). This might be compared to the pre-war instructions given to the Norfolk trained bands, whereof 'the bore thereof shall be justly answerable to the bounds of a round leaden bullet of eleven to the pound', while in 1636 it was ordered 'that you provide for every musketeer within your hundred 3lb of powder, 3lb of lead to make bullets and 3lb of match'.[115] Two years later the Privy Council proposed that each militia soldier in England and Wales should have 3lb of powder, six yards of match and 24 bullets per year for training, although a common complaint was that local troops often lacked the powder for live firing.[116] It seems unlikely that musketeers would have been issued with this amount of ammunition and match together. In armies of both sides issues were collected by senior non-commissioned officers or corporals, who apportioned them out as required. Besides, as Orrery notes, links of match were doled out by corporals to individual soldiers.

The issue of ammunition and match to Captain Brooke's men particularly, raises interesting questions about the typical quantities carried by Civil War musketeers. The Royalist Composition Papers record that in early 1643 Ralph Wood, yeoman, provided a substitute to serve as a foot soldier in the Wigan garrison with 20s., a red coat, musket rest, a pair (or collar) of bandoliers and a knapsack.[117] Similarly, at Oxford in February 1643 a William Riley was engaged 'for the fitting up of 42 pair of bandoliers for His Majesty's present service'. The suggestion here is that singular items were referred to, because the same craftsman was supplied with '40 dozen' lengths of white string for the powder containers at 4d. per dozen.[118] In addition to musket and pistol ammunition, Brereton's army obtained large supplies of artillery ordnance, normally manufactured by provincial founders. In March 1644 shot and mortar rounds were received by the Nantwich garrison from nearby Hough furnace, near Stafford.[119] Similarly, during the siege of Chester in October 1645, the sum of £16 2s. was disbursed to Richard Hopkins of the Mereheath foundry in Staffordshire for 23cwt of bullet at £14 per ton, with an additional £4 'for the workmen that made them, and for making the mould they were cast in'. A further 30cwt was provided from the same source on 14 November at a cost of £26.[120]

Brereton's forces obtained considerable quantities of muskets, musket ammunition and match from London suppliers, as well as more localised sources. On 3 December 1642 the Committee for the Safety of the Kingdom ordered the issue of 400 matchlock muskets and 300 firelocks to Brereton's

115 W. Wrye (ed.), *State Papers Relating to Musters, Beacons, Ship-money, &c. in Norfolk from 1626 chiefly to the beginning of the Civil War* (Norwich, 1907), pp.89, 199–200.

116 *CSPD*, 27 January 1638, p.195.

117 *Royalist Composition Papers*, VI, pp.336–9.

118 Ian Roy (trans. and ed.), *The Royalist Ordnance Papers 1642–1646*, I (Oxfordshire Record Society, 1964), p.202.

119 TNA, SP28/36, fol. 405r.

120 TNA, SP28/35/5, fols 751r., 754r.

forces, while in February 1644 they received a further 1,000 muskets as part of a major cache of arms and equipment for the Cheshire foot.[121] From a combination of centralised supplies and purchases of weapons by officers from local sources, in February 1643 Robert Duckenfield's regiment of foot received muskets and colours costing £9 11s., while 10 months later muskets for Captain William Duckenfield's company and a pistol for the colonel's troop were procured at a cost of £2 2s. 6d., and 30 weapons were supplied to the regiment from the Warrington garrison. In early 1644 Colonel Duckenfield laid out the sum of £80 'for arming and refitting of my foot regiment after the defeat at Middlewich, where I lost above 200 arms'. Moreover, after the fall of Chester in 1646 he received 60 captured Royalist muskets, 20 of which he issued to Captain Booth's men and another 20 to Captain Leadbeater.[122] On 21 November 1644 Captain John Brooke of Colonel Brooke's foot disbursed £2 for muskets and bandoliers.[123]

Johann Jacobi von Wallhausen, *Krijgskunst voor het voet volken krijgskunst voor de cavalerie* (1616), an influential training manual for cavalry. (Amsterdam, Rijksmuseum, CCO 1.0 Universal (CCO 1.0) Public Domain Dedication)

121 *CJ*, II, p.874; *CSPD 1644*, p.26.
122 TNA, SP28/128/10, fols 5r., 8r., 9r., 2r., 4v.
123 BL, MS Add. 2137, fol. 52r.; SP28/208, unfol.

In a letter to Speaker Lenthall, dated 30 October 1644, Sir Thomas Myddelton complained that he had provided 1,000 arms and 28 barrels of powder for the relief of Nantwich earlier in the year, but had received neither replacements 'nor any satisfaction for them'. He requested that the Commons supplied him with '1,500 muskets, and as many swords, belts and bandoliers, with 50 barrels of powder, eight of shot and 150 bundles of match'.[124] During the previous summer Myddelton had brought 40 chests of arms and ammunition to Nantwich upon his commission as commander of the counties of North Wales.[125] The utilisation of arms and equipment seized in combat was essential, although some of the sources recording them may have exaggerated their numbers in order to elevate the level of victory. Following Brereton's success at Middlewich on 13 March 1643 it was reported by Parliamentarian sources that '2 pieces of ordnance, 4 barrels of powder, 2 barrels of match and arms for 500 men' fell into their hands; the storming of Market Drayton in May 1643 resulted in 'many prisoners, horses and arms, that all or most of Nantwich foot soldiers were horsed home, and many of them had two, three, or four muskets and carbines apiece, beside apparel and other goods of theirs'; at Whitchurch on 29 May:

> there was taken about twenty prisoners, one very fair foot colour, four good pieces of ordnance, very many arms, and much money and brave apparel of the Lord Capel's and other gentlemen. Two covered wagons, powder, bullets, match and goods of the soldiers' great store, many drums, one trumpet and many horses, the soldiers having most of the pillage, so that there were scarce any soldiers but be returned back or either horsed, or well-laden with pillage, or both.[126]

Various amounts of muskets, ammunition and other items were reported being taken by the Cheshire soldiers at Cheddleton House on 10 October 1643 and Doddington Hall on 7 February 1644, while later the same month Duckenfield's and Colonel Assheton's Lancashire foot seized 700 muskets at Adlington, and a further 300 at Biddulph Hall.[127] Likewise, an inventory of the weapons and armour taken at Wythenshaw Hall on 25 February 1644 records among other things, 32 muskets with bandoliers and rests, four long fouling pieces, two carbines, one caliver, four cases of pistols with holsters, and 1cwt of powder 'with match and bullets answerable'.[128] Offsetting these figures are the 200 or more muskets lost by Brereton's troops during their defeat at the second Battle of Middlewich on 26 December 1643. Even so, the Cheshire forces appear to have been relatively well equipped with muskets for the Shropshire Committee, in a complaint of 2 May 1645 mentioned that their own soldiers were in want of 400 muskets, and requested that Brereton loan them 200.[129]

124 HMC, *Thirteenth Report*, pp.191–2; *Portland*, I, pp.191–2.
125 Malbon, 71–2.
126 Malbon, pp.41, 52–3; *Cheshire's Successe*.
127 Malbon, pp.41, 53, 58–9, 71, 120, 122.
128 JRL, Tatton Family Papers, 1644 inventory of contents of Wythenshaw Hall in February 1644.
129 BL, MS Add. 11331, fol. 57; *BLB*, I, 401.

Brereton's army obtained match in large quantities and from various sources. In January 1645 Mr Marsh of Stafford supplied an unknown amount at a rate of £2 6s. 8d. per cwt.[130] Contracts were agreed between Richard Worrall – one of Brereton's London treasurers – and various suppliers of match in the city in 1645 and 1646. On 24 November 1645 he disbursed £125 5s. to John Freeman for 72cwt of English match 'sent down to the leaguer [of Chester]'. Additionally, from the same source he had 24 barrels of English powder and 34 cwt of match on 3 February 1646 at a cost of £117 11s., while from another, Thomas Strowton, Worrall bought 26cwt of match for £41 17s.[131] By comparison, one of the chief suppliers of arms and ammunition to the Lancashire Parliamentarians was Henry Wild of Castleton, near Rochdale. He was paid significant sums for match and ball between 1643 and 1645. Wild provided ammunition costing £110 to the Liverpool garrison in November 1643, as well as furnishing 150 bandoliers and 167 muskets to the same soldiers on 14 May 1644.[132] In conjunction with merchants such as William Sunderland and James Wainwright, he played a major role in enabling the Parliamentarian troops in Lancashire to maximise their war effort by providing regular and plentiful supplies of munitions.

Provisions

The procurement, organisation, accounting and transporting of provisions among early modern armies was essential to military operations, and to maintain the effectiveness and morale of the rank and file. Not only did soldiers need to be fed and provided with beverages, but horses and draft animals required large amounts of fodder. Even though troops in garrisons might fare better, benefitting from a more varied and plentiful diet, much depended upon the resources of the locality, in addition to the attitude of the inhabitants who proffered them. During the siege of Chester in 1645 Brereton experienced immense difficulty in provisioning his troops, attributing it to the impoverishment of the area and the hostility of the population.[133] Although it has been suggested that the New Model Army relied more on supplies of rations from London by means of commercial contracts, rather than local sources, provincial forces obtained most of their foodstuffs locally, thus Cheshire had to largely sustain this vital function in support of Brereton's army.[134] Continental armies travelled with huge supply trains – both of ammunition and victuals – the latter controlled by the commissary-general of the victuals, and including assistant commissaries and clerks, as well as bakers, butchers and other victuallers. The Cheshire army of Parliament employed a number of commissaries, who were responsible for extracting

130 TNA, SP28/137, fol. 12v.; SP28/225/4, fol. 697v.

131 TNA, SP28/152/8, fol. 2r; 28/152/9, fol. 2v.

132 TNA, SP28/229, fols 1102r.–v.; SP28/300, fols 1071v., 1076v.

133 *Letter Books of Sir Samuel Luke*, p.1257.

134 Aryeh J.S. Nusbacher, 'Civil Supply in the Civil War: Supply of Victuals to the New Model Army on the Naseby Campaign, 1–14 June 1645', *EHR*, 115: 460 (2000), pp.145–160 (p.145).

the produce they needed for military purposes from the countryside or urban arcas.

Such officials included William Hinde, the commissary general, and his assistant, Robert Lunt.[135] On 27 October 1645 Hinde wrote to Brereton:

> I make bold according to my duty to acquaint you with the present want of provision for the army, which on this Cheshire side is in want of bread and all other provisions, and on the Welsh side bread is our greatest want. If my life lay on it I cannot get one day's provision beforehand of bread, by reason of the great number of horse that lie quartered round about us, which take away all the corn from barns and mills faster than it can be made ready.[136]

William Becket was commissary in Nantwich in 1644–5, while Commissaries Henry Rogers and Roberts are recorded supplying victuals to the garrisons of Nantwich and Tarvin respectively. Moreover, in March 1644 John Miller received quantities of provisions from the Bucklow sequestrators, including 12cwt of cheese and 240 measures of oats 'for the use of the army', while Ralph Metcalfe served as commissary at Beeston Hall in early 1645.[137] Even though every regiment, troop and company was meant to possess a quartermaster, whose duties included overseeing the lodging of soldiers and sometimes distributing their pay, the provost marshal had particular care of victuals. According to Cruso, in addition to punishing wrongdoers:

> he must be an honest man, and content with his fees. He is to look to the weights and measures, and to guard the victuallers (or sutlers) from insolences. Himself or some of his men must always be in the market-place, or where the victuals are sold; and he is to inform himself where and at what price the sutlers buy their victual, that the commissary and auditor may tax them accordingly.[138]

Messrs Noden, Bradley and Ramshaw acted as provost marshals to the Cheshire Parliamentarian army.[139]

Although beef, cheese, bread and beer were the mainstay of the diet of the common soldier, food supplies could vary depending on availability and season, and were contingent on whether units were in garrison or in the field. A warrant for the supply of victuals for the army in Ireland, drawn up on 7 February 1642 directed the commissary for victuals to provide for the magazine at Chester rations 'for 10,000 men for three months, at the rate of 4d. the day for every man, in bread, beef, butter [and] cheese. Wherein you shall be careful of the goodness and wholesomeness of the provision; and likewise

135 BL, MS Harley 2137, fol. 153r.; 2166, fol. 129v.; MS Add.11331, fols 35r., 39r., 52v.–3r., 117v.; 11332, fols 28v., 35r., 39r.; 11333, fols 62v., 118v.; *BLB*, I, 374, 377, 398–9, 472; II, 781, 790, 796, 1104, 1235.

136 BL, MS Add. 11332, fol. 23v.; *BLB*, II, 752.

137 BL, MS Harley MS Harley 2166, fol. 130r.; 1943, fols 7r.–v., 8v.; 2137, fols 105v., 152v.; TNA, SP28/224, fol. 25r.; Malbon, p.168.

138 Cruso, *Military Instructions*, pp.15–16.

139 TNA, SP28/152/8, fols 15r.–18r.

of the prices, that they be as cheap as the markets will afford'.[140] As near as prices would bear, each man was to be supplied daily 1lb of bread, 1lb of beef, or, in lieu thereof, ½lb of cheese, or fish, and ¼lb of butter. Following the first arrival in North Wales of Royalist troops from Ireland, on 20 December 1643 the deputy lieutenants issued warrants for the provisioning of the Cheshire army to each township in the hundreds of Nantwich, Eddisbury, Bucklow, Northwich and Macclesfield, stating:

> Forasmuch as the enemy is now advanced into the bowels of this county, threatening the same hereof with fire and sword which cannot be prevented by a general and universal joining together in arms into the above, and for continuing with cannot be effective and held together, but by a speedy and large supply of victuals. These are to command you immediately upon receipt hereof to repair to all your houses in your said parish, and demand and gather from every householder according to his ability, provisions of bread, butter, beef, bacon, cheese, veals, muttons and other partial provisions ... to require all commissaries are to convey the same to the constables at Sandbach with all possible speed and arrive here by this power to the said commissaries, to press and take carthorses and divers of the said persons for the said service, wherein you are to be hiding and dissenting unto them and hereof fail not [under] pain of imprisonment ... you are likewise to bring in all the able men within your parish with their best arms and every man a week's provisions for himself.[141]

More specifically, in early 1644 Captain John Brooke instructed the constables of Aston to provide victuals for four of his soldiers 'that are upon the guard at Frodsham Bridge, one household loaf, two white loaves and one other to the value of 2s., 3lb of bacon, 2lb of butter, 12d. in ale and as much in small beer'.[142]

The records of the treasurers of the various Cheshire sequestration committees show that at least half of the money received by them (and not sent to the county treasurer) was used to buy provisions for military units and garrisons. Tenants also paid rents in kind, these goods being quickly sent to the soldiers. Much of the task of providing food and other items, such as firewood and straw, fell upon local officials. During the siege of Halton Castle in June and July 1643 Parliamentarian troops were supplied from local sources. The constables of Nether Whitley provided 16s. 6d. 'for provision for the Leaguer at Halton Castle', while their colleagues at Dutton provided victuals to the value of £2 10s.[143] Shortly after the capture of Halton its new Parliamentarian governor issued a warrant to Thomas Woollett and Lawrence Wright, constables of Aston to provide cheese from Aston Hall for the sustenance of his soldiers. Similarly, on 4 December he reminded the constables' assistants that they 'should be aiding and assisting to the constables of your township, in the seizing, taxing and levying of arms and ammunition

140 *CJ*, II, p.417.
141 AA, unlisted warrant, dated 20 December 1643.
142 AA, unlisted warrants, dated 20 December 1643, 7 and 10 April 1644.
143 BL, MS Harley 2137, fols 41v., 149r.

upon the whole township according to your last description, with all equal and substantial division'.[144] The constables of Aston, Aston Grange and other townships were also called upon to supply firewood and hay, and teams of oxen to transport it from Rocksavage park, as well as further teams to haul arms and ammunition from Runcorn dock to Halton Castle.[145]

Cheese was supplied to the army in significant quantities, although Cheshire was a county historically recognised for its production. Examples of payments for this commodity from the sequestrators of Bucklow Hundred include £20 10s. for 14½cwt of cheese issued to Commissary John Miller in March 1643 'for the use of the army in part sent from Dutton demesne'. In mid 1644 Miller received from the sequestered estate of Peter Leycester of Tabley 240 measures of oats at 11d. per measure, costing £11, while at the same time 5cwt of cheese valued at £6 12s. was delivered to Commissary Hinde from the same source. The sum of 1s. 1d. was paid on 19 November 1644 'for carrying 629lb weight of cheese to the garrison of Northwich from Mr Allan in Netherleigh', whereas probably in late 1645 the Bucklow sequestrators provided '120 measures of barley, ground into maize and carried to the Leaguer at Chester', valued at £13, with further delivery of provisions to the value of £54.[146]

Within Northwich Hundred in mid 1643 the constables of Nether Whitley disbursed 16s. 'for two bushels of oats for Northwich garrison and 16s. 6d. on provisions for the Leaguer at Halton Castle', while the constables of Mere paid £2 10s. in May 1644 for a cow for Tarvin garrison.[147] Similarly, on 15 February 1645 the sequestration committee gave 5s. 'to M.F. for two days' service in going into the country by warrant of the council of war to gather provision to it cheese and corn for the relief of the Leaguer, and arms that are before Beeston Castle and Chester, which provision was delivered to the commissary'.[148] On 18 September 1643 51 stone (714lb) of oatmeal was issued to Duckenfield's troop at 8s. 8d. per stone, costing £20 8s. 1d.[149] Additionally, the Lancashire Committee ordered that 500 loads of oats and 20,000lb of oatmeal be sent to Sir William Brereton to feed the Scots at the Chester leaguer in March 1645.[150] Consignments of provisions procured from local suppliers for the troops at the Chester leaguer include 4½ flitches of bacon, one pot of butter, 24 cheeses, seven sides of beef, 16 loaves of bread and bushels of oats (as well as 20 half-pikes) from John Bailiff on 1 March 1645. Moreover a Mr Barrington supplied four veals (costing £6 15s.) on 30 March, along with two muttons (at £3), 12 hens (at £1 4s.) and two bottles of sacke (at 9d. each).[151]

---

144 AA, unlisted warrants, dated *c.* 20 July 1643 and 4 December 1643.

145 AA, unlisted warrants, dated 28 November 1643, 2 December 1643, 16 February 1644, 30 May 1644, 19 July 1644, 5 September 1644, 7 September 1644.

146 BL, MS Harley 2137, fols 55v., 95v., 105v., 199r., 152v.–153r., 203r., 204r.

147 BL, MS Harley 2128, fols 41v., 60v.

148 BL, MS Harley 2166, fol. 130r.

149 TNA, SP28/128/10, fol. 6r.

150 HMC, *Tenth Report*, pp.74–5; CRO, DDX/428, fols 31r.–v.

151 CRO, DDX/428, fol. 1r.; TNA, SP28/225/4, fol. 825r.; *BLB*, I, 22. Barrington had previously (18 December 1644) been employed by the Cheshire forces to mend firelocks and to transport

The isolated Wirral garrisons of Hooton and Puddington suffered from a dearth of victuals, especially during the siege of Chester in 1645. In May the governor of both, Lieutenant Colonel Coote, issued a number of warrants (through the Hooton committee) to local bakers to supply bread for the soldiers.[152] Moreover, on 30 October Commissary Rogers was reimbursed £10 for bread 'for the use of the army'.[153] When a unit was desperate for provisions, the officers might intervene and requisition goods to avoid more serious trouble, even though they had no authority to do this. Whilst quartering in the Wirral in mid 1645 Captain Shepley received hay and peas to the value of £4 10s. from the committee at Hooton. Anxious to obtain provisions for his men, this enterprising officer appropriated land at Burton for the cultivation of crops. Thus, local Parliamentarian officials complained when Shepley's troopers produced 50 measures of oats 'without order' at 12d. per measure, and a further '46 measures of oats not paid for to the state'.[154] Likewise, Captain John Rathbone commanded a company of Wirral foot in Brereton's regiment, which was quartered in various local garrisons. Described by Tony Dyson as 'easily the most prominent Parliamentarian officer in Wirral', and a man of 'combative, even reckless, qualities', Rathbone fell out with local Parliamentarian officials in late 1644 and early 1645, having been accused of 'keeping diverse horses and beats' on its demesne, and requisitioning goods before they could be inventoried and valued. Besides, he grew a field of wheat at Burton.[155] Though Morrill found it odd that Rathbone cultivated crops, it seems probable that he 'was concerned with feeding his men in the face of adverse conditions and an unhelpful bureaucracy'.[156]

Another essential element of a soldier's diet was ale or beer (usually small beer), although purchases by commissaries or local officials appear rarely in documents, probably since brewing was habitually a localised activity and the product would be consumed quickly. Following the capture of Eccleshall Castle in August 1643 it was reported that 40 barrels (124 gallons) of beer, provisions and household goods were delivered to Sir William Brereton.[157] Whilst marching from Adlington to Biddulph Hall between 16 and 20 February 1644, during what was a particularly cold winter, Duckenfield's foot and two Cheshire cavalry troops were given cooked meat and burnt ale (warmed with a hot poker) by the corporation of Congleton, costing a total of £4 1s. 2d.[158] Similarly, in early January 1644, during the siege of Nantwich, £1 7s. 10d. was spent on beer brought to soldiers of Captain Sadler's company at Dorfold. James Croxton disbursed 10s. 'for drinks for my soldiers whom they lay at Beeston', while the sequestrators of upper Wirral Hundred paid £1 7s. in November 1645 to 'several men for ale taken up in the county for

cloth; he seems to have been a local entrepreneur (SP28/225/4, fol. 708v.).

152 BL, MS Harley 1999, fols 62r.–68r.

153 TNA, SP28/224/1, fol. 38r.

154 BL, MS Harley 1999, fols 17r., 69r., 71v.

155 Tony Dyson, 'The Oaths at Woodchurch, 1643–1644: tensions in Civil War Wirral and its aftermath', *THSLC*, 164 (2015), pp.1–20 (pp.15–16); BL, MS Harley 1999, fols 15v., 16r., 71v.

156 Morrill, *Cheshire*, p.110; Dyson, 'Oaths', 17.

157 Malbon, pp.74–5.

158 Anon., 'Extracts from the Corporation Books', pp.367–8.

Hooton garrison'. Also, 4s. 6d. was disbursed for sacke for Lieutenant Colonel Jones at Dodleston in March 1645.[159]

The military operations in North Wales in the spring and winter of 1645 resulted in the procurement of significant quantities of victuals for the Cheshire army of Parliament. In April 1645 Lieutenant Colonel Michael Jones launched an incursion deep into Denbighshire in command of 500 horse and 400 foot, Jones later reporting 'the county was driven by the assent of Sir Thomas Myddelton for the gaining of provisions for the army, which in a manner until that time was provided for by Cheshire, most of which cattle, the whole number of good cows not amounting to 400 nor the sheep 2,000, being not fit to be slain'.[160] The appropriated livestock was turned over to Commissary Hinde, although Sir William Brereton was anxious enough about reports of plundering that he wrote to the deputy lieutenant, William Marbury, on 11 April 1645:

> I was so sensible and so much troubled at the liberty many soldiers had taken to carry away cattle out of Wales that I appointed a guard at Puddington to seize and stay the cattle … I have written also to the Committee of Northwich and to Colonel Brooke to suffer none to pass without my order at Northwich, Frodsham or elsewhere over the river [Weaver] and to make stay of the same aforesaid.'[161]

Three hundred and sixty-six cattle were sold by the commissariat for 29s. each, whilst the 1,700 sheep were either butchered or went for cash. A significant proportion of the moneys received went on provisions for Tarvin and Hoole garrisons. On 1 May it was ordered that:

> a great number of cattle taken from the enemy in Wales should be sold and moneys thereof arising bestowed in provisions for the army and garrisons belonging to this county, and whereas the said cattle are sold unto Commissary Hinde in pursuance of the same order, it is now ordered that £120 of the same due for the said cattle shall be paid unto the treasurer at Tarvin by Commissary Hinde within four days after the date hereof to buy provisions for that garrison (which hath been of late much exhausted) and for the forces at Hoole at the appointment of the Committee at Tarvin. The rest is to be paid unto Mr John Wettenhall, Mr Richard Leicester and Mr [Richard] Egerton to be by them disposed of in making provisions for the army and garrisons as occasion shall require.[162]

According to the 'Order for disposing of money from cattle taken in Wales', it was agreed the following day that £70 was to be distributed to Sir Thomas Myddelton's soldiers, whereas the remaining sums went towards buying provisions:

---

159 TNA, SP28/128/13, fol. 30r.; SP28/224/1, fol. 3r.; SP28/196/1, fol. 9v.; BL, MS Harley 1999, fol. 70v.

160 BL, MS Add. 11331, fols 38r.–v.; Morris, *Siege of Chester*, pp.99–100; *BLB*, I, 375.

161 CRO, DDX/428, fol. 86r.; *BLB*, I, 205.

162 BL, MS Add. 11331, fol. 53v.; *BLB*, I, 398.

> for the supply of the two ships now remaining in the river near Neston, those to the value of £30 for the garrisons of Hooton and Puddington in the Wirral, those to the value of £20 for the garrison at Upton Hall, and the rest for the supplying of the army at Eccleston and Dodleston … and of the garrison of Nantwich as there shall be occasion.[163]

The foray into North Wales by the Cheshire army in the spring of 1645 marginally overshadowed by accusations of plundering by troopers belonging to Captains Vivers and Culme. They were charged with stealing jewels and goods from Plas Tege, near Caergwrle, the home of Sir John Trevor. Although Sir William Brereton later rebuked both officers, it was Jones who remarked that although the jewellery was valued at £7,000 by its owners it was not worth £500, while the Cheshire deputy lieutenants promised 'We shall be careful to take no more of Wales than what is necessary to keep our soldiers alive during the work about Chester.' Brereton, so often sympathetic towards the needs of his soldiers and aware of the wider context, reported to the Committee of Both Kingdoms:

> I must confess some insufferable exorbitances have been committed of late in Wales … I have not had the power to hold the reins of discipline as otherwise had been convenient, when extreme want of all necessities hath inflamed the soldiers' discontents to an unmasterable height. In such a case I humbly appeal to your experience how hard it is to prevent outrages.[164]

The Cheshire Parliamentarian commanders continued to press for supplies from North Wales. From their headquarters in the Chester suburbs on 7 November 1645 Brereton, Brooke and Duckenfield informed Jones, himself an Anglo-Welshman:

> Our country is so much exhausted that it is not possible our army should subsist and be kept together without supply out of North Wales, according as by the Parliament is ordered, and we should be far better content that it were brought in an orderly way than to have it taken from your country by our horse, which we must be forced upon if care not be taken the other way. Therefore it is our earnest desire that you will employ your utmost endeavours to hasten thither what provisions you can and, in especial, beef, mutton and corn. We desire to know from you what we may depend upon and in what time, because our army cannot long subsist without supplies. Whereof we doubt not you will be so sensible that some speedy fruits of your pains may be reaped.[165]

Brereton's activities had been hindered by the recent appointment of Mytton as Parliamentarian commander-in-chief of North Wales. He had local

163 BL, MS Add. 11331, fols 52r., 20v., 25r.; *BLB*, I, 399.

164 CRO, DDX/428, fols 70v.–71r.; BL, MS Add. 11331, fols 20r.–v., 25r., 28r., 35v.; NLW, MS Rhual 115; *BLB*, I, 169–70, 187–8, 352–3, 373; Norman Tucker, *North Wales in the Civil War* (Wrexham: Bridge Books, 1992 edn), pp.46–8.

165 BL, MS Add. 11332, fol. 48v.; *BLB*, II, 831.

connections and possessed different methods to the more direct approach of the Cheshire commander. On 9 November 1645 Mytton expressed to Sir William that he 'did conceive at my departure from the Leaguer that there was satisfaction given concerning the provision out of Wales, which was that there should be several places allotted for their quartering or bringing in to their quarters provisions for so many horse and foot as are on the Welsh side. This, I believe, is as much as can be expected out of those poor, exhausted and daily plundered countries'.[166]

166 HMC, *Portland*, I, p.304; BL, MS Add. 11332, fols 59v., 74r.; *BLB*, II, 840, 847.

7

Standards, Clothing, Arms and Equipment

Military standards, known by contemporaries as cornets for troops of horse, ensigns for companies of foot soldiers and guidons for dragoons, were carried while on the march and on the battlefield, but they were also used for rallying men during or after the chaos of battle. They were constructed from lengths of silk (taffeta or the less expensive sarcenet) and made up by tailors (hence the appearance of cloth and trimmings in tailor's bills), while distinguishing marks in the form of emblematic images and mottos on cornets of horse in particular, were applied by specialist painters. During the Civil Wars standards were observed and recorded for the purpose of estimating the strengths of opposing forces. Soldiers were obligated to 'follow their colours', whereas 'to depart from the colours' (desertion), whether on the march or in battle, elicited the death penalty. Moreover, 'articles of war' produced by both sides insisted that it was 'a disgrace worse than death' to abandon or lose the regimental colours. Standards were also prized trophies of war.

Cornets belonging to troops of horse measured approximately two feet square, and usually contained emblematic devices and religious mottos. According to Markham, the troop officer (with the rank of cornet) bearing his captain's standard:

> shall be armed and horsed in all points both defensive and offensive, like the lieutenant, only instead of the truncheon, he shall carry charged on his right thigh, his captain's cornet, which (being a private captain) should be compounded of colour and metal impaled, that is, the one half colour, the other metal. The substance of the cornet should be damask, and the form must be almost square (only a little longer from the staff then on the staff), and fringed about suitably. The staff should be small like a foot ensign, and not so long as an ordinary lance; it must be headed with steel, and either gilt or silvered; with fair tassels suitable to the cornet. If the cornet belongs to a great officer, it shall then be of one entire colour, of less quantity and full square; and in this cornet, the captain may carry devise or word, or else none, at his own pleasure.[1]

1 Gervase Markham, *The Soldiers Accidence* (London, 1625), p.44.

The majority of devices and mottos portrayed on cornets exemplified spiritual motivation for war. Parliamentarian examples often showed that their owners fought for the reformation of the Church of England and 'the true Protestant religion'.

Table 19: Bill or voucher for trumpet banners and cornets for Sir William Brereton's troop, 30 May 1643 (TNA, SP28/225/1, fol. 3r.)

	£	s.	d.
For the two trumpet banners, black taffeta at £5 apiece	10	00	00
For two pairs of stirrups for the trumpeters at 15s. a pair	01	10	00
For the cornet staff	01	05	00
For the two cornets on black taffeta with silver and black fringe, and taffeta of the same at £5 apiece	10	00	00
Total	17	15	00

Listed above are items purchased for colours for Sir William Brereton's own troop, as well as trumpet banners and stirrups for his trumpeters. Brereton's order for '*two* cornets on black taffeta with silver and black fringe, and taffeta of the same at £5 apiece', is not only unusual, but it offers some problems of interpretation. Given that Brereton was commissioned as captain of a troop of horse on 20 September 1642, his later statements that the unit first saw action at Brentford on 12 November, and that was almost complete in February 1643 (with a full complement of officers), it is probable that his troop had possessed a cornet since the previous autumn. Thus, it is possible that the voucher for the materials for the cornet and associated items for his trumpeters was not produced until May 1643. The document is endorsed in a different hand (presumably one of Sir William's clerks) and signed by Brereton, and instructed James Croxton, the army's London treasurer 'to pay these three matters [doubtless this and two others] out of the moneys which was returned to Sir William Brereton from London and this shall be your discharge, when you have examined the same, 27 August 1644'. Similarly, an endorsement attached to the reverse of a bill for cloth supplied for clothing supplied to Captain William Stukeley's troop, dated 2 October 1643, shows that it was not settled until 29 August of the following year.[2] The trumpet banners and trumpeter's stirrups for Brereton's troop will be discussed later, but cornet staffs were of the design of a tilting lance, but shorter. According to Cruso, they were 'after the manner of a pike, only somewhat thicker at the butt end, the head of it either to be three-edged or otherwise a pike head, made strong and sharp'.[3]

Evidence for the purchase of multiple cornets by other commanders is rare, and it is worth speculating as to why Sir William purchased two of them. Perhaps one was meant as a troop colour and the other a personal recognition symbol as commander-in-chief. The latter notion is not all together unlikely, because leaders of both Parliamentarian and Royalist

2 TNA, SP28/8, fol. 17r.
3 Cruso, *Militarie Instructions*, p.29.

forces, such as the Earl of Essex, Sir Thomas Fairfax and Sir John Hotham (the Parliamentarian governor of Hull) possessed lifeguards, who were clothed in distinctive garb and presumably carried a standard associated with their general. In the latter case, Hotham began purchasing carbines in May 1642, while an account of his later arrest mentions that his men wore red coats 'as being like the Earl of Strafford's lifeguard'.[4] Some part of Brereton's large cavalry troop may have acted in this fashion, even though there is no mention of a 'lifeguard' nor even a separate squadron in any sources. On the other hand, colonels and more senior officers sometimes chose a plain design for the cornet of their own troop, and occasionally these were made of patterned fabric. According to Blount, 'Sir Thomas Fairfax (succeeding Captain-General of the Parliament forces) and General Cromwell, both bear plain colours for their own troops, without any device'.[5] Fairfax's troop cornet in the Northern Association was known to be blue, with a foliated cloth pattern, and this was probably followed into the New Model Army. Essex's captains' cornets seem to have adhered to the same tawny-orange as their colonel's. Myddelton's own troop standard had a green field, with the motto *IN VERITATE TRIVMPHV* ('In truth triumphant'). In April 1644 Captain Enys, one of his cavalry commanders, purchased green taffeta for his cornet, with green and white fringing, and spent 14s. on a staff for it, for his own cornet and trumpet banners, although other captains of this small regiment possessed cornets of other pigments.[6]

The eight known troop cornets belonging to Brereton's horse are all different and indicate that there was no intention of uniformity within the regiment. This might be partly explained by the relative piecemeal development of the Parliamentarian cavalry in Cheshire. On 10 February 1643 Sir William explained the presence of 'near upon five troops of horse in this county, but because they are independent troops and not subjected to command'.[7] Furthermore, perhaps three or more troops were raised in the county within the first few months of the war – Brereton's later claim that he had 'a good regiment of horse a full twelvemonth before I had my commission for that regiment' (that is, by April 1643), confirms that he must have had at least 10 troops by this stage.[8] Moreover, during the general expansion of the Cheshire army in mid 1644 a further four cavalry troops were raised under Jones, Coote, Hawkbridge and Culme.

Ensigns carried by companies of foot were approximately six and a half feet square. On 29 November 1644 Alexander Venn, ensign maker, was contracted by Parliament to provide 'drums, colours, halberds and partizans for the furnishing of Colonel Aldrich's regiment, viz., for eight new ensigns made of blue Florence sarcenet with distinctions of gold-coloured laurels

4 Andrew Hopper, *The Papers of the Hothams, Governors of Hull during the Civil War* (Cambridge: Cambridge University Press, 2011), p.110; *A True Relation of the discovery of a most desperate and dangerous plot, for the delivering up, and surprising of the townes of Hull and Beverley, 4 July* (London: 1643). Thanks to David Evans for this reference.

5 Blount, *Art of Making Devises*, p.77.

6 TNA, SP28/346/1, unfol.

7 HMC, *Portland*, I, pp.94–5.

8 BL, MS Add. 11332, fol. 43r.; *BLB*, II, 809.

with tassels to them … at the rate of 45s. apiece'.[9] Each foot regiment would usually employ similar field colours and designs, but would follow a system of differencing. This system was described by Captain Thomas Venn:

> The colonel's colour in the first place is of a pure and clean colour, without any mixture. The lieutenant colonel's only with a St George's arms in an upper corner next the staff; the major's the same, but in the lower or outer corner with a little stream *blazant*. And every captain with a St George's arms alone, but with so many spots or several devices as pertain to the dignity of their respective places.[10]

In February 1643 Colonel Duckenfield disbursed the sum of £9 00s. 11d. for muskets and colours. Similarly, on 25 March 1644 Captain John Brooke instructed the constables of Aston 'to collect and gather within your township by distress or otherwise, the sum of 10s. for the buying of drums and colours for my company'.[11] A new standard was purchased for Sergeant Major Croxton's company of Brereton's regiment on 29 September 1645, costing £2 10s.[12] By comparison, in February 1643 the Staffordshire Parliamentarian commander, Colonel Jackson spent £2 12s. on having his colours made (for his own company) at Uttoxeter, paying a further 1s. 6d. for the staff and head to mount them on. Moreover, the sum of £14 3s. 6d. was paid out for colours for the newly raised Cheshire regiment under Colonel Lothian in August 1648.[13] Except for perhaps one example, the shade and design of foot standards for the Cheshire forces have yet to be positively identified. On 12 August 1644 *Perfect Diurnall* mentioned that Brereton 'sent a party of 1,500 foot to join the Lancastrians in beleaguering the town of Liverpool'.[14] This was in response to a rendezvous ordered by Sir John Meldrum of Lancashire and Cheshire foot to counter Royalist forces, including the remains of the Northern Horse, retreating from Marston Moor. There was a perceived threat that these troops would cross south into Cheshire. In the contemporary account of the fighting in Lancashire by Edward Robinson, he begins his account of Meldrum's attacks by saying: 'He quartered his army in Preston about Saturday and Sunday. Upon Saturday late at night came up to him a regiment carrying all black colours that came out of Cheshire.'[15]

The Cheshire companies also fought at the skirmish at Ormskirk on 20 August, before marching back across the Mersey at Warrington. It appears likely that most of the Parliamentarian foot that joined Meldrum from Cheshire were from Brereton's own regiment, although they were accompanied by Lancashire soldiers commanded by Colonel John Booth. It is possible then, that the 'regiment carrying all black colours' was Sir William's, a possibility made more likely by the fact that his troop cornet

9 Gerald I. Mungeam, 'Contracts of the Supply of Equipment to the 'New Model Army' in 1645, *JAAS*, 6 (1968–70), pp.53–114 (p.75).

10 Thomas Venn, *Military Observations, Or the Tacticks Put into Practice* (London, 1672), p.181.

11 TNA, SP28/128/10, fol. 4v.; AA, unlisted warrant, dated 25 March 1644.

12 TNA, SP28/35/2, fol. 179r.

13 TNA, SP28/134/2, fol. 23v.; SP28/346/1, unfol.; SP28/128/13, fol. 23r.

14 *Perfect Diurnall*, 12 August 1644; *CWTL*, p.204.

15 Robinson, *Discourse of the War in Lancashire*, p.55.

had a black field. In January 1645 the inhabitants of Warton in West Derby Hundred complained of depravations caused by a 'regiment of black colours', while John Booth is depicted in a portrait wearing a scarf of the same hue.[16]

Surviving evidence for the design and shade of guidons for dragoon units is relatively slight. Probably the same size as cavalry cornets and fringed, they were distinctive on account of their rounded swallow-tail shape. According to Markham, dragoons were only permitted to use banners of this type, but if a unit was promoted to the cavalry the two peaks on the tail were ceremoniously cut off.[17] This might have occurred when Bramhall's Cheshire company was reformed as a troop of horse on 30 April 1644.[18] Guidons seemed to have adhered to the system of differencing used by foot regiments for their ensigns, while known examples (mainly the five belonging to Colonel Wardlaw's Parliamentarian regiment), contain mottos. Wardlaw's standards are uniformly blue and fringed in gold, with a canton containing a St George's cross. Otherwise they are plain, yet each, except for that of the colonel, had a different motto in gold letters.[19] According to Charles Kightly and Anthony Barton, Sir William Waller's dragoons carried yellow guidons differenced by black plates. The only confirmed Royalist dragoon colours are two recorded as being 'taken by the Earl of Essex' at Edgehill in 1642.[20] Both are drawn as if damaged, yet one has an argent (silver or white) field, with a St George's canton, with a blue and white fringe. The second is white with no fringe, but contains five white crescents in the manner of differencing. They could be of the same regiment. The background colour and design of the guidons carried by Brereton's dragoons are unknown, yet it seems likely that they were black, with a black and silver fringe, akin to the cornet and trumpet banners belonging to his troop of horse. Like Wardlaw's, they may also have contained mottos pertaining to each captain.

Coloured scarves or sashes were for the most part limited to officers and cavalrymen, although there is some evidence that they were issued to sergeants and drummers of foot regiments. In July and August 1643 the Earl of Denbigh laid out £22 12s. 10d. on scarves and ribbon for his troops.[21] Moreover, among the items of equipment promised on 22 March 1644 by Sir Thomas Myddelton for the newly raised infantry regiment of his cousin, Sir William were 'scarves for the sergeants and drummers', besides 6d. apiece for ribbons for the said regiment of foot'.[22] Scarves were an essential purchase for captains of cavalry troops alongside the clothing and equipment of trumpeters. The item was vital for battlefield identification and unit identity, even though it is possible that within individual armies there were variations between regiments and even troops, depending on the taste of their commanding officers. In 1636 the captains of troops of the Norfolk

16 LRO, Quarter Sessions Papers 3/93; HMC, *Tenth Report*, *App. VI*, pp.69–70.

17 Markham, *The Souldiers Accidence*, pp.29–30, 33, 44, 46.

18 BL, MS Harley 2128, fols 31v.–32r.

19 *Emblematic Flag Devices*, pp.18, 96, 102, 196, 256.

20 DWL, MS Modern 12.7: 'A list of the colours taken by the Earl of Essex, general of the parliament army at Edgehill, 23 October 1642', fol. 134r.

21 TNA, SP28/34, fols 237r., 250r., 265r., 274v.

22 *CSPD 1644*, p.65.

militia were advised that each trooper should be equipped with 'a scarf of rich crimson taffeta, according as is now used in the war, which is to be two ells in length, cut through the breadth at 15d. a piece'.[23]

The importance of scarves was emphasised by Vernon, who reported:

> Every horseman must wear a scarf of his general's colours, and not leave it off neither in his quarters nor out of his quarters, it being an ornament unto him, besides it will cause him to forbear many unfitting actions, as being thereby distinguished from the vulgar or common soldier, it is likewise a good and visible mark in time of battle to know one another.[24]

The Dutch engraving, 'Ruiter met vaandel' (rider with banner), from *De ruiterschool* (1640) of the workshop of Jacob de Gheyn, in the collection of the Rijksmuseum, Amsterdam, shows a mounted cavalry cornet wearing a flowing scarf suspended from his shoulder and tied at his right hip.[25] According to Peter Young (writing in the late 1960s), 'Earlier in the war a Parliamentarian officer would not have worn a crimson scarf. In 1642 the orange-tawny colours of the Earl of Essex were universally adopted by the roundheads, and crimson scarves were the mark of a Royalist'.[26] This idea has become somewhat of an outdated cliché, however, and at least in the Parliamentarian armies it is evident that other colours were worn. Contemporary portraits of Sir Thomas Myddelton at Chirk Castle illustrate a red or crimson scarf around his arm, while another of Sir Thomas Fairfax in Manchester Art Gallery has him wearing a green one.

His cousin, Sir William Fairfax, and the Lancashire commander Colonel John Booth are each depicted with long and luxurious black scarves, worn over high quality armour and clothing. Although it is possible that Fairfax was painted in September 1642 and the precise date of the Booth portrait is unknown, both men fought at Nantwich in 1644 and after the battle the wounded Fairfax convalesced at Dunham Massey, the Booth family seat. In the same year Captain Henry Westby, commander of a troop of horse under the command of Sir Thomas Fairfax, paid for a 10s. for a 'great black scarf', and 9s. for a second one.[27] Moreover, Nathan Drake's journal of the sieges of Pontefract mentions another Northern Association officer (Colonel Eden of Bright's regiment) in a buff coat and black scarf being killed during a skirmish on 14 April 1645.[28] Given that the previous year Brereton paid 2s. for an ell for silk (see below), Westby's scarves may have been upwards of six yards in length. This appears entirely possible as the item depicted in the William Fairfax portrait is heavily fringed in gold lace and tassels, and appears to hang (even with a large knot) to at least the wearer's knee. Whether Fairfax, Booth, Westby and Eden's use of black scarves was a common feature among

23 *State Papers Relating to Musters*, p.202.
24 Vernon, *The Young Horse-man*, p.8.
25 Amsterdam, Rijksmuseum, *De ruiterschool*, *Jacob de Gheyn (II) (workshop of), after Jacob de Gheyn (II), 1640.*
26 Young, *Edgehill*, pp.27–8.
27 SA, OD/1420. Thanks to David Evans for this reference.
28 George Fox, *The Three Sieges of Pontefract Castle* (Leeds: The Old Hall Press, 1987), p.52.

Parliamentarian officers is uncertain, but there remains a good possibility that such a colour was adopted by officers of the Northern Association, to which each of them belonged.

A voucher of 7 July 1643 records the purchase by Sir William Brereton for his own troop of an ell (45 inches) of crimson scarf silk at 2s. the ell. It remains uncertain how ubiquitous this colour was among the rest of the Cheshire horse and indeed his army.[29] Although evidence from contemporary paintings and bills suggest that officer's scarves were long and trimmed with gilt fringing, those issued to troopers and non-commissioned officers of Brereton's own troop correspond with the dimensions and construction techniques suggested by the instructions given to the pre-war Norfolk militia. In each case this would equate to an item (once both pieces of cloth were sewn together) measuring 90 inches in length and 22½ inches wide, certainly large enough to be positioned about the wearer's body, even over body armour. Although surviving examples from the Civil War period are rare, two in the collection of the V&A are made of tawny-orange taffeta silk, and measure approximately 98½ inches x 27½ inches, and 82½ inches x 18¾ inches respectively.[30]

Common methods of identification also included ribbons or 'favours', lengths of tape or ribbon given by some captains to soldiers of companies and other sub-units, to be sewn onto their coats or caps and thus distinguish them from others. In the summer of 1642 members of the Worcestershire trained bands were provided with 16 yards of broad ribbon, at a cost of 8s., with which to make 'colours', presumably to either decorate their company's standard, or to attach to their hats or clothing.[31] On 22 June 1643 Brereton spent £3 12s. on 'ribbon for colours for soldiers' of the Cheshire Parliamentarian army, while in March 1644 Myddelton agreed to provide (among other items) '6d. apiece for ribbons' for his cousin's recently formed regiment of foot'.[32] Such items could also indicate allegiance to a particular commander. When Thomas Sanders of the Derbyshire horse returned to the county in July 1645 from service under Sir Thomas Fairfax, he reported 'my soldiers wear his Excellency's colours and for that are called rogues and threatened to pull them out of their hats – [Sir John] Gell's soldiers wear his colours and brave it to our faces'.[33]

According to Philip Haythornthwaite, field signs represented 'a visual proclamation of the wearer's allegiance'.[34] Examples include sprigs of foliage worn by Parliamentarians at First Newbury and pieces of white paper employed by some of the New Model's soldiers at Naseby. By their

29 TNA, SP28/8, fol. 15r.

30 Thanks to Ian Dicker for this material and sharing information on his reconstructions.

31 Malcolm Atkin, *Worcestershire under Arms: An English County During the Civil Wars* (Barnsley: Pen and Sword, 2004), p.17.

32 TNA, SP28/196/3, fol. 7r.; *CSPD 1644*, p.65.

33 DRO, D1232/0/40; Ron Slack, 'Colonel Gell and Major Sanders: Internal feuding among the Parliamentary forces in Derbyshire during the Civil Wars of 1642–1646', *Derbyshire Miscellany*, 16 (2) (2001), pp. 34–48.

34 Philip Haythornthwaite, *English Civil War, 1642–1651: An Illustrated Military History* (Worthing: Littlehampton, 1983), p.141.

nature though, such field signs were easily open to misinterpretation and abuse. Also important were 'field words' and passwords. Fighting together created an *esprit de corps* among troops and companies, maybe even within the entire regiment. Battle cries and field words are likely to have solidified these bonds and shored up morale. According to a London-based account of the Parliamentarian triumph at Middlewich on 13 March 1643, 'Their word was *Prince Rupert*, Our's *The Lord of Hosts*, And so you see that *The Lord of Hosts* overcame *Prince Rupert*.'[35] Moreover, in common military practice, pickets and sentries of most armies are likely to have employed local passwords, which were presumably changed on a regular basis. According to the Parliamentarian newsbook *Magnalia Dei,* field words were part of the subterfuge employed by Cheshire and Shropshire troops during the night attack on Moreton Corbet on 8 September 1644, when:

> First, the commander [Lieutenant] Colonel Reinking, seconded by Captain Lord Calvin [of Brereton's foot regiment] gave the word, which was '*Will*' and '*Tom*', with order that if any asked who they were, to answer, '*Will*' and if the other answered not, *Tom,* they should give fire; this being done, he sent drums at a field's distance from the house, with order to beat a march as soon as ever the assault began, which they did accordingly, and thereby made the enemy think that there had been a great strength, when as, indeed, it was no such matter; then presently the lieutenant colonel calling aloud to bring up such a regiment to such a place, and such a regiment to another place (this much daunted the hearts of the enemy at the hearing thereof) and then he sent some to discover the sentry, with an order to tell the sentry that they were friends, and to hold him in discourse until they had notice; which service was so well performed on all parts that before the sentinel knew who we were, our ladders were mounted and we in possession of one of their works.[36]

In terms of clothing it was desirable among Civil War cavalry to wear thick leather coats known as 'buff coats' as protection against sword cuts. Made of ox or bull hide, these tended to be purchased by officers and troopers themselves, although a good-quality officer's coat cost was considerably expensive. Writing in early 1642 the Earl of Bedford had recommended that troopers 'be handsomely furnished [in] comely apparel with coat of buff with long skirts [and a] coat of cloth to keep both himself and furniture from the violence of the weather'.[37] An inventory of the goods of Edmund Jodrell of Yeardsley, Cheshire, taken on 28 April 1643 by Captain-Lieutenant Zankey of Brereton's troop, included two buffcoats valued at £1 13s. 4d. each, 'one bull hide dressed buff-like' and three dressed buckskins, as well as 'two riding coats of broadcloth, the one set with plate [silver-gilt] buttons' at £2 10s. together.[38] Moreover, in 1662 Colonel Brooke left his 'buff doublet' in his will, probably an expensive and substantial item analogous to surviving

35 *Cheshire's Successe*.

36 Vicars, *Magnalia Dei*, pp.24–5.

37 TNA, SP16/492, fol. 49v.

38 JRL, JOD/62c.

examples belonging to Sir Thomas Fairfax and Sergeant Major Thomas Sanders of the Derbyshire horse.[39] In addition to their more general clothing there is evidence to show that cavalry troopers were supplied with riding coats (sometimes referred to in sources as long coats or smock coats) for cold and winter wear. During the siege of Chester Brereton's horse and dragoons were quartered in open terrain to the Welsh side of the city, and constantly engaged in patrolling and picket duty.

On 8 November 1645 Sir William reported to the Speaker that in establishing such *perdues* (outposts) his soldiers had been hampered 'by extreme foul weather which is violent that our men cannot endure out of doors'. Similarly, the following month, Sir Richard Lloyd, the Royalist governor of Holt remarked, 'the river [Dee] is frozen, and can be passed over with horse and foot under this castle', while Brereton recounted on 9 January 1646 that 'Our duty is very hard; the weather extreme and piercing.'[40] Three documentary entries refer directly to the issue of troopers' coats for the Cheshire army of Parliament. During the winter of 1643–4 the Nantwich tailors Peter, John and William Burstow, and Thomas Greenall made 344 infantry coats and 55 troopers' coats, and delivered them to Commissary Hinde on 22 February 1644.[41] Instructions given in a tailor's bill of 2 October 1643 one of Brereton's officials, state: 'we desire you to let Captain Stukeley and his cornet have so much frieze as will make 40 suits and smock coats, and we will see you satisfied for the same'.[42] Colonel Duckenfield disbursed the sum of £41 8s. for '60 and odd new coats for the troop and for other clothes for some of them', in either November 1644 or April 1645 when troop was at Beeston.[43] The 'smock coats' (riding coats) for Stukeley's troop were to be made of frieze, while another bill for 'fabric and trimmings' supplied to the same unit, dated 3 October 1643, included a further 'sixteen yards of frieze at 4s. per yard', costing £3 4s., although it is likely that this went into cassocks or other clothing for his trumpeters.[44]

According to Eric Kerridge, 'Friezes had a hard, rough feel. They were best suited to winter gowns and rough overcoating, but were also used for doublets and jerkins'.[45] They were often written about as being explicitly for winter. In 1549 William Baldwin remarked, 'The coarsest frieze best pleaseth the finest of them in winter', whereas William Stafford in 1581 reflected on serving men being content to go in 'a Kendal coat in the summer, and a frieze coat in winter'.[46] Moreover, Welsh frieze was described by Thomas Fuller in

39 CRO, DBN/D/1/1; Leeds, Royal Armouries Collections, III.4593; York, Castle Museum (uncatalogued).

40 BL, MS Add. 11332, fol. 59v.; 11333, fols 36r., 107r.; *BLB*, II, 840, 1007, 1220.

41 TNA, SP28/49/1, fol. 100v.

42 TNA, SP28/8, fol. 17r.

43 TNA, SP28/128/10, fol. 8r.

44 TNA, SP28/8, fol. 16r.

45 Eric Kerridge, *Textile Manufacturers in Early Modern England* (Manchester: Manchester University Press, 1985), p.19.

46 *The Canticles or Ballads of Salomon, phrase like declared in English Metres, by William Baldwin* (London, 1549), p.4; F.J. Furnival (ed.), *William Stafford's Compendious or Brief Examination of Certain Ordinary Complaints of Divers of Our Country Menin these our days* (London, 1876), p.64.

the 1660s as 'a coarse kind of cloth, than which none warmer to be worn in winter'.[47] A further supply of woollen cloth to Brereton's army came in the form of items delivered by Captain Millington to his servant in April 1645. Millington was involved in the seizure of cattle and cloth from North Wales with other Cheshire troops in April 1645. The batch consisted of 12 yards of gladen (Welsh flannel – *gwlanen*), four yards of coarse gladen, four and a half yards of red cloth, four yards of green cloth, one and a quarter yards of green cloth and three more yards of white gladen in two pieces.[48] Although it is not known how this fabric was subsequently used, it is possible that some of it went on riding coats for the horse or dragoons. The Parliamentarians certainly made use of Welsh cloth. A consignment they captured at Oswestry in June 1644 intended for Rupert's army, instead clothed the Shropshire forces and the Earl of Denbigh's regiment of foot.[49] Cottons in the seventeenth century were cheap woollen fabrics, mainly produced in Wales and the north-west of England. They appear to have been regularly used for riding coats, even among the elite. Conversely, baize was produced largely in the West Country, although it is possible that as much of the cloth supplied to Sir William Brereton's forces derived from Lancashire merchants, they were supplied with quantities of so-called 'Manchester baize'.

According to Kerridge, this was made in and around Rossendale.[50] William Camden, writing in 1610, spoke highly of the clothing industry in Manchester, saying 'it has the best trade of any in these Northern parts … Manchester surpasses the towns hereabouts in woollen manufacture … woollen cloths called Manchester cottons'.[51] Unpublished accounts pertaining to Sir Thomas Aston's regiments of horse and dragoons record the kitting out of his men with 'long' or 'large' coats (riding coats) ordered from local tailors. These coats were unlined, presumably because they were to be worn over doublets and jump coats (a short, buttoned type of soldier's coat), and in some cases were constructed from 2½ to 3 yards of broadcloth, silk, buttons (including a long button) and other items such as loop-lace. Reconstructions of such garments by Ian Dicker, based on a surviving example in Colchester Museum and another in the V&A collection, are of grey broadcloth and flared at the hip to facilitate riding and the wearing of clothing underneath. They also have 24 Turk's head buttons down the front.[52] As for other Royalist mounted units, Sir Thomas Dallison, in command of Prince Rupert's regiment at Welshpool informed the Prince on 4 August 1644:

> I have had 113 coats and caps for foot soldiers in the house of my Lord Powys, a hundred of which are blue, which will serve very well for your Highness's regiment

47 Thomas Fuller, *The History of the Worthies of England* (London, 1840), III, p.485.

48 CRO, DDX/428, fol. 85v.; *BLB*, I, 199–200.

49 *The Perfect Occurrences of Parliament and Chief Collections of Letters*, 28 June–5 July 1644; *CSPD, 1644*, p.429.

50 Kerridge, *Textile Manufactures*, p.104. See also, Norman Lowe, *The Lancashire Textile Industry in the Sixteenth Century*, Chetham Society, 20, 3rd series (Manchester, 1972), pp.25, 29.

51 E. Gibson (ed.), William Camden, *Britannia* (London, 1695), II, p.963.

52 <https://the1642tailor.com/?s=long+coat>. Thanks to Gary Ashby for sharing information on these coats.

> of foot. The rest are green, which may be for Colonel Tillier's regiment. There are also three or four hundred yards of cloth, which may serve to make coats for your Highness's regiment of horse.[53]

Trumpeters were an indispensable part of cavalry troops and armies in general. They acted like heralds in that they negotiated with enemy troops, discussed prisoners, delivered terms of surrender, or acted as messengers. It seems that captains of horse often expended large sums of money on items such as trumpet banners and clothing issued to trumpeters. Markham described the more identifiable aspects of trumpeters:

> The trumpet[er] is not bound to any arms at all, more than his sword, which in former times was not allowed, but with the point broken. He shall have a fair trumpet, with cords suitable to his captain's colours, and to his trumpet shall be made fast a fair banner, containing his captain's full coat armour; he may wear scarf and feather, and all other ordinary accoutrements of a horsemen, and for his horse it shall be a good hackney, with gentleman-like furniture.[54]

The previously mentioned bill of 30 May 1643 records the purchase of trumpet banners and stirrups for the trumpeters of Brereton's troop.[55] On 14 October 1645 Anthony Smith, a London supplier, was paid £4 for a trumpet banner and £2 for a trumpet for the same unit.[56] As per standard practice, Brereton's coat of arms was painted on drums belonging to his foot regiment (and probably his dragoons also). Thus, it is probable that in accordance with Markham's view that trumpeters 'shall have a fair trumpet, with cords suitable to his captain's colours, and to his trumpet shall be made fast a fair banner, his captain's full coat armour', these were likewise depicted on them. This is confirmed by payments made by Captain Enys of Myddelton's horse on 5 April 1644. He had 'two ells of green taffeta for the trumpet banners ... at 12s. an ell', fringed green and white, and expended the impressive sum of 25s. apiece 'for the workmanship on two banners'. Enys's brother officer, Captain Thomas Noakes received £150 a few weeks earlier 'to equip himself and his troop with sufficient horses for service in North Wales'. He had further sums in June 1644 for the pay of two corporals, two trumpeters and 62 troopers, and more in July 1644 for three corporals and 40 soldiers. Noakes himself spent £10 11s. for suits and coats for his trumpeters, another 18s. for hats and bands, £4 10s. for two trumpets, and £7 3s. for trumpet banners and cording.[57]

Surviving documents show that specific payments were made for the clothing of Sir William Brereton's and Captain Robert Stukeley's troops. Included in the bills are a number of items for trumpeters, including the materials for what could be *casaques*:

53 *The True Informer*, 17 August 1644; Phillips, *Memorials*, II, p.195.

54 Markham, *Soldiers Accidence*, pp.44–5.

55 TNA, SP28/225/1, fol. 3r.

56 TNA, SP28/152/8, fol. 3r.

57 TNA, SP28/346/1, unfol.

Table 20: Tailor's bill or voucher for Sir William Brereton's troop, 7 July 1643 (TNA, SP28/8, fol. 15r.)

	£	s.	d.
'Bought of William Brereton for your own troop'			
25½ yards of broad cloth at 10s. [the yard]	12	15	00
27½ yards of narrow at 4s. [the yard]	05	10	00
55 more narrow at 3s. 6d. [the yard]	08	05	00
1 ell of crimson scarf silk at 2s. [the ell]	00	02	00
10lb of black and red thread at 2s. 6. [the lb]	01	06	08
For the trumpeters:			
2 ells of silver parchment at 6s. [the ell]	00	12	00
5 yards of fustian at 14d. per yard	00	05	10
1½ dozen coat buttons at 10d. [each]	00	10	03
7 skeins of silk [thread]	00	00	06
1 yard of coloured buckram	00	01	04
6 yards of tape [and] 1 dozen trussers	00	00	09
4¼ yards of 12d. ribbon	00	04	03
Total	29	04	07

Table 21: Bill or voucher for fabric and trimmings supplied to Captain Robert Stukeley, 3 October 1643 (TNA, SP28/8, fol. 16r.)

	£	s.	d.
16 yards of frieze at 4s. per yard	03	04	00
3 yards of canvas	00	04	00
3 yards of red baize	00	06	00
6 yards of Dutch jean at 1s. 6d. per yard	00	09	00
5 dozen silver and gold buttons	00	12	00
2 collars and 2 pairs of pads	00	01	04
2 dozen trussers	00	00	05
1 quarter of taffeta	00	03	00
6 yards of tape	00	00	06
1 yard silver and gold bobbin [lace]	00	01	00
3 quarters of silk	00	01	09
3 pairs of pockets	00	01	06
2 dozen 6d. ribbon	00	12	00
1 quarter thread	00	01	00
1 yard gold top lace	00	01	00
Total	05	18	09

The 16 yards of frieze purchased for Stukeley's men (above) would imply eight yards per man, and was probably meant to make suits and outer garments. Frieze was a heavier, yet narrower cloth than broadcloth, about 45 inches wide at most. The *casaque* was originally a short garment buttoned along the sleeves and the body under the arms, so that it could be worn as a coat or cloak. Issued to late-Tudor trained bandsmen and workmen, later references to such garments indicate that they had developed into cloak-like outer garments which were often made of expensive cloth, and richly adorned with buttons and lace.[58] These were likely to have been worn over the doublet or buff coat. Such an arrangement is shown in the engraving *Drie trompetters te paard*. The trumpeters' casaques have long-flowing sleeves and shoulder rolls, and are adorned with decorative lace. Another image, *Trompetter te paard*, shows a trumpeter wearing such a garment over body armour, and sporting a sword and pistols. Similarly, a painting by the Dutch artist Gerard ter Borch, *Officer Writing a Letter, with Trumpeter* (*c.* 1648–9) in the Philadelphia Museum of Art, depicts a cavalry trumpeter wearing a blue cassock trimmed with gold and black lace, with open, hanging sleeves and what appear to be loop fastenings at the front.[59] The garment is worn over a sleeved buff coat, while from the trumpeter's left shoulder, suspended from a gold and black cord is his trumpet, and over the right he wears a baldric, in which he has a sword. He also wears thigh-length cavalry boots with rowel spurs and holds a broad-brimmed felt hat.

Specifically issued to footsoldiers and dragoons, soldier's coats – worn over a fitted doublet and breeches – formed the basic item of clothing. Any notion of actual uniformity in the style and shade of clothing issued to Civil War troops is a modern idea, however. There appears to have been no one set pattern for coats, nor construction method, while linings could be entirely arbitrary. Coat colours might also fluctuate, depending upon the availability of batches of cloth and dye stuffs. Issues of clothing to Civil War armies are sometimes referred to as 'suits' or 'uniforms', which could include coats and breeches, and perhaps other items such as caps. In October 1646 'soldiers' suits according to the pattern of cloths shrunk, as they are delivered for Sir Thomas Fairfax's soldiers, at 18s. apiece' were contracted for troops going to Ireland.[60] On 5 April 1645 Colonel Duckenfield paid £85 to John Gaskell, a Manchester draper 'for new uniforms for my regiment'.[61] At the rate of 18s. each, this might compute to over 90 sets of coats and breeches. Moreover, Brereton's dragoon captain, John Bramhall paid various sums to local tailors in May 1643 for the making of suits of clothes for his drummers, as well as laying out £1 4s. 3d. for another suit.[62]

A number of examples exist for the supply of soldier's coats to Brereton's army. Possibly in early 1643 Captain Bramhall received from Commissary Hinde 52 coats for his dragoon company 'which were accordingly disposed of'.[63] Four Nantwich tailors, Peter, John and William Burstow, and Thomas Greenall made 344 infantry coats and 55 troopers' coats during the winter of 1643–4 and delivered them to Hinde on 22 February 1644.[64] They were paid 1s. 2d. per soldier's coat and 1s. 8d. per trooper's coat for their construction and carriage. On 24 December 1644 Brereton paid £100 'to William Barratt

58 Stuart Peachey, *Male Coats and Cassocks*, Clothes of the Common People in Elizabethan and Early Stuart England, 13 (Bristol: Stuart Press, 2014), pp.56–9.

59 Rijksmuseum, *De ruiterschool*; Philadelphia, Philadelphia Museum of Art, The William L. Elkins Collection, E1924-3-21.

60 *CJ*, IV, p.698.

61 BL, MS Harley 2130, fol. 91v.

62 BL, MS Harley 2128, fols 23v., 26v.

63 BL, MS Harley, 2128, fol. 34v.

64 TNA, SP28/49/1, fol. 100v.

of Ridgeway in Cheshire to buy cloth for soldiers' coats in Cheshire, which was accordingly bought and disposed of for the soldiers' coats'.[65] A rough estimate of the number of garments this might have produced is not straightforward, especially as the price of woollen cloth depended largely on its type. However, the frieze purchased to clothe Stukeley's troopers in October 1643 cost 4s. per yard. Given that as a rule of thumb a yard and a half of broadcloth was enough for a soldiers' coat, this could equated to enough fabric to make up in excess of 300 garments. An indication that coat buttons were purchased separately comes from a payment in early 1644 of 6s. 2d. for such items for Lieutenant Colonel Massey's company.[66]

Much of the fabric for clothing appears to have been locally procured. On 19 November 1644 the constables of Aston disbursed £10 to Robert Massey, of Warrington, a local mercer who had previously supplied cloth to Parliamentarian troops in Lancashire.[67] Payments for cloth for Duckenfield's regiment include £5 disbursed to 'Henry Bradshaw, draper in Manchester' for Captain Richard Brereton's company, sometime between 13 November 1643 and 4 July 1644, and a further £30 laid out 'arms to furnish my Irish company and some clothes for them' in March 1644.[68] Some consignments of soldiers' coats for the Cheshire army specify their colour. Between October 1642 and October 1643 the constables of Mere in Northwich Hundred paid the sum of £2 14s. 10d. for grey coats sent to Knutsford garrison, most probably for soldiers under Colonel Leigh.[69] Similarly, in April 1645 the Staffordshire Committee disbursed £30 12s. 11d. for grey coats for Captain Monke's company, belonging to Brereton's own regiment.[70] Three months earlier, the same committee had laid out £9 6s. for the making up soldier's coats, which could have been an earlier batch.[71] In this light, it is possible to suggest that a proportion, if not most of the Cheshire foot were clothed in grey coats. The colour grey was the product of mixing black and white sheep fleeces, or of using dark fleeces unmixed. Grey is often referred to in relation to countrymen, and as it was undyed it may have been cheaper than coloured fabric.

The Yorkshire sheep farmer Henry Best reported that 'three or four black sheep do well in a flock, to furnish one with wool for grey stockings and other uses; but many black sheep in a keeping are neither seemly nor profitable, for their wool is usually hairy, scarce vendible'.[72] Shades of grey would differ considerably depending on the hues of black or white of the original fleeces and the quantities mixed. If Brereton's army obtained significant amounts of cloth and uniforms from north of the Mersey, so did other

65 TNA, SP28/152/7, fol. 16r.

66 TNA, SP28/128/13, fol. 30v.; SP28/224, unfol.

67 AA, unlisted receipt, dated 19 November 1644.

68 TNA, SP28/128/10, fol. 7v.; BL, MS Harley 2130, fol. 89r.

69 BL, MS Harley 2128, fol. 60r.

70 TNA, SP28/134/12, fol. 395r.; Lich. RO, MS Lichfield 24, fol. 83r.

71 TNA, SP28/134/12, fol. 391v.

72 G. Andrews (ed.), Henry Best, *Rural Economy in Yorkshire in 1641: Being the Farming and Account Books of Henry Best, of Elmswell, in the East Riding of the County of York*, SS (Edinburgh: Blackwood, 1857), p.84.

Parliamentarian forces in Lancashire and the Midland counties. As Edwards asserts, 'Lancashire clothiers, especially those from Manchester, supplied Cheshire and Staffordshire forces, as well as their own troops with cloth'.[73] On 25 December 1643 the Staffordshire Committee purchased 118 yards of grey cloth from Thomas Hanson of Manchester at 2s. a yard for soldier's uniforms; in March 1644 they paid the figure of £48 4s. to Yorkshire clothiers, and seven months later £54 14s. was disbursed to Lancashire suppliers.[74] On 2 May 1644 the Staffordshire committee ordered 'that the grey cloth in the treasurer's custody shall be delivered to such as Colonel Rugley shall appoint to make coats forthwith for his regiment. And the treasurer to keep a note of the number of yards delivered'.[75] Moreover, the Staffordshire Order Book records that in May 1645 8½ yards of grey cloth were delivered to Captain Roper's quartermaster.[76]

Similarly, a number of sources, including the testimony of Lucy Hutchinson, mention that Sir Gell's Derbyshire foot regiment was issued with grey coats.[77] It has been suggested that the same were common among northern Parliamentarian regiments. During 1570s Lancashire militia troops sent to Ireland were issued coats variously of 'red, of 6s. 8d. the yard, Gascoigne fashion'; 'of white cloth made of the fashion of a cassock'; and 'broad blue at 8s. the yard, each coat containing one yard and a quarter'.[78] At Beverley on 7 September 1640 it was ordered, 'that whereas the trained band in Yorkshire are to attend His Majesty in the service now intended, that every common soldier for this town shall have a grey coat for the value of 8s. or thereabouts at discretion of Mr Mayor'.[79] Although this was meant for the East Riding trained bands, it is possible that other Yorkshire units were clad in coats of the same colour. On 12 October 1643 the deputy lieutenants of Lancashire ordered the supply of 200 grey coats to Colonel Rigby, but as the same issue included snaphaunces and cartridge boxes the soldiers could have been dragoons.[80] Moreover, the Committee of Both Kingdoms ordered the Lancashire gentlemen on 18 March 1646 to 'clothe Colonel [John] Booth's regiment, and make them fit to march with all expedition' to North Wales, although no there is no indication of what colour the uniforms were meant to be.[81] More certain, however, is the receipt from London manufacturers of 36 red soldier's coats, along with white cloth to make draws and waistcoats by Sir Thomas Myddelton in October 1644.[82]

Outer clothing, such as coats and breeches, were usually made by tailors in their own workshops, although in supplying the Cheshire Parliamentarian

---

73 Edwards, *Dealing in Death*, p.138.

74 TNA, SP28/134/12, fols 357r., 384v.

75 *Committee at Stafford*, p.110.

76 TNA, SP28/134/12, fol. 394v.

77 Lucy Hutchinson, *Memoirs of the life of Colonel Hutchinson* (London: H.G. Bohn, 1863), pp.139, 145; TNA, SP28/226/3, fol. 12v.; SP28/226/2, fol. 2r.

78 LRO, DDKE/Box 122/1, fols 50a, 50d, 55d; *HMC, Fourteenth Report, App. IV*, pp.588–9.

79 RA, BC/II/7/4 (Minute book of the Governors and Beverley Corporation, 1597–1660).

80 HMC, *Tenth Report*, IV, p.67.

81 *CSPD 1645–7*, pp.408–9.

82 TNA, SP28/211, fols 130v.–141r.; SP28/300/1, fol. 93v.; SP28/346/1, unfol.

soldiers a magazine or factory might have been set up (perhaps in Nantwich). Captain Bramhall, possibly a mercer before the war, engaged in producing garments with his mother in the town, charging his soldiers various sums for their supply. This probably involved the purchase of cloth, which was followed by cutting out from patterns, before being made up by tailors or finishers. Charles I established factories at Oxford and Reading, to manufacture clothing for the main Royalist army.[83] In Cheshire, on 20 May 1643 Bramhall disbursed £1 4s. 3d. 'for cloth to make my drummer a suit of clothes' and a further 3s. to a tailor for making it up. He also paid the sum of 11s. 1d. to Thomas Mottershaw for made up uniforms, 5s. 4d. to Henry Meeke for trimming a suit, with a further 9d. for buttons.[84] In April 1644 while Colonel Duckenfield's foot soldiers were at Adlington the sum of £1 was paid to Roger Ridgeway, a local tailor for making up soldiers' coats.[85] In January 1645 the Staffordshire Committee laid out £9 6s. for making coats. These might have been those received by Captain Thomas Monke's company of Sir William Brereton's regiment April 1645, at a cost £30 12s.[86]

Drummers were vital for beating the step and the undertaking of special roles, such as communicating with the enemy. In 1635 William Barriffe stated: 'the drum is the voice of the commander, the spur of the valiant and the heart of the coward, and by it they must receive their directions, when the roaring cannon, the clashing of arms, the neighing of horses, and other confused noise causes than neither captain, nor other officer can be heard'.[87] Drum majors, such as Abraham Butterworth of Duckenfield's regiment, were responsible for the training of drummers and the maintenance of instruments, and were on the strength of the colonel's company. As such, they were paid and treated as non-commissioned officers. As for the supply of drums and drumming equipment, in January1643 Colonel Duckenfield paid 13s. for a drum for his regiment from Thomas Bostock, presumably a local maker, while the sum of 12s. 4d. was spent on drum heads. On an unknown date, Drum Major Butterworth was given the sum of £5 by his colonel, being part of his arrears of pay.[88] The Parliamentarian governor of Leek, Colonel John Bowyer, regularly employed his drum major in the maintenance of his regimental drums, on one occasion sending him to Stafford to purchase parts and make repairs.[89] A drum, valued at £1 6s. 8d. was listed among the belongings of Edmund Jodrell two months later, although going by the cost of other examples and because it was among other sequestered goods it might have been over-priced, although the instruments supplied to the Parliamentarian army in Ireland in October 1646 cost 28*s*. each.[90]

83 David and Hilary Hopkins, *The Tale of a Soldier's Coat: The Story of the Experimental Reconstruction of a 1643 Oxford Royalist Soldier's Coat* (Bristol: Stuart Press, 2000), p.5.

84 BL, MS Harley 2128, fols 26v., 23v., 28v., 31r.

85 TNA, SP28/128/10, fol. 5r.

86 TNA, SP28/134/12, fols 391v., 359r.; Lich. RO, MS Lichfield 24, fol. 83r.

87 William Barriffe, *Military discipline: or, The young artillery man* (London, 1635), pp.11–12.

88 TNA, SP28/128/10, fols 4v, 5v.

89 TNA, SP28/134/5, fols 75v., 79r.

90 JRL, JOD/62c; *CJ*, IV, p.698.

Drummer, fifer and pikemen of the trained bands. (Author's collection)

Similarly, Captain John Brooke instructed the constables of Aston on 25 March 1644 'to collect and gather within your township by distress or otherwise, the sum of 10s. for the buying of drums and colours' for the completion of his company'.[91] On 20 May 1645 Nicholas Higginbottom was reimbursed £2 for 'providing drums and pikes for the garrisons in Wirral, and carriages to carry the said drums to the said garrisons'.[92] In May 1643 'three ensigns, four drums' and various weapons were seized by Brereton's soldiers from Royalist prisoners at Market Drayton, while 'many drums' were among a large haul of ammunition and equipment that fell into Parliamentarian hands at Whitchurch.[93] Sir William paid £4 10s. in July 1643 for the painting of his coat of arms on 20 drums – enough to fit out his entire regiment at two drums per company – while 16 drums were shipped as part of a consignment of arms, equipment and black powder from London to Liverpool for the Cheshire foot in March 1645.[94] Contrastingly, in April 1644 Gyles Smart, a London-based supplier, was contracted for 20 drums for Myddelton's foot.[95] Amongst the items of trained band equipment listed at Wythenshawe on 25 February 1644 was a large drum painted with the device of its Royalist owner, Robert Tatton, as well as three other drums.[96]

It has been assumed that drummers during the Civil Wars in Britain were issued with distinctive or expensive clothing, or at least coats by their commanding officers. Drawing on the Norwich city accounts Peter Young asserted that in 1587–8 'a drummer's coat of green kersey was embellished

91 AA, unlisted warrant, dated 25 March 1644.
92 BL, MS Harley 2130, fols 88r., 91v.
93 Malbon, pp.53, 58–9.
94 TNA, SP28/225/1, fol. 3r.; CRO, DDX/428, fol. 80r.; *BLB*, I, 139.
95 TNA, SP28/346/1, unfol.; SP28/346/2, unfol.
96 JRL, TW/287.

with eleven yards of lace and six yards of 'pointing'. Not only the coats [he said], but the sleeves must, therefore, must have ornamented with lace'.[97] The wearers, however, were hardly faced with the rigours of warfare, and as Neil Younger adds, 'Town governments such as Norwich's often took considerable pride in their military displays.'[98] Direct evidence for the issue of distinctive coats and uniforms to drummers during the 1640s is rather lacking, and it is possible that in most cases they were dressed the same their fellow soldiers. Among the clothing and fabric given to Bramhall's Cheshire dragoons are payments made on 20 May 1643 of £1 4s. 3d. to a mercer of Nantwich 'for cloth to make my drummer a suit of clothes' and a further 3s. to a tailor for making it up. Additionally, on 1 February 1644 the figure of 11s. 3d. was kept back from Drummer Ralph Knowsley's pay for cloth he had been given.[99] In May 1644 treasurer Croxton paid another 3s. 'for making clothes' for one of Bramhall's drummers, and 2s. 6d. for garments for the drummers under Sergeant Major Croxton.[100]

The number of soldier's coats issued to Bramhall's company in early 1643 corresponds with the number of mustered dragoons during this period (50), while considerable quantities of cloth were purchased for officers and non-commissioned officers in December 1642 and January 1643.[101] When Skippon's regiment of Essex's army was raised in November 1642 each of the captain's companies received 107 red lined with yellow coats, enough to include 100 soldiers, two sergeants, three corporals and two drummers.[102] On the weight of this and other evidence, it is possible to confer with Michael Pfiel's view that 'it appears highly questionable if all (up to 20) company drummers did really wear expensive uniforms', and therefore in most cases were issued with ordinary soldier's coats instead.[103]

A persistent difficulty encountered by all Civil War armies was the supply of boots and shoes for its soldiers. Riding boots, issued to the cavalry, and perhaps some dragoons, were more expensive than shoes. A batch of 1,000 pairs of cavalry boots was delivered to the Eastern Association's agents at St Albans in 1644 by the London shoemakers Richard Crofts and Edward Poole. Likewise, though at times Manchester's officers and men obtained footwear and cloth from local suppliers, in late 1644 the army's treasurer employed a number of men to acquire boots and shoes in bulk, which he issued to captains, 'deducting the costs from the sums owed to their companies for pay'.[104] Moreover, 2,000 pairs of boots 'of good neats-leather, well-tanned and waxed' were purchased for troopers sent to Ireland in 1649 at a cost of

97 Peter Young, *Edgehill 1642: The Campaign and the Battle* (Kineton: The Roundwood Press, 1967), p.24.

98 Neil Younger, *War and Politics in the Elizabethan Counties* (Manchester: Manchester University Press, 2012), p.62.

99 BL, MS Harley 2128, fols 23v., 26v., 28r.

100 TNA, SP28/152/3, fol. 8v.

101 BL, MS Harley 2128, fol. 34v.

102 Stuart Peachey and Alan Turton, *Old Robin's Foot* (Leigh-on-Sea: Partizan Press, 1987), p.4; Michael Pfiel, *Drumming in the Civil Wars* (Bristol: Stuart Press, 1997), p.11.

103 Pfiel, *Drumming*, p.11.

104 Holmes, *Eastern Association*, p.152.

14s. 10d. a pair.[105] Shoes worn during the English Civil Wars were low and straight-sided. There is no record of the issue of start-ups (calf-length lace up boots worn by agricultural labourers and servants) to armies of either side, and it is possible that these would have been regarded more as a mark of a lower-class countryman than a soldier. Among the contracts for large numbers of shoes sent to Ireland, one of June 1642 specified that the 10,000 pairs were to be of well-seasoned leather in five sizes (nine to 13).[106] A similar contract for the supply of the New Model Army in January 1645 stipulated:

> 4,500 pair of shoes with good neats-leather with good soles of the several sizes of tens, elevens, twelves and thirteens of each size, a like number of all of them to be punched, and each pair tacked together and marked on the soles with the several marks hereafter mentioned at 2s. 3d. a pair, to be brought into the Tower of London.[107]

The sizes of the thousands of shoes indented for by the New Model in particular, equate roughly to modern British sizes between seven and 10, therefore indicating that to some extent Civil War examples were meant to be both comfortable and practical. Shoes contracted for the Parliamentarian army in Ireland in October 1646 cost 2s. 10d. the pair.[108] Like other Parliamentarian forces, quartermasters and officers of the Cheshire army obtained footwear from a range of sources, some of which were local. While returning from London to Cheshire in June 1644 Sir William Brereton purchased 30 pairs of cavalry boots from Thomas Pendleton at Northampton 'where boots are cheap', and it is possible that Colonel Henry Brooke, who accompanied his commander-in-chief to the capital and back, obtained items for his own troop at the same juncture.[109] It is likely also that bulk orders for cavalry boots were placed in London during the summer and autumn of 1644 for the kitting out of the new troops recruited and equipped with horses there under the command of Anglo-Irish officers such as Captain Hawkbridge. On 1 December 1644 74 pairs of shoes were purchased at Nantwich by Lieutenant Thomas Hunt for Captain Sadler's company.[110] On 5 June 1644 the army's Cheshire treasurer, Richard Worrall, expended 3s. for shoes for William Hickman, a soldier under Lieutenant Colonel Venables' command, while 10 days later a pair of boots costing 8s. and stockings to the value of 1s. 6d. were purchased for the gunner, John Fox.[111]

On 29 September 1645 the Nantwich sequestrators paid John Tench, shoemaker, £3 3s. 6d. 'for boots and shoes for the soldiers'. Moreover, the accounts of the officials of the upper division of Wirral Hundred reveal that in November 1645 they disbursed for the garrison at Hooton £1 10s. for three

105 TNA, SP28/300, fols 700v.–2r.; *CSPD 1649–50*, pp.412, 594.

106 'Minute Book for the Commissioners of Irish Affairs (7 June–14 October 1642)', V.F. Snow and A.S. Young (eds), *The Private Journals of the Long Parliament: 2 June to 17 September 1642* (New Haven and London: Yale University Press, 1992), II, p.388.

107 *CSPD 1649–50*, pp.369, 594, 598.

108 *CJ*, IV, p.698.

109 TNA, SP28/152/7, fol. 6v.

110 TNA, SP28/225/4, fol. 723r.

111 TNA, SP28/152/9, fol. 9r.

pairs of cavalry boots, as well as 5s. 6d. for leather for the making of shoes.[112] At the end of October 1645, outstanding vouchers for the army included '£9 9s. for soldiers' stockings and shoes', while treasurer Croxton disbursed 8s. to John Harper of Stafford on 20 November 1645 for cavalry boots 'for soldiers employed at the Leaguer before Chester'.[113] A direct comparison with prices paid by the Eastern Association for shoes suggests that those issued to the Cheshire soldiers were of a better quality. During 1644 two London cordwainers, Richard Crofts and Edward Poole charged 2s. 6d., 2s. 7d. or 3s. 0d. for the shoes they delivered, including transport costs, whilst the Hertfordshire merchant William Gardiner asked for 2s. 8d. and 3s. 4d. a pair.[114] This range of prices reflects differences in quality and the added price for waxing shoes. They may also have been hobnailed.

Although evidence is limited, the footwear issued to Brereton's dragoons may have included both shoes and boots. Some contemporaries felt that the most commodious footwear for dragoons were shoes rather than boots and spurs, which might snag in the stirrup when mounting and dismounting. Wallhausen, writing in 1616, advocated that 'They shall wear, if they so wish, cassocks and *gamaches* [gaitors] instead of boots, for greater ease in walking when necessary.'[115] Some examples survive for purchases of shoes for Bramhall's dragoons, such as the 3s. paid on 12 August 1643 to John Price, a local cordwainer, 'for one pair of shoes for Samuel Elliot, soldier'. Although no widespread issue of boots to the Cheshire dragoons is known, on 2 March 1643 the sum of 9s. was distributed 'to a soldier of Captain Lea for boots', whereas the clothing and accoutrements provided for a dragoon by the Hollingworth constables included boots and spurs.[116] Even so, without further evidence, the question of whether shoes (possibly worn with leather or canvas gaiters, known as 'cockers', designed to protect shoes and hose from damage) were more regularly issued to the Parliamentarian dragoons in Cheshire must remain open.

In terms of arms and equipment, harquebusiers were issued with defensive armour in the form of a helmet, back and breast plates. They were characterised by the use of a form of carbine, called a harquebus, but their weaponry also included a long-bladed cutting sword and a pair of pistols (both wheellocks and firelocks) carried in holsters. Regarding the type and function of the arms and armour of the horse to be employed in the 1640s, Vernon recommended:

> The harquebuses and carbines arming is chiefly offensive, his defensive arms, as only an open cask or headpiece, a back and breast with buff coat under his arms; his offensive arms are a good harquebus, a carbine hanging on his right side in a belt by a swivel, a flask and cartridge case … and good fire-lock pistols in holsters. At his saddle a good stiff sword sharp pointed.[117]

112 BL, MS Harley 1999, fols 69r., 17r.; 2166, fol. 132v.
113 BL, MS Add. 11332, fols 38r., 99r.; *BLB*, II, 796, 887.
114 TNA, SP28/25, fols 136v., 143v.–4r., 163v., 167r.
115 Wallhausen, *Kriegskunst*, pp.16–17.
116 TNA, SP28/196/3, fol. 14v.; BL, MS Harley 2128, fols 29r., 8r.
117 John Vernon, *The Young Horseman, or, The honest plain-dealing cavalier* (London, 1644), p.8.

According to Orrery:

> I acknowledge I would have every private trooper have his sword, or long tuck, his case of pistols, and carbine; and for defence, his back, breast and pot; at least, I would have the front and flanks of every troop in such armour. For besides the terror it gives to an enemy in his doublet, to fight with men of iron, and the encouragement it gives our own men; none knows what proof the armour is of. And it is most certain, that in combat, as well as pursuit, the sword does most execution; and no armour is less than sword proof.[118]

Cavalry armour contracted for the New Model Army in April 1645 included 400 backs, breasts and pots at 20s. per set.[119]

Brereton complained on a number of occasions about the shortage of money to purchase arms for his army and the haphazard nature of their transportation to Cheshire. On 3 January 1643 his troops intercepted a consignment of 50 cases of pistols intended for the King's forces in Lancashire.[120] Soon after the victory at Middlewich Parliament recommended to the Committee for the Safety that Brereton be granted 20 barrels of powder, with match proportionable, 200 muskets, 40 pair of pistols and 20 carbines.[121] Moreover, he petitioned the Speaker on 21 November 1643 for further arms, stating:

> It is my humble suit that when you send a fleet to clear these coasts [the North West and the port of Liverpool in particular] there may be sent down 100 pair of pistols, 300 muskets and 200 or 300 firelocks. These are not to be procured upon any terms in this country wherein I could raise good store of men if I could arm them.[122]

At Westminster between February and June 1644 Brereton campaigned for a better system of the procurement of arms for his increasingly expanding army. On 2 July he acquired 500 captured muskets from Marston Moor. Sir William's troops briefly joined the siege of the city, before travelling to the magazine at Hull, where he purchased £60 worth of pistols and carbines.[123]

The army's main source of finance, and supply of arms and ammunition outside of Cheshire was through Brereton's London treasurers, who obtained important parliamentary grants. A substantial contribution was £2,125 from the revenue of the Court of Wards and Liveries, which was granted on 7 May 1644. This necessitated the purchase from London suppliers of 500 pairs of pistols, 500 saddles, 500 backs and breasts, and 500 cavalry helmets. From this the gunsmiths received £900 for pistols, and the armourer £390 for weapons, leaving a balance of £835 to be paid to Brereton as reimbursement

118 Orrery, *Treatise of the Art of War*, pp.32–3.
119 Mungeam, 'Contracts', 104.
120 *Mercurius Aulicus*, 3 January 1643, p.4.
121 *CJ*, III, p.19.
122 HMC, *Thirteenth Report*, p.157.
123 Malbon, p.140.TNA, SP28/152/7, fols 8r.–v.; *BLB*, II, 796.

for his former procurement of saddles and weapons (presumably all or part of the 500).[124] This sum of £835 would not be received by him, however, until May 1645.[125] Even so, such a considerable order for cavalry equipment coincides with the expansion of the Cheshire horse during the summer of 1644 (including the completion of some existing troops and formation of new commands under Jones, Hawkbridge and others), and thus we may assume that it was issued around that time. Such a pressing need for weapons and armour is confirmed by instructions sent from the Committee of Both Kingdoms to the committees of Northampton, Coventry and Staffordshire on 3 July 1644, informing them, 'There being a present necessity of arms in Cheshire, William Shakeshaft, carrier, is engaged to carry them into Cheshire to Sir William Brereton'.[126] Further supplies of arms and armour for Brereton's horse were secured from London during the spring of 1645.

Particulars of the July 1644 contract do not appear to have emerged until the following April and directions to the carrier were made a week later, although as Dore suggest, the 1645 document is partly in cypher and might refer to a further consignment of cavalry equipment sent from the capital at that time. A separate shipment of equipment and powder was received from London on the *Sarah Bonaventura*, which landed at Liverpool in March 1645. This included 16 drums, 41 cavalry helmets, 67 carbines, 69 swords and sword belts, 75 infantry helmets and 20 barrels of black powder.[127] In a more local context, in November 1642 Duckenfield's troop was equipped with 63 pairs of pistols, 25 carbines and '63 body armours for so many troopers', which had been purchased in London. A total of £35 6s. 4d. was made over to William Davenport 'for his charges in several journeys to London and providing of arms for my troop', while an additional £5 was paid to Captain John Whitworth 'for carrying down the arms and ammunition from London'. Colonel Duckenfield also had three cases of pistols, 10 carbines and powder worth £20 in January 1643 from Brereton (probably brought from London with him), and paid £2 to Thomas Sydebotham for bullets.[128] Moreover, on 16 June 1643 Captain Stone of the Cheshire army was granted £100 to purchase arms for his newly raised troop.[129]

An outstanding voucher of October 1645 records the payment of £10, which was made at Hull on 9 June 1644 to one of Captain Stanley's trumpeters for the purchase of pistols.[130] Similarly, treasurer Richard Worrall paid John Silke, a London gunsmith the sum of £3 9s. 6d. on 10 February 1646 'for pistols and holsters, and for repairing arms'.[131] By comparison, on 6 June 1643 Myddelton purchased in London 200 carbine belts, 200 swivels, 70 powder flasks and 12 pairs of pistols for his newly raised cavalry.[132] Moreover, on 12

124 *CJ*, III, p.484; *LJ*, VI, p.551.
125 CRO, DDX/428, fols 79v., 94r.; *BLB*, I, 159, 406.
126 *CSPD 1644*, p.305.
127 CRO, DDX/428, fols 79r., 45v., 80r.; *BLB*, I, 406, 472, 87, 139.
128 TNA, SP28/128/10, fols 1r., 2r., 5r., 7v.
129 TNA, SP28/134/12, fol. 332v.; *Committee at* Stafford, p.334.
130 TNA, SP28/152/7, fol. 8r; BL, MS Add. 11332, fols 38–40; *BLB*, II, 796.
131 TNA, SP28/152/9, fol. 2v.
132 TNA, SP28/346/1, unfol.

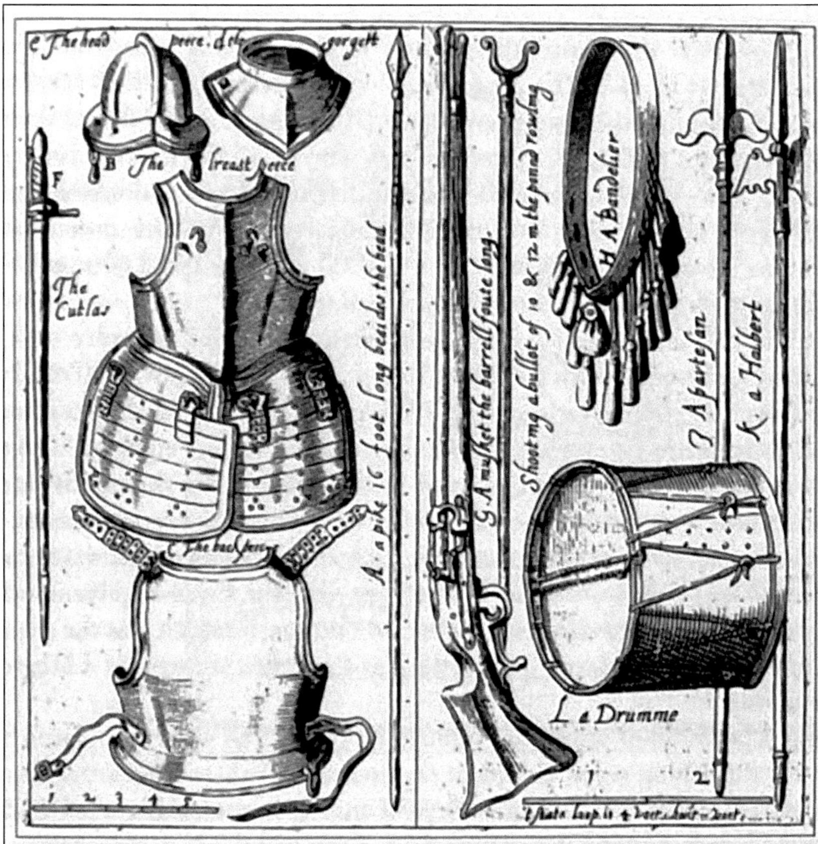

Infantry equipment from Henry Hexham, *The Principles of the Art Military* (1627). (Author's collection)

October 1643 Parliament ordered that '70 pair of pistols and 70 carbines, and the other things belonging to them' were to be delivered to Colonel Ralph Assheton, the Parliamentarian commander in Lancashire.[133]

The supply and retention of good quality troop horses for the cavalry during the Civil War was essential. Cruso stated, 'For the reforming of the cavalry, there is moreover required a singular care, that that the companies be supplied with good horses: wherefore it will be necessary, that when the cavalry is retired from the field, the captains make sale of such horses as be unfit for service, and buy better'.[134] Mounts were a valuable investment, although they were expensive to maintain. In a letter to John Pym on 4 February 1643 Sir William Brereton complained that two of his best horses with their saddles and pistols had been seized at Chester the previous August.[135] Saddle horses for the cavalry 'ideally had to be fifteen hands high, nimble and capable of charging at pace'.[136] The Parliamentarian armies procured many of their mounts on the open market. London (especially

133 HMC, *Tenth Report, App. IV*, p.68.

134 Cruso, *Militarie Instructions*, p.24.

135 HMC, *Portland*, I, p.94.

136 Edwards, 'Turning Ploughshares into Swords', p.68; 'The Supply of Horses to the Parliamentarian and Royalist Armies in the English Civil War', *HR*, 68 (1995), pp. 49–66.

Smithfield) met the heavy demands imposed on it, and a cavalry horse could sell for £10 or £12, a nag for under a pound, although for bulk purchases £6 to £8 was normal. Brereton and Sir Thomas Myddelton obtained horses in the capital in 1643 and 1644, as did the Eastern Association and New Model Army. Regional forces also turned to local suppliers – at Penkridge in Staffordshire the county kept one of the best horse fairs in England, especially for quality saddle mounts. In April 1646 Brereton gave a pass to two studmen at Tutbury stud to travel to Oxford, to bring back three or four stallions, and it is likely that he procured further animals from there for his cavalry.[137]

The Propositions of June 1642 called for the contribution of horses, arms and horsemen, in addition to plate and cash.[138] Parliament's ordinance of 10 May 1643, 'to redress the abuses in taking horses for the supply of the army', authorised the deputy lieutenants and Propositions committees in each county to regulate the acquisition of mounts, while an amendment of 29 May approved the levying of horses by county quota.[139] On 3 December 1642 Parliament ordered that Sir William Brereton should 'have liberty to raise 300 horses in the several counties where they shall be brought in voluntarily, upon Propositions'.[140] A voucher (unpaid receipt) dated 3 June 1645, to Sergeant Major Sankey for £30 for the purchase of horses to complete Brereton's troop of near 100 men relates to original disbursements made in July and September 1644 by him for the same purpose.[141] On 13 January 1645 the troop clerk, John Griffith, paid £12 'for a horse for a trumpeter'.[142] Various mounts were purchased in mid 1644 for the recently formed troop of Michael Jones, including £80 for mounts on 8 June, and payments of £5 and £6 made in August and September respectively for captured animals. In a statement made to the Committee of Accounts on 10 October 1645 Brereton confirmed that they were replacements lost at Malpas, reporting that 'Lieutenant Colonel Jones was wounded and lost very good horses, which was in August 1644.'[143]

Colonel Duckenfield's accounts include a number of payments for horses, equipment and clothing for his troop. Typically, an immediate burden was the provision of cavalry mounts. By May 1643 Duckenfield had disbursed £342 for 43 horses. The various entries illustrate the prices and quantities involved: £80 paid for 'six able horses I put into my troop, valued at £13 6s. 8d. apiece'; another nine mounts, valued at £70; £224 for 32 horses, valued at £7 apiece; and the sum of £48 laid out on 'six horses more put into my troop which I am engaged to pay for at £8 apiece'. Duckenfield later stated, 'All the horses to my knowledge that have served or have been used

---

137 TNA, SP28/134/12, fol. 395r.; LCL, MS Lichfield, fol. 24r.; P. Edwards, *The Horse Trade of Tudor and Stuart England* (Cambridge: Cambridge University Press, 1988), pp.45–6.

138 *LJ*, V, pp.121–2.

139 *LJ*, VI, pp.39–40, 68–9.

140 *CJ*, II, p.874.

141 BL, MS Add. 11332, fol. 38v.; *BLB*, II, 796.

142 TNA, SP28/225/4, fol. 764r.

143 TNA, SP28/152/7, fol. 5r.–v.; SP28/196, fol. 17v.; SP28/225/2, fol. 174r.; BL, MS Add. 11332, fol. 3r.

for my troop which has continued complete about four years has lost the state nothing but as before mentioned, excepting fifteen horses that I had ordered from the deputy-lieutenants for to raise in my neighbourhood about April 1643.'[144] Moreover, the certificate of service for Cornet Richard Brereton, who served in Duckenfield's troop from 27 November 1642 to 13 November 1643, mentions that he constantly mustered three horses of his own completely equipped.[145] Similarly, in early 1644 Duckenfield paid £3 6s. to William Davenport for horses from his Bramhall estate, yet going by this relatively low price they may have been smaller animals rather than expensive cavalry mounts.[146] One complaint about the misuse of horses was submitted by Alexander Hollingworth of Near Hollingworth to the Macclesfield sequestration committee on 15 December 1643:

> Colonel Duckenfield had of me a bay gelding for to be one in his troop, well worth £5 6s. 8d., which continued in his troop until Candlemas after, and then was so spoiled that he was not able to do any more service. After the said horse was so lamed I sent another horse in his room, and a man to ride him, which horse has been in the said troop ever since Candlemas after to this present time: the horse when I put him in was worth £8 10s.[147]

Various payments to the army include references to combinations of mounts and cavalry equipment, some of which were probably brought in via a system of short-term loans. In August or September 1644 the constables of Mere supplied £3 2s. 6d. 'to the sheriff [Colonel Brooke] towards a horse, arms and rider', while the same figure was laid out for a horse and arms for the troop by the neighbouring constables of Lymm.[148] For the same unit Captain-Lieutenant Wynn issued a warrant to the Aston constables on 13 July 1644, requiring them to bring in mounts from their township.[149] During the first months of 1643 Hugh Leigh contributed of a horse worth £8 10s. to Colonel George Booth's troop, while in the year following the sequestrators of Northwich Hundred paid £14 for maintaining seven horses and arms. Likewise, the constables of Lymm accounted for '26 horses [taken] by Colonel George Booth out of the township for his troop, worth £48'; also the sequestration committee for Bucklow furnished two mounts.[150] Similarly, in late 1643 the constables of Mere expended £17 4s. for a 'horse and arms under [the] command of Colonel Leigh'. During the summer of 1644 the same officials supplied a number of cavalry mounts to the troops of Leigh, Coote and Bulkeley.[151] From similar sources about February 1643 Colonel Henry Mainwaring received from the constables of Church Lawton £3 10s.

144 TNA, SP28/128/10, fols. 8r.–v.
145 BL, MS Harley 2128, fol. 73r.
146 TNA, SP28/128/10, fol. 5r.
147 BL, MS Harley 2128, fols 2v.–3r.
148 BL, MS Harley 1970, fols 60r., 49v.; 2137, fol. 200v.
149 AA, unlisted warrant, dated 13 July 1644.
150 BL, MS Harley 2128, fols 43r., 49r., 60r.; 2137, fol. 115r.
151 BL, MS Harley 2128, fols 60v–61r.; SP28/225/3, fol. 924r.

for a mount for his command, with an additional £1 18s. 10d. laid out 'for bridle, saddle and other furniture for [the] said horse'.[152]

At this time Captain Stanley's troop obtained two horses, furniture and arms valued at £12, whereas the constables of Dutton expended £27 for horses on 29 September 1644 'which Captain Bramhall [took] to Montgomery fight and arms upon the designs', as well as a mare lost during the battle, valued at £5. Captain Shepley was paid the same figure for a Royalist horse and pistols captured during the battle.[153] The following year William Davenport of Bramhall complained about the methods employed by various cavalry officers in obtaining mounts from his estate at Bramhall:

> On New Year's Day 1644 Sir William Brereton being about Stockport, Captain Sankey, Captain Francis Duckenfield, with two or three troops, came to Bramhall and went into my stable and took out all my horses, then they drove all they could find out of the park, taking them quite away with them, above twenty in all … Monday 20 May 1644: Being at Woodford with my cousin Davenport [I] had my mare forcibly taken from me by one Robert Norbury, young Deane, Smith and others of Captain Stanley's troop, and had by them some reproachful words given me because I was unwilling to part with her … On Wednesday 22 May came Captain Stanley's lieutenant and a great part of his troop to Bramhall to be quartered; and the next day came up Norbury riding on my saddle with divers others that were at the taking of my mare, but left her behind them at Thomas Taylor's. When I desired that I might have my mare restored to me again, the lieutenant said that he could not do it till he had acquainted his captain therewith, and withal promised that he would either send me the mare again, or his captain's answer by letter. 8 June 1644: Although I had received a letter from Captain Stanley containing many expressions of friendship and that what injury his men had done me in taking my mare from me was without his commission or knowledge, with a promise to have her restored, nevertheless on Saturday 8 June 1644 his troop came hither, his cornet being with them and went into the park, took away all the horses both those that were mine own and others that were laid to the park, to the number of seventeen in all, so not leaving so much as a horse either to ride on or for draught.[154]

After the surrender of Wythenshawe in 1644 the Royalist owner, Robert of Tatton, attempted to prevent three animals being confiscated by Colonel Duckenfield's men. An entry in the inventory of the house mentions prosaically, 'one nag and two mares being taken from Mr Tatton by violence'.[155]

The procurement of quality troop saddles was vital to all armies of the period. Sergeant Major Philip Mainwaring's troop was raised over the winter of 1642–43, with funds being issued in London to purchase saddles.[156] An inventory of the goods of Edmund Jodrell of Wythenshawe,

152 BL, MS Harley 1943, fol. 4r.; 1999, fol. 313v.

153 BL, MS Harley 2128, fols 150v., 60r.; SP28/152/7, fols 6v., 11r.

154 CRO, ZCR/63/2/19, fols 89v.–91r., 93v.

155 JRL,TW/287.

156 TNA, SP28/225/3, fol. 725v.; SP28/263, fol. 154r.

taken by Captain-Lieutenant Zankey of Sir William Brereton's own troop on 28 April 1643 includes two great saddles (valued at £1 15s. apiece), four hackney saddles (at 6s. 8d. each), 'bridles with bits and snaffles', various saddlecloths, three pairs of 'great brass stirrups' and two pistol barrels.[157] Zankey testified that such items were taken into his custody and 'shall forthwith be delivered to my colonel'. Presumably the saddles and tack were appropriated by his troop. In March 1643 Brooke's troop received £30 9s. for the repair of saddles.[158] Similar payments were made for saddles and tack for Duckenfield's troop. In April 1643 £8 was disbursed 'to William Walker, saddler, for saddles for my troop'; payments totalling £9 10s. 4s. were made in May, June and October 1643 for 'saddles and furniture', whereas on 1 November 1643 9s. was given to a Manchester saddler, with a further £3 6s. paid 'to Peter Cork, saddler'. An additional £8 6s. was spent on saddles for the troop on 17 March 1645, while Corporal Johnson of the same troop was reimbursed the sum of £2 8s. 4d. 'for holsters and other necessaries' in April 1643.[159] During the build-up of Myddelton's horse in early 1644 significant quantities of saddles and tack were purchased, including the payment of £65 10s. to William Platt, saddler, for 70 pad saddles, bridles and other tack, while Ellis Parry (going by his name, a local maker) was contracted on two occasions 'for 39 pad saddles with their furniture at 20s. a piece'.[160] Various sums were laid out for the cavalry troop commanded by the former dragoon captain, John Bramhall. For instance, on 18 May 1644 17s. 6d. was given to a farrier 'for shoeing mine and Lieutenant Mainwaring's horses', while on 1 February 1645 the sum of £15 11s. 10d. was disbursed for shoeing the entire command's mounts.[161]

As regards arms and armour for the foot, few examples of issues of pikes to the Cheshire army of Parliament are known. In 1643 the Macclesfield sequestrators disbursed £2 10s. 'for making pikes for the public service', whilst William Duncalfe received £1 4s. for 24 pike-heads at 12d. each. Likewise, on 20 May 1645 Nicholas Higginbottom provided drums and pikes for the Wirral garrisons.[162] Such purchases were procured from local suppliers for Duckenfield's regiment. A batch of 200 pikes was supplied to Myddelton's forces by London manufacturers on 6 June 1643 at a cost of 5s. 6d. each.[163] Moreover, in the spring and summer of 1645 Parliament contracted for such weapons for the New Model Army at between 3s. 10d. and 4s. 2d. apiece – rather cheaper than the 5s. 6d. paid for those sent to Ireland in October 1646.[164] They were supplied in consignments of between 500 and 3,000, and the prices probably reflect a more discounted rate. The 1,500 head-pieces issued to Brereton by London sources in February 1644 are likely to have been pikemen's helmets for they were included with supplies of muskets

157 JRL, JOD/62c; Malbon, pp.245–7.
158 TNA, SP28/196/1, fol. 14v.
159 TNA, SP28/128/10, fols 4v., 5r.–v.; 6r.–v.
160 TNA, SP28/346/1, unfol.; SP28/346/2, unfol.
161 BL, MS Harley 2128, fols 25r., 26r.–v., 27v., 28v.–29r.
162 BL, MS Harley 2130, fols 88r., 91v.
163 TNA, SP28/346/1, unfol.
164 Mungeam, 'Contracts', 74, 81. 97; *CJ*, IV, p.698.

and bandoliers.[165] In mid 1644 the London armourers Thomas Stevens and Nicholas Marshall supplied the Cheshire army with 540 sets of pikemen's armour (including helmets) and 350 spare helmets.[166] Similarly, the Cheshire army received 75 'headpieces for footmen' as part of a larger consignment shipped from London to Liverpool in March 1645.[167]

The procurement of such items would suggest that from the outset, Brereton's pikemen were fully equipped with defensive armour. Glenn Foard postulates that the lack of purchases of back and breast plates, and helmets to the fledgling New Model Army in April 1645 'supports the argument that armour was no longer issued to pikemen by this time in the war, although some soldiers may have brought such equipment from old armies'.[168] Musketeers were commonly issued with the smoothbore, muzzle-loading matchlock musket (often supplied early in the war with a rest), bandolier and sword. Instructions issued in 1636 for arming the English and Welsh militia declared that muskets were meant to be of one standard bore (12 bullets to the pound) and that each musketeer 'shall be furnished with a sufficient whole musket, the barrel thereof shall be four feet in length and no more', the total length of the weapon being five feet two inches.[169] Moreover:

> Every such person appointed to serve with a full musket shall be further furnished and armed with a good bandolier, and with fifteen good and serviceable charges of turned wood, covered with leather and fastened there unto. Also with a good primer, worm and scourer, and a bullet bag annexed unto it, with a mould to cast such bullets as aforesaid.

They were also to be equipped with a headpiece, sword, rest, girdle and hangers. During spring 1645 matchlock muskets costing 10s., 11s. and 11s. 6d. were purchased for the New Model Army, while in 1646 Parliament contracted for 'English matchlock muskets and bandoliers, at 14*s.* per weapon for its forces in Ireland'.[170]

A list for 'provision of arms and other necessaries for his Majesty's store [in Ireland]', dated 20 September 1642, mentions 'Boxes according to fifteen to the pound for decayed bandoliers for musketeers, 90,000; and primers for every fifteen boxes of that number, 6,000; and girdles to supply decayed bandoliers, 6,000.'[171] Various quantities of bandoliers were issued to the Cheshire army. Fixed contributions by the constables of Church Lawton in Nantwich Hundred included the maintenance of two soldiers at 1s. a week, while in late 1642 they paid 15s. 8d. 'for a sword and belt, and

165 *CSPD 1644*, p.26; *LJ*, VI, p.446.

166 TNA, SP28/168/2, unfol.

167 CRO, DDX/428, fol. 80r.; *BLB*, I, 139.

168 Foard, *Naseby*, p.61.

169 Wrye, *State Papers Relating to Musters*, p.89; David R. Lawrence, *The Complete Soldier: Military Books and Military Culture in Early Stuart England, 1603–1645* (Brill: Leiden, 2008), p.189.

170 Mungeam, 'Contracts', pp.106, 112, 114; *CJ*, IV, p.698.

171 James Hogan (ed.), *Letters and Papers Relating to the Irish Rebellion Between 1642–46* (Dublin: The Stationery Office, 1936), p.134; *CJ*, II, pp.576, 793, 807.

bandolier for one or two trained band soldiers'.[172] Moreover February 1644 1,500 bandoliers were purchased from London sources for Brereton's foot, while a large number of these items must have captured from the enemy (including the '32 muskets with bandoliers and rests' seized at Wythenshaw Hall).[173] London manufacturers supplied enormous quantities of bandoliers and associated leather wear to the Parliamentarian forces. In October 1644 Myddelton bought 300 sets at 1s. 2d. each, as well as 300 knapsacks from James Goffe, a leading London-based supplier of leatherware.[174] The price of these bandoliers compares with those supplied to Fairfax's army in early 1645, which were got for between 12d. and 20d. each (mostly the latter).[175]

Knapsacks or snapsacks, sausage-shaped bags worn over the shoulder and largely made of leather, were important pieces of equipment issued to Civil War soldiers, especially the foot and dragoons. They were used for carrying rations, spare clothing and personal items. In 1627 the Ordnance Office paid 15d. apiece for leather knapsacks, while the same items 'large and of good leather' were purchased for the New Model in 1645 at 8s. per dozen (8d. each).[176] In addition to the 300 supplied to Myddelton (above), on 6 June 1643 a further 2,000 knapsacks were purchased by him at 6d. each, possibly from the same manufacturer.[177] Myddelton never raised more than 2–300 foot, but the endorsement at the foot of the bill mentions 'the several forces abovementioned', which must be taken to mean the Parliamentarian troops of North Wales, Cheshire and Shropshire that were 'brigaded' together during the operations in Shropshire and the Welsh borders. It seems likely therefore that Brereton's foot and dragoons benefitted from this issue.

When the war began dragoons were generally issued with matchlock muskets, but as the war progressed, these were often replaced with flintlocks (snaphance or dog-lock muskets). The use of muskets by dragoons is described by Vernon in *The Young Horse-man*:

> The dragoon's arming is only offensive, having a good fire and cock musket something, a wider bore, then ordinary hanging in a belt by a swivel at his side, with a good sword and ordinary horse, it being only to expedite his march, for he must perform his service on foot, the ordinary marching is usually ten a breast, and when they come in service, nine of them alight casting the bridle over the next sideman's horse's neck, and for one in ten serves to keep their horses, the rest perform the service; it is a good and special principle, to have our soldiers both horse and foot well chosen, well-armed, and well disciplined.[178]

Although such weapons possessed certain advantages over matchlocks they were more expensive. Hence in April 1645 Parliament contracted with two London gunsmiths, William Watson and Edward Burrows for

172 BL, MS Harley 1943, fols 2r., 3r., 6r., 8r.
173 *CSPD 1644*, p.26; *LJ*, VI, p.446; JRL, TW/287.
174 TNA, SP28/346/2, unfol.
175 Mungeam, 'Contracts', pp.90, 102.
176 TNA, WO49/55, fol. 174r.; Mungeam, 'Contracts', p.100.
177 TNA, SP28/346/1, unfol.
178 Vernon, *The Young Horse-man*, pp.8–9.

200 'snaphance muskets English full bore and proof', at 15s. 6d. each, while in October 1646 17s. was paid for them.[179] Brereton's dragoons were often referred to by contemporaries as 'firelocks', owing to their association with these weapons, and it seems likely that most (if not all) of these soldiers were issued with them from the outset. There is evidence that Sir Thomas Aston's four dragoon companies were armed with both matchlocks and firelocks, although he was purchasing snaphance locks of the 'new fashion' suitable for dragoons in late 1641.[180] On 3 December 1642 Parliament ordered the delivery of 300 snaphances (as well as 400 matchlocks for the foot) to Brereton, 'to be employed for the safety of the county of Chester', while Sir William petitioned Speaker Lenthall on 21 November 1643 to send by sea 100 pair of pistols, 300 muskets and 200 or 300 firelocks, adding 'These are not to be procured upon any terms in this country wherein I could raise good store of men if I could arm them.'[181]

Bramhall's accounts show that his company was supplied with 20 firearms in London, and a further 30 in Leek and Nantwich, although a total of 82 weapons were 'lost upon service'. Moreover, in July and August he disbursed a total of 17s. 2d. for restocking firelocks.[182] We might assume that some of the bandoliers supplied to Brereton's forces were meant for the dragoons. In April 1645 Colonel Okey's New Model dragoons were issued with 1,050 snaphances, while archaeological surveys of the Naseby battlefield have revealed quantities of powder boxes from bandoliers around Okey's deployment about Sulby Hedges.[183] Cartridge boxes, worn about the waist, were an alternative to the bandolier, although there are no records of these being given to Brereton's men. Such items were issued to Lancashire soldiers, however. On 12 October 1643 the county's deputy lieutenants ordered that '100 snaphance muskets and the 200 grey coats, and the portmanteaus [leather shoulder bags], knapsacks, and other small things, that is, cartridges and belts belonging to those snaphances shall be delivered to Colonel Rigby, he paying for the carriage of them.'[184] Regarding the usefulness of bandoliers and cartridge boxes Orrery observed, 'I am also on long experience an enemy to the use of bandoliers, but a great approver of boxes of cartridges; for then, but by biting off the bottom of the cartridge, you charge your musket for service with one ramming. I would have these cartridge boxes of tin, as the carbines use them, because they are not so apt to break as the wooden ones are, and do not in wet weather, or lying in the tents, relax.'[185]

When riding, the dragoon probably secured his musket by a sling, as depicted in Wallhausen's *Kriegskunst*. Like their brothers-in-arms in the

179 Mungeam, 'Contracts', p.107; *CJ*, IV, p.698.

180 Thanks to Gary Ashby for this information.

181 *CJ*, II, p.874; HMC, *Thirteenth Report*, p.157.

182 BL, MS Harley 2128, fols 25r., 34r.–35r. 500 snaphances were purchased for the army on 29 February 1644, but it seems likely that these were cavalry carbines because on 7 May a further 500 pairs of pistols, 500 saddles, 500 backs and breasts, 500 cavalry helmets, as well as saddle and pistols were acquired from London suppliers (*CJ*, III, p.484; *LJ*, VI, pp.446, 551).

183 Foard, *Naseby*, pp.59–64, 247–9.

184 HMC, *Tenth Report, App. IV*, p.67.

185 Orrery, *Treatise of the Art of War*, p.31.

foot, these soldiers were also commonly issued with the tuck, a cheaper and lighter version of the cavalry sword and employed in close-quarter combat with musket butts. Instructions issued to the trained bands in 1626 referred to 'A good strong and serviceable sword, the blade thereof not to be above three foot in length, in a good scabbard with belt or girdle and hangers fitted thereunto'. Similarly, in 1635 they were to be issued with 'a good sword of three foot long, cutting, stiff-pointed, with girdle and hangers'.[186] In April 1645 Parliament contracted with the London cutler, Daniel Judd, to supply '400 swords and belts Dutch blades at 4s. 6d. each'.[187] At Hopton Heath on 19 March 1643 Bramhall's dragoons were reported by Sir William Brereton as fighting 'so long, and so fiercely, until all their powder and bullet was spent. Afterwards they joined, and fell to it pell mell, one upon another, with the stocks of their muskets'.[188]

Dragoons during the English Civil War were supplied with inferior horses and comparatively simple equipment, and were cheaper to recruit and maintain than the expensive regiments of horse. In mid 1645 Parliament contracted with London suppliers for dragoon saddles for the New Model Army priced between 6s. 6d. and 7s. 6d., somewhat cheaper than cavalry saddles, which were procured for between 16s. and 18s.[189] In Cheshire, during the winter of 1643–4 the constables of Aston were directed to provide two 'scout horses' for Captain Littler's company, while around April 1644 the constables of Mere laid out £2 9s. 4d. for 'a horse, men and arms' for the same unit.[190] Similarly, the constables of Nether Whitley expended £8 16s. on 1 October 1643 'for one horse, and horse furniture and apparel for a dragoon by warrant of Sir William Brereton', and a further £4 'for riding the horse'. Moreover, between 1 October 1643 and 1 October 1644 the same officials paid 18s. 'for maintaining a man, horse and arms for three weeks at the first voyage into Wales under command of Captain Goldegay'. In late 1642 or early 1643 the same officer received two mounts with furniture and arms from the constables of Mere at a cost of £6, while in 1644 the collectors at nearby Lymm disbursed the sum of £11 3s. for three dragoon horses and three soldiers in his company. In either 1643 or 1644 the constables of Hollingworth in Macclesfield Hundred fully kitted out a dragoon, except for his musket. This included a horse, costing £5, and 'a saddle, bridal, stirrups, boots, spurs, sword, girdle and other furniture for a rider to the said horse', at a total cost of £4. Items of equipment purchased for Bramhall's company on 1 February 1644 include a bridle costing 4s. and six girths at a cost of 2s., while 3s. was paid for the mending of spurs and bridles.[191]

186 Wrye, *State Papers Relating to Musters*, pp.90, 200.

187 Mungeam, 'Contracts', p.107.

188 *History and Antiquities of Staffordshire*, I, p.59.

189 Mungeam, 'Contracts', pp.66, 80–1, 103–5, 111–13.

190 AA, unlisted warrant, dated 20 November 1643 x 2 February 1644; BL, MS Harley 2128, fols 166r., 60v.

191 BL, MS Harley 2128, fols 41v., 42r., 48v., 60r., 8r., 25r., 27v.

Part III

Military units of the Cheshire Army of Parliament

8

Sir William Brereton's Regiment of Horse

Sir William Brereton's commission as colonel of a regiment of harquebusiers dates from 1 March 1643 to 16 April 1644, and of a regiment of horse from 16 April 1644 to 24 June 1645.[1] He later reported to the Committee of Accounts, 'I had a good regiment of horse a full twelvemonth before I had my commission for that regiment', but he was probably referring to his second commission of 16 April 1644.[2] Brereton arrived in Cheshire in January 1643 with two troops of horse (one being his own, the other under his close associate Captain William Edwards). He was joined on his arrival by three other newly raised cavalry units from the county, although perhaps two or more others had already been formed by Colonels Duckenfield and Brooke by the close of 1642. On 10 February 1643 Sir William informed Captain Rowe in London that with him were five troops of horse, although a sergeant major was much required to organise them into a regiment, and taking the opportunity to request that 'some officers of foot [be] sent down, for we have a great need of them, a lieutenant-colonel and sergeant major of foot and some lieutenants of foot … some old soldiers for sergeants would do wonderous well'.[3] This mounted force of perhaps 300–400 men formed the nucleus of the Cheshire horse, which at its peak in 1645 numbered up to 1,000 officers and troopers.

Brereton's regiment of horse (ostensibly a 'double regiment') was akin to Cromwell's Ironsides, his regiment of the Eastern Association, which in early 1644 numbered 14 troops). The question of Brereton's insistence that all cavalry troops serving in the Cheshire army were brought under his command as part of his regiment of horse, is not entirely clear. His social and religious similarities with Cromwell have been discussed alluded to in this book, yet Sir William may have preferred the advantages offered by a potent regional mounted force, flexible and capable enough to prosecute

1 TNA, SP28/152/7, fol. 20r.; SP28/35/1, fols 164r.–165v.; BL, MS Add. 11332, fol. 43r.; *BLB*, II, 809.

2 TNA, SP28/35/1, fol. 168r.; BL, MS Add. 11332, fol. 43r.; *BLB*, II, 809.

3 HMC, *Portland*, I, pp.94–5.

his war aims as commander-in-chief over a wide strategic area. In terms of command and control, Brereton could and did rely on some talented and energetic subordinate officers, such as Michael Jones and Jerome Zankey, as well as a number of experienced professional soldiers. Given the resistance in some quarters to his command by the Booth faction in particular, but also from the Staffordshire Committee, it is worth conjecturing that the retention of a single regiment was meant to prevent any diminution of arguably his greatest military asset into either two or more smaller commands, perhaps under the command of less 'committed' leadership, a problem which the Lancashire forces had struggled with. Perhaps this was one of the reasons for the breach between Sir William Brereton and Colonel Henry Mainwaring.

Henry had raised a troop of horse and regiment of foot, and was the Parliamentarian commander in Cheshire until Brereton's arrival in January 1643. Although Mainwaring's troop was still operating in March 1644, the one raised by his associate, Thomas Stanley, had disbanded or been put under another captain by before 1645, with his son no longer holding a commission and Stanley himself in opposition to Sir William on the County Committee.[4] Colonel Mainwaring was removed from his military commands and role as deputy lieutenant at Sir William Brereton's suggestion in May 1644. When Brereton relinquished his military commands under the Self-Denying Ordinance of April 1645, control of his regiment of horse passed to his lieutenant colonel, Michael Jones. Upon his return to the Cheshire army to supervise the capitulation of Chester and the final military operations in the Midlands, Brereton did not recommence control of the regiment, although part of his own troop served with him at Lichfield Close.

Sir William Brereton's Own Troop

Brereton received a commission as captain of a troop of horse from the Lords and Commons for the Safety of the Kingdom on 20 September 1642:

> By virtue of an Ordinance of the Lords and Commons in Parliament authorizing us, we do constitute and appoint you to be captain of a troop of horse harquebusiers, consisting of 60 besides officers with power to raise both the said horses and riders in Cheshire or in any other county, and to command the same being raised, as captain. These are therefore to will and require you to make your present repair in the said county and having levied the said troop to take it into your charge as captain thereof by virtue of this commission given, and to receive pay therefore out of the moneys there brought in upon the Propositions, and taking charge thereof diligently to lead and exercise the same in arms for the service of the King, Parliament and Kingdom, commanding all inferior officers of the same troop to obey you, and likewise you to obey us, or the Lord General the Earl of Essex, or the deputy lieutenants of that county as ordered shall be given your according to the disciplines of war.[5]

4 *CSPD 1644*, p.41; *BLB*, II, 796, note 6.

5 JRL, TW/262.

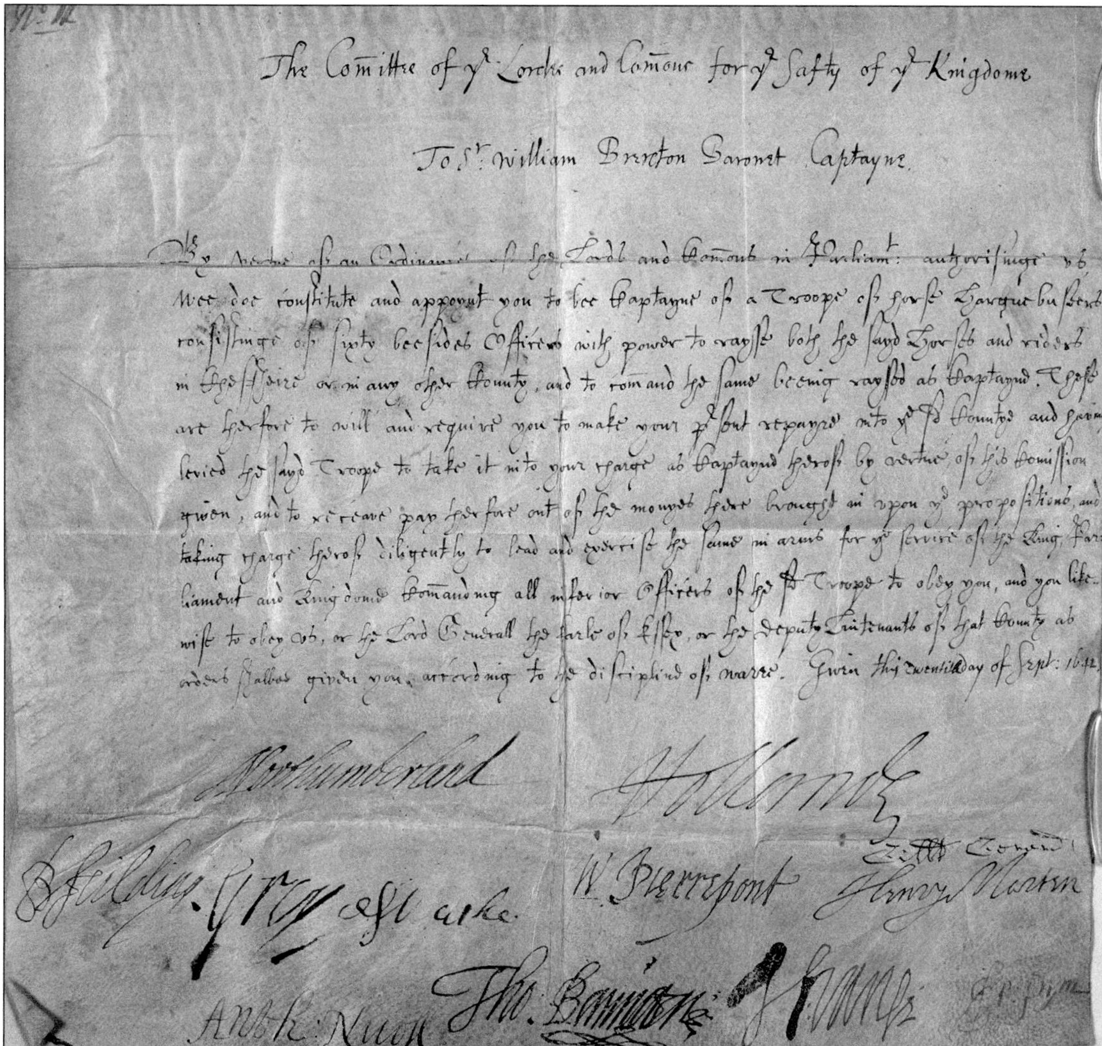

The Comittee of ye Lords and Comons for ye Safty of ye Kingdome

To Sr. William Brereton Baronet Captayne

By vertue of an Ordinance of the Lords and Comons in Parliamt: authorising us Wee doe constitute and appoynt you to bee Captayne of a Troope of horse Harquebusiers consisting of sixty besides Officers with power to rayse both the sayd horses and riders in Cheshire or in any other County, and to command the same being raysed as Captayne. These are therfore to will and require you to make your present repayre unto the sd Countyes and having levied the sayd Troope to take it into your charge as Captayne thereof by vertue of this Comission given, and to receave pay therfore out of the moneys there brought in upon the propositions, and taking charge thereof diligently to lead and exercise the same in armes for the service of the King, Parliament and Kingdome Commanding all inferior Officers of the sd Troope to obey you, and you likewise to obey us, or the Lord Generall the Earle of Essex, or the Deputy Lieutenants of that County as orders shalbe given you, according to the discipline of warre. Given this twentieth day of Sept: 1642.

Northumberland

Holland

W. Pierrepont

Henry Marten

Anth: Nicoll

Tho. Barrington

Sir William Brereton's commission as captain of a troop of harquebusiers, dated 20 September 1642 John Rylands Library, JRL, TW/262. (Copyright of The University of Manchester)

As the above document indicates, the nucleus of Brereton's troop of horse was formed in London (between September and November 1642), although he was authorised to raise horses and troopers in Cheshire or elsewhere. Like similar units, it is likely that some of his close associates and estate tenants were also among its ranks. Miles Edwards (possibly a second son of Captain William Edwards) was the troop's first captain-lieutenant until the arrival of Zankey in February or March 1643. Similarly, Francis Duckenfield, a younger brother of Sir William Brereton's close associate Colonel Robert, served as a trooper before transferring to Duckenfield's troop, where he acted as cornet and captain-lieutenant until mid 1644, when he took command of a company of foot in his brother's regiment.[6] Brereton's command is certain to have contained officers and troopers of similar religious zeal to himself

6 TNA, E121/5/7/43, fols 1v.–2r., 114r.

– Zankey was known for his ardent religiosity, and acted as Sir William's personal chaplain and captain-lieutenant to his troop. Brereton's troopers participated in the skirmish at Brentford and the defence of the city, before embarking for Cheshire.[7] On 17 January 1643 the command joined with Derbyshire forces under Gell and Lord Grey in capturing the town of Ashby-de-la-Zouch, although their planned assault of the Royalist held fortified church and castle was thwarted by a report that Prince Rupert was marching from Banbury to relive it.[8] Gell's account reports 'Sir William Brereton was likewise to meet him [Sir John] with some 40 horse'.

This number is confirmed by payments by Brereton's secretary, Richard Stelfox on 19–20 January to 'Brereton's troop having marched down from London about Derby, consisting of 47 men'.[9] During its two-week stay in the town a number of complaints were made against Grey's troops for plundering, yet the Cheshire soldiers drew no such rebuke. The Royalist source *Mercurius Aulicus* reported on 3 January 1643 that Sir William's troops intercepted a consignment of 50 cases of cavalry pistols intended for the King's forces in Lancashire.[10] Brereton reported to John Pym on 4 February, 'I am in want of some 20 pair of pistols, which if they were supplied I hope I should make my troop near 100'.[11] For most of the war he maintained this ideal establishment of a colonel's troop. Thus it numbered that many on 30 April 1645, although the troop strength on October 18 1645 was 120 troopers. On 4 August 1646 Sir William obtained pay for a quartermaster, one trumpeter, three corporals and 57 troopers, who had served with him at Lichfield Close.[12] Needless to say, Brereton's command was at the forefront of military operations throughout Cheshire and beyond between 1642 and 1646, including active service at various sieges. The troop was still acquiring arms and horses at beginning of March 1643 when William Davenport of Bramhall reported:

> About which time Sir William Brereton, sending his cornet with part of his troop to be quartered with me, next morning, came to Bramhall himself, attended by the whole of his troop and John Brereton with him, and then disarmed me of all the arms I had my house (leaving only a piece for my keeper) viz: eight muskets, eight corslets, besides my horse.[13]

In May 1643 two sources described Brereton's troop as cuirassiers during the Parliamentarian assault on Stafford Castle. *Certain Informations* mentioned 'his own troop of cuirassiers' being sent to back the Moorlanders against the

7 Sir William reported to the Committee of Accounts on 3 November 1645: 'The first time I was out with my troop upon service was at Brentford' (TNA, SP28/35/1, fol. 168r.; BL, MS Add. 11332, fol. 43r.; *BLB*, II, 809).

8 DRO, D803/MZ9/fol. 52r.; *Mercurius Aulicus, 21 January 1643;* Brian Stone, *Derbyshire in the Civil War*, p.26.

9 TNA, SP28/196/1, fol. 1v.

10 *Mercurius Aulicus*, 3 January 1643, p.4.

11 HMC, *Portland*, I, p.94.

12 TNA, SP28/196/1, fols 1v.–2r.; SP28/261/5, fol. 20v.; SP16/513/1, fol. 93r.; BL, MS Add. 11331, fol. 45v.; 11332, fol. 3v.

13 CRO, ZCR/63/2/19, fol. 92r.

town of Stafford, while the author of *Certain special and remarkable passages* reported Sir William despatched 'some cuirassiers and dragoons'.[14] Both accounts probably derived from the same source, while the compiler(s) were unlikely to have witnessed the events themselves and employed inaccurate terminology. Brereton's commissions clearly refer to harquebusiers, there is no other evidence to corroborate the notion that he ever commanded any cuirassiers and no purchases of closed helmets, gorgets, pauldrons or similar items are known. When Brereton's regiment of horse was reduced in late 1646 Jerome Zankey reformed the troop as the 'county troop', and led it until 2 February 1648, when it was disbanded with £600 in arrears of pay.[15] Receiving pay with Brereton's own troop on 19–20 January and 12 March 1643 were:

Captain-Lieutenant Miles Edwards
Cornet William Sergeant
Quartermaster Thomas Elcock[16]

Captain-Lieutenant/Sergeant Major Jerome Zankey

Son of Richard Zankey, rector of Hodnet, Shropshire, matriculated Trinity College, Cambridge in 1637, migrated to Clare Hall in 1640, awarded a BA 1641 and MA 1644. Jerome was, according to Richard Gough, 'a person of a mean stature, mild disposition, and accounted a very religious man', whereas he was noted in Royalist propaganda as a preaching captain and nicknamed 'the little pope'.[17] Dore described Zankey as 'a colourful and energetic man who had a remarkable career'.[18] Exactly when he joined Brereton's troop is unclear – various payments to 'Mr Zankey' and 'Captain Zankey, minister' occur in February 1643. He appears as captain-lieutenant of the troop in an acquittance, dated 3 April 1643, for forced contributions towards Brereton's forces, while on 28 April 1643 he compiled an inventory of the goods of Edmund Jodrell of Yeardsley. The record includes a detailed list of saddlery and tack, and clearly illustrates Zankey's knowledge of equine paraphernalia.[19] There has been considerable confusion over the supposed role of his brother Robert in Brereton's horse. Dore (following Wanklyn) thought that he was commissioned the regiment's major, but soon afterwards 'died or left the service'.[20]

Although he provided no actual evidence for this, in 1940 J.E. Auden wrote that:

14 *Certain Informations, 18 May 1643; A Continuation of Certain special and remarkable passages*, 18–25 May 1643'

15 TNA, SP28/124/1, fols 160v., 58v.–65r.; SP28/257, unfol.; SP28/51/1, fol. 118r.

16 TNA, SP28/196/1, fols 1v., 3r., 4r.

17 P.E. Razzell (ed.), Richard Gough, *The History of Myddle* (Pittsburgh, PA: Caliban Books, new edn, 1979), p.220; *Mercurius Aulicus*, 3 July 1643.

18 *BLB*, I, 186, n.1.

19 TNA, SP28/196/1 fols 1v., 10v., 12r., 497r.; JRL: Jodrell of Yeardsley correspondence and papers, *c*. 1642–97, unfol.; Malbon, *Memorials*, pp.245–7.

20 *BLB*, I, 186, note 1.

> Colonel [*sic* – Major] Robert Zankey apparently died soon after receiving his commission, and without being mentioned for his army services, though he must have been a prominent leader to have gained such an early position at the head of a regiment, unless indeed he had raised it himself, for he is described as "Major Commandant of the regiment of horse of Chester".[21]

Similarly, Carr and Atherton, seemingly following Dore, state: 'He [Jerome] was first captain in Brereton's regiment of horse under his brother Major Robert Zankey, and then succeeded as major on his brother's death, retaining that command when Brereton's horse effectively transferred to Michael Jones.'[22] None of this, however, is supported by documentary evidence. Jerome was captured at Hanmer on 20 June 1643, but had been exchanged before the following August when he fought at Tarvin (where Royalist cavalry reportedly 'were pursued gallantly by that valiant Captain Zankey, who commands Sir William Brereton's own troop, within pistol shot of the walls of Chester and Malpas').[23] He was wounded at Christleton on 18 January 1645, where Lord Byron's force marching to relieve Beeston was defeated. Brereton reported that 'Captain Zankey, who is a very valiant man, and commands my own troop, being without his armour, was wounded in the body, but we hope not mortally.'[24] He had recovered and was on active service again by 26 March, by which time he had been promoted to sergeant major. During the spring of 1646 Zankey led 400 Cheshire horse in North Wales under Colonel Mytton and on 4 June he acted as a commissioner at the surrender of Caernarfon.[25] Jerome later served with distinction in Cheshire and Ireland, rising to the rank of colonel. He was elected MP in 1656 and was knighted by Richard Cromwell on 16 November 1658.

Lieutenant Burroughs

Burroughs appears to have replaced Miles Edwards, and is included in pay warrants for Brereton's troop in April and May 1643, although his commission ended on 31 July 1644.[26] He may be the Lieutenant Ralph Burroughs who had served previously in Bramhall's dragoons.

Cornet Gervase Dodson

He had previously served as cornet to Captain Robert Farrer, an English captain in Myddelton's brigade. Pay warrants place him in Brereton's troop on 2 June 1645. Cornet Dodson was wounded in the arm and captured in late 1645, held at Chester and released on 4 January 1646.[27]

---

21 J.E. Auden, 'Sir Jerome Zankey (or Sankey), of Balderton Hall, co. Salop, and of Coolmore, co. Tipperary', *Transactions of the Shropshire Archaeological Society*, 50 (1940), pp.171–8 (p. 172).

22 *CWS*, p.21, n. 3.

23 *A True Relation of two great Victories*; *The Success of Our Cheshire Forces The Success of Our Cheshire Forces*; Phillips, *Memoirs*, II, pp.196, 199–200.

24 *Perfect Passages,* 22 January 1645; Lancaster, *Narrative*, p.12; Phillips, *Memoirs*, II, p.226.

25 BCA, MS 595611, pp.24, 26, 67–7.

26 TNA, SP28/152/7, fols 5r., 7v., 9v.

27 TNA, SP28/225, fol. 365v., SP28/346/171; MS Add. 11333, fols 4, 101; *BLB*, I, 369.

Quartermaster Phillip Peake

Present on 2 June 1645, but had been replaced by Quartermaster Cooper by 23 April 1646, possibly John Cooper who had been promoted from corporal.[28]

Clerk John Griffith

Mentioned with John Chadwick, surgeon to Brereton's troop on 14 August 1644. Further references include: '13 January 1645 received by Major Zankey through John Griffith, clerk to Brereton's troop, £12'; and 'paid to John Griffith, clerk of my troop for a horse for a trumpeter £12'.[29] It can be assumed that Griffith served as clerk throughout most of the war, and by all accounts he was vital to Brereton. In 1647 he acted as quartermaster to the reformed troop under Zankey, probably based around the core of the previous unit. It is possible that this Griffith, and the Captain John who was an important Parliamentarian officer in Cheshire and North Wales during the Interregnum were one and the same. According to Gough, he came from Myddle in Shropshire, and was an apothecary and relative of his.[30] If Captain John Griffith had been Brereton's troop clerk, the fact that Jerome Zankey was from nearby Hodnet makes it more likely.

John Bealey, groom to Sir William Brereton.[31]

Surgeon John Chadwick
Corporal John Cooper
Corporal Nathaniel Hilton
Corporal Dudley[32]
Trumpeter Ranulf Smallwood
Trumpeter Ralph Burgess[33]
Saddler John Grovenborough – appears in a list of prisoners for exchange, dated 4 January 1646.[34]
Mr Dury, gentleman of the troop – mentioned with the command at the Battle of Tarvin on 21 August 1644.[35]

Trooper Radcliffe Bennett – given £5 on 18 May 1646 'to buy a horse for the said troop on service in Staffordshire, he having dismounted in service' (that is, his horse was either killed or deemed unfit for service).[36]

On 4 August 1646 Brereton's troop was paid for its service at Lichfield Close at the rate of 30s. per trooper, being one month's arrears of pay. The corresponding muster roll lists half of the unit being present:

28 TNA, SP28/30/7, fol. 775v.; BCA, MS 595611, pp.67–8.

29 BL, MS Add. 11332, fols 38v.–40r.; TNA: SP28/152/7, fol. 17; SP28/225/4, fol. 764r.; *BLB*, II, 796

30 Gough, *Myddle*, p.167. For a wider discussion of Griffith, see *BLB*, II, 796 n. 9, 838, n. 1.

31 TNA, SP28/196/3, fol. 14.

32 BL, MS Harley 2136, fol. 68v.

33 TNA, E121/7/25, unfol.; E121/5/7, unfol.; SP28/124/1, fols 58v.–65r.

34 BL, MS Add. 11333, fol. 95v.; *BLB*, II, 1180.

35 *True Relation of a great Victory*.

36 TNA, SP16/513/1, fols 92v.–3r., 83r.

Quartermaster Thomas Egerton
Corporal Thomas Topp
Corporal John Mottershead [senior]
Corporal John Mottershead
Trumpeter Ralph Burgess
57 troopers.[37]

Lieutenant Colonel Michael Jones's Troop

Michael Jones was the second son of Lewis Jones, the Welsh preacher and Bishop of Killaloe, County Clare. His father's Puritan tendencies were deplored by Archbishop Laud, but he stayed in his post until his death in 1646. Michael entered Trinity College, Dublin, in 1621, and Lincoln's Inn in 1631, began a legal career, and was admitted to the King's Inns in Dublin in November 1640. With his brothers, Oliver and Theophilus, he took up arms against the Catholic confederates. Michael Jones served in the Earl of Kildare's regiment, rising to the rank of sergeant major. A staunch Protestant, Jones was suspicious of the Charles I's negotiations with the confederates and refused to fight for the Royalists when the Cessation of Arms was signed in 1643.[38] When the King's army returned to England Jones defected to the Parliamentarian forces in Cheshire. He distinguished himself on a number of occasions and was wounded twice. Jones was a highly experienced officer who served as lieutenant colonel of the Cheshire horse, taking command (with promotion to colonel) when Sir William Brereton was recalled to Westminster in the summer and autumn of 1645. One recent commentator notes that Jones 'had a high opinion of his own ability, and was frequently impatient with what he saw as his superior's over-cautious approach'.[39] One thing that is not in doubt though is his fighting ability, which was observed by various contemporaries.

Jones's role as commander-in-chief of the Cheshire forces during Brereton's absence is worthy of mention. The first petition of the deputy lieutenants (dominated by the Booth faction and mainly civilian) to the Committee of Both Kingdoms of 3 May 1645, and later revisions, called for the appointment of a professional soldier, eventually requesting that Sir John Meldrum 'or other such commander in chief for our military affairs as the lord lieutenant of this county'.[40] In later petitions the deputy lieutenants refrained from asking for the Scots commander, asking simply 'an able soldier to command in chief', although they appear to have favoured Michael Jones and he had actually been appointed commander of the Cheshire horse when Brereton had gone back to London.[41] Morrill concluded, 'It is clear that although he and Brereton were on close terms up to Brereton's departure, Jones was subsequently won over by the deputy lieutenants.'[42] There is, however, evidence to show that the conduct of Jones during this

37 TNA, SP16/513/1, fol. 92r.
38 Carte, *Ormond*, III, pp.96, 104.
39 Barratt, *The Great Siege of Chester*, p.67.
40 BL, MS Add. 11331, fols 54r.–v., 67r.–v.; *BLB*, I, 408–9; Morrill, *Cheshire*, pp. 155–8.
41 Bod. Lib., MS Tanner, 60, fol. 220v.; *CJ*, IV, p.139; *LJ*, VII, p.367.
42 Morrill, *Cheshire*, p.158.

affair caused some bitterness among some of his brother officers. On 15 March 1646 Lieutenant Colonel Chidley Coote (a fellow Anglo-Irishman) complained of 'your large and undigested expressions against Sir William Brereton whom you are so much tied to honour by all the ties of gratitude that can be expressed for his many respects from time to time shown to you and yours; many much admire at and I for my part ingenuously confess unto you that I can no way approve of it, neither can I imagine that a blessing may follow it'.[43] In a note the copyist added:

> Colonel Jones did afterwards acknowledge to Colonel Coote his rashness in his expressions towards Sir William Brereton, and did acquaint Colonel Coote that no man more loved and honoured him than he did, and that he did intend to go to Ireland with the Lord Lisle, but would never depart the kingdom until he were friends with Sir William Brereton; and also Colonel Jones wrote to Sir William Brereton and acknowledged his rashness, desired his affection and that he would pass by what was past.

On 10 April 1646 Brereton's associate, John Swinfen, reported from London:

> Colonel Jones came to town last night. I have not seen him nor can I hear what his business is, but I will so soon as I can. By your last and the copy of Colonel Jones to Major Zankey, [neither being in the letter book] he seems to abate some things of his former heat and if he takes entertainment under the Lord Lisle I could wish you did part fairly.[44]

Captain-Lieutenant Grant

Named in a pay warrant for the troop, dated 2 August 1645.[45] He was killed in action at Rowton Heath, a pension of £8 being awarded to his widow Elisabeth on 22 November 1648.[46]

Captain-Lieutenant Cusack

He was serving in Jones' troop in Cheshire by 1646. A pay warrant dated 17 October to Captain-Lieutenant Cusack was meant for the satisfaction of his officers and soldiers (gratuity and pay). The order relates to a letter of 10 November 1646 from the deputy lieutenants of the county to disburse sums specified in a later warrant to Cusack for the use of the commands of Jones and Captain John Glegg, 'these being both designed for Ireland … and likewise to free the country from further free quarter, and so to go on with other troops to whom there is the like engagement, as you shall be supplied with monies'.[47]

---

43 BCA, MS 595611, pp.78–9; *CWS*, 8.

44 BCA, MS 595611, p.15; *CWS*, 21.

45 BL, MS Harley, 2128, fol. 92r.

46 TNA, SP28/224/2, fol. 72r. For her petition see SP28/224/3, fols 249r.–v.

47 TNA, SP/28/224, fols 163r., 181v.

Corporal William Atkinson[48]

Trooper Marsh – known from a payment by the constables of Burton and Puddington of 10s. to his widow by order from Lieutenant Colonel Jones and the committee at Hooton, her husband having served in his troop and killed at the siege of Chester.[49] Jones's quartermaster and one of his trumpeters were prisoners of war at Denbigh Castle in April 1645.[50] The command mustered 70 troopers on 30 April 1645 and 60 on 18 October 1645.[51]

Sergeant Major John Browne's Troop

Brereton's request on 10 February 1643 that 'there may be a major sent down, and honest and conscionable man. We are much disadvantaged for want of such an officer, who is able to order a regiment of horse', raises some important questions about its early leadership. In June 1643 a Sergeant Major John Browne joined the Cheshire horse, and by his own account he remained for 13 months.[52] This officer seems to have previously served in Lord Brooke's regiment of foot of the Earl of Essex's army, which fought at Edgehill and Brentford, before its disbandment at the end of 1642. On 20 April 1644 'Christopher Robinson a trooper under Major Browne', who was a prisoner of war at Chester, was exchanged for a Royalist cornet under a Major Walton.[53] Browne received various payments as major in the Cheshire horse in July and August 1643, and was in arrears on 20 June 1644 at Coventry, when he was given £3.[54] An undated warrant refers to 'Major Browne's troop of Brereton's regiment'. Nathaniel Hilton served as cornet to Browne's troop (having previously served under the Staffordshire officer Lieutenant Colonel Peter Shepkins), and as trooper and corporal to Brereton's own troop.[55] However, Sergeant Major Browne's service in Cheshire remains somewhat obscure as he appears in no narrative accounts or letters of the period, unlike other senior officers of the Cheshire Horse, such as Zankey and Jones. The end of Browne's service in the county in July 1644 coincides with the promotion of Captain-Lieutenant Jerome Sankey to sergeant major, and the arrival of Lieutenant Colonel Jones as second in command of Brereton's regiment of horse. Browne later served under Colonel Thomas Rainsborough in the New Model Army in 1645–6.[56]

48 TNA, E121/5/7/351, fol. 50v.

49 BL, MS Harley 1999, fol. 68v.

50 BL, MS Add. 11331, fol. 5v.; *BLB*, I, 297.

51 BL, MS Add. 11331, fol. 45r.; 11333, fol. 3r.

52 TNA, SP28/264, fol. 289r.; SP28/220, unfol.

53 *Committee at Stafford*, p.100. For Dore's comments about this officer, see *BLB*, II, 796, note 1.

54 TNA, SP28/196/1, fols 16v.–18r.; SP28/152/7, unfol. (payment included in the vouchers wanting for Brereton's army, dated late October 1645 – BL, MS Add. 11332, fol. 38; *BLB*, II, 796).

55 TNA, E121/5/7/351, unfol. Shepkins (who later rose to colonel) was highly active in Civil War Staffordshire and Cheshire, and commanded a cavalry troop from January 1644 to January 1645 (SP28/43/2, fol. 259; Pennington and Roots, pp.lxiii, 57, 86, 176, 316).

56 Sprigge, *Anglia Rediviva*, pp.125–6; Charles Firth and Godfrey Davies, *The Regimental History of Cromwell's Army* (Oxford: Clarendon Press, 1991 edn), pp.419–21.

Colonel Robert Duckenfield's Troop

Robert Duckenfield received a commission as 'captain of a troop of harquebusiers from 26 November 1642 until 2 October 1646, when my troop was disbanded'. Robert's initial entitlement of £140 advance money ('mounting money for myself') remained in arrears in 1647. His command was active in Cheshire and Lancashire in late 1642, and was completed by April 1643 at the latest. As an integral part of the Cheshire horse it was in constant and arduous service throughout the war, including the sieges of Beeston and Chester. Between November 1642 and June 1644 a total sum of £644 15s. 10d. in pay was distributed to his troop in pay from localised sources, including £37 15s. 'to Quartermaster Hurst for my troop' on 27 September 1643 and £64 disbursed to the troopers from goods taken from Adlington House in January 1644. Additionally, Robert claimed that his troop of horse and regiment of foot received the sum of £2,148 19s. 7d. from James Croxton, treasurer in London 'at several times as of his account'.[57] In April 1645 Colonel Duckenfield reported to Sir Samuel Luke:

> My troop was the first served in these parts of the kingdom for the parliament and have continued a complete troop above two years and a half until this present, for very little pay which is on account, for the last twelvemonth they have received £215 14s. from the public and no more, Sir William Brereton allows his own troop double pay to the rest which is contrary to an ordinance of parliament especially my men who have served so long.[58]

Whilst at the Chester leaguer on 18 December 1645 Duckenfield's troop was included in a wider payment to 'the officers and soldiers of the Cheshire horse, who have been constant upon duty and received no pay since August last 1645'.[59] Robert's own final arrears of pay as captain of a troop of horse, having served for 1,405 days at 39s. per day, amounted to £2,739 15s.[60]

Captain-Lieutenant Francis Duckenfield

Of Stockport, brother of Colonel Robert and Captain William Duckenfield (of Duckenfield's foot regiment). Francis served briefly as a trooper in Colonel Brereton's troop, before transferring to Duckenfield's, where he acted as cornet and captain-lieutenant until mid 1644.[61] 'Captain Francis Duckenfield of Stockport' was present at Bramhall on 1 April 1644 with Sir William Brereton, Captain-Lieutenant Sankey and two or three troops of Cheshire horse.[62]

57 TNA, SP28/128/10, fols 4r.–9r. Croxton's accounts record a total disbursement of £2,283 7s. 3d. (SP28/128/13, fol. 16r.).

58 BL, MS Egerton 787/3, fol. 48; *Letter Books of Sir Samuel Luke*, p.505; *Cheshire and Lancashire Historical Collector*, pp.95–6.

59 BL, MS Add. 11333, fol. 30r.; *BLB*, II, 1040.

60 TNA, SP28/128/10, fol. 9v.

61 TNA, E121/5/7/43, fols 1v.–2r., 114r.

62 BL, MS Harley 2012, fol. 52r.

Captain-Lieutenant Samuel Smith

A number of references place him in command of the troop by June 1645.[63] This is confirmed by a surviving warrant of 17 November 1646, directing payment to Captain-Lieutenant Smith 'for satisfaction of officers and men of Colonel Duckenfield's troop for gratuity due to them for service at leaguer of Chester and pay under the New Model'.[64] In computing the amount, treasurer Croxton named Smith, and mentioned a cornet, a quartermaster, three corporals, one trumpeter, a clerk of the troop and 53 troopers. Samuel Smith signed the acquittance (receipt) for same on 29 December 1646.

Captain James Afflecke

Provost-marshal to Duckenfield's regiment of foot, he was paid on 6 October 1645 in temporary command of the troop.[65]

Cornet Richard Brereton

His relationship to Sir William is uncertain. Richard's record suggests a degree of interchangeability between some of the units in the Cheshire army, particularly the horse, and perhaps illustrates an especial closeness between the war aims and religious sensibilities of the Brereton and Duckenfield families. Richard's certificate of service states that he was cornet to Duckenfield's troop from 27 November 1642 to 13 November 1643, during which time he constantly mustered three horses of his own completely equipped. He left the troop on 1 December 1643 when he was commissioned captain of a company of foot under 'under Sir William Brereton's command'.[66]

Cornet George Hurst progressed from trooper, corporal and quartermaster to cornet of the troop; he was paid as quartermaster on 4 August 1643 and cornet on 18 September 1643.[67] The remaining non-commissioned officers can be gleaned from a number of sources:

Quartermaster Whitworth
Sergeant Jeffrey Alcocke
Corporal John Johnson
Corporal Burke
Corporal William Bonnison[68]
Surgeon Thomas Harrington
Clerk Bibby
Clerk Isaac Turner
Clerk Peter Newton

Trooper Robert Hully was paid £1 4s. on 18 September 1643. Among pensioners listed in 1653 is 'Ellen Benetson, whose husband, William Benetson, of Duckenfield, a soldier in Colonel Duckenfield's troop, was wounded in the right shoulder at the siege of Chester, and died'.[69]

63 TNA, SP28/30/7, fol. 671v.; SP28/224/1, fols 32v.–3r.; E121/5/7/351, fols 2r.–4r.; E121/5/7/misc., unfol.; BL, MS Harley 2128, fol. 92r., MS Add. 11333, fols 30r, 110v.

64 TNA, SP28/224/1, fols 178v.–80r.

65 TNA, SP28/152/8, fol. 1v.

66 BL, MS Harley 2128, fols 73r.–78r.;

67 TNA, E121/5/7/43, fols 4v.–5r; SP28/128/10, fol. 6r., 8v.

68 TNA, SP28/225/4, fol. 747r.; SP28/128/10, fols 5v.–6r.; SP28/128/2/11, fol. 1v.; SP28/225/4, fol. 747r.; SP28/121/A, fol.645r.; BL, MS Harley 2128, fol. 92r.; E121/5/7/351, fol. 2v.

69 TNA, SP28/128/10, fol. 6r.; Earwaker, *East Cheshire*, I, p.69.

Duckenfield's troop numbered 63 troopers fit for duty on 26 November 1642, 57 on 10 October 1644, 60 on 30 April and 18 October 1645, and 53 on 17 November 1646.[70]

Lieutenant Colonel Chidley Coote's Troop

Chidley was the third son of Sir Charles Coote, head of a prominent Irish Protestant family. He was an experienced officer, having served with his brothers in pacifying the Confederates in Offaly and Laois. In March 1644 Chidley Coote published the influential pamphlet *Ireland's Lamentation for the Late Destructive Cessation*, in which his pro-militaristic stance condemned the Royalist administration in Dublin.[71] Like Michael Jones and others, he refused to serve the King when the Cessation of Arms was signed and crossed to England to take up arms for the Parliament. Lieutenant Colonel Coote appears to have joined the Cheshire forces by 15 June 1644 when he acted as a co-signatory to an intelligence report with Sir William Brereton and other senior officers at Stourbridge on the movements of Prince Rupert.[72] He began forming a troop of horse for the Cheshire army in September 1644, but this failed to materialise and he took over the newly formed command of Captain Francis Farrington, 'who came from Shropshire'.[73] This reference is from a payment to Farrington, dated 31 July 1644.

His later service in unclear, though he was paid with the Cheshire army on 12 October and 2 December 1644 and may have stayed with the unit until the appearance of Lieutenant, later Captain Thomas Garnet in early 1645. Sometime later the treasurer, James Croxton disbursed the sum of £101 9s. 1d. 'to Captain Farrington for himself, officers and troop'.[74] Coote seems also to have absorbed recruits raised by Francis' brother, Captain Samuel Farrington, who had been attempting to build a company of foot in August 1644.[75]

Lieutenant Colonel Coote's troop and company of foot are likely to have been augmented by Irish soldiers who defected from the siege of Liverpool in October and November 1644.[76] Although Coote was assigned to the Shropshire Committee in mid 1645 he remained under the operational command of Brereton at the siege of Chester, predominantly on the Wirral and Welsh side of the city. The context of his transferral was the modification in the partnership between the Shropshire Committee and

70 TNA, SP28/128/10, fol. 2r.; SP28/121/A, fols 645r., 819v.; SP28/224, fols 178v.–80r.; BL, Add. 11331, fol. 45r.; 11332, fol. 3v.

71 *Ireland's lamentation for the late destructive cessation* (London, 1644). This copy is annotated '1 March 1643'. See also, Eamon Darcy, *The Irish Rebellion of 1641 and the Wars of the Three Kingdoms* (Woodbridge: Boydell, 2013), pp.124–5.

72 *CSPD 1644*, pp.237–8.

73 TNA, SP28/152/7, fol. 9r.

74 TNA, SP28/225/3, fol. 504r.; SP28/152/7, fol. 10v.; SP28/128/13, fol. 15v.

75 Samuel was paid an unspecified amount at Stafford on 4 December 'towards what he has laid out towards raising a company of dragoons' (TNA: SP28/225/4, fol. 742v.). On 1 March 1645 he received a commission from the Shropshire Committee as captain of a company of foot, serving in that capacity until 31 July 1646 (SP28/174/1 – Farrington's account book).

76 TNA, SP21/17, fols 63v.–5r.

Brereton, occasioned by the appointment of Mytton as commander-in-chief for North Wales, replacing his brother-in-law Myddelton on 12 May 1645.[77] Coote's association with the Shropshire Parliamentarian war effort may have originated the previous year with his absorption into his troop of soldiers raised by the Farrington brothers, but by 1645 other Cheshire officers and units were seconded to the county.

Coote claimed pay as troop commander in the Cheshire army from 20 October 1644 to 10 August 1645, at which date he took command of the Shropshire horse, being promoted to colonel on 8 November 1645 and serving with it until 31 July 1646.[78] In November 1645 the committee at Hooton disbursed 5s. to his men, while the troop was remunerated £23 out of the £100 received by Coote from Sir William Brereton for the Shropshire forces and the leaguer of Chester.[79] On 15 November 1645 Lieutenant Colonel Coote and Major Thomas Croxton took the surrender of the Royalist garrison at Beeston, and he was appointed as a commissioner for the surrender of Chester. Coote's troop of horse mustered 50 troopers on 3 April, and 60 troopers on 18 October. In July 1646 he was contracted to raise a regiment for service in Ireland.[80]

Lieutenant Thomas Garnet

Garnet was paid with the troop in early 1645. He appears as a signee of a petition and letter as one of the commanders of the Shropshire horse to Brereton about the end of October 1645 and on 7 November 1645 respectively.[81]

Cornet Clay[82]
Trooper George Hilton
Trooper John Cornwall
Trooper William Dennis – these three are included in a list of Parliamentarian prisoners of war held at Hawarden, dated 14 April 1645. Coote subsequently petitioned for their exchange.[83]

Colonel Henry Brooke's Troop

This may have been formed as early as 1642, although it existed by March 1643.[84] On 7 May 1644 Parliament granted Henry Brooke £1,000 for the

77 *BLB*, II, p.20.
78 TNA, SP28/225/3, fol. 770r.; SP28/196/1, fols 506v., 510r.; *BLB*, II, p.20.
79 BL, MS Harley 1999, fol. 71r.; MS Add. 11332, fol. 62v.; *BLB*, II, 808.
80 BL, MS Add. 11331, fols 90r., 100v.; MS 11333, fols 30r., 45r., 48v.–9r., 57v., 59v., 128v.; TNA, SP28/267/2, fols 1r.–v.; *CSPI, 1633–47*, p.514; *BLB*, II, 868, 885, 1040, 1063, 1072, 1087–8, 1091, 1260.
81 TNA, SP28/30/7, fol. 688v.; MS Harley, 2128, fol. 91r.; E121/5/7/43, fol. 2r.; BL, MS Add. 11332, fols 40v., 61v.; *BLB*, II, 795, 833.
82 TNA, SP28/30/7, fol. 688v.
83 BL, MS Add. 11331, fol. 9v.; *BLB*, I, 236.
84 TNA, SP28/196/1, fol. 14v.

completion of his troop and regiment of foot.[85] The troop was led throughout the war by Captain-Lieutenant Robert Wynn. He may have been a professional soldier brought by Brooke from his wife's native Nottinghamshire to help organise and lead his troop. During the siege of Chester Colonel Brooke's troop was quartered for much of the time at small outposts to the south and south-west of the city. These were both isolated and at times, vulnerable to enemy attack. Thus on 11 January 1645, whilst quartering at Aldford, his men were surprised by an attack from Chester, during which a number horses and arms were lost, and Captain Warburton and Captain Stukeley, serving as gentleman troopers were captured.[86] Like the rest of the Cheshire horse, Colonel Henry Brooke's men received pay from a range of sources. For instance, on 29 September 1644 the constables of Weston provided them with £1 14s. 10d., while on 20 February 1644 the constables of Aston were ordered to supply the sum of £5 13s. 4d. and to render a further six weeks' pay at 13s. each week per trooper.[87] Correspondingly, in 1643 and 1644 the constables of Church Lawton accounted for £2 6s. paid to Brooke's troop fortnightly; the sequestrators for Northwich Hundred disbursed £1 10s. on 1 October 1644 'to maintain the riders in the high sheriff's troop', whereas John Wettenhall, sequestration agent for Broxton, paid the sum of £65 to Captain-Lieutenant Robert Wynn for Brooke's troop during the siege of Beeston Castle on 2 August 1645.[88] The unit mustered 50 troopers on 30 April and 18 October 1645. Lieutenant Leighton distributed pay to the troop in April 1643 and January 1645, and may have acted as its adjutant.[89]

Cornet John Brooke

John was the fifth son of Sir Richard and Katherine Brooke of Norton, and thus younger brother to the officers Henry and Richard. By early 1643 he had been commissioned as captain in Colonel Brooke's infantry regiment, although later records of his service state that he had also served as a 'cornet of horse'. Moreover, in 1645 John received payment of £31 0s. 0½d. as cornet and captain of a company of foot.[90] The assumption must be that he acted as cornet to his brother's troop of horse before obtaining his commission as captain.

Cornet Lawrence Hyde

Probably the eighth son of Robert Hyde of Norbury, in 1656 Lawrence married Dorothy, a sister of Colonel Henry Brooke. If John Brooke had served as cornet to Brooke's troop, then Lawrence certainly succeeded him in the early months of 1643. Cornet Hyde signed an acquittance for £5, dated 13 July 1646, being the gratuity for his part in the siege of Chester. It was followed by a letter to the Committee of Accounts in Cheshire from Colonel Brooke, urging its payment

85 *CJ*, III, p.484.
86 Malbon, p.154.
87 BL, MS Harley 1970, fol. 150r.; Aston archive, unlisted warrant, dated 20 February 1644.
88 BL, MS Harley 1970, fols 44r., 92r.; 1943, fol. 6r. See also MS Harley 1970, fols 60r., 49v.; 2137, fols 200v.–201r.; MS Add. 11333, fols 30, 118; TNA, SP28/208, unfol.; SP28/224, fol. 168r.
89 BL, MS Add. 11331, fol. 45r.; MS Add. 11333, fol. 3r.; TNA, SP28/196, fol. 16v.
90 TNA, E121/1/5, fol. 307v.; E121/5/7/95, fol. 1r.–v.

and recommending 'his quality and fidelity', whilst adding in a postscript that a Mr Atkinson of Northwich 'has stolen a nag from my cornet'.[91]

Edward Birtle served as trooper and quartermaster to Brooke's troop, and later as lieutenant to Captain Robert Wynn's company in Colonel Brooke's militia regiment in 1650–1.[92]

Corporal John Doane	Trooper Adam Earl
Trooper Joseph Hale	Trooper William Darnell
Trooper Thomas Millington	Trooper Phillip Newson
Trooper Tobias Lowe	Trooper Robert Wood
Trooper Roger Harrison	Trooper Brian Sixsmith[93]

Colonel George Booth's Troop

Probably raised in September or October 1642, it was one of the Cheshire army's earliest cavalry units. Colonel Booth's command served at the First Battle of Middlewich and throughout 1643, but may have disbanded at the end of 1644 when he briefly resigned his commission as colonel of his regiment of foot. During the first months of 1643 Booth's troop obtained a horse worth £8 10s. from the sequestrated Hugh Leigh, while in the year following the collectors for Northwich Hundred paid £14 for maintaining seven horses and arms. Likewise, the constables of Lymm accounted for '26 horses [taken] by Colonel George Booth out of the township for his troop, worth £48'; also the sequestration committee for Bucklow furnished two mounts.[94] At an unspecified date, but probably in 1645–6 Booth's command was included in a larger payment of £554 8s. 3d. by treasurer Croxton with his own foot regiment and the cavalry troop under Sergeant Major John Bramhall.[95] The following served in Booth's troop:

Captain-Lieutenant Loughton

The troop's first captain-lieutenant, he received pay in that role on 8 May 1643. Loughton appears to have been succeeded by Quartermaster Wood before the end of the year.[96]

Cornet Vaudrey[97]
Corporal Hurior – serving in the troop by 15 March 1643.[98]

91 TNA, SP28/224/1, fols 152r.–153v.
92 TNA, E121/ 5/7/351, fol. 32v.
93 BL, MS Add. 11331, fol. 9v.; 11333, fol. 110r.; TNA, SP28/196, fol. 17v.; E121/5/7/351, fols 22r., 23v., 50v., 53r., 61r., 65r. Trooper Millington was reported among Parliamentarian prisoners of war at Hawarden Castle on 14 April 1645, while Lowe and Harrison were prisoners of war in Chester in January 1646.
94 BL, MS Harley 2128, fols 43r., 49r., 60r.; 2137, fol. 115r.
95 TNA, SP28/128/13, fol. 17v.
96 TNA, SP28/196/1, fols 6v., 12v.; SP28/152/4, fol. 13r.
97 TNA, SP28/128/13, fol. 26r.
98 TNA, SP28/196/1, fol. 3v.

Colonel John Leigh's Troop

Raised by late 1643 when the constables of Mere expended £17 4s. for a 'horse and arms under [the] command of Colonel Leigh'. During the summer of 1644 the same officials supplied a number of cavalry mounts to the troops of Leigh, Coote and Bulkeley, and on 19 October and in November of that year Colonel John's soldiers were in receipt of arrears of pay.[99] The troop was attacked at Tattenhall on the night of 9 January 1645, on which occasion the Royalists 'took many of Colonel Leigh's horses, arms, and some men of his troop, being of the parliament side in their quarters, and took them to Chester'.[100]

Captain-Lieutenant Samuel Leigh

Younger brother to Colonel John, he received pay 'as captain of his brother's troop' on 15 December 1645.[101] The command was unaccountably omitted from Brereton's army list of 30 April 1645, but not from his regiments of horse and foot, dated 18 October, when it had 60 troopers.

Colonel Henry Mainwaring's Troop

The troop was in existence by February 1643. Shortly afterwards the constables of Church Lawton, William Rowley and Thomas Shaw spent 3 10s. for a mount for the command, with an additional £1 18s. 10d. laid out 'for bridle, saddle and other furniture for [the] said horse'. Moreover, on 15 December 1643 Mainwaring received the sum of £10 for his troopers. The troop also benefitted from an overall payment made to it and Colonel Henry Mainwaring's regiment of foot from central sources of £244 19s. 8d.[102] On 8 March the Committee of Both Kingdoms ordered 'Colonel Henry Mainwaring and his brother for their horse' to go to the relief of Wem with other Cheshire forces.[103] Philemon Mainwaring, half-brother to Henry was paid as cornet to the troop, and probably served as its leader following the imprisonment of Captain-Lieutenant Dutton by order of the Stafford Committee in March 1644 for allegedly plundered horses in Staffordshire.[104] Owing to the later service of Philemon as lieutenant to Captain William Carter's troop, it seems likely that Colonel Henry's horse survived under this captain's command, probably from mid to late 1644 onwards. It is possible that Sir William Brereton's insistence that all the troops of horse in the county were brought under his command as part of his regiment of horse was one of the reasons for the breach between him and Henry Mainwaring. The commands of Philip Mainwaring and Stanley of Alderley were operating in a

99 BL, MS Harley 2128, fols 60v–61r.; TNA, SP28/225, fol. 924r.; SP28/152/7, fol. 12v.

100 Malbon, p.154.

101 TNA, SP28/225/3, fol. 578v.

102 TNA, SP28/196/1, fol. 13; SP28/128/13, fol. 16v.; SP28/208, unfol.; BL, MS Harley 1943, fol. 4r.; 1999, fol. 313v.

103 *CSPD 1644*, p.41.

104 TNA, SP28/30/7, fol. 694r.; Pennington and Roots, *Committee at Stafford*, p.84.

similar fashion to Colonel Henry's in 1644, but these too had disappeared by the time of Brereton's army lists of April and October 1645. In the case of the latter, Stanley's son Peter no longer held a commission and Stanley himself was in opposition to Sir William on the county committee.

Sergeant Major Philip Mainwaring's Troop

Philip Mainwaring was of an ancient family of Over Peover and Baddiley. He had served as sheriff of Cheshire in 1638 and encountered considerable opposition towards the payment of ship money within the county. Mainwaring was also a deputy lieutenant, assessments commissioner and one of the leading opponents of Brereton in Cheshire between 1643 and 1645.[105] His troop of horse was raised over the winter of 1642–43, with funds being issued in London to purchase saddles for it in January 1643.[106] The sum of £20 was disbursed to Captain Philip Mainwaring on 25 September 1643, yet by 23 April 1644 he had been promoted, when all the profits of the lands of the sequestered Lawrence Wynington of Armitage were granted to his troop. Besides, in 1644 Mainwaring received from the Tabley estate £33 6s. 8d. out of the £100 owing him, while Robert Wittingham of Over complained that there had been 'taken by Major Mainwaring's and Major Croxton's soldiers 12 cows and three heifers, and one calf and a chain which the calf was tied with to the value of £40'.[107] Mainwaring's arrears of pay amounted to £34 2s., which were settled at a later date by treasurer Croxton.[108] His troop of horse appears to have been disbanded sometime in 1644.

Captain John Hawkbridge's Troop

This officer's origins are uncertain, but he was in London and the Midlands with Michael Jones during the summer of 1644, raising a troop for the Cheshire army. He was paid as captain on 7 June and had probably completed his command by 7 September.[109] Hawkbridge participated in a council of war at Hawarden on 16 May 1645, and his troop participated in the siege of Chester and other operations into 1646.[110]

Lieutenant Betts

Paid with Hawkbridge on 7 June 1644 and probably came with him from London. He seems to have been recommended to Brereton by the Reverend Hugh Peter, the army chaplain and well-known independent preacher, who wrote to Sir William on 20 March 1645:

---

105 *Acts and ordinances of the interregnum, 1642–1660*, ed. Firth, C.H. and Rait, R.S. (London: HMSO, 1911), I, pp.90, 147; Morrill, *Cheshire*, pp.28–9, 86.

106 TNA, SP28/225/3, fol. 725v.; SP28/263, fol. 154r.

107 BL, MS Harley 1999, fol. 313r.; 2126, fol. 19v.; SP28/225/3, unfol.

108 TNA, SP28/128/13, fol. 26r.; SP28/224/1, unfol.

109 TNA, SP28/152/7, fol. 12v.; SP28/196, fol. 20v.

110 BL, MS Add. 11331, fol. 113; *BLB*, I, 551.

> I am also bold to become a suitor unto you in behalf of Lieutenant Betts whom I commended unto you and hope he deserves it. Let him be not forgotten for a place amongst those on whom you cast a gracious eye and to whom you intend preferment, though I know I need not add spurs to your readiness to do and deal righteously. Yet I cannot tell whether the modesty of my friend may not be something prejudicious. I hope one word will serve and hereby you will make me more your obliged servant in Christ.[111]

John Brooke received pay as lieutenant to Hawkbridge's troop in June and October 1645. Payments to Cornet Francis Cooke and Quartermaster Gelson were made at the same time.[112] The troop mustered 50 troopers on 30 April 1645 and 18 October 1645.

Captain Henry Stone's Troop

Henry Stone was a Walsall merchant and member of the Staffordshire Committee. He was commissioned captain in Sir Richard Houghton's regiment of foot in Staffordshire in May 1643.[113] Following the Royalist storming of Burton-on-Trent, of which Houghton was the governor, his regiment dispersed. By 16 June Captain Stone had taken command of a troop of horse, which was probably recruited in Staffordshire, and for which he was granted £100 to purchase arms.[114] This was nominally part of the Cheshire army, but it was also paid occasionally and directed by the Staffordshire Committee. Stone was one of Brereton's main supporters in the county, yet his chief value was as governor of Eccleshall and Stafford. Moreover, Henry's intelligence reports to the Cheshire commander, as well as the Committee of Both Kingdoms, were invaluable, none more than during various stages of 1645, when Chester, the Welsh marches and the Midlands were threatened by the King, Prince Rupert and other Royalist commanders. As Dore suggests, 'in January 1643 was the absolute necessity in creating a Parliamentarian presence in north Staffordshire whose border with Cheshire was only a few miles from Nantwich, his recently acquired H.Q., and lay across the vital link through the midlands with London'.[115] Such a presence was established in August 1643 when, with the assistance of the Cheshire army, Eccleshall and Stafford Castles had been captured, and a county committee was created at Stafford.

An indication as to how highly Sir William Brereton regarded Captain Stone and his soldiers can be gleaned from his letter to the Committee of Both Kingdoms, dated 13 March 1645, following the officer's appointment by him as governor of Stafford:

---

111 TNA, SP28/152/7, fols 5r., 12v.; BL, MS Add. 11331, fol. 79; *BLB*, I, 88.

112 TNA, SP28/35/2, fol. 295v.; SP28/152/8, fol. 1v.

113 TNA, SP28/267/4, fols 101r.–114v.

114 TNA, SP28/134/12, fol. 332; *Committee at Stafford*, p.334.

115 *BLB*, I, p.18.

> You were pleased to command me to take care of Stafford, a place of great strength and concernment, and to confirm Captain Stone in the charge and due government thereof. You commanded him to remain there until further order, where he hath, in obedience to your commands, performed very good service and reduced the garrison to as good order and government as in any kingdom. The well-affected inhabitants are so well satisfied that they apprehend themselves in a more secure condition, although they want five or six companies, now with me, that were in the town when he took the command. And I dare affirm that his single troop of horse, belonging to Eccleshall Castle, hath done as much service as any in England.[116]

Lieutenant George Hill

Of Walsall, he was serving in the troop on 12 November 1644. Hill received the sum of £1 on 20 November 1645 for carrying despatches from Stafford to Coventry.[117]

Cornet Casteele[118]
Saddler Roger Boulton[119]

The unit contained 100 troopers on 30 April 1645, 80 on 19 May 1645 and 100 on 18 October 1645.[120]

Captain John Vivers' Troop

This troop may have begun life under Captain Robert Vivers of Colonel Goodwin's regiment in Essex's army in August 1642. In a letter to his father, the Parliamentarian Nathaniel Fiennes mentioned a 'Captain Vivers', a brother of Robert's who had delivered a despatch to him on the eve of the Battle of Edgehill, fought on 23 October.[121] Captain Robert was subsequently taken prisoner, but seems to have been paroled by early 1645. It is probable that his brother John took command of the troop because the last recorded payment to it, dated December 1643, was signed for by him.[122] In May 1644 members of Captain John Vivers' troop were quartered in Middlesex and paid with others of Brereton's own troop which had travelled with Sir William to London following the Parliamentarian victory at Nantwich in January 1644.[123] The commander-in-chief was raising other cavalry troops at that time, including those of Jones, Coote and Hawkbridge, as well as

116 CRO, DDX/428, fol. 56; *BLB*, I, 151.
117 TNA, SP28/ 196/1, fol. 22v.; SP28/152/7, fol. 15v.; BL, MS Add. 11332, fol. 99; *BLB*, II, 887.
118 TNA, SP28/152/9, fol. 5r.
119 TNA, SP28/152/7, fol. 17r.
120 BL, MS Add. 11331; fol. 45v.; 11332, fol. 133v.; 11333, fol. 3r.
121 *A most true and exact relation of both the battels fought by his excellency and his forces against the bloody cavaliers* (London, 9 November 1642).
122 TNA, SP28/11/232, fol. 20v.; SP28/21/267, fol. 88r.
123 TNA, SP28/198/1, fols 1v.–5v.

eliciting substantial quantities of money and arms for the expansion of the Cheshire army. Presumably Vivers's troop was taken into his service at this time. It reached Cheshire by 24 June 1644 and numbered 56 troopers among its ranks.[124] Captain John Vivers' troop appears to have been completed by 23 October 1644.[125]

Vivers also appears to have commanded the remains of Bulkeley's troop between 29 April 1645 and January 1646. John Vivers's troop mustered 50 troopers on 30 April 1645 and (combined with Bulkeley's) 120 troopers on 18 October 1645. From central sources James Croxton disbursed a total of £563 9s. 6d. to 'Captain Vivers for himself, officers and troop'.[126] In April 1645 troopers under the command of Captains Vivers and Culme were charged with plundering jewels. In a postscript to a letter of 7 April from Brereton and Myddelton to bother officers, the latter appealed to John Vivers: 'if restitution be not made of these goods your brother, Colonel Vivers, will be much dishonoured and questioned. As I shall be much troubled for him, consider therefore and vindicate him and yourself and loving friend, William Brereton.'[127] Trumpeter Abraham Nicholas was paid with the troop on May 1644.[128]

Captain Robert Stukeley's Troop

Two references place Captain Robert Stukeley in Cheshire in June and October 1643.[129] Wanklyn asserts that he was a professional soldier who raised a foot company in the spring of 1644 at the same time as Captain Hugh Whitney.[130] Yet the manuscript entry simply mentions a payment to Stukeley, rather than his company, while Whitney had commanded a company in Colonel George Booth's regiment since September 1643, and perhaps as early as the previous February.[131] Clothing bills, dated to 3 and 25 October 1643, show that Captain Stukeley raised and kitted out a troop of horse in Cheshire during this time.[132] What became of the command is unclear, however. He was captured whilst serving as a gentleman trooper with Brooke's troop at Aldford on 11 January 1645 and may have left the army following his release.

124 TNA, SP28/225/924, fol. 44r.; SP28/144, fol. 6v.
125 TNA, SP28/152/7, fol. 12v.
126 TNA, SP28/128/13, fol. 15v.
127 CRO, DDX/428, fol. 70v.–r.; *BLB*, I, 168. For the entire affair and inventories of items taken, see BL, MS Add. 11331, fols 28r., 35v., 116v.; CRO, DDX/428, fol. 71v.–r.; NLW, MS Rhual 115; *BLB*, I, 169–70, 187–8, 373; Tucker, *North Wales in the Civil War*, pp.46–8.
128 TNA, SP28/152/7, fol. 12v.
129 TNA, SP28/45, fol. 67r.–v.
130 Wanklyn, 'Landed Society' (citing CRO, DAR/1/56).
131 BL, MS Harley 1999, fol. 60r.
132 TNA, SP28/8, fols 17r., 16r.

Captain William Shepley's Troop

Probably of Stockport, William Shepley had formed his troop by late summer 1643. About this time Shepley demanded arrears of pay for his men from the constables of Aston in Bucklow Hundred.[133] During operations in Shropshire in July 1644 a number of troops of horse from the Cheshire army acted in support of the forlorn hope during the Parliamentarian assault on Montford Bridge.[134] Shepley's troop fought at Montgomery, following which he was paid £5 for a captured horse and a pair of pistols.[135] Whilst quartering in the Wirral in mid 1645 William received hay and peas to the value of £4 10s. from the Committee at Hooton. Seemingly desperate to obtain provisions for his men, this enterprising officer appropriated land at Burton for the cultivation of crops. Thus, local Parliamentarian officials complained when Shepley's troopers produced 50 measures of oats 'without order' at 12d. per measure, and a further '46 measures of oats not paid for to the state'.[136] There is evidence that William Shepley was captured on 15 October 1645. An intercepted letter from the Royalist Thomas Rogers of Llanasa, dated the following day mentions, 'For this present time our horse sallied out [from Chester] to Eccleston, killed and took threescore and seven of theirs, took Shepley's horse and some light horse besides.'

Captain Shepley's incarceration is confirmed by an undated payment from treasurer Croxton of £4 'to Major Bramhall, to be given Captain Shepley, prisoner at Salop'.[137] William had been released by 29 December, however, when he was present with his own troop and that of Glegg, and a small body of Cheshire foot guarding Lache, some two miles south-west of Chester. Shepley's was one of three Cheshire troops of horse diverted from operations in North Wales to the siege of Lichfield Close (Brereton's and Carter's being the others) on 16 April 1646.[138] The total paid to William Shepley 'and his officers and troop' from central funds between 1643 and 1646 was £1,018 19s. 8d.[139] Lieutenant Hyber Scott, Shepley's second in command, was serving by 1644 and in April 1646 he took custody of the munitions and arms taken at the capture of Tutbury Castle, which he delivered to the Parliamentarian stronghold at Eccleshall. On 21 April Scott was paid £2 'to defray [his] charges being employed to take charge of the guns, arms and materials of war taken at Tutbury Castle to convey them to Eccleshall Castle', and a further sum for the same in November 1646 of £5 0s. 5d.[140] Shepley's troop mustered 60 troopers on 3 October 1645 and 50 on 18 October 1645.

---

133 Aston archive, unlisted warrant from Captain William Shepley, undated, possibly *c.* October 1643.

134 *Great Victories obtained by the Earl of Denbigh at Shrewsbury, Chulmely and other parts of Cheshire* (London, 1644); *CWTC*, pp.123–4.

135 TNA, SP28/152, 7, fol. 6v.; BL, MS Add. 11332, fol. 39v.

136 BL, MS Harley 1999, fols 17r., 69r., 71v.

137 BL, MS Add. 11332, fol. 97v.; TNA, SP28/128/13, fol. 26r; *BLB*, II, 680.

138 BL, MS Add. 11333, fol. 78v.; BCA, MS 595611, p.35; *BLB*, I, 1140; *CWS*, 55.

139 TNA, SP28/128/13, fol. 18v.

140 TNA, SP28/224/1, fol. 185r.; SP16/513/1, fols 73r., 81r.; BCA, MS 595611, p.69; *CWS*, 110.

Captain Humphrey Bulkeley's Troop

Humphrey Bulkeley of Cheadle was the head of the senior branch of the Cheshire Bulkeleys. He was commanding a troop of Cheshire horse by 1 March 1643, and is mentioned by Malbon as participating in the action at Hanmer on 20 June.[141] In August 1644 Captain Bulkeley was granted the rents and goods of the parsonage of Cheadle, with its glebe lands, as well as a dwelling and the demesne of Peel for the use of his officers and men by the sequestration committee of Macclesfield Hundred.[142] He was captured with a large part of his troop near Wrexham on 29 April 1645 by Royalists from Denbighshire. In his post-war accounts Bulkeley mentioned that himself, his cornet, two corporals, two trumpeters were taken.[143] The cornet in question was Humphrey Milton; on 5 July 1645 a warrant was issued to pay Trumpeter John Fletcher, Clerk Thomas Lindley and 21 troopers of Bulkeley's who had recently been released.[144] Captain Bulkeley was held at Ruthin Castle before being transferred to Chester. On 5 May a clearly vexed Sir William Brereton reported, 'Wherein of late they have plagued and infested our out-quarters, wherein they have taken (29 April in the night) Captain Bulkeley and about 40 of his troop, and ten of my firelocks.'[145] During mid 1645 in particular, the various isolated Parliamentarian outposts on the Welsh side of the Chester leaguer were highly susceptible to attack, poorly provisioned and difficult to reinforce if threatened. On 6 May Colonel Trevor with 500 horse and foot surprised a small force of Montgomeryshire troops in Wrexham. During a desperate fight, the Royalists seized 60 prisoners, including 19 gentlemen and officers. Brereton offered his support to Sir Thomas Myddelton's commanders, although he had few resources to send them.[146]

On 30 October 1645 it was related by Brereton that a trooper belonging to Captain Bulkeley 'went forth to scout and most treacherously betrayed those of his fellow soldiers into the hands of the enemy'.[147] The unnamed trooper subsequently deserted and took up arms for the King, before being recaptured by his former comrades. Thus, despite various proposals by Humphrey Bulkeley, Brereton rejected them, and it seems he was in no hurry to have him exchanged. Dore reasonably suggests 'As Bulkeley was in charge of a troop of horse that should have given alarm at the approach of the Royalist forces, Brereton may well have blamed him for the setbacks near Wrexham.'[148]

Corporal Henry Sidebottom
Trumpeter John Fletcher
Clerk Thomas Lindley[149]

141 TNA, SP28/196/1, fol. 11v.; Malbon, p.62.
142 BL, MS Harley 2130, fol. 3r.
143 NLW, Bangor University, GB 0222 BHILL/38.
144 TNA, SP28/30/7, fol. 747r.; SP28/224/1, fol. 6v.
145 BL, MS Add. 11331, fol. 80v.; *BLB*, I, 439.
146 BL, MS Add. 11331, fols 63v.–5v.; *BLB*, I, 433–6.
147 BL. MS Add. 11332, fol. 29r.; *BLB*, II, 786.
148 *BLB*, I, 1164, n. 1. For Bulkeley's appeals for parole, see BL, MS Add. 11331, fols 80v., 73r., 76r., 119v.; *BLB*, I, 439, 455, 539. Captain Bulkeley was finally exchanged on 13 January 1646 (TNA, SP28/196/1, fol. 11r.).
149 TNA, E121/5/7/351, fol. 38v.

Captain John Glegg's Troop

The son of William Glegg of Gayton in the Wirral, and brother of Captain Edward Glegg, a company commander in Sir William Brereton's regiment of foot. John raised his troop in late 1644, while in January 1645 the Parliamentarian committee at Hooton disbursed 'to Captain John Glegg by order from Sir William Brereton towards raising of a troop of horse, in barley 27 measures valued at £3 6s'.[150] On 9 June 1645 Glegg and his command was attacked by a sortie from Chester, intent on disrupting various Parliamentarian garrisons about the besieged city. They were rescued by the intervention of a task force from Tarvin led by Lieutenant Colonel Venables.[151] On 20 November 1646 Glegg's troop were paid with Jones's command, 'being both designed for Ireland'.[152] Glegg probably died there. His Cheshire troop numbered 40 troopers on 30 April 1645 and 18 October 1645.

Captain Hugh Culme's Troop

An Anglo-Irishman, related by marriage to Lieutenant Colonel Michael Jones, Hugh served as captain from 11 December 1644, but was killed at Rowton Heath on 25 September 1645.[153] His troop was subsequently led by his lieutenant, John Ely, before being taken over by Captain Richard Brereton on 9 November 1645, who served in that capacity until 10 October 1646.[154] Richard had previously acted as cornet to Duckenfield's troop until 1 December 1643, when he received a commission as captain of a company of foot 'under Sir William Brereton's command', which he led until 4 July 1644. He was subsequently a reformado, before replacing Captain Culme and serving until October 1646. Richard served at the Leaguer of Chester and with the Cheshire forces at Lichfield until the disbandment of Sir William Brereton's regiment of horse. Whilst at Lichfield on 30 May 1646 Captain Brereton received £20 in pay, and in the September his troop received £83 4d. Sergeant Major Zankey later supported his claims that when Sir Thomas Fairfax ordered him to go to Cheshire from Leighton Buzzard on 30 July 1647, Richard volunteered himself and his men 'and engaged himself as far as in him lay to observe whatever orders I should receive' from the general, and continued under Sankey's command until his troop was disbanded on 9 January 1648.[155]

On 14 May 1645 the junior and non-commissioned officers of the troop were:

150 BL, MS Harley 1999, fol. 70r.

151 Lancaster, p.15; Malbon, pp.172–3.

152 TNA, SP28/224/1, fols 163r., 181v.

153 TNA, SP28/252/1, fol. 1v.; Lancaster, p.52.

154 BL, MS Harley 2128, fol. 77r.; TNA, SP28/225/3, fol. 775v.; SP28/225/4, fols 873r.–v.; SP28/38, fol. 183r.

155 TNA, SP16/513/1, fol. 87r.; SP28/40/40.

Lieutenant John Ely	Corporal Wood
Cornet Carter	Corporal Booth
Quartermaster Johnson	Corporal Cork[156]

Muster rolls show that the troop was substantially reformed after Rowton Heath, and was disbanded on 10 October 1646.[157] The following were present on 15 April 1646:

Captain Richard Brereton	Corporal Leigh
Lieutenant John Ely	Corporal Francis Clenton
Cornet Johnson	Trumpeter William Ridgeway
Quartermaster Alcocke	Trumpeter Edward Acton
Sergeant Elliot	Surgeon Elias Preston.[158]
Corporal Moore	

The troop mustered 50 troopers (with Edwards) on 30 April 1645, 19 on 14 May 1645, 40 on 18 October 1645 and 54 on 15 April 1646.[159]

Captain William Edwards' Troop

William was the younger brother of the Royalist Evan Edwards of Rhualt, Flintshire. He was a pre-war merchant, alderman and mayor of Chester in 1636, and a close friend of Sir William Brereton. Captain Edwards' troop was raised in London by October 1642, and accompanied Brereton's horse to Cheshire the following January.[160] The command was a stalwart of the Cheshire army and participated in numerous operations. On 12 January 1645 it was quartered at Barrow, near Chester, where during a night attack it became 'suddenly surprised, and many of his men, horse and arms taken and carried away to Chester'.[161] Command of the troop seems to have passed to William Edwards' son, William, by 2 August 1645.[162] It mustered 41 troopers on 17 December 1644, 50 on 30 April 1645 and 40 on 18 October 1645. On 17 December 1644 the junior and non-commissioned officers were:

Lieutenant John Wynn	Corporal Parker
Quartermaster Bayfield	Trumpeter Parker
Corporal Richard	Trumpeter Bonner[163]
Corporal Earle	

156 TNA, SP28/28/3, fol. 283r.
157 BL, MS Harley 2128, fol. 77r.
158 TNA, SP28/123/3, fols. 381v.–87r.
159 BL, MS Add. 11331, fol. 45r.; 11333, fol. 3r.; TNA, SP28/28/3, fol. 283v.; SP28/123, fol. 1r.
160 HMC, *Portland*, I, pp.94–5.
161 Malbon, pp.154–5.
162 BL, MS Harley 2128, fol. 92r.; TNA, SP/28/224, fol. 214v.
163 TNA, SP28/121/A, fol. 645r.; BL, MS Add. 11331, fol. 45; 11332, fol. 3.

Captain William Carter's Troop

Carter was from Cotton, near Chester. Although he may have possessed a commission as captain by August 1643, there is evidence that he took command of Colonel Henry Mainwaring's troop following his removal by Parliament in early 1644 for disloyalty, although it remains unclear when Mainwaring laid down his military commission.[164] On 8 March the Committee of Both Kingdoms issued an order for 'Colonel Henry Mainwaring and his brother for their horse' to march with other Cheshire forces to Wem.[165] He also led his foot regiment at Stockport in May and the operations in Shropshire in August 1644. Henry's 'brother' referred to in the order to march the troop to Wem in March 1644 was Philemon Mainwaring of Great Warford, half-brother to the colonel. He was paid at an unspecified date as cornet to his troop, and owing to his appearance here as second-in-command to Henry, he had probably been promoted to lieutenant by early 1644.[166]

Lieutenant Philemon Mainwaring later served under Captain Carter. William Carter actively commanded the troop in Broxton Hundred area and the Chester leaguer in April and May 1645 alongside those of Jones, Coote and Duckenfield.[167] The Royalist Colonel Trevor reported that on the evening of 15 May at Farndon 'a party of ours took seven of his [Carter's] men and had taken himself and all the rest but for the goodness of their horses'.[168]

The precariousness of the various forward Parliamentarian outposts was exhibited again, when in the early hours of 15 October 1645 William Carter's troop was surprised at Eccleston when a body of Royalist horse sallied out and 'beat up a quarter of the rebels and took one horse colours and a trumpet, and Carter's lieutenant, and four troopers and about eight horses and some foot arms and (as they say) killed 30 upon the place'.[169] The identity of the lieutenant is confirmed in a letter of Lieutenant Colonel Peter Griffith, written two days later, as Philemon Mainwaring. Randle Holme's later account of the action adds: 'On Wednesday 15 October Captain Dutton and Captain Crosby fell upon the enemy's quarters at Eccleston, slew a cornet with about 20 or 30 of their foot. They bring in Captain Carter's lieutenant and four troopers prisoner with his trumpet and colours.'[170]

Mainwaring was misidentified by Dore as Captain Bulkeley's lieutenant, because he assumed that the troop which was attacked when Mainwaring was captured was Colonel John Carter's. This mistake was the cause of another one, as Colonel Carter was an officer of Sir Thomas Myddelton's, whose men were involved round Wrexham, which is where Bulkeley and

164 TNA, SP28/196/2, fol. 496v.; SP28/144, fol. 7v.

165 *CSPD 1644*, p.41.

166 TNA, SP28/30/7, fol. 694r.

167 CRO, DDX/428, fol. 79v.; BL, MS Add. 11331, fols 112v.–13r.; *BLB*, I, 181, 509, 558.

168 BL, MS Add. 11331, fol. 112v.; *BLB*, I, 541.

169 BL, MS Add. 11332, fol. 84r.; *BLB*, I, 684.

170 BL, MS Harley 2155, fol. 24v.; MS Add. 11332, fol. 96r.; *BLB*, II, 686; Morris, *Siege of Chester*, App. I. 'Owen William, trumpeter to Captain Carter' is further listed as prisoner of war in Chester on 8 November 1645 (MS Add. 11331, fol. 1r.; *BLB*, II, 842).

his troop were taken.[171] James Gibson replaced the unnamed cornet killed at Eccleston with Captain Carter's troop; he later served in Ireland and was paid as cornet to Colonel Sankey's own troop on 14 June 1650. A list of prisoners of war in Chester on 8 November 1645 identifies Carter's trumpeter as Owen William.[172] William Carter received £14 8s. in pay from the sequestrators of the upper division of Wirral Hundred on 23 May 1645, while his troop was mentioned as being in distinct arrears with other Cheshire horse and Captain Joseph Holt's dragoons on 6 November 1645.[173] 40 troopers mustered on 30 April 1645, 60 on 18 October 1645 and 22 and 23 April 1646.[174] A probably earlier (undated) figure of 15 troopers clearly reflects the sudden decrease in numbers, and indicates that the depleted troop had hardly recovered by April 1646.[175]

Muster roll of the troop, undated (probably late 1645):

Lieutenant Philemon Mainwaring	Corporal Samuel Barry
Cornet James Gibson	Corporal William Hulme
Quartermaster George Hough	Trumpeter John Workman
Corporal John Moss	Trumpeter Thomas Wollam
Corporal Thomas Hussey	15 troopers listed[176]

Captain Edward Hyde's Troop

Edward was from a well-established Presbyterian family, of Norbury, Cheshire. He was a deputy lieutenant, brother-in-law to Colonel Henry Brooke of Norton and close associate of Colonel Robert Duckenfield. Edward was active in the early months of war, raising his troop and company of foot (in Duckenfield's regiment) by September 1642. Captain Hyde's troop participated in the defence of Manchester, and was present at the actions at Nantwich on 30 January 1643 and Middlewich on 13 March.[177]

Sergeant Major John Marbury's Troop

From Marbury, Cheshire, John was brother of Thomas Marbury and half-brother to the William Marbury, deputy lieutenants for Cheshire. Wanklyn (taken up uncritically by Dore) suggests that at some point John held a commission as major in Colonel Brooke's regiment.[178] There is no contemporaneous evidence

171 See *BLB*, II, 686 n. 4.

172 TNA, E121/4/6, fol. 96r.; BL, MS Add. 11331, fol. 1r.; *BLB*, II, 842.

173 BL, MS Add. 11332, fol. 105v.; *BLB*, II, 897.

174 BL, MS Add. 11331, fol. 45r.; 11332, fol. 3r.; SP28/123/1, fol. 97r.

175 TNA, SP28/123/1, fol. 122v.

176 TNA, SP28/ 123/1, fols 122v.–3r.

177 *News from Manchester* (London, 24 September 1642); *A True and Faithful Relation of the besieging of the town of Manchester* (London, 1 October 1642); Malbon, pp.36, 40–3; *Military Proceedings in Lancashire*, pp.45, 53.

178 Wanklyn, 'Landed Society', p.239, n. 3; *BLB*, I, 267, n. 1; II, 837, note 2.

for this, whereas an undated warrant refers to 'Major Marbury's company in Colonel [George] Booth's regiment in the county of Chester'.[179] Malbon records that a troop of horse under 'Captain Marbury' was part of the force of Cheshire horse and foot that rendezvoused with Sir William Brereton at Nantwich during the first week of February 1643, and soon afterwards fought at Middlewich.[180] As neither of his relatives, William and Thomas Marbury, are known to have held military commissions he must have meant John. A pay warrant of 22 April 1644 refers to 'Captain Marbury's troop', while on 18 June John held the rank of sergeant major when his troop, numbering three officers, three corporals, two trumpeters, one quartermaster, one clerk and 58 troopers received pay.[181] For some reason the unit is not listed in Brereton's regiment on 30 April 1645 – a strange occurrence as it is mentioned in a letter from Lieutenant Colonel Michael Jones to Sir William Brereton with those of Leigh, Holford, Duckenfield, Coote and Carter on the Cheshire side of the Chester leaguer on 13 May.[182] Sergeant Major John Marbury's military career ended in November 1645 when on the recommendation of the Commons Committee for Examinations, he was cashiered for disloyalty to Sir William Brereton with Captains Hugh Whitney and George Massey.[183]

Sergeant Major John Bramhall's Troop

Bramhall served as captain of a company of Cheshire dragoons from 21 November 1642 to 20 August 1643, and as major of dragoons from 20 August 1643 to 30 April 1644. His commission as major of a troop of horse ran from 30 April 1644 to his resignation on 5 February 1645. On the day of its disbandment (or more likely, coming under the command of another officer) the troop mustered one lieutenant, one cornet, one quartermaster, three corporals, two trumpeters and 50 troopers.[184] Bramhall's former lieutenant, Thomas Mainwaring, took up a commission in the troop, and it is possible that a number of his soldiers either followed him or enlisted in other dragoon units. A number of payments by Bramhall and others offer some insights into the supply, pay and expenses of his troop. On 18 May 1644 17s. 6. was given to the farrier Abraham Lindop 'for shoeing mine and Lieutenant Mainwaring's horses', while the sum of £15 11s. 10d. was disbursed to Randle Walton for shoeing the entire command's mounts on 1 February 1645. Bramhall's men were paid £21 on 18 December 1644 'upon muster by the treasurer at Beeston Castle', and on the same day he received an additional £13 'at Shrewsbury for the diet of my officers and soldiers'. Around mid 1646 his officers and troopers were remunerated £19 0s. 6d. in arrears of pay by James Croxton, the army's treasurer.[185]

179 TNA, E121/5/7, 351, fol. 4r.
180 Malbon, pp.36–7.
181 TNA, SP28/225/2, fol. 413r.; SP/28/196/1, fol. 21v.
182 BL, MS Add. 11331, fol. 96r.; *BLB*, I, 509.
183 BL, MS Add. 11333, fol. 96v.; *BLB*, II, 837.
184 BL, MS Harley 2128, fols 31v.–32r.
185 BL, MS Harley 2128, fols 26r.–v., 27v., 29r.

Captain Peter Stanley's Troop

The son of Thomas Stanley of Alderley, deputy lieutenant and member of the County Committee for Cheshire. According to his testimony, Peter served as a captain of a troop of horse from 28 February 1643 to 28 April 1644, and as captain of dragoons from 28 April 1644 to 6 May 1645.[186] According to Dore his troop was 'disbanded or put under another captain' sometime before April 1645', yet there is evidence to suggest that it was transferred to the Shropshire Committee it was paid by it soon afterwards, and appears among Shropshire forces remunerated at the Chester leaguer on 18 December.[187] The following served in the unit:

Lieutenant Burton
Cornet Lely
Clerk Thomas Doane[188]

Captain John Holford's Troop

There appears to have been more than one Captain Holford active in Cheshire during the First Civil War. Dore suggests that:

> Holford's horse is also spoken of by Jones but the confusion concerning this name – a well-known one in Cheshire – is almost total. There appears to have been a Captain Thomas, a Captain John and a Lieutenant Richard, brother to John. John and Richard, being of Lostock Gralam, nr Northwich, seem likely to be linked to Colonel Leigh, but his troop of horse is also mentioned by Jones in the same sentence with Holford's and Marbury's. Richard writes a letter while guarding a passage near Tarvin, but whether the Captain Holford whose presence at the siege of Beeston the Cheshire Committee desired … and the commander of Holford's horse are one and the same person and whether Thomas or John is unknown.[189]

Captain John Holford is first alluded to in January 1643 when he was paid £2 2s. for assisting Colonel Duckenfield at Stockport. Holford was associated with Colonel John Leigh – between 1643 and early 1644 his troop was paid and received provisions as part of the Northwich garrison with its governor, Lieutenant Colonel Gerard, and may have been raised from that part of Cheshire.[190] Captain Holford was commended for his 'good service' during the storming of Cholmondley House on 8 July 1644. His command was mentioned by Michael Jones in April and May 1645 as being at Knutsford, Beeston, Dodleston and the Welsh side of the Chester leaguer. On 24 November 1645 a warrant instructed the deliver to Captain Holford's officers and troopers one

186 TNA, SP28/46, fol. 19v.
187 TNA, SP28/46/19, 91r.; BL, MS Add. 11333, fol. 30r.; *BLB*, II, 1040.
188 TNA, SP28/152/7, fol. 5v.; SP28/225/4, fol. 748v.; CRO, ZCR/63/2/19, fol. 91r.
189 *BLB*, I, 385, note 1.
190 BL, MS Harley 2137, fols 152v., 114r.

month's pay upon the list to be given Captain John Whitworth.[191] Moreover, under a similar arrangement Holford's troop received a month's pay on 4 November 1646 'for gratuity promised them at the taking of Chester'.[192] The following junior officers served with the command:

Lieutenant Richard Holford

Brother to John, he commanded pickets at Farndon and Tarvin in early February and May 1645.

Quartermaster William Davies[193]

Captain Richard Blackwell's Troop

Blackwell served as captain of a troop of horse from 10 December 1644 to 21 July 1645.[194] He was captured at Christleton on 18 January 1645. In his account of the action to the Committee of Both Kingdoms, Brereton reported Blackwell as missing, while on 19 March 1645 he wrote to Sir Marmaduke Langdale, 'Captain Blackwell is now upon his parole to London for an exchange.'[195] Richard spent the remainder of his brief service in custody and on parole in London. He was exchanged on 18 August, but does not appear to have returned to the army, although on 4 February 1645 Lieutenant John Birkenshaw delivered £6 'for the use of Captain Richard Blackwell'.[196] Moreover, his troop appears to have avoided being broken up as Lieutenant William Sergeant took service with it on 7 February 1645 and 'continued for his twelve month warrant'.[197] Sergeant had previously served as cornet to Brereton's troop. He was succeeded by Lieutenant John Birkenshaw – on 4 February 1645 this officer received the sum of £6 'for the use of his captain, Captain Richard Blackwell'.[198]

Birkenshaw previously appears to have been a supernumerary officer. On 1 July 1643 he received £5 from the Macclesfield Hundred sequestration committee by the appointment of Sir William Brereton. Birkenshaw also acted as the bearer of a letter from Brereton to Major Croxton on 13 May 1645.[199] Moreover, Blackwell's troopers received pay on 9 March 1645.[200]

---

191 *Great Victories obtained by the Earl of Denbigh*; CRO, DDX/428, fol. 88v.; BL, MS Add. 11331, fol. 96v.; TNA, SP28/128/10, fol. 7v.; *BLB*, I, 202, 509.

192 TNA, SP28/224, fol. 175v.

193 BL, MS Add. 11331, fol. 72r.; TNA, SP28/224/1, fol. 75v; E121/5/7/351, fol. 31r; E121/5/7/43, fol. 2r.

194 TNA, E315/5, fol. 83v.

195 *Perfect Passages*, 22 January 1645; CRO, DDX/428, fol. 25; Phillips, *Memoirs*, pp.225–6; Morris, *Siege of Chester*, p.71. For further correspondence surrounding Blackwell's parole and exchange, see BL, MS Add. 11331, fols 61r.–v., 122; 11332, fol. 11r.; *BLB*, I, 77, 420, 422, 426, 496; II, 664.

196 TNA, SP28/128/10, fol. 5v.; SP/28/225/3, fol. 689r.

197 TNA, SP28/28/3, fol. 347r.

198 TNA, SP28/225/3, fol. 689r.

199 TNA, SP28/128/10, fol. 5v.; BL, MS Add. 11331, fol. 88r.; *BLB*, I, 514.

200 TNA, SP28/225/2, fol. 372v.

As for Captain Blackwell's origins, Dore suggests, 'From the absence of any local family of the name Blackwell, from his non-appearance in the records of the war in Cheshire prior to January 1645 and from his having gone to London during his parole, it can be deduced that he was not a Cheshire man and had become an officer in Brereton's army late in the war.'[201]

201 *BLB*, I, 420, n. 1. Dore, however, does not seem to have aware of the entry in TNA, E315/5 (above), which provides his service dates.

9

Sir William Brereton's Regiment of Foot

Sir William Brereton's commission from the Earl of Essex as colonel of a regiment of foot dates from 20 September 1642 to 24 June 1645.[1] Before its issue, however, he had already appointed his field officers and a number of captains. In comparison to the other five Parliamentarian infantry regiments in Cheshire, which tended to be officered by local gentlemen and raised from the general area of their estates, Brereton's own (described in April 1645 as being ready 'upon instant duty') appears to have been more broadly recruited and less locally based. Like the Cheshire horse, the regiment underwent a significant build-up in 1644 with the addition of new companies under the commands of Lieutenant Colonel Coote and Captains Calvin, Rathbone, Greene, William and Richard Coventry, and Davies. As articulated in Brereton's army list of April 1645, it was by far the largest regiment in the army at 1,520 common soldiers (essentially a double regiment) in 19 companies, although this figure requires some caution as 210 of these were dragoons. On 18 October there were 1,080 soldiers in 14 companies.

The commands of Coote and Calvin benefitted from the recruitment of Royalist soldiers from Ireland who had surrendered at Liverpool, while the rest consisted of volunteers, impressed men and country companies from hundreds of Wirral and Broxton. Given this, it might be assumed that before this Sir William's own regiment developed from its original core of 180–220 men to perhaps 800–900. The unit also included some highly experienced and capable officers, such as Robert Venables, Chidley Coote and Thomas Croxton. As such, Brereton's was perhaps the only foot regiment in the Cheshire army that was not roughly drawn from a particular locality or hundred, although it had some trained band and former militia soldiers amongst its ranks. Benjamin Hinde acted as quartermaster to the regiment.[2]

1 TNA, SP28/152/7, fol. 20r.
2 TNA, SP28/152/8, fol. 1v.

Sir William Brereton's Own Company

The colonel's company appears to have been initially raised in Cheshire during the summer of 1642 and was completed in London before marching north in January the following year. The original captain-lieutenant, John Baskerville, was from of Withington, near Stockport, and the other officers were local to the county. In November 1645 Brereton informed the Committee of Accounts, 'As for my foot regiment I had my field officers and divers captains before the date of my commission. So had I also my own company consisting near of nine score or two hundred divers months before the date of my commission [20 September 1642], before which time as also before my coming down, they did perform good service.'[3] Baskerville was paid £10 for the forming of his own company in Mainwaring's regiment on 19 May 1643 and was replaced as captain-lieutenant by Robert Venables.[4] Sir William Brereton's company was at the forefront of the fighting in Cheshire, Staffordshire and Shropshire during the spring and summer of 1643, and was among other Cheshire foot at Cholmondeley on 25 August 1643 when it was paid the sum of £506, being three months' pay in arrears.[5] Muster rolls for that date and 9 September 1643 record the following personnel:

Captain-Lieutenant Robert Venables
Lieutenant Lewis Griffith
Ensign Thomas Davies
Quartermaster Samuel Lawton
Sergeant Jennings
Sergeant Foden
Corporal Davenport
Corporal Hilton
Drummer John Workington
Drummer Robert Fallows[6]

Captain-Lieutenant/Lieutenant Colonel Robert Venables

Of Antrobus near Northwich, his military service began in late 1642 as captain of a company of volunteer foot. In his *Narrative*, Venables later stated:

> among others myself (as conscience and judgement guide me) adhered to the parliament, upon such grounds, reasons and engagements … which cause I promoted to my utmost ability against all discouragements and enable me the better I sold a tenement of about forty pounds a year, with the money to raise arms and to maintain a company of foot in that service, which I did, and served with the same in Lancashire without any pay … My service in England I shall not mention but leave others to speak of, both in Lancashire and Cheshire, Yorkshire, Salop and North Wales, in the siege of Nantwich, fight at Lee Bridge, Christleton and Montgomery, besides other services of lesser importance.[7]

3 BL, MS Add. 11332, fol. 43r.; *BLB*, II, 809.
4 TNA, SP28/196/1, fol. 7r.
5 BL, MS Harley 1999, fol. 61v.
6 TNA, SP28/124/1, fols 25r.–30v.
7 BL, MS Add. 12429, fol. 7r.; MS Add. 11410, fols 56v.–7r.; *Narrative of General Venables*, pp.1–2.

Lieutenant Colonel Robert Venables (*c.* 1613–87). L.P. Townshend, 'Some Account of General Robert Venables of Antrobus and Wincham, Cheshire (with an engraving from his portrait at Wincham); together with the autobiographical memoir, or diary, of his widow, Elizabeth Venables', *CS*, 83 (Manchester, 1871), pp.1–28.

On 16 December 1642 his company, with Lancashire men under Captain Bradshaw (together numbering around 250 soldiers) came under Royalist attack during their march from Bolton to Wigan. Venables and a number of his men were taken prisoner, he being held at Lathom House for 'some months'.[8] During the following summer he became captain-lieutenant to the colonel's company of Brereton's regiment. Details of his war service and pay arrears are revealed in his accounts, in which he stated:

> I took up employment in the parliament cause under Sir William Brereton in Cheshire as captain on 1 July 1643 until 1 March 1646, being 1338 days without pay – total due: £1,003 10s. I have served as Lieutenant Colonel as by Lord Fairfax's commission from 14 February 1644 until 1 March 1646, being 1,109 days without any pay – total due: £831 15s. 6 March 1644 I was appointed governor of Tarvin, which was taken up 1 July 1645 until 8 January 1646, at £5 5s. 8d. per day – total due: £278 10s. Full total pay due: £2,113 15s.'

Robert further received from Cheshire sources £1,554 10s. 1d. in pay. Included in this figure was £40 for his free quarter for a year for himself and one horse, and quarter for two years for two horses. Additionally, sometime in 1644 he purchased £30 worth of books and other items from the sequestrators of Broxton Hundred and was subsequently granted an order that these should be credited against £30 of arrears. By 1647 Robert Venables had received £561 out of £2,113 owing to the soldiers of Brereton's company.[9]

Venables served at the vanguard of the Cheshire foot, fighting with distinction at the siege of Nantwich, operations in Shropshire (including the defence of Wem) and the Battle of Montgomery in 1644. Following his promotion to lieutenant colonel he was appointed governor of Brereton's newly established garrison at Tarvin, the centre of operations for the siege of Chester. In addition, Robert played a prominent role in directing the siege of Chester, and was a signatory of the articles of surrender in February 1646. It has been suggested that Venables served as lieutenant colonel to Duckenfield's regiment during the First Civil War. According to Wanklyn, 'The five new regiments of foot were probably raised during the winter of 1643. Robert Duckenfield's commission as colonel was granted by the Earl of Essex in November; his field officers, Robert Venables and Henry Bradshaw,

8 *The latest printed News from Chichester, Windsor, Winchester, Chester and Manchester* (London, 1642); *The Great Civil War in Lancashire, 1642–1651*, ed. Ernest Broxap (Manchester University Press, 1910), p.61.

9 BL, MS Harley 1999, fols 58v.–63r.; TNA, SP28/224/1, fol. 232v.

received theirs early in the following year'.[10] Yet this is difficult to accept. As previously noted, Venables later stated that he had acted as captain 'under Sir William Brereton in Cheshire' from 1 July 1643 and as lieutenant colonel from 14 February 1644, but references in his accounts to service in Duckenfield's command during this period are lacking.

Venables' own accounts show that he was in command of Brereton's company at Cholmondeley house on 27 August 1643, thus suggesting further that his service in Cheshire began in this capacity. Likewise, although Robert Venables was appointed to the Macclesfield Hundred sequestration committee on 7 May 1644 (a body which made numerous payments to Colonel Duckenfield's troops), the only evidence to his direct association with Duckenfield's regiment are an outlay of £24 for firewood for the soldiers at Adlington, and two small payments of wages, one to Duckenfield himself and the other to Captain John Whitworth.[11] Before June 1647 Venables received a total of £3,641 19s. 10d. in pay 'for himself, and the officers and soldiers of the Macclesfield Hundred trained and freehold bands'. His command is confirmed by a warrant of 30 December 1647, authorising a payment to Thomas Davies, who is stated to have 'served commendably in Cheshire as ensign to the freehold band, or company, of Macclesfield under the command of Lieutenant Colonel Venables'.[12]

Conceivably, after 1646 this unit was commanded by Venables as part of Colonel Duckenfield's 'county regiment'. On 26 January 1648, as lieutenant colonel to the regiment, the following were disbursed: '£600 upon account towards the payment of Duckenfield's regiment of foot', and 'payment of £642 to Lieutenant Colonel Venables towards Colonel Duckenfield's regiment'.[13] The following year Venables became colonel of a newly raised regiment of foot from Cheshire which crossed to Dublin and participated in the victory at Rathmines. Venables led the second storming of the breach at Drogheda in September 1649, while his soldiers played a crucial role in seizing the drawbridge across the River Boyne, which allowed the Parliamentarian army to enter the northern part of the town. Robert spent another five years in Ireland, but in 1655 he was made major general of the land forces of Cromwell's expedition to the West Indies.

Lieutenant Lewis Griffith

Griffith is identified by pay warrants dating from August and September 1643 as lieutenant to Sir William Brereton's own company under the command of Captain-Lieutenant Robert Venables. He also appears consistently in muster rolls until at least March 1646.[14] On 16 December, when he had received a posting to Ireland, Griffith was described as 'much in arrears of pay for his service in this county [of Cheshire], and whereas he is now engaged in this

---

10 Wanklyn, 'Landed Society', p.239. This was followed by Dore in *BLB*, I, 144 note 1; 385 note 3; *CWS*, 69 n. 5.

11 *CJ*, III, p.484; TNA, SP28/128/10, fols 1r., 7r.

12 TNA, SP28/128/13, fol. 16v.; SP28/125/3, fol. 313r.; SP28/224, fol. 276v.

13 TNA, SP28/50/1, fol. 70v.; SP28/50/3, fol. 356v.

14 BL, MS Harley 2128, fol. 61v.; TNA, SP28/124/1, fols 25r.–30v.

present expedition for Ireland and wants monies for his necessaries: treasurer to pay him £30 in full satisfaction of all his arrears, he having been in constant service for the space of four years in this county'.[15] Thus, his service under Sir William Brereton must have begun in the autumn or winter of 1642.

Ensign Thomas Davies

From Ashton, near Tarvin, Thomas was a younger brother of Captain William Davies, company commander in Brereton's foot regiment. He emerges in pay warrants from August and September 1643, March 1644 and the muster roll of 9 September 1643 as ensign of Captain Robert Venables' company of the garrison of Cholmondeley House. In June or July 1644 he received the sum of £6 from Sir William Brereton, possibly in recompense for money laid out by him for weapons for the command.[16] He appears to have left the unit before 17 March 1646, however (being replaced by Ensign Brereton), although a warrant dated 30 December 1647, authorising a payment of £29 15s. 6d. to Thomas Davies confirms that he had served commendably in Cheshire as ensign to the freehold band, or company, of Macclesfield under the command of Lieutenant Colonel Venables.[17] Muster rolls dated to between 17 and 23 March 1646 record that Brereton's own company mustered the following:

Lieutenant Colonel Robert Venables	Corporal Henry Moore
Lieutenant Lewis Griffith	Corporal Bisson
Ensign Brereton	Drummer Richard Watson
Sergeant Strothall	Drummer Thomas Younger
Sergeant Hoden	Arnold Baxter and
Sergeant Randle Hall	James Whitley} gentlemen of the company
Corporal Ratcliffe	Clerk Thomas Chetham[18]

Brereton's company numbered 120 common soldiers fit for duty on 8 June 1644, 150 on 30 April 1645, 140 on 18 October 1645, 90 on 30 October 1645, 89 between 17 and 23 March 1646, 130 on 15 August 1646, 85 on 4 November 1646 and 132 on 1 April 1647.[19]

Lieutenant Colonel Chidley Coote's Company

Following his appearance in Cheshire in the summer of 1644 Coote acted as lieutenant colonel to Brereton's foot regiment. His command was being completed in early September 1644 when Sir William Brereton responded to requests from the committee at Wem and the Committee of Both Kingdoms for the loan of troops to the Shropshire Parliamentarians. On 8 September the

15 TNA, SP28/224/1, fol. 203v.

16 BL, MS Harley 2128, fol. 61v.; MS Add. 11332, fol. 40; *BLB*, II, 796.

17 TNA: SP28/125/3, fol. 313r.; SP28/224, fol. 276v.

18 TNA: SP28/124/1, fols 25r.–30v.; E121/5/7/351, fol. 46r.

19 TNA: SP28/196/1, fol. 21v.; SP28/124/1, fol. 29r.; SP28/123/3, fols 463r.–v., 495v.; SP28/123/4, fol. 640r.–v.; BL, MS Add. 11331, fol. 45v.; 11332, fols 3v., 32r.

forward elements of this force (which consisted of the uncompleted Cheshire companies of Coote, and Captains Calvin, Spicer and Finch) assisted in the capture the important Royalist stronghold of Moreton Corbet Castle.[20] Calvin's and Spicer's commands remained in Shropshire, leaving Coote's foot and Finch's dragoons to return to Cheshire. Lieutenant Colonel Coote's company was bolstered by Irish soldiers who came over to him and Michael Jones from the siege of Liverpool in the autumn of 1644.[21] From late 1644 until the summer of 1645 Lieutenant Colonel Coote acted as governor of the garrisons of Hooton and Puddington, where special committees had been established by Brereton with the responsibility for the organisation and collection of contributions and taxations in Wirral Hundred. These isolated garrisons were also pivotal to the maintenance of the fords over the Dee into Wales, and to that end, Coote supplied Sir William with regular intelligence reports on the situation there.

Although his soldiers regularly quartered at Hooton and Puddington, other commands (mostly 'country' companies) were brought up to operate from them when required. Whilst at Hooton on 21 April 1645 Chidley confided in Brereton that he had not replied to his commander's letters as he was 'so sick and full of pain', although a week later he had recovered enough for Sir William to compel him (in a set of instructions issued by Brereton to troops appointed to guard the ford across the Dee) 'to assist with his soldiers the effectual observation of this order'.[22] Towards the end of the month Coote petitioned Brereton on behalf of his foot soldiers 'to give some competent satisfaction for our past service and what we cannot have at present – the remainder if our arrears – may be settled and assured to us, according to the power of the ordinance granted to you, out of papists' and malignants' estates'.[23] These unfortunate men not only suffered from lack of pay, but victuals too. In May 1645 Coote issued a number of warrants (through the Hooton committee) to local bakers to supply bread for them.[24]

Around this period Lieutenant Colonel Coote, with the troop and company under his command, was seconded to the Shropshire Committee on a more permanent basis, although they continued to play an important role in the siege of Chester and military operations in the area. This seemingly necessitated the relinquishment of his governorship of the Wirral strongholds because on 19 July the deputy lieutenants of Cheshire issued the following order:

> In regard Lieutenant Colonel Coote hath earnestly moved this board to provide a governor for Hooton House in Wirral. It is therefore ordered that Captain Edward Glegg and Captain Birkenhead shall forthwith repair to the said garrison with their companies, and take the charge thereof, and of the provision there, and shall carefully keep and provide for the said garrison until order to the contrary.[25]

20 BL, MS Add. 11333, fol. 3; *CSPD, 1644,* pp.462–3, 484–5; Malbon, *Memorials*, p.146.
21 TNA: SP21/17, fols 63v.–5r.
22 BL, MS Add. 11331, fols 7, 26; *BLB*, I, 308, 368.
23 BL, MS Add. 11331, fol. 29; *BLB*, I, 387.
24 BL, MS Harley 1999, fols 62r.–68r.
25 BL, MS Harley 2128, fol. 174r.

In November 1645 the Shropshire Committee appealed somewhat tersely to Brereton for pay for Coote's soldiers, saying they would 'take especial favour if you will pay £50 of it [the sum of £100 that Sir William had borrowed from them and repaid before going to London] to [Lieutenant] Colonel Coote's company, whom we know not otherwise how to supply'.[26] During the same month the sequestrators of the upper division of Wirral Hundred paid his men 5s., while the following year the overall funds disbursed by James Croxton to 'Lieutenant Colonel Coote for himself, officers and soldiers' amounted to £428 17s. 8d.[27] His company mustered 100 common soldiers on 30 April 1645 and 80 on 18 October 1645.

Sergeant Major Thomas Croxton's Company

Of Ravenscroft, near Northwich, Thomas was captain of the Northwich Hundred trained bands before the war and was serving under Brereton by February 1643.[28] He was promoted to sergeant major and appointed as deputy lieutenant for Cheshire on 7 May 1644. Croxton also acted as the governor of Nantwich, the army's headquarters until the beginning of 1647.[29] His company was quartered semi-permanently at Nantwich, although it participated in a number of operations, including the defence of Wem during the autumn of 1643. Whether Brereton's regiment possessed a sergeant major's company from the start is open to question. It might not have been deemed necessary until the expansion of the unit during the summer and autumn of 1644 (hence Croxton's promotion). Wanklyn has it that James Lothian was the regiment's 'major' before his capture on 17 December 1643, stating 'was also a prisoner of the Royalists for some months early in 1644, and Brereton, probably thinking that he had also gone for good, chose Thomas Croxton of Ravenscroft to take his place'.[30] This is hard to substantiate though, as Lothian was released in July 1644, and although he was referred to as 'sergeant major' he took operational command of the Cheshire foot and there is no evidence that he ever led a major's company in Brereton's regiment. In April 1645 Lothian was attempting to complete a company of foot from the Broxton Hundred trained and freehold bands.[31]

Amongst the army officers and deputy lieutenants Thomas Croxton was deeply loyal to his commander-in-chief. Reflecting his key importance to the Parliamentarian war effort in the county Croxton became a colonel in late 1645, while in 1651 he raised a regiment of Cheshire foot that fought at the Battle of Worcester. In 1659, as governor of Chester, Thomas held the castle against Booth's Rising. Croxton's arrears of pay as 'captain and major of foot in the county of Chester' amounted to £1,648 12s. 6d., of which he received £1,103 10s. 10½d. on 5 December 1651 and a further £558 9s. 3d.

26 BL, MS Add. 11332, fols 111, 100; *BLB*, II, 903.

27 BL, MS Harley 1999, fol. 71r.; SP28/128/13, fol. 15v.

28 BL, MS Harley 2119, fols 211v.–13r.

29 *CJ*, III, p.484; *BLB*, I, p.29; Morrill, *Cheshire*, pp.81–3, 235–6.

30 Wanklyn, p.241.

31 CRO: DDX/428, fol. 79; MS Add. 11331, fol. 45; TNA: SP28/128/13, fol. 17v.; *BLB*, I, 181 n. 2; 385 n. 4.

on 6 August 1652.[32] Sergeant Major Croxton's company was drawn from the Nantwich Hundred Trained Bands and was quartered in the town. The total disbursement in pay from London sources to the command was £1,243 19s.[33] His men were highly experienced and dependable, and served in a number of operations in Cheshire and elsewhere.

Lieutenant Chambers

Received pay with Croxton's company on 27 February 1643.[34]

Lieutenant Samuel Ratcliffe

He had replaced Chambers by 16 May 1645 when he deliberated at a council of war outside Hawarden Castle on whether the Parliamentarian forces should continue mining the Royalist defences or rendezvous together and march into Wales. Ratcliffe's service as lieutenant to Croxton is confirmed by a pay warrant issued on 8 November 1645 'for officers and soldiers in Northwich Hundred, from a list of names under the hand of Lieutenant Ratcliffe'. He also appears in a muster roll for the company, dated 4 March 1646.[35]

Ensign Lindsey

Paid as ensign to the company on 11 July 1643.[36]

Ensign Pearson

Paid as sergeant to the company on 26 December 1644 but had been promoted to ensign by 10 November 1645.[37]

Ensign Joseph Smallwood

Included in disbursements made by Croxton to his officers between 26 December 1644 and 26 December 1645.[38]

The following junior and non-commissioned officers were listed on 10 November 1645 and 4 March 1646:

Lieutenant Samuel Ratcliffe
Ensign Pearson
Sergeant Bostock
Sergeant Worsley
Sergeant Widdows
Corporal Smallwood
Corporal Higginson
Corporal Perrin
Corporal Cramager
Drummer Edward Griffith
Drummer Edward Walmsley
Clerk William Culcheth
Surgeon Humphrey Pearson[39]

32 TNA: E121/3/1, fol. 287v.
33 TNA: SP28/128/13, fol. 17r.
34 TNA: SP28/122/3, fol. 443r.
35 BL, MS Add. 11331, fol. 113; TNA: SP28/224, fols 47v., 49v.–50r.; SP28/123/4, fol. 676v.; *BLB*, I, 552.
36 TNA: SP28/196/1, fol. 17r.
37 TNA: SP28/124/1, fol. 4r.; SP28/123/4, fol. 676v.
38 TNA: SP23/71, p.609; SP28/224, fols 3r., 4r.; BCL: MS 595611, pp.120–1.
39 TNA: SP28/152/7, fol. 8r.; SP28/122/3, fols 432r.–43r.

Other company non-commissioned officers were Sergeant Ralph Milton (killed during the assault on Cholmondeley House on 7 July 1644); Corporal Kent (promoted to sergeant by 8 January 1646); Corporals Potts, Riversley and Shrigley (listed in a muster roll at Lichfield on 11 June 1646).[40]

Croxton's company mustered 160 common soldiers fit for duty on 30 April 1645, 140 on 18 October 1645, 172 (131 fit, 41 unfit) on 10 November 1645, 173 on 8 January 1646, 116 on 4 March 1646 and 62 on 28 March 1647.[41]

Captain Lord James Calvin's Company

James, second Lord Calvin of Culross was an Anglo-Scots officer who seems to have resided in Ireland from 1640 onwards. He probably took up arms against the Irish Rebellion and (like Jones and Coote), subsequently declined to accept the Cessation. He was leading a company of foot in Sir William Brereton's regiment by August or September 1644.[42] Calvin's men participated in the capture of Moreton Corbet in Shropshire on 8 September 1644 and the capture of Shrewsbury in February 1645. On 30 April it was listed as 'about 100' common soldiers, but soon afterwards was transferred to the Shropshire Committee. From June 1645 Calvin acted successively as governor of Stoke-on-Tern, Moreton Corbet and Broncroft Castle.[43] In 1646 he crossed to Ireland and saw service there under Colonel Michael Jones.

Captain John Sadler's Company

A Nantwich yeoman, Sadler first distinguished himself defending Acton Church during the siege of Nantwich in January 1644.In February 1645, together with part of Colonel Mainwaring's regiment, Captain Sadler's soldiers engaged in siege operations at Holt and Farndon, and later played an important role in the surrender of the castle, of which he became governor.[44] Although his company was nominally part of Brereton's regiment in October 1645, following the seizure of Chester the following spring Sadler appears to have transferred to Mytton's command in North Wales, where he was promoted to sergeant major. The total outlay to 'Captain Sadler for himself, his officers and soldiers' from central sources amounted to £80 19s. 8d.[45]

---

40 Malbon, *Memorials*, p.139; TNA: SP28/123/2, fol. 316r.; SP28/122/3, fol. 443r.–v.; SP16/513/1, fol. 89r.

41 BL, MS Add. 11331, fol. 45.; 11333, fol. 3.; TNA: SP28/123/2, fol. 316v.; SP28/123/4, fol. 676r.; SP28/122/3, fol. 443r–v.; SP28/123/3, fol. 509v.

42 Carte, *Collection*, III, p.349. For brief discussions of Calvin, see *BLB*, I, 11, n. 1; II, 1000, note.

43 BL, MS Add. 11331, fol. 45; 11333, fols 16, 41; *BLB*, I, 963; II, 956, 1049; Malbon, *Memorials*, p.146; F.S. Acton, *The Garrisons of Shropshire during the Civil War, 1642–48* (Shrewsbury: Leake and Evans, 1867), pp.21, 49, 84.

44 Malbon, *Memorials*, pp.98–9; CRO: DDX/428, fol. 107; *BLB*, I, 290.

45 TNA: SP28/128/13, fol. 17v.; SP28/224, unfol.

Lieutenant Thomas Hunt
Ensign John Roberts
Sergeant Lancelot Lewis
Corporal Edward Bath
Corporal John Brown[46]

70 common soldiers mustered on 30 April 1645 and 60 on 18 October 1645.[47]

Captain Thomas Monke's Company

Monke's company was formed by 1 May 1643. Thomas and his soldiers were from Staffordshire, although by mid 1645 they were among the forces directed to join Brereton in Cheshire. Captain Monke's command appears on the strength of Sir William's regiment of foot in his lists of 30 April 1645 and 18 October 1645, but although it was active with the Cheshire forces at the siege of Chester, and operated in Staffordshire, Shropshire and North Wales it also came under the auspices of the Staffordshire Committee.[48] Captain Monke commanded 150 Staffordshire foot that participated in the Whitchurch–Denbigh Green campaign in December 1645, and marched to Hawarden Castle with his own company on 6 January 1646.[49] Furthermore, his soldiers received pay with the Staffordshire foot on 18 December, 20 December 1645 and 12 January 1646 'in service in the Leaguer before Chester'. [50] Following the surrender of the city in early February 1646 Monke's company acted as part of combined force of 1,800 foot and 1,200 horse under Brereton's command at Lichfield Close. On 23 May 1646 the unit mustered with the force of Cheshire companies, where it consisted of a captain, a lieutenant, two drummers, two corporals and 36 soldiers.[51] Like most of the other commands listed, the fairly low strength of Monke's company appears indicative of the not inconsiderable losses it sustained during previous operations.

On 20 May 1644 Captain Monke was assigned the weekly pay of the Staffordshire townships of Blynhill, Brynton, Higham, Pladwicke and Pillington 'towards the augmentation of his soldiers' and officers' pay'.[52] During the siege of Lichfield the company obtained desperately needed arrears of pay from the £3,000 sent to Brereton by the Committee of Both Kingdoms. On 21 March Monke's common soldiers received £40, whilst on 30 May the same amount was paid to 'Captain Thomas Monke for his foot company'. Similarly, on 12 June 1646 Lieutenant Pargiter had £5 12s. and Ensign Millward (missing from the muster a week previously) received the sum of £4 4s., being a month's pay in arrears. The final disbursements,

46 TNA: E121/1/5/7, fols 394v., 1r.; E121/5/7/351, fols 34r., 51v.–2r., 43r.
47 BL, MS Add. 11331, fol. 45; 11333, fol. 3v.
48 BL, MS Add. 11331, fol. 44; 11332, fol. 3; CRO: DDX/428, fol. 116; *BLB*, I, 300, 385 and note 3; II, 703; *Committee at Stafford*, pp.307–8.
49 BL, MS Add. 11333, fols 45, 109; *BLB*, II, 1112, 1212.
50 BL, MS Add. 11333, fols 30, 32, 118; *BLB*, II, 1040, 1057, 1235.
51 BCL: MS 595611, p.253; *CWS*, p.271.
52 *Committee at Stafford*, p.118.

made in November 1646 included £5 and £3 10s. to Pargiter and Millward respectively, while Captain Monke himself received £10 10s.[53]

Lieutenant Monke

Either a brother or son of Captain Thomas Monke. He was paid with him on 1 May 1643, but was replaced by Lieutenant Pargiter sometime before 23 May 1646.[54]

Ensign Izat

Serving on 20 December 1645, but replaced by Ensign Millward before 23 May 1646.[55]

Monke's company returned 60 common soldiers on 30 April 1645, 50 on 18 October 1645, 60 on 8 January 1646 and 36 on 23 May 1646.[56]

Captain Henry Greene's Company

Of Poulton Lancelyn in Bebington parish, he allegedly gave a horse to the Earl of Derby in 1644, although he was later exonerated.[57] He commanded a company of Wirral countrymen 'who maintained the garrison at Hooton', and numbered 120 common soldiers on 30 April and 100 on 18 October 1645. No muster rolls or pay warrants for the company have come to light.

Captain Edward Glegg's Company

Brother of John Glegg, one of Sir William Brereton's captains of horse. Edward Glegg's company of the Trained Bands of Wirral Hundred is referred to in Brereton's army list of 30 April 1645 as 'now disposed of', his soldiers having been recently combined with Captain Birkenhead's men. Twenty days previously the deputy lieutenants at Nantwich had reported that most of his soldiers had deserted for lack of pay and that Glegg had laid down his commission.[58] The actions of Captain Glegg's soldiers were especially problematic because the company was stationed at Tilston, an important garrison located six miles south-west of Beeston. Evidence suggests, however, that Glegg retained his commission. On 19 July 1645 he and Captain Birkenhead were instructed to take charge of the garrison of Hooton, where his soldiers remained until at least the October.

53 TNA: SP16/513/1, fols 74, 70, 91, 72; *CWS*, pp.330, 325, 328, 330, 354.

54 TNA: SP28/196/1, fol. 5r.; MS 595611, p.253.

55 BL, MS Add. 11333, fol. 32; MS 595611, p.253.

56 BL, MS Add. 11331, fol. 45; 11333, fols 3v., 109v.; BCL: MS 595611, p.253; *BLB*, II, 212; *CWS*, p.271.

57 *Calendar of proceedings of the Committee for the Advancement of Money*, ed. Mary Green (London: HMSO, 1888), III, p.1210; Morrill, *Cheshire*, p.215; Tony Dyson, 'Colonel Moore's Offensive Against Wirral, November 1643', *THSLC*, 162 (2013), 29–48 (p.43).

58 CRO: DDX/428, fol. 88r.; *BLB*, I, 202.

In early March 1646 the Cheshire commissioners ordered that Glegg's command should receive a month's wages and a further month's pay (being its bounty due on the fall of Chester) when it reached Nantwich, nonetheless, the county treasurer found that 'because money was wanting' there was only enough to pay the common soldiers.[59] Glegg's and Captain Whalley's companies refused to march to Lichfield without pay, yet by 13 May they had joined Brereton's forces at the siege. The total money disbursed to 'Captain Edward Glegg for himself, and his officers and soldiers' by treasurer Croxton amounted to £683 19s. 4d.[60] While at Chester on 21 April 1646 Glegg's company had reported the following:

Lieutenant Nathaniel Swettenham
Ensign Robert Hall
Sergeant Henry Waring
Sergeant Edward Bennet
Sergeant Alexander Barnet
Clerk Thomas Bennet
Corporal Lawrence Cooke
Corporal Richard Jones
Corporal John Merson
Drummer Andrew Parrot
Drummer Richard Beddow[61]

Swettenham had replaced Lieutenant Symonds, who was paid as second-in-command of the company on 29 December 1644 and 3 August 1645. On 23 May Captain Glegg's command mustered one captain, one lieutenant, one ensign, three sergeants, two corporals, one drummer, one clerk and 69 common soldiers.[62] The company mustered 160 common soldiers (with Birkenhead's) on 30 April 1645, 120 (with Rathbone's) on 18 October 1645, 67 on 23 November 1645, 73 on 5 January 1646, 74 on 12 February 1646, 78 on 30 March 1646, 50 on 21 April 1646, 69 on 23 May 1646 and 70 on 30 May 1646.[63]

Captain Henry Birkenhead's Company

Henry Birkenhead was from Backford in the Wirral. He and his father (Henry senior) were noted lawyers; they both promoted the Cheshire Remonstrance in 1642 and thus were apprehended when Charles I visited Chester. Henry Birkenhead junior was a county magistrate and lieutenant colonel of the regiment raised by Colonel Duckenfield in 1650, MP for Cheshire in 1653 and with Duckenfield he presided at the trial of the Earl of Derby.[64] Birkenhead's company, raised from Wirral Hundred, was quartered at the important Wirral garrison of Hooton in July 1645, and Hooton and

59 TNA: SP28/43/7, fols 863v.–4r.; SP28/123/4, fol. 618v.

60 TNA: SP28/128/13, fol. 18r.; SP28/224/1, unfol.

61 TNA: SP28/123/2, fols 242v.–4r.; SP16/513/1, fols 71v., 88r.

62 TNA: SP28/196/1, fol. 24v.; SP28/32/1, fol. 46r.; BCL: MS 595611, p.253.

63 TNA: SP28/123/4, fols 674r., 703r.; SP28/43/7, fol. 863r.; SP28/123/2, fol. 243r.; SP28/123/2, fol. 244v.; SP16/153/1, fol. 86r.; SP28/122/3, fol. 474v.; MS Add. 11331, fol. 45; 11332, fol. 3; BCL: MS 595611, p.253.

64 *BLB*, I, 288 n.; *CWS*, p.257, n. 6.

Lache (south-east of Chester) in January 1646.[65] Gregory Rowlins, a common soldier of Captain Birkenhead's company was exchanged as a prisoner of war at Chester on 4 January 1646.[66] The total outlay from central funds to 'Captain Birkenhead for himself, and the officers and soldiers of the Trained and Freehold Band of Wirral Hundred' was £1,718 18s.[67] On 22 July 1646 the junior and non-commissioned officers of the company were:

Lieutenant John Astbrook	Corporal Thomas Dausley
Ensign William Rathbone	Corporal John Harrison
Sergeant William Woolmer	Drummer John Davy
Sergeant Thomas Worford	Drummer James Davy[68]
Corporal George Harrison	

Birkenhead's command mustered 160 common soldiers(with Glegg's) on 30 April 1645, 100 on 18 October 1645, 89 on 30 March 1646, 68 on 28 April 1646, 94 on 28 May 1646, 96 on 22 June 1646, 90 on 22 July 1646 and 78 on 9 December 1646.[69]

Captain Thomas Hulse's Company

Thomas Hulse was a Nantwich man. During much of 1645 his company was quartered at Cholmondeley House, and following the capture of the Parliamentarian governor (Hulse's brother officer, Captain Anthony Brereton) in the October, he was appointed in his stead. Upon the fall of Beeston Castle to Brereton's army a month later, Captain Hulse was also made commander-in-chief there.[70] The company reported 60 soldiers on 30 April 1645 and 80 soldiers (with Captain Brereton's men) on 18 October 1645.[71]

Captain John Rathbone's Company

Of Irby, described by Tony Dyson as 'easily the most prominent Parliamentarian officer in Wirral', and a man of 'combative, even reckless, qualities'.[72] Rathbone first appears among a group of persons found guilty of disturbing the peace at Nantwich on 18 July 1643, although by late 1644 he had raised a company of Wirral volunteers, which was quartered in various local garrisons. At Puddington in late 1644 and early 1645 Captain John

65 BL, MS Add. 11333, fols 105, 113–4; *BLB*, II, 1210, 1240–1.

66 BL, MS Add. 11333, fol. 95; *BLB*, II, 1180.

67 TNA: SP28/128/13, fol. 18v.; SP28/224, unfol.

68 TNA: SP28/123/2, fol. 343v.

69 BL, MS Add. 11331, fol. 45r.; 11332, fol. 3.; TNA: SP28/123/1, fols 181r., 170v., 33v.; SP28/123/2, fols 352v.–r., 343r., 371r.

70 *BLB*, I, 287 note.

71 MS Add. 11331, fol. 45r.; 11332, fol. 3v.

72 Tony Dyson, 'The Oaths at Woodchurch, 1643–1644: tensions in civil-war Wirral and its aftermath', *THSLC*, 164 (2015), pp.1–20 (pp.15–16).

Rathbone fell out with local Parliamentarian officials, having been accused of 'keeping diverse horses and beats' on its demesne, and requisitioning goods before they could be inventoried and valued. Moreover, he grew a field of wheat at Burton.[73] Though Morrill found it odd that Rathbone cultivated crops, it seems probable that he 'was concerned with feeding his men in the face of adverse conditions and an unhelpful bureaucracy'.[74]

During the spring of 1645 Captain Rathbone's company was stationed Upton House, an important communications point north of Chester and an important link between the Leaguer and Parliamentarian army's supply port of Liverpool (Rathbone had suitably received instructions to report on the arrival at the latter of a ship carrying rations, powder and other items). The garrison had been established after the retirement of Prince Maurice from Chester the previous month and not, as Morris asserts, in December 1644.[75] On 2 April a Royalist night attack on the strongpoint was reported upon by the governor of Hooton, Lieutenant Colonel Coote:

> Three hours before this day morning the enemy came out of Chester towards Upton House, and thought to have surprised the garrison and cut our men to pieces. They came, every man with a match in his hat and a white cloth of distinction about his right arm to know themselves from our men. When they were about their intended butchery, out horse scouts descried them. After which they marched openly and demanded of our men to deliver up the house upon fair quarter. Our men answered they would have no quarter at their hands; so they fell upon and shot. Many of them were wounded; two of their men lay dead close by the door, and 16 more slain and taken off. Upton garrison is within a mile of Chester, newly garrisoned and maintained by Captain Rathbone, a Wirral man.[76]

Following the end of the siege of Chester in February 1646 Captain John Rathbone's company marched with Brereton's Cheshire forces to Staffordshire and its ultimate objective of the campaign, the siege of Lichfield. On 16 January 1646 its junior and non-commissioned officers comprised:

Lieutenant Phillip Browne
Ensign Thomas Watmough
Sergeant John Sarton
Sergeant Hugh Carter
Sergeant Arthur Lowe
Corporal George Honney
Corporal Christopher Derbyshire
Corporal Robert Ball
Drummer John Stackhouse
Drummer John Caldy
Clerk Robert Shirley[77]

On 23 May 1646 one captain, one lieutenant, one ensign, three sergeants, three corporals, two drummers and one clerk (Richard Eccleston) mustered.[78]

73 BL, MS Harley 1999, fols 15v., 16r., 71v.
74 Morrill, *Cheshire*, p.110; Dyson, 'Oaths', 17.
75 Malbon, p.169; Morris, *Siege of Chester*, p.70. This is further confirmed by the document below.
76 CRO: DDX/408, fol. 60v.; *BLB*, I, 158.
77 TNA: SP28/123/4, fol. 617.
78 BCL: MS 595611, p.252; TNA: SP16/531/1, fol. 87v.

In June 1646 Rathbone was 'dangerously wounded' at Lichfield, yet although he was clearly a valuable officer he was ordered by Brereton in the December to pay off his soldiers and safeguard that they disbanded and dispersed.[79] The overall sum distributed to 'Captain John Rathbone for himself, officers and soldiers' was £704 4s. 4d.[80] Rathbone's company numbered 80 common soldiers fit for duty on 30 April 1645, 120 (with Glegg's) on 18 October 1645, 71 on 9 November 1645, 47 on 16 January 1646, 61 on 24 March 1646 and 60 on 23 May 1646.[81]

Captain John Hardware's Company

Hardware came from Bromborough in the Wirral. Raised in 1644, his soldiers were part of the Tarvin garrison and on 8 March 1645 the sum £5 was made to Hardware 'towards paying the volunteers of my company'.[82] John's command was active at the Chester leaguer – in late October 1645 it joined Leadbeater's company in the siege lines opposite the city's Pikegate and the Bars in Foregate Street, on which occasion 40 common soldiers were present.[83] On 18 January 1646 James Henley of Hardware's company was one of 16 Parliamentarian prisoners of war exchanged at Chester.[84] The command received the sum of £159 4s. from treasurer Croxton later in the year.[85] On 12 November 1645 the following junior and non-commissioned officers were present:

Lieutenant Christopher Ball	Corporal Daniel Mather
Ensign Samuel Hardware	Corporal William Grimsdale
Sergeant Richard Bakewell	Drummer Thomas Rathbone
Corporal James Whitley	Clerk John Johnson[86]

Hardware's company mustered 60 common soldiers on 30 April 1645, 80 on 18 October 1645, 40 on 31 October 1645 and 45 on 12 November 1645.[87]

Captain Francis Spicer's Company

Francis Spicer served as captain of a company of foot in Sir William Brereton's regiment from 10 May 1644 to 14 September 1644, and as captain and

79 TNA: SP28/224/1, fols 149r., 193v.–94r.
80 TNA: SP28/128/13, fol. 17r.; SP28/224/1, unfol.
81 BL, MS Add. 11331, fol. 45r.; 11332, fol. 3v.; TNA: SP28/123/4, fols 686v., 617r.; SP28/3/7/1, fol. 103r.; BCL: MS 595611, p.252.
82 TNA: SP29/196/1, unfol. For a letter of Jones urging that company and others from Colonel George Booth's regiment march from there on 27 December 1656 see BL, MS Add. 11332, fol. 22r.; *BLB*, II, 748.
83 BL, MS Add. 11332, fols 31v.–2r.; *BLB*, II, 777, 791.
84 MS Add. 11333, fol. 110r.; *BLB*, II, 1214.
85 TNA: SP28/128/13, fol. 18v.
86 TNA: SP28/122/3, fol. 431r.
87 BL, MS Add. 11331, fol. 45; 11332, fols 3, 32; TNA: SP28/122/3, fol. 431r.

governor of Lilleshall under the Shropshire Committee from August 1645 to 31 July 1646.[88] He was posted with his company to Shropshire, and although his soldiers formed the Lilleshall garrison, they remained in Brereton's regiment. From Lilleshall Spicer provided his commander-in-chief with vital intelligence reports during Royalist activity in Shropshire in December 1645. The company reported 40 common soldiers on 30 April 1645 and 50 on 18 October 1645.[89]

Lieutenant Shield

Received pay with the company on 8 January 1645.[90]

Captain William Coventry's, Captain Richard Coventry's and Captain George Ball's Companies

The volunteer companies of Captains William Coventry, Richard Coventry and George Ball are listed in Brereton's regiment in April 1645, but they appear to have been disbanded by the end of the year. Little is known of their service, and the companies probably spent most of their short service billeted at Wirral garrisons such as Puddington and Hooton, although Ball's men were paid £1 18s. as 'trained soldiers' whilst quartering at Frodsham.[91] William Coventry of West Kirby was accused of taking the oath of loyalty to the King and of providing support to Royalist troops, but such charges were dismissed in October 1652 for lack of evidence against him. Captain George Ball is likely to have been a son of William Ball of Irby, and related to Lieutenant Christopher and Ensign Robert Ball under the command of Hardware and Glegg respectively. The problems encountered by many Wirral officers is illustrated by the case of Ball and Richard Coventry, who during 1643 and 1644 were compelled to take an oath of association at Woodchurch, when the area was under Royalist control. Upon Brereton's arrival in the Wirral in the autumn of 1644 they 'did immediately declare themselves for him; and have, ever since been trusted and employed in the Parliament's service, and discharged the same faithfully'.[92] In 1651 Ball and Coventry were charged with delinquency, but acquitted.

Captain William Davies's Company

Of Ashton-juxta-Tarvin, William Davies was a member of the Tarvin Committee. He was commissioned as captain of a company of foot by Sir William Brereton on 9 September 1644, and he served in that capacity until

88 TNA: SP28/253A/Letter Book B/case 152. For his service, see also MS Add. 11333, fols 16, 48–9, 91; *BLB*, II, 703, 965, 979, 1072, 1159.

89 MS Add. 11331, fol. 45r.; 11332, fol. 3v.

90 TNA: SP28/152/7, fol. 16v.

91 BL, MS Harley 1999, fol. 75r. For the scant information on these officers and their companies, see *BLB*, I, 385, n. 3.

92 *CJ*, VII, pp.61–2; Dyson, 'Oaths', 4–6.

'the latter end of September 1645'.[93] His commission, granted by Brereton as commander-in-chief, states:

> To Mr William Davies, captain by virtue of authority derived from the parliament, I do by constitute and appoint you to be captain of one company of foot soldiers consisting of 100 men to be raised by you within the several townships of Tarvin, Ashton, Alvanley and Hartford, and anywhere your talents within the county of Chester, to serve in my own regiment of foot for the service of protestant religion, the king, parliament and kingdoms, which the company being raised as aforesaid, you shall by virtue of this commission given you to receive into your care, charge and command as captain thereof receive the same diligently to lead and otherwise in arms for the said service of king and parliament, diligently attending the duty of the said place, hereby commanding all inferior officers and soldiers of the said company to obey you as their captain, and you yourself to obey and follow such orders and directions as from time to time you shall receive from myself and the superior officers of the army according to the discipline of war. Given under my hand and seal at arms, this ninth day of September 1644.

Moreover, Captain Davies' testament of service, dated 10 July 1649 and endorsed by Lieutenant Colonel Robert Venables, says:

> These are to certify all whom it may concern, that Captain William Davies did raise a foot company according to his commission, which was ever ready on all occasions for the public service both at Eaton and other places, and from the date of his commission, being 9 September 1644 until the latter end of September 1645, performed duty in this garrison of Tarvin (where I was governor), and at all times when required for which service neither he nor they did receive any satisfaction that I know of. Witness my hand and seal, 10 July 1649.

Captain Anthony Brereton's Company

From Edge, near Malpas, Anthony (often given as Andrew) Brereton commanded one of a number of companies raised from Broxton Hundred. He acted as governor of Cholmondeley, although by 27 October 1645 he had been captured and taken to Denbigh Castle. Brereton was exchanged at Holt shortly afterwards.[94] On 20 December 1645 he commanded a body of 60 foot at Chester, whilst on 12 January 1646 Captain Brereton was paid £39 18s. 8d. 'for himself, his officers and soldiers in service in the Leaguer before Chester'.[95] They later participated in the siege operations at Holt Castle (January 1646 to 13 January 1647) with Major Lothian's company. On 16 May 1646 the deputy lieutenants and the committee at Chester informed Sir William Brereton that:

93 BL, MS Harley 1970, fols 73v.–74r.

94 BL, MS Add. 11332, fols 3v., 28v., 85v.–6r.; *BLB*, II, 703 n. 8, 759, 841, 858.

95 BL, MS Add. 11333, fols 45r., 118r.; *BLB*, II, 1063, 1235.

> we have provided pay for Captain Brereton's company who (being something full) have undertaken to keep the bridge and Farndon Church where they now are, and are about to build a mount in the face of the castle on Cheshire side, and with the help of some horse doubt not to keep Broxton Hundred safe, which is to the good content of the neighbourhood there and as there shall be occasion all assistance we are able shall, God willing, be given to that leaguer, and to the preservation of that hundred as you desire.[96]

Captain Anthony Brereton's company received the sum of £138 16s. 8d. from treasurer Croxton in 1646.[97] On 22 April the following junior and non-commissioned officers mustered for pay:

Lieutenant John Brereton	Corporal Thomas Rowe
Ensign Edward Rathbone	Corporal Robert Stephens
Sergeant John Evans	Drummer Edward Brereton[98]
Sergeant Ralph Bathoe	

Captain Brereton's company mustered 80 common soldiers (with Hulse's) on 18 October 1645 and 44 on 22 April 1646.[99]

Sergeant Major John Holford's Company

Holford's company of foot appears in a muster roll dated 6 March 1646 amongst others from the Cheshire Parliamentarian army. Whether this was the officer of the same name who commanded a troop of horse in Brereton's regiment is uncertain, however. John Holford was commissioned captain of foot of Colonel Thomas Croxton's Cheshire militia regiment on 22 August 1650. In July 1651 he was paid £25 to convey to Chester the 100 men impressed within Cheshire for service in Ireland.[100]

The following were listed on 6 March 1646:

Lieutenant Elias Holford	Corporal Robert Manchester
Ensign John Brandon	Corporal William Rossiter
Sergeant Robert Brown	Drummer William Emes
Sergeant Richard Job	Drummer Robert Hill
Corporal William Dace	63 common soldiers[101]

96 BCL: MS 595611, p.197; *CWS*, 220.
97 TNA: SP28/128/13, fol. 18r.; SP28/224, unfol.
98 TNA: SP28/123/1, fol. 87r.
99 BL, MS Add. 11332, fol. 3; SP28/123/1, fol. 87r.
100 TNA: SP28/224/2, fol. 330v.
101 TNA: SP28/123/1, fols 252v.–3r.

10

Colonel George Booth's Regiment of Foot

George was the son of William Booth, and grandson of the leading deputy lieutenant, Sir George Booth of Dunham Massey. His uncle, Colonel John Booth, commanded a Lancashire regiment of foot and was Parliamentarian governor of Warrington. The Booths were one of the most powerful Presbyterian families in Cheshire. Colonel George Booth was an early deputy lieutenant and raised one of the first troops of horse from the county. He took an active part in early military operations, leading his troop at the First Battle of Middlewich, as well as raising and commanding a regiment of foot in Cheshire and Shropshire throughout 1643 and 1644. George played a decisive part in the relief of Nantwich against Byron's Royalists, and personally led his soldiers in action at Wem, Oswestry and Cholmondeley. It has been suggested that the young Colonel George (20 years of age on the outbreak of war) was the governor of Nantwich during the siege of 1643–4, but this appears unlikely. The answer sent to Lord Byron's summons to surrender signifies that it came from 'George Booth', meaning either the 78-year-old baronet and deputy lieutenant, or his grandson.[1] Dore suggests that 'In some ways the older man would have been more suitable, as he would have had much administrative and diplomatic work to do as well as military.'[2] Booth senior was very active throughout the war and the Committee of Both Kingdoms placed him in charge of the important garrison of Warrington in 1645. Additionally, Malbon lists a Colonel Booth among the commanders who came to the rescue of Nantwich, but as Colonel John Booth had been named previously, this could only be young George.[3]

Colonel George Booth, described by Sir John Meldrum in September 1644 as 'a young gentleman of great expectation', was a capable officer, but his increasing opposition to Brereton eroded his military and administrative effectiveness, and he resigned his commission in April or May 1645.[4] His

1 *CWTC*, p.104.
2 *BLB*, II, p.64.
3 Malbon, p.117.
4 *CSPD 1644*, p.543.

activities in the spring of 1645 are unclear, although on 26 February he was reported as being in London with some of his captains, undermining his commander-in-chief's authority.[5] Yet on 12 April he was at Leicester, where he recorded that the defences were in 'weak condition', an observation that he noted was 'most obvious to the un-observing eye'.[6] Although the Committee of Both Kingdoms ordered a significant improvement of the size of the garrison, earthworks and dilapidated medieval walls, the town was sacked by Rupert's forces on 30 May 1645. Booth continued to serve on the county committee, and he sat as MP for Cheshire in 1645, 1654 and 1656, yet vigorously opposed the Protectorate. In 1659 George led the Cheshire Rising, a failed attempt to restore a free parliament, but at the Restoration he was rewarded with the title of Baron Delamer of Dunham Massey.

Colonel George Booth (1622–84). (Copyright of National Portrait Gallery)

Colonel Booth's regiment was raised by late 1642 or early 1643, partly from the region near to the Booth estates at Dunham Massey, but also from Nantwich town and hundred. In April 1645 the regiment contained 710 common soldiers in 10 companies. In response to a petition to Parliament, on 28 March 1643 £1,000 was granted to Booth for the recruitment and pay of soldiers. The Commons further ordered 'that it be referred to the Committee of Cheshire, to consider the furnishing of Colonel George Booth with arms, according to his desire', to which end, on 7 May 1644 it was determined that £300 was advanced out of the Court of Wards for the supply of arms to his regiment.[7] During the summer of 1644 Booth's regiment was integral to the composition and effectiveness of the Cheshire foot, which operated at the forefront of Parliamentarian operations in Shropshire and the Welsh borders.

Several of the officers under his command (notably Lieutenant Colonel Massey, Sergeant Major Daniell, and Captains George and Thomas Malbon) were known for their skill and courage on the battlefield. Yet the general conduct of others created difficulties within the regiment. The friction experienced between this group – Colonel Booth, John Daniell, and Captains George Massey and Hugh Whitney in particular – and Sir William Brereton led to their open disloyalty in 1645. In April or May Booth laid down his commission, although his regiment survived under the command of his lieutenant colonel, William Massey. Confirmation of this comes from a letter from Lothian to Brereton, dated 26 October 1645, which mentions 'the six

5 CRO, DDX/428, fol. 61r.; *BLB*, I, 19.

6 James Hollings, *The History of Leicester during the Great Civil War* (Combe and Crossley: Leicester, 1839), p.38; *BLB*, I, 478 note 1.

7 *CJ*, III, p.484; II, p.439.

companies of Colonel Massey's'.[8] This figure must have omitted two of the three commands of Captains Cartwright, Wright and Whitney then serving in Shropshire, as well as the country companies of Alcocke and Grantham. The likelihood of this enhanced by a subsequent letter of Colonel Booth, written on 4 December, which suggests that the latter two commands were quartered at or near Dunham Massey.[9]

It seems likely that Colonel George Booth's resignation affected the cohesion of at least part of his regiment – by the spring of 1645 there appears to have been a significant reduction in the size of the colonel's company. The most immediate problem during this period was the habitual lack of pay, which may have affected recruitment and the retention of soldiers within the regiment. In early 1645 various companies, quartered across Cheshire and Shropshire were close to mutiny. Their whereabouts in April and May can be ascertained from marginal notes in Brereton's list of Cheshire regiments made on 30 April, as well as contemporary letters to and from the commander-in-chief.[10] Although cited as 'dissolved', Booth's former company, now under the command of his captain-lieutenant, Sergeant Major John Daniell, was billeted at Tarvin, while Lieutenant Colonel Massey's troops were quartered at Nantwich with the townsmen under Captains George and Thomas Malbon. The companies of Captains Cartwright, Wright and Whitney had been detained in Shropshire. Furthermore, the country companies under Alcocke and Grantham were residing in the Altrincham–Wilmslow area. By 8 May increasing discontent among some of the soldiers caused the deputy lieutenants in Nantwich to hastily inform Brereton that:

> Ensign Cheshire came this day purposely to acquaint us that the regiment formerly under Colonel Booth (who hath resigned his commission) are in great discontent. Major Daniell's company, being commanded to Tarvin from the rest of the regiment and receiving no pay, desire to be commanded with the rest of the same regiment where they now are, or that they may have such pay and accommodation within this county as other soldiers have and they will be as ready to be commanded upon any service. You may be assured that, unless care be speedily taken, the regiment will be lost and become unserviceable to this county. Captain George Malbon's company refuse to march this night and it is likely the other [Captain Thomas Malbon's] will do the like when occasion is afforded. The reason is because the officers have received pay and the soldiers have none.[11]

Following Brereton's request, Daniell's company had been ordered by the Shropshire Committee on 14 April 1645 to march from Shrewsbury to return to Cheshire, while 13 days later it was reported that Daniell had been placed in command of five companies of foot (including his own and four from Staffordshire) that had marched from Shrewsbury to Tarvin.[12] On 8 May

8 BL, Add. 11332, fol. 15v.; *BLB*, II, 734 and n. 1.
9 BL, MS Add. 11332, fol. 119r.; *BLB*, II, 931.
10 BL, MS Add. 11331, fol. 44v.; *BLB*, I, 385.
11 BL, MS Add. 11331, fol. 66r.–v.; *BLB*, I, 441.
12 CRO, DDX/428, fol. 103r.; BL, MS Add. 11331, fol. 33v.; *BLB*, I, 235, 360.

Sir William Brereton replied to the 'Gentlemen at Nantwich' from Tarvin garrison, indicating his concern and sympathy for the plight of the soldiers:

> Touching Major Daniell's company. I am informed that, whilst they were at Tarvin they were so well paid that they have no cause to complain and, whilst they were at Shrewsbury, they had the like pay the others had. So long as they and the rest of that regiment do serve as others do, you shall have my assistance and endeavours to provide pay and accommodation for them as for others, and keep them together for the service of the county, so as they shall have no just cause at all to complain. Whereas you write that Captain George Malbon's company deny to watch, for that their officers are paid and not the common soldiers, and that you doubt [not] the rest will do the like if they not be paid. I am of your opinion. For it cannot be expected that soldiers should do duty without money, and I believe it will hardly be answered to the parliament by them that should have provided money out of the Excise, which hath often been ordered to be put into execution and is hitherto much neglected. I desire you, therefore, for their better pay and accommodation to countenance and assist the speedy putting the Excise into execution.[13]

In a postscript, Brereton added:

> Since the writing of this letter Major Daniell is come hither and tells me that nothing hindered more the coming up of his men to do service than Colonel John Booth's interposition in the town[ships] where his men are raised and his listing of the major's men. Which I leave to your consideration whether we can have any great hopes of good by the soldiers thus abused.

The above highlights the continuing problem of Colonel John Booth and his agents, who continued to draw finance and resources from local townships, against the express wishes of Parliament and the deputy lieutenants of Cheshire throughout 1644 and 1645. Sir William Brereton appears to have acted swiftly by appointing William Massey as colonel of the regiment, and obtained immediate pay for the soldiers. Such expedients, coupled with the cashiering of Captains Massey and Whitney in November 1645 pulled the remaining officers into line and effectively saved the regiment. Its want of pay, seemingly acute during mid 1645 must have been alleviated to some extent by the payment of £167 11s. by the sequestration committee for Bucklow Hundred 'from mid-summer rents in Ashley, Bowden, Timperley, Hale and Altrincham'.[14]

Colonel George Booth's Own Company

The colonel's company was raised by late 1642 or early 1643 from the areas in Bucklow and Macclesfield Hundreds near to his family's Dunham Massey estates. The captain-lieutenant, John Daniell, was the son of John Daniell of

13 BL, MS Add. 11331, fol. 68r.; *BLB*, I, 443.
14 BL, MS Harley 2137, fol. 204v.

Daresbury, senior, a sequestration commissioner for Bucklow Hundred, and also one of the leaders of the anti-Brereton movement. Captain-Lieutenant, later Sergeant Major Daniell was in command of Booth's company by April 1643, and served in that capacity until the end of the First Civil War.[15] Ensign, later Lieutenant John Cheshire was another local gentleman, who was a son or kinsman of Thomas Cheshire of Hallwood, near Halton, who had been bailiff of the castle during the early months of the war. The company survived the resignation of Colonel Booth in May 1645 and it was still active in November 1646. As might be expected, the colonel's company was at the forefront of the regiment's operations throughout the war. From the country treasurer, 'Major Daniell and his officers and soldiers' received a total of £1,033 1s. 86.[16] In early April 1645 Booth's company was quartered at Shrewsbury, where it comprised the following:

Sergeant Major John Daniell
Lieutenant John Cheshire
Ensign Alexander Shifnall
Sergeant John Hallmark
Sergeant Alexander Basnett
Corporal John Smallhurst
Corporal Ralph Sanders
Corporal Richard Foson
Drummer John Jones
Drummer Ralph Knowsley
Clerk Robert Harrington[17]

Drum Major William Stafford served in Booth's regiment, and later under Colonels James Lothian and William Massey.[18] The company reported 70 common soldiers on 30 April 1645.[19]

Lieutenant Colonel William Massey's Company

Of Moss House, Audlem, William Massey had been commissioned captain of a company of foot by 10 April 1643 and promoted to lieutenant colonel before 25 September 1643. He took command of Colonel George Booth's regiment following his resignation around April 1645 and was promoted to colonel. Massey was a valuable and highly competent field officer, particularly during the siege of Chester, where his company operated on the Welsh side of the city. In January 1646 he commanded a force of Cheshire and Montgomery foot besieging Hawarden Castle. Between 1646 and 1649 William served on the county committee and was governor of the city during the 1647 army mutinies.[20] Lieutenant Colonel Massey's company was drawn from the Nantwich Hundred trained and freehold bands, although it operated virtually as a 'frontline' unit from its base in the Nantwich garrison. The total funds disbursed to its officers and soldiers from London sources was £4,197

15 TNA, SP28/152/7, fol. 4r.
16 TNA, SP28/128/13, fol. 16v.; SP28/208, unfol.
17 TNA, SP28/123/1, fol. 98v.
18 TNA, SP28/124/1, fol. 5v.; E121/5/7/351, fol. 62r.
19 BL, MS Add. 11331, fol. 45v.
20 BL, MS Add. 11332, fol. 31r.; 11333, fols 30r., 101v.–2r., 118r.; *BLB*, II, 776, 1040, 1063, 1235; Morrill, *Cheshire*, pp.200–1.

5s. 10d.[21] On 28 June 1645 the following officers and non-commissioned officers mustered:

Captain-Lieutenant George Massey	Corporal Peter Sutton
Ensign Thomas Rutter	Corporal Thomas Hawsley
Sergeant Roger Warburton	Drummer Ralph Burton
Sergeant Richard Wilson	Drummer Thomas Worrall[22]
Corporal Ralph Maddon	

Captain-Lieutenant Browne can be identified among pay warrants dated 11 June and 8 November 1645 as leading a company of foot from Nantwich Hundred, which was probably Massey's.[23] Lieutenant Clark is referred to in a warrant of 27 May 1645 with the command, while Thomas Massey was serving as company clerk on 2 August 1645 and was promoted to ensign in the trained bands before 28 June 1647.[24]

Massey's company mustered 160 common soldiers fit for duty on 30 April 1645, 140 on 18 October 1645, 136 on 30 November 1645, 98 on 15 January 1646 and 80 on 28 June 1646.[25]

Sergeant Major John Marbury's Company

While Marbury raised an early troop of horse in Cheshire, he also commanded a company in Colonel Booth's regiment. It has been conjectured by Wanklyn (followed by Dore) that John was commissioned sergeant major in Brooke's regiment of foot in 1643, although corroborating evidence for this is lacking.[26] Yet an undated warrant refers to 'Major Marbury's company in Colonel Booth's regiment in the county of Chester'.[27] It would be reasonable to assume that the Colonel Booth referred to was Colonel *George* Booth, because two contemporaneous warrants exist in the same source for 'Colonel John Booth's regiment in the county of Lancaster'. On 27 August 1643 whilst at Cholmondeley House with Captain Whitney's company of Booth's regiment, Captain John Marbury's soldiers were paid 4s. for finding spent lead for remoulding into bullets.[28] It seems more likely that infantry soldiers would be more anxious to replenish their stock of ammunition than troopers of horse would be.

Marbury had been promoted to sergeant major by May 1644; perhaps this coincided with the elevation around the previous September to lieutenant colonel of Captain William Massey, the second in command of Booth's regiment. Marbury's military career ended in November 1645,

21 TNA, SP28/128/13, fols 17r., 25v.; SP28/208, unfol.
22 TNA, SP28/124/1, fols 10r., 88r.
23 TNA, SP28/224/1, fols 47v., 49v.–50r.
24 TNA, SP28/30/7, fols 698r., 758v.; SP28/124/1, fol. 80v.; BL, MS Harley 2128, fol. 91r.
25 BL, MS Add. 11331, fol. 45v.; 11332, fols 3r., 99r.–v.; TNA, SP28/224, fols 10v., 88v.
26 Wanklyn, 'Landed Society', p.239 and note 3; *BLB*, I, 267, note 1; II, 837, note 2.
27 TNA, E121/5/7/351, fols 4r., 31v.–32r.
28 BL, MS Harley 1999, fol. 60r.

however, when on the recommendation of the Commons Committee for Examinations, he was cashiered for disloyalty to Sir William Brereton with Captains Hugh Whitney and George Massey, both company commanders in Colonel George Booth's regiment and members of the group opposed to Sir William Brereton in mid 1645, led by the Booths and many of their associates.[29] John Marbury's 'misconduct' might also have been due to the influence of his brother and half-brother, Thomas and William, both deputy lieutenants for Cheshire. Dore suggests that William Marbury 'does not joined whole-heartedly in the campaign the Booths waged in the county itself through the Knutsford Petitions … but he was a deputy lieutenant and, critical of the conduct of his colonels. Possibly he had drawn his brothers into anti-Brereton activities.'[30]

Captain Edward Alcocke's Company

From Ashton-upon-Mersey, near Sale, Alcocke was leading his country company by 16 June 1643.[31] With Captain Richard Grantham (below) he later served as captain in Colonel Henry Bradshaw's regiment in 1650–1, including the Battle of Worcester, and sat at Lord Derby's court martial. During the siege of Chester, particular difficulties occurred with the mustering, and conditions of service and payment of the country companies of Alcocke and Grantham. In early April 1645 the Committee at Tarvin was tasked by Brereton to call in various companies to cover the leaguer in the absence of the Parliamentarian forces that had recently marched into Wales. Writing to Sir George Booth on 4 April they stated:

> We are commanded by Sir William Brereton to let you know that the army is marched into Wales and intends to block up that side of Chester, and expects you will summon in the country, especially all that are enlisted or well-armed, to be at Crabtree Green on Thursday next, there to receive orders the better to keep them on this side. Every man is to bring in provision with him, which I hope will cheerfully be done, for that it is the most likely way to put a speedy end to the distractions of this county. If you please write to the captains that are absent from the army to do their duty herein, and to the constables to apprehend all soldiers that absent themselves from their colours and bring them to Nantwich to be tried by council of war it might much advance their work.[32]

The next day, Booth expressed his concerns about bringing in Alcocke's and Grantham's soldiers to Colonel John Leigh, the deputy lieutenant and member of the Tarvin council. Leigh's volunteer regiment of foot was also largely raised in the Knutsford and Altrincham area. Sir George wrote:

---

29 BL, MS Add. 11333, fol. 96v.; *BLB*, II, 837.
30 *BLB*, II, 837 n. 2.
31 TNA, SP28/31/4, fol. 429v.
32 CRO,DDX/428, fol. 87r.–v.; *BLB*, I, 162.

> [I] have written to Captains Alcocke and Grantham to call their companies together and make their appearance. But for raising the country people I forbear, in regard they are making their seedings, as also they have so often been called together and to so little purpose that they grow sensible that the country is burdened and opportunities offered neglected, and no return made of them. I send the letter to you that, if your captains are not on service, you will send them in.[33]

Again, in early November 1645 these countrymen refused to march from their home parishes, causing Sir George Booth to report to Sir William Brereton from Dunham Massey on 9 November:

> Touching preparations for that service and supply to the siege of Chester, I cannot but give you some knowledge thereof, as also by whom I have met with opposition. First, for my endeavours to advance the service, for which purpose I made several journeys to Wilmslow to complete a company for Captain Alcocke and to proportion the charge, as also in Bowdon parish to set forth Captain Grantham. And for such people as have refused to go upon service and thereby given ill example, when I know the parties I shall desire some example may be made.[34]

Arrears of pay and the methods employed in distributing it were high on their agenda. On 4 December 1645 Colonel George Booth endorsed their grievances to Brereton:

> Captains Grantham and Alcocke have given us here [at Dunham Massey] intimation that their companies having done the same duty other auxiliaries of the county have, yet you have been pleased to allow money to others, none to them. As I conceive it was not the Parliament's intention this poor county should be charged more than what is included in the Model, and if I be not very much deceived, all without, though of our own county, are as properly auxiliaries than strangers, I therefore entreat you that no particular disgust may draw on partiality, and, since Colonel Duckenfield's men have had a fortnight's pay, that Grantham's and Alcocke's, behaving themselves as others, may have a competency.[35]

When Alcocke's and Grantham's troops did join the army outside Chester, they appear to have been effective. On 29 October 1645 they were hastened to man the works before the Northgate with other Cheshire companies, while on 12 January 1646 both captains, with their officers and soldiers were paid £102 8s. 8d. whilst at the leaguer.[36] On 30 April 1646 the combined strength of their commands was 100 common soldiers; they also mustered 70 men at Chester on 20 December 1645.[37] On 28 June 1646 Captain Alcocke's company reported the following officers and non-commissioned officers:

33 CRO, DDX/428, fol. 87v.; *BLB*, I, 163.

34 BL, MS Add. 11332, fol. 71r.; *BLB*, II, 846.

35 BL, MS Add. 11332, fol. 119v.; *BLB*, II, 931. Sir William replied the following day that both companies had subsequently been paid (MS Add. 11332, fol. 120r.; *BLB*, II, 933).

36 BL, MS Add. 11332, fol. 31r.; 11333, fol. 45v.; *BLB*, I, 38; II, 1063.

37 BL, MS Add. 11331, fol. 44; 11333, fol. 118v.; *BLB*, II,

Lieutenant Edward Alcocke jnr

He was serving in his father's company by 13 June 1644, but had probably been in the unit for some time. He acted in the same position in Colonel Henry Bradshaw's militia regiment of foot in the Cheshire brigade at the Battle of Worcester.[38]

Ensign William Alcocke

He served as ensign to his father's company, and with his brother Edward junior, he held the same rank in Bradshaw's regiment in 1650–1, but was wounded at Worcester.

Sergeant John Key
Sergeant Robert Alcocke
Corporal John Smith
Corporal George Burgess
Corporal Richard Royle
Drummer Richard Wyatt
Drummer William Woodhall[39]

Captain Richard Grantham's Company

Richard Grantham, a yeoman of Hale, near Cheadle was listed commanding a company in Booth's regiment in the spring of 1645. Among the other country companies raised in the area of the Booth family estates and other parts of eastern Cheshire, Captain Grantham's soldiers were often reluctant to assemble and obey orders. On 5 April Sir George Booth ordered Grantham to muster his command, which reluctant to march to the Chester leaguer owing to lack of pay. Moreover, he related his 'endeavours to advance the service' to Brereton from Dunham Massey on 9 November, in attempting to muster Captain Alcock's soldiers at Wilmslow and Captain Grantham's men in Bowden parish, and to muster 200 of his tenants 'by covenants in their leases' under their assigned captains.[40] On 28 June 1646 Grantham's company comprised:

Lieutenant Thomas Smith
Ensign Edward Harper
Sergeant John Hough
Sergeant Matthew Cookson
Corporal William Peake
Corporal William Speakman
Corporal Ralph Openshaw
Drummer James Neild
Drummer Robert Owen[41]

Captain George Massey's Company

George was the ninth son of the Presbyterian John Massey of Coddington and younger brother of Major General Edward Massey, governor of Gloucester

38 TNA, SP28/196/1, fol. 16r.; Earwaker, *East Cheshire*, p.68.
39 TNA, SP28/124/1, fol. 1r.
40 BL, MS Add. 11332, fol. 71v.; CRO, DDX/428, fol. 88v.; *BLB*, I, 182; II, 846.
41 TNA, SP28/124/1, fol. 1v.

and commander-in-chief of the Western Association. By 18 August 1643 George was part of the besieged garrison of Gloucester, participating in a sally which disabled Royalist artillery. A few weeks later he was wounded, yet by December 1644 he had been appointed governor of Sudeley Castle in Gloucestershire. When the garrison mutinied over pay, Massey killed or wounded the ringleader (depending on which account is followed), and according to Sir Samuel Luke 'whereupon there arose such a mutiny in the castle that he was forced to fly to his brother at Gloucester for relief'.[42]

Such impetuosity (somewhat like that possessed by his brother) could be the reason why George took up a commission in Brereton's army, perhaps in late 1644. On 30 April 1645 he was listed with his company as part of Colonel George Booth's regiment of foot. Soon afterwards, however, Sir William reported to the Committee of Both Kingdoms that 'Captain Massey, brother to the governor of Gloucester, and near 20 gentlemen and officers and about 40 common soldiers were taken in and about Wrexham by the Welsh forces under the command of Colonel Trevor'.[43] In the margin of an earlier letter, dated 6 May, Brereton wrote 'Officers lost: Captain Massey, Mr Pierce, Lieutenant Knightsbridge, Lieutenant Williams, four sergeants'.[44] On 9 October, having been exchanged, George Massey led his company in the great assault on the new breach at Chester's Newgate. He and Lieutenant Colonel Robert Venables were reported among the wounded.[45] Captain Massey was an ardent Booth supporter, and on 7 November 1645, alongside Major Marbury and Captain Whitney he was relieved of his command on charges of disloyalty.[46] Roger Bickerton received pay under Massey as corporal and sergeant.[47]

Captain Cartwright's Company

Captain Cartwright was from near Audlem, Cheshire. Little is known of his company, other than it was raised from Nantwich Hundred and was listed as 100 men co-commanded by Captain George Massey on 30 April 1645.[48] Lieutenant Taylor was paid under Captain Cartwright on 9 August 1645.[49]

Captain Matthew Wright's Company

Of Crewe-by-Farndon, he was serving with his company by 21 August 1643. It is likely that Wright came from a well-known Nantwich family

42 Stuart Peachey and Alan Turton, *The Fall of the West* (Stuart Press, 1994), 6, pp.644–6; *Letter Books of Sir Samuel Luke*, p.117.
43 BL, MS Add. 11331, fol. 80v.; *BLB*, I, 439.
44 BL, MS Add. 11331, fol. 63r.; *BLB*, I, 433.
45 Lancaster, p.22.
46 BL, MS Add. 11333, fol. 96; *BLB*, II, 837.
47 TNA, E121/5/7/351, fols 58v., 50v.
48 BL, MS Add. 11331, fol. 44; *BLB*, I, 385.
49 BL, MS Harley 2128, fol. 91v.

of merchants and was buried at Nantwich on 22 November 1645.[50] His command spent most of 1645 in Shropshire, although Captain Wright was at Dodleston garrison on 13 May, passing on intelligence to Lieutenant Colonel Michael Jones.[51]

Lieutenant John Hay.[52]

Captain Hugh Whitney's Company

From Coole Pilate, Nantwich Hundred. He may have raised his company by early 1643, although on 27 August he received 6s. for the provision of Parliamentarian soldiers in Whitchurch from Sir William Brereton and Captain Thomas Croxton out of the money raised at Cholmondeley.[53] Located 11 miles south-west of Nantwich, Whitchurch had served as the base for the Royalist commander, Lord Capel, but on 30 May 1643 Brereton bypassed his field army and in a bitter fight defeated the garrison, consisting of the Prince of Wales's Lifeguard of Foot, under the command of the governor, Sir Michael Woodhouse.[54] On an unspecified date Captain Hugh Whitney received the sum of £7 10s. for his officers and soldiers from treasurer James Croxton.[55] Whitney's alignment with the Booth party against Sir William Brereton is illustrated by his presence in London with his colonel and other fellow officers in February 1645, when he reportedly complained about Sir William's financial methods and conduct. According to a testimony of Mr Goldsmith, a London merchant, sent to Brereton on 26 February 1645:

> I, seeing Captain Whitney upon the Change [Royal Exchange] saluting him and asking him of the affairs in Cheshire, he answering that it was in a reasonable good condition but that a great want of pay was amongst the soldiers, I asked him where the fault was and what was become of London moneys. He answered the soldiers had but little pay. I made answer I did believe Sir William Brereton was a godly honest man. He made answer 'as any in hell'. For Colonel George Booth, Colonel John Booth, Colonel Mainwaring and Colonel Massey, and himself were come to complain of Sir William Brereton and had procured a warrant from the Committee of Accounts to examine his accounts and all money received in Lindon, Essex etc.[56]

Hugh Whitney was cashiered for disloyalty with John Marbury and George Massey, the Commons Committee for Examinations informing the sheriff,

50 *BLB*, I, 385 note 5.
51 BL, MS Add. 11331, fol. 96v.; *BLB*, I, 509.
52 TNA, SP28/225/3, fol. 682r.
53 BL, MS Harley 1999, fol. 60r.
54 HMC, *Twelfth Report, App. IX*, p. 40; W.A. Day (ed.), *The Pythouse Papers: Correspondence Concerning The Civil War, the Popish Plot and a Contested Election in 1680* (Bickers & Son, 1879), p.16.
55 TNA, SP28/128/13, fol. 26r.; SP28/224/1, unfol.
56 CRO, DDX/428, fol. 61r.; *BLB*, I, 19.

Colonel Henry Brooke on 7 November, 'it appears they are dangerous and do much disturb the peace of the county'.[57] The precise charges against these three officers is unknown, but Whitney's actions in the capital appear to have been symptomatic of a more general belligerence shown towards his commander-in-chief, whereas George Massey's previous conduct in the West Country suggests that he was something of a hothead. Captain Whitney's company served with Booth's regiment during its many operations in 1643 and 1644, but was seconded to the Shropshire Committee in late 1645. Drummer Richard Allot was paid with it during this time.[58] Whitney was commissioned as captain in Colonel Thomas Croxton's Cheshire militia regiment of foot on 22 August 1650.[59]

Captain George Malbon's Company

The eldest son of Thomas Malbon of Bradley, near Nantwich, the Cheshire lawyer and annalist, and brother of Captain Thomas (below). Both of the companies under command of the Malbon brothers were at the forefront of the Parliamentarian assaults on Cholmondeley House and Oswestry during the summer of 1644, and served with vigour and reliability at the Chester leaguer. Neither sibling seems to have played any part in the Booth–Brereton affair. In 1650 George acted as major in Colonel Thomas Croxton's regiment of foot. Captain George Malbon's company of Nantwich townsmen may have originally been raised and led by his cousin, Captain Richard Clutton, probably the Mr Clutton, 'an active gentleman' who defied the commissioners of array when they entered Nantwich in September 1642.[60] He was reported to have:

> disarmed the under-sheriff's man, who came from the cavaliers, who would not hear talk of any parley, but gave express command to the townsmen of his own company to give fire as soon as the cavaliers shall come within shot, and not to admit of any parley; but other gentlemen persuaded the contrary, lest it should be fired, whereupon they came to parley.

A lieutenant, five corporals and 86 common solders are listed under Captain George Malbon on 31 October 1644, although in the army list of April 1645 his company is given as a combined figure of 200 with that of his brother.

Lieutenant John Acton – named as lieutenant to the company in pay warrants of 24 and 27 December 1644. On 21 March 1645 the following were also remunerated for their service:

57 BL, MS Add. 11333, fol. 96v.; *BLB*, II, 837.
58 TNA, E121/1/5, fol. 394r.
59 *CSPD 1650*, p.509.
60 Malbon, p.238;

Corporal William Mirkflood
Corporal Roger Davies
Corporal Thomas Marchant
Corporal Richard Pemberton
Corporal Thomas Birch[61]

Captain Thomas Malbon's Company

It is possible that the company of Thomas Malbon junior was originally formed in early 1643 under the command of Captain Edward Minshall. He died and was interred at Nantwich on 14 July 1643. The commissioners for stating of accounts and giving forth debentures for Cheshire noted on 8 July 1650 that Lieutenant William Burscough was owed £120 17s., having served 143 days (at 18d. per day) as sergeant in Minshall's company of foot; for serving 736 days (at the same rate) as sergeant in Captain Thomas Malbon's command; and for serving 528 days (at 4s.) as lieutenant in Captain John Crew's company (force unknown).[62] In Brereton's army list, dated 30 April 1645 the 'Two Nantwich companies of townsmen under Captains George and Thomas Malbon' possessed a combined strength of 200 men, and quartered in the said town.[63] In an undated pay warrant (probably late 1645) Randle Sparrow was paid as ensign to Thomas Malbon's company.[64] Thomas later served as captain in Croxton's regiment.

Captain Jones Lownes's Company

The earliest warrant for pay to Captain Lownes dates from 6 February 1643.[65] Upon the capture of Cholmondeley House in July 1644 he was appointed joint-governor, while on 29 October led his foot company in a raid from Nantwich on Farndon with other Cheshire forces.[66] In 1646 treasurer Croxton disbursed the sum of £13 12s. 6d. 'to Captain John Lownes, and his officers and soldiers'.[67] It is possible that Lownes commanded an independent company, although given the Cholmondeley connection it appears more likely that it was part of Colonel George Booth's regiment (Booth having led his men in person at the storming of both this and Oswestry days earlier), and was quartered for much of its time in Nantwich. As it is unlisted in Brereton's Cheshire forces in April 1645, it may have been disbanded by then, or Lownes had left the army and his soldiers dispersed under other captains.

61 TNA, SP28/21/294, fol. 295r.; SP28/225/3, fol. 503r.
62 Malbon, p.256; SP28/224/1, fol. 327r.
63 BL, MS Add. 11331, fol. 44r.; *BLB*, I, 385.
64 TNA, SP28/225/3, fol. 473v.
65 TNA, SP28/196/3, fol. 1v.
66 BL, MS Harley 1999, fol. 61r.; TNA, SP28/196/1, fol. 2r.; Malbon, pp.138, 150.
67 TNA, SP28/128/13, fol. 15r.

11

Colonel Henry Brooke's Regiment of Foot

Henry Brooke was the head of an important Presbyterian family of Norton, near Runcorn. He was a significant figure in the Parliamentarian war effort in Cheshire and the struggle for power within it. The Brookes were the only major Parliamentarian supporters in upper Bucklow Hundred, being direct neighbours of Earl Rivers of Rocksavage, Sir Thomas Aston of Aston and Robert Needham, Lord Kilmorey, who owned land at Frodsham and Weston. Rivers and Aston raised forces for Charles I during the early months of the war from the local area. There is some evidence that Henry Brooke resided at the home of his wife at Selston Hall, Nottinghamshire before the war. In 1639 John Aston mentioned meeting him with his brother Sir Thomas at Nottingham Castle whilst travelling to rendezvous with the King's forces during the First Bishops' War.[1] Moreover, in 1642 Henry was in the process of settling his wife's dowry in the presence of his father-in-law, Timothy Pusey and brother-in-law William Willoughby of South Muskham.[2] Nottinghamshire was chaotic during the beginning of the war – in June 1642, as at Manchester, the townsmen of Nottingham refused to allow the local Royalists to seize the magazine, and only submitted when Charles I himself arrived to raise his standard on 22 August. Also, both sides actively recruited in the county during the latter part of the year.

Henry Brooke was an early deputy lieutenant in Cheshire and actively promoted the Parliamentarian war aims in the county during the winter of 1642–3, some months before Sir William Brereton arrived from London with his military forces. With Brereton's support, Henry was placed on the original county Committee for Assessment and Sequestration. He raised a troop of horse and regiment of foot, and on 28 March 1644 petitioned Parliament, presumably for funds for the completion of his military commands. On 7 May 1644 Brooke was granted £1,000 towards the completion of his regiment

1 BL, MS Add. 28566, unfol.; Hodgson, J.C. (ed.), John Aston, 'Iter Boreale, Anno Salutis 1639 et Dissidae inter Anglos at Scotos Inchoatus 1 Aprilis finitum 29 Junii', *Six North Country Diaries*, SS, 118 (1910), 124 (1915), p.3.

2 CRO, DBN/B/2/8.

of foot and troop of horse. Henry's authority increased on 13 September 1644 when he was appointed high sheriff of Cheshire by parliamentary ordinance.[3] He was constantly with Brereton, endorsing his letters and instructions, whilst serving with ability and loyalty. It is possible that with the deputy lieutenant Roger Wilbraham, Colonel Brooke headed a 'middle party' in May 1645, which modified the anti-Brereton Knutsford Petition. As Dore suggests, 'It is difficult to avoid the conclusion that Brereton aided this build-up of the influence of the Brooke family to act as a counter-weight to the Booths.' In 1645 or 1646 Henry was reimbursed the £298 3s. 0d. he had spent 'in the public service', while his final arrears of pay amounted to £1,195 12s. 6d. for which he was later granted the manor and castle of Halton by Parliament.[4] In March 1646 Brooke, members of his family and tenants gave evidence before the Bucklow Hundred sequestration committee against the conduct of their former neighbour, Earl Rivers.[5] After the war Henry acted as a magistrate and MP for Cheshire, and supported the Booth Rebellion in 1659.

Colonel Henry Brooke's regiment of foot was recruited almost entirely from upper Bucklow Hundred and contained three members of his family among its senior officers. Another brother, Thomas, held a commission as lieutenant in the Cheshire army. Thomas was mortally wounded at the Battle of Nantwich on 25 January 1644 and buried in the town three days later. On 3 October 1646 his widow, Jane, was granted £20 due to her late husband 'for provision by him brought into Norton house for the use of the soldiers there when the same was a garrison'.[6] Given the family connection and reference to provisioning the garrison of Norton, it is likely that Lieutenant Thomas Brooke served in his brother Henry's regiment of foot (perhaps in the colonel's own or one of the Nantwich town companies of Captains Delves and Bramhall, or as a supernumerary officer). Wanklyn suggests that Colonel Brooke's foot originally ('in the spring and summer of 1643') consisted of seven companies, and was the 'only regiment with any degree of social exclusiveness', meaning that four of those companies were commanded by officers from 'middling landowning families'.[7] On 30 April 1645 Brooke's regiment mustered 570 common soldiers in seven companies. With officers and non-commissioned officers the complete strength is likely to have been upwards of 650.

Although the regiment was not completed until mid 1644, various companies were active by early 1643 in establishing Parliamentarian authority in north-west Cheshire, and serving in Brereton's field army both in the county and beyond. Richard and John Brooke were probably commissioned by February–March 1643, when they were drawing pay for their soldiers, while Captain-Lieutenant John Church may have been a professional,

3 *JHC*, III, pp.439, 484, 610; *A&O*, I, pp.503–5.

4 TNA, SP28/196/1, fol. 26r.; E121/1/5, fol. 43v.

5 CRO, DCH/X/15/14.

6 Malbon, p.257; TNA, SP28/225/3, fol. 519r.In his mother's will, dated 21 April 1651, Thomas is referred to as 'my late son', while Jane was bequeathed a silver watch, and their son Richard and daughter Katherine were left £30 and £20 respectively (TNA, PROB 11/220/237).

7 Wanklyn, 'Landed Society', p.239 and n. 3.

brought in by Henry Brooke to command the colonel's company around this time. During the first half of 1643 Brooke's soldiers acted in the successful defence of Norton House and the siege of Halton Castle. On 20 July Henry accepted the surrender of the Royalist stronghold, appointing his brother, Captain (later Lieutenant Colonel) Richard Brooke as governor of the new garrison.[8] Thus, the regiment was detached from the main Cheshire army during this period, one in which Parliamentarian control of the locality was established and maintained for the remainder of the war.

Some indication of the importance of maintaining the security of the upper Bucklow area for the Parliament is suggested by the location of Norton itself – its close proximity to Halton Castle meant that it was part of a wider strategic network of defences on the Mersey at Hale Ford and Warrington, defensive positions at Frodsham Bridge and ditch, a ford at Dutton and for the safeguarding of Runcorn dock, an important link in the supply chain between the port of Liverpool and the army in Cheshire. The Aston warrants illustrate that during Prince Rupert's advance through Cheshire in May 1644 Colonel Brooke placed the bulk of his regiment (and possibly his cavalry troop) at Halton and Norton, while locally raised dragoons patrolled what was considered by the Parliamentarians as a 'safe area'. Moreover, in April 1645 Sir William Brereton, anxious to apprehend soldiers of his army who were guilty of pillaging, informed the deputy lieutenant, William Marbury, 'I have written also to the Committee of Northwich and to Colonel Brooke to suffer none to pass without my order at Northwich, Frodsham or elsewhere over the river [Weaver] and to make stay of the same aforesaid.'[9]

The Cheshire foot regiments commanded by Colonels Brooke and George Booth suffered particularly from recruiting problems, as well as the procurement of supplies and pay due chiefly to an order from the Council of War at Nantwich, made in late 1643, which permitted the Lancashire colonel, John Booth to draw money raised in the 29 townships of the upper division of Bucklow Hundred to be diverted towards his soldiers. John Booth's regiment formed the Parliamentarian garrison of Warrington, with responsibility for securing the eastern part of West Derby Hundred, as well as assisting Brereton in Cheshire.[10] On 12 October 1643 the hundred of West Derby was made liable for the upkeep of the garrisons of Liverpool and Warrington, while the leys and taxations raised within five South Lancashire parishes were allotted to the latter.

However concerned Sir William Brereton might have been that the Lancashire Committee (of which he was a member) took complete responsibility for the maintenance of the Warrington garrison, its Cheshire neighbours remained liable for substantial contributions. The accounts of Thomas Warburton, treasurer to the Bucklow sequestration committee, show that up to the end of April 1644 he paid £328 18s. 2d. to Colonel John Booth, almost half the total received from sequestrations in the whole hundred

8 HLJO, HL/PO/JO/10/1/224.

9 CRO, DDX/428, fol. 86r.; *BLB*, I, 205.

10 *CJ*, III, p.157; HMC, *Tenth Report*, App. IV, p.68; *BLB*, I, 19n.

during the same period.[11] Additionally, in the summary of his accounts, made on 28 June 1645, Warburton highlighted the difficulty of maintaining garrisons at both Warrington and at Halton, in north-west Cheshire, as well as funding the various military units raised from the area. He and his collectors, he said, had been 'much obstructed in the service of sequestrators within the division ordered for the garrison of Warrington, and that there hath been great sums seized for the use of the garrison of Halton … and that several soldiers have seized goods without our order, we conceive it cannot be, but something may be committed and some mistaken'.[12] Although payments to Booth ceased, following an order of 2 March 1644 by Sir Thomas Fairfax (nominally commander-in-chief while Brereton was in London, that all sequestration money was to be paid directly to the county treasurer) and parliamentary ordinance of 7 May 1644, evidence shows that money, recruits and supplies continued to be appropriated well into the following year.

Perhaps due to the difficulties of obtaining recruits in northern Cheshire, Colonel Henry Brooke's regiment was augmented by two companies of Nantwich men under the command of Captains John Delves and Francis Bramhall. This build-up probably occurred after May 1644 when Colonel Brooke was granted £1,000 for the completion of his regiment of foot and troop of horse. The accounts of the constables of Lymm record that they maintained 'three soldiers in the trained bands at Nantwich under Colonel Brooke' in 1643, 1644 and 1645, costing them respectively £54 12s., £46 4s. and £19 5s.[13] Furthermore, in a letter to Sir William Brereton, penned by three of his Cheshire colonels in December 1645, a 'country company of Colonel Brooke's' was described as being among troops occupying the eastern suburbs of Chester.[14] But as Henry Brooke's regiment does not have 'country' opposite any of its companies in Brereton's army list of 31 October 1645, it is likely that the troops alluded to above were from either the command of 'Captain Delves and Captain Bramhall both of Nantwich Hundred'. These men quartered in the town, and as Dore suggests, thus mistaken for militia or country companies who by their nature 'although on permanent call for duty, the men were quartered in their own homes'.[15]

Colonel Henry Brooke's Own Company

The colonel's company is likely to have been recruited from the '80 volunteers' (largely gentlemen and tenants) who defended Norton against Earl Rivers in February 1643. In April 1645 there were 140 common soldiers – forming one of the largest companies in the Cheshire army – which might be accounted for by the necessity on the part of Brooke and Brereton to maintain a sizeable force of foot in upper Bucklow until the summer of 1644 onwards, when

11 TNA, SP28/208, unfol.; BL, MS Harley 2137, fols 56v., 60v.–61r.

12 BL, MS Harley 2137, fol. 161r.

13 BL, MS Harley 2128, fol. 48v.

14 BL, MS Add. 11333, fol. 57r.–v.; *BLB*, II, 1088.

15 *BLB*, II, 1088, note 2.

Cheshire was more secure after the departure of Rupert's forces from the North West. Henry Brooke's own company was led from the outset by Captain-Lieutenant John Church, who was promoted to sergeant major by 12 April 1644. Church penned a series of letters to Thomas Warburton between July and September 1644, requesting pay and provisions for his soldiers.[16] In the list of Cheshire forces, dated 30 April 1645, Church is stated to have been from Bucklow Hundred, but it seems more likely that like Captain-Lieutenant Robert Wynn of Brooke's cavalry troop, he was a professional soldier who was brought in either in the autumn of 1642 or the early months of 1643, to help in the establishment and training of the fledgling regiment.[17] Church continued to lead Colonel Brooke's company in a number of operations until its disbandment in 1646.

Dore suggests that 'As a result [of defending Norton and limiting the activities of the Royalist garrison at Halton Castle in 1643 the Brookes] … played no part in Brereton's victorious campaign on the southern borders of Cheshire or in the defence of Nantwich against the army from Ireland and the subsequent victory outside the town.'[18] There might be some truth in this, although evidence points to Colonel Henry Brooke's company being part of the Nantwich garrison from November 1643, if not earlier. A warrant issued by the army's commanders to the constables of Aston on 23 November (in the form of a standing order and endorsed by Captain-Lieutenant John Church), required them to 'levy and gather in your constableship by distress or otherwise the same of the sum of 28s. for a month's pay for the trained soldiers your township stands charged with, and you are to pay the sum together with 3s. more that you are behind of old over unto Captain Church or his assignees upon Monday next without deferring the time of payment any longer'.[19] From its base at Nantwich a detachment under Captain-Lieutenant Church formed part of an outpost of 'about forty soldiers' at Doddington Hall.[20]

This was part of the defensive operations designed to counter the movements of Rupert, whose forces were joined on their march from Shrewsbury, via Audlem, Sandbach and Stockport en route to Lancashire in May 1644 by Lord Byron with four regiments of horse and four of foot from Chester. Warrants indicate that during this period, the bulk of Colonel Brooke's regiment of foot, and possibly his troop of horse, were concentrated in the Halton-Norton area, presumably to defend it against Royalist attack. During most of this time Church and his men received various amounts of pay from the Bucklow sequestrators. Between 26 July 1644 and 2 April 1645 John benefitted from personal payments totalling £124 3s. 9d. On 15 October the sum of 10s. was disbursed to 'four of Captain Church's soldiers for bringing of cattle' from the sequestered estates of Thomas Leigh and others. Likewise, John Church received £16 10s. towards the pay of three of

16 TNA, SP28/225/2, fols 58v., 53v.–5r.
17 BL, MS Add. 11331, fol. 45v.; *BLB*, I, 385, n. 6.
18 *BLB*, I, 260, n. 1.
19 AA, unlisted warrant, dated 23 November 1643.
20 Malbon, pp.129–30.

his soldiers from the Tabley estate, and a further £15 5s. 1d. 'for the soldiers of his company'.[21] The command was one of those singled out for its part in the actions fought at Malpas on 26 August and Montgomery on 18 September 1644.[22] During 1645–6 Colonel Brooke's own company saw constant service at the Chester leaguer. In December 1645 it participated in the Whitchurch march, an important operation designed to relieve pressure on the Chester siege lines. The accounts of James Croxton, treasurer to the army, includes an undated disbursement of £27 7s. 0d. to 'Captain John Church, and his officers and soldiers'.[23]

Ensign Richard Heath

A Frodsham yeoman, Heath received pay for the company in early 1643, although soon afterwards he was promoted to lieutenant and transferred to Captain William Daniell's command.[24]

Ensign Robert Hyde

He is likely to have been a younger brother of Captain Edward Hyde, deputy lieutenant and brother-in-law to Henry Brooke. In 1644 he received pay from the Rocksavage estate with Lieutenants Johnson and Heath, while two years later he was in arrears of pay as ensign to the company of Captain John Brooke which became the Bucklow Hundred trained band. Robert still held the rank on 21 January 1648, when he was reimbursed the sum of £2 5s. 4d., which he and Lieutenant Johnson had laid out in June 1645 for powder and match for guarding Frodsham Ditch Ford on the River Weaver. On 22 August 1650 Robert Pike was commissioned captain in Henry Brooke's militia regiment of foot.[25]

Mr Dunlop

Paid as 'surgeon to Colonel Brooke's regiment'.[26]

Lieutenant Colonel Richard Brooke's Company

Richard Brooke, third son of Sir Richard Brooke of Norton, served as captain and lieutenant colonel in his brother's regiment, governor of Halton Castle and sequestrator for Bucklow Hundred. By his own admission, he was one of the earliest officers to declare for Parliament in north-west Cheshire, others having not done so because of Earl Rivers' presence in the

21 BL, MS Harley 2137, fols 52v., 55v., 57v–92v., 153r.

22 *The Success of Our Cheshire Forces, as they came Related by Sir William Brereton's own pen to a Minister of note and eminency in the City ... To which is added, late good newes from Lancashire, etc.* (26 August 1644); Phillips, *Memoirs*, II, p.198. The events of the action and its aftermath are related by Malbon, pp.143–5.

23 TNA, SP28/128/13, fol. 25v.; SP28/208, unfol.

24 TNA, E121/5/7/351, fol. 62v.

25 BL, MS Harley 2137, fol. 144r.; SP28/224, fol. 218v., SP28/225/3, fols 524r.–v.; *CSPD 1650*, p.509.

26 TNA, SP28/225/4, fol. 714v.

area. The Brookes were particularly ill-disposed towards Thomas Savage, their Royalist neighbour, who had not only held sway in and recruited men from upper Bucklow in 1642 and early 1643, but had attacked Norton, and plundered their estates and tenants. Later in the war Richard Brooke poured scorn on his previous enemy, stating 'it was wonderful to all who knew his lordship's former voluptuous life, how he became so unexpectedly active and industrious', also claiming that Rivers' regiment was 'miserably routed and broken at Edgehill' (although the latter was an exaggeration).[27] Richard Brooke had raised his company by February 1643, and from an early stage he engaged in local military operations. During mid 1643 as captain he led the storming of Rocksavage House, claiming its goods as a prize.[28]

These were inventoried by sequestration officials and exploited to provide money, provisions and other resources for Richard's company in particular. How damaged the fabric of the structure was is uncertain, but at a later date Brooke's ensign, Thomas Davenport was reimbursed by the sequestrators of Bucklow Hundred the sum of £30 13s. 4d. 'for the repair of Rocksavage House', while a further £35 9s. was allowed towards his pay.[29] In early 1645 'arrears of meadowing and demising in Rocksavage the last year' were disbursed by the Bucklow sequestration agents – it was recorded that 'Lieutenant Johnson and his party in the meadowing and demesne land had all or most of the cattle plundered by the army.' Moreover, Brooke's soldiers received £84 13s. 4d. in pay out of the Rocksavage rents, whilst in arrears for 1645 and 1646 a number of officers of Colonel Brooke's regiment obtained recompense from the same source, including Henry and Richard Brooke, who received £42 and £21 16s. each.[30]

By mid 1644 Richard Brooke been promoted to lieutenant colonel. On 21 August 1644 his company fought with the Cheshire foot at the Battle of Tarvin.[31] The accounts of James Croxton, county treasurer, record 34 payments to Richard Brooke's company between February and July 1645, with a further disbursement of £248 4s. 2d. in pay to Richard 'and to his officers and soldiers'.[32] His final outstanding remuneration as 'captain of a foot company and as Lieutenant Colonel to the regiment of Henry Brooke, as governor of Halton Castle, and as captain as a foot company in [the] said castle' amounted to £297 0s. 8d. In lieu of this sum Richard was granted the Lancashire manor of Cuerdley on 25 September 1650.[33] The only recorded strength Lieutenant Colonel Brooke's company is that of 60 common soldiers who mustered on 30 April 1645.[34]

27 CRO, DCH/X/15/14, fol. 1.

28 BL, MS Harley 2128, fol. 201r. For a description of the house by William Webb in 1622 see Daniel King, *The History of Cheshire: containing King's Vale-Royal entire* (Chester, 1656), I, pp.242–3.

29 BL, MS Harley 2128, fol. 201r. For the full inventory of Earl Rivers' goods, see fols 98r.–v.

30 BL, MS Harley 2128, fols 144r.–v.; 2137, fol. 200v.

31 *A True relation of two great Victories*; Malbon, p.142.

32 TNA, SP28/208, unfol.; SP28/128/13, fol. 18r.

33 TNA, E121/1/5, fol. 204r.–v.

34 BL, MS Add. 11331, fol. 45; *BLB*, I, 385.

Lieutenant Humphrey Johnson

Lieutenant Johnson of Newton, near Frodsham, and Ensign Davenport are included in three payments with Captain Richard Brooke in mid 1643, and both acted as co-issuers of warrants to the constables of Aston with him and Captain William Daniell at Halton Castle in July 1644.[35] On 14 January 1647 Johnson was reimbursed for arrears due serving in Captain John Brooke's company of volunteers before it became the trained band of Bucklow Hundred. He is probably the same Humphrey Johnson mentioned in a receipt of 21 January 1648, when the sequestrators of Bucklow were instructed to repay monies to him and Ensign Pike that they had spent on powder and match for their soldiers for the guarding of Frodsham Ditch Ford on 7 June 1645.[36]

Ensign Thomas Davenport

Thomas Davenport began his service in Richard Brooke's company from mid 1643, if not earlier. He later served as captain-lieutenant to Colonel William Daniell's own company in the garrison of Perth. In June 1657 Daniell reported 'He has been under my command almost fourteen years and hitherto demeaned himself in good order'. Davenport converted to Quakerism at about that time, which led to his discharge from the army.[37]

Corporal Richard Smith
Clerk Humphrey Clayton

Common soldiers:

Robert Gregg
John Sharples
Robert Broughill
Jonathan Pickering
Noah Pickering[38]

During the summer of 1648 Brooke was ordered to regarrison Halton Castle, the hundreds of Bucklow and Eddisbury being allotted to paying £9 per week for the maintenance of one sergeant, one drummer and 30 soldiers 'until instructed otherwise'.[39]

Captain John Brooke's Company

The youngest brother of Henry Brooke, John appears to have returned from his studies at Oxford in the autumn of 1642 to take up arms. He served as cornet to Colonel Henry Brooke's troop and captain in his regiment of foot.[40]

35 BL, MS Harley 2137, fols 144r., 200r.
36 TNA, SP28/224, fol. 218v.; SP28/225, fol. 524r.–v.
37 *Regimental History of Cromwell's Army*, II, pp.493–4; *Cromwell's Army*, pp.341–2.
38 TNA, E121/5/9/351, fols 51v., 65r., 67r.; BL, MS Harley 2137, fols 124r., 199v.
39 TNA, SP28/225/3, fol. 520v.
40 TNA, E121/5/7/95, fol. 1r.; E121/1/5, misc. fol. 307v.

John Brooke received his commission as captain of a company of foot from Ferdinando, Lord Fairfax, major general of the Northern Association. In a warrant written on 2 March 1644 to the constables of Aston, Brooke stated:

> By virtue of an original commission to me granted by the right honourable Lord Fairfax, general of these counties, for the speedy raising of my company to lie in the garrison of Northwich, or in what other place shall be, by the general thought convenient. These are therefore strictly to command you, to warn all those who are to send men and arms under me according to my commission, that they repair to Norton Hall upon Tuesday next, being the fifth day of this present March by twelve of the clock and there to appear with their complete arms'.[41]

On paper at least, Cheshire was part of the Northern Association (and thus Fairfax's authority) from 17 November 1642 to 16 February 1643, hence John's commission must have been issued during this period. He received £5 for his own pay on 22 March 1643, while on 8 August 1643 a further disbursement was made to 'Captain Brooke's volunteers', although some of the Aston warrants refer to the mustering and equipping of 'trained soldiers', thus indicating that in 1643 and 1644 at least, part of the company was made up of trained bandsmen.[42] For much of 1643 and 1644 his company was located in Norton, Frodsham and the local area, but during the Chester leaguer it garrisoned Bridge Trafford.

During the winter of 1643 and spring of 1644 Captain John Brooke appears to have been anxious to complete his command. On 25 March 1644 he instructed the constables of Aston 'to collect and gather within your township by distress or otherwise, the sum of 10s. for the buying of drums and colours for my company'.[43] Furthermore, on 21 November 1644 Brooke disbursed £2 for muskets and bandoliers.[44] As already noted, the raising of recruits, finance and equipment was problematic for the Brookes before mid 1643 owing to Royalist influence in the Bucklow area and the activities of Colonel John Booth on behalf of the Warrington garrison. By early 1644 it was possible for Henry Brooke to petition Parliament for more resources and the local sequestration committee to divert more funds away from Booth. Significantly, on 13 December 1643 Captain John Brooke directed the constables of Aston and Aston Grange to ensure that all trained soldiers they were liable to maintain within their townships should muster fully armed at Daresbury:

> By virtue of commission from the honourable deputy lieutenants and the militia for this country to meet at Daresbury for the speedy raising of men and arms to be in readiness in *extremis exigence* and urgent necessity within divers townships, and your townships of Aston and Aston Grange, the right worthy it is hoped we

41 AA, unlisted warrant, dated 2 March 1644.

42 TNA, SP28/196/1, fols 15v., 18v.

43 AA, unlisted warrant, dated 25 March 1644.

44 BL, MS Add. 2137, fol. 52r.; TNA, SP28/208, unfol.

> shall be found able with god's blessing to resist the enemy who otherwise will be ready to make much intrusion, waste and spoil in the country, as formerly they have done when they have had power and ability for that purpose and forasmuch as you all men are warned by the same commission to be ready with their arms within one fortnight after warning ... that you warn all the inhabitants within your townships who hold the value of whole ploughs, half ploughs, or any other ability in personal estate, as also all those who hold and possess to the value of £5 a year freehold, freefarm or copyhold, to appear with their arms which they have heretofore directed and appointed, to find there to be equipped and trained in martial discipline, giving further notice that whosoever shall be found failing in his arms at that time is to find the same by Saturday at furthest, or to be treated an enemy to the high court of parliament, and forasmuch contended thereof and the constables presumed to make their presentments the day resuming their appearance, which thing was hindered in some townships by the forwardness of some who stand malignantly affected.[45]

John Brooke was promoted to sergeant major in 1646 and commanded the Bucklow trained bands in May and August 1648 during the campaign against Royalist rebellions in North Wales.[46] In August 1650 served as lieutenant colonel in his brother Henry's regiment of foot, formed from Eddisbury Hundred, and parts of Bucklow and Northwich. Although perhaps only Bradshaw's regiment subsequently fought against the Royalist–Scots army at Worcester on 3 September 1651, the majority of the Cheshire forces were engaged in skirmishes at Warrington Bridge, Sandbach and Congleton.[47] Lieutenant Colonel John Brooke continued to serve with the Cheshire forces throughout the 1650s. On 30 January 1651 he purchased land in Hawarden from John Griffith of Hawarden, gentleman, while in payment of his final arrears as cornet of horse and captain of a company of foot in the Cheshire army, which amounted to £418 0s. 4d., John Brooke was granted the manor of Middlewich by Parliament on 25 September 1651.[48]

Like others, Captain Brooke and his company received pay from a combination of sources. On 22 March 1644 he was paid £5 for himself by Richard Stelfox. John received from the county treasurer payments of £10 on 19 November and 17 December 1644, and a further £1 was obtained, probably in 1645.[49] Similarly, on 18 December 1645 Captain William Daniell and Captain John Brooke had each £10 'this being besides their ordinary pay, according to the Cheshire Model, they having been constantly upon

45 AA, unlisted warrant, dated 13 December 1643. See similar warrants, dated 5, 19 and 22 March 1644, directing musters at Norton and Daresbury.

46 BL, MS Harley 2137, fol. 201r. ('paid to Major Brooke for grass taken by Captain Lathom's troop – £42'); TNA, SP28/124, fol. 198r.; SP28/208, unfol.

47 *Mercurius politicus, communicating the chief transactions of, and advertisements from the three kingdomes, England, Scotland, and Ireland*, 3–9 September 1651; *The weekly intelligencer of the Commonwealth faithfully communicating the affaires of these three nations*, 3–9 September 1651; Thomas Helsby (ed.), George Ormerod, *History of the County Palatine and City of Chester* (London: Routledge, 2nd edn, 1874), II, pp.xxxix, xl; III, pp.60–1.

48 NLW, Hawarden Deeds/325; E121/1/5, fol. 307v.

49 TNA, SP28/196/1, fol. 15r.; SP28/208, unfol.; SP28/128/13, fol. 29r.; BL, MS Harley 2137, fol. 52r.

service in the Leaguer before Chester'.[50] The final arrears owing to John by Parliament were assessed on 15 September 1650 at £418 0s. 4d. In return for the payment of his arrears, he was able to purchase the manor of Middlewich under the Act of 16 July 1649, which disposed of Crown lands in order to raise £600,000 to pay the army.[51] In January 1651 Brooke further purchased properties in Hawarden from John and Thomas Griffith for the sum of £100.[52] The total pay disbursed by Croxton by 1647 to 'Captain John Brooke and his officers and soldiers' came to £1,260 4s. 8d.[53]

During 1643 and 1644 various companies from Colonel Brooke's regiment were quartered in north-west Cheshire. In August 1643 Robert Ragin of Frodsham was paid 8d. by the Bucklow sequestration committee for billeting two soldiers under Richard Brooke's command for a day and a night, while Thomas Modshall had 1s. 4d. for accommodating two men of Captain John Brooke's company for two days and two nights. On the same occasion Captain Daniell's company received £65 18d. in pay whilst being quartered in the same town.[54] How many of John Brooke's soldiers were billeted on the townships of Aston and Aston Grange at any one time is unclear, although on 3 June 1644 he charged the constables of Aston 'to quarter in your township twelve of my soldiers without delay'. They were also expected to provide each night 'four able men with a horse for to work and keep sentry whereof they will be appointed'. In particular, these officials had the responsibility of constructing, manning and victualling a sentry post at Frodsham Bridge, which formed the western boundary of Bucklow Hundred. Captain Brooke was ordered by the council of war at Nantwich on 1 July 1644 to bring in his company for a rendezvous at Norton garrison.

The reasoning for this was the earlier concentration of the four volunteer companies of Colonel Henry Brooke's regiment of foot within the Halton–Norton area during the summer of 1644 to maintain the defence of the area against the threat of the march of Prince Rupert and his forces through Cheshire towards Lancashire and the north the previous month. Henry's own warrant to the constables of Weston, Runcorn, Sutton, Halton, Norton, Aston and Aston Grange, ordering them to appear at Halton Castle 'to conclude how to put the country in a defensive posture', issued on 11 July was fundamental to the Parliamentarian strategy in the locality. John Brooke's command received its marching orders once more on 30 September 1644 – 'by virtue of a general order from my colonel [he directed the Aston and Aston Grange constables] for the speedy calling in of my company upon pain of death at the rendezvous at Tarvin tomorrow by 12 of the clock' ... [to that affect they were] 'to notify all soldiers quartering in their townships to join their colours'.[55] On 19 December 1644 the sum of £2 4s. was paid by Ralph Judson to 'Captain John Brooke, whose resolute guard

50 BL, MS Add. 11333, fols 30r., 118r.; *BLB*, II, 1040, 1235.

51 TNA, E121/1/5, fol. 307v.

52 NLW, Hawarden Deeds/325.

53 TNA, SP28/128/13, fol. 16v.

54 BL, MS Harley 1999, fols 75v., 78r.

55 AA, unlisted warrants, dated *ibid.*, dated 3 June 1644, 20 November 1643, 28 March 1644, 7 April, 1, 11, 18 July, 30 September 1644.

at Bridge Trafford, in want of pay', while in Brereton's army list of 30 April 1645 his command is recorded as the garrison there.[56] Moreover, Brooke's soldiers saw active at the siege of Chester, particularly on the Welsh side of the city. On 20 or 21 March 1645 the company was ordered to rendezvous with Colonel Robert Duckenfield's regiment and elements of the Cheshire horse at Mold, during an operation to counter Royalist activity in the area. Additionally, one of Captain Brooke's men was wounded by musket shot during an attack on the Parliamentarian siegeworks to the south-west of Chester on 12 October 1645.[57]

Lieutenant John Witter

John was a son of William Witter of Frodsham, and brother of Ensign Joseph Witter of Captain William Daniell's company in Brooke's regiment. He began as cornet of dragoons under Captain Richard Littler, before serving as ensign to Sergeant Major John Trevis of Colonel Leigh's regiment of foot. On 17 September 1645, Lieutenant John Witter received money for 'Lieutenant Colonel Richard Brooke's company at Halton Castle in need of pay'. However, before January 1646 Witter had transferred to Captain John Brooke's command, and by the following year seems to have been succeeded by Humphrey Johnson, formerly of Richard Brooke's company.

Ensign Henry Warburton

Sergeant James Parkson	Drummer Robert Grindleton
Sergeant Richard Maddow	Drummer Owen Brereton
Corporal Richard Millington	Corporal John Moores
Corporal Arthur Key	Clerk George Leicester[58]

Captain John Brooke's company mustered 70 common soldiers fit for duty on 30 April 1645, 92 on 14 January 1646, 118 on 25 January 1646, 80 on 17 March 1646, 124 on 9 April and 28 May 1646, 123 on 27 July 1646, 105 on 18 September 1646, 111 on 19 November 1646 and 107 on 16 March 1647. A muster roll for 1 April 1647 is entitled 'Captain John Brooke's company before such time as they were made the trained Bands of Bucklow Hundred'.[59]

Captain William Daniell's Company

William was the third son of Peter Daniell of Over Tabley, near Knutsford, head of an established Cheshire gentry family. Peter was MP for the county in 1625, while his wife Christian was the daughter of Richard Grosvenor, himself a member for Cheshire between 1621 and 1629. The loyalties of the Daniell family were divided during the Civil War. Two of William's brothers

56 TNA, SP28/152/7, fol. 15r.; BL, MS Add. 11331, fol. 44r.; *BLB*, I, 385.

57 BL, MS Add. 11331, fol. 7r.–v.; 11332, fol. 31r.; *BLB*, I, 309; II, 775.

58 TNA, SP28/224/1, fol. 54r.

59 BL, MS Add. 11331, fol. 44; TNA, SP28/124/1, fol. 54r.; SP28/224/1, fol. 228v.; SP28/124/1, fol. 49v.; SP28/123/4, fols 712r., 664r., 695r., 630v.; SP28/123/3, fols 538v., 524r.

were officers in Earl Rivers' regiment – Lieutenant Thomas Daniell was killed at the storming of Brentford on 12 November 1642, whilst Captain Peter Daniell was wounded at Gloucester in August 1643 and later died in Oxford.[60] Furthermore, three of the Daniell sisters married Royalists, and the fourth, Mary, wed a captain in Brereton's army. William Daniell was a highly competent and industrious officer, who held a commission in Brooke's regiment by early 1643. Although some of his inferior officers were Frodsham men, his company was formed predominately from Bucklow Hundred.

During the early part of the fighting in Cheshire William's command operated in and around the local area. In August 1643 it was quartered in Frodsham, wherein the constables of the township disbursed £65 18s. in pay to Captain Daniell 'and to his clerk and soldiers under his command'.[61] From June 1644 it was quartered at the forward garrison of Tarvin (of which William was probably deputy governor). About this time the constables of Lymm disbursed the sum of £44 4s. 4d. 'for maintaining fourteen foot soldiers under Major Daniell at Tarvin for 28 weeks at 3s. a week for every soldier'.[62] Conceivably this entry could refer to John Daniell's command of Booth's regiment, given the not uncommon problem of assigning imprecise ranks by often overworked scribes, or those unfamiliar with particular officers and units, although it seems unlikely. For one thing, Colonel Booth's regiment (including the colonel's company led by John Daniell) was active elsewhere in Cheshire and Shropshire during this period, while the earlier entry recording the payment by the constables of Frodsham referred anachronistically to 'Major William Daniell' and his men. During the subsequent military operations in Cheshire occasioned by Rupert's march northwards during that summer, Daniell marched his men to the relative safety of the Halton garrison. In the first week of July he joined other officers of Colonel Brooke's regiment in delivering warrants to the constables of Aston, demanding outstanding payment of rents from the estates of Sir Thomas Aston.

Throughout 1645 and early 1646 Captain Daniell's company participated almost as a 'frontline unit' in the siege of Chester and military operations in North Wales. As such, William was particularly commended for his actions leading one of the two bodies of commanded musketeers at the Parliamentarian victory at Rowton Heath on 24 September 1645.

On 20 December 1645 Captain William Daniell attended a council of war that determined to intercept Royalist attempts to relieve the siege of Chester, his company duly participating in the march to Whitchurch. Six days later it was ordered to march with Adjutant Lothian's command to strengthen the guards on the Dee at Lache, while on 8 January 1646 Captain Daniell's company was part of a joint force of Cheshire, Staffordshire and Montgomeryshire foot commanded to march to Hawarden Castle. Soon afterwards, it assisted in the blocking up of Holt by Parliamentarian troops; there on 14 January Daniell was reminded by Sir William Brereton that 'We

60 CRO, QJB 3, fols 176r., 136v.–7r., 205r.; SP29/68 (Earl Rivers and Anthony Thelwall).

61 BL, MS Harley 1999, fol. 75v.

62 BL, MS Harley 2128, fol.48v.

have had many shot for want of blinds and many by over-careless wandering. I shall entreat your care in causing blinds to be made, and use your advice to the soldiers not to hazard themselves indiscreetly and without cause.' Furthermore, during this period he was entrusted with leading negotiations with the Royalist garrison in Chester for the exchange of prisoners of war.[63] William was promoted to sergeant major in April 1646 whilst at the siege of Lichfield. The exact date is unclear, owing to the somewhat ambiguous nature of the documents. He is referred to in this rank by his fellow Cheshire officer Captain John Whitworth in a letter to Sir William Brereton, dated 13 April; in correspondence on 16 April Brereton mentions 'Captain Daniell'; William Daniell referred to himself as sergeant major to his commander-in-chief in a letter on 29 April, while on 16 May Sir Thomas Tyldesley, deputy-governor of Lichfield, wrote that one of his officers 'should meet Major Daniell this afternoon.'[64] Perhaps more certainly, William is listed as holding the rank in pay accounts, dated 23 and 30 May 1646.[65]

Lieutenant Richard Heath

He had previously acted as ensign to Colonel Brooke's own company, but by mid 1645 was lieutenant under Captain William Daniell. A later, undated reference to Heath mentions him as 'lieutenant in Major Daniell's company in Brooke's regiment and also Colonels Lothian, Jones and Duckenfield's regiments.' In May 1650 Richard accepted a commission as captain in Daniell's regiment, and by the summer of 1656 he was serving as a major in Scotland.[66]

Ensign Joseph Witter

Younger brother of Lieutenant John Witter, Joseph began as sergeant in Sergeant Major Trevis's company in Leigh's regiment, before taking a commission as ensign under William Daniell. He received a commission as captain in his regiment in 1650. Captain Witter became governor of Dunstaffnage in 1657, but two years later declared for Monck, and was rewarded with promotion first to major and then to lieutenant colonel.[67]

A total of 89 common soldiers reported for duty under Captain William Daniell on 29 March 1646; 107 including officers on 5 May 1646; one major, one lieutenant, one ensign, three sergeants, two drummers, three corporals, and 92 soldiers on 30 May 1646, while in December 1646 it mustered 46 common soldiers.[68] On 13 April 1646 Daniell's command was listed as the only volunteer company among 600 Cheshire foot in Chester (the others being five trained band units). Within a month, however, the company

63 BL, MS Add. 11333, fols 45v., 69r., 109v., 117v., 101v.–2r.; *BLB*, II, 1063, 1113, 1200–1, 1212, 1247.

64 BCL, MS 595611, pp.30, 40, 114–5, 209; TNA: SP16/513/1, fols 74r, 86v.; *CWS*, 36, 61, 221.

65 BCL, MS 595611, p.252; TNA, SP16/513/1, fols 74r, 86v.; *CWS*, 240.

66 TNA, SP28/30/7, fol. 684r.; SP16/513/1, fols 91v., 72v., 74v.; *CJ*, VII, pp.762–3; Firth and Davies, *Regimental History*, pp.489–96.

67 TNA, E121/5/7/95, fols 61r.–5r.; Firth and Davies, *Regimental History*, pp.489, 492, 495–6.

68 TNA, SP28/123/1, fol. 98r.; SP28/38, fol. 201v.; SP16/513/1, fols 74r., 86v.; BCL, MS 595611, p.252.

had joined the siege of Lichfield, where it was engaged in constructing and manning a breastwork with Lieutenant Colonel Gerard's company on the Beacon Hill side of the city.[69] Whilst at Lichfield on 30 May 1646 Major William Daniell's soldiers were paid with the rest of the Cheshire foot a month's arrears of £85 17s. 4d., being 18s. 6d. per man; later, on 5 June the non-commissioned officers received payment 'according to the New Model' of £11 12s., their names being listed as:

Sergeant Richard Smith	Corporal Hugh Sling
Sergeant Thomas Banner	Corporal William Copperk
Sergeant John Rodes	Drummer Edward Hill
Corporal William Davenport	Drummer William Barratt
Corporal Thomas Garratt	Clerk Hugh Davenport[70]

Further disbursements to the company included £5 12s. to Lieutenant Richard Heath and £4 4s. to Ensign Joseph Witter respectively, made on 12 June, £16 to Major William Daniell in November and a further £30 given to 46 common soldiers at 10s. per man.[71] The overall sum disbursed from central funds in pay to Daniell 'for himself, and officers and soldiers' was £1,210 15s. 9s.[72] His final arrears of pay as 'lieutenant, captain and major of foot in the several regiments of Colonel Brooke, Lothian, Jones and Duckenfield' amounted to £598 3s. 1½d.[73] William Daniell's later military career was no less ordinary. In 1648 he was given command of Chester Castle, but in May 1650 he was promoted to colonel of a regiment of Cheshire and Lancashire foot, which was initially intended for Irish service, instead marched to Scotland. Daniell's regiment (which contained a number of officers and men who had previously served under him during the First Civil War) fought at Dunbar on 3 September, and remained active north of the border throughout the 1650s. Colonel Daniell acted as governor of Perth and various other garrisons from 1651 to 1659. As a staunch Cromwellian, he was dismissed in 1659, but even though William returned briefly under Monck, he ended his career at the Restoration.[74]

Captain John Delves' Company

An illegitimate son of Sir Thomas Delves of Doddington, John was a leading citizen of Nantwich both before and after the Civil War. His volunteer company may have been raised during mid 1644 and was quartered in the town. The following are recorded as serving in its ranks:

69 BCL, MS 595611, pp.30, 99, 114–15, 209.

70 TNA, SP16/513/1, fols 70r.–71r., 86v.–87r.; E121/5/7/351, fols 64v.–5r. Copperk later served as sergeant in Colonel Leigh's own company.

71 TNA, SP16/513/1, fols 91v., 72v., 74v.

72 TNA, SP 28/128/13, fol. 19r.; SP28/224, unfol.

73 TNA, E121/5/7/43, fol. 2r.

74 Firth and Davies, *Regimental History*, pp.489, 494.

Corporal Barker
Corporal Astle
Corporal Collier
Corporal Edward Pike
Corporal William Johnson[75]

The company numbered 99 common soldiers for duty on 4 September 1644, 98 on 14 September 1644, 100 on 26 September 1644, 98 on 29 November 1644 and 80 on 30 April 1645.[76]

Captain Francis Bramhall's Company

Bramhall was a Nantwich townsman. His volunteer company was quartered there (perhaps by 1643) and turned out 80 common soldiers on 30 April 1645.[77]

Captain Thomas Touchet's Company

Thomas was probably the second son of William Touchet of Nether Whitley. He raised his company from Bucklow Hundred and probably possessed a commission by the summer of 1643. He was paid the sum of £4 on 14 March 1644.[78] He is erroneously listed as lieutenant in Brereton's list of the army, dated 30 April 1645, while his command of 80 common soldiers was said to be 'dissolved'. Around two weeks previously Colonel John Booth, the governor of Warrington complained that Captain Touchet and others had been allowed to gather men and provisions from upper Bucklow, with Booth's officers forcibly disbanded bodies of recruits.[79] On 11 March 1644 Thomas received £4 in pay, while between 1 October 1644 and 20 July 1645 the constables of Nether Whitley disbursed £3 'to two soldiers under Captain Touchet'. Similarly, the constables' accounts for Dutton township for All Saints' Day 1644 to 25 July 1645 note that they disbursed £3 5s. 4d. to 'Captain Touchet's soldiers' for pay on seven occasions.[80]

Lieutenant Holt

Ensign Holt is listed with Captain Touchet in August 1643 and February 1644, while on 22 March 1644 he received pay the sequestration committee of Bucklow Hundred to the sum of £13 6s. 8d. An officer of that name commanded a detachment of foot at Farndon Bridge in January and February 1645.[81]

---

75 TNA, SP28/225/3, fols 470v., 491r.; E121/5/7/43, fol. 4r.
76 TNA, SP28/225/3, fols 491v.–2r., 499v.; SP28/225/4, fol. 703r.; BL, MS Add. 11331, fol. 44.
77 BL, MS Harley 1999, fol. 328v.; 2126, fol. 35v.; MS Add. 11331, fol. 44v.
78 BL, MS Harley 2137, fol. 94r.; TNA: SP28/208, unfol.
79 BL, MS Add. 11331, fol. 14r.; *BLB*, I, 245.
80 BL, MS Harley 2137, fol. 52v.; 2128, fols 44r., 151r.–v.
81 TNA, SP28/196/1, fols 3r., 12r.; BL, MS Harley 2137, fols 52v., 94r.; CRO, DDX/428, fols 12r.–v.; *BLB*, I, 2.

12

Colonel Robert Duckenfield's Regiment of Foot

Robert Duckenfield of Duckenfield Hall, near Stockport, was a Congregational Independent who raised and led a troop of horse and regiment of foot in the service of Parliament. As one of Sir William Brereton's closest associates he was among the most important officers in the Cheshire army. Duckenfield was commissioned by the Earl of Essex as captain of a troop of horse from 26 November 1642 to 2 October 1646, as captain of a company of foot from 25 September 1642 to 7 November 1643, and colonel of a regiment of foot from 7 November 1643 to 19 February 1646.[1] Robert mustered a company of foot on Whit Tuesday 1642, but had to provide for it from his own pocket as he had not yet received a commission as captain. Similarly, the rest of his regiment had been raised and seen action on various occasions before his commission as colonel was issued in November 1643, although by his own admission, he had raised all of his companies by then. He led his own company and troop of horse during the operations around the siege of Manchester in September 1642. Duckenfield and other gentlemen from the Tame valley, running from Manchester and Stockport towards the Pennines, were outside the authority of the commissioners of array, so they were able to recruit, train and arm troops for the Parliamentarian cause from an early stage.

A certificate produced in May 1645 by the leading deputy lieutenants of Cheshire in support of Robert's petition to the Committee for Sequestrations outlines his service:

> Colonel Robert Duckenfield, esquire, has had the command of a complete troop of horse and a full foot company ever since the beginning of the troubles within this county of Chester until this present, which were raised and recruited by him, and have been kept full and in good order, and have done very good service, the said foot company being brought to the relief and assistance of the town of Manchester when it was besieged by the Earl of Derby's force. And since the beginning of November *Anno Domini* 1643 the said Colonel Duckenfield has commanded

1 TNA, SP28/128/10, fol. 9v.; SP/20/10/63, fol. 161r.

> a regiment of foot, raised within the said county, sometimes consisting of ten companies but now of seven or eight full companies, which have also done very good service, especially at raising the siege of Nantwich, Montgomery, Middlewich and other places, and formerly by securing part of Derbyshire and a great part of our county of Chester from the invades of the Earl of Newcastle his army for a long time together by keeping a forward guard upon the border of Yorkshire.[2]

Duckenfield was particularly active in east Cheshire (besieging and capturing the Royalist strongholds of Adlington and Wythenshawe Halls in early 1644). He fought at the Battle of Nantwich, and on 25 May, with Colonel Henry Mainwaring, attempted to defend Stockport against Prince Rupert. Later in the year Duckenfield was active at Beeston Castle and commanded his regiment at Montgomery. During the summer of 1645 at the siege of Chester he served as governor of the suburbs in Brereton's absence, and was one of the commissioners for the city's surrender. Robert Duckenfield was fiercely loyal to his soldiers, and on a number of occasions petitioned various commanders (including Sir Thomas Fairfax), complaining about their conditions and arrears of pay, which were severe (although on one occasion, he was rebuked by Brereton for his reluctance to obey orders). He was governor of Chester in 1648, and commissioned captain of the county troop of horse and colonel of a militia regiment of foot in 1650. During the following year Robert sat at Lord Derby's trial and took the surrender of the Isle of Man. In 1655 he became MP in the Nominated Parliament, but refused to support the Protectorate by declining a commission as colonel of a regiment of horse. In later life Duckenfield was responsible for establishing nonconformist chapels at Stockport and Duckenfield Hall, where he had installed the fiery separatist Samuel Eaton as his chaplain.[3]

Colonel Duckenfield's command, described by Dore as 'the most vigorous and reliable regiment in Cheshire', was raised from the area of Stockport and Macclesfield Hundred.[4] On 6 March 1644 Robert informed Sir Thomas Fairfax, 'I received an order from the Council of War before Michaelmas last past, that my regiment should first be paid out of the sequestration in Macclesfield Hundred, but neither myself nor my soldiers have received 6d. from them since that time; and now they demand their pay, or part thereof, from me; and the sequestrators are ordered to pay the money into the treasury in Nantwich, which deprives them of all hope of pay'.[5] By the time Duckenfield received a commission as colonel in November 1643 his regiment had been in existence for a year. The majority of his officers (including his two brothers) were local gentlemen and yeomen. At its height the regiment fielded 10 companies, although by April 1645 it numbered 580 common soldiers (around 650 when officers and non-commissioned officers

2 TNA, SP/20/10/63, fol. 163r.

3 BL, MS Add. 18979; Robert Bell, *Memorials of the Civil War: comprising the correspondence of the Fairfax family* (London, 1849), pp.79–80, *Letter Books of Sir Samuel Luke*, p.505;*CSPD, 1650*, pp.507 509; *BLB*, I, 91, note 1; CWS, p.133.

4 Dore, *Civil Wars in Cheshire*, p.64.

5 BL, MS Add. 18979; Bell, *Memorials of the Civil War*, pp.79–80.

are added) in seven companies under one captain-lieutenant, one sergeant major and five captains.

A payment made in March 1644 by Colonel Duckenfield of £30 'for arms to furnish my Irish company and some clothes for them', suggests that a number of veterans of the wars in Ireland were recruited into his regiment following their recent capture and change of sides at Nantwich.[6] Robert had fought against such soldiers at Middlewich the previous December and in the relief of Nantwich, and clearly held them in high regard. Under whose captaincy these veterans served remains uncertain, although William Duckenfield, one of Colonel Robert's brothers is one contender. He served as captain of a company of foot from March 1643 to March 1645. Colonel Duckenfield's soldiers possessed an enviable fighting record, but their regiment was badly mauled during the Second Battle of Middlewich on 26 December 1643. The colonel's company and that of Captain William Duckenfield sustained a significant portion of the losses.[7]

Although Colonel Duckenfield's men served with the Cheshire army in most of its operations, much of their time during 1645 was spent at the sieges of Chester (the regiment's headquarters being at Hoole Hall) and Beeston. In a letter to Sir Samuel Luke on 5 April 1645 Robert reported:

> my regiment hath passed upon very hard duty for this twelvemonth, especially last winter at the siege of Beeston Castle, and in Wirral where many of my men were lost and maimed, for all which service they have received but a month's pay and now they begin to mutiny and will break presently, unless some competent means be allowed them.[8]

Duckenfield's regiment was employed in some of the most challenging and hazardous duties, and was considered to be the most experienced of the Cheshire foot regiments. Given its conditions, pay arrears and the effects of two regiments of Yorkshire horse quartered on its soldiers' homes for a time, the complaints expressed by Colonel Robert and his officers seem reasonable. The regiment contained at least two executive officers, whose responsibilities included the distribution of pay, victuals and equipment to soldiers, and verifying accounts. Captain James Afflecke acted as provost marshal to Duckenfield's foot. In September 1645 he obtained £32 'over and above what he has received of others for his service'. Afflecke is likely to have left the Cheshire army sometime in 1646, as on 14 October 1647 James Duckenfield, one of Brereton's officials, attested that the residue of his pay was disbursed 'above a year after he left the command of Colonel Duckenfield'.[9] Lieutenant William Heritage is described in two undated warrants as 'marshal' to Colonel Duckenfield.[10]

---

6 TNA, SP28/128/10, fol. 7v.

7 *Ibid.*, fols 8r., 9r.

8 BL, MS Egerton 787/3, fol. 48r.; *Letter Books of Sir Samuel Luke*, p.505; *Cheshire and Lancashire Historical Collector*, pp.95–6.

9 BL, MS Harley 2128, fols 73r.–78r.; TNA, SP28/128/10, fols 7v., 8r., 10r.

10 TNA, SP28/128/2/11, fol. 3v.; SP28/128/10, fol. 6v.

Heritage vouched for his colonel's service from the raising of his first foot company onwards, and disbursed various sums of money to Duckenfield's troopers and soldiers from his colonel, alongside those elicited by the commissioners for Macclesfield Hundred. Whilst at Gawsworth on 14 June 1643 Lieutenant Heritage had £5 for his own pay, and 15 days later paid £6 to Duckenfield's soldiers out the £30 4s. received from Alderman Deane. He was at the siege of Adlington Hall in February 1644, where he was paid for keeping a guard, and the following month he disbursed from its captured goods the sum of £64 to Colonel Duckenfield's troop and a further £64 to his foot company. Likewise, Lieutenant Heritage obtained £8 6s. from William Barrett, collector for Macclesfield Hundred, for saddles on 17 March 1645.[11]

Colonel Robert Duckenfield's Own Company

A company under Colonel Duckenfield's command was mustered for service on Whit Tuesday 1642 at Brinnington Moor, Stockport. His commission as dates from 25 September 1642 to 7 November 1643.A number of payments to Duckenfield's soldiers were made at Woodhead, Adlington, Gawsworth and Stockport in 1643 and 1644. These illustrate some of the activities of the company, especially in reducing Royalist strongholds in the east Cheshire area. A detachment of 30 men under the command of Captain Adams besieged Wythenshawe Hall between 21 November 1643 and 27 February 1644.[12] Colonel Duckenfield's own company was at the forefront of this active and experienced regiment. Its officers and non-commissioned offers were:

Captain-Lieutenant Francis Acton

Son of Richard Acton of Over Alderley, Francis served as captain-lieutenant to the command. He was present at Brereton's council of war at Hawarden in May 1645, while on 12 January 1646 he received £60 1s. 4d. in pay for himself and his company 'in service at the Leaguer before Chester'.[13]

Captain-Lieutenant Samuel Smith

He is probably the same officer who had commanded Duckenfield's troop between mid 1645 and December 1646. Smith was paid as captain-lieutenant to the colonel's company as part of the Chester garrison in 1647.[14]

Lieutenant Pendleton

Pendleton received regular pay on behalf of the company between late 1642 and 1644. In January and February1643 the sum of £45 6s. 4d. was disbursed to 'Lieutenant Pendleton and [Duckenfield's] company', while in March

11 TNA, E121/5/7/351, fol. 1r.; SP28/128/11, fols 1r.–2r. ('Accounts of Lieutenant William Heritage, February–September 1643); SP28/128/10, fols 6v., 5r., 8v.; SP28/152/7, fol. 6r.

12 TNA, SP28/128/10, fols 4v., 6v.; JRL, Tatton of Wythenshawe Papers, deposition of James Brownhill, October 1646; Groves, *Impact of Civil War on a Community*, pp.11–16.

13 BL, MS Add. 11331, fols 113r., 118v.; *BLB*, I, 327, 437–8, 522.

14 TNA, SP28/30/7, fol. 671v.; SP28/224/1, fols 32v.–3r.; E121/5/7/351, fols 2r.–4r.; E121/5/7/misc., fols 59r.–v.; BL, MS Harley 2128, fol. 92r., MS Add. 11333, fols 30r, 110v.

'Lieutenant Pendleton and other officers of the same company' received £3 in pay. From local sources the company also had £10 raised by the inhabitants of Prestbury and another £15 from the Macclesfield sequestrators.[15]

Lieutenant John Upton

He may have succeeded Pendleton, for on 27 October 1644 he was ordered by Colonel Duckenfield to distribute £30 'to my foot company out of the [Mottram in] Longdendale rents by Sir William Brereton's order'.[16] He later served in the same rank in Lieutenant Colonel Alexander Newton's company in Colonel Bradshaw's Cheshire militia regiment of foot at the Battle of Worcester.

The company mustered the following on 7 April 1644:

Ensign Samuel Lawton	Sergeant William Cork
Sergeant Booth	Corporal Thomas Cork
Sergeant Edmund Birch	Corporal William Matley
Sergeant John Hay	Corporal John Rider[17]

Drum-major Abraham Butterworth[18]
James Ashton – gentleman of the arms[19]

120 common soldiers were mustered on 30 April 1645.[20]

Sergeant Major Henry Bradshaw's Company

Bradshaw was from Marple Hall, near Macclesfield, and elder brother of John, the MP and regicide. Henry was a sequestration commissioner for Macclesfield Hundred, and as evidenced by his own accounts, served as:

> captain of a company of foot soldiers in the regiment of Colonel Robert Duckenfield, in actual service for the parliament from the thirteenth day of May 1643 to the tenth day of March the same year, being 301 days; he was sergeant major to the foresaid regiment from the said tenth of March, by virtue of a commission from the late Ferdinando, Lord Fairfax until the third day of February 1645[6], being 695 days, and was in both these commands in actual service'.

Bradshaw asserted that he had not received more than £50 in pay for both offices.[21]

15 TNA, SP/28/128/10, fols 7r.–v.
16 TNA, SP28/128/10, fol. 7r.
17 TNA, E121/5/7/351, misc., fols 3r., 22v., 33r.–v., 37v.
18 TNA, SP28/128/10, fol.5v.
19 TNA, E121/5/7, fol. 39v.
20 BL, MS Add. 11331, fol. 44v.; *BLB*, I, 385.
21 Bod. Lib., MS Top Cheshire e 3, fols 1r.–v.; A. Craig Gibson, 'Every-Day Life of a Country Gentleman of Cheshire in the Seventeenth Century', *THSLC*, 15 (1862–1863), pp. 67–92 (p. 71).

During 1645 Sergeant Major Bradshaw co-petitioned with his colonel on behalf of the regiment. On 9 May, writing from Hoole garrison at the Chester leaguer, he complained bitterly to Brereton:

> There is divers of our neighbours purposely come hither to certify in what condition they have left our parts, which hath so increased the complaints of most of our regiment, that, crying out upon me, they say they expect no other that their parents, friends and families will be undone. They allege also that, whilst they themselves are upon duty here and have nothing, strangers, having pay, doing no service, devour that which should sustain both them and theirs at home. Therefore, seeing their petition disregarded, and no hope of relief and hearing of the many outrages done by the Yorkshiremen and in as much as they and theirs are so continually opposed, they are resolved to endeavour to help themselves. What thereupon may [ensue] I leave to your wisdom, being assured that to continue our regiment longer here is above my power.[22]

Bradshaw was present at the council of war for summoning Chester on 6 January 1646.[23] The following month, after the fall of the city, he became lieutenant colonel to Colonel Assheton's regiment of Lancashire foot. Henry commanded one of the four regiments of Cheshire infantry raised in 1650 as colonel; the regiment participated in the Battle of Worcester, where he was wounded. In 1652, Bradshaw sat with Robert Duckenfield and other local officers at the court martial of the Earl of Derby. Between 1646 and 1659 he was one of the most active justices of the peace in Cheshire. In August 1659, faced with the Booth Rebellion, the Rump Parliament commissioned Colonel Bradshaw to command a regiment of volunteer foot, 'on consideration of his past fidelity and good services', although he remained neutral, protesting to Booth that he had not acted against him and objecting to the search of his house for arms.[24]

Listed in a muster roll of 21 December 1644 are the following junior and non-commissioned officers:

Lieutenant John Jackson

Sequestration agent for Macclesfield Hundred, he also served as captain-lieutenant to Colonel Bradshaw's own company in 1650–1.[25]

Ensign William Sidebottom

Paid with Bradshaw's company on 27 March 1645.[26]

22 BL, MS Add. 11331, fol. 70v.; *BLB*, I, 453.
23 BL, MS Add. 11333, fol. 102r.; *BLB*, II, 1197.
24 *CSPD 1659–1660*, p.74.
25 BL, MS Harley 2130, fol. 40v.
26 TNA, SP28/128/10, fol. 7r.

Quartermaster John Wharmby

On 27 March 1645 he received £100 for the officers of Duckenfield's regiment, and on 11 April 1645 the sum of £10 was disbursed 'to Quartermaster Wharmby for Bradshaw's company'.[27]

Sergeant John Nickson	Corporal John Swindells
Sergeant John Astle	Corporal Richard Gresling
Sergeant Henry Swindells	Drummer Henry Collier
Sergeant Peter Sidebottom	Drummer Robert Partington
Corporal John Robinson	Drummer Edmund Swindells
Corporal William Ernsworth	Clerk Thomas Elcock[28]

Major Bradshaw's company numbered 140 common soldiers on 30 April 1645. John Low, James Dealt and William Goddard, common soldiers under Henry Bradshaw were exchanged at Chester on 8 January 1646.[29]

Captain Ralph Arderne's Company

Of an ancient gentry family of Harden Hall, north of Stockport. Ralph engaged in the early fighting in Cheshire and Lancashire, participating in the defence of Manchester in September 1642. He saw further service at the First Battle of Middlewich and the siege of Warrington the following year. Between October 1642 and April 1643 his company received £29 13s. 6d. in pay, while a further £14 was disbursed 'to Lieutenant Jolly for Captain Arderne's company'.[30] Ralph Arderne appears to have been captured during mid 1643, probably in Shropshire or Staffordshire; he was exchanged at Worcester on 6 September.[31] His command was also part of the regiment under Colonel Robert Duckenfield that operated in the Midlands under the Earl of Denbigh during the summer of 1644. In March and June 1644 the sum of 14s. was paid to wounded soldiers of Arderne's company.[32] Captain Arderne was appointed to the Macclesfield Hundred sequestration committee on 7 May 1644, and he seems to have left the army soon afterwards.[33]

Captain Edward Hyde's Company

Hyde's company was formed by September 1642. In October 1642 and January 1643 he received separate payments amounting to £19 for his command. The company was also paid on 11 February and 22 February 1643.[34] Captain

27 TNA, TNA: SP28/128/10, fols 7r., 6v.
28 TNA, SP28/225/4, fol. 712r.
29 BL, MS Add. 11333, fol. 110r.–v.; *BLB*, II, 1214.
30 TNA, SP28/128/10, fols 4r., 8r.; SP28/152/4, fol. 10; SP28/208, fols 20v.–1r.
31 *JHC*, III, p.230.
32 TNA, SP28/128/19, fol. 4v.
33 *CJ*, III, p.484.
34 TNA, SP28/128/10, fols 4r., 8r.; SP28/125/3, fol. 2v.; SP28/196, fol. 13v.

Hyde's soldiers took part in the abortive attack on Cholmondeley House on 11 April 1643, during which a number of them were wounded. A list of pensioners taken at Stockport in 1653 includes 'Elizabeth Small, whose husband was slain at Cholmondeley under command of Captain Hyde', and John Sydebotham, a soldier in his company who had received a wound to the right arm at the same time.[35]

Captain Anthony Booth's Company

Booth was an alderman and mayor of Macclesfield for 1640–1, 1645 and 1649–50. His company was probably established by early 1643. Captain Booth's men served with Duckenfield's regiment throughout the war. His men participated at the second Battle of Middlewich on 26 December 1643, Anthony later being reimbursed the sum of 2s. 'for the expending of shot and powder for the first work at Acton Bridge'.[36] In May 1645 Captain Booth's men received a week's wages at Chester, and another at Beeston, although this appears to have been resented by other members of their regiment, who were themselves suffering from lack of pay. On 26 May Colonel Robert Duckenfield duly grumbled to Sir William Brereton:

> I did meet my company of foot at Mottram this day and I could not prevail with them to march to Barlow Moor this day for divers reasons ... My company and divers others of my regiment do allege that you have paid to Captain Booth's company a week's pay last week and another week's pay at Beeston Castle since the rest of them received any pay. They conceive that the company under Captain Booth deserve least pay of all the rest by much. They mover me this day to inform you that they desired you would show them as much favour, and afford them as much pay and encouragement as you did to the aforesaid and to other companies, and then they would be more ready to observe you.[37]

Again, this time on 25 November 1645, Brereton felt compelled to alleviate the distress which Booth's soldiers were experiencing, wrote from his headquarters at Tarvin, 'Seventy four common soldiers of Captain Anthony Booth's company have been upon constant service in this Leaguer. To James Croxton, treasurer, you are required to pay unto Captain Anthony Booth and his officers and soldiers fourteen days' pay according to the New Model. These are upon service against Chester.'[38] This note was added to a muster roll of the company, which lists its composition:

Lieutenant Phillip Platt	Corporal Thomas Spacey
Ensign John Lely	Corporal Francis Warrington
Sergeant Thomas Pownell	Drummer John Barr

35 Malbon, pp.49–50; Earwaker, *East Cheshire*, I, p.69.
36 BL, MS Harley 2128, fol. 43r.
37 BL, MS Add. 11331, fol. 170v.; *BLB*, I, 638.
38 TNA, SP28/122, fol. 553r.

Sergeant William Parkinson Surgeon Edmund Granger
Corporal Roger Grayling

During the later phase of the Parliamentarian siege of Chester Captain Anthony Booth's company was located with Captain Hancock's soldiers in the eastern suburbs of the city, being particularly mentioned manning the area of The Bars in Foregate Street, the battery at St John's Church and the bridge of boats on the Dee. In November and December 1645 Booth lodged a woman 'messenger' (that is, 'spy') in his quarters. On 11 December she reported to Brereton that she had been sent to Royalist held Worcester in the guise of a bringer of news, and spoken to the governor, Colonel Sandys, Sir William Vaughan and Prince Maurice.[39]

Captain Booth's company mustered 70 common soldiers on 30 April 1645 and 60 on 31 October 1645.[40] Sometime in early 1646, possibly following the fall of Chester on 3 February, the command appears to have been reduced in size and amalgamated with that of Captain John Leadbeater. An entry in the accounts of their colonel, Robert Duckenfield, mentions a receipt from Sir William Brereton of '60 muskets I received of the storehouse at Chester, presently after the taking of that city, 20 of these last are in Captain Booth's and Captain Leadbeater's hands, and the rest are in Nantwich undisposed of'.[41] During April 1646 while serving with the Cheshire foot at the siege of Lichfield Close, the soldiers 'in Lichfield Leaguer' under the command of these officers sent a petition to Sir William Brereton, once more complaining about lack of pay and threatening to disband:

> Humbly showing that whereas formerly your petitioners had masters from whom they received due pay according to the service they performed and now are as they understand by the committee in Cheshire taken away from them and debarred that privilege in so much that now they know not where to demand one penny which makes them bold to carve your honour's consideration and loving assistance to your servants in this mean condition, who are as unwilling to leave this service or gain your displeasure as to loose themselves. Although in regard of the family charges many of them be tied to maintain they are forced to let your honour know that without present supply of money, they shall be constrained to leave your service and leaguer whereof they being so unwilling. Humbly intreat your honour as they have served you in love hitherto, so they may still continue in the same, and for the present either receive pay here for their late service, and an assurance of it for the future, or else a free discharge according to their voluntary willingness.[42]

39 BL, MS Add. 11332, fols 31v.–2r., 105r.; 11333, fol. 43r.; *BLB*, II, 777, 791, 897, 983.

40 BL, MS Add. 11331, fol. 44v.; 11332, fol. 32r.; SP28/122, fol. 562v.

41 TNA, SP28/128/10, fol. 2r.

42 BCL, MS 595611, p.10; *CWS*, 24. Date unknown, but enclosed in Brereton's letter of 11 April 1646 to William Ashurst and John Swinfen (MS 595611, p.7; *CWS*, 25). In the letter Sir William reported: 'The Cheshire men are now come up to the number of 700 and are very willing to do service, but I fear unless speedily prevented by supply of money there may be an evil precedent given, for those that came up first begin to murmur and threaten to go home if they receive not money, speedily for they must not have any out of their own county for service they do here'.

When the Cheshire Foot mustered for pay on 23 May the mutual command of Captains Booth and Leadbeater consisted of the following:

> Captain Booth, 1 sergeant, 1 drum, 2 corporals and 48 common soldiers.
> Captain Leadbeater, Lieutenant Norbury, Ensign Banniell, 1 sergeant, 1 drum, 2 corporals and 33 common soldiers.[43]

Subsequently, on 5 June 1646 within the sum disbursed 'to the sergeants, drums and corporals of the aforesaid Cheshire companies one month's pay', the command received £1 8s. for the drum major, £1 5s. apiece to the sergeants and clerk, while the corporals and drummers had £1 4s. The non-commissioned officers under Booth were Sergeant William Jackson, Drummer Richard Normanshall, and Corporals Frederick Warren and George Bread. Leadbeater's men were Sergeant Thomas Kelshall, Drummer John Normanshall, the corporals being John White and William Newton. A week later, payments of £5 12s. and £4 4s. were made to 'Lieutenant Norbury as lieutenant to Captain Booth [and] his ensign Banniell'. However, by the November Anthony Booth's junior officers had been replaced by Lieutenant Pargeter and Ensign Millward. Finally, in November and December 1646, while still at Lichfield, Booth himself received personal payments of £10 10s. and £15 respectively.[44]

Captain William Duckenfield's Company

A brother of Colonel Robert and Captain Francis Duckenfield, he served as captain of a company of foot from March 1643 'for two years'.[45] Captain William Duckenfield's company was noted for its service at the first and second battles of Middlewich, the defence of Stockport, service under the Earl of Denbigh in Shropshire in 1644, and the Battle of Montgomery. On 22 September 1643 William's soldiers received £2 15s. in pay, while during December they had a further £2 15s. in money and a batch of muskets. On Christmas Day 'at Sandbach the day before Middlewich fight' Captain Duckenfield was remunerated £21 4s. 'for 58 soldiers besides his officers'. About this time his lieutenant received £4 in pay. Moreover, in August 1644: Colonel Duckenfield's and Captain William Duckenfield's companies benefitted from £52 15s. 'upon the petty care at Stockport, being a week's pay'.[46] When William Duckenfield's commission expired in March 1645 he was replaced by Captain William Smith, a former tenant of William Davenport, who with William Siddall had refused enlistment for the King. John Hay served in the company as corporal and sergeant, although he was killed in

43 Next to which the clerk wrote: 'these two make but one company and officers and allowed accordingly' (BCL, MS 595611, pp.252–3; *CWS*, 240).

44 TNA, SP16/513/1, fols 71r., 72r., 88r., 91r., 74r.

45 TNA, SP28/196, fol. 13v. Moreover, an undated payment appears in Colonel Robert Duckenfield's accounts for £50 'allowed besides to my brother, Captain William Duckenfield for quarter for himself, man and horses two years' (SP28/128/10, fol. 9r.).

46 TNA, SP28/128/10, fols. 4r.–4v., 8r., 5r., 6v.

March 1644, the sum of 14s. being found for his burial and the treatment of some of Captain Arderne's company of Duckenfield's regiment.[47]

Captain Francis Duckenfield's Company

Of Stockport, brother of Colonel Robert. Francis served briefly as a trooper in Colonel Brereton's troop, before transferring to Duckenfield's, where he acted as cornet and captain-lieutenant until mid 1644, when he took command of a company of foot in his brother's regiment.[48] Francis was present at Bramhall Hall on 1 April 1644 with Sir William Brereton, Captain-Lieutenant Zankey and two or three troops of Cheshire horse. On 24 June 1645 he was paid the sum of £10 'by Sir William Brereton's order'.[49] Lieutenant Symonds, 'lieutenant to Captain Duckenfield at the Leaguer of Beeston' received pay on 22 November 1645.[50]

Captain William Watson's Company

From Macclesfield, he was mayor from 1643 to 1644 and sequestrator of Macclesfield Hundred. Watson had received his commission as captain and raised his company of foot by 25 January 1643.[51] He served under Robert Duckenfield throughout the First Civil War and commanded a company in Colonel Bradshaw's regiment in 1650–1. An undated list (probably from 1644) of Captain Watson's company includes:

Lieutenant Thomas Mottershead	Corporal Adam Jackson
Ensign Robert Barlow	Corporal John Baddiley
Sergeant William Rowbotham	Corporal John Warren
Sergeant Robert Moss	Drummer John Brown[52]

Captain William Siddall's Company

Siddall was a tenant of William Davenport of Bramhall, who with 24 others refused Royalist service in September 1642.[53] These men enlisted under Captain Edward Hyde and were at the defence of Manchester. Captain Siddall was also a sequestrator for Macclesfield Hundred.

47 TNA, SP28/196/1, fol. 4v.
48 TNA, E121/5/7/43, fols 1v.–3r., 114r.
49 BL, MS Harley 2012, fol. 52r.; TNA: SP28/128/10, fol. 7r.; E121/5/7/351, fol. 39v.
50 TNA, SP28/152/8, fol. 1v.
51 TNA, SP28/31/4, fol. 428r.
52 BL, MS Harley 2128, unfol.
53 CRO, ZCR63/2/19, fol. 88; J.S. Morrill, 'William Davenport and the Silent Majority of Early Stuart England', *JCAS*, 58 (1974), pp.115–29 (pp. 128–9).

Captain Edmund Shelmerdine's Company

Shelmerdine hailed from Etchells, Northenden parish. On 12 May 1644, under orders from the sequestration commissioners for Macclesfield Hundred, he carried out an inventory of William Davenport's goods at Bramhall Hall. According to Davenport, 'they, in a most strict and severe manner performed, going into every room of the house, narrowly searching every corner, causing all chests and boxes to be opened, which otherwise they threatened to break up, being in the meantime guarded with a company of musketeers who stood in the park and all about the house with their matches lighted'.[54] On 14 May 1645 the officers of Captain Shelmerdine's company were Lieutenant Miller and Ensign Palden, while one clerk, one quartermaster, two sergeants, three corporals, one drummer and 60 soldiers were also listed. One of the sergeants was Francis Booth.[55]

Captain Alexander Newton's Company

Captain Alexander Newton was the son of George Newton of Newton Hall. As one of the sequestrators for Macclesfield Hundred he was responsible for the payment of troops, and expenditure on arms and equipment. In October 1642 payment was made 'several times for the foot company under his command', while on 18 September 1643 Newton had £1 for his own pay. In January 1644 he was present with his company at Bramhall Hall.[56]The company was not listed among Brereton's forces on 30 April 1645, although Captain Newton attended a council or war at Dodleston 20 days earlier, while at least a detachment of his soldiers were at Hawarden under Lieutenant Randle Radman on 16 May.[57]

Captain Ralph Miller's Company (possibly)

Miller appears in various payments made on 12 November 1645 to him, and to other officers and soldiers of Bradshaw's company. He also received specific sums for himself, officers and soldiers fourteen days' pay, 'for his service in the leaguer before Chester' and as part of Colonel Duckenfield's regiment.[58] He may be the Lieutenant Ralph Miller who received pay at Nantwich on 12 September 1643 and is listed in Captain Shelmerdine's company on 14 May 1645.[59]

54 CRO, ZCR63/2/19, fol. 90r.

55 *Ibid.*, fols 90v.–1r.; TNA, SP28/30/1, fol. 79r.; BL, MS Harley 2130, fol. 268v.

56 TNA, SP28/128/10, fols 6r., 7r; SP28/152/4, fol. 10v.

57 TNA, SP28/225/1, unfol.; CRO,DDX/428, fol. 83; BL, MS Add. 11331, fol. 113v.; *BLB*, I, 197, 552.

58 TNA, SP28/224/1, fols 57r.–v.

59 CRO, ZCR63/2/19, fols 90v.–1r.; BL, MS Harley 2130, fol. 121v.; TNA, SP28/30/1, fol. 79r.

13

Colonel John Leigh's Regiment of Foot

John Leigh esquire, of Norbury Booths, near Knutsford, raised a troop of horse, company of dragoons and regiment of foot for the service of Parliament in Cheshire. In February 1643 he briefly became governor of Northwich, while on 13 September 1643 John was appointed deputy lieutenant for Cheshire. The following May he was placed on the county committee for sequestrations.[1] With Colonel Robert Duckenfield, Leigh was one of the closest associates of Sir William Brereton, and appears to have been a proficient officer. As sheriff of Cheshire during the 1650s John supported the Cromwellian parliaments and may have been a republican.

Colonel Leigh's regiment of foot was formed at Northwich in early 1643 from volunteers from the hundreds of Northwich, Bucklow and Eddisbury. It also contained the Eddisbury Hundred trained and freehold Bands (being 'country companies' under Captains John Acton, Thomas Whalley, and Lieutenant/Captain Hugh Birtles). Colonel Leigh's regiment distinguished itself in the defence of Northwich and the Battle of Tarvin on 21 August 1644 (during which its major, John Trevis led the Cheshire Foot with valour).[2] In Brereton's army list of April 1645 the command contained 520 common soldiers in six companies, although the volunteer company under Major Trevis appears to have been disbanded by then. Except for Lieutenant Colonel Gilbert Gerard's men, who were located at Tarvin from mid 1644 onwards, Leigh's regiment was mainly quartered in Northwich town and Hundred, owing to its preponderance of townsmen and trained band soldiers.

The town of Northwich was fortified by a system of earthworks and garrisoned for the Parliament in early 1643. During this time the constables of Nether Whitley contributed 4s. 'for making of mud walls at Northwich'.[3] The garrison there was largely maintained by payments from the sequestration committees of the hundreds of Northwich and Bucklow, as well as the constables of nearby townships. Between 1 October 1643 and mid 1644 numerous

1 *CJ*, III, p.484; Morrill, *Cheshire*, p.83.
2 *A True Relation of two great Victories*; Malbon, p.142.
3 BL, MS Harley 2128, fol. 43r.

payments were received by Colonel Leigh's regiment from the former, while the Nether Whitley officials expended 16s. on 'two bushels of oats brought to the Northwich garrison'.[4] Additionally, the Bucklow committee complied with a standing order from the deputy lieutenants by granting some of the profits of the sequestered goods of Peter Leycester of Tabley to Lieutenant Colonel Gerard and Captain Holford for the use of the soldiers. Similarly, £9 15s. 3d. was disbursed out of the estate of Peter Venables of Marston to 'Captain Wright for the Northwich garrison', while on 19 November 1644 629lb of cheese was delivered to it from the township of Netherleigh.[5]

A letter from Sir William Brereton to the Speaker, dated 8 November 1645 mentions that the large number of Royalist prisoners taken at Denbigh Green 'doth much add to our trouble and charge, having not only so many as all our prisons and garrisons are capable of, but we are forced to disburse them to several towns and parishes upon open quarters, as in Stockport, Grappenhall, Middlewich, Northwich and Congleton'.[6] This suggests that Northwich was no longer garrisoned at this stage. The tenure of its governor, Lieutenant Colonel Gerard, ceased on 2 February 1644 and his command was posted to Tarvin, although according to marginal notes in Brereton's army list, Captain Richard Pigott's company of townsmen were still located in Northwich in April 1645.[7] Even so, the unit fulfilled various roles at the Chester leaguer in October and November 1645, and was still mustered on 29 October 1646.[8]

Colonel John Leigh's Own Company

This was established by early 1643 from volunteers of the town of Northwich, and spent much of its service in that garrison. Leigh received various payments to the sum of £49 7s. 6. for his company from the Bucklow sequestrators between 4 April 1644 and 22 May 1645.[9] His command numbered 44 common soldiers on 25 November 1643, 44 between 17 December 1643 and 20 April 1644, 60 on 4 May 1644 and 100 on 30 April 1645.[10] The following inferior and non-commissioned officers were listed on 22 March 1643:

Captain-Lieutenant Newton
Ensign Cartwright
Sergeant Henley
Sergeant Taylor
Corporal Grimshaw
Corporal Roxtall
Corporal Davenport
Drummer William Newton
Clerk Humphrey Burgess[11]

4 BL, MS Harley 2128, fols 42r., 41v.
5 BL, MS Harley 2137, fols 55v., 95v., 114r., 151r.–v., 152v.
6 HMC, *Portland*, I, p.304; MS Add. 11332, fol. 59r.
7 TNA, SP28/152/4, unfol.; SP28/208, fols 33v.–4r.
8 TNA, SP28/40/2, fol. 190v.; E121/5/7/351, fol. 22v.; BL, MS Add. 11332, fols 14r.–15r., 20v., 31v., 35r.
9 TNA, SP28/40/2, fols 57r., 92r.–v.
10 TNA, SP28/152/9, fol. 15r.
11 TNA, SP28/35/2, fol. 258v.

The following appear in undated pay warrants for the company:

Quartermaster Boden	Surgeon William Ludlow
Clerk Thomas Robinson	Corporal John Baxter[12]

Sometime before late 1645 Captain-Lieutenant Newton was replaced by Hugh Birtles. Probably from Birtles, near Macclesfield, he is listed as lieutenant in command of a country company in the list of Cheshire forces on 30 April 1645, but this must be a scribal error. Payments to 'Captain-Lieutenant Birtles of Leigh's company' on 12 December 1645, and 'Colonel Leigh and Lieutenant Birtles for the officers of his foot company in service in the Leaguer of Chester', dated 21 January 1646, indicate that Hugh was serving as captain-lieutenant to Colonel Leigh's own volunteer company by late 1645.[13] Like Captain Thomas Whalley's command from Leigh's regiment, Hugh Birtles's own company served at the siege of Lichfield Close during much of 1646. On 23 May, with the rank of captain, his command (listed among the other Cheshire volunteer companies) comprised himself, Ensign Cartwright, two sergeants, one drummer, two corporals, one clerk and 52 common soldiers. A week later the common soldiers under Birtles were paid £48 11s. 6d., being a month's wages at 18s. 8d. apiece.[14]

Whether these were actually Colonel John Leigh's soldiers, or a mixture of two or more units is unclear, as Ensign Cartwright and some of the non-commissioned officers had previously served with Birtles in Colonel Leigh's company in Cheshire. Besides, a payment made on 12 June 1646 of £4 4s. was made to 'Captain-Lieutenant Birtles for his Ensign Cartwright'.[15] Unlike each of the other captain's companies in the Lichfield musters, no Lieutenant appears under Birtles' command. On 5 June the company comprised:

Ensign Cartwright	Corporal Davenport
Sergeant Hindley	Corporal Bradshaw
Sergeant Taylor	Drummer William Newton.[16]
Clerk Newton	

Captain Hugh Birtles appears to have taken command of the Eddisbury Hundred Trained and Freehold Bands by 1648, while he later served as captain in the foot regiment of Colonel William Daniell at the Battle of Dunbar in 1650.

12 TNA, SP28/152/4, fols 10v., 12r.–13r.; E121/5/7/35, fol. 64v. (undated).
13 TNA, SP28/35/2, fol. 262v.; BL, MS Add. 11333, fol. 118; *BLB*, II, 1235.
14 BCL, MS 595611, pp.252–3; SP28/513/1, fols 70r., 71r., 87r.
15 TNA, SP28/513/1, fol. 91r.
16 BCL, MS 595611, p.253; TNA, SP28/513/1, fol. 87r.

Lieutenant Colonel Gilbert Gerard's Company

Of Crewood, near Kingsley, Gilbert Gerard was head of a minor branch of the Royalist Lancashire Gerards. Described as an 'Anabaptist fanatic', Gilbert was regarded as one of the most religiously radical of the Cheshire Parliamentarian officers. He acted as head constable for Eddisbury Hundred before the war and was involved in the petitioning campaign of 1641, instigated by his neighbour, Sir Thomas Aston. Gerard's wartime accounts show that he served as captain of a company of foot in Colonel John Leigh's regiment from 14 February 1643 to 30 November 1644; as Lieutenant Colonel of foot from 30 November 1644 to 14 November 1646; as governor of Northwich between 1 March 1643 and 15 December 1643; and as captain of dragoons from 20 November 1643 to 2 February 1644.[17] He was promoted to lieutenant colonel, probably in late 1644. Gilbert served as lieutenant colonel of the Cheshire foot at the siege of Lichfield Close in 1646, and he was a leading commissioner for the surrender of the Royalist garrison. He was a highly capable officer and talented administrator. Throughout the 1650s Gerard acted as a vigorous magistrate, and remained loyal to the Commonwealth and Protectorate.

In early 1643 Gilbert Gerard received the sum of £20, the first of similar annual payments from six gentlemen who acted as his personal sponsor. Likewise, the accounts of William Leftwich, constable of Northwich Hundred record various payments to the officer between September and 12 December 1643 amounting to £73 4s.[18] His foot company was composed of volunteers from the town of Northwich. Before his promotion the constables of Frodsham township paid Captain Gerard £3 for arms for three of his men, and the same for the monthly pay of trained soldiers, seemingly a portion of the exactions placed upon them for the support of the army. Several sums were also disbursed to inhabitants of Frodsham for quartering Gerard's soldiers.[19] On 18 January 1644 £5 5s. was received by Richard Starkey, clerk to Gerard's company from the Bucklow committee for pay for the soldiers, and the figure of £11 6s. 8d. went to 'Captain Gerard and delivered to Colonel Leigh's clerk'.[20]

On 20 November 1643, when quartered at Tarvin, the company was attacked a Royalist force attempting to cross Stamford Bridge on the road from Chester. Following exchanges of musketry, troops from Cholmondeley House arrived and assisted Gerard's soldiers in repelling the enemy as far as the Gorse Stacks to the north-east of Chester. In the words of Malbon, the Parliamentarians 'slew some of them, and marched back to Tarvin without loss of any, only one a little wounded'.[21] As is insinuated by the annotation 'Tarvin' next to the name of Gerard's company in Brereton's army list of 30 April 1645, the command acted as part of the garrison of the town throughout the siege of Chester. In the spring of 1645, however, some of Lieutenant Colonel Gerard's men became embroiled in the ongoing dispute surrounding the taking of

17 TNA, SP28/152/4, unfol; SP28/208, fols 33v.–4r.

18 BL, MS Harley 1999, fols 75v., 313r.

19 *Ibid.*, fols 76v.–91v.

20 BL, MS Harley 2137, fols 54r., 94r.

21 Malbon, p.88.

money and goods by Colonel John Booth for the Warrington garrison from upper Bucklow Hundred. Like Colonel Henry Brooke's regiment, Gerard's company and much of Leigh's command were also maintained by this and the neighbouring hundreds of Northwich and Eddisbury. On 1 April the sequestrators for Bucklow wrote to Sir William Brereton from Daresbury:

> We send you here enclosed a copy of a letter from Colonel John Booth [dated the previous day, threatening the head sequestrator, Thomas Warburton], occasioned as we conceive, by the signing of some of us of an order for levying £50 out of delinquents' estates within the townships formerly assigned for the maintenance of the garrison of Warrington. This order was given to Richard Starkey, clerk to Lieutenant Colonel Gerard, and certain of his soldiers for the payment of the £50 ordered by you to his officers. But on the execution of the said order by the said Starkey, notice being given thereof to Colonel John Booth, a number of soldiers were sent out of Warrington, the cattle rescued from them [Starkey's men] and they carried prisoners to Warrington and our order taken from them by the said colonel. Sir, if our collectors shall suffer so long imprisonment as they have done in another county, for yielding obedience to the orders of parliament, and our agents shall be resisted with violence and we so much vilified, and so often threatened to be imprisoned and plundered for our endeavours to perform the best service to the Commonwealth and yet there be no vindication of justice, we may judge ourselves in as evil a case as Israel was under the taskmasters of Pharoah.[22]

A number of muster rolls survive for Gerard's company between 1643 and 1646, listing the following:

Strength	Date	Strength	Date	Strength	Date
44	25 Nov. 1643	100	30 Apr. 1645	109	27 Mar. 1646
44	17 Dec. 1643	123	21 Oct. 1645	130	23 May 1646
60	4 May 1644	123	7 Feb. 1646	124	9 Aug. 1646[23]

The distinct increase in the size of Gerard's company by the spring of 1645 is probably related to his promotion as lieutenant colonel, and also the disbandment and probable re-distribution of the regiment's major's company around that time. On 21 October 1645 the following junior and non-commissioned officers were present in Lieutenant Colonel Gerard's company:

Lieutenant Edward Barker
Ensign William Holt
Sergeant Anthony Hitchins
Sergeant George Spencer
Sergeant Richard Southall
Corporal Adam Hulmes
Corporal Joshua Grimes
Corporal Thomas Basnett
Drummer John Catchpoll
Drummer Henry Williamson
Clerk Richard Starkey[24]

22 CRO, DDX/428, fol. 72v.; *BLB*, I, 148, 156.
23 TNA, SP28/152/4, fol. 15v.; SP28/123/2, fols 190v., 196r.; SP28/123/1, fols 38r., 50r.; BL, MS 11331, fol. 44r.; BCL, MS 595611, p.253.
24 TNA, SP28/123/2, fol. 190v.

In April 1646, following the fall of Chester, Lieutenant Colonel Gilbert Gerard's soldiers spent seven weeks besieging Hawarden Castle with others under the overall command of Colonel Lothian.[25] The muster of Cheshire forces at Bacon Hill facing Lichfield Close on 23 May 1646 shows that by this time Gerard led a company of trained bandsmen, which had been modified from a volunteer command since the fall of Chester a few months previously. However, as subsequent pay documents dated 11, 12 and 21 June illustrate, the former command structure of officers and non-commissioned officers remained (minus the reduction in one of its drummers – John Catchpoll), alongside a cadre of 19 volunteer soldiers.[26] Such accounts must be treated with caution, however, as they can present a confused picture, while among the more specific sections (fols 86v.–91r.) the payments to the common soldiers of Leadbeater's, Booth's and Monke's companies are omitted, as are the disbursements to Daniell's and Monke's officers.

On 30 May 'Lieutenant Colonel Gerard's volunteers', were among the 'common soldiers of the Cheshire volunteer companies of foot and dragoons at 18s. 8d. a man, there being no pay allowed them during the said leaguer of Lichfield'. Moreover, a separate payment of £17 14s. 8d. was given to the 19 volunteers in Gerard's trained band company 'over and above the number of the trained men that have their settled pay from the country', in other words, the remainder of the men who had previously served under Gilbert as volunteers had all been paid off, and either disbanded or re-enlisted as trained bandsmen. Whilst serving in the siege lines at Bacon Hill on 25 May 1646 Gerard was reimbursed £5 which he had given workmen 'to work about the sconces and mounts against the Close', while on 12 June he marched his company to Coventry to carry £500 which Sir William Brereton had borrowed for the payment of troops at the Leaguer.[27]

At an undetermined date (possibly 1643) the following were also paid with Gerard's company:

Sergeant Haigh
Surgeon Nathaniel Burrows[28]

Sergeant Major James Chantrell's/Sergeant Major John Trevis's Company

Probably from West Derby Hundred, Lancashire, James Chantrell aided the defence of Manchester as captain in September 1642 and commanded a company in Colonel Leigh's regiment. He may have left the regiment around August 1643, and was replaced by Major John Trevis. Chantrell was commanding Wirral troops as lieutenant colonel in the Chester suburbs in October 1645, although two months later he was paid with the Lancashire

25 NLW, MS Rhual 136.
26 TNA: SP28/16/513/1, fol. 70r.
27 *Ibid.*, fols 71r., 89r., 90r., 91r., 84r.
28 TNA: SP28/208, fol. 20v.

foot (being lieutenant colonel to Colonel Richard Holland's regiment) at the Leaguer.[29] A pay warrant of 4 November 1646 directed payment of £30 to Major John Trevis, in part of his pay for service done as major to Colonel Leigh in the garrison of Northwich and elsewhere (which probably began in the autumn of 1643), £10 of which was 'to be paid in convenient time, the rest when the army is disbanded'.[30] He commanded the Cheshire foot at the Battle of Tarvin in August 1644, but by the following spring he appears as an emissary to Sir William Brereton, a role he kept for the remainder of the war. Major Trevis's company must have been disbanded by then because it is not listed in the regiment on 30 April 1645, although a payment appears in James Croxton's accounts of £41 4s. 8d. 'to Major John Trevis, and his officers and soldiers'.[31]The brothers Ensign John Witter and Sergeant Joseph Witter, who later served in Colonel Brooke's regiment as Lieutenant and Ensign respectively, were paid with Major Trevis in 1643.[32]

Captain John Acton's Company

From Nantwich, Acton commanded one of three companies that constituted the Eddisbury Hundred trained and freehold bands. On 26 January and 8 November 1645 pay warrants refer to 'Captain John Acton, and his officers and soldiers'.[33] In October 1645 Acton's men garrisoned Brewers' Hall Mount, located to the west of the city of Chester and the Dee to cover the absence of Cheshire troops at the Battle of Denbigh Green. The company mustered 60 common soldiers on 30 April and 30 October 1645.[34] The accounts of the county treasurer include a total disbursement of £1,273 11s. 2d. to the officers and soldiers trained bands of Eddisbury. Corporal Richard Hawkeshead was paid with the company in 1645.[35]

Captain Thomas Whalley's Company

Possibly a yeoman from Shipbrook in Northwich Hundred, he was leading a company of the Eddisbury Hundred Trained and Freehold Bands by 1 July 1643. Whalley's company contained 60 common soldiers in April 1645. He acted as commander of the besieging Parliamentarian force at Beeston in November 1645.[36] On 4 April 1646 the deputy lieutenants of Cheshire wrote to Sir William Brereton informing him of their failed attempts to get troops

---

29 TNA: SP28/208, fol. 18r.; E121/5/7/351, fol. 42v.; BL, MS Add. 11332, fols 23r., 30v.–2r.; 11333, fols 30r., 118r.; *BLB*, II, 775n., 777, 791, 1040, 1235.

30 TNA, SP28/224/1, fol. 173r.

31 TNA, SP28/128/13, fol. 17v.; BL, MS Add. 11331, fols 33r., 97r.; 11332, fol. 121r.–v.; 11333, fol. 23v.; *BLB*, I, 372, 528–9; II, 894, 919, 1011.

32 TNA, E121/5/7/43, fol. 4r.; E121/5/7/351, fol. 63v.

33 TNA, SP28/35/2, fols 261r., 264r.

34 BL, MS Harley 1999, fol. 283r.; MS Add. 11331, fol. 45v.; 11332, fol. 32r.; *BLB*, II, 791.

35 TNA, SP28/128/13, fol. 16r.; E121/5/7/351, fol. 59v.

36 TNA, SP28/128/13, fol. 13v.; BL, MS Add. 11332, fol. 102v.; *BLB*, II, 872.

to march from Chester to Lichfield. This was part of an ongoing dispute, initially involving Captain Edward Glegg's company over unpaid arrears, and in particular, promises of bonuses on the capture of Chester which had not been completely honoured. A week later Brereton reported to his London agents that soldiers under the command of Glegg and Captain Thomas Whalley 'will not march without money'.

Whilst in Staffordshire on 13 May 1646 Whalley acted as a signatory to a letter from the 'Cheshire commanders at Lichfield' to Sir William, dated informing him not only about the severe conditions experienced by their men, but increasing pay arrears which were causing some of them desert their colours.[37] Ten days later, Captain Thomas Whalley's company mustered three officers, two sergeants, one drummer, two corporals and 36 soldiers. The muster of 23 May was for the purpose of paying the troops, hence on 30 May the sum of £33 12s. was disbursed 'for the private soldiers of his company consisting of 36 men at 18s. 8d. a man according to the muster roll annexed'. Along with the rest of the Cheshire foot they had 'one month's pay, there being several months due to them in arrears'.[38] The moneys to pay such sums were from £500 borrowed by Sir William Brereton for the payment of his troops, which had been transported to Lichfield the previous day by the companies of Captains Whalley and Gimbert. Additionally, on 5 June the non-commissioned officers of both units also had a month's pay 'according to the new model', while in December 1646 Captain Whalley's command received a further £16.[39] On 5 June 1646 his company contained the following:

Lieutenant Cheany Bostock
Ensign Bradford
Sergeant John Bostock
Sergeant John Riley
Corporal William Nixon
Corporal Thomas Read
Drummer John Stubbs[40]

Whalley received overall payments from treasurer Croxton from London sources for his officers and soldiers of £336 10s. 6s.[41] In 1650 Thomas served as captain in the Cheshire regiment raised by Colonel Thomas Croxton.

Captain Richard Pigott's Company

Captain Richard Pigott was 'of the town of Northwich' and as Dore suggests, he might have been Master of Witton School in 1643 and Master of Shrewsbury in 1646, 'dates that would just allow for his military career'.[42] In October 1643 the constables of Nether Whitley remunerated Pigott to the sum of £36, being

37 BCL, MS 595611, pp.6, 9, 203 *CWS*, 17, 27, 211.
38 BCL, MS 595611, pp.70–1, 86.
39 *Ibid.*, pp.74, 86–7.
40 *Ibid.*, MS 595611, p.87.
41 TNA, SP28/128/13, fol. 17v.
42 *BLB*, I, 385, n. 8.

an annual outlay from four of his sponsors. A similar system helped fund Gilbert Gerard of the same regiment.[43] A pay warrant, this time from central funds, exists for Captain Pigott's soldiers for 11 February 1645.[44] His large volunteer company of 120 common soldiers was formed from Northwich townsmen in early 1643, and habitually served in the town's garrison.

When expedient, for instance, during the autumn and winter of 1645, Pigott's soldiers were engaged at the Chester leaguer – on 26 October the Committee of Tarvin requested Sir William Brereton 'to remember to send to Captain Pigott for his company to march with speed'. Three days later his command was included with 800 Cheshire foot located in the suburbs of Chester before the Eastgate, which had fallen to Parliament following the bombardment and great assault on the city on 9 October 1645. Moreover, with 60 of his men he manned the garrison of Eccleston in the absence of the force consisting of 1,200 horse and 1,500 foot led by Lieutenant Colonel Michael Jones and Adjutant James Lothian that defeated Sir William Vaughan's troops at Denbigh Green on 1 November.[45]

On 23 December Colonels Brooke, Duckenfield and Leigh reported to Sir William Brereton from the Chester suburbs, 'Captain Pigott's company are unwilling to advance further than Tarvin, supposing you commanded them no further. So that the hard duty that our forces here are put upon will not be endured by the soldiers without more assistance speedily.'[46] The immediate context of this was the seizure of the eastern suburbs of Chester by the Cheshire army and calling out of the trained bands on 26 October to relieve volunteer companies at Chester for their subsequent march to Whitchurch and Denbigh Green. Although militarily beneficial, this also served to exacerbate the increasing need of pay and provisions by the Cheshire foot in particular. During his return journey to the county following the extension of his commission in Westminster due to the Self-Denying Ordinance, Brereton received reports from Jones, Lothian and Commissary William Hinde about the mutinous state of the unpaid and poorly supplied soldiers under his command.[47] Captain Richard Pigott's company was still mustered, however, on 29 October 1646 when Corporal John Butler was among its ranks.[48]

43 BL, MS Harley 2128, fol. 42r.; 1999, fol. 75v.

44 TNA: SP28/35/2, 266r.

45 BL, MS Add. 11332, fols 14r.–15r., 20v., 31v., 35r.; *BLB*, II, 733–4, 775, 790–1.

46 BL, MS Add. 11333, fol. 57r.; *BLB*, II, 1088.

47 BL, MS Add. 11332, fols 28r., 25v., 23v.; *BLB*, II, 757, 760, 752.

48 TNA, SP28/40/2, fol. 190v.; E121/5/7/351, fol. 22v.

14

Colonel Henry Mainwaring's Regiment of Foot

Colonel Henry Mainwaring of Kermincham, near Sandbach, was a leading deputy lieutenant and Presbyterian colonel in the Cheshire army of Parliament from the outset of the war. According to Morrill, he was:

> an active colonel throughout 1643 and the early months of 1644, he was the only senior officer who did not owe his appointment to Brereton, and there is some evidence of mutual dislike and jealousy. He was ordered to be dismissed from all his offices by Parliament in the spring of 1644 (this was during Brereton's period in London). He was in fact sacked as a deputy lieutenant and committee-man, and though his name appears on Commissions of the Peace as late as the end of 1648, there is no evidence that he ever exercised authority as a magistrate in the years 1645–8. The evidence surrounding the continuation of his military commission is ambiguous and confusing.[1]

Mainwaring raised a troop of horse and regiment of foot, and was military commander in Cheshire until the arrival of Sir William Brereton in January 1643. In December 1642, at the head of 5,000 Manchester and Cheshire militia troops he countered Royalist forays into the county by forces under the Earl of Derby and Colonel Thomas Leigh. With his own company he attacked Adlington and Wrinehill Halls, seizing 120 arms from each, while on 10 December he fortified Northwich with 1,000 soldiers.

As suggested above, Henry Mainwaring's loyalties had become problematic by 1644. He was married into the Royalist Fitton family of Gawsworth, and evidently – like other officers associated with Colonel George Booth – attempted openly to weaken Brereton's position as commander-in-chief of the Cheshire forces and deputy lieutenant. There is also the possibility that Brereton's insistence that all the troop of horse in the county were brought under his command as part of his regiment of horse, was one of the reasons for the breach between him and Henry Mainwaring. Although Colonel

1 Morrill, *Cheshire*, pp.215–6.

Mainwaring's troop was still operating in March 1644, the raised by Thomas Stanley of Alderley had disbanded or been put under another captain by before 1645, in his son no longer holding a commission and Stanley himself was in opposition to Sir William on the county committee.[2] Mainwaring was removed from all military commands and role as deputy lieutenant at the prompting of Brereton on 7 May 1644, the Commons resolving that:

> Henry Mainwaring, and Henry Vernon, esquires, two deputy lieutenants of Cheshire, in regard of their disservice to the parliament in many particulars, be forthwith discharged and removed from their said places, and other power of command in any military way, in or gathering or receiving monies: and that all horses, arms, ammunition, and money, now under their or either of their commands, belonging to the state, be, upon demand, delivered up to Sir William Brereton, to be by him disposed of and employed for the said service of king and parliament: and that the said persons be called to account for what monies, arms, and ammunition they have; and accordingly to restore the same for the public service.[3]

No reasons are given for such 'disservice', although doubts about his loyalty were pursued when Mainwaring found himself facing sequestration as a delinquent, although he was cleared of any charges. Henry's position after this, though, is unclear. He led his regiment in person at Stockport on 25 May and at Oswestry on 2 July, although as Dore notes in regard to the former, that this could have been due to the uncertainty of Rupert's arrival in Cheshire and Lancashire.[4] Yet although Mainwaring's regiment of foot continued to be listed under his command in April and May 1645 there is nothing indicating that he was still serving with the army by that time. In 1659 Henry contributed to the Booth Rising, charged as a colonel with recruiting in Northwich Hundred.

Colonel Henry Mainwaring's regiment was perhaps raised as early as 1642 from Northwich Hundred. Four of its company commanders were from the Sandbach–Holmes Chapel area. Although the regiment served throughout 1643 and 1644, by early 1645 it had been reduced to 160 men in four 'country' companies (the parts of the Nantwich Hundred trained bands not commanded by Thomas Croxton). Yet it is obvious that Mainwaring's foot must have been considerably stronger in earlier times. Both the colonel's and major's companies had been disbanded by 1645, leaving command of the regiment to Major Robert Jackson, then probably after this officer's death in late February 1645 to James Stockport, captain-lieutenant of Colonel Mainwaring's own company. Mainwaring's regiment was a highly active one and regularly in the thick of the action in Cheshire and elsewhere. Thus, his men fought at Middlewich in December 1643 and the Battle of Nantwich on 25 January 1644. On 25 May Mainwaring's and Duckenfield's regiments were

2 *CSPD 1644*, p.41; *BLB*, II, 796, note 6.
3 *CJ*, III, p.484.
4 *BLB*, I, 385, note 9.

unable to stop Prince Rupert's advance at Stockport, seeking refuge in the Manchester garrison.

However, a month later Colonel Mainwaring's soldiers rendezvoused with George Booth's regiment and other Cheshire foot, under the temporary command of Denbigh and Myddelton, participating in operations in Shropshire. Mainwaring's regiment served also with the Cheshire forces at the Battle of Montgomery on 18 September, and was active in 1645 at Farndon Bridge and Hawarden Castle, as well as the Chester leaguer. It can be assumed that Mainwaring's regiment had been considerably larger than its 160 common soldiers listed in April 1645. Additionally, if as seems likely, the 'countrymen' under the command of Mainwaring's captains were part of the earlier regiment, what remained of them by the end of the war had a good record of service.

Colonel Henry Mainwaring's Own Company

Mainwaring raised his own company in late 1642 with volunteers from Northwich Hundred. It was led by Captain-Lieutenant James Stockport of Saltersford, near Macclesfield. Dore suggests that with Mainwaring's disgrace and Major Jackson's death in early 1645, Stockport may have commanded what remained of the regiment. Stockport appears to have led the four companies of Mainwaring's regiment at Holt Bridge in April 1645 alongside two units of Cheshire dragoons, and he was given responsibility for accounting for cattle appropriated from the vicinity of Holt Castle. A letter from Sergeant Major Thomas Croxton, governor of Nantwich garrison, dated 18 April relates to this, but it is also revealing about the activities of the regiment during this period:

> It is this day ordered that Captain Stockport shall give to the captains hereafter named a particular account of the cattle mentioned in the note hereunto annexed and the valuation thereof, and of the disbursements for Major Jackson's funeral, and shall pay for the price of the cattle to Captain Leadbeater, and his sergeant and men for their service and care of the magazine at Holt Bridge, five pounds more when they did so bravely maintain the bridge, and for the seven men that adventured their lives for the taking of a parcel of the cattle near Holt Castle five marks, and the remainder of the price of the cattle to be equally divided to Captains Baskerville, Cotton, Stockport, Sadler, Leadbeater and Hancock. Given under my hand at Nantwich the day aforesaid.[5]

This and an earlier letter from Lieutenant Richard Holford, commanding a Parliamentarian picket before the bridge, relate to a series of attacks when the Royalist commander Prince Maurice arrived at Chester in February 1645.[6] The possession by the King's forces of Holt Castle, half a mile from the medieval bridge, crossing of the Dee into Wales, made efforts by Brereton's

5 CRO, DDX/428, fol. 107v.; *BLB*, I, 290.
6 CRO, DDX/428, fol. 12r.–v.; *BLB*, I, 2.

troops to block it off very difficult. In December 1644 the Parliamentarians had constructed a fort at the Cheshire end of the bridge, yet events connected to the siege of Chester would soon involve it once more in determined fighting by both sides. On 23 February 1645 a composite of the remaining companies of Booth's regiment was at the forefront of the action fought at Farndon against Prince Maurice's troops.[7] Captain-Lieutenant Stockport received from central funds the final part of £279 for the pay of the officers and soldiers of the company on 30 December 1646.[8] The ensign, sergeants and clerk of the unit remain known, however, in mid 1644 the remaining non-commissioners and men were:

Corporal Thomas Stubbs	Drummer William Moores
Corporal Thomas Pownall	Drummer John Berry
Corporal Thomas Read	

And 32 common soldiers:

John Tomkinson	Peter Eaton	William Strongitharm
Thomas Bowyer	John Frimlet	Henry Bradshaw
Thomas Compton	William Dowleys	William Dale
Lester Smith	Thomas Wharmby	John Bramhall jnr
Peter Bramhall	William Booke	Francis Moores
Edward Starke	Robert Newell	Thomas Hayes
Thomas Burrows	John Bramhall sen.	Edward Barlow
John Bonston	Hugh Bonston	Thomas Carter
William Bosford	Thomas Hill	Robert Stockport
Henry Jackson	Thomas Adams	Adam Marks[9]
Peter Wright	Edward Berry	

There is evidence that Stockport also commanded a unit dragoons in late 1645 to early 1646. He was commissioned captain in Duckenfield's militia regiment in 1650, and sat on the court martial of the Earl of Derby in 1651. He later served in Ireland, and acquired extensive estates in Dublin and various counties across the country.

Sergeant Major Robert Jackson's Company

No local origins have come to light for Jackson, therefore according to Dore 'presumably he was from outside the county, perhaps a professional soldier'.[10] This would not be unusual for the Cheshire army of Parliament, given that Brereton, Brooke and probably Duckenfield brought in professionals to organise, train and lead parts of their military commands. On 28 December

7 Vicars, *Magnalia Dei*, p.122.
8 TNA, SP28/128/13, fol. 18r.; SP28/224/1, fol. 208r.
9 TNA, SP28/121A, fol. 1v.
10 *BLB*, I, 385, n. 9.

1644 a payment was made to 'Major Jackson, Colonel Mainwaring's major'. He was killed in action at Farndon on 23 February 1645 buried at Nantwich, his funeral costing £11 3s. 2d.[11] Jackson's company was presumably raised in either late 1642 or early 1643, although by early 1645 it had either been disbanded or absorbed into other commands.

Captain John Leadbeater's Company

Leadbeater was probably from Gawsworth, where he took the Covenant on 24 November 1644. His militia company was drawn from Macclesfield Hundred and served regularly at the Chester leaguer until at least February 1646, being particularly mentioned with Mainwaring's regiment defending Farndon Bridge in April 1645, as well as protecting the Pikegate and Bars on the eastern side of the city on 29 October 1645, and as part of a body of Cheshire and Montgomeryshire foot that was ordered to march to Hawarden Castle on 8 January 1646.[12] Soon the fall of Chester to Parliamentarian forces on 3 February 1646 Captain Leadbeater's command was transferred to Colonel Robert Duckenfield's regiment and amalgamated with the company of Captain Anthony Booth. An entry in Duckenfield's accounts mentions '60 muskets I received of the storehouse at Chester, presently after the taking of that city, 20 of these last are in Captain Booth's and Captain Leadbeater's hands, and the rest are in Nantwich'.[13]

About 11 April 1646 whilst at Lichfield Close both officers petitioned Sir William Brereton on behalf of their beleaguered soldiers: '[We] humbly entreat your honour as they have served you in love hitherto, so they may still continue in the same, and for the present either receive pay here for their late service, and an assurance of it for the future, or else a free discharge according to their voluntary willingness.' On 23 May the combined command mustered one lieutenant, one ensign, two sergeants, two drummers, four corporals and 81 common soldiers – next to the muster roll the clerk wrote: 'these two make but one company and officers and allowed accordingly'.[14] Captain John Leadbeater still held a commission on 16 November 1646 when he was paid the sum of £20 by William Barret, collector for Macclesfield Hundred to be given to the sequestered Lady Felitia Fitton of Gawsworth.[15] On 9 February 1645 Leadbeater's company mustered the following:

11 TNA, SP28/196/1, fol. 24r.; SP28/152/7, fol. 16r.; CRO, DDX/428, fol. 107v.; *BLB*, I, 291.

12 BL, MS Add. 11331, fol. 44v.; 11332, fols 31v.–2r.; 11333, fols 57r., 109r.; CRO, DDX/428, fol. 107v.; TNA, SP28/43/7, fols 861v.–2r.; SP28/128/10, fol. 2r.; SP28/123/2, fol. 324r.; *BLB*, I, 290; II, 777, 791, 1088, 1212; Earwaker, *East Cheshire*, II, p.589.

13 TNA, SP28/128/10, fol. 2r.

14 BCL, MS 595611, pp.10, 252; *CWS*, 24, 240. The breakdown as per the muster roll is as follows: Captain Booth, one sergeant, one drummer, two corporals and 48 common soldiers; Captain Leadbeater, Lieutenant Norbury, Ensign Banniel, one sergeant, one drummer, two corporals and 33 common soldiers.

15 BL, MS Harley 2130, fol. 92v.

Lieutenant Randle Norbury | Sergeant John Banniel
Ensign William Whilton | Sergeant John Low
Quartermaster William Leadbeater | Sergeant Richard Ironmonger[16]

The remaining non-commissioned officers recorded serving on 5 June 1646 were:

Corporal John White | Drummer John Normanshall[17]
Corporal William Newton

This country company contained:

Strength	Date	Strength	Date
50	9 Feb. 1645	52	7 Feb. 1646
60	31 Oct. 1645	81 (with Booth's)	23 May 1646.[18]

Captain Thomas Cotton's Company

Of Cotton Hall, near Holmes Chapel, Thomas Cotton commanded a company of foot by mid 1644. He was present with Colonel Mainwaring's regiment throughout operations in Cheshire, Shropshire and the Chester leaguer. In May 1645 Captain Cotton's company was listed among a taskforce of Cheshire foot led by Major James Lothian that was sent to Leicestershire to intercept Charles I's Oxford Army. Although Lieutenant Colonel Michael Jones spoke disparagingly of militia companies such as Cotton's, Baskerville's and Hardware's 'whose men may prove well in houses, though not in the field', they were described as 'well armed men' when they mustered at Chester on 26 October 1645.[19]

Captain John Baskerville's Company

John Baskerville of Withington, near Stockport, was the first captain-lieutenant of Sir William Brereton's own company. On 19 May 1643 he was paid £10 'to raise a company of his own' in the regiment of Colonel Henry Mainwaring.[20] It might be assumed that this contained volunteers and impressed men, yet by spring 1645 Captain Baskerville was listed as commanding a small company of countrymen.

16 TNA, SP28/122/3, fols 766v.–7r.
17 TNA, SP16/513/1, fol. 88r.; E121/5/7/351, fol. 54v.
18 TNA, SP28/122/3, fols 767r.; SP28/123/2, fol. 324r.; BL, MS Add. 11332, fol. 32r.; BCL, MS 595611, p.252.
19 BL, Add. 11131, fols 96v., 165r.–v.; 11332, fol. 15v.; CRO: DDX/428, fol. 107r.; *BLB*, I, 509, 654; II, 734.
20 TNA, SP28/196/1, fol. 7r.

Captain John Hancock's Company

Hancock was a clergyman from Odd Rode, near Sandbach. He commanded his company throughout the war and in 1648 took up a commission as captain in Colonel James Lothian's regiment of foot, participating in the suppression of the Royalist uprising in North Wales. According to the account of Schoolmaster Williams of the Parliamentarian attack on Beaumaris town and castle on 1 October 1648 Captain John Hancock, with his lieutenant and ensign were killed by musket fire.[21] Hancock's company mustered 40 common soldiers on 31 October 1645 and 64 on 2 September 1648. Later in the month the following junior and non-commissioned officers were recorded:

Lieutenant John Walton
Ensign John Thompson
Corporal William Harrison
Sergeant Randle Kent
Sergeant William Meeker
Corporal Richard Mottershead
Corporal William Harrison
Corporal John Carter
Drummer John Bramhall[22]

21 Edward Parry, *Royal Visits and Progresses to Wales* (Chester, 1850), pp.388–9; Norman Tucker, *North Wales in the Civil War* (Wrexham: Bridge Books, 1992 edn), p.111.

22 BL, MS Add. 11332, fol. 32; TNA, SP28/124, fol. 238v.; SP28/224, fol. 318r.

15

Sir William Brereton's Regiment of Dragoons

Sir William Brereton's commission as colonel of a regiment of dragoons dates from his first appearance in Cheshire in January 1643 to 24 June 1645.[1] On 3 November 1645 he informed the Committee of Accounts, 'I raised and took down with me in December [1642] these companies of dragoons: Captain Bramhall, Captain Goldegay and Captain Lea which, together with my horse and all the force with me, were put upon service by the way and the first night after we came into Cheshire'.[2] Sir William's commission as colonel of dragoons ended when he gave up his command under the Self-Denying Ordinance. It is likely that the dragoon companies were reasonably well equipped when they arrived in Cheshire in January 1643. On 3 December 1642 Parliament had ordered the delivery of 400 muskets and 300 firelocks for Brereton and Alderman William Edwards, 'to be employed for the safety of the county of Chester'. Moreover, Bramhall's soldiers had been supplied with 20 firearms and 60 mounts in London, and a further 14 'on arrival in Cheshire'.[3]

Initially raised in London and Cheshire, the dragoons participated in the defence of the capital in November 1642. Upon their arrival in Cheshire they soon saw action during the skirmish against Sir Thomas Aston's troops at Nantwich and the First Battle of Middlewich, before participating in Sir William Brereton's operations in Staffordshire and the fight at Hopton Heath in March 1643. Three companies of Cheshire dragoons took part in the capture of Eccleshall Castle on 30 August, while the soldiers under the command of Captains Bramhall, Lea and Cheswis benefitted from the sale of the goods of the garrison with other Cheshire and Staffordshire troops.[4] Despite some initial battlefield inexperience, the Cheshire dragoons developed into versatile and highly specialised troops who were accustomed

1 TNA, SP28/152/7, fol. 20r.

2 BL, MS Add. 11332, fol. 43v.; *BLB*, II, 809.

3 *CJ*, II, p.874; MS Harley 2128, fols 34r.–35r.

4 CRO, ZCR63/2/702, fol. 24r. This is also referred to in a petition of the widow of the Royalist governor, Captain Thomas Bird, who was killed during operations there (*HMC Seventh Report*, p.121).

to hazardous service. Furthermore, they were commanded by resourceful and experienced officers, who for the most part were professional soldiers (some of whom had previously served in the Irish wars).

Like some of their Royalist counterparts, in terms of equipment, tactics and leadership Brereton's firelocks seem to have been 'sufficiently different' to the rest of the army and towards the forefront of an evolution in the role of dragoons in seventeenth-century warfare. Owing to battlefield attrition, the capture, reassignment and promotion of officers, and the influx of recruits from the Royalist army from Ireland, in 1644 Brereton's dragoons were reorganised into three companies, led by Captains Finch, Gilbert and Holt, although other commands and detachments are known from later in the war under different officers. Thus, Sir William spoke more than once of 'three to four' companies of dragoons under his command. Like other Parliamentarian forces in Shropshire and the borderlands of Wales, those of Cheshire were bolstered by soldiers from the English army in Ireland who had changed sides after the Battle of Nantwich and the siege of Liverpool in 1644.

Perhaps as many as 600 of the 1,500 soldiers captured on 25 January took service with Brereton's army. Some of these might have served previously in the firelock companies of Captains Sandford and Francis Langley. Nothing is known of the latter's fate, but Sandford played a leading role in the capture of Hawarden Castle and with eight of his men took Beeston Castle in a surprise operation. He was killed leading Byron's unsuccessful attack on Nantwich on 17 January 1644. According to Malbon, papers outlining plans for the assault were found in his pockets.[5] Brereton later described his dragoons 'which were soldiers in Ireland' as 'very serviceable' and 'well-accommodated'. He also informed Lord Leven on 22 May 1645, 'I can bring no more foot than one regiment and some choice dragoons – firelocks which were soldiers in Ireland lately mounted'.[6] Three dragoon companies (numbering 210 soldiers collectively) were listed with Brereton's foot regiment in April 1645, but the reason for this remains uncertain.

Sergeant Major John Bramhall's Company

The son of widow Bramhall of Nantwich, John is likely to have been a mercer before the war. His first service was as captain in Colonel John Hampden's regiment of foot in the Earl of Essex's Army, which had been formed in July and August 1642, and saw action at Edgehill, Brentford (against Prince Rupert's horse) and Turnham Green. During November 1642 Bramhall joined Sir William Brereton as captain of one of three companies of dragoons

---

5 HMC, *Fourteenth Report, App. VII*, pp.124, 131, 143; Malbon, *Memorials*, pp.91–109. See also Lowe, 'The Campaign of the Irish Royalist Army', pp.62, 65); Ian Ryder, *An English Army for Ireland* (Partizan Press, 1987), p.31; John Barratt, 'What Sanford's Firelocks Did Next', *English Civil War Notes & Queries*, 50 (Partizan Press, 1995), 18–21; Andrew Hopper, *Turncoats and Renegadoes: Changing Sides during the English Civil Wars* (Oxford University Press, 2012), pp.89–90.

6 HMC, *Fourteenth Report, App. IV*, p.62; BL, MS Add. 11331, fol. 142v.; *BLB*, I, 610.

raised in the capital for the Cheshire forces. His detailed accounts begin with 'A particular of such moneys paid to my soldiers after I came out of my Lord General's army during my stay in London until I came upon the service in Cheshire'.[7] They provide much detail about Bramhall's service and expenditure, as well as the equipping, provisioning and activities of his command. John Bramhall held a commission as captain of a company of dragoons from 21 November 1642 to 20 August 1643, as sergeant major of dragoons from 20 August 1643 to 30 April 1644, and sergeant major of a troop of horse from 30 April 1644 to 5 February 1645. He was an energetic and talented officer who was constantly in action with Brereton during the period November 1642 to autumn 1643, being engaged with his company at Nantwich, Stafford, Middlewich and Hopton Heath, among others.[8]

Following his company's participation in the reduction of Eccleshall Castle in August, Captain Bramhall was captured with some of his junior officers and dragoons at Loppington in north Shropshire a month later.[9] Bramhall's accounts show that 30 firelocks and 24 mounts were also lost in the battle, suggesting that nearly half of his company was taken.[10] John was exchanged in April 1644, but by then Brereton's dragoons were beginning to be remodelled. He thus received command of a troop of horse, although with his former position as dragoon leader gone and being seemingly at odds with his commander-in-chief's war aims, Bramhall resigned his commission in early February 1645. This is borne out by his appearance as a signatory to the anti-Brereton petition three months later. In August 1650 Major John Bramhall was commissioned sergeant major in Colonel Henry Brooke's militia regiment of foot.[11] Whether he saw action with the unit at the Battle of Worcester the following year remains unclear.

Bramhall's company was raised in London in November and December 1642, although going by the names present in its first complete muster roll, he is likely to have had some Cheshire men with him already. During the first recruitment period, between 21 November and 2 December, one captain, one lieutenant, one cornet, two sergeants, three corporals, one drummer, one clerk and 57 soldiers were mustered. The company officers were paid the sum of £19 10s. in stages from 21 November to 15 December. Before departing from London in the first week of December, Captain John Bramhall purchased horsemeat for his soldiers at a cost of £157s. 4d., with an additional 19s. spent on 'the diet of my officers'. Leaving the capital for the march to Cheshire, 20 of Bramhall's soldiers reached Abbots Langley in Hertfordshire on 2 December, where they were paid £29 18s. 6d. Between Saturday 11 and Wednesday 15 December the remaining 37 dragoons received £2 15s. 6., having marched with Sir William Brereton's other forces to Watford. John Bramhall's accounts show his initial outlay in pay for his officers and men to have been £53 15s.

7 BL, MS Harley 2128, fols 20r.–35v.

8 Shaw, *History and Antiquities of Staffordshire*, I, pp.80–1; Malbon, p.54.

9 Malbon, pp.76–7; *Shropshires misery and mercie, Manifested in the defeat given to the Lord Capels ravenous and devouring Armie, by the forces of Cheshire and Shropshire* (November 1643), pp.2–3.

10 BL, MS Harley 2128, fols 34r.–v. ('where my officers and soldiers [were] captured').

11 *CSPD, 1650*, p.509.

Having marched to Northampton, his cornet and two sergeants had £1 4s. in pay, while 15s. 8d. was laid out for hay and corn for their horses. The first complete muster roll of Bramhall's company dates from 24 January 1643:

Captain John Bramhall	Corporal John Picket
Lieutenant Ralph Burrows	Corporal Henry Birkenshaw
Cornet Thomas Mainwaring	Corporal John Cooke
Sergeant John Turner	Drummer Owen Wollam
Sergeant Thomas Parry	Clerk John Higginson

Dragoons:

John Mottershaw	John Morrison	Humphrey Ellesmere
John Hesketh	Richard Sadler	Walter Frimley
Ralph Reeve	Henry Mercer	Hugh Colley
John Sillitoe	Peter Wooley	John Bridle
William Reeve	Richard Carter	John Derbyshire
Francis Green	John Lea	Arthur Comberbach
William Goodyear	William Braddock	Thomas Braddock
Isaac Johnson	Henry Meeke	Peter Platt
Richard Gleave	Randle Kent	Thomas Bentley
Henry Kendrick	Nicholas Sherman	Robert Dymond
John Gibson	John Price	John Ball
John Wright	Samuel Elliot	Richard Bradbury
Richard Cliffe	Robert Lunt	Samuel Elliot
Robert Scott	John Johnson	Edward Butterworth
Richard Style	Richard Morris	Thomas Mainwaring
Richard Lawton	William Betts	Thomas Comberbach
John Jackson	Stephen Fisher	John Jackson
John Croxton	Thomas Leigh	Ralph Finney
George Brookes	Ralph Knowsley	John Wildgoose[12]

Bramhall further claimed pay for 53 dragoons between 24 January and 31 March 1643, and 60 between 31 March and 20 May 1643.On 20 May 1643 one captain, one lieutenant, one cornet, one quartermaster, two sergeants, three corporals, two drummers one clerk and 80 men mustered for service. Among the junior and non-commissioned offers there had been some promotion from the ranks, perhaps due to casualties sustained during the early stages of the fighting in Cheshire and transfers to other commands. For instance, Malbon reported that at Nantwich on 28 January 1643 the Parliamentarians 'had many wounded', while Brereton reported that on the afternoon of 12 March, the day before the First Battle of Middlewich, he sent 'betwixt two and three companies of dragooners' on a probing attack, probably to ascertain the strength and dispositions of Aston's troops.[13] Hence, on 20 May the nominal roll of Bramhall's command listed:

12 BL, MS Harley 2128, fols 20v.–21r., 31v.

13 Malbon, p.36; *Cheshire's Successe*.

Captain John Bramhall	Corporal Thomas Mottershaw
Lieutenant Thomas Mainwaring	Corporal Thomas Comberbach
Cornet John Turner	Drummer Owen Wollam
Sergeant Thomas Parry	Drummer Ralph Knowsley
Sergeant John Picket	Clerk John Higginson
Corporal John Corke	

Moreover, between 20 August 1643 and 30 April 1644 (the date upon which it was disbanded) Bramhall's command mustered 60 soldiers.[14]

As far as the sources allow, it is possible to trace the service history of some members of Bramhall's dragoons. Lieutenant Ralph Burroughs, who appears to have left the company by 20 May, could be the 'Lieutenant Burroughs' included in warrants for Sir William Brereton's own troop of horse in March and April 1643, before his commission ended on 31 July 1644.[15] Perhaps after the loss of Sergeant Major Bramhall and his officers at Loppington, Burroughs returned to lead the remainder of their dragoons. Thomas Mainwaring, the company's original cornet, is listed in the 20 May muster roll as lieutenant, although Malbon assigned him his former rank in his narrative of the Loppington fight on 28 September 1643. Mainwaring (who is also listed as lieutenant in Bramhall's accounts) was held in Shrewsbury, and was still there on 18 December. He had evidently been released by 6 March 1644 when he received £15 10s. in pay, while in April 1644 John Bramhall expended the sum of £3, to be 'left in the hands of Lieutenant Mainwaring at my coming out of prison to give to my soldiers'. Furthermore, on 28 September Mainwaring was given £5 by the same 'to pay his fees when he was a prisoner in Shrewsbury'. It is evident that Thomas later served as lieutenant to Sergeant Major Bramhall's troop of horse. On 18 May 1644 both his and Bramhall's mounts were included in a payment to a farrier for shoeing mounts, whereas he received pay as a member of the troop on 23 October 1644.[16]

John Turner began as sergeant in Bramhall's dragoons, but going by the muster roll above he been promoted to cornet by 20 May 1643. After his release as prisoner of war in late 1643 or early 1644 Turner was promoted to lieutenant, serving later in that rank under Captain Godfrey Gimbert in the Cheshire army, receiving pay until at least July 1647.[17] Similarly, Thomas Comberbach began his service in Bramhall's company as a dragoon, but he was a corporal by May 1643 and had been promoted to sergeant by August, when the recently promoted major's mother sent her son £30 to discharge his soldiers' quarters by Cornet Turner and Sergeant Comberbach, following the capture of Eccleshall Castle. He was paid as cornet on 12 August 1644, but this was under the auspices of Bramhall's troop of horse, which had recently been formed. On 2 November 'Lieutenant Comberbach' received £5 for Bramhall's troopers. He also appears in a pay warrant of 7 June 1645 for the

14 BL, MS Harley 2128, fols 23v., 32r.
15 TNA, SP28/152/7, fols 5r., 7v., 9v.
16 BL, MS Harley 2128, fols 25r., 26r.; TNA, SP28/30/7, fol. 648v.
17 TNA, SP28/124/1, fols 72r.–78r., 114r.

unit.[18] Dragoon Ralph Knowsley was promoted to drummer before 20 May 1643 and on 9 June was paid 8s. 'to mend his drum'. He later acted as corporal in the company of Captain Gimbert.[19]

Table 22: Horses received from the State and lost in service by Sergeant Major Bramhall's Company (BL, MS Harley 2128, fols 34r.–v.)

Received:	
In London	60
On arrival in Cheshire	14
From Sir George Booth	14
Total	88
Lost upon service:	
At Salt Heath [Hopton Heath]	34
At Hanmer	8
At Tern Hill	6
At Loppington	27
At Leigh Bridge	4
At Longford	24
At Kelsall	12
To mount Scottish officers that came under Brereton's command	9
Lost as draught horses	4
Total	128

Table 23: Arms (firelocks) received from the State and lost in service by Sergeant Major Bramhall's Company (BL, MS Harley 2128, fol. 35r.)

Received:	
In London	20
At Nantwich	10
Out of Sir Thomas Myddelton's store	14
At Leek	6
Total	50
Lost upon service:	
At Salt Heath	8
At Tern Hill	16
At Hanmer	14
At Loppington	30
At Longford	24
Total	82

Captain Gwilliam (William) Goldegay's Company

Goldegay, probably a professional soldier, led one of the companies of dragoons that Brereton brought from London to Cheshire during December 1642 and

18 BL, MS Harley 2128, fols 25r., 26v., 28r.

19 BL, MS Harley 2128, fols 21r., 23r.–25r., 28v.; TNA, SP28/124/1, fols 72v.–78r.

January 1643. A copy of a letter from Goldegay to Sir William Brereton on 16 December 1645 has his Christian name, though somewhat illegibly written, as *Gwilliam* (William) or *Gawen* (Gavin), probably indicating his Welsh identity. Additionally, an extract in the Ottley MSS gives his forename as *William*, while it seems in other letters in which he is referred to he is named *George*, but it appears likely that this represents a misunderstanding on the part of Brereton's copyist.[20] Thus, on the weight of the evidence, it would be reasonable to assign the Christian name of *Gwilliam* to the officer. His earliest appearance in the documents is in a warrant of November 1642, in which as quartermaster (perhaps in the army of the Earl of Essex) he was tasked to conduct three sakers from the Tower of London to Reading.[21] Goldegay was commissioned captain of a company of Cheshire dragoons on 6 December 1642, and he with his men was listed in London where the unit was recruited. Lieutenant Monkes and Cornet John Marum were paid with the command on 15 April 1643, whilst a warrant for Captain Goldegay's pay from Ralph Judson is dated 19 August of the same year.[22]

Captain Goldegay's dragoons played an important part in winning the small victory outside Nantwich that allowed Brereton control of the town and enable him to establish his headquarters there. During the skirmish the Parliamentarians, consisting of Sergeant Major James Lothian, with 50 dragoons led by Captains Captain Bramhall and Goldegay, arrived in the town before Sir Thomas Aston. Clearing a lane of Aston's troops, 'Captain Goldegay dismounted his dragooners, and turned his horses upon them, which brought them into confusion, and charged upon them very sore'.[23] During the action Goldegay was wounded, and his lieutenant (Joseph Banbury) and two soldiers were killed. Showing their inexperience, the dragoons neglected to leave anyone to hold their mounts – which were taken by the Royalists for charging cavalry – but it was a sound beginning. Captain Goldegay was absent from duty for most of the year, recovering from his wounds, but he reappeared under the command of the Shropshire Committee in October 1643, and claimed pay on 1 November. Although it is not clear if he had any troops under him, William was a sergeant major at Wem in October 1644, and by November 1645 he had risen to lieutenant colonel, operating in North Wales with Mytton, and Cheshire forces under Jones and Lothian.[24] Goldegay's former dragoon company was probably dissolved in 1644, and its officers and soldiers dispersed to other commands.

20 BL, MS Add. 11332, fol. 36; Ottley Papers, 206; *BLB*, II, 800 and note 1; Wanklyn, 'Landed Society', pp.242–3.

21 TNA, WO55/1937 (warrants relating to stores).

22 TNA, SP28/225/3, fols 865v.–866r.; SP28/208, fol. 20v.; SP28/196/1, fols 16v., 12v.

23 *Cheshire's Successe*; Malbon, p.20.

24 BL, MS Add. 11332, fol. 75r.–v.; *BLB*, II, 1224–5.

Captain John Lea's Company

The certificate of John Lea, gentleman of Stafford states: 'Captain Lea hath been a very faithful servant to the parliament, engaging not only on several engagements, freely endangering his life (being once shot through the body). And also we further certify that the aforesaid Captain John Lea was in actual service from 7 November 1642 until 12 November 1643'. It further records that his pay arrears 'for the above service, for 370 days due £370. Paid £50 in London, total due to him £320'.[25] He evidently received his commission in London and must have raised his company in the city. In the words of Dore:

> he held it for the whole of that remarkable period after Brereton's return to the North-West when, against all the odds, the Parliamentarians gained control of Lancashire, most of Cheshire, North Staffordshire and North Salop. Brereton's statement that Lea was with him [in a letter of 3 November 1645] 'the first night when we came into Cheshire' (which was when Aston was defeated and Nantwich captured), taken with the frequent mention of dragoons in the accounts of Malbon and others of the raids, surprises and minor battles that followed and the testimony of the certificate that Lea 'upon several engagements freely adventured his life' leave little doubt that Lea must have played a useful part.[26]

After the taking of Eccleshall Castle on 30 August 1643 Captain Lea and his soldiers were rewarded with £15 from the profits of the sale of its goods.[27] Lea's absence from the records after this, and the mention in his certificate of him being 'once shot through the body' (probably indicating a severe wound), suggests that he did not return to military service after November 1643. Captain Simon Finch, a Royalist officer who changed sides after the relief of Nantwich in February 1644, appears to have taken control of Lea's company.

Captain John Cheswis's Company

John Cheswis was commissioned captain of dragoons by Sir George Booth on 5 November 1642.[28] His company was raised for service in Cheshire by the spring of 1643. Warrants dated 17 April, 10 May, 18 June and 8 August 1643 relate to his pay.[29] He was captured during operations in Shropshire (perhaps at Loppington on 11 September 1643), although he is mentioned as being a prisoner of war in Shrewsbury in March 1644. On his release in April Captain Cheswis took command of a troop of horse (this may have been a new unit or his dragoons were upgraded). He was paid on five occasions around this time, which could have been associated with the paying and

25 TNA, SP28/252/1, fol. 184v.; SP28/265/1, fols 68r.–v., 70r.
26 *BLB*, II, 809, note 2.
27 CRO, ZCR/63/2/702, fol. 24r.
28 TNA, SP28/267/3, fols 112v.–117r.
29 TNA, SP28/196/1, fols 6v., 14r., 18r., 21v.

equipping of this new troop.[30] During the summer of 1644 he was involved with the Cheshire horse in a number of operations. According to Malbon, 'Upon Thursday 8 May 1644 Captain Cheswis, with a few horse, issued forth of the town [of Nantwich], and near Cholmondeley Hall he took five men and horse with their arms, and slew one, which five he brought prisoners to Nantwich.'[31] John Cheswis was killed in action at Oswestry on 20 July 1644, his widow, Lady Leigh, being provided with a pension of £50 per annum on the authority of the Council of War and deputy lieutenants.[32] The following served in his dragoon company and possibly his later troop:

Lieutenant James Geirn
Corporal Jeremiah Clough
Corporal James Gibson[33]

Captain Gilbert Gerard's Company

Captain Gilbert Gerard raised a company of dragoons under the command of Captain Richard Littler in early 1643. It appears to have been recruited in north-west Cheshire (and probably more specifically, the town of Northwich and its environs). Littler may have been a local man, but going by Sir William Brereton's other dragoon captains, he was more likely a professional soldier. The company's role seems to have included the safeguarding of the strategically important area of upper Bucklow Hundred, including the Parliamentarian garrisons of Halton and Norton, and in particular patrolling the various passes over the River Mersey at Runcorn, the Weaver at Frodsham Bridge, the ford on the salt marshes at Frodsham Ditch, and perhaps Acton Bridge and ford to the south. As such, Gerard's–Littler's dragoons received pay, horses and equipment from local sources in particular. During late 1643 the constables of Mere laid out £2 9s. 4d. for 'a horse, men and arms under Captain Littler', while their colleagues at Dutton provided pay to the company.[34]

Similarly, two undated warrants relate to the supply of dragoon mounts and food. Captain Richard Littler instructed Thomas Woollett, one of the constables of Aston township 'to provide Sergeant Hall [with] two horses, one of your own, the other from George Guest, for scout horses this night for our safeties and the safety of this township'. Also, the constables of Bucklow Hundred charged those of Aston and Aston Grange with bringing each day two horse load of oats to Great Budworth, presumably for the dragoon horses. The township of Aston was also responsible for finding pay for Litter's soldiers. A warrant issued by Colonel Henry Brooke on 2 September 1643

30 TNA, SP28/31/4, fol. 431v.; SP28/196/1, fols 3v.–4r., 6v., 18r., 21r.

31 Malbon, p.128.

32 TNA, SP28/196/3, fol. 490v.; SP28/267/3, fol. 115r.; SP28/128/13, fol. 26r.; BL, MS Harley 2166, fol. 130r.

33 TNA, SP28/225/3, fol. 682v.; E121/3/1, fol. 287v.; E121/5/7/351, fol. 31r.

34 BL, MS Harley 2128, fols 166r., 60v.

informed the officials, 'I formerly sent out several leys to them for collecting of moneys for the dragoons and as you are, as appears, behind with your payment. These are henceforth to charge and command you that you are besides with and withal four weeks' pay more at 6s. 6d. per week, which you are to supply at Norton before 7 [September] 1643 to my clerk.'[35]

The command was taken over by Captain William Wright following Richard Littler's death on 2 February 1644. Wright had served as lieutenant to the company, being paid with Sergeant James Harwood on 25 November 1643.[36] The testament of Captain Wright, dated 12 August 1647, states that he received his commission on 11 April 1644, serving in command of the company until he was stood down by Sir William Brereton on 30 September 1644.[37] During the Spring of 1644 the Bucklow sequestration committee disbursed the sum of £9 15s. 3d. to 'Captain Wright for the Northwich garrison', thus confirming his connection to Colonel John Leigh, Gilbert Gerard (by then lieutenant colonel) and the town itself.[38] During the period of its service, the dragoon company consisted of three officers, two sergeants, three corporals and 36 soldiers. John Witter, son of a Frodsham yeoman, acted as cornet before taking up a commission as ensign to Sergeant Major John Trevis of Colonel Leigh's foot regiment, whilst later serving as lieutenant to Lieutenant Colonel Richard Brooke in 1645 and Captain John Brooke in early 1646.[39]

Captain Simon Finch's Company

Simon Finch came over to England with the Royalist army from Ireland in November 1643 as a captain in Sir Michael Ernle's regiment of foot. He was captured on 25 January 1644 following the defeat at Nantwich and brought by Sir William Brereton to London where he was imprisoned at Southwark. Finch consequently joined the forces of Parliament, although his younger brothers continued to serve in the Royalist Anglo-Irish regiments. A deposition of William Wilbraham (presumably a Parliamentarian agent), dated 13 May 1644 states:

> that about a month since this examinant being in London fell into company with one Captain Finch as he informed this deponent was a captain in one of the regiments that came out of Ireland and was taken prisoner near Nantwich in service for His Majesty. Who told the examinant that he was taken prisoner near Nantwich and was brought to Acton Church where his money was taken from him from where he was brought prisoner to Nantwich, and that since he hath accepted of a commission to be captain of a troop of Horse under Sir William Brereton, which Commission captain Finch showed this deponent and further said not.

35 AA, unlisted warrants, dated 20 November 1643 x 2 February 1644, 2 September 1643.
36 TNA, SP28/152/9, fol. 15r.
37 BL, MS Harley 2128, fol. 166r.; TNA: SP28/208, fol. 33v.; E121/351, fols 63r.–v.
38 BL, MS Harley 2137, fol. 151r.–v.
39 TNA, SP28/224/1, fol. 24v.; SP28/124/1, fols 40v.–54r.; E121/5/7/351, fols 63v., 65v.; E121/5/7/43, fol. 44r.

The following day Simon's brother, Captain John Finch signed a receipt for:

> the several goods hereafter named which said goods were left there in the custody of the said Elizabeth, being late the goods of Captain Simon Finch under Sir Michael Ernle's regiment; which said Simon was taken prisoner at Nantwich in the county of Chester, in His Majesty's service. But since that time hath forfeited the said goods by taking up arms against His Majesty under the command of Sir William Brereton as it doth appear upon oath taken before the said mayor and others, as also by good testimony to the right honourable Lord Byron, lord field marshal-general, who by his warrant under his hand and seal hereunto annexed, hath given to me the said John Finch all the said goods so remaining in their custody. An old pair of spurs, fifteen points, a little white pitcher, a plush jump with silver clasps, a taffeta doublet and cloth breeches, a cloak lined with plush, a pair of shammy sleeves, a red scarf, three coarse linen towels, an old trunk and £15 in money, which said goods were all praised to £3 8s. 2d., besides the money, which made up in the whole £19 13s. 2d. All which said goods and money, I John Finch do acknowledge to have received, of the said Randle Holme, and Elizabeth his wife, by virtue of the said warrant from the said Lord Byron and thereof of every part and parcel thereof. I do hereby acquit and discharge them the said Randle Holme and Elizabeth his wife their and either of their executors and administrators from the said goods. And I do promise and assume hereby, both for myself and Robert Finch, lieutenant under Captain Edmund Langley who is to have part thereof, both by my Lord Byron's direction and my promise to the said Lord Byron.[40]

Finch was a highly valued officer who distinguished himself on a number of occasions. On 31 January 1645 the Shropshire Committee wrote to Brereton from Wem, 'We desire Captain Finch and his company to be in the party you send, for he is well known to us.'[41] After the fall of Chester Finch led his dragoons into North Wales with the forces under Colonel Mytton. With Captain Gimbert's men they participated in the siege of Holt Castle, which proved an arduous task. Mytton clearly placed much value on the effectiveness of these experienced and skilled troops, hence reporting on 8 April 1646:

> The siege of Holt hath of late been of great difficulty and hazard to those few men I have there, for the drawing off of the Cheshire firelocks from that service without my privity gave the enemy an advantage to burn the guard the firelocks kept (which cost the country much to fortify), and about forty dwelling-houses more in the town, and exposed my men (who lay in open quarters, and fewer in number than the enemy within were) to their power, which necessitated my men to be upon continual duty.[42]

By then the siege operations against Lichfield Close had begun. Companies of the Cheshire foot under Sir William Brereton's command at Lichfield were

40 BL, MS Harley 2135, fols 69v.–71r.

41 BL, MS Add. 11331, fol. 137r.; *BLB*, I, 1.

42 Phillips, *Memoirs*, II, p.302; Tucker, *North Wales and Chester in the Civil War*, p.92.

badly in arrears of pay, including an unpaid bounty promised for their part in the capture of Chester. On 14 April 1646 Captains Finch and Gimbert received between them £102 18s. 'for pay for their companies that came upon service at Lichfield in discharge of the month's gratuity upon taking Chester'.[43] As Carr and Atherton suggest:

> These were the only companies where this money came from Brereton, although payment was made to other individuals, and may indicate some competition between Brereton and the Cheshire committee for the service of these elite troops who had spearheaded most of the operations against Chester. The rest of the Cheshire foot were paid their gratuity by the county committee and sent on their way to Lichfield piecemeal as it secured the money.[44]

Sir William was in much need of the dragoons, who had served so effectively at various other sieges. On 1 April Lieutenant John Turner of Gimbert's company travelled from Holt to Lichfield 'on special service' and was reimbursed his expenses by Brereton. It is likely that Finch's and Gimbert's entire commands did not arrive until early May, however, as Captain Gimbert, six officers and 10 of his dragoons were paid at Holt from Cheshire, while both captains received a month's wages there on 21 April from the same source.[45] On 13 May Finch signed a letter with Gimbert and the 'Cheshire Commanders at Lichfield' to Sir William Brereton, complaining about lack of pay. Even so, his company was evidently much involved in the siege operations. On 25 May Brereton had reported to John Swinfen, one of his associates in Westminster, the details of a recent 'desperate sally' by the Royalist garrison upon the Parliamentarian earthworks, during which (among others) 'five or six of Captain Finch's firelocks [were] wounded'. Moreover, its junior officers were described on 12 June as 'being upon guard'.[46] Among the muster rolls of the Cheshire forces at the siege, drawn up 10 days later, present under Captain Finch were one lieutenant, one cornet, two sergeants, one drummer, three corporals and 76 dragoons. On 30 May, and 5 and 12 June 1646 payments were made to the following:[47]

Lieutenant Mather	Corporal James More
Ensign Sydes	Corporal Darby Malone
Sergeant Robert Lathom	Drummer Richard Hawkes
Sergeant Henry Dayes	Drummer John Carter
Corporal Hugh Stanley	Clerk Henry Wilkes

It is probably unsurprising that the later military career of Simon Finch was an active one. He became an officer of the Chester garrison in 1647, commanding a company of foot that from the evidence of a contemporary

43 TNA, SP16/513/1, fol. 79v.
44 *CWS*, p.59.
45 TNA, SP28/37/639–40, unfol.
46 BCL, MS 595611, p.231; TNA: SP16/513/1, fol. 91r.
47 BCL, MS 595611, pp.203, 252–3; TNA: SP16/513/1, fols 70r., 72r., 87v.

muster roll contained a number of officers and dragoons formerly under his command.[48] On 22 August 1650 Finch received a commission as major in Colonel Robert Duckenfield's militia regiment of Cheshire foot, and at the Battle of Worcester, as its lieutenant colonel, he was singled out for his actions. When Duckenfield's militia regiment disbanded Simon took command of five companies to be posted to Ireland to reinforce Sir Hardress Waller's regiment of foot (four of which were led by officers who had previously served with Finch in Brereton's army). In 1651 he also sat at Lord Derby's court martial. By December 1656 Finch was serving in Ireland and continued there until 1659.[49]

The following also appear in undated (but possibly 1645) pay warrants:

Cornet Walton	Corporal Thomas Wilson
Cornet Randle Hall	Corporal Hugh Stanley
Sergeant John Walker	Drummer John Normansell
Corporal Thomas Warren	Drummer John Berry[50]

Captain Godfrey Gimbert's Company

Captain Godfrey Gimbert was probably a professional soldier and may have previously served in Ireland. He began his service in Cheshire as cornet of dragoons, and had received a commission as captain by December 1643 when he was paid in that rank by Richard Stelfox, Sir William Brereton's clerk. On 18 July 1644 Godfrey was paid the sum of £10 for the completing of his company.[51] Gimbert is listed in command of 60 firelocks (dragoons) in April 1645, who early the following month were engaged in besieging Beeston Castle. As commander of 'Fort Royal', the Parliamentarian blockhouse situated opposite the fortress's outer gates, on 9 May Gimbert received a letter of defiance from the Royalist governor, Captain William Vallett. Lord Byron, the governor of Chester would later report of the officer 'Beeston Castle, commanded by Captain Vallet, formerly an officer in my regiment of horse, both which places [Lathom House in Lancashire and Beeston] were defended with as much gallantry and resolution as possibly could be expected, and not rendered till forced thereunto by the uttermost of extremities'.[52] Vallett's letter to Gimbert is reproduced below:

> I understand by the bearer that you intend to burn the house. Indeed it should not have been left for you to have done it, that I did commiserate a poor widow and two poor orphans in so much that I was content rather to shew that extremity

48 TNA, E121/5/7/misc., fols 59r.–v.

49 *CSPD, 1650*, p.509; *1651–2*, pp.117–8; *CSP Ireland, 1647–1660*, p.289; C.H. Firth (ed.), *The Memoirs of Edmund Ludlow, Lieutenant-General of the Horse in the army of the Commonwealth of England, 1625–1672* (Oxford: Clarendon Press, 1894), I, p.323; Firth and Davies, *Regimental History*, I, pp.357–8; II, p.446.

50 TNA, SP28/225/4, fol. 753v.; E121/5/7/351, fols 46v., 52v.

51 TNA, SP28/196/1, fol. 13r.; SP28/152/7, fol. 8v.; E121/5/7/43, fol. 1r.

52 Byron, 'Account of the Siege of Chester', 23.

> to suffer it to be a den of thieves and traitors. But if you take this course you prevent that which I might, upon good reasons, do myself and I shall make it such a precedent as the surveyors of your works – Aldersey, Spurstow, Metcalf *cum multiisaliis* of your traitorous faction shall repent. And whereas you flatter yourself with hopes of taking this place, I scorn your threats and attempts, and the forces of your best general, for all his great ram's head.[53]

To this Gimbert replied:

> From my royal fort which stands for the confusion of a den of traitors in Beeston Castle. Governor, I have received your civil expressions in a scandalous paper. You said you delighted in civility; it appears in your beastlike expressions. You told me you would not be tied to conditions. And do you think to tie [me] that am at liberty, and that by you whom I keep close prisoner amongst your anti-Christian, Babylonian crew and will wait to expend my dearest blood upon the destruction of such traitors to king and state as that den of blasphemers are whereof you are chief. You cause me to burn the house by your expressions. For your scandals to my general, you put it upon him whose shoes you are not worthy to clean. But I suppose you take the counsel to write this letter with the asses whom you took prisoners.

The 'house' that the two commanders were bickering over was evidently located between the castle and the siegeworks, rather than Beeston Hall which Rupert had set fire to in March 1645. Malbon offers the most likely culprit in his description of how in November 1644 a sally from the garrison surprised the Parliamentarian guard, 'being in one Owen's house standing at the foot of the castle hill at dinner and very careless'.[54]

Of Gimbert's later military career, he was an officer in the Chester garrison during the early months of 1647. In November of the following year, orders were given to pay him £20 towards his arrears from money owed for the Royalist Colonel Robert Werden's ransom. He had been captured defending Chester on 18 January 1645 and compounded for delinquency. However, the money was still unpaid on 9 July 1650 when Gimbert was recorded as dead. Colonel Robert Duckenfield wrote to the committee for compounding asking for the money to be paid to his widow, whom he described as 'very poor and having lost her husband in the service of the state'.[55]

In spring 1646 Captain Gimbert's dragoons, with those of Finch's company, participated in besieging Holt Castle, but by mid May they had joined the remaining Cheshire forces at Lichfield Close. Whilst at Holt on 14 April Gimbert's men received their Chester gratuity (their captain getting his bonus of £51 2s.), and 10 days afterwards they had a month's pay.[56] The company had arrived at Lichfield Close by 21 May 1646. On 23 May,

53 BL, MS Add. 11331, fol. 101r.–v.; *BLB*, I, 459–60.

54 Malbon, p.153. See also Dore, 'Beeston', p.111; John Barratt, *"Civil War Stronghold": Beeston Castle at War 1642–45* (Birkenhead: Caracole, 1995), p.7.

55 TNA, SP28/224/2, fol. 267r.; *Calendar of Committee for Compounding*, I, p.269; *CJ*, VII, p.39.

56 TNA, SP28/37/639–40, unfol.; SP16/513/1, fol. 79v.

assembled with the rest of the Cheshire forces at the siege the command mustered:

Lieutenant John Turner	Corporal Richard Osman
Cornet John Urmston	Corporal John Ball
Quartermaster Thomas Bentley	Corporal John Forshall
Sergeant Leigh	Drummer Richard Bradbury
Sergeant Arthur Dickinson	65 dragoons[57]

Captain Joseph Holt's Company

Like other Parliamentarian dragoon commanders in Cheshire Joseph may have been a professional soldier. He was probably the Cornet Holt who received pay with Bramhall's dragoons on 22 July 1643; the Hugh Holt who was reimbursed for a payment of cloth whilst at Northampton in December is likely to have been the company's first quartermaster, and later received a commission as captain of pioneers in the army.[58] A warrant for pay to Captain Joseph Holt dates from 22 June 1644,[59] and it is conceivable that he took command of the dragoons of Gerard's company when the commission of its officer commanding, Captain William Wright ended on 30 September 1644. On 10 February the sequestrators of Bucklow Hundred paid the sum of £1 6s. 8d. to Holt for pasturing two horses in Dutton Park.[60] Gerard's dragoons had been previously supplied with weapons, pay, provisions and mounts by the constables of the Bucklow townships of Mere, Dutton, Aston and Aston Grange, possibly in the form of standing orders.[61] On 30 April 1645 Joseph Holt was serving as captain of a company of 80 firelocks in the Cheshire Parliamentarian army.

Captain Holt was further listed on 27 May 1645 as leading a detachment of 25 dragoons, being part of a force of Cheshire soldiers assembled by Major James Lothian in readiness for a rendezvous with the New Model Army in Leicestershire following the Battle of Naseby.[62] His company saw action at Denbigh Green on 1 November 1645 against a Royalist force commanded by Sir William Vaughan. As Lancaster reported, 'they [the Parliamentarians] were in a lane flanked by the enemy's horse and dragoons, so that they were forced to make good that pass with the forlorn hope and Cheshire dragoons, under the command of Captains Finch and Holt, stout and resolute men. These with the forlorn hope behaved themselves gallantly and maintained the pass until the foot came up'.[63] On 18 December 1645 Captain Holt's

57 BCA, MS 595611, pp.252–3.
58 BL, MS Harley 2128, fols 27v., 20r.; MS Add. 11331, fol. 113.
59 TNA, SP28/225/3, fol. 673r.
60 BL, MS Harley 2137, fol. 200r.
61 BL, MS Harley 2128, fols 60v., 166r.
62 BL, MS Add. 11331, fols 45v., 165v.; *BLB*, I, 385, 654.
63 *A True Relation of a Great Victory obtained by the Parliament Forces, &c., against the King's Forces, &c., near Denbigh*; BL, MS Add. 11332, fol. 76; *BLB*, II, 801; Tucker, *North Wales and Chester in the Civil War*, pp.61–2.

soldiers received pay with the two other companies of Cheshire firelocks, and following the fall of Chester he and his company received gratuities for their part in the siege. Moreover, the total sum disbursed to 'Captain Joseph Holt, and his officers and soldiers' by treasurer Croxton was £811 5s. 10d.[64] The company was still drawing pay on 26 November 1646 when Lieutenant John Reading signed a receipt for it as 'Lieutenant to Captain Joseph Holt'.[65] Undated warrants also exist for Sergeant/Cornet Thomas Canary and Sergeant Hugh Jordaine.[66]

Captain Kempton's Company

On 15 and 24 July 1643 the Cheshire Parliamentarian collector Ralph Judson made payments to 'Captain Kempton's soldiers'.[67] Evidence that Kempton served as a captain of dragoons in the Cheshire forces comes from references to his clerk, John Urmston, who had been involved in paying dragoons at the beginning of 1643, and listed as 'cornet to Captain Kempton' in warrants dated 15 July and December of the same year. Although Kempton is not directly stated to be a dragoon officer, Cornet Urmston later served in Captain Godfrey Gimbert's company at the siege of Holt Castle in April 1646 and later with the Cheshire forces at Lichfield Close.[68] However, a list of pensioners made at Stockport on 8 December 1653 includes Randle Cartwright, 'a soldier under Captain Kempton, wounded in the right arm at Hanmer'.[69] The action in question occurred on 20 June 1643 when according to Malbon, 'Colonel Brereton's troop, Captain Bulkeley and many other troopers and dragoons' from Nantwich were ambushed and defeated by Royalist forces with the loss of a number of officers and men. Although it is evident that Captain John Bramhall's company were present (losing eight horses and 14 firearms), such references suggest that Captain Kempton commanded the remaining dragoons in Flintshire.[70]

Captain/Captain-Lieutenant James Stockport's Company

Two references associate this officer with the Cheshire firelocks. A pay warrant to John Berry describes him as 'drummer in Captain James Stockport's company of dragoons in Colonel Michael Jones's regiment'.[71] In June 1645 Jones succeeded Brereton as colonel of his regiment of horse following his recall to Parliament, and it would seem he retained his colonelcy when Sir

64 BL, MS Add. 11333, fols 30r.–v., 118v.; TNA, SP28/224, fol. 202v.-r.; SP28/128/13, fol. 18r.; *BLB*, II, 1040, 1235.
65 TNA, SP28/224/1, fol. 184v.
66 TNA, E121/5/7/351, fols 33r., 39r., 55v.
67 TNA, SP28/196/1, fol. 11v.
68 TNA, E121/5/7/351, fols 28v.–29r.; BCL, MS 595611, pp.252–3.
69 Earwaker, *East Cheshire*, II, p.69.
70 Malbon, pp.62–3; BL, MS Harley 2128, fols 34r.–35r.
71 TNA, E121/5/7/351, fol. 53r.

William returned to active military service later in the year. This included the short campaign in North Wales which culminated in the Parliamentarian victory at Denbigh Green on 1 November. A Drummer John Berry served in Captain Joseph Holt's dragoons, and perhaps Stockport temporarily took command of this company between the wounding of Holt at Chester on 21 September 1645 and his recovery by Denbigh Green, when he was commended for his conduct.

Nevertheless, on 12 January 1646 the county treasurer disbursed the sum of £466 6s. 'to the Cheshire dragoons as appeareth under the hands of Captains Finch, Gimbert and Holt, with £50 paid to Captain Stockport for his dragoons'.[72] This implies that the latter had a company, or at the least a detachment under his command, although this might have been a temporary appointment as he appears nowhere else in this role. As no other officer of that name is known to have served with the Cheshire army, this must have been Captain-Lieutenant James Stockport, who had spent much of the war leading Colonel Henry Mainwaring's own company of foot, and in early 1645 probably the remains of his regiment during fighting at Farndon Bridge against troops under Prince Maurice, who were attempting to relieve Chester. If so, his record shows that he was a highly experienced and trusted officer.

Captain Collinson's Company

A payment of £8 10s. was made by Richard Stelfox on 12 March 1643 to 'Captain Collinson's dragoons'.[73] Nothing more is known of this officer, although it is possible that he took temporary command of Captain William Goldegay's company following his absence from duty for most of year owing to wounds received during the Nantwich skirmish in January 1643.

Sergeant Major Morris's Company

On 23 December Sir William Brereton disbursed the sum of £20 'to Major Morris for his company of firelocks'.[74] The identity of this officer is uncertain and he appears in no other references in connection with the Cheshire forces. A John Morris served in the royal army in Ireland, then came to England, but defected to Parliament after the fall of Liverpool on 1 November 1644. He joined the Northern Army as sergeant major and was promoted to lieutenant colonel in May 1645 during the siege of Pontefract, only to change sides again three years later.[75] If it was him, he may have been (like Captain Finch and others) an able and experienced officer whose services Brereton was keen to retain, if only briefly.

---

72 BL, MS Add. 11333, fol. 118v.; *BLB*, II, 1236.

73 TNA, SP28/196/3, fol. 4r.

74 TNA, SP28/152/7, fol. 16r.

75 Jennifer Jones, 'The War in the North: The Northern Parliamentary Army in the English Civil War, 1642–1645', PhD thesis (York University, Toronto, 1994), pp.394–5.

Colour Plate Captions & Commentaries

Plate A Ensign of the Cheshire Foot

The ensign carries the furled colour belonging to a company of one of the six regiments of the Cheshire foot, and wears a collar or gorget, denoting his status as a commissioned officer, about his neck. References describe a 'regiment of all black colours' marching into Lancashire from Cheshire in August 1644, which on other evidence, could have been Sir William Brereton's own. This officer's black silk scarf is conjectural, but given that the army was nominally part of the Northern Association in early 1643, and some officers received their commissions directly from Lord Fairfax, it is possible that (even temporarily) they wore such devices in similar fashion to known examples of men of that association from Yorkshire and Lancashire.

Plate B Trooper of Sir William Brereton's Own Troop

The trooper is dressed in the requisite apparel and accoutrements of a harquebusier, complete with sleeved buffcoat, broadsword and carbine. He is identified as a member of Brereton's own troop by his crimson taffeta scarf, worn about his body. Whether other parliamentarian troops raised in Cheshire wore scarfs of the same hue is unknown, although it is entirely possible. This mounted soldier wears a riding coat, constructed of heavy frieze wool, 'to keep both himself and [horse] furniture from the violence of the weather'. Such items were commonly issued to the Cheshire horse, while quantities of green, red and yellow Welsh flannel were obtained by Brereton's men in 1645.

Plate C Musketeer

The foot represented the mainstay of most seventeenth-century armies. This musketeer is dressed in a soldiers' coat of grey russet cloth, which were issued in some quantity to Sir William's infantry. Armed with a matchlock musket, he carries a bandolier, sword and knapsack, and marches 'at the shoulder' with lighted match. He may possibly have been issued with 3lbs of powder, 12 yards of match and 60 bullets 'in marching order' as per some of his colleagues. The quality of the musketry of Brereton's infantry regiments was remarked upon by various commanders.

Plate D Dragoon

By all accounts Brereton's dragoons were well-armed, equipped and mounted, as befitted their specialized role. The example here wears a short grey soldiers' coat, buttoned at the front, and is equipped with a doglock/snaphaunce musket, which were given to Bramhall's company at least in November 1642. The weapon is fitted with a sling for carrying on horseback and ease of deployment when in enemy contact. It is possible that like the cavalry, dragoons were issued riding coats. For riding, this soldier wears leather gaiters with shoes, although there is no direct evidence for the supply of the former to the Cheshire parliamentarian dragoons, and one issue of boots with spurs is known.

Notes on cavalry cornets by Dr Lesley Prince

The colours carried by cavalry units of all the armies during the civil wars that raged over the British Isles, *c.* 1642–1651, followed a pattern used in the Thirty Years' War on the Continent. These flags, called cornets (as were the officers that carried them), were generally around two feet square, and were painted and fringed. From what evidence we have, the fringes used in the British Isles tended to be parti-coloured, one of the colours reflecting the field colour. Although the cavalry was regimented, the cornets did not always reflect regimental affiliation. The ones that did, such as Cromwell's double regiment, the 'Ironsides' (which all had red fields whilst in the Eastern Association Army, and blue fields when transferred to the New Model Army), and the Earl of Essex's cavalry (all carrying orange tawny fields), seem to have been the exception. Most units, it seems, comprised a motley of cornets, the designs reflecting the choice of the commanding captain. The designs, similarly, were varied. From what evidence we have, Parliamentarian captains favoured religious or political slogans on simple designs comprising scrolls. Others, however, were much more elaborate, often including punning slogans and comprising elaborate images. Royalists often favoured scurrilous or insulting slogans, such as the famous 'Come Out You Cuckold' cornet of Sir Horatio Cary, otherwise their designs reflected the same sort of designs as the Parliamentarians. Scottish units preferred designs referring to the Solemn League and Covenant, and used heraldic elements far more than their English counterparts. From what little we know of Irish cornets, these tended to favour Catholic imagery.

Plate E Cornet of Sir William Brereton

'*Sable semee* [covered all over or strewn with small charges] with stars *or*; in fess, a label *fleched*, its points turned, and endorsed, forming two Cs, motto: *DEVS NOBISCVM* ['God be with us']; fringed *sable* and *argent*'.

(BL, MS Add. 5247, fol. 19a; DWL, MS Modern 12.7, fol. 11r.; NAM 6208-1: 'Standards Taken in the Civil Wars', p.149; John Thomas Blount, *The Art of Making Devises* (London: 2nd edn, 1655), p.78; John Prestwich, *Prestwich's Respublica* (London, 1787), p.33; Alan R. Young (ed.), *The English Emblem Tradition: Volume 3: Emblematic Flag Devices of the English Civil Wars, 1642–1660* (University of Toronto Press, 1995), p.42.

Plate E Cornet of Lieutenant Colonel Michael Jones

[Erroneously ascribed as 'Colonell Jones of Shropshire' in Turmile]: 'argent on a scroll of three folds, its points forming two Cs, indorsed all of gold, and thereon in Roman sable letters *VERITAS ERIT VICTRIX*'('Truth be victorious').

(DWL, MS Modern 12.7, fol. 48r.; Prestwich, *Respublica*, p.40).

Plate F Cornet of Colonel Robert Duckenfield

'Argent on a scroll of three folds, its points forming two Cs, indorsed all of gold, and thereon in Roman sable letters *VERITAS ERIT VICTRIX*' ('Truth be victorious').

(DWL, MS Modern 12.7, fol. 40r.; Prestwich, *Respublica*, p. 40).

Plate F Cornet of Colonel George Booth

'Gules, on a plain vert; on a white horse trotting, comparisoned or, with an armed knight, his face in profile, in his helmet a plume of yellow feathers; over his right shoulder, and under his left arm, a sash of the same; in his right hand a dagger held in pale, hilted as the last; over all, in chief, a scroll, and thereon, *NON SINE CAUSA*; fringed or and sable' ('Not without cause').

(Prestwich, *Respublica*, p.33).

Plate G Cornet of Colonel Henry Mainwaring

'Gules; in bend, in letters of gold, in one line, *PRO RELIGIONE ET PATRIA*, fringed or and gules' ('For country and religion').

(DWL, MS Modern 12.7, fol. 61r.; Prestwich, *Respublica*, p. 34).

Plate G Cornet of Captain John Hawkbridge

'Of sable, extending from the dexter corner and upwards, and ascending as in bend, above the sefs point to the sinister side, a representation of rugger and ragged cliffs proper; near a base of which, as if in trouble and anguish, a man in armour in profile, issuant from the cliffs; from the thigh upwards has left hand downwards placed on the rock; his right arm embowed, and his right hand placed as on his left breast; in his steel cap, on the head thereof, and in front, a plume of five feathers argent and gules; out of his mouth a label, ascending in bend, sinister argent, and thereupon, in Roman sable letters, *TRANSIBIT*; from the *dexter* angle thick and dark clouds, with others yellow or enlightened, and out of these a representation of a shower, all over and in bend; in the clouds on a label argent, shaded crimson, in Roman sable letters, *PRO DOLOR* ['Pass for pain']; fringed argent and gules'.

(DWL, MS Modern 12.7, fol. 82r.; Prestwich, *Respublica*, pp. 68–9).

Plate H Cornet of Captain John Vivers

'Orange; on a scroll with three folds of gold, one folio in-chief, each side turned in as to the middle, then swelling from the side, and so rounded at bottom, the ends turning to the centre, and thereby forming two human hearts, united, and in Roman sable letters: *VITA VERITATI OMNIAQVU* ['Life and truth is all']; fringed orange and argent'.

(DWL, MS Modern 12.7, fol. 106r.; Prestwich, *Respublica*, p.60).

Plate H Cornet of Captain William Edwards

'Argent; on a scroll of three folds, its points forming two Cs endorsed, all of gold, and thereon in Roman sable letters: *QVIS CONTRA NOS* ['Who would be against us?']; fringed sable and argent'.

(DWL, MS Modern 12.7, fol. 47r.; Prestwich, *Respublica*, p. 40).

Bibliography

Manuscript Sources

Aberystwyth, The National Library of Wales
Hawarden Deeds/325
MSS Rhual 115, 136

Amsterdam, Rijksmuseum
De ruiterschool, Jacob de Gheyn (II) (workshop of), after Jacob de Gheyn (II), 1640

Aston, Cheshire
Aston Archive, unlisted warrants and receipts, 1643–5

Bangor University
GB 0222 B/HILL/38

Beverley, East Riding Archives
BC/II/7/4

Birmingham, City Archives
MS 595611

Chester, Cheshire Archives
DBN/B/2/8, DBN/D/1/1,DCC/26, DCH/X/15/14, DDX/428, QJB 3, ZCR63/2/19, ZCR/63/2/702

Lichfield, Lichfield Cathedral Library
MS Lichfield

Lichfield, Lichfield Record Office
MS Lichfield 24

London, Dr Williams's Library
MS Modern 12.7 'Parliamentary army officers' colours and standards':
(a) The colours, or standards, and armorial bearings of certain officers in the Parliamentarian army 1642, drawn by Jonathan Turmile, fols1r.–117r.
(b) A list of the colours taken by the Earl of Essex, general of the parliament army at Edgehill 23 October 1642,fols 129r.–136r.

London, House of Lords, Journal Office
HL/PO/JO/10/1/224

London, National Army Museum
NAM 6208–1

London, The British Library
MS Egerton 787/3
MSS Add. 11331–3,11410, 18979,12429, 28566, 34253, 36913
MSS Harley 1970, 1999, 2012, 2119, 2125, 2126, 2128, 2130, 2135, 2137, 2155,2166, 6804

London, The National Archives
E121/3/1, E121/4/43, E121/1/5, E121/5/7/43, E121/5/7/95, E121/5/7/351, E121/5/7/misc., E121/5/9/351, E121/7/25, E121/351, PROB 11/220/237, SP16/381/66, SP16/409/216, SP16/492, SP16/513/1, SP20/10/63, SP20/253A/40, SP21/17, SP23/71, SP23/197/39, SP24/15/8, SP24/74, SP28/3/7/1, SP28/8, SP28/11/232, SP28/21/267, SP28/21/294, SP28/25, SP28/27/398, SP28/28/3, SP28/30, SP28/32/1, SP28/35/2,SP28/35/5, SP28/37/639–40, SP28/38, SP28/40/40, SP28/42, SP28/43/2, SP28/43/7,SP28/46, SP28/46/19, SP28/49/1, SP28/51/1, SP28/121/A, SP28/122, SP28/128/2/11, SP28/128/10–11, SP28/128/13, SP28/134/2, SP28/134/4–5, SP28/134/10, SP28/134/12, SP28/137, SP28/144, SP28/152/3–4, SP28/152/7–9, SP28/168/2, SP28/196/1–3, SP28/198/1, SP28/198/1, SP28/208, SP28/211, SP28/223/1–3, SP28/224/1–4, SP28/225/1–4, SP28/225/924, SP28/226/2–3, SP28/229, SP28/252/1–3, SP28/253A/Letter Book B/5, SP28/261/5, SP28/263, SP28/300, SP28/346/1–2, SP29/68, WO49/55, WO55/1937

Manchester, Chetham's Library
Bridgewater Scrapbook no. 248

Manchester, John Rylands Library (The University of Manchester Library)
Jodrell of Yeardsley correspondence and papers, *c.* 1642–97
Tatton Family papers, 1644 inventory of Wythenshall Hall
Tatton of Wythenshawe papers, deposition of James Brownhill, October 1646
TW/262

Matlock, Derbyshire Record Office
D258/30/9, D252/60/26c, D258/34/10, D258/60/59, D803/MZ9, D1232/0/40, D3287/1043/4

Oxford, Bodleian Library
MS Top Cheshire e 3, MS Firth C7, MS Tanner 60

Philadelphia, Philadelphia Museum of Art
The William L. Elkins Collection, E1924-3-21

Preston, Lancashire Record Office
Quarter Sessions Papers 3/93

Sheffield, Sheffield Archives
OD/1420

Stafford, Staffordshire Record Office
D100/1

Printed Primary Sources

Contemporary Newsbooks
Certaine Informations from severall parts of the Kingdome, for the satisfaction of all sorts of people that desire to be truly informed, 30 May 1643
Kingdom's Weekly Intelligencer, 24–30 April 1644
Mercurius Aulicus, 3 January 1643, 25 June 1643, 2 June 1644
Mercurius Civicus, 15 August 1644
Perfect Diurnall, 29 May–5 June 1643, 9–16 September, 4–11 November 644, 1–8, 8–15 December 1645
Perfect Occurrences, 28 August 1644
Scottish Dove, 17–23 April 1644
The Latest Remarkable Truths, 29 October 1642

The London Post, 10 September 1644, 24 September 1644
The Parliament Scout, 26 January–2 February 1644
The True Informer, 10–17 August 1644, 2 October 1644
The Weekly Account, 6–13 May 1646
The Weekly Intelligencer of the Commonwealth faithfully communicating the affaires of these three nations, 3–9 September 1651

Contemporary Tracts and Pamphlets

A Copy of a Letter sent from Sir Thomas Myddelton (London, 10 July 1644)
A Relation of some of the Remarkable Passages before the Siege of Nantwich, during the continuance of it, and at the happy raising of it by the victorious Gentlemen, Sir Thomas Fairfax, and Sir William Brereton, and the Lancashire Gentlemen, and Forces with them (London: 1643)
A True and Exact Relation of the Great Victories Obtained by the Earl of Manchester and the Lord Fairfax Against the Earl of Newcastle's Army in the North (London: 1643)
A True and Fuller Relation of the battle fought at Stow on the Wold (London: 1646)
A True Relation of a great Victory obtained by the Parliament's Forces against the Cavaliers near Chester (London: 27 November, 1643)
A True Relation of a great Victory obtained by the Parliament's Forces in Cheshire, under Sir William Brereton, against the King's Forces under Sir William Vaughan, near Denbigh (London: 1 November 1645)
A True Relation of the great Fight and Routing the Kings forces on Rowton Heath (London: September 1645)
A True Relation of two great Victories obtained of the enemy: the one by Sir William Brereton in Cheshire, etc. (London: 30 August 1644)
Cheshire's Successe Since their Pious and truly Valiant Collonel Sir William Brereton, came to their Rescue (London: 1643)
Copy of a Letter sent from Sir Thomas Myddelton, to the Honourable, William Lenthal Esq; Speaker of the House of Commons, Concerning the Siege of Oswestree (London: 3 July 1644)
Exceeding Joyful News out of Lancashire (London: 1643)
Great victories obtained by the Earle of Denbigh at Shrewsbury, Chulmely, and other parts in Cheshire (London: 9 July 1644)
Ireland's lamentation for the late destructive cessation (London: 1644)
Lancashire's Valley of Achor (London: 1643)
Letters from Sir William Brereton, Sir Thomas Myddelton, Sir John Meldrum, of the Great Victory (by God's providence), given them in raising the siege from before Montgomery Castle (London: 18 September 1644)
Orders Concluded by the Lord Strange and his adherents at Preston in the county of Lancaster, with some Queries concerning the late differences at Winchester (London: 29 December 1642)
Shrewsbury Taken. A copie of Sir William Brereton's letter to the Parliament (London: 1645)
Shropshire's Miserie and Mercie. Manifested in the defeat given to Lord Capel's Armie by the forces under Sir William Brereton, Sir Thomas Middelton and Colonel Mitton. (London: 16 October 1643)
The Advice and Direction of Both Houses of Parliament, to Sir William Brereton, and to the rest of the Deputy Lieutenants, for the County of Chester (London: 9 January 1643)
The King's forces totally routed by the Parliaments army, under the command of Major Generall Poyntz and Cheshire-Forces, on Routon-Heath, within two miles of Chester (London: 24 September 1645)
The latest printed News from Chichester, Windsor, Winchester, Chester and Manchester (London: 22 December 1642)
The Success of Our Cheshire Forces, as they came Related by Sir William Brereton's own pen to a Minister of note and eminency in the City … To which is added, late good newes from Lancashire, etc. (London: 26 August 1644)
Two Great Victories: On[e] Obtained by the Earl of Denbigh as Oswestry […] The Other by Colonel Mytton (London: June 1644)
Two Letters of Great Consequence to the House of Commons: the one from Aylesbury in Buckinghamshire … The other from Sir William Brereton to a Member of the House of Commons, of a Great Victory he obtained the 15 of March, at a town called Middlewich (London: 24 March 1643)
Wareham taken by the Parliament Forces. Also Colonel Mytton's valiant Exploits certified by two several Letters dated at his Quarters (London: 1644)

Books and Edited Collections

Andrews, G. (ed.), Henry Best, *Rural Economy in Yorkshire in 1641: Being the Farming and Account Books of Henry Best, of Elmswell, in the East Riding of the County of York*, SS (Edinburgh: Blackwood, 1857)

Atkinson, James, *Tracts Relating to the Civil War in Cheshire, 1641–1659* (Manchester: CS, 1909)

Baldwin, William, *The Canticles or Ballads of Salomon, phrase like declared in English Metres, by William Baldwin* (London, 1549)

Barriffe, William, *Military discipline: or, The young artillery man* (London, 1635)

Beamont, William (ed.), Robinson, Edward, *A Discourse of the War in Lancashire*, CS, Old Series, 62 (1864)

Blount, J.T. *The Art of Making Devises* (London: 2nd edn, 1655)

Boyle, Roger, Earl of Orrery, *A Treatise of the Art of War dedicated to the King's Most Excellent Majesty* (1677)

Byron, Lord, 'Account of the Siege of Chester', Rawlinson MS 210 in Bodleian Library, reprinted as 'John Byron's Account of the Siege of Chester 1645–1646', *CS*, 4th series, 6 (1971), 1–25

Calendar of the State Papers relating to Ireland, of the reign of Charles I, 4 vols (London: HMSO, 1900–3)

Carr, Ivor and Atherton, Ian (eds), *The Civil War in Staffordshire in the Spring of 1646: Sir William Brereton's Letter Book, April–May 1646*, Collections for a History of Staffordshire, Fourth Series, 21 (SRS, 2007)

Carte, Thomas, *A collection of original letters and papers, concerning the affairs of England, from the year 1641 to 1660, found among the Duke of Ormonde's papers*, 2 vols (London: J. and P. Knapton, 1735)

Carte, Thomas, *The Life of James, Duke of Ormond*, 5 vols (Oxford: Oxford University Press, 1851)

Coates, W.H. (ed.),*The Journal of Sir Simonds D'Ewes, from the first recess of the Long Parliament to the withdrawal of King Charles from London* (New Haven: Yale University Press, 1942)

Cruso, John, *Militarie Instructions for the Cavallrie* (Cambridge: 1632)

Day, W.A. (ed.), *The Pythouse Papers: Correspondence Concerning The Civil War, the Popish Plot and a Contested Election in 1680* (Bickers & Son, 1879)

Dore, R.N. (ed.), *The Letter Books of Sir William Brereton*, 2 vols, RSLC, 123, 128 (1984, 1990)

Fairfax, Thomas, 'A Short Memorial of the Northern Actions in which I was engaged (1642–4)', *JSAHR*, 5 (1926), 119–25 and 160–74

Firth, C.H. and Rait, R.S. (eds), *Acts and Ordinances of the Interregnum, 1642–1660*, 3 vols (London: HMSO, 1911)

Firth, C.H. (ed.),*The Memoirs of Edmund Ludlow, Lieutenant-General of the Horse in the army of the Commonwealth of England, 1625–1672* (Oxford: Clarendon Press, 1894)

Firth, C.H. (ed.), *The Narrative of General Venables* (London: Longmans, 1900)

Fuller, Thomas, *The History of the Worthies of England*, 3 vols (London, 1840)

Furnival, F.J. (ed.), *William Stafford's Compendious or Brief Examination of Certain Ordinary Complaints of Divers of Our Country Menin these our days* (London, 1876)

Gibson, E. (ed.), William Camden, *Britannia* (London, 1695)

Green, M.A. Everett (ed.),*Calendar of Proceedings of the Committee for the Advancement of Money*, 3 vols (London: HMSO, 1888)

Hall, James, *A history of the town and parish of Nantwich, or Wich-Malbank, in the county palatine of Chester* (Nantwich, 1883)

Hall, James (ed.), *Memorials of the Civil War in Cheshire and the adjacent counties by Thomas Malbon, of Nantwich, Gent., and Providence improved by Edward Burghall* Lancashire and Cheshire Record Society, 19 (1889)

Hamilton, W.D. and Bruce, J. (eds), *Calendar of State Papers Domestic: Charles I, 1625–49*, 23 vols (London: HMSO, 1858)

Hey, David (ed.), Gough, Richard, The History of Myddle (London: Penguin, new edn, 1981)

Hinds, A.B. (ed.), *Report on the manuscripts of the Marquess of Downshire, preserved at Easthampstead Park, Berks*, 5 vols (London, HMSO, 1921)

Hodgson, J.C. (ed.), Aston, John, 'Iter Boreale, Anno Salutis 1639 et Dissidae inter Anglos at Scotos Inchoatus 1 Aprilis finitum 29 Junii', *Six North Country Diaries*, SS, 118 (1910), 124 (1915)

Hogan, James (ed.), *Letters and Papers Relating to the Irish Rebellion Between 1642–46* (Dublin: The Stationery Office, 1936)

Hutchinson, Lucy, *Memoirs of the life of Colonel Hutchinson* (London: H.G. Bohn, 1863)

Hyde, Edward, Earl of Clarendon, *The History of the Rebellion and Civil Wars in England*, ed. Macray, W.D., 6 vols (Oxford: Clarendon Press, 1888)
Journals of the House of Commons, 1547--1687, 9 vols (London, 1742)
Journals of the House of Lords, 1509–1681, 13 vols (London, 1771)
Kempe, A.J. (ed.), *The Loseley Manuscripts* (London: J. Murray, 1836)
Lewis, John (ed.), *The Siege of Chester: Nathaniel Lancaster's Narrative* (Nottingham: Raider Books, 1987)
Long, C.E. (ed.), *Diary of the Marches of the Royal Army during the Great Civil War; kept by Richard Symonds*, CS, Old Series, 74 (1859)
Macray, W.D. (ed.), Clarendon, Edward, Earl of, *The History of the Rebellion and Civil Wars in England*, 6 vols (Oxford: Clarendon Press, 1888)
Markham, Francis, *Five Decades of Epistles of Warre* (London, 1622)
Markham, Gervase, *The Soldiers Accidence* (London, 1625)
McKenna, Joseph (ed.), *A Journal of the English Civil War: The Letter Book of Sir William Brereton, Spring 1646* (Jefferson, NC: McFarland and Co., 2012)
Ormerod, George (ed.), *Tracts Relating to Military Proceedings in Lancashire during the Great Civil War* (Manchester: CS, 1844)
Parkinson, R. (ed.), *Life of Adam Martindale*, CS, Old Series, 4 (1845)
Pennington, D.H. and Roots, I.A. (eds and intro.), *The Committee at Stafford, 1643–1645* (Manchester: Manchester University Press, 1957)
Rushworth, John, *Historical Collections of Private Passages of State*, 8 vols (London: D. Browne, 1722)
Snow, V.F. and Young, A.S. (eds), *The Private Journals of the Long Parliament: 2 June to 17 September 1642*, 2 vols (New Haven and London: Yale University Press, 1992)
Sprigge, Joshua, *Anglia Rediviva or England's Recovery* (London, 1647)
Stanning, J.H. (ed.), *The Royalist Composition Papers: being the proceedings of the Committee for Compounding, A.D. 1643–1660, so far as they relate to the County of Lancaster*, 6 vols (Manchester, 1891–1942)
Tibbut, H.G. (ed.), *The Letter Books of Sir Samuel Luke* (London: HMSO, 1963)
Roy, Ian (trans. and ed.), *The Royalist Ordnance Papers 1642–1646*, 2 vols (Oxfordshire Record Society, 1964 and 1969)
Ryves, Bruno, *Mercurius Rusticus* (London: 1685)
Venn, Thomas, *Military Observations, Or the Tacticks Put into Practice* (London, 1672)
Vernon, John, *The Young Horseman, or, The honest plain-dealing cavalier* (London, 1644)
Vicars, John, *Gods Ark overtopping the World's Waves* (London, 1646)
Vicars, John, *Magnalia Dei Anglicana, or England's Parliamentary Chronicle* (London, 1646)
Wallhausen, Johann Jacobi von, *Kriegskunst zu Pferd* (Frankfurt, 1616)
Warburton, Eliot, *Memoirs of Prince Rupert and the Cavaliers*, 3 vols (London: S. & J. Bentley and Henry Fley, 1849)
Whitelocke, Bulstrode, *Memorials of the English Affairs*, 4 vols (Oxford: Oxford University Press, 1853)
Wrye, W. (ed.), *State Papers Relating to Musters, Beacons, Ship-money, &c. in Norfolk from 1626 chiefly to the beginning of the Civil War* (Norwich, 1907)
Young, Alan R. (ed.), *The English Emblem Tradition: Volume 3: Emblematic Flag Devices of the English Civil Wars, 1642–1660* (Toronto: University of Toronto Press, 1995)

Reports of the Historical Manuscripts Commission

Third Report (1872)
Fourth Report, I (1874)
Seventh Report (1879)
Tenth Report, Appendix IV (1885)
Twelfth Report, Appendix IX (1890)
Thirteenth Report, Appendix I (1891)
Fourteenth Report, Appendix IV (1893)
Fifteenth Report, Appendix II (1899)
The Manuscripts of His Grace the Duke of Portland, I (1891)

Secondary Sources

Books and Reports

Abram, Andrew, *The Battle of Montgomery 1644* (Bristol: Stuart Press, 1993)
Abram, Andrew, *The Brookes at Norton: The Civil War and After 1642–1660* (Norton Priory Museum Trust, 1994)
Acton, F.S., *The Garrisons of Shropshire during the Civil War, 1642–48* (Shrewsbury: Leake and Evans, 1867)
Atkin, Malcolm, *Worcestershire under Arms: An English County during the Civil Wars* (Barnsley: Pen and Sword, 2004)
Barlow, T.W. (ed.), *The Cheshire and Lancashire Historical Collector* (Manchester, 1853)
Barratt, John, *A Rabble of Gentility: The Royalist Northern Horse, 1644–45* (Solihull: Helion & Co., 2017)
Barratt, John, *Cavaliers: The Royalist Army at War 1642–1646* (Stroud: Sutton, 2000)
Barratt, John, *"Civil War Stronghold": Beeston Castle at War* (Birkenhead: Caracole Press, 1995)
Barratt, John, *The Battle of Nantwich 1644* (Bristol: Stuart Press, 1993)
Barratt, John, *The Great Siege of Chester* (Stroud: Tempus, 2003)
Barratt, John, *The Last Army: The Battle of Stow-on-the-Wold and the end of the Civil War in the Welsh Marches, 1646* (Solihull: Helion & Co., 2018)
Barratt, John, *The Siege of Liverpool and the Lancashire Campaign of 1644* (Bristol: Stuart Press, 1993)
Barratt, John, *The Siege of Manchester 1642* (Bristol: Stuart Press, 1993)
Beamont, William, *A History of the Castle of Halton and the Priory or Abbey of Norton* (Warrington: Percival Pearse, 1873)
Bell, Robert, *Memorials of the Civil War: comprising the correspondence of the Fairfax family* (London, 1849)
Brighton, T.J., *Royalists and Roundheads in Derbyshire* (Bakewell: Bakewell and District Historical Society, 1981)
Broxap, Ernest (ed.), *The Great Civil War in Lancashire, 1642–1651* (Manchester: Manchester University Press, 1910)
Bull, Stephen, *'The Furie of the Ordnance': Artillery in the English Civil War* (Woodbridge: Boydell, 2008)
Burne, A.H. and Young, Peter, *The Great Civil War: A Military History of the First Civil War, 1642–1646* (London: Eyre & Spottiswoode, 1959)
Chandler, George, *Liverpool under Charles I* (Liverpool, 1965)
Clayton, Howard, *Loyal and Ancient City: The Civil War in Lichfield* (Lichfield: Abbotsford, 1987)
Coates, Ben, *The Impact of the English Civil War on the Economy London, 1642–50* (London: Routledge, 2004)
Darcy, Eamon, *The Irish Rebellion of 1641 and the Wars of the Three Kingdoms* (Woodbridge: Boydell, 2013)
Donagan, Barbara, *War in England 1642–1649* (Oxford: Oxford University Press, 2008)
Dore, R.N., *The Civil Wars in Cheshire* (Chester: Cheshire Community Council, 1966)
Earwaker, J.P., *East Cheshire: past and present*, 2 vols (London, 1877–80)
Edwards, Peter, *Dealing in Death: The Arms Trade and the British Civil Wars, 1638–52* (Stroud: Sutton, 2000)
Edwards, Peter, *Horse and Man in Early Modern England* (London: Bloomsbury, 2007)
Edwards, Peter, *The Horse Trade of Tudor and Stuart England* (Cambridge: Cambridge University Press, 1988)
Firth, Charles and Davies, Godfrey, *The Regimental History of Cromwell's Army* (Oxford: Clarendon Press, 1991 edn)
Fletcher, Anthony, *The Outbreak of the English Civil War* (London: Edward Arnold, rev. edn 1985)
Foard, Glenn, *Naseby: The Decisive Campaign* (Barnsley: Pen & Sword, 2004 edn)
Gaunt, Peter, *A Nation under Siege: The Civil War in Wales 1642–48* (London: HMSO, 1991)
Gaunt, Peter, *The English Civil Wars 1642–1651* (Oxford: Osprey, 2003)
Gentles, Ian, *The English Revolution and the Wars in the Three Kingdoms, 1638–1652* (London: Pearson, 2007)
Gratton, J.M., *The Parliamentarian and Royalist War Effort in Lancashire 1642–1651* (Manchester: CS, 2010)
Greenslade, M.W. and Baugh, G.C. (intro.), *The History and Antiquities of Staffordshire, by Stebbing Shaw*, 2 vols (East Ardsley: E.P. Publishing, 1976)

Groves, Jill, *The Impact of Civil War on a Community: Northenden and Etchels in Cheshire 1642–1660* (Sale: Northern Writers Advisory Services, 1992)

Gruber von Arni, Eric, *Justice to the Maimed Soldier: Nursing, Medical Care and Welfare for Sick and Wounded Soldiers and their Families during the English Civil Wars and Interregnum, 1642–1660* (London and New York: Routledge, 2001)

Haythornthwaite, Phillip, *English Civil War, 1642–1651: An Illustrated Military History* (Worthing: Littlehampton, 1983)

Hazell, Martin, *Fidelity and Fortitude: Lord Capel his regiments and the English Civil War* (Leigh-on-Sea: Partizan Press, 1987)

Helsby, Thomas (ed.), George Ormerod, *History of the County Palatine and City of Chester*, (London: Routledge, 2nd edn, 1874)

Hollings, James, *The History of Leicester during the Great Civil War* (Leicester: Combe and Crossley, 1839)

Holmes, Clive, *The Eastern Association in the English Civil War* (Cambridge: Cambridge University Press, 2008)

Hopkins, David and Hilary, *The Tale of a Soldier's Coat: The Story of the Experimental Reconstruction of a 1643 Oxford Royalist Soldier's Coat* (Bristol: Stuart Press, 2000)

Hopper, Andrew, *Black Tom: Sir Thomas Fairfax and the English Revolution* (Manchester: Manchester University Press, 2007)

Hopper, Andrew, *Turncoats and Renegadoes: Changing Sides during the English Civil Wars* (Oxford: Oxford University Press, 2012)

Hutton, Ronald, *The Royalist War Effort, 1642–46* (Upper Saddle River, NJ: Prentice Hall Press, 1984)

Kerridge, Eric, *Textile Manufacturers in Early Modern England* (Manchester: Manchester University Press, 1985)

Kishlansky, Mark A., *The Rise of the New Model Army* (Cambridge: Cambridge University Press, 1979)

Laurence, Anne, *Parliamentary Army Chaplains, 1642–51* (Woodbridge: Royal Historical Society, 1990)

Lawrence, David R., *The Complete Soldier: Military Books and Military Culture in Early Stuart England, 1603–1645* (Leiden: Brill, 2008)

Lawson, P.H. (ed.), Morris, Rupert H., *The Siege of Chester, 1643–1646* (Chester: G.R. Griffith, 1924)

Lenihan, Pádraig, *Confederate Catholics at War, 1641–49* (Cork: Cork University Press, 2001)

Lowe, Norman, *The Lancashire Textile Industry in the Sixteenth Century*, CS, 20, Third Series (Manchester, 1972)

Mahler, Margaret, *The History of Chirk Castle and Chirkland* (London: G. Bell and Sons, 1912)

Malcolm, Joyce, *Caesar's Due: Loyalty and King Charles, 1642–46* (London: RHS, 1983)

Maltby, Judith, *Prayer Book and People in Elizabethan and Early Stuart England* (Cambridge: Cambridge University Press, 1998)

Matthews, H.C.G., and Harrison, B. (eds), *Oxford Dictionary of National Biography*, 40 vols (Oxford: Oxford University Press, 2004)

McNeil, Robina, *Halton Castle: A Visual Treasure*, North West Archaeological Trust, Report No. 1 (1987)

Morrill, J.S., *Cheshire 1630–1660: County Government and Society during the 'English Revolution'* (Oxford: Oxford University Press, 1974)

Peachey, Stuart, *Male Coats and Cassocks*, Clothes of the Common People in Elizabethan and Early Stuart England, 13 (Bristol: Stuart Press, 2014)

Peachey, Stuart, and Turton, Alan, *Old Robin's Foot* (Leigh-on-Sea: Partizan Press, 1987)

Peachey, Stuart, and Prince, Lesley, *ECW Flags and Colours 1: English Foot* (Leigh-on-Sea: Partizan Press, 1991)

Pfiel, Michael, *Drumming in the Civil Wars* (Bristol: Stuart Press, 1997)

Phillips, J.R., *Memoirs of the Civil War in Wales and the Marches, 1642–1649*, 2 vols (London: Longmans, 1874)

Porter, Stephen and Marsh, Simon, *The Battle for London* (Stroud: Amberley, 2010)

Richardson, R.C. (ed.), *Town and Countryside in the English Revolution* (Manchester, Manchester University Press, 1992)

Roberts, Keith, *Cromwell's War Machine: The New Model Army, 1645–1660* (Barnsley: Pen & Sword, 2005)

Ryder, Ian, *An English Army for Ireland* (Leigh-on-Sea: Partizan Press, 1987)

Shay, Jonathan, *Odysseus In America: Combat Trauma and the Trials of Homecoming* (New York: Scribner, 2002)

Shercliff, W.H. (ed.), *Wythenshawe: A History of the Townships of Northenden, Northen Etchells and Baguley*, 2 vols (Didsbury, 1974)

Sherwood, Roy, *The Civil War in the Midlands 1642–1651* (Stroud: Sutton, 1992 edn)

Slack, Ron, *Man at War: John Gell in His Troubled Time* (R. Slack, 1997)

Solt, Leo F., *Saints in Arms: Puritanism and Democracy in Cromwell's Army* (Stanford: Stanford University Press, 1959)

Stone, Brian, *Derbyshire in the Civil War* (Matlock: Scarthin Books, 1992)

Stoyle, Mark, *Soldiers and Strangers: An Ethnic History of the English Civil War* (New Haven, CT: Yale University Press 2005)

Tucker, Norman, *North Wales in the Civil War* (Wrexham: Bridge Books, 1992 edn)

Ward, Simon, *Excavations at Chester: Civil War Siegeworks 1642–46* (Grosvenor Museum Chester, 1987)

Webb, J. and T.W., *Memorials of the Civil War between Charles I and the Parliament as it Affected Herefordshire and the adjacent counties*, 2 vols (London: Spottiswoode, 1879)

Williams, John, *Ancient and Modern Denbigh* (Denbigh: J. Williams, 1856)

Worton, Jonathan, *The Battle of Montgomery, 1644: The English Civil War in the Welsh Borderlands* (Solihull: Helion & Co., 2016)

Worton, Jonathan, *To Settle the Crown: Waging Civil War in Shropshire, 1642–1648* (Solihull: Helion & Co., 2016)

Young, Peter, *Edgehill 1642: The Campaign and the Battle* (Kineton: Roundwood Press, 1967)

Younger, Neil, *War and Politics in the Elizabethan Counties* (Manchester: Manchester University Press, 2012)

Articles and Chapters

Anon., 'Extracts from the Corporation Books of the Borough of Congleton, Cheshire', *JCAS*, Old Series, 2 (1864), pp.365–8

Auden, J.E., 'Sir Jerome Zankey (or Sankey), of Balderton Hall, co. Salop, and of Coolmore, co. Tipperary', *TSAS*, 50 (1939–40), pp.171–8

Barratt, John, 'The Battle of Rowton Heath, 1645', *JSAHR*, 54:220 (1976), pp.208–224

——, 'What Sanford's Firelocks Did Next', *ECWNQ*, 50 (Leigh-on-sea: Partizan Press, 1995), pp.18–21

Beats, Lynn, 'The East Midland Association 1642–1644', *MH*, 4:3 (1978), pp.160–174

Bennett, Martyn, '"My Plundered Townes, My Houses Devastation": *The Civil War in North Midland Life, 1642–1646, MH,* 22:1 (1997), pp.35–50

Dore, R.N., 'Beeston Castle in the Great Civil War, 1643–46', *TLCAS*, 75–6 (1965–6), pp.103–22

Dore, R.N., 'Sir Thomas Myddelton's Attempted Conquest of Powys, 1644–5', *MC*, 57 (1961–2), pp.91–118

Dore, R.N., 'Sir William Brereton's siege of Chester and the campaign of Naseby', *TLCAS*, 67 (1957), pp.17–44

Dore R.N., '1642: the coming of the Civil War to Cheshire: conflicting actions and impressions', *TLCAS*, 87 (1991), pp.39–6

Dore, R.N., and Lowe, John, 'The Battle of Nantwich, 25 January 1644', *THSLC*, 113 (1961), pp.97–124

Dore, R.N., 'The Early Life of Sir William Brereton', *TLCAS*, 63 (1953), pp.1–8

Dore, R.N., 'The Sea Approaches: the importance of the Dee and the Mersey in the Civil War in the North West', *THSLC*, 136 (1987), pp.1–26

Dore, R.N., 'The Garrisons at Hooton and Puddington', *THSLC*, 159 (2010), pp.45–62

Dore, R.N., 'The Oaths at Woodchurch, 1643–1644: tensions in civil-war Wirral and its aftermath', *THSLC*, 164 (2015), pp.1–20

Dyson, Tony, 'Colonel Moore's Offensive against Wirral, November 1643', *THSLC*, 162 (2013), pp.29–48

Edwards, Peter, 'Turning Ploughshares into Swords: The Arms and Military Equipment Industries in Staffordshire in the First Civil War, 1642–1646', *MH*, 27 (2002), pp.52–79

Gaunt, Peter, 'Barthomley Church and the Civil War', *CH*, 35 (1995–96), pp.16–21

Gaunt, Peter, 'Chester's role in the Civil War', *Cromwelliana*(1995), pp.8–21

Gaunt, Peter, 'Cromwellian Britain VII: Barthomley Church', *Cromwelliana* (1994), pp.66–70

Gaunt, Peter, 'Four Churches and a River: The Civil War in Cheshire', *Cromwelliana*, Second Series, 5 (2008), pp.31–48

Gaunt, Peter, 'Barthomley Church and the Civil War', *CH*, 35 (1995–96), pp.16–21
Gaunt, Peter, 'Chester's role in the Civil War', *Cromwelliana* (1995), pp.8–21
Gaunt, Peter, 'Cromwellian Britain VII: Barthomley Church', *Cromwelliana* (1994), pp.66–70
Gaunt, Peter, 'The Parliamentary War Effort in Cheshire', *CH*, 32 (1993), pp.6–14
Gaunt, Peter, '"Wedged up in the church like billets in a woodpile": New light on the battle of Middlewich, 13 March 1643', Pells, I. (ed.), *New Approaches to the Military History of the English Civil War*, Proceedings of the First Helion and Company 'Century of the Soldier' Conference, 2015 (Solihull: Helion & Co., 2016), pp.27–56
Gibson, A. Craig, 'Every-Day Life of a Country Gentleman of Cheshire in the Seventeenth Century', *THSLC*, 15 (1862–1863), pp.67–92
Gratton, J.M., 'Liverpool under parliament: The anatomy of a civil war garrison, May 1643 to June 1644', *THSLC*, 156 (2007), pp.51–74
Gratton, J.M., 'The Earl of Derby's Catholic Army', *THSLC*, 137 (1988), pp.25–54
Higgins, G.P., 'The militia in early Stuart Cheshire', *JCAS*, 61 (1978), pp.39–49
Hudson, Geoffrey, 'Northern Civil War atrocity at Barthomley Church, 1643, Revisited', *NH*, 46:2 (2009), pp.329–32
Hughes, Ann, 'Militancy and Localism: Warwickshire Politics and Westminster Politics, 1643–1647', *TRHS*, 5th Series, 31 (1981), pp.51–68
Hughes, Ann, 'The King, the Parliament, and the Localities during the English Civil War', *JBS*, 24:2 (April 1985), pp.236–63
Hutton, Ronald, 'The Failure of the Lancashire Cavaliers', *THSLC*, 129 (1980), pp.47–57
Johnson, A.J., 'Politics in Chester during the Civil Wars and Interregnum 1640–62', Clark, Peter and Slack, Paul (eds), *Crisis and Order in English Towns, 1500–1700* (Oxford: Routledge, 1972), pp.204–36
Kightley, Charles and Barton, Anthony (illustrator), 'Standards of the English Civil Wars: The Parliamentary Cavalry', *Military Modelling*, 7:12 (December 1977), pp.851–3
Holmes, Clive, 'The County Community in Stuart Historiography', *JBS*, 19:2 (1980), pp.54–73
Lowe, John, 'The Campaign of the Irish Royalist Army in Cheshire, November 1643–January 1644', *THSLC*, 111 (1959), pp.49–76
Malcolm, Joyce, 'All the King's Men: The Impact of the Crown's Irish Soldiers on the English Civil War', *IHS*, 21 (1979), pp.239–64
Marsh, Simon, 'A Case of Drakes – James Wemyss and Artillery Innovation in the Civil War', Jones, Serena (ed.), *A New Way of Fighting: Professionalism in the English Civil War, Proceedings of the 2016 Helion and Company 'Century of the Soldier' Conference* (Solihull: & Co., 2017), pp.91–107
McDonald, Mary Catherine, 'Haunted by a Different Ghost: Re-thinking Moral Injury', *Philosophy Faculty Publications*, 35 (2017), pp.1–16
Morrill, J.S., 'Brereton, Sir William, first Baronet (1604–61)', *ODNB*, 7, pp.471–3
Morrill, J.S., 'Mutiny and Discontent in English Provincial Armies 1645–1647', *P&P*, 56:1 (1972), pp.49–74
Morrill, J.S., 'Sir William Brereton and England's Wars of Religion', *JBS*, 24:3 (1985), pp.311–32
Morrill, J.S., 'William Davenport and the Silent Majority of Early Stuart England', *JCAS*, pp.58 (1974), 115–29
Mungeam, Gerald I., 'Contracts of the Supply of Equipment to the 'New Model Army' in 1645, *JAAS*, 6 (1968–70), 53–114
Newman, P.R., 'Aspects of the Civil War in Lancashire', *TLCAS*, 82 (1983), pp.113–120
Nusbacher, Aryeh J.S., 'Civil Supply in the Civil War: Supply of Victuals to the New Model Army on the Naseby Campaign, 1–14 June 1645', *EHR*, 115 (2000), pp.145–160
Townshend, L.P., 'Some Account of General Robert Venables of Antrobus and Wincham, Cheshire (with an engraving from his portrait at Wincham); together with the autobiographical memoir, or diary, of his widow, Elizabeth Venables', *CS*, 83 (Manchester, 1871), pp.1–28
Phillips, C.B., 'Landlord-Tenant Relationships 1642–1660', Richardson, R.C. (ed.), *Town and Countryside in the English Revolution* (Manchester, Manchester University Press, 1992), pp.224–50
Slack, Ron, 'Colonel Gell and Major Sanders: Internal feuding among the Parliamentary forces in Derbyshire during the Civil Wars of 1642–1646', *Derbyshire Miscellany*, 16:2 (2001), pp.34–48

Unpublished Theses

Bennett, Martyn, 'The Royalist War Effort in the North Midlands 1642–1646', PhD thesis (Loughborough, 1986)

Gratton, Malcolm, 'The Parliamentarian and Royalist War Effort in Lancashire 1642–1651', PhD thesis (Manchester, 1998)

Jones, Jennifer, 'The War in the North: The Northern Parliamentary Army in the English Civil-War, 1642–1645', PhD thesis (York University, Toronto, 1994)

Wanklyn, Malcolm, 'Landed Society and Allegiance in Cheshire and Shropshire in the First Civil War', PhD thesis (Manchester, 1976)